5795

SOCIAL
MEANINGS
OF NEWS

To Holly, Ben and the Princess

Dan Berkowitz

SOCIAL MEANINGS OF NEWS

A Text-Reader

SAGE Publications
International Educational and Professional Publisher
Thousand Oaks   London   New Delhi

For information address:

SAGE Publications, Inc.
2455 Teller Road
Thousand Oaks, California 91320
E-mail: order@sagepub.com

SAGE Publications Ltd.
6 Bonhill Street
London EC2A 4PU
United Kingdom

SAGE Publications India Pvt. Ltd.
M-32 Market
Greater Kailash I
New Delhi 110 048 India

Printed in the United States of America

Library of Congress Cataloging-in-Publication Data

Main entry under title:

Social meanings of news: A text-reader / editor, Dan Berkowitz
    p. cm.
  Includes bibliographical references (p.) and index
  ISBN 0-7619-0075-6 (acid-free paper). —ISBN 0-7619-0076-4
(pbk.: acid-free paper)
    1. Journalism—Social aspects. I. Berkowitz, Daniel A. (Daniel Allen)
PN4749.S64   1997
302.23—dc21   96-51208

This book is printed on acid-free paper.

99 00 01 02 10 9 8 7 6 5 4 3

Acquiring Editor:	Margaret Seawell
Editorial Assistant:	Renée Piernot
Production Editor:	Astrid Virding
Production Assistant:	Denise Santoyo
Typesetter& Designer:	Andrea D. Swanson
Indexer:	Cristina Haley
Cover Designer:	Lesa Valdez

Contents

Acknowledgments

This volume represents a collective effort, even though only one person's name appears on the cover. Much of what I have learned about the study of news and newswork comes from teaching this material to graduate students over the years. Some students had been journalists, and this body of literature required great bravery to reconcile with their work experiences. Some were new to graduate school and had never faced the challenge of reading research from a variety of approaches, grappling with the new ideas, and then presenting their interpretations to their peers or putting their ideas on paper. Other students had no exposure whatsoever to the world of journalism and frequently had to ask for explanations about concepts that other students took for granted. Yet a few others latched onto these ideas quickly and left me scrambling in their dust.

Besides my former students, there are several other people who I need to thank for their contributions to this volume. First of all, I must thank the authors and publishers whose work is presented here. Without them, the pages would be empty. A project like this cannot be done in isolation, either, and I need to thank Dave Pritchard and John Soloski for reading over my lists of readings and talking with me about the project at its various stages. Graduate student Jim TerKeurst seemed like a coeditor at times, carefully reading many of the new potential selections under consideration and providing thoughtful feedback about their concepts and merits. I also want to thank research assistants Ralph Beliveau and Luis Rivera, who helped collect copies of the selections and obtain permissions.

This book would not have happened at all without Sophy Craze, former editor at Sage Publications in California, who talked with me about the project and encouraged me to develop it. Margaret Seawell helpfully jumped in as editor to bring closure to the last stages of this project after Sophy's departure from Sage's U.S. operations. I also need to thank the reviewers, who provided helpful feedback on my initial proposal to Sage, especially regarding the incorporation of more "culturologically" oriented studies. These people also provided helpful ideas for the final manuscript. Looking back several years, I must give credit to the patient journal editors and reviewers, who took the time to help me develop a better understanding of this literature as I worked to publish my own research articles.

Finally, I need to thank my family for their patience in providing me the time to wrap up the project at its final stages and for allowing me to play the blues when my sanity was waning.

Overview

Why a "Social Meanings of News" Perspective?

The study of news is much like viewing a hologram. A person can get closer or farther away. A person can stand in different places. Each new perspective will reveal a different aspect of the same holographic picture. There is no way, though, that a person can find a single vantage point where the entire hologram can be viewed all at once.

As it turns out, some vantage points are not particularly productive for understanding the nature of news. This book thus starts by discarding three ideas that often frame discussions about the nature of news in journalism schools and in the working world of journalists. First, the idea must be discarded that news is something tangible "out there" that good journalists know when they see it. That is, although journalists learn to think about news as an ongoing "parade" of stories that can be captured intact and conveyed to a waiting audience, this is not exactly what goes on. More realistically, news exists because journalists apply mutually agreed on work procedures to observe, interpret, and represent occurrences in society. These occurrences do not really have any time or space limits: Those limits are humanly imposed as an occurrence unfolds.

A second idea to discard is that news naturally contains values making some occurrences newsworthy and other occurrences not so. That is, as journalists observe the news parade, they imagine each story conspicuously displaying its news values for all good journalists to see. From a social perspective, though, values are human constructions that have evolved through an informal consensus among journalists and others over time. On their own, stories do not actually contain news values.

A third idea to discard rests at the very foundation of journalistic practice: that journalists can be objective about the world they observe and on which they report. This point does not argue that journalists are incapable of *trying* to remove their personal beliefs from the news stories they produce. Rather, it suggests that if news is the result of social processes, then journalists can never discard their socially learned beliefs about society and how the world works. In sum, news can never be value free, because social values are embedded in everyday activities and the ways that people manage them.

These three discarded ideas all belong to what could be called "the ideology of journalism," those beliefs about the nature of news that are sometimes challenged by journalists, scholars, and news critics yet tend to set the boundaries of discussion. A new point of departure for thinking about news can now be offered that allows a more analytic approach to the study of news: News is a human construction that gains its characteristics through the social world from which it emerges. This view requires new answers to two long-standing questions:

— What is news?
— Why does news turn out like it does?

From a traditional journalistic perspective, answers to "What is news?" focus on what people need to know and what they should know about their community, their country, and their world. When the nature of news is explored from a social perspective, however, the "need to know" and "should know" answers become only a small part of the answer. The emphasis now shifts to the social processes by which journalists decide what is news and the social forces that influence and limit how journalists gather and assemble news from raw materials into a journalistic product. News becomes the product of the practicalities and constraints of the process by which it is created. It becomes the product of economic systems and political systems, and the press systems that result from them. And it becomes the product of unspoken cultural values and beliefs by which people manage their daily lives.

For example, when a television assignment editor begins to plan a daily newscast, journalistic judgment becomes only one decision-making factor. That editor also must consider the number of available reporters and photographers, the difficulty of filling the newscast, and the likely audience appeal that might result from choosing certain stories over others. That editor also must consider how much time and travel each story will take to report on and how difficult it will be to edit the videotape into a coherent package.

Similarly, when a newspaper reporter leaves the newsroom to cover a story, that reporter begins to subconsciously draw on social values that define how the story will be cast, including the actors and institutions that are to be included and the social lessons that will be learned. Pressures from powerful local officials also come into play. Consciously or unconsciously, the reporter factors in expectations from local advertisers that help pay both salaries and bills, as well as the expectations of community members who form the subscriber base that shapes and justifies advertising rates.

Suddenly, answers to "Why does news turn out like it does?" become more complex. The kind of answer a person gives now depends heavily on the theoretical orientation applied (consciously or subconsciously), as well as on the social elements that a particular theory considers. In sum, unlike the traditional journalistic perspective, a social perspective on news offers no single or simple answer to the question, "What is news?"

The purpose of this book, then, is to cast aside conventional answers about the nature of news and begin a fresh series of explorations. Many plausible answers to "What is news?" will surface, so that the question becomes more elusive as one viable alternative is replaced with another. The more one explores the nature of news from a social perspective, the less any single answer feels acceptable as *the* answer. In a way, ignorance is bliss.

About the Use and Organization of This Book

The readings that appear here represent a blend of classic studies and lesser-known pieces that combine to make important points. By no means is this a comprehensive collection of readings about news and newswork, but it is reasonably representative of important threads in the literature. Selections have been drawn from several methodologies and approaches, and readers should challenge themselves to glean ideas from all. Rather than arguing for certain answers, the hope is to lead toward better-informed questions. In fact, several interpretations of this book's readings could be viable, depending on a person's interests in the study of news. A reading by another person or even by the same person for a different purpose would yield yet another emphasis on key points.

It follows that gaining maximum benefit from this book requires an open-minded yet analytic approach. Rather than looking for holes to reject a study's argument, a reader should try to unearth the utility of a particular perspective. In some cases, a reader might disagree with an author's assertions, yet still find valuable insights from the counterpoint an article provides. The quest for connections among these readings also becomes challenging because different research traditions tend to discuss their ideas through different terms. For example, a psychologist's *schema* is similar to a sociologist's *typification*, and both have some correspondence to a critical scholar's *ideology*.

The 30 readings in this book are organized into seven sections that emphasize different aspects of news and newswork. In turn, the seven sections fit into three broader topical parts. Each section introduction serves as a guide to key points in that section's readings. Rather than analyzing and critiquing the readings, these introductions are primarily designed to highlight the selections' arguments so that the reader can assess their utility.

Part I provides a framework for studying news. One task is to identify different *paradigms*—ways of seeing and interpreting—for the study of news. A second task is to introduce the concept of *levels of analysis*, the idea that studies can focus on different degrees of social aggregation—individual, organizational, institutional, and societal.

Together, these tools provide an organized way of approaching the rest of the readings and analyzing their concepts.

Part II contains four sections that highlight news as a result of its production processes at several levels of analysis. The readings in Part II progress from lower levels of analysis, that is, the role of the individual, to higher levels of analysis, including the organization, the profession, and the media as a social institution.

Part III centers on a more macrolevel of analysis by examining news texts in relation to society and culture, portraying news as both the result of social cultures and the maintainer of those cultures. The first of the two sections in Part III considers news as social narrative, and how news represents the telling and retelling of cultural stories. The second section focuses on the ideological aspects of news, aspects that convey information about social values, social beliefs, and social power.

Collectively, the readings in this book develop the argument that journalists are not objective bearers of truth, but are instead makers of a product shaped through a variety of social forces. By keeping in mind the framework concepts from the first section, ideas across sections will become cumulative and intellectual bridges can be built across research perspectives.

However, one of the challenges in working with the readings in this book is that the literature of news and newswork is somewhat circular and very large. To understand fully the implications of the classic readings requires knowledge of organizing frameworks written many years later. At the same time, many of the more recent approaches become difficult to grasp without an understanding of the thinking and beliefs that preceded them. Although this book offers an organizing scheme that helps the reader turn the selections into a cohesive whole, there really is no clear point of entry into this literature. Some readers might want to start at another point, perhaps at the paradigm and level of analysis with which they are most familiar. Regardless of where a person begins, though, an ongoing bibliography can be drawn from this book's readings to both build greater depth and develop finer nuance about the social meanings of news.

PART I: Introduction

A Framework for
Thinking About News

If we are to reject the notion that news simply represents journalists' best efforts to seek truth and serve as society's watchdogs, other specific perspectives must be offered in its place. That is the purpose of this section, which is accomplished through three selections that summarize key alternative perspectives about news. The selections also provide a broad synthesis of the literature about news and newswork, helping to put selections from the next six sections into a common context.

Each of these alternative perspectives explicitly considers how news is shaped by the interaction within and among the journalism workforce, media organizations, and society. For some readers, these perspectives will seem obvious and reasonable. For many readers with working experience in journalism, though, these framework pieces likely will be dissonant and jarring to a journalistic ideology that casts newswork as a logical and natural process for learning about occurrences in society and presenting information to media audiences.

Michael Schudson's "The Sociology of News Production" begins to develop our framework by clarifying the concept of *making news,* a term that refers not to fabrications and falsehoods—as in *making up* news—but instead emphasizes that news is the outcome of work accomplished in a social environment. News organizations thus become bureaucratic organizations, and news becomes the outcome of a routine, bureaucratic process.

Schudson summarizes three research traditions that contrast with the beliefs of textbook journalism. The first, *political economy,* examines the relationship between the funding of media organizations and the constraints that as a result affect the production of news content. A second thread brings a *sociological* emphasis to study how working arrangements within news organizations and occupational beliefs shape expectations for accomplishing news. A third thread considers *culturological* approaches, where news emerges from the relationship between occurrences and a culture's symbolic system. Schudson adds that although comparative and historical approaches have not been applied to the study of news as frequently, they nonetheless add a crucial dimension for understanding news as a dynamic cultural product.

In "Has Communication Explained Journalism?" Barbie Zelizer contends that the nature of news cannot truly be understood until journalists are studied within the cultural context of their craft. This requires a conception of news beyond that of a "sociological problem" to be studied through its visible elements: news texts, news-gathering settings, and news audiences. Zelizer argues that understanding the cultural context of journalism requires going beyond these surface elements to learn how dimensions of authority and power are constructed and maintained.

The chapter presents four alternative frames for understanding journalism. The first considers *journalism as performance*, an approach that places emphasis on journalists' roles as actors in the unfolding of news occurrences. *Journalism as narrative* sees a commonality among journalists within the news stories that they tell, repeat, and alter to construct the world they observe. *Journalism as ritual* focuses on interaction within the culture of journalists and how the terms of that culture are restated and placed into action. Finally, *journalism as interpretive community* takes the stance that journalists are united by the interpretations of reality that they share in their work.

In sum, Zelizer calls for an understanding of news based on what news and newswork means from within the culture of journalism rather than studying it from the outside through its cultural artifacts.

James S. Ettema and D. Charles Whitney (with Daniel B. Wackman) present a broad integration of studies in "Professional Mass Communicators." They begin by emphasizing the same point as the previous two selections: to understand news and journalism as a cultural product rather than through an evaluative perspective. By taking this route, studies of news avoid applying a particular normative standard, looking instead at relationships between journalistic production processes and the social contexts in which they are enacted.

A key contribution of this selection is how the question of whether truth can be known and told given the social context of journalism is organized through three levels of analysis: *individual and small group, media organizations,* and *industrial and institutional.* For analysis to be most effective, the authors argue, these levels' influence on news should not be considered distinctly. Instead, interactions across levels should be considered as well, because the influence of one level on another cannot be easily separated.

At the industrial and institutional levels, evidence from previous studies suggests that journalists' work patterns are clearly shaped by the economic necessities of a media organization in its particular socioeconomic system.

At the organizational level, news becomes the outcome of bureaucratic activity where journalists learn work routines and strategies for meeting organizational expectations and constraints. At the individual level, questions about news focus on how a journalist's predispositions and personal characteristics relate to the news that person produces—often these individual-level influences have been reinterpreted as stemming from higher-level influences.

Bringing their analysis together, Ettema and Whitney define news as the result of the tension between the search for truth and the constraints coming from organizational and institutional constraints.

Taken together, the three chapters in this section form a framework for understanding the readings that follow. For example, Schudson's discussion of research traditions could pinpoint the general area where a study is located, such as sociological or culturological. This information helps the reader understand the basic conceptual framing that has been applied. Similarly, Zelizer's discussion of alternative frames for understanding journalism can help a reader reinterpret an article's framing to make explicit what might have been overlooked in an author's original framing. The journalism-as-ritual approach, for example, might be applied to reconsider a study framed more simply around journalistic work routines. The concept of levels of analysis discussed by Ettema and Whitney can help a reader rethink a study's argument to reach different conclusions for another level of analysis, or even to recognize how an author's choice of analysis level led toward the conclusions that they did.

In sum, building an explicit understanding of research approaches and levels of analysis can lead to new questions and understandings of long-standing articles.

Thus, the framework introduced here is important, because it can make a reader aware of a researcher's implicit assumptions that shaped both initial arguments and final outcomes. As a result, a reader can develop a sharper, more systematic critique of an article's main arguments, along the way building a keener understanding about the social meanings of news.

CHAPTER **1**

The Sociology of
News Production

Michael Schudson

Social scientists who study the news speak a language that journalists
mistrust and misunderstand. They speak of "constructing the news," of
"making news," of the "social construction of reality." "News is what newspapermen make it" (Gieber, 1964: 173). "News is the result of the methods
newsworkers employ" (Fishman, 1980: 14). News is "manufactured by journalists" (Cohen and Young, 1973: 97). Even journalists who are critical of the
daily practices of their colleagues and their own organizations find this talk
offensive. I have been at several conferences of journalists and social scientists where such language promptly pushed the journalists into a fierce
defence of their work, on the familiar ground that they just report the world
as they see it, the facts, facts, and nothing but the facts, and yes, there's
occasional bias, occasional sensationalism, occasional inaccuracy, but a responsible journalist never, never, never fakes the news.

That's not what we said, the hurt scholars respond. We didn't say
journalists *fake* the news, we said journalists *make* the news:

From *Media, Culture & Society*, 1989, Vol. 11, pp. 263-282. Copyright © 1989 Sage
Publications, Ltd.

> To say that a news report is a story, no more, but no less, is not to demean
> the news, not to accuse it of being fictitious. Rather, it alerts us that news,
> like all public documents, is a constructed reality possessing its own
> internal validity. (Tuchman, 1976: 97)

In the most elementary way, this is obvious. Journalists write the words that
turn up in the papers or on the screen as stories. Not government officials,
not cultural forces, not "reality" magically transforming itself into alphabetic
signs, but flesh-and-blood journalists literally compose the stories we call
news. Once this is granted, social scientists say, all the rest follows. (Would
you say that of science? the journalist might respond. Would you say that
scientists "make" science rather than "discover" it or report it? Yes, the
conscientious scholar must answer, we would say precisely that, and sociologists of science do say precisely that.)

   This is not a point of view likely to make much headway with professional journalists. "News and news programmes could almost be called
random reactions to random events," a reporter told sociologist Graham
Murdock. "Again and again, the main reason why they turn out as they do
is accident—accident of a kind which recurs so haphazardly as to defeat
statistical examination" (1973: 163). The study of the generation of news aims
to find and make plausible an order behind this sense of accident (and to
understand as ideology journalists' failure to recognize such an order).

   The sociology of the generation of news goes back some years. Max
Weber wrote of the social standing of the journalist as a political person:
Robert Park, an ex-journalist himself, wrote about the generation of news
and news itself as a form of knowledge, and Helen MacGill Hughes wrote
an early study of human interest stories. But the formal study of how news
organizations produce news products dates to the American studies in the
early 1950s of "gatekeepers."

   Social psychologist Kurt Lewin coined the term "gatekeeper," and several social scientists (White, 1950; Gieber, 1964) applied it to journalism.
David Manning White studied a middle-aged wire editor at a small midwestern newspaper. He decided which wire service stories would run in the paper
and which would not. For one week, "Mr. Gates" (as White called him) made
available to the researcher every piece of wire copy, both those he rejected
and those he selected to print in the paper. He then wrote down a reason for
rejection on every story he rejected. Some of these reasons were not very
illuminating—"not enough space."

   Others were technical or professional—"dull writing" or "drags too
much." Still others were explicitly political—"propaganda" or "He's too
Red." These last greatly influenced White's interpretation of gatekeeping
although, in fact, explicitly political, opinionated reasons for rejection amounted
to just 18 out of 423 cases. Mr. Gates admitted that he did not like Truman's
economic policies, that he was anti-Catholic, and that his views on these
subjects affected his news judgement. So there was reason for White to
conclude that "we see how highly subjective, how based on the 'gate-

keeper's' own set of experiences, attitudes and expectations the communication of 'news' really is." Can Mr. Gates's judgement be attributed to personal subjectivity? If so, we would expect some variation among wire editors if a larger sample were studied. Walter Gieber found otherwise in a 1956 study of 16 wire editors in Wisconsin (Gieber, 1964). All selected news items in essentially the same way. Gieber found the telegraph editor to be preoccupied with the mechanical pressures of his work rather than the social meanings and impact of the news. His personal evaluations rarely entered into his selection process; the values of his employer were an accepted part of the newsroom environment.

The telegraph editor, then, was not practising politics in selecting the news. He was doing a rote task. He was, as Gieber reported, "concerned with goals of production, bureaucratic routine and interpersonal relations within the newsroom" (1964: 175).

The term "gatekeeper" is still in use and provides a handy, if not altogether appropriate, metaphor for the relation of news organizations to news products. A problem with the metaphor is that it leaves "information" sociologically untouched, a pristine material that comes to the gate already prepared; the journalist as "gatekeeper" simply decides which pieces of prefabricated news will be allowed through the gate. The gatekeeper's job, then, is necessarily quantitative, reducing the amount of information available to a sum that fits the size of a paper or length of a news show. Moreover, the metaphor individualizes a bureaucratic phenomenon and implicitly transforms organizational bias into individual subjectivity, as Gieber's study points out. Gieber's analysis is actually a refutation of White's.

A "gatekeeper" needs some criteria for selecting which items of information to let through the gate, which to hold back. But this underestimates the complexity of the situation; news items are not simply selected but constructed. The gatekeeper metaphor describes neither this nor the feedback loops in which generators of information for the press anticipate the criteria of the gatekeepers in their efforts to get through the gate, like teenagers trying to figure out how best to talk and look in order to get admitted to X-rated movies or establishments that serve liquor. How do you "pass" as an adult? How do you get a piece of information to "pass" as news? The whole industry of public relations, which after the First World War emerged as a major intermediary between government and business on the one hand, and journalism on the other (Schudson, 1978), trades on its expertise in knowing how to construct items that "pass."

If the gatekeeper model is ultimately as confused as it is suggestive, what approaches might work better? Three perspectives on the topic are commonly employed. The first is the view of political economy that relates the outcome of the news process to the economic structure of the news organization. Everything in between is a black box that need not be examined to understand the fundamental consonance between profit-seeking industry and conservative, system-maintaining news. This view appears in its most theoretically sophisticated and self-critical form in British media studies (Murdock, 1982).

The second approach is that of mainstream sociology, the study of social organization and the sociology of occupations and occupational ideology that, unlike the standard political economy perspective, takes as the central problem the journalists' professed autonomy and decision-making power and tries to understand how journalists' efforts on the job are constrained by organizational and occupational routines.

Third, but rarely explicitly developed, there is a "culturological" or anthropological approach, if you will, one that emphasizes the constraining force of broad cultural symbol systems regardless of the details of organizational and occupational routines. There are also semiotic analyses of journalism and journalistic ideologies that might well fit under this rubric but they often fail to make precise what their explanatory scheme actually is.

All three of these approaches have strengths and weaknesses I want to discuss here. All of them, even taken together, have thus far fallen short of a comparative and historical social science of news production.

The Political Economy of News

This perspective is often characterized and caricatured as "conspiracy theory" or as a rather simpleminded notion that there is a ruling directorate of the capitalist class that dictates to editors and reporters what to run in the newspapers. (Note that sociologists of news have examined almost exclusively news in capitalist societies. This is obviously a limitation to any comprehensive understanding of news.) Since this ignores the observable fact that reporters often initiate stories of their own, that editors rarely meet with publishers, and that most working journalists have no idea who sits on the board of directors of the institutions they work for, in this form the political economy perspective is easily dismissed. However, its more sophisticated versions not only add to but are essential to an understanding of the generation of news.

Here, as elsewhere, a key issue is what aspect of "news" one wants to explain or understand. Is it the conservative, system-maintaining character of news? This is more often than not the feature of news that political economy scholars focus on—but there are many other possibilities. One of them, of course, appears to be the exact opposite—the press has sometimes been characterized as adversarial or even nihilistic, system attacking or system denigrating, government toppling or crime promoting. In other cases, there are finer features of news that analysts want to understand. Why does news seem to focus on individuals rather than systems and structures? Why does news appear to be so heavily dependent on official sources? Or analysts may focus on features of the literary character of news—why is there a "summary lead" rather than a chronological opening to a news story? Why is a television sound bite in American network news usually no more than 10 or 15 seconds long? Why do city hall reporters summarize the highlights of official meetings rather than report the whole, often disorganized and desultory proceedings—and what consequences are there to thereby "rationalizing" the portrait of the political process? (Paletz et al., 1971). Perhaps the most complex question of "what to explain" concerns whether one should find distressing, and try to explain, the deviation of the media from "fair" and "objective" reporting or, instead, should find disturbing and try to understand how it is that "fair," "objective" reporting presents a portrait of the world in tune with the view of dominant groups in society. Thus critics have objected to the Glasgow Media Group's studies for its castigation of television news for bias when the more important point may be that broadcast news programmes "achieve their ideological effectivity *precisely through* their observation of the *statutory* requirements of balance and impartiality" (Bennett, 1982: 306).

The "political economy" approach generally does not attend to fine-grained questions but looks at the big picture. This is both its strength and its weakness. The link between the larger political economy of society and day-to-day practices in journalism is, as Graham Murdock has observed, "oblique." Still, he concludes, and despite journalistic autonomy, "the basic definition of the situation that underpins the news reporting of political events, very largely coincides with the definition provided by the legitimated power holders" (1973: 158).

For an American, that kind of conclusion was a lot easier to come to before Watergate than after. As Peter Dreier (1982) observes, much of the interest in institutional- or organizational-level analysis of the news emerged in the late 1960s because "instrumental" perspectives from political economy did not seem to describe current media activism. While one can still argue that the outcome of Watergate was just what legitimated power holders in some circles wanted, it stretches the concept of "legitimated power holders" to the breaking point if a two-term president at the centre of political life in Washington for two decades, is not among the power holders. (It is also a problem, as Dreier, 1982, observes, to understand why, if the large corporations and the media work hand-in-glove, the corporations in the early 1970s should have been aghast at the media coverage of politics, the environment, and business.) At the same time, there is normally little problem in demonstrating that, at least in broad terms, news "coincides with" and "reinforces" the "definition of the political situation evolved by the political elite" (Murdock, 1973: 172). The behavior of the American press in questioning the Vietnam War can be understood as happening only because the political elite was divided much more profoundly than it ordinarily is. Even then, the press seems largely to have gone about its normal business of citing official leaders; it just so happened that the officials were at odds with one another (Hallin, 1986).

For understanding the broad outlines of the news product, economic or political-economic explanations are often well suited. Curran et al. ask why elite and mass-oriented newspapers provide such different fare, when reader surveys find that different classes in fact prefer to read very similar materials. Their explanation centres on the value to advertisers of advertising in papers that attract a small, concentrated elite audience. The expense of having an ad reach what American advertisers now call an "upscale" audience is lower if a concentration of this audience can be found in one publication—without having to pay the cost of reaching thousands of extraneous readers.

It is true that American media corporations are interlocked with other major corporations (Dreier and Weinberg, 1979). It is equally true that fewer and fewer corporations control more and more of the American news media (Bagdikian, 1983; Compaine, 1979). In these circumstances it would be a shock to find the press a hotbed of radical thought. But, then, critical or radical thought in any society at any time is exceptional. That there could be a moment of critical upheaval in American society and in the American media in the late 1960s raises doubts about any political-economic perspective that attributes power of Orwellian proportion to the capitalist class. The abilities of a capitalist class to manipulate opinion and create a closed system of discourse are limited; ideology in contemporary capitalism is "contested territory," as many analysts have observed.

The most recent and comprehensive statement of a political-economic perspective in the United States is Edward S. Herman and Noam Chomsky's *Manufacturing Consent* (1988). They offer what they call a "propaganda model" of the mass media, the view that the media "serve to mobilize support for the special interests that dominate the state and private activity" (1988: xi). For them, news serves established power and, although they recognize some variability in the American press, they do not locate any essential difference between the role of leading news institutions in the United States and *Pravda* in the Soviet Union (judging from half a dozen instances where they directly liken the American press to *Pravda*). For them, this follows necessarily from the fact that the news is produced by a relatively concentrated industry of several dozen profit-making corporations, that the industry is dependent on advertising for its profits, that it is dependent on government officials for its sources, that it is intimated by right-wing pressure groups, and that it is imbued with anti-communist ideology. Their "propaganda model" is a rather blunt instrument for examining a subtle system, a system with more heterogeneity and more capacity for change (however limited that capacity) than they give it credit for. Their documented examples of American foreign affairs reporting distorted by an anti-communist consensus remain quite powerful, although not so careful, it seems to me, as Daniel Hallin's evidence that news coverage of Central America (one of the key cases Herman and Chomsky take up) has been less dominated by an anti-communist frame of reference than foreign affairs reporting a generation earlier (Hallin, 1983).

If there is serious ideological contestation (as Herman and Chomsky would deny), how does it take place? What institutional mechanisms or cultural traditions or contradictions of power provide room for debate and revision? The political economy perspective typically does not say. Intent on establishing connections among different key social institutions, political economy generally fails to describe formally what the disconnections are. In contrast, Daniel Hallin, borrowing from the work of Jürgen Habermas, has argued that the media are formally "disconnected" from other ruling agencies because they must attend as much to their own legitimation as to furthering the legitimation of the capitalist system as a whole (Hallin, 1985). If they fail to attend to their own integrity and their own credibility with audiences, they may in fact "simply become ineffective ideological institutions." This, I suspect, is exactly what has happened to official media in eastern Europe; readers there are famous for recognizing that the only reading worth doing is reading "between the lines." In any event, the weaknesses in the political economy perspective lead necessarily to greater scholarly attention to the social organization of the newswork and the actual practices of creating the news product.

The Social Organization of Newswork

In an influential essay (1974), Harvey Molotch and Marilyn Lester created a typology of news stories according to whether a news "occurrence" is planned or unplanned, and whether the planners of the occurrence are or are not also the promoters of it as news. If an event is planned and then promoted as news by its planners, this is a "routine" news item. If the event is planned but promoted by someone different from the agent of the occurrence, it is a "scandal." If the event is unplanned and then promoted as news by someone other than its hapless instigator, it is an "accident."

This typology defines news by the way it comes to the awareness of a news organization. In none of the three news types is the occurrence a spontaneous event in the world that the news media discover on their own by surveying the world scene. For Molotch and Lester, it is a mistake to try to compare news accounts to "reality" in the way journalism critics ordinarily do, labelling the discrepancy "bias." Instead, they seek out the purposes that create one reality instead of another. The news provides a "reality" that is "the political work by which events are constituted by those who happen to currently hold power" (1974: 111). Molotch and Lester reject what they call the "objectivity assumption" in journalism—not that the media are objective but that there is a real world to be objective about. For Molotch and Lester, newspapers reflect not a world "out there" but "the practices of those who have the power to determine the experiences of others" (1974: 54).

In what might these practices consist?

Mark Fishman conducted a participant-observation study of newspaper work in a California newspaper with a daily circulation of 45,000 and a full-time editorial staff of 37 (Fishman, 1980). He finds that journalists are highly attuned to bureaucratic organizations of government and that *the world is bureaucratically oriented for journalists*" (1980: 51). That is, the organization of "beats" is such that reporters get the largest share of their news from official government agencies. "The journalist's view of the society as bureaucratically structured is the very basis upon which the journalist is able to detect events" (1980: 51). One of the greatest advantages of dealing with bureaucracies for the journalist is that the bureaucracies "provide for the continuous detection of events" (1980: 52). The bureaucrat provides a reliable and steady source of news.

One study after another comes up with essentially the same observation, and it matters not whether the study is at the national, state, or local level—the story of journalism, on a day-to-day basis, is the story of the interaction of reporters and officials. Some claim officials generally have the upper hand (Gans, 1979: 116; Cohen, 1963: 267). Some media critics, including many government officials, say reporters do (Hess, 1984: 109). But there is little doubt that the centre of news generation is the link between reporter and official, the interaction of the representatives of the news bureaucracies and the government bureaucracies. This is clear especially when one examines the actual daily practices of journalists. "The only important tool of the reporter is his news sources and how he uses them," a reporter covering state government told Delmer Dunne (1963: 41).

Stephen Hess confirms this in his study of Washington correspondents that found reporters had conducted 3,967 interviews for 865 stories sampled and that Washington reporters "use no documents in the preparation of nearly three-quarters of their stories" (Hess, 1981: 17-18). Hess does not count press releases as documents—these are, of course, another means of communication directly from official to reporter. Knowing sources, Gaye Tuchman observed, is a mark of professional status for a reporter. She cites one reporter as saying of another, "He's the best political reporter in the city. He has more sources than anyone else" (1978: 68). It is clear that the reporter-official connection makes news an important tool of government and other established authorities. The corollary is that "resource-poor organizations" have great difficulty in getting news coverage (Goldenberg, 1975). If they are to be covered, as Todd Gitlin's study of SDS indicated, they must adjust to modes of organizational interaction more like those of established organizations (Gitlin, 1980).

There has been much more attention to reporter-official relations than to reporter-editor relations, a second critical aspect of the social organization of newswork. Despite some suggestive early work on the ways in which reporters engage in self-censorship when they have an eye fixed on pleasing an editor (Breed, 1955: 80), systematic sociological research has not been especially successful in this domain. Certainly case studies of newswork regularly note the effects—usually baleful—of editorial intervention (Crouse, 1973: 186; Gitlin, 1980: 64-65; Hallin, 1986: 22). But studies rarely look at the social relations of newswork from an editor's view. Most research focuses on the gathering of news rather than on its writing, rewriting, and "play" in the press.

This is particularly unfortunate when research suggests that it is in the *play* of a story that real influence comes. Hallin (1986), Herman and Chomsky (1988), and Lipstadt (1986) all argue that in the press of a liberal society like the United States, lots of news, including dissenting or adversarial information and opinion, gets into the newspaper. The question is *where* that information appears and how it is inflected. Hallin interestingly suggests there was a "reverse inverted pyramid" of news in much Vietnam reporting. The nearer the information was to the truth, the farther down in the story it appeared (1986: 78).

If one theoretical source for the sociology of news has been symbolic interactionism or social constructionist views of society (as in the work of Molotch and Lester, Tuchman, and others), a complementary source has been organizational or bureaucratic theory. If, on the one hand, the creation of news is seen as the social production of "reality," on the other hand it is taken to be the social manufacture of an organizational product, one that can be studied like other manufactured goods. This latter point of view is evident, for instance, in Edward Jay Epstein's early study (1973) that grew out of a political science seminar at Harvard on organizational theory. That seminar took as its working assumption that members of the organization "modified their own personal values in accordance with the requisites of the organization" (1973: xiv). One needed then to understand organizations, not individuals, to analyse the "output" of organizations—in this case, news. Epstein's study, based on fieldwork at national network news programmes in 1968 and 1969, emphasized organizational, economic, and technical requirements of television news production in explaining the news product. Epstein's study, like many others, finds the technical constraints of television news particularly notable. These, of course, have changed radically and rapidly in the past two decades—a serious historical account of this technological revolution remains to be written.

Who are the journalists who cover beats, interview sources, rewrite press releases from government bureaus, and rarely (but occasionally) take the initiative in ferreting out hidden or complex stories? If the organizational theorists are generally correct, it does not matter who they are or where they come from; they will be socialized quickly into the values and routines in the daily rituals of journalism. Still, there is great interest among some scholars in determining what the social backgrounds of media personnel may be as clues to the kind of bias they will bring to their work. In the United States this has led to controversy over whether newsworkers are (too) "liberal," in the peculiarly American sense of that term, or not. Studies by S. Robert Lichter, Stanley Rothman, and Linda S. Lichter, culminating in *The Media Elite: America's New Powerbrokers* (1986) make the case that news in the United States is "biased" in a liberal direction because journalists at the elite news organizations are themselves liberal. Their survey of 240 elite journalists finds a pattern familiar from earlier work—that many of these journalists describe themselves as liberals and tend to vote Democratic. They argue that these national journalists are a "homogeneous" liberal, cosmopolitan band with growing wealth and power.

"Homogeneous," however, does not describe a group in which 54 percent describe themselves as liberal, 46 percent as moderate or conservative (Lichter et al., 1986: 28). The group is more socially liberal (53 percent say adultery is not wrong) than economically liberal (only 13 percent think government should own big corporations). The journalists are not the "liberals" that the Lichters and Rothman sneeringly suggest. They fully accept the framework of capitalism although some of them wish it had a human face. They may be better termed, as Herbert Gans characterized them in his own participant-observation study of elite journalists, "Progressive" (1985).

The real problem in Rothman and the Lichters' approach is that it offers no convincing evidence that the news product reflects the personal views of journalists rather than the views of officials whose positions they are reporting (Gans, 1985). Journalists are avowedly and often passionately committed to their ideology of dispassion, their sense of professionalism, their allegiance to fairness or objectivity as it has been professionally defined. They have a professional commitment to shielding their work from their personal political leanings. Moreover, their political leanings may be weak. Several observers find leading American journalists not so much liberal or conservative as apolitical. Robinson and Sheehan (1983) interviewed CBS and UPI reporters and found that most seemed to be moderates or just not very political. Stephen Hess came to a similar conclusion in studying Washington reporters: "Washington reporters are more apolitical than press critics contend. The slant of Washington news is more a product of the angle from which it is observed than from ideology" (1981: 115).

What is fundamental in organizational approaches, as opposed to the social-compositional approach of Rothman and the Lichters, is the emphasis on (a) constraints imposed by organizations despite the private intentions of the individual actors and (b) the inevitability of "social construction" of reality in any system. The latter point is crucial. Many (though not all) analysts from a social-organizational perspective abandon any strong claim that there is a "reality" out there that journalists or journalistic organizations distort. News is not a report on a factual world; news is "a depletable consumer product that must be made fresh daily" (Tuchman, 1978: 179). It is not a gathering of facts that already exists; indeed, as Tuchman has argued, facts are defined organizationally—facts are "pertinent information gathered by professionally validated methods specifying the relationship between what is known and how it is known. In news, verification of facts is both a political and a professional accomplishment" (1978: 82-83).

Culturological Approaches

For Molotch and Lester and Tuchman, the fact that news is "constructed" suggests that it is *socially* constructed, elaborated in the interaction of the news-making players with one another. But the emphasis on the human construction of news can be taken in another direction. Anthropologist Marshall Sahlins has written in a different context that "an event is not just a happening in the world; it is a *relation* between a certain happening and a given symbolic system" (1985: 153). Molotch and Lester, Tuchman, and others who emphasize the "production of culture" do not focus on the "cultural givens" within which everyday interaction happens in the first place. These cultural givens, while they may be uncovered by detailed historical analysis, cannot be linked to features of social organization at the moment of study. They are a part of culture—a given symbolic system, within which and in relation to which reporters and officials go about their duties.

This "cultural" perspective on the news has not been codified nor established as any sort of "school." Indeed, I think that most understandings of the generation of news merge a "cultural" view (or submerge it) with the social organization view. It is, however, analytically distinct. Where the organizational view finds interactional determinants of news in the relations between people, the cultural view finds symbolic determinants of news in the relations between ideas and symbols. This does not mean that the culturologist must repair to universal categories—although this is one possibility. Frank Pearce, for instance, in examining media coverage of homosexuals in Britain (1973), takes as a theoretical starting point anthropologist Mary Douglas's view that societies like to keep their cultural concepts clean and neat and are troubled by "anomalies" that do not fit the preconceived categories of the culture. Homosexuality is an anomaly in societies that take as fundamental the opposition and relationship of male and female; thus homosexuals provide a culturally charged topic for story-telling that seeks to preserve or reinforce the conventional moral order of society—and its conceptual or symbolic foundation. News stories about homosexuals, Pearce says, may be moral tales, "a negative reference point . . . an occasion to reinforce conventional moral values by telling a moral tale. Through these means tensions in the social system can be dealt with and 'conventionalized' " (1973: 293).

If Mary Douglas is one theoretical reference point for Pearce, Sigmund Freud is another (though unstated). Pearce cites R. D. Laing's observation that people enjoy reading the kind of material to be found in the sensational press because it enables them vicariously to experience pleasurable feelings they are otherwise forbidden to discuss or imagine. "These pleasurable sensations that we have denied but not annihilated," Pearce writes, "may be lived through again by means of the sensational newspaper" (1973: 291).

Incidentally, this sort of observation brings into the analysis the news institutions' sense of their audience, something relatively rare in the sociology of news. Of course, there is a large literature in communication studies on the "uses and gratifications" audiences get from the mass media. But these studies are rarely invoked by analysts to explain why we get the sort of news we do. Is this an important omission? Perhaps not, because journalists typically know very little about their audience. Herbert Gans found that the reporters and editors at news weeklies and network television programmes he studied

> had little knowledge about the actual audience and rejected feedback
> from it. Although they had a vague image of the audience, they paid

little attention to it; instead, they filmed and wrote for their superiors and for themselves, assuming that what interested them would interest the audience. (1979: 230)

(But this may be an area where more research would help.)

Paul Hartmann and Charles Husband find it important for their analysis of mass media coverage of racial conflict to note that "the British cultural tradition contains elements derogatory to foreigners, particularly blacks. The media operate within the culture and are obliged to use cultural symbols" (1973: 274). This is presumably true regardless of the ownership of the media or the social relations of reporters and officials. This is a cultural, rather than social, line of explanation.

A culturalist account of news would seem relevant when trying to understand journalists' vague renderings of how they know "news" when they see it. Stuart Hall, in his essay on news photographs, tried to define the indefinable "news values" or "news sense" that journalists regularly talk about. He writes:

"News values" are one of the most opaque structures of meaning in modern society. All "true journalists" are supposed to possess it: few can or are willing to identify and define it. Journalists speak of "the news" as if events select themselves. Further, they speak as if which is the "most significant" news story, and which "news angles" are most salient are divinely inspired. Yet of the millions of events which occur every day in the world, only a tiny portion ever become visible as "potential news stories," and of this proportion, only a small fraction are actually produced as the day's news in the news media. We appear to be dealing, then, with a "deep structure" whose function as a selective device is un-transparent even to those who professionally most know how to operate it. (1973: 181)

This seems to me exactly right. And Gaye Tuchman is equally correct when she writes that "news judgment is the sacred knowledge, the secret ability of the newsman which differentiates him from other people" (1972: 672). The question is what to make of it. It seems to me too simple, though common now, to label this as "ideology" or the "common sense" of a hegemonic system. It makes of human beliefs and attitudes a more unified, intentional, and functional system than they are. Many beliefs that ruling groups may use for their own ends are rooted much more deeply in human consciousness and are to be found much more widely in human societies than capitalism or socialism or industrialism or any other modern system of social organization and domination. Patriarchal and sexist outlooks, for instance, may well be turned to the service of capitalism, but this does not make them "capitalist" in origin nor does it mean that they are perfectly or inherently homologous to capitalist structures or requirements for their preservation.

A specific example may illustrate the many dimensions of this problem. Why, Johan Galtung and Mari Ruge (1970) ask, are news stories so often "personified"? Why do reporters write of persons and not structures, of individuals and not social forces?

They cite a number of possible explanations, some of which are "cultural." There is cultural idealism—the Western view that individuals are masters of their own destiny, responsible for their acts through the free will they exercise. There is the nature of storytelling itself, with the need in narrative to establish "identification." There is also what they call the "frequency factor"—that people act during a time span that fits the frequency of the news media (daily) better than do the actions of "structures" that are much harder to connect with specific events in a 24-hour cycle.

This last point is particularly interesting. Is it a "social structural" or a "cultural" phenomenon? In some respects it is structural—if the media operated monthly or annually rather than daily, perhaps they would more customarily speak of social forces. Indeed, examining journalism's "year-end reviews" would very likely turn up more attention to social trends and structural changes than the daily news. But, then, is the fact that so much of the press operates on a daily basis for the most part structural or cultural? Is there some basic primacy to the daily cycle of the press, of business, of government, of sleeping and waking, that makes the institutions of daily journalism essentially human and person-centred in scale and inescapably so?

Or might there be some more or less universal processes of human perception that leads to an emphasis on the individual? Does this have less to do with something peculiarly American or Western or capitalist than it does with what psychologists refer to as the "fundamental attribution error" in human causal thinking—attributing to individuals in the foreground responsibility or agency for causation that should be attributed to background situations or large-scale trends or structures?

One need not adopt assumptions about universal properties of human nature and human interest (although it would be foolish to dismiss them out of hand) to acknowledge aspects of news-generation that go far beyond what political, economic, or sociological analysis of news organizations can handle. Richard Hoggart has written that the most important filter through which news is constructed is "the cultural air we breathe, the whole ideological atmosphere of our society, which tells us that some things can be said and others had best not be said" (Bennett, 1982: 303). That "cultural air" is one that in part ruling groups and institutions create but it is in part one in whose context their own establishment takes place.

The cultural air has both a form and content. The content—the substance of taken-for-granted values—has often been discussed. Gans (1979) arrived at a list for American journalism that includes ethnocentrism, altruistic democracy, responsible capitalism, small town pastoralism, individualism, and moderatism as core, unquestioned values of American news. They are the unquestioned and generally unnoticed background assumptions through which the news is gathered and within which it is framed. If these elements of content fit rather well conventional notions of ideology or the common sense of a hegemonic system (Gans calls them "para-ideology"), aspects of form operate at a level more remote from ideology as generally understood.

By "form," I refer to assumptions about narrative, storytelling, human interest, and the conventions of photographic and linguistic presentation that shape the presentation of all of the news the media produce. Weaver (1975) has shown some systematic differences between the inverted-pyramid structure of print news and the "thematic" structure of television news; Schudson (1982) has argued that the inverted-pyramid form is a peculiar development of late 19th-century American journalism and one that implicitly authorized the journalist as political expert and helped redefine politics itself as a subject appropriately discussed by experts rather than partisans; Hallin and Mancini (1984) demonstrate in a comparison of television news in Italy and the United States that formal conventions of news reporting often attributed to the technology of television by analysts or to "the nature of things" by journalists in fact stem from peculiar features of the political culture of the country in question. At any rate, sociological work that recognizes news as a form of literature makes an important contribution, demonstrating that one key resource that journalists work with is the cultural tradition of storytelling and picture-making and sentence construction they inherit, with a number of vital assumptions about the world built in.

Conclusions

The approaches to the study of news I have reviewed are often inclined to ignore the possibilities for change in the nature of newswork. When William Rivers studied Washington correspondents in 1960, a generation after Leo Rosten had studied them, asking some of the same questions Rosten had asked, he found significant differences. Most important, he found reporters more free from directives from their home offices than they had been in the 1930s.

When Leon Sigal studied changes in the front pages of the *New York Times* and the *Washington Post* he found that from the 1950s to the early 1970s news stories were significantly more likely to be based on more than one source and to include material gathered from (sometimes disaffected or dissident) bureaucrats lower down in the organizational hierarchy. My own research found that in the 1880s news stories of presidential addresses did not try to summarize the key points of a speech but that by 1910 a "summary lead" was a standard form, an assertion, in a sense, of the authority of the press to *define* the key political reality of the day. Anthony Smith (1980) found major changes in the nature of newswork in British journalism in his review of changes in journalistic values and practices. In general, historical studies of the press reveal significantly different patterns of newsgathering and newswriting over time that are rarely referenced or accounted for in contemporary sociological studies of news.

All three approaches reviewed here tend to be indifferent to comparative as well as to historical studies. Even the Anglo-American interchange this journal has helped to foster is reluctant to engage in truly comparative work. Comparative research is cumbersome, of course, even in the age of word processors and computer networking. Moreover, media studies are genuinely linked to national political issues—they are an academic metadiscourse on the daily defining of political reality. The motive for research, then, is normally conceived in isolation from comparative concerns. If this strengthens the immediate political relevance of media studies, it weakens its longer-term value as social science.

References

Bagdikian, B. (1983) *The Media Monopoly.* Boston: Beacon.

Bennett, T. (1982) "Media, 'Reality,' Signification," pp. 287-308 in M. Gurevitch, T. Bennett, J. Curran, and J. Woollacott (eds.), *Culture, Society and the Media.* London: Methuen.

Breed, W. (1952, 1980) *The Newspaperman, News and Society.* New York: Arno.

Breed, W. (1955) "Social Control in the Newsroom: A Functional Analysis," *Social Forces,* 33: 326-335.

Cohen, B. C. (1963) *The Press and Foreign Policy.* Princeton, NJ: Princeton University Press.

Cohen, S. and J. Young (eds.) (1973) *The Manufacture of News: A Reader.* Beverly Hills, CA: Sage.

Compaine, B. (1979) *Who Owns the Media?* White Plains, NY: Knowledge Industry Publications.

Crouse, T. (1973) *The Boys on the Bus.* New York: Ballantine.

Curran, J., A. Douglas and G. Whannel (1980) "The Political Economy of the Human-Interest Story," pp. 288-342 in Anthony Smith (ed.), *Newspapers and Democracy.* Cambridge, MA: MIT Press.

Dreier, P. (1982) "Capitalists vs. the Media: An Analysis of an Ideological Mobilization Among Business Leaders." *Media Culture and Society,* 4: 111-132.

Dreier, P. and S. Weinberg (1979) "Interlocking Directorates," *Columbia Journalism Review,* November/December: 51-68.

Dunne, D. D. (1969) *Public Officials and the Press.* Reading, MA: Addison-Wesley.

Epstein, E. J. (1973) *News From Nowhere.* New York: Random House.

Fishman, M. (1980) *Manufacturing the News.* Austin: University of Texas Press.

Galtung, J. and M. Ruge (1970) "The Structure of Foreign News: The Presentation of the Congo, Cuba and Cyprus Crises in Four Foreign Newspapers," pp. 259-298 in J. Tunstall (ed.), *Media Sociology: A Reader.* University of Illinois Press.

Gans, H. J. (1979) *Deciding What's News: A Study of CBS Evening News, NBC Nightly News, Newsweek and Time.* New York: Pantheon.

Gans, H. J. (1985) "Are U.S. Journalists Dangerously Liberal?" *Columbia Journalism Review,* November/December: 29-33.

Gieber, W. (1964) "News Is What Newspapermen Make It," in L. A. Dexter and D. Manning, *White People, Society and Mass Communications.* New York: Free Press.

Gitlin, T. (1980) *The Whole World Is Watching.* Berkeley: University of California Press.

Goldenberg, E. (1975) *Making the Papers.* Lexington, MA: D. C. Heath.

Gurevitch, M., T. Bennett, J. Curran and J. Woollacott (eds.) (1982) *Culture, Society and the Media.* London: Methuen.

Hall, S. (1973) "The Determination of News Photographs," pp. 176-190 in S. Cohen and J. Young (eds.), *The Manufacture of News: A Reader.* Beverly Hills, CA: Sage.

Hallin, D. C. (1983) "The Media Go to War—From Vietnam to Central America," *NACLA Report on the Americas,* July/August.

Hallin, D. C. (1985) "The American News Media: A Critical Theory Perspective," pp. 121-146 in J. Forrester (ed.), *Critical Theory and Public Life*. Cambridge, MA.

Hallin, D. C. (1986) *"The Uncensored War": The Media and Vietnam*. New York: Oxford University Press.

Hallin, D. C. and P. Mancini (1984) "Speaking of the President: Political Structure and Representational Form in U.S. and Italian Television News," *Theory and Society*, 13: 829-850.

Hartmann, P. and C. Husband (1973) "The Mass Media and Racial Conflict," pp. 270-283 in S. Cohen and J. Young (eds.), *The Manufacture of News: A Reader*. Beverly Hills, CA: Sage.

Herman, E. S. and N. Chomsky (1988) *Manufacturing Consent*. New York: Pantheon.

Hess, S. (1981) *The Washington Reporters*. Washington, DC: Brookings Institution.

Hess, S. (1984) *The Government/Press Connection*. Washington, DC: Brookings Institution.

Hughes, H. M. (1940) *News and the Human Interest Story*. Chicago: University of Chicago Press.

Lichter, S. R., S. Rothman and L. S. Lichter (1986) *The Media Elite: America's New Powerbrokers*. Bethesda, MD: Adler and Adler.

Lipstadt, D. (1986) *Beyond Belief: The American Press and the Coming of the Holocaust 1933-1945*. New York: Free Press.

Molotch, H. and M. Lester (1974) "News as Purposive Behavior: On the Strategic Use of Routine Events, Accidents, and Scandals," *American Sociological Review*, 39: 101-112.

Murdock, G. (1973) "Political Deviance: The Press Presentation of a Militant Mass Demonstration," pp. 156-175 in S. Cohen and J. Young (eds.), *The Manufacture of News: A Reader*. Beverly Hills, CA: Sage.

Murdock, G. (1982) "Large Corporations and the Control of the Communications Industries," pp. 118-150 in M. Gurevitch, T. Bennett, J. Curran and J. Woollacott (eds.), *Culture, Society and the Media*. London: Methuen.

Paletz, D., P. Reichert and B. McIntyre (1971) "How the Media Support Local Governmental Authority," *Public Opinion Quarterly*, 35: 80-92.

Park, R. E. (1923) "The Natural History of the Newspaper," *American Journal of Sociology*, 29: 273-289.

Pearce, F. (1973) "How to Be Immoral and Ill, Pathetic and Dangerous, All at the Same Time: Mass Media and the Homosexual," pp. 284-301 in S. Cohen and J. Young (eds.), *The Manufacture of News: A Reader*. Beverly Hills, CA: Sage.

Rivers, W. (1962) "The Correspondents After 25 Years," *Columbia Journalism Review*, 1: 4-10.

Robinson, M. J. and M. A. Sheehan (1983) *Over the Wire and on TV*. New York: Russell Sage.

Sahlins, M. (1985) *Islands of History*. Chicago: University of Chicago Press.

Schudson, M. (1978) *Discovering the News: A Social History of American Newspapers*. New York: Basic Books.

Schudson, M. (1982) "The Politics of Narrative Form: The Emergence of News Conventions in Print and Television," *Daedalus*, 111: 97-113.

Sigal, L. V. (1973) *Reporters and Officials*. Lexington, MA: Lexington Books.

Smith, A. (1980) *Newspapers and Democracy*. Cambridge, MA: MIT Press.

Tuchman, G. (1972) "Objectivity as Strategic Ritual: An Examination of Newsmen's Notions of Objectivity," *American Journal of Sociology*, 77: 660-679.

Tuchman, G. (1976) "Telling Stories," *Journal of Communication* 26 (Fall): 93-97.

Tuchman, G. (1978) *Making News: A Study in the Construction of Reality*. New York: Free Press.

Weaver, P. (1975) "Newspaper News and Television News," in D. Cater and R. Adler (eds.), *Television as a Social Force*. New York: Praeger.

Weber, M. (1921, 1946) "Politics as a Vocation," pp. 77-128 in H. Gerth and C. W. Mills (eds.), *From Max Weber: Essays in Sociology*. New York: Oxford University Press.

White, D. M. (1950) "The 'Gate Keeper': A Case Study in the Selection of News," *Journalism Quarterly*, 27: 383-390.

CHAPTER **2**

Has Communication Explained Journalism?

Barbie Zelizer

Regardless of one's view of the discipline of communication, journalism has occupied a central place in it. Communication researchers have long used journalism to explain how communication works, and journalists' visibility in mediated discourse has made them a target for scholars seeking to understand the work of communication practitioners and the communication process. But has communication done its job? Has communication scholarship provided the tools necessary to explain how and why journalism works? Has it explained why publics let reporters present themselves as cultural authorities for events of the "real world"? In short, has communication adequately explained journalism and journalistic authority?

This article argues that it has not. Journalism researchers, I contend, have allowed media power to flourish by not addressing the ritual and collective functions it fulfills for journalists themselves. The article argues for a more interdisciplinary approach to journalism scholarship to provide a fuller account of media power. It also briefly considers the notions of *performance, narrative, ritual,* and *interpretive community* as alternative frames through which to consider journalism.

From *Journal of Communication*, 1993, Vol. 43, No. 4, pp. 80-88. Used by permission of Oxford University Press.

Power of the Fourth Estate

Media power is one of the outstanding conundrums of contemporary public discourse, in that we still cannot account for the media's persistent presence as arbiters of events of the real world. Audiences tend to question journalistic authority only when journalists' versions of events conflict with the audience's view of the same events. And while critical appraisals of the media should be part of everyday life, journalistic power burgeons largely due to the public's general acquiescence and its reluctance to question journalism's parameters and fundamental legitimacy.

In part, this has had to do with the rather basic fact that journalists do not invite or appreciate criticism. The media, Lule recently argued, "engage in critical evaluation of every institution in society except [themselves]" (1992, p. 92). Journalists ignore criticism leveled at them in journalism reviews, academic conferences, books, and the alternative press, trying to maintain a stance of autonomous indifference both vis-à-vis the events of the real world and that world's most vocal inhabitants, their critics.

Yet scholars studying journalism have also been partly responsible for the public's inability to grasp fully the power of journalists. News has been approached primarily by communication researchers "as a sociological problem" (Roshco, 1975, p. 2). Inquiry has favored examining the dominant rather than deviant form of practice. It has addressed the identifiable and relatively finished products—news text (Fowler, 1991; Glasgow University Media Group, 1980; van Dijk, 1988), news-gathering setting (Fishman, 1980; Gans, 1979; Gitlin, 1980; Tuchman, 1978), or news audience (Graber, 1988; Robinson & Levy, 1986)—rather than the continuous negotiation toward such products. It has generated linear notions of media power that have explained it as a dominance over the weak by the strong, supporting the view, recently voiced by sociologist Dennis Wrong, that power "is the capacity of some persons to produce intended and foreseen effects on others" (1979/1988, p. 2). In adopting a sociological tenor in their scholarship, journalism researchers have thereby fashioned a view of journalism that fits neatly within sociology, but perhaps nowhere else in the academy. Given journalism's complex and multifaceted dimensions, this may mean we have missed much of what constitutes journalism. Reporters' burgeoning authority underscores the degree to which we have understated journalists' consolidation of the power derived from reporting any given event. We thereby need to explore other lenses for examining the trappings of journalism and to consider how authority and power function as a collective code of knowledge for journalists.

Humanistic Inquiry Into Journalism

An alternative view of media power and authority is supported by humanistic inquiry. Rather than conceptualize power only as the influence of one group over another, humanistic inquiry supports a view of power as also having ritual or communal dimensions. These communal dimensions have prompted certain communication scholars to consider the limitations imposed by our preference for sociological inquiry (Carey, 1975; Hirsch & Carey, 1978; Park, 1940; Schlesinger, 1989; Schudson, 1991). These scholars, and others, have produced work that addresses the collective codes by which journalism constitutes itself (Carey, 1974; Hardt, 1990; Nord, 1988; O'Brien, 1983; Schudson, 1988, 1992). But humanistic inquiry has not made sufficient inroads into journalism scholarship, generating concerns about how to capitalize on what the inquiry offers—a way to examine journalism through its own collectivity in addition to its influence on others. In such a view, authority and power become a construct of community, functioning as the stuff that keeps a community together.

Four notions employed in humanistic fields of inquiry suggest this explicit address to journalism as a collectivity: performance, narrative, ritual, and interpretive community. Each provides an alternative frame for explaining journalism, a frame that regards journalistic practice as a way to connect journalists with each other as well as to relay news. Thus in different ways each frame addresses the basic yet overlooked fact that journalists use news to achieve pragmatic aims of community.

Journalism as Performance

Within folklore, anthropology, and particularly performance studies, the notion of performance has generated widespread interest as a way of explaining practice (Bauman, 1986; Schechner, 1985). The performance frame signifies both accomplishment and artfulness, and it has been used to reference both small theatrical productions and large-scale public events (Abrahams, 1977; Bauman, 1989; MacAloon, 1984; Turner, 1982; Zelizer, 1989). In anthropologist Victor Turner's words, performance is a circumstance of "making, not faking" (1982, p. 93). It offers group members a way to negotiate their internal group authentication (Abrahams, 1986).

Generally contrasted with *text*, performance suggests a fluid, less fixed frame for understanding practice (Bauman, 1986; Fine, 1984). In its most fundamental form, text refers to the actual script of a play, performance to how it is acted out. Within this frame, journalism scholars have begun to examine the unfolding of news rather than the finished product, an aim called for by Bauman (1989). Ettema (1990) and Wagner-Pacifici (1986) used the performative dimensions of the social drama to consider media coverage of, respectively, Chicago's Cokely affair and the Aldo Moro kidnapping. Dayan and Katz (1992) analyzed the media event as a type of performance. When seen as performance, news is understood as a situationally variant process that is neither static nor fixed. Reporters negotiate their power across a variety of situations, allowing analysts to map out the patterns of cultural argumentation by which an event becomes news. Given a news event's inherently unstable meaning, this frame may turn out to be particularly useful for considering journalism.

Journalism as Narrative

Journalism as narrative is another way to account for journalism's commonality. Borrowed from literary studies, this frame indexes a group's ability to consolidate around codes of knowledge by examining which narratives are upheld, repeated, and altered. In this view, narrative helps us construct our view of the world, by allowing us to share stories within culturally and socially explicit codes of meaning (Barthes, 1977, 1979). Narrative gives us a way to challenge or interrupt a community's so-called master discourses (Bhabha, 1990). In social history and historiography, narrative is seen as a strategic way of remembering and representing the past (Halbwachs, 1950/1980; Kammen, 1991). Hayden White (1981) in particular has argued that over time narratives offer narrators ways of reconfiguring their authority for events.

Narrative has received considerable attention from communication scholars during the past decade (Fisher, 1987; Lucaites & Condit, 1985). News scholarship has produced discussions of common narrative frames and themes (Barkin & Gurevitch, 1987; Bennett & Edelman, 1985; Campbell & Reeves, 1989; Carragee, 1990) and "narrativizing" strategies (Bird & Dardenne, 1988; Mander, 1987; Schudson, 1982). An issue of the journal *Communication* focused on the theme of "news as social narrative" (Carey & Fritzler, 1989). Recent interest in collective memory has also generated interest in narrative, whereby oft-repeated narratives are seen as offering speakers a way to compete for a place in public discourse about the past (Schudson, 1992; Zelizer, 1992b).

Narrative helps us explain journalism by stressing elements that are formulaic, patterned, finite, yet mutable over time. In this sense, news as narrative offers analysts a way to account for change within predictable and defined patterns of news presentation. Not only does this focus on how narratives are repeated in conjunction with certain events, but it also suggests that narratives change and thereby affect the power of their narrators, the journalists.

Journalism as Ritual

Yet another way of viewing journalism is through the frame of ritual. Taken from anthropology and folklore, rituals are seen as offering "a periodic restatement of the terms in which [people] of a particular culture must interact if there is to be any kind of a coherent social life" (Turner, 1968, p. 6). Rituals provide moments for individuals to question authority and consolidate themselves into communities (Turner, 1969).

Certain work within communication and journalism scholarship has called for an examination of ritual (e.g., Glasser & Ettema, 1989; Rothenbuhler, n.d.). Rothenbuhler provided an extended discussion of the efficacy of ritual as a communication concept; he characterized ritual as "communication without information" or communication that had more to do with meaning-making than with informing. Glasser and Ettema (1989) examined the way in which rituals in journalistic work helped promote cultural change. Press rites were explored for the ways in which they allowed reporters to flex their muscles (Elliot, 1982; Manoff & Schudson, 1986; Tuchman, 1972). Press criticism was found to function symbolically for reporters, who use media criticism not so much to generate real debate over appropriate journalistic practice as to uphold and maintain the larger canon of objective journalism (Lule, 1992). Such "allowed" critiques constitute journalism's way of under-scoring its own apparent reflexivity. Looking at news as ritual suggests a way of examining patterned behavior that emerges through collectivity, for rituals do not work without solid support behind them. This again allows us to examine journalism via its own commonality, rather than merely accounting for its influence on others.

Journalism as Interpretive Community

The idea of the interpretive community has long been of interest in literary studies, anthropology, and folklore. Hymes defined "speech commu-nities" as groups united by shared interpretations of reality (1980, p. 2). In literary studies, Fish defined interpretive communities as those that produce texts and "determine the shape of what is read" (1980, p. 171). Scholars have examined "communities of memory," where group members create shared interpretations over time (Bellah, Madsen, Sullivan, Swidler, & Tipton, 1985). Each view suggests that communities arise through patterns of association derived from the communication of shared interpretation.

In communication, the idea of the interpretive community has been invoked most avidly in audience studies (Lindlof, 1987; Radway, 1984). But it is possible to examine communicators themselves as an interpretive com-munity (Zelizer, 1993). Journalists, in this view, create community through discourse that proliferates in informal talks, professional meetings and trade reviews, memoirs, interviews on talk shows, and media retrospectives. Through discourse, journalists create shared interpretations that make their profes-sional lives meaningful; that is, they use stories about the past to address dilemmas that present themselves while covering news.

The idea of the interpretive community has been the thrust of certain journalism scholarship. It is implied in Schudson's (1991) recent discussion of the "culturological" studies of news, which chart the flow of informal discourse among reporters; also in Pauly's (1988) examination of journalistic rhetoric about the tabloid, used by reporters to establish standards of "good" journalism; and it can be observed in journalists' reliance on shared interpre-tive strategies to address the Janet Cooke affair (Eason, 1986). The prescriptive parameters that underlie journalistic textbooks similarly reflect consensual assumptions about the kinds of gendered voices that have been permitted and barred from news (Steiner, 1992). Journalists functioned as an interpre-tive community in shaping the tale of John F. Kennedy's assassination into a story about the legitimation of television news, in fashioning stories of the

Gulf War into celebrations of CNN, or in recasting stories about Watergate and McCarthyism into moral tales about appropriate journalistic practice (Zelizer, 1992a, 1992b, 1993). In examining journalism as an interpretive community, we see a group united by its shared discourse and collective interpretations of key public events. The shared discourse that they produce thus offers a marker of how journalists see themselves as journalists.

Alternative Explanations

The principal thrust of this article has been to argue for a more interdisciplinary approach to journalism. This is a necessary corrective to our commonly held view of journalism—that it is foremost a sociological problem—for that view has prompted us to examine journalism in narrowly defined ways. In considering these alternative frames for examining journalism, this article suggests a broader understanding of journalism that addresses both how news functions *for journalists* as well as for audiences. Adopting such a focus may help us achieve one of communication scholarship's most pragmatic aims: how to predict and control for the work of communication practitioners, by understanding their collective aims in practice. By recognizing our dependence on sociologically motivated inquiry, we may find we have thus far missed much of journalism's essence. And considering journalism's central role in explaining general communicative practice, this may mean we have missed much of the essence of communication as well.

References

Abrahams, R. (1977). Toward an enactment-centered theory of folklore. In W. R. Bascom (Ed.), *Frontiers of folklore* (pp. 79-120). Boulder, CO: Westview.

Abrahams, R. (1986). Ordinary and extraordinary experience. In V. Turner & E. Bruner (Eds.), *The anthropology of experience* (pp. 45-72). Urbana: University of Illinois Press.

Barkin, S., & Gurevitch, M. (1987). Out of work and on the air: Television news of unemployment. *Critical Studies in Mass Communication, 4,* 1-20.

Barthes, R. (1977). Introduction to the structural analysis of narrative. In *Image, music, text* (pp. 79-124). New York: Hill and Wang.

Barthes, R. (1979). From work to text. In J. Harari (Ed.), *Textual strategies* (pp. 73-81). Ithaca, NY: Cornell University Press.

Bauman, R. (1986). *Story, performance, and event.* Cambridge, England: Cambridge University Press.

Bauman, R. (1989). American folklore studies and social transformation: A performance-centered perspective. *Text and Performance Quarterly, 9*(3), 175-184.

Bellah, R., Madsen, R., Sullivan, W., Swidler, A., & Tipton, S. (1985). *Habits of the heart.* Berkeley: University of California Press.

Bennett, W. L., & Edelman, M. (1985). Toward a new political narrative. *Journal of Communications, 35*(4), 156-171.

Bhabha, H. (1990). *Nation and narration.* London: Routledge.

Bird, S. E., & Dardenne, R. W. (1988). Myth, chronicle and story: Exploring the narrative qualities of news. In J. W. Carey (Ed.), *Media, myths, and narratives: Television and the press* (pp. 67-87). Newbury Park, CA: Sage.

Campbell, R., & Reeves, J. L. (1989). Covering the homeless: The Joyce Brown story. *Critical Studies in Mass Communication, 6*(1), 21-42.

Carey, J. W. (1974). The problem of journalism history. *Journalism History, 1*(1), 3-5, 27.

Carey, J. W. (1975). A cultural approach to communication. *Communication, 2,* 1-22.

Carey, J. W., & Fritzler, M. (Eds.). (1989). News as social narrative. *Communication, 10*(1), 1-92.

Carragee, K. M. (1990, February). Defining solidarity: Themes and omissions in coverage of the Solidarity trade union movement by ABC news. *Journalism Monographs, 119.*

Dayan, D., & Katz, E. (1992). *Media events: The live broadcasting of history.* Cambridge, MA: Harvard University Press.

Eason, D. (1986). On journalistic authority: The Janet Cooke scandal. *Critical Studies in Mass Communication, 3,* pp. 429-447.

Elliot, P. (1982). Press performance as political ritual. In D. C. Whitney, E. Wartella, & S. Windahl (Eds.), *Mass communication review yearbook* (Vol. 3, pp. 583-619). Beverly Hills, CA: Sage.

Ettema, J. S. (1990). Press rites and race relations: A study of mass-mediated ritual. *Critical Studies in Mass Communication, 7*(4), 309-331.

Fine, E. (1984). *The folklore text: From performance to print.* Bloomington: Indiana University Press.

Fish, S. (1980). *Is there a text in this class?* Cambridge, MA: Harvard University Press.

Fisher, W. R. (1987). *Human communications as narration: Toward a philosophy of reason, value, and action.* Columbia: University of South Carolina Press.

Fishman, M. (1980). *Manufacturing the news.* Austin: University of Texas Press.

Fowler, R. (1991). *Language in the news: Discourse and ideology in the press.* London: Routledge.

Gans, H. (1979). *Deciding what's news.* New York: Pantheon.

Gitlin, T. (1980). *The whole world is watching.* Berkeley: University of California Press.

Glasgow University Media Group. (1980). *More bad news.* London: Routledge and Kegan Paul.

Glasser, T. L., & Ettema, J. S. (1989). Investigative journalism and the moral order. *Critical Studies in Mass Communication, 6*(1), 1-20.

Graber, D. (1988). *Processing the news.* White Plains, NY: Longman.

Halbwachs, M. (1980). *The collective memory.* New York: Harper and Row. (Original work published 1950)

Hardt, H. (1990). Newsworkers, technology, and journalism history. *Critical Studies in Mass Communication, 7,* 346-365.

Hirsch, P., & Carey, J. W. (Eds.). (1978). Communication and culture: Humanistic models in research. *Communication Research, 5*(3).

Hymes, D. (1980). Functions of speech. In *Language in education: Ethnolinguistic essays* (pp. 1-18). Washington, DC: Center for Applied Linguistics.

Kammen, M. (1991). *Mystic chords of memory.* New York: Alfred A. Knopf.

Lindlof, T. (Ed.). (1987). *Natural audiences.* Norwood. NJ: Ablex.

Lucaites, J. L., & Condit, C. (1985). Reconstructing narrative theory: A functional perspective. *Journal of Communication, 35*(4), 90-108.

Lule, J. (1992). Journalism and criticism: The *Philadelphia Inquirer* Norplant editorial. *Critical Studies in Mass Communication, 9,* 91-109.

MacAloon, J. (1984). *Rite, drama, festival spectacle: Rehearsals toward a theory of cultural performance.* Philadelphia: ISHI Publications.

Mander, M. S. (1987). Narrative dimensions of the news: Omniscience, prophecy and morality. *Communication, 10,* 51-70.

Manoff, R., & Schudson, M. (1986). *Reading the news*. New York: Pantheon.

Nord, D. P. (1988). A plea for journalism history. *Journalism History, 15*(1), 8-15.

O'Brien, D. (1983, September). The news as environment. *Journalism Monographs, 85*.

Park, R. (1940). News as a form of knowledge. *American Journal of Sociology, 45*, 669-686.

Pauly, J. P. (1988). Rupert Murdoch and the demonology of professional journalism. In J. W. Carey (Ed.), *Media, myths, and narratives: Television and the press* (pp. 246-261). Newbury Park, CA: Sage.

Radway, J. (1984). *Reading the romance*. Chapel Hill: University of North Carolina Press.

Robinson, J. P., & Levy, M. R. (1986). *The main source: Learning from television news*. Beverly Hills, CA: Sage.

Roshco, B. (1975). *Newsmaking*. Chicago: University of Chicago Press.

Rothenbuhler, E. (n.d.). *Ritual as a communication concept*. Unpublished manuscript, University of Iowa.

Schechner, R. (1985). *Between theater and anthropology*. Philadelphia: University of Pennsylvania Press.

Schlesinger, P. (1989). Rethinking the sociology of journalism: Source strategies and the limits of media-centrism. In M. Ferguson (Ed.), *Public communication: The new imperatives* (pp. 61-83). London: Sage.

Schudson, M. (1982). The politics of narrative form: The emergence of news conventions in print and television. *Daedalus, 3*(4), 97-112.

Schudson, M. (1988). What is a reporter? The private face of public journalism. In J. W. Carey (Ed.), *Media, myths, and narratives: Television and the press* (pp. 228-245). Newbury Park, CA: Sage.

Schudson, M. (1991). The sociology of news production revisited. In J. Curran & M. Gurevitch (Eds.), *Mass media and society* (pp. 141-159). London: Edward Arnold.

Schudson, M. (1992). *Watergate in American memory: How we remember, forget and reconstruct the past*. New York: Basic Books.

Steiner, L. (1992, October). Construction of gender in newsreporting textbooks: 1890-1990. *Journalism Monographs, 135*.

Tuchman, G. (1972). Objectivity as a strategic ritual. *American Journal of Sociology, 77*, 660-679.

Tuchman, G. (1978). *Making news*. Glencoe, IL: Free Press.

Turner, V. (1968). *The drums of affliction*. Oxford, England: Clarendon.

Turner, V. (1969). *The ritual process*. Ithaca, NY: Cornell University Press.

Turner, V. (1982). *From ritual to theatre*. New York: Performing Arts Journal Publication.

van Dijk, T. A. (1988). *News as discourse*. Hillsdale, NJ: Lawrence Erlbaum.

Wagner-Pacifici, R. (1986). *The Moro morality play*. Chicago: University of Chicago Press.

White, H. (1981). The value of narrativity in the representation of reality. In W. J. T. Mitchell (Ed.), *On narrative* (pp. 1-23). Chicago: University of Chicago Press.

Wrong, D. H. (1988). *Power: Its forms, bases, and uses*. Chicago: University of Chicago Press. (Original work published 1979)

Zelizer, B. (1989, May). *"All the world's a stage": "Performance" as interdisciplinary tool*. Paper presented at annual meeting of International Communication Association, San Francisco.

Zelizer, B. (1992a). CNN, the Gulf War, and journalistic practice. *Journal of Communication, 42*(1), 68-81.

Zelizer, B. (1992b). *Covering the body: The Kennedy assassination, the media, and the shaping of collective memory*. Chicago: University of Chicago Press.

Zelizer, B. (1993). Journalists as interpretive communities. *Critical Studies in Mass Communication, 10*(3), 219-237.

CHAPTER **3**

Professional Mass Communicators

James S. Ettema
D. Charles Whitney
with Daniel B. Wackman

Studies of professional mass communicators that could be fairly termed "communication science" date back at least to Rosten's (1937) survey of Washington correspondents. Such studies have, however, been much enriched since the early 1970s by several developments. One is the infusion of ideas from cognate fields of study, particularly sociology. Sociology of knowledge, for example, while not new to mass communication (e.g., Park, 1940), has lately revitalized the critique of journalistic objectivity (e.g., Tuchman, 1972, 1973, 1978). Similarly, the sociology of complex organizations has reshaped the study of popular culture. In drawing up a prospectus for "production of culture" research, Peterson (1976) urged a focus on organizational structures and processes by which the "creation, manufacture, marketing, distribution, exhibiting, inculcation, evaluation and consumption" (p. 10) of symbol systems are accomplished.

From C. H. Berger and S. H. Chaffee (Eds.), *Handbook of Communication Science*, 1987, pp. 747-780. Copyright © 1987 Sage Publications, Inc.

Interest in professional mass communicators has also been intensified by the blossoming of cultural and critical perspectives within communication scholarship. While a variety of approaches—cultural anthropology, social history, political economy—are pursued under the cultural and critical banners, they share an interest in the meaning of mass media symbol systems and in the processes that yield those meanings. From a cultural perspective, for example, Newcomb and Alley (1983) emphasize the transformatory potential of television as ritual. Television, they argue, like the "in-between" phase of an initiation rite in tribal society, provides a release from sociocultural constraint and an opportunity to envision alternatives. The alternative visions are often unrealistic, and even monstrous, but this may make them all the more compelling as deconstructions of the commonsensical and the taken-for-granted. Television provides commentary on social reality by constructing *unreality*. Newcomb and Alley search for the source of these visions in the work of the producer who often originates the TV series concept and who manages series production.

Those working from a critical perspective, on the other hand, emphasize the confirmatory potential of popular culture. Gitlin (1979), for example, recognizes that television does confront social issues but in a way that "domesticates" them. The issues of race, gender, and class may be raised on television but the prevailing arrangements of capitalist consumer society are typically confirmed as offering the solution to such "social problems." This is Gitlin's interpretation of the concept of "hegemony," finding on television not social commentary but social control. Theorists in this tradition urge attention to how, for example, occupational cultures of professional communicators mediate the relationship between "the ruling ideology" and media content (Murdock & Golding, 1977).

These perspectives are at odds with an attempt to develop a sociology of cultural production that is analytic rather than evaluative in goal. Peterson's (1976) vision of such a sociology sets aside the idealist/materialist debate—whether culture creates social structure or vice versa—to study the production and reproduction of culture. Such a sociology would hold in abeyance the evaluation of cultural forms and focus on the mechanisms that reproduce these forms. But this, argue the cultural and critical theorists, is impossible. Writing from a materialist position, Tuchman (1983) argues that much "production of culture" research is a brand of organizational sociology that takes for granted contemporary capitalism and thus "obscure[s] the historicity of cultural products" and how such products are "implicated in the creation of ideology" (p. 332). She urges attention to how ideology is "embedded" in organizational process. Writing from an idealist position, Jensen (1984) argues that the production of culture perspective fails to recognize cultural production as a truly cultural enterprise—one "encompassing both the producers and the audience for which they create" (p. 110). She urges viewing popular culture not as "a container of messages processed along a line from sender to receiver" but rather as "the means through which people construct meaningful worlds in which to live" (p. 108). These critics are unwilling to hold the study of meaning in abeyance, arguing that the study of message formulation without a theory of meaning is, indeed, meaningless.

There is substantial merit in these arguments. The social science approach to the study of professional mass communicators has only recently begun to come to terms with the critique of news as ideology (see Hackett, 1984). It still does not emphasize the relationships between production process and social setting that yield particular themes, songs, stories, or images in popular entertainment. Instead it emphasizes more global dimensions of media content such as degree of content diversity within a medium. But the approach need not be "meaningless." For example, Peterson and Berger's (1975) analysis of the relationship between recording industry concentration and musical diversity is informed by an appreciation of the content of postwar popular music. Similarly, Schatz (1981) begins his history of film genre with a review of the organizational functions of genre in the old Hollywood studio system. These authors do not reduce the meaning of popular music and film genre to market structure or organizational routine but rather enumerate some conditions necessary for particular meanings to be formulated. Meaning cannot be reduced to economic, industrial, organizational, or psychological processes, and yet mass-mediated meaning cannot exist without these processes. Still, the social science approach is more attuned to how symbols are produced than to what they mean and more attuned to industrial and organizational context than to the text itself. In outlining a "communication science" of professional mass communicators that emphasizes structures and processes of message production we can, then, provide only part—albeit an important part—of what should be said about the form, content, and meaning of mass communication.

Mass Communicators in Context

Mass-mediated symbol systems—news, popular music, television, and film—are, at one level of analysis, the work of individual or small groups of media professionals. At another level of analysis, however, they are the products of complex organizations; at still another, higher level they reflect the economic arrangements of media industries and institutions. The work of individual mass communicators cannot be understood outside these organizational, industrial, and institutional contexts (Dimmick & Coit, 1982; Whitney, 1982). For example, Hirsch's (1977) reanalysis of White's (1950) classic gatekeeper study, as well as data collected by Whitney and Becker (1982), suggest that influences on news selection that have been traced to individual or professional values must also be traced to organizational routines that partly cue news selection by wire editors. The analysis of symbol formulation and diffusion via the mass media must, then, be pursued on several levels of analysis, and yet the activities at each level so interpenetrate these other levels that it is difficult to disentangle them. . . .

Journalism and Truth

If the search for creative opportunity is a central issue in the production of popular entertainment, knowing and telling the truth is the corresponding goal in journalism. Whether truth can be equated with fact or differentiated from value and how it can be known at all are old and enduring issues of the craft (e.g., Hutchins, 1947; Lippmann, 1922). Even so, practitioners and critics alike regularly affirm the *possibility* of truth through journalism ("Can the press tell the truth?" 1985; Epstein, 1975). Gitlin (1979) acknowledges, if grudgingly, that journalism does seek "truth—partial, superficial, occasion- and celebrity-centered truth, but truth nevertheless" (p. 263). Our focus on truth in journalism does not, then, deny the ancient philosophical problems surrounding truth, but as we held in abeyance the materialist/idealist debate in the study of culture, we set aside this problem by assuming that *as a practical matter* there is truth to be known and told. In this section, then, we assess the prospects for knowing and telling that truth given what is known about how journalism works.

Industrial and Institutional Levels:
The Political Economy of Journalism

Analysis of the extent to which—or whether at all—journalism can approximate truth begins with the political economy of the craft. From a variety of (typically British) materialist (e.g., Murdock, 1982; Murdock & Golding, 1977) and cultural Marxist (e.g., Hall, 1977, 1980, 1982) positions, mass communication is viewed as a means for legitimation and maintenance of socioeconomic stratification. These authors see more than simple determin- ism between the prevailing economic order and the practice of journalism. Murdock and Golding (1977) maintain that while Marx "saw the basic economic relations of capitalism as structuring the overall framework and 'general process' of intellectual life, within these general limits he allowed a good deal of room for intellectual autonomy and innovation" (p. 16).

Authors in this critical tradition, like social historians and organizational theorists, argue that the relationship between capitalist ownership of the means of mass communication and the day-to-day practice of journalism is mediated by a journalistic "culture of objectivity." (On the rise of this culture and what Carey, 1969, calls "the purely commercial motives" behind it, see Roshco, 1975; Schiller, 1981; Schudson, 1978.) This culture of objectivity does allow—indeed it prizes—autonomy, as evidenced by occasional clashes with corporate and governmental authorities. But it also demands fairness and balance within the limits of the "consensus" (Schlesinger, 1978) or the "com- mon sense" (Hartley, 1982) of liberal capitalism. The partisan bias of an earlier era is reduced considerably, but this culture is subject to biases of its own— biases not so much *in* the news as biases *of* the news. Gitlin (1980), for example, argues that journalistic devotion to hard fact and editorial balance led to coverage of the Vietnam-era antiwar movement that emphasized confrontation with authorities rather than analysis of issues and portrayed the movement as operating beyond the bounds of reasonable dissent.

If journalism is a tool of social control, and one need not be a Marxist to argue that it is, that tool is used with considerable subtlety and restraint. Dreier (1982) interrelated memberships on the boards of directors of the 25 largest U.S. newspaper-owning firms with other affiliations and argues that at this top corporate level, these media firms are intimately tied to the U.S. power structure. These firms, Dreier suggests, embody a "corporate liberal" perspective more concerned with stability of the entire system than with more conservative or parochial interests often identified with large corporations.

Few current political-economic approaches, then, suggest that big-industry news media work to stifle dissent entirely. Most, if not all, suggest instead that the primary effect is either to direct and shape political dialogue or to limit the diversity of opinion and information that is expressed. On diversity, we shall have more to say later. On shaping the news, we must add to Gitlin (1980) a variety of literature that suggests that corporate-capitalist ownership of news media predisposes news to routinely uncritical treatment of corporate and governmental power sources (e.g., Bennett, 1983). This is seen most clearly when ruptures in the normal webs of coverage, such as accidents, scandals, and disasters, occasion "repair work" by the powerful (Molotch & Lester, 1974) or by the news media themselves (Bennett, Gressett, & Haltom, 1985).

Across the news industry scarcity of resources promotes efficiency in news gathering, particularly in ways of conceptualizing newsworthiness that make for predictability and economy. The beat system, for example, disperses reporters to where news is most likely to occur—usually centers of institutional power (Tuchman, 1978). Television network news is geographically biased; that is, when news occurs in places where its production and distribution is cheaper, it is more "newsworthy" or at least more likely to be transmitted as news (Dominick, 1977; Epstein, 1974; Whitney, Fritzler, Jones, Mazzarella, & Rakow, 1985).

On diversity, scholars who argue that news media *are* diverse usually point to the number, variety, and competitiveness of media outlets either nationally or in particular markets (e.g., Compaine, 1982, 1985). Those who argue that they are not, point instead to a lack of direct competition within a particular medium in a particular market. For example, only about 30 U.S. cities have two separately owned daily newspapers (Bagdikian, 1985). Competition in a media market may be related to organizational differentiation in news gathering by its daily newspapers (DuBick, 1978), but the evidence that direct newspaper competition is reflected in news or editorial diversity is far less compelling (Entman, 1985).

Studies comparing the content of competitive versus noncompetitive media rarely find significant differences. Why? It may be that the "logic" of news in a market economy is itself standardized, as suggested above. Or competition itself may breed standardization rather than diversity, as Dominick and Pearce (1976) have argued for prime-time television entertainment, and as Crouse (1973) and Dunwoody (1980) document for beat reporters. It may be that the news values of journalists overlap so much that "diversity" does not show up in content analysis categories. Finally, it may be that only a few news sources—the television networks, the wire services, and a few major newspapers—either supply the bulk of news or set the agenda for news production (Breed, 1959; Gold & Simmons, 1965; Hirsch, 1977; McCombs & Shaw, 1977; Whitney & Becker, 1982).

A number of noneconomic institutional factors are also related to journalistic performance. Two important categories are community or market structural differences and industry sector differences. Tichenor and his colleagues (Donohue, Olien, & Tichenor, 1985; Olien, Donohue, & Tichenor, 1968; Tichenor, Donohue, & Olien, 1980) have identified several predictors of the amount of coverage devoted to social conflict by smaller dailies. Such reporting is positively associated with community size, community pluralism, location of the newspaper publisher *outside* the community power structure, and absentee ownership. (In larger cities, newspapers whose publishers are *inside* the power structure report more conflict.) In regard to industry sector differences, how do newspapers, magazines, radio, and television differ in news content and process? In terms of content, the visual nature and more limited capacity of television as compared to the newspaper "news hole" may explain why Robinson (1976) found that television news is more devoted to conflict and negativity than newspaper news. Patterson (1980), however, was struck by the similarity across the two media (and news magazines as well) in how presidential campaign news is presented. In terms of process, Tuchman (1969) demonstrates that local television and local newspaper news production, while sharing a logic of "objectivity," differ markedly in news handling. Compared to newspaper reporters, television reporters have less autonomy in the selection of stories, but there is a greater likelihood that television reporters' stories will appear as the reporters have prepared them (see also Bantz, McCorkle, & Baade, 1980; Weaver & Wilhoit, 1986). Several surveys of American journalists (Becker, 1982; Johnstone, Slawski, & Bowman, 1976; Weaver & Wilhoit, 1986) reveal both structural and attitudinal differences between newspaper and broadcast journalists. Newspaper journalists are more likely to engage in beat reporting and to value interpretive and adversarial news; broadcast journalists are more mobile and experience greater job satisfaction.

Turow (1985) argues that an understanding of what becomes news requires an appreciation of the differences between "mainstream" and "peripheral" media and of the role served by "linking pin" organizations. The mainstream media's constant need for information and ideas that are new and "progressive" can lead them to adapt material from peripheral media that stands in "remedial opposition" to established interests. However, the linking pin activities of wire services, public relations firms, syndicators, and integrated media conglomerates "are counter-elements in the structure of mass communication that act as an ironic brake on the breadth, depth and diversity" of news (Turow, 1985, p. 150). For Turow, then, news reflects a tension between journalism's historical definition of news and the counterelements in the structure of the industry.

In related research, Strodthoff, Hawkins, and Schoenfeld (1985) have shown via content analysis of general- and special-interest media coverage of one social movement—environmentalism in the 1960s and 1970s—that the "diffusion of ideology" is complex but patterned. News coverage of the issue begins in special-interest media and is early marked by "disambiguation," or establishment of the doctrinal tenets of various positions on the issue. This is followed by a period of "legitimation" in which gatekeepers come to recognize that information about the issue is valid news, and then a period of "routinization," in which regular allocations of time, budget, and space are devoted to news about the issue (see also Tichenor et al., 1980).

In sum, a considerable body of research supports the argument that inter-organizational- and institutional-level forces, realized in a journalistic culture of "objectivity," fostered by, and in the service of, progressive liberal capitalism, constrain what journalists report. News thus exhibits an identifiable and widely shared form and a content broadly consonant with the social structures and values of its political-economic context. To understand these uniformities—but also the differences—we must move to the organizational level of analysis where the culture of journalism is enacted and news is made.

Organizational Level: Making News

News media, like entertainment firms, have devised organizational structures and processes to cope with uncertainties. Focusing on the organizational level highlights (1) the bureaucratic nature of news production, (2) the routines and conventions by which work is accomplished, and (3) the management of organizational conflict.

News is the product of bureaucratically structured organizations. The work of gathering, assembling, and selecting news is left primarily to workers who are relatively low in the hierarchy but who, in Western industrialized countries, are considered professionals and given substantial autonomy. Several observers have noted that remarkably little task-related discussion accompanies newswork (Schlesinger, 1978; Tuchman, 1972). Exceptions occur when news is truly nonroutine (Bailey & Lichty, 1972; Robinson, 1970) or is "close to home" (Bowers, 1967) and when the news has direct relevance to the organization's revenues (Donohew, 1967). In such situations, decision making may shift upward in the hierarchy. In larger newspapers there tends to be less "publisher power" in directing news decisions (Bowers, 1967; Olien et al., 1968).

The limited character of intraorganizational communication under normal conditions is evidence of the importance of routines in news organizations. But, as many researchers have pointed out (Dimmick, 1974; Gans, 1979; Tuchman, 1973, 1978), newsworkers see their environment as highly uncertain in several respects. Far more "news" is available at a given time than most organizations can reproduce as "their" news. Moreover, uncertainty underlies the generation of news: The organization must make a priori decisions about where news is likely to occur. When news breaks out in unexpected places (e.g., accidents, disasters, conflict) decisions about reallocating staff resources become necessary. Organizations deal with such uncertainties by routinization: typifications, reliance on routine sources, allocation of personnel to places where news is most likely, and adherence to organizational policy. We examine each of these in turn.

Tuchman (1973, 1978) has suggested that newsworkers employ "typifications" of potential news stories (e.g., spot news versus continuing news, hard news versus soft news) in an effort to routinize the unexpected features of events as news. These newsroom terms are applied to stories to define appropriate modes of coverage and scheduling. These terms, for example, help identify stories that demand the "rituals of objectivity"—covering "both sides," adducing supportive evidence, judiciously using quotation marks. In other words, the organization knows how to define unknown news in terms of known forms and modes of production.

Reliance on routine news sources shapes news in several ways. Almost all news media depend for the bulk of their news content on other news suppliers, selecting from among the offerings of wire services and syndicators (Breed, 1955a; Turow, 1985). This dependence leads to content standardization. But even for their own news product, media depend on other organizations as sources. According to Sigal (1973), such "pseudoevents" as press conferences and news releases account for about two-thirds of *Washington Post* and *New York Times* coverage of national and international news. Moreover, in developing their own news, organizations deploy their reporters on news beats. Tuchman (1978) likens a beat to a "news net" designed to "catch" information offered by some individuals and organizations—especially those in government—but to let other information slip through (see also Gans, 1979). Sigal (1973) found that almost four-fifths of *New York Times* and *Washington Post* news emanates from official sources. Not only do official and institutional sources predominate, but they are given favorable treatment, because journalists either consider them legitimate spokespersons (Paletz & Dunn, 1969; Paletz, Reichert, & McIntyre, 1971) or are accustomed to and accept administrative procedures routinely employed by official sources. Fishman (1980, 1982) suggests that government and police reporters become so tied to "bureaucratic phase structures" that public activities only become news "events" at times when formal action is taken. A crime only becomes a story, for example, at the time of initial police reports and at the times of arrest, arraignment, trial, and sentencing—and at no other.

Organizational policy provides an uncertain guide to understanding a news organization's behavior. As most studies following Breed's (1955b) lead have suggested, policy tends to be unwritten and informal, accessible to newsworkers only through organizational socialization—except for formal written policies concerning nonroutine occurrences that news organizations tend to adopt *after* experiencing major news events, such as serious accidents and natural disasters (Kueneman & Wright, 1975). However, as Siegelman (1973) has noted, socialization may be an informal process in which reporters and editors internalize "rules" inferred from the treatment of stories but policy is still sufficiently transparent that journalists are aware of it before they go to work in a news organization. Further, there are instances of newsroom policy that do make a substantial difference in content selection and play of news. Lester

(1980), for example, notes that for policy reasons one newspaper does not employ the typifications identified by Tuchman (1973).

Despite typifications, routines, and socialization, organizational conflict still occurs. Within news organizations, several kinds of conflict are apparent: conflict between business and professional norms, between partisan and ideological factions, and between neutral and participant news values. These disputes usually involve hierarchical role conflict, where management is more conservative (i.e., more oriented toward business and entertainment, conservative and neutral values) than are the journalists responsible for most newswork (Bantz, 1985). While management clearly has an upper hand in such disputes, newsworkers are not without informal power. Their major weapon is journalism's canons of professionalism, most especially objectivity. Objectivity becomes, in Tuchman's (1972) felicitous phrase, a "strategic ritual" by which a journalist questioned about a particular news story may defend it by demonstrating that the account is factually veridical, that it confines statements of opinion to legitimate news sources, or that it contains no "unjustified" adjectives and adverbs. Journalists may also attempt to negotiate questioned news reports by referring to their individual expertise, talent, or ability (Breed, 1955a; Roshco, 1975; Stark, 1962).

Another sort of conflict in news organizations is for "turf." Tuchman (1978) documents internal disputes between news desks, as between the city desk and the state government desk when a "state" story occurs within the city. She suggests that these issues are disputed with shared news values as the coin of the realm: Each desk attempts to claim high-value stories as it own while attempting to palm off low-value ones. Sigal (1973) documents an equal accommodation of international, national, and local news desks on the *New York Times* and *Washington Post,* whereby editorial management apportions almost identical space on the front news page to each desk over time. In other words, newsworthiness of international, national, and local news is defined by policy as equivalent, reducing endemic conflict.

In sum, news organizations' attempts to routinize the production of news provide the news with much of its character and content. Even so, there is still some validity to the notion that news is what journalists make it (Gieber, 1964). It is thus to the individual level of analysis that we turn.

Individual Level: News as Work

While more than one individual may be required to move a news story from inception to publication (particularly in television), the reporting and writing of news accounts usually falls to a single person or at most a few collaborators. The issue at this level of analysis is whether, or to what extent, individuals' attitudes, values, cognitions, demographic characteristics, and the like influence what they report and write. This has been studied in four somewhat overlapping streams of research: (1) perceptions of audiences and sources, (2) news values and news cognitions, (3) personal characteristics and ideological biases, and (4) objectivity as a personal value.

Do journalists "know their audience," and to what extent do images of that audience shape what they write or how they edit? From depth interviews of journalists and experiments with journalism students, Pool and Shulman (1959) argued that journalists' "fantasies" about their audiences did influence newswriting and, further, that when student journalists held views discrepant from those of the perceived audience, they tended to write less accurate or favorable stories. This study has been criticized on conceptual and methodological grounds (Darnton, 1975; Whitney, 1982, pp. 248-249), primarily because it ignores organizational and institutional reality. Routine organizational practice (editing) does tend to smooth out any deviation from "objective" copy, a point that Pool and Shulman (1959) acknowledge:

> The author's private fantasies are clearly not the only things that affect the character of what he writes. An experienced professional newsman will have acquired great facility in turning out a standard product for each of the many kinds of routine story of which so much of the news consists. (p. 150)

In other words, news is first and foremost an organizational product born of routines.

More recent investigators have expressed surprise at how little newsworkers seem to know about their audiences (Burgoon, Burgoon, & Atkin, 1982; Gans, 1979; Schlesinger, 1978). Gans's (1979) observational study of national newsmagazine and network television journalists is illustrative:

> I . . . paid close attention to how the journalists conceived of and related to their audience. I was surprised to find, however, that they had little knowledge about their actual audience and rejected feedback from it. Although they had a vague image of the audience, they paid little attention to it; instead, they filmed and wrote for their superiors and for themselves, assuming . . . that what interested them would interest the audience. (p. 230)

Audience images seem to have minor influence on journalistic performance relative to other potential influence sources. Flegel and Chaffee (1971) found that among eight sources of perceived influence, journalists ranked readers' opinions seventh. An unexamined premise in the research on journalists' perception of the audience is that professional mass communicators should have one; that it should be accurate; and that if it were, content would somehow change. There is little to support this premise, however, and the most compelling writing on the topic is still among the oldest. News, George Herbert Mead (1964) once wrote, could serve an "aesthetic function" if it could "interpret to the reader his experiences as the shared experiences of the community of which he feels he himself to be a part" (p. 302). Presumably this would indeed demand a keener sense of the reader and the community than journalists typically have.

Another stream of research on journalists concerns news values and news cognitions. Journalism textbooks characteristically begin by attempting to define news usually by reference to characteristics, elements, or values of news. The list of such values usually includes timeliness, consequence or significance, proximity, known principals, conflict, and human interest. Journalists are said to invoke such values in deciding whether stories are to be covered or selected for use. A number of studies (e.g., Buckalew, 1969; Dimmick, 1974) have examined this but generally they explain little selection variance among journalists, less than can be accounted for by organizational- or institutional-level variables.

The agenda-setting concept has been applied to journalists, to suggest that they are influenced by issue priorities in the media on which they themselves rely. Fresh looks at the classic "Mr. Gates" study (White, 1950) by McCombs and Shaw (1977) and Hirsch (1977), for example, dispute White's original conclusion that the gatekeeper's personal bias in news selection was a principal news determinant. Both studies argued instead that wire services' priorities, as reflected by proportions of content in standard news categories, were an important news determinant. This result was confirmed experimentally by Whitney and Becker (1982). Fishman (1978, 1980) has shown that reporting on crimes against the elderly was generated more by other reporting on the topic than by any change in the rate of crime against older persons. Similarly Protess, Leff, Brooks, and Gordon (1985), in a study of one Chicago newspaper's extensive coverage of rape, found virtually no agenda-setting effect on the public, on the newspaper's audience, or on policymakers. Following the series on rape, however, the newspaper featuring the series gave more prominent attention to rape while neither the incidence of rape in the city nor coverage of the crime in other city newspapers changed.

Still another stream of research concerns the personal attributes of journalists. In the original gatekeeper study, White (1950) concluded,

> Through studying his overt reasons for rejecting news stories from the press associations, we see how highly subjective, how based on the "gatekeeper's" own set of experiences, attitudes and expectations the communication of "news" really is. (p. 390)

Subsequent interpretations of the data from this study as we noted have undercut this conclusion but the notion that what becomes news is dependent on the attitudes of individual journalists continues to have force in the literature. Lichter and Rothman (1981) describe individuals within U.S. "elite" news media organizations as more liberal politically and socially than a comparison sample of executives of major businesses. They also described them as of disproportionately high social and economic status, white, and not religiously observant. Most of these trends are also evident in more representative surveys of U.S. journalists (Associated Press Managing Editors, 1985; Lewis, 1985; Weaver & Wilhoit, 1986) but to a lesser degree, particularly in regard to political and social liberalism. Critics of the Lichter and Rothman study (Clancey & Robinson, 1985; Gans, 1985; Robinson, 1983, 1985; Schneider & Lewis, 1985) have noted the absence of any evidence that a liberal bias enters news presentations. Content analyses of the 1980 and 1984 presidential elections (Robinson, 1983, 1985) indicate biases in treatment against the incumbent and against minority parties in coverage, but no left/right or majority partisan bias at all in primary and election coverage. Clarke and Evans's (1983) analysis of congressional campaigns found a pronounced bias in favor of the incumbent but no partisan bias. There was much less tendency to endorse Republicans for Congress than is the case in presidential elections; local newspapers mostly endorse their local incumbent representatives in Washington. Mainstream news media bias is not so much toward one party as toward powerful individuals and institutions in general.

The final stream of research we consider here concerns journalistic objectivity as a personal value set. Clearly the set of values motivating journalistic performance is broader than the news values previously discussed. In an argument that crosses all three levels of analysis, Nord (1984) traces the development of a modern journalistic ethic emphasizing public service and public responsibility, community, consensus, and social order among major Chicago newspapers in the late 19th century—before such values emerged as important concepts in the Progressive Movement and despite the fact that, while sharing these values, the Chicago papers could hardly have differed more sharply in their news and editorial treatment of the great labor disputes of the day. Moreover, in discussions concerning the professional status of journalists (Singletary, 1982) a critical issue has been the proper role of the news media in society and of the journalist in gathering news. Researchers typically contrast conflicting values: participant versus neutral (Johnstone, Slawski, & Bowman, 1973), or gatekeeper versus advocate (Janowitz, 1975). However, in their survey of American journalists, Johnstone and colleagues (1976) found *both* the neutral and participant orientations were embraced by majorities of newsworkers; there were relatively few pure neutral or participant cases. Participant values were associated with working for elite media, being younger, and socializing with other journalists. A replication by Weaver and Wilhoit (1986) found less adherence to participant values and suggested that three roles (adversarial, interpretive, and disseminator) better characterize journalistic ideologies.

How do these values relate to actual practice? Ettema and Glasser (1985) argue that the more participant-oriented investigative journalists may employ an epistemology quite different from that of neutralists. Because truth claims by sources used in investigative reporting, unlike those by the representatives of established institutions used in daily reporting, are often problematic, the investigative reporter may be at great pains to justify the claims made in a story. Investigative reporters may, then, devise elaborate procedures—the "test of moral certainty" for example—to render the story credible to readers, to superiors, and to themselves. Levy (1981) suggests that there is an important interaction between journalists' personal views as to the worth of a news story, of competition for that story, and of competing journalists' assessment of their story. Where journalists see a story as important and also expect competition, Levy argues, they produce an "objective" story. Where they see competitive pressure as high *and* believe the story somehow *tainted*, the result, particularly if they believe other journalists share these assessments, is the "disdained" story, which is presented in such a way as to distance reporters from what they are reporting. Truth operates for journalists at two levels: They can report the "objective" truth about an event (e.g., accurately reproduce what was said at a news conference) while distancing themselves from the truth of what was said (see also Hallin & Mancini, 1984). Journalists deal as best they can with the fact that accurate and objective stories are not necessarily true.

Truth and Constraint

What, then, can be said of the prospects for knowing and telling the truth through journalism? If we are willing to stipulate that there is such a thing as truth to be known and told—a key stipulation, we admit—then we can formulate the issue of truth in journalism much as we formulated the issue for creativity in popular entertainment and much as journalists themselves sometimes formulate it ("Can the press tell the truth?" 1985): as a tension between the search for truth and the organizational and institutional constraints upon that process.

According to the ethic of professional journalism, an ethic that blurs truth and objectivity, constraints on the search for truth are *imposed on* journalistic practice either by the power of other institutions (particularly government) or by the human limitations of individual journalists. Normative journalistic ethics codes thus celebrate freedom of the press and yet urge restraint on the part of the reporter. This formulation of the threat to truth in journalism is reflected, for example, in White's (1950) emphasis on the failure of Mr. Gates to be very vigilant against personal bias.

More recent scholarship, however, has drastically reformulated the issue as one of constraints imposed *by* journalistic practice rather than *on* it. In this reformulation, the threats to truth are raised by organizational process and institutional arrangement, shifting research attention to higher levels of analysis. Cognitions of individual journalists are still of interest but they are now seen to reflect the "phase structures" of the bureaucracies to be covered. Similarly, the value of objectivity itself is seen as an organizational routine or ritual that serves the corporate drive to make news an efficiently produced commodity. In this formulation, then, it is not the attempt of individuals to make sense of their world that threatens truth but rather the constraints upon that attempt imposed by the social organization of journalism. Carey (1969) expresses this concern compellingly, though perhaps with a bit too much nostalgia for 19th-century journalism:

> With the rise of "objective reporting" in the latter part of the 19th century, the journalist went through a process that can be fairly termed a "conversion downwards," a process whereby a role is de-intellectualized and technicalized. . . . In this role he does not principally utilize an

intellectual skill as critic, interpreter and contemporary historian but a
technical skill at writing, a capacity to translate the specialized language
and purposes of government, science, art, medicine and finance into an
idiom that can be understood by a broader, more amorphous, less
educated audience. (p. 32)

The finding that many journalists do express participant, adversarial, or
interpretive values as part of their personal value systems suggests, however,
that at the individual level there is at least the desire to utilize intellectual as
well as technical skill and to find release from the constraints of objectivity.
The prospects for truth in journalism, much like the prospects for creativity
in popular entertainment, it seems, turn on the willingness and skill of
individuals to work within, around, and through the organizational and
institutional constraints to achieve their goals. The difference is that for
popular entertainment we emphasize "through" while for journalism we
may wish to emphasize "around" such constraints.

Lest our celebration of the individual journalist as truth teller gets out
of hand, we must acknowledge that, of course, journalists live and work
within an encompassing social and cultural context that powerfully and
implicitly informs their attempts to make sense of the world. Journalists have
no alternative but to draw upon the intellectual tools—theory and concept,
myth and metaphor—of their place and time in the world. Very much as
memoirists drew upon the cultural resource of irony to interpret the great
wars of their times, so, for example, journalists draw upon widely shared
understanding of nuclear weapons and strategy to report on the great war
that may yet come. William Dorman's (1985) critique of press performance
in the nuclear age begins with the problem of establishing independence of
journalistic vision and voice:

Since Hiroshima, journalism, like most other aspects of society, has been
held in nuclear thrall. The prospects of absolute warfare against the
homeland (and species) created the national-security state, and journalism has proved no more independent of it than national government,
education, the church or business. (p. 119)

Dorman concludes by asking the peace community to help reinvent journalism, but while some other journalism might be more critical of American
nuclear policy, it is not at all clear that any other journalism could be
independent of theory or interest. The knowledge-creating machinery of
professional journalism reviewed here has a particular social location with
particular political ramifications. But is it not so that *any* process of knowledge creation must have *some* location with political ramifications of its own?
And if this is so, then should not media access and diversity be our goals?
But do such goals imply that truth, after all, is not really a useful concept?
We find ourselves back to the ancient questions that we attempted to set aside
to study the sociology of journalism. Much as the research on the production

of culture cannot ultimately resolve questions of the role and meaning of culture materials in human life, so the research on newsmaking cannot finally resolve questions of knowledge and truth. The social science of professional mass communicators, their organizations, and institutions can, however, help define the terms and enrich the vocabulary used in the ongoing discussion of these enduring questions.

References

Associated Press Managing Editors. (1985). *Journalists and readers: Bridging the credibility gap.* San Francisco: APME Credibility Committee.

Bacharach, S. B., & Lawler, E. J. (1980). *Power and politics in organizations.* San Francisco: Jossey-Bass.

Bagdikian, B. H. (1985). The U.S. media: Supermarket or assembly line? *Journal of Communication, 35,* 97-109.

Bailey, G., & Lichty, L. W. (1972). Rough justice on a Saigon street. *Journalism Quarterly, 42,* 221-238.

Bantz, C. R. (1985). News organizations: Conflict as cultural norm. *Communication, 8,* 225-244.

Bantz, C. R., McCorkle, S., & Baade, R. C. (1980). The news factory. *Communication Research, 7,* 45-68.

Barnouw, E. (1978). *The sponsor: Notes on a modern potentate.* New York: Oxford University Press.

Becker, L. B. (1982). Print or broadcast: How the medium influences the reporter. In J. S. Ettema & D. C. Whitney (Eds.), *Individuals in mass media organizations: Creativity and constraint.* Beverly Hills, CA: Sage.

Becker, H. S. (1982). *Art worlds.* Berkeley: University of California Press.

Bennett, W. L. (1983). *News: The politics of illusion.* New York: Longman.

Bennett, W. L., Gressett, L. A., & Haltom, W. (1985). Repairing the news: A case study of the news paradigm. *Journal of Communication, 35,* 50-68.

Bennis, W., & Nanus, B. (1985). *Leaders: The strategies for taking charge.* New York: Harper & Row.

Blau, J. R., & McKinley, W. (1979). Ideas, complexity and innovation. *Administrative Science Quarterly, 24,* 200-219.

Bowers, D. R. (1967). A report on activity by publishers in directing newsroom decisions. *Journalism Quarterly, 44,* 43-52.

Breed, W. (1955a). Newspaper "opinion leaders" and the process of standardization. *Journalism Quarterly, 32,* 277-284.

Breed, W. (1955b). Social control in the newsroom: A functional analysis. *Social Forces, 33,* 326-335.

Brown, R. L. (1968). The creative process in the popular arts. *International Social Science Journal, 20,* 613-624.

Buckalew, J. K. (1969). A Q-analysis of TV news editors' decisions. *Journalism Quarterly, 46,* 135-137.

Burgoon, J. K., Burgoon, M., & Atkin, C. K. (1982). *The world of the working journalist.* New York: Newspaper Advertising Bureau.

Can the press tell the truth? (1985, January). *Harper's,* pp. 37-51.

Cantor, M. G. (1971). *The Hollywood television producer.* New York: Basic Books.

Cantor, M. G. (1979). The politics of popular drama. *Communication Research, 6,* 387-406.

Cantor, M. G. (1980). *Prime-time television: Content and control.* Beverly Hills, CA: Sage.

Carey, J. W. (1969). The communications revolution and the professional communicator. In *The sociology of mass media communicators* (Sociological Review Monograph No. 13, pp. 23-38).

Cawelti, J. (1969). The concept of formula in the study of popular literature. *Journal of Popular Culture, 3,* 381-403.

Cawelti, J. (1976). *Adventure, mystery, and romance.* Chicago: University of Chicago Press.

Clancey, M., & Robinson, M. J. (1985, December/January). The media in Campaign '84: General election coverage. *Public Opinion*, pp. 49-54, 59.

Clarke, P., & Evans, S. H. (1983). *Covering campaigns*. Stanford, CA: Stanford University Press.

Compaine, B. (Ed.). (1982). *Who owns the media?* White Plains, NY: Knowledge Industry.

Compaine, B. (1985). The expanding base of media competition. *Journal of Communication, 35*, 81-96.

Coser, L. A., Kadushin, C., & Powell, W. (1981). *Books: The culture and commerce of publishing*. New York: Basic Books.

Crouse, T. (1973). *The boys on the bus*. New York: Random House.

Darnton, R. (1975). Writing news and telling stories. *Daedalus, 104*, 175-194.

DiMaggio, P. (1977). Market structure, the creative process and popular culture: Toward an organizational reinterpretation of mass culture theory. *Journal of Popular Culture, 11*, 436-452.

DiMaggio, P., & Hirsch, P. (1976). Production organization in the arts. *American Behavioral Scientist, 19*, 735-749.

Dimmick, J. (1974, November). The gate-keeper: An uncertainty theory. *Journalism Monographs, 37*.

Dimmick, J., & Coit, P. (1982). Levels of analysis in mass media decision making. *Communication Research, 9*, 3-32.

Dominick, J. (1977). Geographic bias in network TV news. *Journal of Communication, 27*, 94-99.

Dominick, J., & Pearce, M. C. (1976). Trends in network prime time programming, 1953-1974. *Journal of Communication, 26*, 70-80.

Donohew, L. (1967). Newspaper gatekeepers and forces in the news channel. *Public Opinion Quarterly, 31*, 61-68.

Donohue, G. A., Olien, C. N., & Tichenor, P. J. (1985). Reporting conflict by pluralism, newspaper type and ownership. *Journalism Quarterly, 62*, 489-499.

Dorman, W. A. (1985, August). The media: Playing the government's game. *Bulletin of the Atomic Scientists*, pp. 118-124.

Downs, W. G., & Mohr, B. L. (1976). Conceptual issues in the study of innovations. *Administrative Science Quarterly, 21*, 700-714.

Dreier, P. (1982). The position of the press in the U.S. power structure. *Social Problems, 29*, 298-310.

DuBick, M. A. (1978). The organizational structure of newspapers in relation to their metropolitan environments. *Administrative Science Quarterly, 23*, 418-433.

Dunwoody, S. L. (1980). The science writing inner club. *Science, Technology & Human Values, 5*, 14-22.

Emery, F. C., & Trist, E. L. (1965). The causal texture of organizational environment. *Human Relations, 18*, 21-31.

Epstein, E. J. (1974). *News from nowhere*. New York: Vintage.

Epstein, E. J. (1975). *Between fact and fiction*. New York: Vintage.

Entman, R. M. (1985). Newspaper competition and First Amendment ideals: Does monopoly matter? *Journal of Communication, 35*, 147-165.

Espinosa, P. (1982). The audience in the text: Ethnographic observations of a Hollywood story conference. *Media, Culture & Society, 4*, 77-86.

Ettema, J. S. (1980). The role of educators and researchers in the production of educational television. *Journal of Broadcasting, 24*, 487-498.

Ettema, J. S. (1982). The organizational context of creativity: A case study from public television. In J. S. Ettema & D. C. Whitney (Eds.), *Individuals in mass media organizations: Creativity and constraint*. Beverly Hills, CA: Sage.

Ettema, J. S., & Glasser, T. L. (1985). On the epistemology of investigate journalism. *Communication, 8*, 183-206.

Ettema, J. S., & Whitney, D. C. (1982). Introduction: Mass communicators in context. In J. S. Ettema & D. C. Whitney (Eds.), *Individuals in mass media organizations: Creativity and constraint*. Beverly Hills, CA: Sage.

Faulkner, R. R. (1971). *Hollywood studio musicians.* Chicago: Aldine.

Faulkner, R. R. (1982). Improvising on a triad. In J. Van Maanen, J. M. Dabbs, Jr., & R. R. Faulkner, *Varieties of qualitative research.* Beverly Hills, CA: Sage.

Fishman, M. (1978). Crime waves as ideology. *Social Problems, 25,* 531-543.

Fishman, M. (1980). *Manufacturing the news.* Austin: University of Texas Press.

Fishman, M. (1982). News and nonevents: Making the visible invisible. In J. S. Ettema & D. C. Whitney (Eds.), *Individuals in mass media organizations: Creativity and constraint.* Beverly Hills, CA: Sage.

Flegel, R. C., & Chaffee, S. H. (1971). Influences of editors, readers and personal opinions on reporters. *Journalism Quarterly, 48,* 645-651.

Gans, H. J. (1957). The creator-audience relationship in the mass media: An analysis of movie making. In B. Rosenberg & D. M. White (Eds.), *Mass culture: The popular arts in America.* New York: Free Press.

Gans, H. J. (1979). *Deciding what's news.* New York: Pantheon.

Gans, H. J. (1985, November/December). Are U.S. journalists dangerously liberal? *Columbia Journalism Review,* pp. 29-33.

Gieber, W. (1964). News is what newspapermen make it. In L. A. Dexter & D. M. White (Eds.), *People, society and mass communications.* New York: Free Press.

Gitlin, T. (1979). Prime-time ideology: The hegemonic process in television entertainment. *Social Problems, 26,* 251-266.

Gitlin, T. (1980). *The whole world is watching.* Berkeley: University of California Press.

Gitlin, T. (1983). *Inside prime time.* New York: Pantheon.

Gold, D., & Simmons, J. L. (1965). News selection patterns among Iowa dailies. *Public Opinion Quarterly, 29,* 425-430.

Goldman, R. (1982). Hegemony and managed critique in prime-time television. *Theory and Society, 11,* 363-388.

Griff, M. (1960). The commercial artist. In M. R. Stein, A. J. Vidich, & D. M. White (Eds.), *Identity and anxiety.* New York: Free Press.

Hackett, R. A. (1984). Decline of a paradigm? Bias and objectivity in news media studies. *Critical Studies in Mass Communication, 1,* 229-259.

Hall, S. (1977). Culture, the media and the "ideological" effect. In J. Curran, M. Gurevitch, & J. Woollacott (Eds.), *Mass communication and society.* London: Edward Arnold.

Hall, S. (1980). Encoding and decoding in the television discourse. In S. Hall et al. (Eds.), *Culture, media, language.* London: Hutchinson.

Hall, S. (1982). The rediscovery of "ideology": Return of the repressed in media studies. In M. Gurevitch, T. Bennett, J. Curran, & J. Woollacott (Eds.), *Culture, society and the media.* London: Methuen.

Hallin, D. C., & Mancini, P. (1984). Speaking of the president: Political structure and representational form in U.S. and Italian television news. *Theory and Society, 13,* 829-850.

Hartley, J. (1982). *Understanding news.* London: Methuen.

Hickson, D. J., Hinings, C. R., Lee, C. A., & Schenck, R. E. (1971). A strategic contingencies theory of intra-organizational power. *Administrative Science Quarterly, 16,* 216-229.

Hirsch, P. M. (1972). Processing fads and fashions: An organization-set analysis of cultural industry systems. *American Journal of Sociology, 77,* 639-659.

Hirsch, P. M. (1975). Organizational effectiveness and the institutional environment. *Administrative Science Quarterly, 20,* 327-344.

Hutchins, R. M. (1947). *Commission on freedom of the press: Toward a free and responsible press.* Chicago: University of Chicago Press.

Intintoli, M. J. (1984). *Taking soaps seriously: The world of "Guiding Light."* New York: Praeger.

Janowitz, M. (1975). Professional models in journalism: The gatekeeper and the advocate. *Journalism Quarterly, 57,* 618-626, 662.

Jensen, J. (1984). An interpretive approach to culture production. In W. D. Rowland, Jr., & B. Watkins (Eds.), *Interpreting television: Current research perspectives.* Beverly Hills, CA: Sage.

Johnstone, J. W. C., Slawski, E., & Bowman, W. (1973). The professional values of American newsmen. *Public Opinion Quarterly, 36,* 522-540.

Johnstone, J. W. C., Slawski, E., & Bowman, W. (1976). *The news people: A sociological portrait of American journalists and their work.* Urbana: University of Illinois Press.

Kaminsky, S. M. (1985). *American film genres.* Chicago: Nelson-Hall.

Kanter, R. M. (1983). *The change masters: Innovations for productivity in the American corporation.* New York: Simon & Schuster.

Kueneman, R. M., & Wright, J. E. (1975). News policies of broadcast stations for civil disturbances and disasters. *Journalism Quarterly, 52,* 670-677.

Lester, M. (1980). Generating newsworthiness: The interpretive construction of public events. *American Sociological Review, 45,* 984-994.

Levy, M. R. (1981). Disdaining the news. *Journal of Communication, 31,* 24-31.

Lewis, I. A. (1985). *The news media: Los Angeles Times Poll No. 94.* Los Angeles: Los Angeles Times.

Lichter, S. R., & Rothman, S. (1981, October/November). Media and business elites. *Public Opinion,* pp. 42-46, 59-60.

Lippmann, W. (1922). *Public opinion.* New York: Macmillan.

Lowell, A. (1930). *Poetry and poets.* Boston: Houghton Mifflin.

March, J. G., & Simon, H. A. (1958). *Organizations.* New York: John Wiley.

McCombs, M. E., & Shaw, D. L. (1972). The agenda-setting function of the mass media. *Public Opinion Quarterly, 36,* 176-187.

McCombs, M. E., & Shaw, D. L. (1977). Structuring the "unseen environment." *Journal of Communication, 27,* 18-22.

Mead, G. H. (1964). The nature of the aesthetic experience. In A. J. Peck (Ed.), *The selected writings of George Herbert Mead.* Indianapolis, IN: Bobbs-Merrill.

Molotch, H., & Lester, M. (1974). News as purposive behavior: On the strategic use of routine events, accidents and scandals. *American Sociological Review, 39,* 101-112.

Montgomery, K. (1981). Gay activists and the networks. *Journal of Communication, 31,* 49-71.

Murdock, G. (1982). Large corporations and the control communications industries. In M. Gurevitch, T. Bennett, J. Curran, & J. Woollacott (Eds.), *Culture, society and the media.* London: Methuen.

Murdock, G., & Golding, P. (1977). Capitalism, communication and class relations. In J. Curran, M. Gurevitch, & J. Woollacott (Eds.), *Mass Communication and Society,* London: Edward Arnold.

Newcomb, H. M., & Alley, R. S. (1982). The producer as artist: Commercial television. In J. S. Ettema & D. C. Whitney (Eds.), *Individuals in mass media organizations: Creativity and constraint.* Beverly Hills, CA: Sage.

Newcomb, H. M., & Alley, R. S. (1983). *The producer's medium.* New York: Oxford University Press.

Newcomb, H. M., & Hirsch, P. M. (1984). Television as a cultural forum: Implications for research. In W. R. Rowland, Jr., & B. Watkins (Eds.), *Interpreting television: Current research perspectives.* Beverly Hills, CA: Sage.

Nichols, B. (1976). *Motives and methods.* Berkeley: University of California Press.

Nord, D. P. (1980). An economic perspective on formula in popular culture. *Journal of American Culture, 3,* 17-31.

Nord, D. P. (1984). The business values of American newspapers: The 19th century watershed in Chicago. *Journalism Quarterly, 61,* 265-273.

Olien, C. N., Donohue, G. A., & Tichenor, P. J. (1968). The community editor's power and the reporting of conflict. *Journalism Quarterly, 45,* 243-252.

Owen, B. M. (1975). *Economics and freedom of expression: Media structure and the First Amendment.* Cambridge, MA: Ballinger.

Owen, B. M., Beebe, J. H., & Manning, W. G., Jr. (1974). *Television economics*. Lexington, MA: Lexington Books.

Paletz, D., & Dunn, R. (1969). Press coverage of civil disorders: A case study of Winston-Salem, 1967. *Public Opinion Quarterly, 33*, 328-345.

Paletz, D., Reichert, P., & McIntyre, B. (1971). How the media support local government authority. *Public Opinion Quarterly, 35*, 80-92.

Park, R. E. (1940). News as a form of knowledge. *American Journal of Sociology, 45*, 669-686.

Patterson, T. (1980). *The mass media election*. New York: Praeger.

Pekurny, R. (1982). Coping with television production. In J. S. Ettema & D. C. Whitney (Eds.), *Individuals in mass media organizations: Creativity and constraint*. Beverly Hills, CA: Sage.

Perrow, C. (1979). *Complex organizations: A critical essay* (2nd ed.). Glenview, IL: Scott, Foresman.

Peters, S. K., & Cantor, M. G. (1982). Screen acting as work. In J. S. Ettema & D. C. Whitney (Eds.), *Individuals in mass media organizations: Creativity and constraint*. Beverly Hills, CA: Sage.

Peterson, R. A. (1976). The production of culture: A prolegomenon. *American Behavioral Scientist, 19*, 7-22.

Peterson, R. A., & Berger, D. G. (1975). Cycles in symbol production: The case of popular music. *American Sociological Review, 40*, 158-173.

Pool, I., & Shulman, I. (1959). Newsmen's fantasies, audiences and newswriting. *Public Opinion Quarterly, 23*, 145-158.

Powell, W. W. (1982). From craft to corporation: The impact of outside ownership on book publishing. In J. S. Ettema & D. C. Whitney (Eds.), *Individuals in mass media organizations: Creativity and constraint*. Beverly Hills, CA: Sage.

Protess, D. L., Leff, D. R., Brooks, S. C., & Gordon, M. T. (1985). Uncovering rape: The watchdog press and the limits of agenda setting. *Public Opinion Quarterly, 49*, 19-37.

Robinson, G. J. (1970). Foreign news selection is non-linear in Yugoslavia's Tanjug agency. *Journalism Quarterly, 47*, 340-351.

Robinson, M. J. (1976). Public affairs television and the growth of political malaise. *American Political Science Review, 70*, 409-432.

Robinson, M. J. (1983, February/March). Just how liberal is the news? 1980 revisited. *Public Opinion*, pp. 55-60.

Robinson, M. J. (1985, February/March). The media in Campaign '84, Part II: Wingless, toothless and hopeless. *Public Opinion*, pp. 43-48.

Roshco, B. (1975). *Newsmaking*. Chicago: University of Chicago Press.

Rosten, L. C. (1937). *The Washington correspondents*. New York: Harcourt Brace Jovanovich.

Ryan, J., & Peterson, R. A. (1982). The product image: The fate of creativity in country music songwriting. In J. S. Ettema & D. C. Whitney (Eds.), *Individuals in mass media organizations: Creativity and constraint*. Beverly Hills, CA: Sage.

Sanders, C. R. (1982). Structural and interactional features of popular culture production: An introduction to the production of culture perspective. *Journal of Popular Culture, 16*, 66-74.

Schatz, T. (1981). *Hollywood genres: Formulas, filmmaking and the studio system*. Philadelphia: Temple University Press.

Schiller, D. (1981). *Objectivity and the news*. Philadelphia: University of Pennsylvania Press.

Schlesinger, P. (1978). *Putting "reality" together: BBC news*. London: Constable.

Schneider, W., & Lewis, I. A. (1985, August/September). Views on the news. *Public Opinion*, pp. 6-11, 58-59.

Schudson, M. (1978). *Discovering the news*. New York: Basic Books.

Siegelman, L. (1973). Reporting the news: An organizational analysis. *American Journal of Sociology, 79*, 132-151.

Sigal, L. V. (1973). *Reporters and officials*. Lexington, MA: D. C. Heath.

Singletary, M. (1982). Commentary: Are journalists "professionals"? *Newspaper Research Journal, 3*, 75-78.

Stark, R. (1962). Policy and the pros: An organizational analysis of a metropolitan newspaper. *Berkeley Journal of Sociology, 7*, 11-31.

Stinchcombe, A. L. (1959). Bureaucratic and craft administration of production: A comparative study. *Administrative Science Quarterly, 4*, 168-187.

Strodthoff, G. G., Hawkins, R. P., & Schoenfeld, A. C. (1985). Media roles in a social movement: A model of ideology diffusion. *Journal of Communication, 35*, 134-153.

Thompson, J. D. (1967). *Organizations in action.* New York: McGraw-Hill.

Tichenor, P. J., Donohue, G. A., & Olien, C. N. (1980). *Community conflict and the press.* Beverly Hills, CA: Sage.

Tuchman, G. (1969). *News, the newsman's reality.* Ph.D. dissertation, Brandeis University.

Tuchman, G. (1972). Objectivity as strategic ritual. *American Journal of Sociology, 77*, 660-679.

Tuchman, G. (1973). Making news by doing work: Routinizing the unexpected. *American Journal of Sociology, 79*, 110-131.

Tuchman, G. (1974). Assembling a network talk-show. In G. Tuchman (Ed.), *The TV establishment: Programming for power and profit.* Englewood Cliffs, NJ: Prentice Hall.

Tuchman, G. (1978). *Making news: A study in the construction of reality.* New York: Free Press.

Tuchman, G. (1983). Consciousness industries and the production of culture. *Journal of Communication, 33*, 330-341.

Turow, J. (1977). Client relationship and children's book publishing: A comparative study of mass media policy in two marketplaces. In P. M. Hirsch, P. V. Miller, & F. G. Kline (Eds.), *Strategies for communication research.* Beverly Hills, CA: Sage.

Turow, J. (1978). Casting for television: The anatomy of social typing. *Journal of Communication, 28*, 18-24.

Turow, J. (1979). *Getting books to children.* Chicago: American Library Association.

Turow, J. (1982). Unconventional programs on commercial television: An organizational perspective. In J. S. Ettema & D. C. Whitney (Eds.), *Individuals in mass media organizations: Creativity and constraints.* Beverly Hills, CA: Sage.

Turow, J. (1984a). *Media industries: The production of news and entertainment.* New York: Longman.

Turow, J. (1984b). Pressure groups and television entertainment: A framework for analysis. In W. D. Rowland, Jr., & B. Watkins (Eds.), *Interpreting television: Current research perspectives.* Beverly Hills, CA: Sage.

Turow, J. (1985). Cultural argumentation through the mass media: A framework for organizational research. *Communication, 8*, 139-164.

Weaver, D. H., & Wilhoit, G. C. (1986). *The American journalist: A portrait of U.S. news people and their work.* Bloomington: Indiana University Press.

White, D. M. (1950). The "gate keeper": A case study in the selection of news. *Journalism Quarterly, 27*, 383-396.

Whiteside, T. (1981). *The blockbuster complex.* Middletown, CT: Wesleyan University Press.

Whitney, D. C. (1982). Mass communicator studies: Similarity, difference and level of analysis. In J. S. Ettema & D. C. Whitney (Eds.), *Individuals in mass media organizations: Creativity and constraint.* Beverly Hills, CA: Sage.

Whitney, D. C., & Becker, L. B. (1982). "Keeping the gates" for gatekeepers: The effects of wire news. *Journalism Quarterly, 59*, 60-65.

Whitney, D. C., Fritzler, M., Jones, S., Mazzarella, S., & Rakow, L. (1985, August). *Geographic and source biases in network television news 1982-1984.* Paper presented at Association for Education in Journalism, Memphis, TN.

PART II: News as Social Production

Selecting News

The Individual Gatekeeper

At the individual level of analysis, news represents the outcome of a reporter's expert judgment and personal motivation. Without interference from manipulative sources or demanding news organizations, this perspective might argue, reporters should be able to produce a newspaper or newscast that accurately represents a well-rounded look at the day's events. The gatekeeping tradition has its roots in these beliefs, focusing on the gatekeeper's ability to exercise professional news judgment.

Although the gatekeeping tradition has essentially been abandoned by media scholars, it nonetheless provides a good point of entry for a reader making the transition away from conventional beliefs about the production of news and toward a more socially based approach.

Pamela J. Shoemaker's "A New Gatekeeping Model" puts the individual level of analysis into its broader social context. Three diagrams and their accompanying discussion clarify how social forces shape decisions made by individual journalists. Levels included in this scheme include the broad societal level (ideology and culture), the everyday working environment (communication routines and organizational characteristics), and the socially shaped mind of the journalist (intraindividual).

In all, these three levels are similar to the scheme outlined by Ettema and Whitney in Chapter 3. Here, they provide an explicit, systematic framework for considering the other selections in this section, which move from the individual level to the organizational and community levels of analysis.

David Manning White's classic 1950 "The 'Gate Keeper': A Case Study in the Selection of News" introduced the gatekeeping metaphor to mainstream inquiry about the nature of news. He depicted news selection as a rational individual-level process where a gatekeeping editor pits core beliefs

about newsworthiness—such as the mix of story topics and the importance
of the stories—against a gatekeeper's personal preferences and values.

The study was based on research with one male wire editor in his
mid-40s who worked at a newspaper with a circulation of 30,000 in a city of
100,000. By tallying characteristics of the pool of news stories Mr. Gates
considered, and then interviewing Mr. Gates about his choices, White concluded that basic journalistic beliefs were involved in decisions, but the
process was rather subjective and depended on the gatekeeper's experiences,
attitudes, and expectations.

Glen L. Bleske's 1991 replication of White's original study, "Ms. Gates
Takes Over," offers several comparative dimensions, including gender, journalism experience, historical time period, news technology differences, and
organizational size. For the most part, though, none of these dimensions
seems to produce meaningful differences between news selection choices of
the two gatekeepers. As before, the bulk of selected stories were those that a
newspaper could not gather economically on its own: human interest, international politics, and national politics.

Reading between the lines of White's and Bleske's studies, both gatekeepers saw their job as the implementation of journalistic judgment in the
face of organizational constraints. In fact, other aspects of these gatekeepers'
work was clearly shaped by higher levels of analysis. For example, the fact
that Ms. Gates did not emphasize stories about women's issues illustrates
the homogenizing effect of the news organization and journalistic professionalism on journalists' behavior. Similarly, Ms. Gates chose stories partly
because one wire service's timing and story form offered a better opportunity
for predictable accomplishment of her work.

"Refining the Gatekeeping Metaphor for Local Television News" places
news selection beyond the individual level. Here, news values played a small
part, but a much greater effect surfaced from the work routines and organizational constraints that gatekeepers faced.

Overall, the news organization needed to choose stories that could be
gathered and produced expediently. Like many other television stations and
some newspapers, gatekeeping was accomplished through group decision
making that varied by the dynamics of the group members involved on any
particular day. This finding significantly recasts the concept of gatekeeping,
both in terms of the nature of the job and the nature of the social forces that
shape its outcomes.

Community and organizational levels of analysis stand out in G. A.
Donohue, C. A. Olien, and P. J. Tichenor's "Structure and Constraints on
Community Newspaper Gatekeepers." From this vantage point, the gatekeeper's job involves managing the intersection of organizational constraints
with those constraints stemming from the nature of the media organization's
community. Within organizations, gatekeepers face constraints from professional values, resource limits, personnel structures, and management concerns. Within the community, the degree of pluralism becomes key. Most
simply, pluralism refers to the centrality of a community's power structure.

This intersection of media and community affects both news content and news procedures. For example, small town editors face greater economic constraints, which in turn influence staff size and work routines. In larger communities, part of an editor's responsibilities are delegated to others on the larger staff. Donohue and colleagues tested these ideas through a survey of daily and weekly newspaper editors. Although they found that pressures related to advertising and organizational management varied by level of community pluralism, beliefs about news judgment were quite similar across different social contexts.

This point about professional values spans the studies by White, Bleske, and Berkowitz in this section of the book, showing how journalists' comments reflect a common view about the nature of news. Thus, this section documents the evolution of the gatekeeping concept, moving from its simple roots to its place in broader social contexts.

CHAPTER **4**

A New Gatekeeping Model

Pamela J. Shoemaker

Simply put, gatekeeping is the process by which the billions of messages that are available in the world get cut down and transformed into the hundreds of messages that reach a given person on a given day. Gatekeeping studies have most often looked at the selection of news items within the mass media, but gatekeeping can involve more than just selection. Donohue, Tichenor, and Olien (1972) have suggested that gatekeeping be defined as a broader process of information control that includes all aspects of message encoding: not just selection but also withholding, transmission, shaping, display, repetition, and timing of information as it goes from the sender to the receiver. In other words, the gatekeeping process involves every aspect of message selection, handling, and control, whether the message is communicated through mass media or interpersonal channels.

On a more microscopic level of analysis, gatekeeping also can be thought of as the process of reconstructing the essential framework of an event and turning it into news. People who see an event occur pass along some details and not others (Schramm, 1949a). Analysts provide interpretation and can emphasize some aspects while downplaying others. Communicators pick some elements of a message and reject others. The elements selected are evaluated according to their importance, with the most important elements being displayed most prominently and presented most quickly and/or frequently. One day's news represents the effects of many gatekeepers at many gates. It is probably not an overstatement to say that all communication workers are gatekeepers to some degree, for gatekeeping is an integral part of the overall process of selecting and producing messages. Not only is it impossible for everything to be transmitted, but it also is impossible to transmit something without in some fashion shaping it.

Although gatekeeping research in the field of communication has most commonly involved the mass media, the gatekeeping metaphor can be applied to any decision point involving any bit of information, whether transmission is expected to occur through mass or interpersonal channels. Schramm (1949b, pp. 175-176), for example, distinguished between "media chains" and "interpersonal chains"—both channels through which messages can pass from sender to receiver, via gatekeepers. Diffusion studies, for example, could be said to involve gatekeeping, with every person in a social system acting as a potential gatekeeper for others (Greenberg, 1964).

The usual definition of gatekeeping involves an activity performed by a communication organization and its representatives. Our discussion of gatekeeping will start at the point at which a communication worker first learns about an actual or potential message and it will stop at the point at which a subset of those messages is transmitted to a receiver. A gate is an "in" or "out" decision point, and messages come to the communication organization from a variety of channels. For example, some messages may come from routine channels (e.g., from wire services or as the result of a news beat), some may come unsolicited (e.g., press releases), and others may be sought out by a communication worker (e.g., following up a possible news story) or even created by the communication worker (e.g., investigative reporting). . . .

Figures 4.1, 4.2, and 4.3 summarize and integrate what is known about gatekeeping, based on the theoretical approaches we have discussed. Figures 4.2 and 4.3 are not independent models but represent enlargements of portions of Figure 4.1. The overall process is shown in Figure 4.1 but without detail within communication organizations and within individual gatekeepers. Figure 4.2 shows the gatekeeping processes within a communication organization, and Figure 4.3 shows the intraindividual psychological processes within one gatekeeper. In Figure 4.1 (see Figures 4.2 and 4.3 for more detail), circles represent individual gatekeepers, vertical bars in front of gatekeepers are gates, and the arrows in front of and behind each gate represent the forces that affect a message's entrance into the gate and what happens to it afterward. The large squares are communication organizations, and small rectangles represent social and institutional factors. One or more channels lead to and from each gate and gatekeeper, each carrying one or more messages or potential messages.

The process starts with a variety of potential messages traveling through multiple channels to any of several types of communication organizations, such as a wire service, a public relations agency, a newspaper, or a television network. An organization may have multiple staff members operating in boundary-role input positions, each with the power to control which potential messages actually enter the organization and the power to shape the message.

Moving to the organizational enlargement (Figure 4.2), we see that, within a complex organization, the boundary-role gatekeepers in charge of

(Text continues on p. 62)

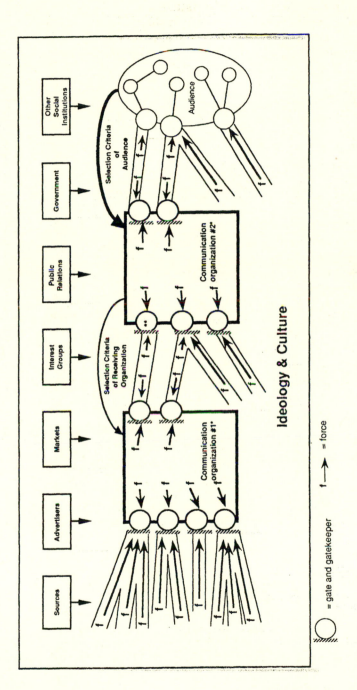

Figure 4.1. Gatekeeping Between Organizations Is Embedded in Social System Ideology and Culture and Is Influenced by Social and Institutional Factors

NOTE: As an example, communication organizations could include wire services, public relations agencies, television networks, or newspapers.
*See Figure 4.2 for a detailed version of gatekeeping within an organization.
**See Figure 4.3 for a detailed version of gatekeeping within an individual.

60

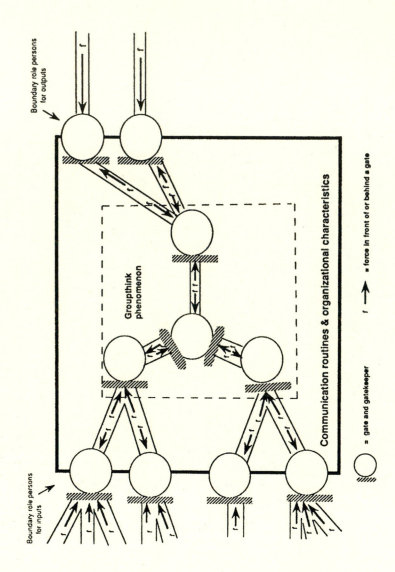

Figure 4.2. Gatekeeping Within an Organization Is Embedded in Communication Routines and Organizational Characteristics
NOTE: See Figure 4.3 for intraindividual gatekeeping processes.

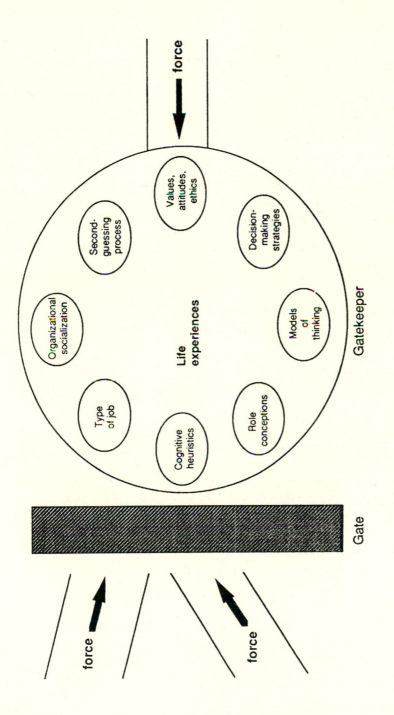

Figure 4.3. Intraindividual Gatekeeping Processes

NOTE: Intraindividual-level variables are embedded in life experiences.

61

inputs may channel selected messages to one or more internal gatekeepers, who may exert their own selection processes and who also may shape the message in a variety of ways. The surviving, shaped messages are then transmitted to boundary-role gatekeepers for final shaping, selection, and transmission directly to the audience or to another communication organization (see Figure 4.1). As the feedback loop from Organization 2 to Organization 1 (and from the audience to Organization 2) indicates, selection of messages for outputting is heavily influenced by the selection criteria of the receiver. As Figure 4.2 shows, the gatekeeping processes internal to the organization are embedded in the organization's communication routines and characteristics, which affect the decisions organizational gatekeepers make. Figure 4.2 also provides for the "groupthink" phenomenon (Janis, 1983), particularly among socially cohesive groups of gatekeepers.

Figure 4.3 identifies various psychological processes and individual characteristics that can affect the gatekeeping process, including cognitive heuristics, models of thinking, socialization, second-guessing, values, attitudes, decision-making strategies, role conceptions, and type of job. Just as the broader gatekeeping model (Figure 4.1) is embedded in social system ideology and culture, within-organization gatekeeping (Figure 4.2) is embedded in communication routines and organizational characteristics, and individual-level gatekeeping processes (Figure 4.3) are embedded in the individual's life experiences.

Thus we see the complexity of the gatekeeping process. The individual gatekeeper has likes and dislikes, ideas about the nature of his or her job, ways of thinking about a problem, preferred decision-making strategies, and values that all impinge on the decision to reject or select (and shape) a message. But the gatekeeper is not totally free to follow a personal whim; he or she must operate within the constraints of communication routines to do things this way or that. All of this also must occur within the framework of the communication organization, which has its own priorities but also is continuously buffeted by influential forces from outside the organization. And, of course, none of these actors—the individual, the routine, the organization, or the social institution—can escape the fact that it is tied to and draws its sustenance from the social system.

References

Donohue, G. A., Tichenor, P. J., & Olien, C. N. (1972). Gatekeeping: Mass media systems and information control. In F. G. Kline & P. J. Tichenor (Eds.), *Current perspectives in mass communication research* (pp. 41-70). Beverly Hills, CA: Sage.

Greenberg, B. S. (1964). Person-to-person communication in the diffusion of news events. *Journalism Quarterly, 41,* 489-494.

Janis, I. L. (1983). *Group think: Psychological studies of policy decisions and fiascoes.* Boston: Houghton Mifflin.

Schramm, W. (1949a). The nature of news. *Journalism Quarterly, 26,* 259-269.

Schramm, W. (1949b). The gatekeeper: A memorandum. In W. Schramm (Ed.), *Mass communications* (pp. 175-177). Urbana: University of Illinois Press.

CHAPTER 5

The "Gate Keeper"

A Case Study in the Selection of News

David Manning White

It was the late Kurt Lewin, truly one of the great social scientists of our time, who applied the term "gate keeper" to a phenomenon which is of considerable importance to students of mass communications. In his last article,[1] before his untimely death, Dr. Lewin pointed out that the traveling of a news item through certain communication channels was dependent on the fact that certain areas within the channels functioned as "gates." Carrying the analogy further, Lewin said that gate sections are governed either by impartial rules or by "gate keepers," and in the latter case an individual or group is "in power" for making the decision between "in" or "out."

To understand the functioning of the "gate," Lewin said, was equivalent to understanding the factors which determine the decisions of the "gate keepers," and he rightly suggested that the first diagnostic task is the finding of the actual "gate keepers."

The purpose of this study is to examine closely the way one of the "gate keepers" in the complex channels of communication operates his "gate."

Wilbur Schramm made an observation central to this whole study when he wrote that "no aspect of communication is so impressive as the enormous

From *Journalism Quarterly*, 1950, Vol. 27, pp. 383-396, published by the Association for Education in Journalism and Mass Communication.

AUTHOR'S NOTE: The author acknowledges the suggestions of Dr. Wilbur Schramm during the preparation of this article, also the assistance of Mr. Raymond Stewart.

number of choices and discards which have to be made between the formation of the symbol in the mind of the communicator, and the appearance of
a related symbol in the mind of the receiver." [2] To illustrate this in terms of a
news story let us consider, for example, a Senate hearing on a proposed bill
for federal aid to education. At the hearing there will be reporters from the
various press associations, Washington correspondents of large newspapers
which maintain staffs in the capital, as well as reporters for local newspapers.
All of these form the first "gate" in the process of communication. They have
to make the initial judgment as to whether a story is "important" or not. One
has only to read the Washington stories from two newspapers whose general
editorial attitudes differ widely on such an issue as federal aid to education
to realize from the beginning of the process the "gate keepers" are playing
an important role. The appearance of the story in the Chicago *Tribune* and
the Chicago *Sun-Times* might well show some differences in treatment. It is
apparent that even the actual physical event of the Senate hearing (which we
might call the *criterion event*) is reported by two reporters in two different
perceptual frameworks and that the two men bring to the "story" different
sets of experience, attitudes and expectations.

Thus a story is transmitted from one "gate keeper" after another in the
chain of communications. From reporter to rewrite man, through bureau
chief to "state" file editors at various press association offices, the process of
choosing and discarding is continuously taking place. And finally we come
to our last "gate keeper," the one to whom we turn for the purpose of our
case study. This is the man who is usually known as the wire editor on the
non-metropolitan newspaper. He has charge of the selection of national and
international news which will appear on the front and "jump" pages of his
newspaper, and usually he makes up these pages.

Our "gate keeper" is a man in his middle 40s, who after approximately
25 years' experience as a journalist (both as reporter and copy editor) is now
the wire editor of a morning newspaper of approximately 30,000 circulation
in a highly industrialized midwest city of 100,000. It is his job to select from
the avalanche of wire copy daily provided by the Associated Press, United
Press and International News Service what 30,000 families will read on the
front page of their morning newspapers. He also copyedits and writes the
headlines for these stories. His job is similar to that which newspapermen
throughout the country hold in hundreds of non-metropolitan newspapers.[3]
And in many respects he is the most important "gate keeper" of all, for if he
rejects a story the work of all those who preceded him in reporting and
transmitting the story is negated. It is understood, of course, that the story
could have "ended" (insofar as its subsequent transmission is concerned) at
any of the previous "gates." But assuming the story has progressed through
all the "gates," it is obvious that this wire editor is faced with an extremely
complicated set of decisions to make regarding the limited number of stories
he can use.

Our purpose in this study was to determine some preliminary ideas as
to why this particular wire editor selected or rejected the news stories filed

by the three press associations (and transmitted by the "gate keeper" above him in Chicago) and thereby gain some diagnostic notions about the general role of the "gate keeper" in the areas of mass communications.

To this end we received the full cooperation of "Mr. Gates," the above-mentioned wire editor. The problem of finding out what Mr. Gates selected from the mass of incoming wire copy was not difficult, for it appeared on the front and "jump" pages of his newspaper each morning. Actually, we were far more concerned with the copy that did not get into the paper. So for the week of February 6 through 13, 1949, Mr. Gates saved every piece of wire copy that came to his desk. Instead of throwing the dispatch into the waste basket once he had decided not to use it, he put it into a large box next to his desk. Then at one o'clock when his pages were made up and his night's work through, Mr. Gates went through every piece of copy in the "reject" box and wrote on it the reason why he had initially rejected it, assuming that he could recall the reason. In the cases where no ascertainable reason had occurred to him he made no notations on the copy. Although this meant that Mr. Gates had to spend between an hour and a half and two hours each night at this rather tedious phase of the project, he was perfectly willing to do this throughout the entire week.

When Mr. Gates had turned over the raw material of his choices for the week period, we tried to analyze his performance in terms of certain basic questions which presented themselves. These questions are applicable not only to this particular "gate keeper," but with modifications to all of the "gate keepers" in the communications process. Thus, after determining what wire news came in during the week in terms of total column inches and categories, we measured the amount of wire news that appeared in the papers for that period.

Assuming that five lines of wire copy are equivalent to a column inch in a newspaper, Mr. Gates received approximately 12,400 inches of press association news from the AP, UP and INS during the week. Of this he used 1,297 column inches of wire news, or about *one-tenth*, in the seven issues we measured. Table 5.1 shows a breakdown by categories of the wire news received and used during the week.

It is only when we study the reasons given by Mr. Gates for rejecting almost nine-tenths of the wire copy (in his search for the one-tenth for which he has space) that we begin to understand how highly subjective, how reliant upon value-judgments based on the "gate keeper's" own set of experiences, attitudes and expectations the communication of "news" really is. In this particular case the 56 wordings given may be divided into two main categories: (1) rejecting the incident as worthy of being reported, and (2) selecting from many reports of the same event. (See Table 5.2.)

Thus we find him rejecting one piece of wire copy with the notation, "He's too Red." Another story is categorically marked "Never use this." The story dealt with the Townsend Plan, and because this "gate keeper" feels that the merits of the Townsend Plan are highly dubious, the chances of wire news about the plan appearing in the paper are negligible. Eighteen pieces of copy

Table 5.1 Amounts of Press Association News Mr. Gates Received and Used
During Seven-Day Period

Category	Wire Copy Received		Wire Copy Used	
	Column In.*	% of Total	Column In.*	% of Total
Crime	527	4.4	41	3.2
Disaster	405	3.4	44	3.4
Political				
State	565	4.7	88	6.8
National	1,722	14.5	205	15.8
Human interest	4,171	35.0	301	23.2
International				
Political	1,804	15.1	176	13.6
Economic	405	3.4	59	4.5
War	480	4.0	72	5.6
Labor	650	5.5	71	5.5
National				
Farm	301	2.5	78	6.0
Economic	294	2.5	43	3.3
Education	381	3.2	56	4.3
Science	205	1.7	63	4.9
Total	11,910	99.9	1,297	100.1

*Counting five lines of wire copy as one column inch.

were marked "B. S."; 16 were marked "Propaganda." One interesting notation on a story said, "Don't care for suicides." Thus we see that many of the
reasons which Mr. Gates gives for the rejection of the stories fall into the
category of highly subjective value-judgments.

The second category gives us an important clue as to the difficulty of
making choices of one piece of copy over another. No less than 168 times, Mr.
Gates makes the notation "No space." In short, the story (in his eyes) has
merit and interest, he has no "personal" objections to it, but space is at a
premium. It is significant to observe that the later in the evening the stories
came in, the higher was the proportion of the "no space" or "would use" type
of notation. As the evening progresses the wire editor's pages become more
and more filled up. A story that has a good chance of getting on the front
page at 7:30 or 8 o'clock in the evening may not be worth the precious
remaining space at 11 o'clock. The notation "Would use" is made 221 times,
and a similar one "Good—if space" is made 154 times. Other reasons which
fall into the mechanical category are "Used INS—shorter" or "Used UP—this
is late." Even in this category, though, we find subjective value-judgments
such as "Used AP—better story" or "Used INS—lead more interesting."

Now that we have some preliminary knowledge of the manner in which
Mr. Gates selects or rejects news for his front and "jump" pages, it might be
interesting to examine his performance for a specific day. In Table 5.3 the
amount and type of news which appeared on the front and "jump" pages

Table 5.2 Reasons for Rejection of Press Association News Given by Mr. Gates During Seven-Day Period

Reason		No. of Times Given
Rejecting incident as worthy of reporting		423
Not interesting (61); no interest here (43)	104	
Dull writing (51); too vague (26); drags too much (3)	80	
No good (31); slop (18); B. S. (18)	67	
Too much already on subject (54); used up (4); passed—dragging out;* too much of this; goes on all the time; dying out	62	
Trivial (29); would ignore (21); no need for this; wasted space; not too important; not too hot; not too worthy	55	
Never use this (16); never use (7)	23	
Propaganda (16); he's too red; sour grapes	18	
Wouldn't use (11); don't care for suicide stories; too suggestive; out of good taste	14	
Selecting from reports of the same event		910
Would use if space (221); no space (168); good— if space (154); late—used up (61); too late—no space (34); no space—used other press service; would use partially if space	640	
Passed for later story (61); waiting for later information (48); waiting on this (33); waiting for this to hatch (17); would let drop a day or two (11); outcome will be used— not this; waiting for later day progress	172	
Too far away (24); out of area (16)	40	
Too regional (36)	36	
Used another press service: Better story (11); shorter (6); this is late; lead more interesting; meatier	20	
Bannered yesterday	1	
I missed this one	1	

*In this and other cases where no number follows the reason, that reason was given only once.

edited by Gates for February 9, 1949, is presented. Table 5.4 shows the total number of dispatches (classified as to type of story) received but not used.

During this particular week the Cardinal Mindszenty trial was receiving wide play from newspapers throughout the land and the press associations were filing many stories covering all phases of the case. So in making a comparison of the dispatches received and the stories which appeared, it should not be surprising to note that human interest news was used most. Yet even in his treatment of the Mindzenty case, Mr. Gates used highly subjective reasons in his selection of stories. Particularly interesting in this connection is his remark on an Associated Press story which he rejected with the comment *"Would pass, propaganda itself."* The story dealt with a statement by Samuel Cardinal Stritch, who said, "It is very unfortunate that our news agencies are not giving their sources of information in their day-by-day reports on the trial of Cardinal Mindszenty. It should be made clear that

Table 5.3 Column Inches Devoted to Content Categories in February 9, 1949, Issue*

Category	Front Page	and Jump
Local		3.50
Crime		5.00
Disaster		9.75
Political		41.25
Local	9.75	
State	19.50	
National	12.00	
Human interest		43.75**
International		23.00
Political	11.50	
Economic	11.50	
War	—	
National		24.25
Labor	19.25	
Farm	—	
Economic	5.00	
Education		—
Science		6.00***

*Banner not included.
**About one-half of this amount were Cardinal Mindszenty stories, which, because of the human appeal, were classed as human interest.
***Three-column picture not included.

restrictions have been made on the few American correspondents who have been present at the trial." It is obvious that Mr. Gates resented the implication by Cardinal Stritch that the press associations were not doing all they could to tell the Mindszenty story. The comment which Mr. Gates put on a United Press story dealing with Cardinal Stritch's statement, "No space—pure propaganda," illustrates his sensitivity on this particular point. And when the story came to his attention for the third time that evening as an International News Service dispatch he again rejected it, this time with the statement "Would pass." Perhaps his feeling of anger against the story had cooled by this time, but Mr. Gates still considered the story worthless.

Political news enjoyed the second largest play. Here we begin to have an indication of preference, as political news ranked only fifth in the "dispatches received" department. Political news seems to be a favorite with Mr. Gates, for even if we subtract the almost ten inches given to a local political story it ranks second in play.

While a total of 33 crime stories was received, only five column inches of crime appeared on the front and "jump" pages of Mr. Gates's paper. The obvious conclusion is that crime news, as such, does not appeal to this wire editor. But it should be noted that no "big" crime stories broke that day.

As one examines the whole week's performance of Mr. Gates, as manifested in the stories he chose, certain broad patterns become apparent. What

Table 5.4 Number of Pieces of Press Association Releases Received but Not Used
February 9, 1949

Category	Received Before Front Page Was Made Up	Received After Front Page Was Made Up	Total Received for Day
Local	3		3
Crime	32	1	33
Disaster	15		15
Political			22
Local	1	2	
State	10	2	
National	6	1	
Human interest	65	14	79
International			46
Political	19	5	
Economic	9	1	
War	10	2	
National			37
Farm	2		
Labor	13	1	
Economic	17	4	
Education	3	2	5
Science	5	2	7
Total for day	210	37	247

do we know, for example, about the kinds of stories that he selected in preference to others from the same category? What tests of subject matter and way-of-writing did Mr. Gates seem to apply? In almost every case where he had some choice between competing press association stories Mr. Gates preferred the "conservative." I use this expression not only in terms of its political connotations but also in terms of the style of writing. Sensationalism and insinuation seemed to be avoided consistently.

As to the way-of-writing that he preferred, Mr. Gates showed an obvious dislike for stories that had too many figures and statistics. In almost every case where one news agency supplied a story filled with figures and statistics and the competing agency's story was an easier going, more interpretative than statistical type of story, the latter appeared in the paper. An indication of his standards for writing is seen in Table 5.2, where 26 stories were rejected as being "too vague," 51 rejected for "dull writing" and 61 for being "not interesting."

Another question that should be considered in this study (and subsequent ones) is: Does the category really enter into the choice? That is, does the wire editor try to choose a certain amount of crime news, human interest news, etc.? Are there some other divisions of subject matter or form which he chooses in this manner, such as a certain number of one-paragraph stories?

Insofar as this "gate keeper" is representative of wire editors as a whole, it does not appear that there is any conscious choice of news by categories.

During this particular week under examination an emphasis on the human interest type of story was seen mainly because of the large news appeal of the Cardinal Mindszenty story. It would be most interesting and valuable to ascertain how a wire editor determines what one issue or type of story is "the" story of the week. Many times that decision is made by "gate keepers" above him, or by "gate keepers" in competing media. Can a wire editor refuse to play a story "up" when his counterpart in the local radio station is playing it to the hilt? Likewise, can a wire editor play down a story when he sees competing papers from nearby metropolitan areas coming into his city and playing up the story? These factors undoubtedly have something to do in determining the wire editor's opinion as to what he should give the reading public the next morning. This brings up the rather obvious conclusion that theoretically all of the wire editor's standards of taste should refer back to an audience who must be served and pleased.

Subsequent to Mr. Gates's participation in the project to determine the "reasons" for selecting or rejecting wire stories during a week, he was asked to consider at length four questions which we submitted. His answers to these questions tell us much about Mr. Gates, particularly if they are collated with the "spot" reasons which came under the pressure of a working night.

Question 1: "Does the category of news affect your choice of news stories?"

The category of news definitely enters into my choice of stories. A crime story will carry a warning as will an accident story. Human interest stories provoke sympathy and could set examples of conduct. Economic news is informative for some readers and over the heads of others. I make no attempt to hold a rigid balance in these selections but do strive for variety. The category of news suggests groups that should be interested in a particular story, that is, teachers, laborers, professional people, etc. Wire service reports can't keep a strictly balanced diet and for this reason we could not attempt it. For the most part, the same thinking applies in the selection of shorts, although some are admittedly filler material.

Question 2: "Do you feel that you have any prejudices which may affect your choice of news stories?"

I have few prejudices, built-in or otherwise, and there is little I can do about them. I dislike Truman's economics, daylight saving time and warm beer, but I go ahead using stories on them and other matters if I feel there is nothing more important to give space to. I am also prejudiced against a publicity-seeking minority with headquarters in Rome, and I don't help them a lot. As far as preferences are concerned, I go for human interest stories in a big way. My other preferences are for stories well-wrapped up and tailored to suit our needs (or ones slanted to conform to our editorial policies).

Question 3: "What is your concept of the audience for whom you select stories and what sort of person do you conceive the average person to be?"

Our readers are looked upon as people with average intelligence and with a variety of interests and abilities. I am aware of the fact we have readers with above average intelligence (there are four colleges in our area) and that there are many with far less education. Anyway, I see them as human and with some common interests. I believe they are all entitled to news that pleases them (stories involving their thinking and activity) and news that informs them of what is going on in the world.

Question 4: "Do you have specific tests of subject matter or way of writing that help you determine the selection of any particular news story?"

The only tests of subject matter or way of writing I am aware of when making a selection involve clarity, conciseness and angle. I mentioned earlier that certain stories are selected for their warning, moral or lesson, but I am not inclined to list these reasons as any test of subject matter or way of writing. The clarity trio is almost a constant yardstick in judging a story, especially when I often have three of a kind, AP, UP and INS. Length of a story is another factor (or test) in a selection. The long-winded one is usually discarded unless it can be cut to fill satisfactorily.

It is a well-known fact in individual psychology that people tend to perceive as true only those happenings which fit into their own beliefs concerning what is likely to happen. It begins to appear (if Mr. Gates is a fair representative of his class) that in his position as "gate keeper" the newspaper editor sees to it (even though he may never be consciously aware of it) that the community shall hear as a fact only those events which the newsman, as the representative of his culture, believes to be true.

This is the case study of one "gate keeper," but one, who like several hundred of his fellow "gate keepers," plays a most important role as the terminal "gate" in the complex process of communication. Through studying his overt reasons for rejecting news stories from the press associations we see how highly subjective, how based on the "gate keeper's" own set of experiences, attitudes and expectations the communication of "news" really is.

Notes

1. Lewin, Kurt, Channels of Group Life, *Human Relations*, Vol. 1, No. 2, p. 145.

2. Schramm, Wilbur, *Mass Communications*, U. of Illinois Press, Urbana, 1949, p. 289.

3. By far the majority of the approximately 1,780 daily newspapers in this country are in the smaller cities not on the main trunk wires of the press associations. Their reliance on the single wire "state" operations which emanate from the larger cities thus places great responsibility in the hands of the wire editor.

CHAPTER 6

Ms. Gates Takes Over

An Updated Version
of a 1949 Case Study

Glen L. Bleske

About 40 years ago, David Manning White studied the way a newspaper wire editor, dubbed Mr. Gates, selected and rejected news stories sent by wire services.[1]

Today, Ms. Gates, a wire editor at a midsized Southern daily, makes decisions similar to those of Mr. Gates, even though her background varies from Mr. Gates's and she works in an electronic newsroom. She opens and closes electronic copies of stories instead of ripping paper dispatches off the wire machine. The satellite dish has replaced the trunk wire that sent dispatches to Mr. Gates. And modern concepts such as packaging and modular layouts guide the news selection decisions that Ms. Gates makes.

The purpose of this case study is to revisit a newsroom using the techniques pioneered by White. The wire editor in this case is a woman; her supervisor, an assistant managing editor, is a woman, as is the editor of the newspaper. Ms. Gates is in her early 30s and has five years of journalism experience. She graduated with a bachelor's degree in English from a large Southern public university. Her knowledge of journalism and its values has come mainly from on-the-job training. She has held her current job for almost three years.

From *Newspaper Research Journal*, 1991, Vol. 12, pp. 88-97.

Her newspaper has a daily circulation of 90,000, about three times larger than the Midwest newspaper Mr. Gates worked for in 1949. It is a morning newspaper, published seven days a week. Ms. Gates is responsible for reading and deciding the fate of about 90 percent of the news stories moved by the newspaper's three wires.

Personally, Ms. Gates enjoys gardening and traveling. She characterizes herself as a heavy reader of "everything." She is a nonsmoker and participates in no activities in her community, a small town of about 20,000 on the fringes of her newspaper's circulation area. She belongs to no church. Her husband is a reporter for the same newspaper. They have no children.

According to White, Mr. Gates was in his middle 40s and had 25 years' journalism experience. Snider, who revisited Mr. Gates in 1966, noted that the wire editor had earned his bachelor's degree from a small private liberal arts college, where he had no journalism training.[2] He had two children and four grandchildren, read few books, was an ardent fisherman, smoked nonfiltered Camels, and was a church deacon.

Purpose

Lewin first used the term "gatekeeper" to describe someone who decides which news items would continue to flow through communication channels.[3]

In 1949, White, in what he called an experimental study, examined the decisions of a wire editor who chose what international and national news appeared in a nonmetropolitan newspaper. White's goal was to find some preliminary ideas on how his Mr. Gates selected or rejected news stories.

White's Mr. Gates was highly subjective in his selection of news. Snider found similar results: Mr. Gates continued to pick the stories he liked and believed his readers wanted.

Although Mr. Gates discounted the effects of news categories on his choices, later researchers such as McCombs and Shaw were struck by the phenomenal Spearman's rho rank correlation between the proportion of wire stories sent in a category and the proportion of that category Mr. Gates selected to appear in the newspaper.[4] Whitney and Becker suggested that unbalanced news categories sent by the wire services cue gatekeepers who uncritically accept the wire service pattern of emphasis for their newspapers.[5] Wire service editors set a news agenda for newspapers by suggesting the proper news mix, said Whitney and Becker.

The purpose of this case study was to answer the following questions:

1. What are the differences and similarities between two gatekeepers, 40 years apart?
2. What influences the story mix selected by Ms. Gates?
3. What role might the gender of the gatekeeper play in the selection of news stories?

Method

The format for this study followed the work of White. To collect data for this case study, Ms. Gates made electronic copies of wire stories, used her editing computer to measure the length of each story, and transferred each story to a storage queue. After her shift, Ms. Gates printed out a long directory listing the length of each story, its wire service headline, and the lead.

Ms. Gates marked each story as to why she did not use it. She also marked each story that was used and why. The actual wire content of the newspaper for five days, November 20-24, 1989, was categorized and measured.

The stories were categorized according to the seven topics (along with subcategories for national, international, and political news, for a total of 13 categories) developed by White. The column inch used was the standard six-column measurement, about 12.3 picas wide.

Stories measured were only those that passed through Ms. Gates's VDT. Not included were weather data and news moved on wires controlled by other editors: sports, business, opinion, and features.

The newspaper computer sorts the incoming wire news into categories according to wire service coding. Ms. Gates was responsible for selecting news from the national wire, the Washington wire, the state wire, and the international wire of the Associated Press. She also was responsible for wire stories sent to separate queues by the New York Times Wire Service and the Los Angeles Times/Washington Post Wire Service.

In nearly all cases, the policy of Ms. Gates's newspaper dictates the use of the latest, most complete version of a wire story that is available at deadline. When the wire service sent multiple copies of a story or partial stories, data for this study include only the final, most complete copy reviewed by Ms. Gates. Stories sent on the wire's PM cycle were not counted.

To measure output, the content analysis data include stories that appeared in the "A" or main wire section of the newspaper. Also measured were some of the wire pages that appeared in other sections.

A number of limitations have affected this study. Ms. Gates works for a paper nearly triple the size of Mr. Gates's newspaper, and she appears to have less control over news content than he did because of that size difference.

Equipment differences pose problems in comparing column inches in each category. White considered a column inch to be "five lines" of wire type. This type of measurement is no longer possible, which skews any direct comparison of total column inches sent by the wires.

If the five lines of wire type equaled a column inch in Mr. Gates's newspaper, it seems probable that the column inch used by Mr. Gates—in an era of 9- and 8-column newspapers—is smaller than that used by Ms. Gates.

Another problem is that White used seven days of data in his study. This study uses five days of data, as did Snider's 1966 study. Major limitations in data comparison are the effects of changes in technology, production, and evolving professional values, especially electronic editing and microwave transmission of copy.

Table 6.1 Comparison of Wire Input and Output Content Categories, Ranked, 1949 and 1989, in Percentages

		1989		
Rank		Wire Copy Input		Output in Paper
1.	Human interest	23.8	Human interest	26.9
2.	International politics	19.8	International politics	17.0
3.	National politics	19.5	National politics	16.5
4.	Crime	9.0	Science	10.6
5.	Science	7.4	Crime	7.6
6.	International war	6.6	International war	6.2
7.	National economics	5.0	State politics	3.9
8.	International economics	2.6	International economics	2.9
9.	Education	1.9	Education	2.6
10.	Disaster	1.8	Labor	2.3
11.	Labor	1.3	National economics	1.9
12.	State politics	0.7	Disaster	1.6
13.	Farm	0.6	Farm	0.0

		1949*		
Rank		Wire Copy Input		Output in Paper
1.	Human interest	35.0	Human interest	23.2
2.	International politics	15.1	National politics	15.8
3.	National politics	14.5	International politics	13.6
4.	Labor	5.5	State politics	6.8
5.	State politics	4.7	Farm	6.0
6.	Crime	4.4	International war	5.6
7.	International war	4.0	Labor	5.5
8.	International economics	3.4	Science	4.9
9.	Disaster	3.4	International economics	4.5
10.	Education	3.2	Education	4.3
11.	Farm	2.5	Disaster	3.4
12.	National economics	2.5	National economics	3.3
13.	Science	1.7	Crime	3.2

*1949 data from White.

Findings

In four decades some things do not change. In 1949, three categories—human interest, international politics, and national politics—accounted for 65 percent of the input from three wire services (see Table 6.1). In 1989, those same three categories accounted for 63 percent of the input. Those categories represented 53 percent of Mr. Gates's output, 60 percent for Ms. Gates.

The top seven categories of news in the 1949 study represented 90 percent of the news received by Mr. Gates, and the same seven categories represented 85 percent of the news received in 1989. Post-White researchers noted the strong rank-order correlation between the proportion of each

Table 6.2   Percentages of Available Wire Copy Used by Mr. Gates and Ms. Gates, 1949 and 1989

Content Category	1989	1949*
Human interest	10	7
Crime	8	8
Disaster	8	11
International politics	8	10
National politics	8	12
State politics	50	16
International economics	10	15
National economics	4	14
International war	9	15
Labor	16	11
National farm	0	26
National education	13	15
National science	13	31
Total	9.1	10.8*

NOTE: Total wire copy available: 1949/7 days: AP, UP, INS—11,910 inches; 1989/5 days: AP, NYT, Wash. Post/LA Times—18,897 inches.
*1949 data from White.

category of wire input and Mr. Gates's output. The Spearman rank correlation between wire input in each category and the output of Ms. Gates is .86. When the categories are reduced to the seven main categories (national, international, politics, human interest, disaster, crime, and labor), McCombs and Shaw noted a Spearman's rho of .64 for White's study when comparing the rank of wire copy received and the rank of the copy used. For Ms. Gates, the correlation between copy categories received and used equaled .96.

These strong relationships can be found across time. The rank-order correlation between the proportions of categories of wire copy sent in 1949 and 1989 is .53. When the ranks of copy used by Mr. Gates and Ms. Gates are compared, rho = .66 for all 13 categories. When collapsed to the seven main categories as suggested by McCombs and Shaw, the rho comparing wire copy received in 1949 and 1989 is .85; for wire copy used, rho = .85.

As Table 6.2 indicates, in five days, Ms. Gates processed 37 percent more news than Mr. Gates did in seven days in 1949. While it may not be possible to exactly compare column inch to column inch over the four decades, it is obvious that the simultaneous nature of microwave transmission allows the wire services to not only dump wire copy faster but also to send longer stories.

In 1949, Mr. Gates, with three wire machines to choose from, rejected 1,333 stories in seven days, about 190 stories a day. Ms. Gates rejected about 188 stories a day. But the average length of a rejected story in 1989 was about 18 column inches, compared to about 8 column inches in 1949.

Mr. Gates and Ms. Gates agree that the No. 1 reason to reject a story was lack of news hole. Ms. Gates marked 44 percent of her rejected stories with "no room" or "would use." In 1949, Mr. Gates marked the same reasons on 48 percent of his rejections. But by merely listing why a story is rejected or selected, Ms. Gates and Mr. Gates provide little insight into why one story is considered newsworthy and another is not.

No significant patterns could be related to the possible effects of a female gatekeeper. Only 18 stories selected by Ms. Gates were directly about women's issues or featured women as the main news subject or as the main source of the news. Data collected were not adequate for analyzing the total number of wire stories received that dealt with women.

The 142.25 inches of "women's news" equaled 8.5 percent of the news selected during the five days of this study. The pattern appears to support Whitlow's contention that there is a deep-rooted prejudice against women as newsmakers in society and among gatekeepers.[6] Because White made no attempt to assess gender in Mr. Gates's choices, no comparison can be made with the choices of Ms. Gates.

Ms. Gates Speaks

White asked Mr. Gates four questions. Snider, in his replication, asked the same questions and added the fifth. Ms. Gates was asked to answer the five questions and a sixth.

Q1: Does the category of news affect your choice of news stories?

A1: Like Mr. Gates, Ms. Gates said, "Not at all."

Q2: Do you think that you have any prejudices which may affect your choice of news stories?

A2: Again, Mr. Gates and Ms. Gates agree: They admit they have prejudices and favorites, but they say they try to remain neutral.

Q3: What is your concept of the audience for whom you select stories and what sort of person do you conceive the average person to be?

A3: Again agreement: Mr. Gates and Ms. Gates acknowledge that they strive for balance that appeals to a wide range of readers.

Q4: Do you have any specific tests of subject matter or way of writing that help you determine the selection of any particular news story?

A4: Ms. Gates said she chooses AP for inside pages, where space is limited, because it arrives soonest, it is easiest to cut and it is the shortest. On stories for the front page, she selects stories that have the best writing. Mr. Gates cited clarity, conciseness, and story angle as his main criteria.

Q5: How would you define news?

A5: News is a story that has great impact in the realms of economic, political, or human interest, said Ms. Gates. News is anything that piques her interest or that she thinks will pique anyone else's interest. Mr. Gates said news is a daily report of events and personalities that is varied.

Q6: Do you believe that your gender plays any role in your selection of news stories? If so, please describe.

A6: Not usually, said Ms. Gates, noting that she is more likely to run a story about women instead of men when last-minute extra space opens in the newspaper.

Discussion

Despite differences in newspaper size and gatekeeper gender, background and experience, news categories and the importance of those categories remained consistent in the Mr. Gates's and Ms. Gates's studies.

In noting the rank-order correlation between categories of wire received and wire used in the Mr. Gates's studies, researchers such as Whitney and Becker have suggested that the wire services cued Mr. Gates into what proportions of news to select. But both Mr. Gates and Ms. Gates deny having any knowledge of the proportions sent by the wire services, and they say they have a strong, critical interest in the content of the news.

In theory, gatekeepers should be expected to focus on the broad categories of human interest and international and national politics. The explanations for most relationships between wire news received and used are probably multidimensional and complex:[7] random chance, influence of the wire mix, and a combination of economic, social, and personal reasons.

As researchers have tried to understand news judgment and selection, they have recognized that professional, organizational, technological, and cultural influences frame and shape the news.[8] The case studies of Mr. Gates and Ms. Gates may not explain much about why a gatekeeper selects a particular story, but the studies taken as a whole convey a sense of the role of wire service news in the selections of two gatekeepers, separated by 40 years of sweeping technological and social changes.

Some of the possible reasons for the predominance of human interest and political news in gatekeeper studies include:

1. Wire editors are trained to use professional standards that accent a mix of stories to interest readers.[9] Although a wire editor may not know what interests readers, both Mr. Gates and Ms. Gates say they seek stories that are interesting to a large and varied audience.
2. Coverage of political events is a well-known professional norm and duty.
3. An agenda-setting effect is at work. To paraphrase Bernard Cohen,[10] the wire services may not be successful in telling gatekeepers what stories to select, but they are amazingly successful in telling gatekeepers what types of stories to consider selecting. To understand the rank-order correlations found in this study, it may be useful to think of gatekeepers as an audience influenced by an agenda-setting effect.

From the data in this study, no conclusion can be drawn about the effect of gender on a gatekeeper. The male domination of the content selected by

Ms. Gates suggests that prejudice against women cannot be overcome just by assuring that women assume leadership roles in newsrooms.[11]

Summary

Instead of focusing on random samples of individuals, researchers may find value in a population of gatekeepers for macro studies of agenda-setting and gatekeeping.[12] Lowery and DeFleur noted that agenda-setting is part of a complex process that produces gatekeeping and audience response.[13] It seems reasonable that if researchers expect to find in society a media effect such as agenda-setting, they should be able to find the effect within social organizations that produce media messages.

Newspaper gatekeepers read and assess about 1,000 stories a week. They are usually experienced journalists who have spent many years reading news stories sent by the wire services, which in turn have gatekeepers with similar experiences. Gatekeepers learn to select news by being gatekeepers.[14] As a group, gatekeepers—to do and keep their jobs—share high exposure, acceptance, and comprehension of the same media messages every day.

An analysis of data from Ms. Gates and Mr. Gates supports the idea that U.S. newspapers classify news in predictable ways. Wire news selection is subjective yet consistent when broad categories of news content are measured in these case studies. Apparently, the system allows for choice in stories by individual gatekeepers, who often disagree on which particular stories to select,[15] but the system also suggests to the population of gatekeepers the importance of various news categories.

Notes

1. David Manning White, "The 'Gate Keeper': A Case Study in the Selection of News," *Journalism Quarterly*, Fall 1950, 27:383-390.

2. Paul B. Snider, "Mr. Gates Revisited: A 1966 Version of the 1949 Case Study," *Journalism Quarterly*, Fall 1967, 44:419-427.

3. Kurt Lewin, "Psychology Ecology." In *Field Theory in Social Sciences* (New York: Harpers, 1943).

4. Maxwell E. McCombs and Donald L. Shaw, "Structuring the 'Unseen Environment,'" *Journal of Communication*, Winter 1976, 26:18-22.

5. Charles D. Whitney and Lee B. Becker, " 'Keeping the Gates' for Gatekeepers: The Effects of Wire News," *Journalism Quarterly*, Spring 1982, 59:60-65.

6. S. Scott Whitlow, "How Male and Female Gatekeepers Respond to News Stories of Women," *Journalism Quarterly*, Fall 1977, 54:573-579.

7. John Dimmick, "The Gate-Keeper: An Uncertainty Theory," *Journalism Monographs*, 37 (1974).

8. McCombs and Shaw, *op. cit.*

9. Dimmick, *op. cit.*

10. Bernard Cohen, *The Press and Foreign Policy* (Princeton, NJ: Princeton University Press, 1963), p. 13.

11. Suzanne Pingree and Robert Parker Hawkins, "News Definitions and Their Effects on Women." In Laurily Keir Epstein (ed.), *Women and the News* (New York: Hastings House, 1978), pp. 116-136.

12. Donald F. Roberts and Nathan Maccoby, "Effects of Mass Communication." In Gardner Lindzey and Elliot Aronson (eds.), *Handbook of Social Psychology*, 3rd ed. (New York: Random House, 1985), pp. 539-583.

13. Shearon A. Lowery and Melvin L. DeFleur, "The Agenda-Setting Function of the Press: Telling Us What to Think About." In *Milestones in Mass Communication Research*, 2nd ed. (New York: Longman, 1988), pp. 327-353.

14. Gaye Tuchman, *Making News: A Study in the Construction of Reality* (New York: Free Press, 1978).

15. Guido H. Stempel III, "Gatekeeping: The Mix of Topics and the Selection of Stories," *Journalism Quarterly*, Winter 1985, 62:791-796, 815.

CHAPTER 7

Refining the Gatekeeping Metaphor for Local Television News

Dan Berkowitz

In presenting the news each day, journalists apply a variety of schemes for selecting from among the pool of news stories they have gathered (Dimmick, 1974). That process has been a focus of mass communication research ever since the early studies of gatekeeping and news selection in the late 1940s and 1950s (e.g., Breed, 1955, 1956; White, 1949).

This study examined the gatekeeping process in local television news by applying content analysis techniques to observational research. Data were collected in a network-affiliate station's newsroom in Indianapolis, IN. One purpose of the study was to explore how stories are selected in local television news from a pool of potential news items. The focus, though, is not on

From *Journal of Broadcasting & Electronic Media*, 1990, Vol. 34, pp. 55-68, published by the Broadcast Education Association.

AUTHOR'S NOTE: The author thanks Doug Adams, John Erickson, and John Soloski of the University of Iowa, and David Pritchard of Indiana University for many helpful comments. Also, thanks go to Hemant Shah of the University of Wisconsin–Madison for help with the coder reliability checks. This manuscript was accepted for publication October 1989.

gatekeeping in the usual sense of studying individual journalists' news judgments, because this interpretation does not match the findings of many studies of newswork. A second purpose of this study, then, is to refine the metaphor of the news "gate," reshaping the notion of gatekeeping to provide a closer match to local television news.

Studies of newswork have found that news selection involves more than an evaluation of stories according to their news merits. Some researchers have pointed out the role of ideology in news decision making (Gitlin, 1980; Shoemaker, 1987; Soloski, 1989; Tuchman, 1978). Others have focused on the role of the news organization—its demands, limitations, and resource availabilities—in shaping what is published or aired (Altheide, 1976; Bantz, McCorkle, & Baade, 1980; Epstein, 1973; Fishman, 1982). Yet others emphasize the role of news sources in the news creation process (Gandy, 1982; Sigal, 1973; Turk, 1986). In addition, several studies have found that television news decision making is a group process instead of one made by individual gatekeepers (Epstein, 1973; Tuchman, 1978). These and other forces make news decisions a more complex task than that portrayed by the gatekeeping literature.

Studies focusing directly on gatekeeping have looked both at gatekeepers' decision-making processes and news content that is the outcome of those processes. Several researchers have focused on the issue of newscast quality (Carroll, 1985, 1989; Dominick, Wurtzel, & Lometti, 1975; Roberts & Dickson, 1984; Wulfemeyer, 1982a, 1982b). That debate generally examines the relative roles of hard news and show business in shaping newscasts. Many of these studies have concluded that news-related values are a stronger determinant of content than are show business-related values. Some studies, however (e.g., Carroll, 1989), have found differences among media organizations in different market sizes, with major market stations likely to devote more attention to soft news than medium- or small-market stations.

Another way of examining the outcome of gatekeeping has been to look at topic categories. Ryu (1982), for example, found that community-based stories or government news stories appeared less commonly on three Cincinnati, OH, stations' newscasts than sensational or human interest stories. Other studies have found government and crime stories to be among the most commonly covered topics (Berkowitz, 1986; Roberts & Dickson, 1984).

A third way of analyzing the outcome of the gatekeeping process has been to focus on coverage of planned events. Often, these studies have found that half or more of newscasts were built on stories about planned events (Berkowitz, 1987; Carroll, 1985; Smith, 1979). In some studies, though (e.g., Carroll, 1989), stations have been found to cover a greater proportion of breaking stories than planned events.

Studies observing the work of gatekeepers often look at specific news values by which potential content can be evaluated, such as timeliness, proximity, and known principals. Some research has found evidence for the importance of these news values in gatekeeping decisions (Buckalew, 1969, 1970; Dimmick, 1974). Other studies have found that news decisions were not based on these kinds of specific news values, but rather on subjective judgments (e.g., Staab, 1989; White, 1949). Yet others report a middle ground, where news judgments are based on broader news value categories such as level of audience interest or degree of social importance (Gans, 1979; Tuchman, 1973).

In general, the literature has suggested several patterns related to gatekeeping, although these patterns have not been consistent across studies. Some key factors that have been examined include types of stories (hard news vs. entertainment), event-related stories, story topics, and specific news values. At least in part, journalists' news selections seem to be the result of schemes for deciding what news is and is not. Decisions also appear to favor certain types of stories—planned-event stories, for example—that help journalists accomplish their work within the constraints of a media organization. This research focused on two research questions that address news selection in local television:

1. Is there a systematic pattern in the selection (aired) and rejection (unaired) of potential news content in local television?
2. What aspects of the selection process lead to certain kinds of news stories being chosen more often than others?

Method

Data for this study came from a combination of qualitative and quantitative observation techniques at a network-affiliate television station in Indianapolis, IN, the nation's 24th largest television market. More than 220 hours were spent talking with and observing journalists during 7 weeks in October and November 1987 (Berkowitz, 1989b). Research began with 2 weeks of familiarization with the newsroom and the station's news process. During the next 4 weeks, each story that journalists considered for airing was coded according to several decision-making criteria. Finally, after coding was completed, interviews were conducted with journalists over a 1-week period. All of these efforts focused on the content of the station's early evening newscasts at 5 o'clock and 6 o'clock.

A brief description of the news department and the journalists who worked there helps put this study into context. The news department staff included 15 reporters, 4 anchors, 15 photographers, and 4 tape editors. There were six key decision makers for the two evening newscasts: the news director, assistant news director, assignment editor, managing editor, 5 p.m. news producer, and 6 p.m. news producer. These six people averaged 16 years of experience in the profession, ranging overall from 7 to 33 years. The median age of the decision makers was 37 years, although the two producers were somewhat younger at 27 and 30 years old.

A typical news day began with an 8:30 a.m. story conference that reviewed preplanned stories from the assignment editor's news budget.

Other stories were also introduced during these story conferences. The conference typically ended at 9:30 a.m. Later in the day, breaking stories were discussed for inclusion in the newscasts. Each producer typically created two or three versions of newscast lineups during the news day.

Data collection followed this decision-making sequence, with a focus on three types of stories: (1) planned, event-related stories; (2) non-event stories concerning local issues and trends; and (3) breaking stories that newsworkers actively considered putting on the air. Stories that fit the station's definition of local news (if they took place within about an hour's drive of the station) were coded. Magazine-like elements of the newscasts (such as regular consumer and medical segments, sports, weather, and commentaries) were not coded because the process for creating those segments was different—planning for those stories took place on a different day and did not involve the regular news decision makers and reporters.

A related study (Berkowitz, 1989a) found that 77.5% of potential stories were discarded by the assignment editor before the news day began. A majority of the remaining stories ended up on the morning news budget. Coding sheets were completed at about noon each day for stories introduced during morning conferences; later-breaking stories were coded as they came up. Local newspapers were consulted to better understand potential stories and decision makers' discussions about those stories. Occasionally, short conversations with decision makers helped to clarify selection considerations. Copies of producers' preliminary newscast lineups ensured that all relevant stories were coded. Finally, stories were coded each evening as to whether they had aired. This information was based on final newscast lineups and observation from the producer's bench while newscasts were under way.

In all, eight measures were coded for each potential story. Three concerned the kind of story being considered. Five others came from a representative group of traditional textbook news values. The measures were defined as follows:

Type of story was developed from the literature concerning the quality of local television newscasts (e.g., Wulfemeyer, 1982a). "Issues" stories related to improving daily living, guiding people's decisions, and providing information about ongoing community debates. "Unexpected events" included stories about crime, accidents, and disasters. "Entertainment" concerned soft news stories, human interest stories, and personality profiles.

Story topic categories were derived from the author's earlier work (Berkowitz, 1986), which adapted Deutschmann's (1959) original categories. Coding was based on the actual topic of a potential story, rather than the news source originating the item. In all, 14 categories were created: government/politics, crime, disaster/accident, labor/unions, business/economy, public moral problems, health, welfare, education, arts, science/inventions, energy/environment, religion, and miscellaneous.

The event-related story was chosen to assess findings that local television news has a tendency to cover planned-event stories over other types of news. The "planned event" category concerned stories about meetings, rallies, news conferences, and special community events. The other category, "non-event or unplanned event," included stories about accidents, disasters, and crimes, as well as other stories not related to planned events.

Five measures of newsworthiness were chosen, with each news value coded as 0 for "low" and 1 for "high." The following measures were used:

Conflict was defined as verbal or physical clashes between story principals. By this definition, conflict required at least two parties engaged in an active dispute.

Timeliness, most simply, meant recent happenings or fresh stories. To be coded as high, a coder would have to answer "no" to the question, "Could this story just as easily have been arranged to happen on another day?" This definition of timeliness was created to favor spot news and eliminate most pseudo-events from being considered as timely.

Proximity was coded as high for stories taking place within the city of Indianapolis. Regional or out-of-state stories were considered as low proximity.

Significance rated whether a story topic was likely to have a direct effect—immediate or long term—on a large portion of the viewing audience. High significance meant that a news item would likely have audience impact.

Known principal was based on the familiarity of persons, institutions, or issues. High familiarity was coded as 1.

All quantitative data were coded by one person, although a second coder assisted in a reliability check.[1] The Scott's pi coefficients were: type of story, 1.00; topic, .71; event-related, .92; conflict, .89; timeliness, .52; proximity, .79; significance, .52; known principal, .68.

After all the quantitative data were collected, interviews were conducted with 10 key decision makers (producers, news directors, editors) at the station. These interviews ranged in length from about 30 minutes to more than an hour. Interviews were taped, transcribed, and studied before the quantitative data were analyzed.

Results

Quantitative Analysis

A total of 391 potential stories were coded in the newsroom during the 4-week period. Slightly more than half of them (57.8%) aired, a proportion higher than if all news items received at the television station had been coded. This was because coding focused on items that had passed the assignment editor's first filtering of the mail, which weeded out items with little news potential.

Analysis of items by story type found that 56.6% of issue-related stories aired, 66.7% of unexpected-event items aired, and 53.7% of entertainment items aired. Chi-square analysis showed these differences were not significant.

Table 7.1 presents a chi-square analysis of story topics by whether they were aired. Stories about government/politics, accidents/disasters, and

Table 7.1 Percentages of Topics in Stories Selected or Not Selected

Topic Category	Selected (aired)	Not Selected (unaired)	No. of Stories
Accidents and disasters[a]	73.4	26.6	64
Government and politics	62.0	38.0	79
Crime	60.7	39.3	61
Miscellaneous[b]	54.9	45.1	71
Business and economics	52.0	48.0	50
Education	45.0	55.0	20
Health and welfare[c]	41.3	58.7	46
Total	57.8	42.2	391

NOTE: $\chi^2(6, N = 391) = 14.6, p < .05$, Cramer's $V = .19$.
a. This category is somewhat inflated because a large portion of 2 days' newscasts were devoted to a plane crash story.
b. Several original categories were collapsed into the "miscellaneous" category because each contained fewer than 5% of the total stories. These categories included labor/unions, public moral problems, arts, science/inventions, energy/environment, and religion.
c. This category does not include stories from a regular medical segment.

crime were aired more frequently than the 42.2%-57.8% split in the marginals. These were also the most common potential topics from which journalists chose.

Analysis of event-related stories found a greater tendency to air stories in the non-event or unplanned-event category (66.0%) than in the planned-event category (49.5%). Although statistically significant, $\chi^2(1, N = 391) = 10.3, p < .001$, the phi statistic (.17) suggests a low degree of association.

The analysis scheme for the five news values used discriminant analysis. The five news values were coded on a zero-one scale corresponding to low and high values, and these can be treated as interval-level independent variables (Nie, Hull, Jenkins, Steinbrenner, & Bent, 1975); the unaired/aired variable represents two distinct groups of stories and can be considered a dichotomous dependent variable. In addition, some studies (e.g., Dimmick, 1974) suggest that decisions based on news values involve a multivariate process, making the analysis theoretically reasonable.

Table 7.2 presents the results of the discriminant analysis for the five news values. Examining the standardized discriminant function coefficients, timeliness (.85) was most closely associated with potential stories airing. The significance news value was somewhat less so (.46), but also important. The other three measures showed weaker associations with potential stories airing. In all, the five criteria accounted for only 19.4% of the variance in why potential news stories were aired.

Qualitative Analysis

The first research question asked if there might be a systematic pattern in the selection (aired) and rejection (unaired) of potential news content. The

Table 7.2 Standardized Discriminant Function Coefficients for Five News Values and Airing of News Items

Discriminator Variables	Airing of News Items	
	Function Coefficients	r
Timeliness	.85	.36
Significance	.46	.22
Proximity	.25	.12
Known principal	.24	.10
Conflict	.15	.09

NOTE: $N = 391$
Canonical correlation = .44 Significance level, $p < .001$
Eigenvalue = .25 Group centroids
Wilks's lambda = .80 Aired group = .42
Chi-square = 85.24 Unaired group = −.58
Degrees of freedom = 5 Percentage correctly classified, 70.3

findings here were somewhat mixed. An examination of potential stories by story type (issues, unexpected events, entertainment) did not reveal any pattern. The analysis of items by topic, however, did find some patterns in the potential stories that were aired, with a tendency to select stories about government/politics, accidents/disasters, and crime more frequently than other topic categories. The analysis of event-related stories found a pattern favoring non-event or unplanned-event stories over planned-event stories. This finding was in agreement with the work of Carroll (1989) that found larger-market media organizations were more likely to cover spontaneous news stories than were small-market stations. The discriminant analysis of news values shows that timeliness, a characteristic of spontaneous news, was most closely associated with airing of potential stories. The amount of variance in story selection accounted for by this analysis was relatively low, however, suggesting that more might be at play in story selection than news values alone. The low degree of association in the other analyses also suggest this might be the case.

The second research question further probed this possibility, asking about particular aspects of the news selection process that lead to some kinds of news stories being chosen over others. One aspect that stood out in the selection process was the group nature of decision making. Group dynamics were likely a reason for the large proportion of unexplained variance and relatively modest associations. Unlike the portrayal of individual decision makers appearing in several gatekeeping studies, news decision making at this station was a group process based on discussion that began with a morning story conference and continued in the newsroom throughout the day. The assignment editor highlights this point:

> It's done by committee and it's done for a lot of reasons. A lot of people play into this. It isn't like a newspaper where your city editor says, "This is the news hole and here's how we're going to shape it."

One producer explained that although decision making was a group process, it wasn't a fully balanced group process and, therefore, had some inherent unpredictability:

> If you're sitting in the news conference, whatever the news director says is going to carry a lot of weight. The person with the most influence is going to dictate what is covered. Producers or the managing editor will be influential if the news director isn't at the conference.

That the examination of potential stories by story type found no meaningful differences between the unaired and aired stories also points to process elements other than news values, such as the formula of the newscast format. Interviews with journalists found that they chose among the three story types according to quotas in the format. Here is the assistant news director's explanation:

> A newscast should have all of the above [issues, spot news, entertainment]. Just because we've got 14 car accidents, we can't do a whole newscast of auto accidents and call it a newscast. A newscast, to me, should be well-rounded. Tell me some things that are useful for survival, tell me some things that are interesting. Sometimes, though, some stories might get in if there aren't enough of some kind.

The analysis of story topics unaired/aired in Table 7.1 found a mix typical of most television stations or even many newspapers. A closer look, though, leads to some inferences about the news selection process. The first three topics had a greater chance of airing, and they have something in common: They concern relatively concrete kinds of information. Especially in the case of accidents/disasters and crime, these stories required less research effort and less expertise to develop into an airable story. Law enforcement authorities were usually at an accident scene; politicians often set up news conferences to make their announcements. In addition, the resource commitment needed to develop one of these stories was basically a one-shot proposition: The reporter gathered basic facts, the photographer shot representative video of the scene, and the story was ready for assembly.

Common threads among the second group of topics (business/economics, health/welfare, education) also suggest a pattern. These topics are more abstract, requiring greater knowledge from a reporter and more time away from the newsroom gathering facts. A reporter also would need more time to find appropriate expert sources to interview than for an accident story or for a news conference. Journalists at the station, however, didn't envision story topic selection as guided by these constraints, accepting the constraints as a natural element of television newsgathering. During interviews, some decision makers explained that national trends (often appearing in USA Today stories) were an important consideration for topic selection. The news director named other sources of trend information—market research and perceived audience interests—that shaped the topic mix. The assignment editor explained that his sense of audience needs was a guiding factor:

> We all read national magazines and are impressed with trends, whether it's hot tubs or tanning parlors. . . . But we have to place that editorially where it belongs, give it the weight that it should have, and not let that override something that our viewers need to know.

In sum, there seemed to be more than one reason why particular story topics were chosen over others, many of them distinct from an evaluation of each story on its own merits. One explanation relates to the demands of reporting a story. Other rationales concern audience interests and audience needs. Evaluations of story topics also addressed aspects of news items distinct from the item's topic, such as whether a story involved a planned event. One producer described the link this way:

> Planned events are a lot easier to cover than enterprise stories, so if planned events fall into the topics we're interested in, we're more likely to cover them as opposed to trying to scrape up something on our own.

In contrast to the producer's comments, however, the quantitative analysis of planned-event stories found a greater tendency to select non-event or unplanned-event stories over preplanned events. The rejection rate of planned-event items might be somewhat inflated, though, because stories based on news releases formed the bulk of discussion in morning story conferences. Later, these planned-event stories were dropped as spot news emerged. The assignment editor explains:

> If an unplanned event comes up, it may weigh more journalistically than two news conferences we have coming up. I wouldn't say there's a trend though [toward planned- or non-event stories], because we fill out the show early [with planned events] and then we begin to plug in spot news that's unscheduled. Some of the planned items then get bumped.

The 5 p.m. news producer saw a tendency toward selecting planned events, but he believed that avoiding them was an ideal:

> There's a whole world out there that doesn't revolve around a 10:30 [a.m.] news conference. We feel too often that we rely on the daily [news] budget, that we come in with blinders on. . . . At some stations, we've covered proclamations. Here, we've never covered proclamations.

The discriminant analysis of news values found that timeliness and significance were the best predictors of aired/unaired stories of the five news values (timeliness, significance, proximity, known principal, conflict), but the analysis provided only a partial explanation for how news stories were chosen. During interviews, several decision makers named timeliness as important, but at the same time, these people pointed out other elements, such as logistics and resource constraints, that ended up nearly as important of considerations, what the assignment editor called "the tipping balance." In general, the journalists didn't think in terms of specific newsworthiness criteria but took a gut-level approach. The assignment editor, for example, called traditional newsworthiness criteria "laudable, nice for a J-school student." Occasionally, the assignment editor suggested, news values had little to do with story selection:

> A producer, if he's looking at his computer and he sees he's got "X" number of minutes left that aren't filled, that's going to guide him into selecting a story, rather than necessarily the editorial content of the story.

Most often, though, when asked to explain news values in specific terms, decision makers described a balance among importance, interest, and visual impact. The night producer explained his approach this way:

> Think of importance and visual impact, and try to achieve a balance of the two. The more visual a story, the less important it needs to be to get on the air; the less visual, the more important it has to be. That's generally the see-saw I use.

The assistant news director worked within an interest-importance framework instead. Importance, as he defined it, translated to the news value of "significance" used by this study:

> [It depends on] how interesting the story is, judged on how interesting I think the story is, or how interesting the viewer will think the story is. That's the primary one. How important do I think it is that the viewer knows about this story? That's secondary.

Just as frequently as they spoke about the importance-interest-visual triad, however, newsworkers expressed a specialized sense of local television newsworthiness. One producer distinguished between this sense of newsworthiness and traditional newsworthiness:

> Newsworthiness used to be associated with the word "importance," and I think television has done a lot to redefine that. Something may be newsworthy, but it might not be important. It might tell people something about the world they live in or the life they lead, or it might just be fun—we're an entertainment medium.

The producer continued on, presenting a rationale for the shift in the meaning of newsworthiness:

> You have to be careful in TV news not to show people that this is a bad, depressing world, that they'll die in a fire, and that prices are expensive.

You have to make sure that you balance that with the more positive aspects of life.

Conclusion

Data from this case study suggested that news selection decisions were based on several considerations in addition to news values. News content seemed to be built from information that was easy to explain, that would provide a good audience draw, and that could be assembled with efficiency of effort. Rather than consciously relying on textbook news values, news-workers said they used their instincts about what made a good newscast. When asked about their decision-making framework in specific terms, news-workers spoke of interest, importance, and visual impact. Surprisingly, visual impact of potential stories was rarely mentioned during story conference discussions.

The structure of the newscast format had almost as much to do with story selection as did news merits of the potential stories. This helps explain why gatekeepers do not always agree on specific stories, but they do tend to agree on the kinds of stories that constitute a balanced news mix (Stempel, 1985). The newscast format here called for an approximate quota of stories from a variety of categories.

Reconsidering the metaphor of "the gate" as a way of envisioning news selection, this study found that decision making didn't fit the traditional mold of a lone wire editor sitting next to a pile of stories and making decisions based on either newsworthiness or personal preferences. Three main differences stand out. First, decision making seemed to be a group process; content, therefore, was shaped by group dynamics—the gates were not controlled by just one person, or even by the same group of people on different days. Second, the keys to the lock—interest, importance, visual quality—were different than the keys searched for by past studies of newspaper wire editors or those taught in journalism classes. Whether these keys could even be used was partly dictated by organizational demands such as resource constraints and newscast formats. Third, the metaphor of opening and closing a gate to allow individual news items through didn't provide a close fit to what was observed in the newsroom. Stories that passed through one gate faced still other gates on their way toward being broadcast. Spot news closed the gate on planned-event stories. Resource constraints and logistical problems sometimes closed the gate on spot news stories.

Notes

1. Assessing the reliability of observational data presented a more difficult task than assessing reliability for analysis of newspapers or videotapes of newscasts. One of the greatest difficulties was that the universe of content was harder to define. A pretest found

that two coders could not take identical notes or even draw together an identical pool of stories. Therefore, a less orthodox approach had to be devised. Before data collection began, a second person spent one full day in the newsroom. A few days later, the second person coded potential news items based on a discussion of the first coder's observation notes from one reasonably typical day. In all, 25 potential stories were coded during three 2-hour sessions.

2. Discriminant analysis provides standardized discriminant function coefficients that allow interpretation similar to beta weights in multiple regression (McLaughlin, 1980). Although independent variables coded as 0 or 1 do not strictly meet the assumptions for discriminant analysis, McLaughlin (1980, p. 185) reports that results will be only "slightly less efficient." Norusis (1985, p. 109) similarly states that although binary independent variables do not produce optimal results in discriminant analysis, "most evidence suggests that the linear discriminant function often performs reasonably well."

References

Altheide, D. L. (1976). *Creating reality: How TV news distorts events.* Beverly Hills, CA: Sage.

Bantz, C. R., McCorkle, S., & Baade, R. C. (1980). The news factory. *Communication Research, 7,* 45-68.

Berkowitz, D. (1986, August). *Television news sources and news channels: A study in agenda-building.* Paper presented at the annual convention of the Association for Education in Journalism and Mass Communication, Norman, OK.

Berkowitz, D. (1987). TV news sources and news channels: A study in agenda-building. *Journalism Quarterly, 3,* 508-513.

Berkowitz, D. (1989a, August). *Information subsidy and agenda-building in local television news.* Paper presented at the annual convention of the Association for Education in Journalism and Mass Communication, Washington, DC.

Berkowitz, D. (1989b). Organization influences, ideology, and the creation of local television news (Doctoral dissertation, Indiana University, 1988). *Dissertation Abstracts International, 49,* 2854A.

Breed, W. (1955). Social control in the news room: A functional analysis. *Social Forces, 33,* 326-355.

Breed, W. (1956). Analyzing news: Some questions for research. *Journalism Quarterly, 33,* 467-477.

Buckalew, J. K. (1969). A Q-analysis of television news editors' decisions. *Journalism Quarterly, 46,* 135-137.

Buckalew, J. K. (1970). News elements and selection by television news editors. *Journal of Broadcasting, 14,* 47-54.

Carroll, R. L. (1985). Content values in TV news programs in small and large markets. *Journalism Quarterly, 62,* 877-882.

Carroll, R. L. (1989). Market size and TV news values. *Journalism Quarterly, 66,* 49-56.

Deutschmann, P. J. (1959). *News content of twelve metropolitan dailies.* Cincinnati, OH: Scripps-Howard Research.

Dimmick, J. (1974). The gatekeeper: An uncertainty theory. *Journalism Monographs, 37.*

Dominick, J. R., Wurtzel, A., & Lometti, G. (1975). Television journalism vs. show business: A content analysis of eyewitness news. *Journalism Quarterly, 59,* 213-218.

Epstein, E. J. (1973). *News from nowhere: Television and the news.* New York: Random House.

Fishman, M. (1982). News and nonevents: Making the visible invisible. In J. S. Ettema & D. C. Whitney (Eds.), *Individuals in media organizations: Creativity and constraint* (pp. 219-240). Beverly Hills, CA: Sage.

Gandy, O. H. (1982). *Beyond agenda-setting: Information subsidies and public policy.* Norwood, NJ: Ablex.

Gans, H. J. (1979). *Deciding what's news: A study of CBS Evening News, NBC Nightly News, Newsweek and Time.* New York: Pantheon Books.

Gitlin, T. (1980). *The whole world is watching: Mass media in the making and unmaking of the New Left.* Berkeley, CA: University of California Press.

McLaughlin, M. L. (1980). Discriminant analysis in communication research. In P. R. Monge & J. N. Cappella (Eds.), *Multivariate techniques in human communication research* (pp. 175-204). New York: Academic Press.

Nie, N. H., Hull, C. H., Jenkins, J. G., Steinbrenner, K., & Bent, D. H. (1975). *SPSS: Statistical package for the social sciences* (2nd ed.). New York: McGraw-Hill.

Norusis, M. J. (1985). *SPSS-X advanced statistics guide.* New York: McGraw-Hill.

Roberts, C. L., & Dickson, S. H. (1984). Assessing quality in local TV news. *Journalism Quarterly, 61,* 392-398.

Ryu, J. S. (1982). Public affairs and sensationalism in local TV news programs. *Journalism Quarterly, 59,* 74-78.

Shoemaker, P. J. (1987). Building a theory of news content: A synthesis of current approaches. *Journalism Monographs, 103.*

Sigal, L. V. (1973). *Reporters and officials.* Lexington, MA: D. C. Heath.

Smith, R. R. (1979). Mythic elements in television news. *Journal of Communication, 29*(1), 75-82.

Soloski, J. (1989). News reporting and professionalism: Some constraints on the reporting of the news. *Media, Culture, and Society, 11,* 207-228.

Staab, J. C. (1989, May). *The concept of news factors in news selection: A theoretical reconsideration.* Paper presented at the annual conference of the International Communication Association, San Francisco.

Stempel, G. H. (1985). Gatekeeping: The mix of topics and the selection of stories. *Journalism Quarterly, 62,* 791-796.

Tuchman, G. (1973). Making news by doing work: Routinizing the unexpected. *American Journal of Sociology, 79,* 110-131.

Tuchman, G. (1978). *Making news: A study in the construction of reality.* New York: Free Press.

Turk, J. V. (1986). Information subsidies and media content: A study of public relations influence on the news. *Journalism Monographs, 100.*

White, D. M. (1950). The gate-keeper: A case study in the selection of news. *Journalism Quarterly, 27,* 383-390.

Wulfemeyer, K. T. (1982a). A content analysis of local television newscasts: Answering the critics. *Journal of Broadcasting, 26,* 481-486.

Wulfemeyer, K. T. (1982b). Developing and testing method for assessing local TV newscasts. *Journalism Quarterly, 59,* 79-82.

CHAPTER **8**

Structure and Constraints on Community Newspaper Gatekeepers

G. A. Donohue
C. N. Olien
P. J. Tichenor

Editors are often seen as having a "buckstopping" role in the gatekeeping process. In the midst of a flow of information from a variety of sources and directions and in multiple forms, the editor must make the final decision about where, when, and how messages will be published.

As a gatekeeper, the editor operates within a structural context. Structure presents a variety of constraints, such as community pluralism, type of newspaper and form of ownership, which may affect the outcome of the gatekeeping process. This is a report of an exploratory study of some of these constraints as they are perceived by a sample of Minnesota community newspaper editors.

From *Journalism Quarterly*, 1989, Vol. 66, pp. 807-812, published by the Association for Education in Journalism and Mass Communication.

AUTHORS' NOTE: The research is supported by Projects 27-18 and 27-19, Minnesota Agricultural Experiment Station.

Constraints: Values, Routines and Organizational Management

Among the constraints which may impinge upon media organizations are:

1. Professional values which serve as standards for use, nonuse, modification and layout of news, including (a) the major priorities of gatekeepers and (b) their professional ethics;
2. Constraints arising from implementation of standards in the routines of news selection, including pressures of time and space; and
3. Organizational structure for personnel recruitment, management and change.

Priority questions include the relative degree of concern with information, as contrasted with maintaining economic support of the newspaper through advertising or circulation. Since journalism is presumably based on the primacy of information generation and distribution, one would expect that deciding what to publish would be a foremost value for all editors. Such a primary value becomes a standard for criticism, especially the contention that obsession with profits often deters gatekeepers from concentrating on their main job of gathering, interpreting and distributing information.[1]

Ethical constraints in journalism include fairness and balance in reporting controversial issues, with respect for the individuals and groups being reported. Such constraints have been stated formally in journalism, as in all professions, for decades.[2] Greater recent focus on ethics may in part be related to increased conflict in the system with respect to special interest groups and the ensuing litigation. Anderson, for example, regards media ethics as having been "on the backburner" of public attention from World War II through the early 1970s. He concludes that interest in ethics has increased, as suggested by the finding that three-fourths of a recent sample of 96 daily newspaper managing editors had issued memos on ethical issues and about two-thirds had held meetings or seminars on these topics.[3]

Constraints arising from implementation of standards through news routines are a basic part of the journalist's environment, as Johnstone, Bowman and Slawski found.[4] Gieber pointed to the "strait jacket of mechanical details" accompanying some editing positions.[5] Whitney concluded that organizational inflexibility could produce strains in the organization under both "information overload" and "underload" conditions. The organizations were expected to send a rigidly specified amount of information "through the gate" on any given day, and a flow above or below an optimum level would lead to coping problems.[6]

Organizational structures for recruitment, management and change present recurring problems in news organizations, as documented in the Johnstone, Bowman and Slawski study.[7] Conflicts between reporters and editors were central to Breed's analysis of social control in the newsroom,[8] and to Stark's interpretation of the "trouble maintaining a staff" faced by the editors of a metropolitan newspaper.[9]

Impact of Community Structure on Constraints

Some values can be expressed more easily in one community structure than in another. While rugged individualism is steeped in American tradition, it is more widely expressed in small towns than in urban settings, where high interdependence requires one to be a "group person" rather than one who is self-sufficient in all realms of life. Autonomy in urban areas is born of interdependence rather than self-sufficiency and rests on more formalized statements of professional conduct.

Editors of locally owned papers in small consensus-oriented communities play multiple roles, including reporting, advertising and management. Such editors are acutely concerned about economic survival and hence would be expected to emphasize advertising, circulation and operating profit. The routine for getting the paper out is a formidable task under any conditions, but it is especially complex in a small town newspaper that has a staff of four persons or less with minimal specialization. Daily editors, with their large staffs and division of labor, specialize in news and information while others in their organizations make decisions about advertising, profit and loss. One might speculate that corporate ownership of newspapers, through increasing the scale of operations, is an additional factor in maintaining such specialization and reducing role conflict for the individual.[10]

Ethical constraints might well be perceived more frequently in small, homogeneous communities which create a moral conflict resulting from simultaneously knowing (a) the professional obligation to report a bid-rigging charge filed in local court against a council member of personal acquaintance and (b) the personal loyalty to a friend who also may be part of the power structure. This is not a question of community difference in orientation, since personal loyalty to power figures may occur in New York and Los Angeles as well as in Pine City, Minn. or Clinton, Tenn. The secondary nature of urban relations, however, and the balancing of power groups constrain the urban editor to report the charge in spite of the question of personal loyalty. In both the urban and rural community, the editor shares the value orientation of the power group. The difference is that in the pluralistic urban setting, the conflict among power groups is more likely to result in public reporting of individual deviances as well as group differences. The small town editor has a restricted community of advertisers, whereas the urban daily editor could lose one furniture advertiser and still have other advertisers in the same product area. Furthermore, the furniture dealer in the urban center may well have a greater *need* to advertise to reach the target audience. Such factors typify the ways in which pluralism insulates an editor from pressure by any one source, including a personal acquaintance.

Intra-organizational constraints such as managerial problems may be perceived more frequently as constraints by editors of daily newspapers than by editors of weeklies in small communities. This outcome results from bureaucratization, which produces more specialized subgroups, staff meeting procedures and formalized recruiting and dismissal procedures. Specialized bureaucratic arrangements may also contribute to lower satisfaction of journalists as found by Samuelson and Johnstone, Bowman, and Slawski.[11] By contrast, newspapers in smaller, more homogeneous and consensual communities tend to have small staffs with individuals having multiple responsibilities and operating on a face-to-face informal basis. Given this logic, one might expect less strain from organizational problems to be reported by editors of weeklies. In these more authoritarian structures, editors make decisions by fiat and, therefore, would be less likely to perceive constraints.

To summarize, four hypotheses were tested.

1. Editors of locally owned weekly papers in small, less pluralistic communities will be more likely than editors of dailies in larger, more pluralistic communities to perceive a high priority for advertising.
2. Editors of locally owned weekly papers in small, less pluralistic communities will be more likely than editors of dailies in larger, more pluralistic communities to perceive constraints associated with treatment of negative news about individuals.
3. Editors of locally owned weekly papers in small, less pluralistic communities will be more likely than editors of dailies in larger, more pluralistic communities to perceive constraints associated with routine problems of news selection and display.
4. Intraorganizational constraints are more likely to be mentioned by editors of corporate-owned dailies in larger, more pluralistic communities than by editors of locally owned weekly newspapers in small, more homogeneous communities.

Research Methods

Editors of 155 community newspapers, including 59 weeklies in Minnesota and 96 dailies in six Midwestern states, were interviewed by telephone in 1985. The sample was restricted to nonmetropolitan communities of 60,000 or less, and each newspaper was in a different county.

Two measures of editor perceptions of constraints were employed. One is a measure of editors' views of their responsibilities. Editors were asked to rank production, circulation, advertising and news-editorial from most to least important as "concerns for decisions you make on your paper." The assumption is that this item taps perceptions of a constraint which rests on the fundamental value of news as governing the gatekeeping role.

A second measure of constraints is an open-ended question framed in terms of difficult decisions:

> In all of the decisions that you need to make as an editor, what kinds of
> decisions would you say are the toughest ones to make?

Table 8.1 Average Rankings of Editor Concerns by Editors of Weekly and Daily
Newspapers, 1985

	Minnesota Weeklies (N = 58)	*Midwestern Dailies* (N = 93)
News and editorial	1.43	1.08*
Advertising	2.08	2.96*
Production	3.05	2.96
Circulation	3.32	2.89

NOTE: The lower the number, the higher the rank.
*Difference between groups, *t* test.
p < .001.

Responses to this item were placed in one or more of six categories,
including fairness in reporting about individuals, news selection and display,
pressure from individuals and groups, organizational problems, legal problems and business.

Community pluralism was measured by an index based on proportion
of labor force outside agriculture, per capita income, distance to a metropolitan area, community population and county population. Newspapers were
categorized as local and independent, owned by a group with headquarters
in Minnesota or owned by a group with headquarters outside the state. The
assumption is that those with outside headquarters tend to have a more
bureaucratized form of organization. Newspapers were categorized as dailies or weeklies, with the latter category including six newspapers published
semiweekly.

Results

Pluralism and Ranking of Advertising

The average rankings for the four different parts of the newspaper
operation, for dailies and nondailies, are shown in Table 8.1. All editors
ranked news and editorial at the top, although daily newspaper editors gave
that function a higher absolute rating than did editors of weeklies. This
ubiquity of the news-editorial function indicates that it is a value of great
import. But because of structural variation, the information function is more
apparent among editors of dailies.

There is support for the first hypothesis, that advertising will rank higher
as a concern among editors of weekly newspapers in small, homogeneous
communities than among editors of corporate-owned daily newspapers in
larger, more pluralistic communities. Among nondailies under in-state ownership in the low-pluralism communities, the advertising ranking is 1.97,
higher than for any other group. On the other hand, the very lowest ranking,

Table 8.2 Average Ranking of Advertising According to Pluralism, Frequency of
Publication and Ownership

	Low Pluralism		High Pluralism	
	Nondaily	Daily	Nondaily	Daily
In-state ownership	1.97**	2.43	2.35*	2.95*
	(33)	(7)	(20)	(37)
Out-of-state ownership	2.00	2.00	—	3.23**
	(4)	(7)		(39)

*$p = .035$.
**Difference between groups, $p < .001$, t test.

3.23, is among dailies under out-of-state ownership in high-pluralism communities. These differences provide direct support of the hypothesis.

One might ask from these data which is the most important variable.
Under conditions of low pluralism, out-of-state ownership makes no significant difference in ranking of advertising. Also, the observed differences
according to ownership among dailies under out-of-state ownership are not
significant statistically. These results therefore do not support the contention
that corporate ownership by itself is a factor in increasing editor concern with
advertising at the expense of news, even though earlier analyses indicate that
ownership is related to increased *reporting* of business.

Negative News, Selection and Organizational Problems

Among the editors as a whole, the most frequent categories of response
to the "toughest decisions" question were negative news about individuals,
44%; news selection and display, 33%; pressure from individuals and groups,
23%; organizational and personnel problems, 19%; legal reporting, 9%; and
business concerns, 8%.

Typical responses coded as problems of "negative news about individuals" were:

. . . where someone you know could be hurt. In a small community
everyone knows everybody, so community matters like these are important.

. . . as editor . . . sensitive issues involving people you've known all your
life . . . e.g., . . . a story on a man indicted in bid-rigging is in today's
paper. It's hard to differentiate between what's your obligation to report
and any loyalty you might have for that person.

. . . whether to tear somebody apart who really deserves it. The ex-
mayor was trying to create a job for himself . . . that's tough because I've
known him a long time.

Coded as "news selection" and display, were:

What to leave out when I am short of space.

What to include, exclude.

Which pictures can get in, using space effectively.

It should be pointed out that in terms of gatekeeping processes, the "negative news" concern is a special case of news selection in that it is a matter of deciding whether to publish the item causing consternation. These two categories dominated the responses to the "toughest decisions" questions, and that other issues which might have been expected from the literature on journalism ethics were virtually nonexistent in the responses. There were no mentions of reporter deception, for example, or of problems with unnamed sources or questionable methods of information gathering. It may well be that such problems are more likely to be perceived by journalists in the largest, most diversified and specialized media organizations of metropolitan areas where public conflict occurs more routinely and "investigative journalism" is more likely to be seen as an ongoing part of the media operation.

Also, it may be noted that writing editorials was mentioned as among the "toughest decisions" by only 4 of the 155 editors, and only 2 referred specifically to problems of getting "in-depth" coverage or "investigative news" into their papers. The foremost professional problems of negative news about individuals and more general concerns with news selection were seen as the "toughest decisions" rather than concern about whether to comment editorially. The implication is that editorializing, which about 9 editors in 10 reported doing, may in fact be a rather routine and noncontentious activity. Such a finding is somewhat surprising, in that the idea of editors being troubled about writing editorials is not supported.

Coded as "pressure from individuals and minorities" were mentions of specific local purposive communicators, individuals or groups, who seek either to have information placed in, or kept out of, the newspaper.

Typical responses coded as "organizational problems" were:

Keeping the publisher happy.

Hiring is one. It takes so much time to do it right. Managing the newsroom while trying to do many other things—[including] resolving conflicts among staff.

Personnel decisions. We have gone through tremendous changes—refinement of newsroom structure . . . you're tampering with people's lives. Some will get good jobs, some worse and some will have no job.

Structure and "Toughest Decisions"

Problems of "fair treatment" of individuals were mentioned with similar frequency regardless of type of newspaper, ownership, or pluralism. The findings do not support the second hypothesis, that editors of locally owned weekly papers in small, less pluralistic communities would be more likely than editors of dailies in larger, more pluralistic communities to perceive constraints associated with treatment of negative news about individuals. There are no significant differences in mention of this concern according to pluralism, frequency of publication or ownership. Also, there are no differences according to whether the community had undergone substantial change in population growth or decline in agriculture in the past decade.

The third hypothesis, that problems of news selection and display would be more frequently mentioned by editors of weeklies under local ownership in less pluralistic communities, was also not supported. Rather, this category was mentioned in about the same proportion of cases regardless of community pluralism or whether the newspaper was a daily or nondaily. Nor were there differences by ownership. It appears that for the most part, problems with negative news about individuals and more general concerns about selecting and displaying the news are fundamental to newspaper journalism regardless of the structural factors studied here.

A related aspect of the findings suggests that editors in small communities do not necessarily depend more on overt pressure from purposive communicators than do editors in more pluralistic communities. While the differences are not significant, it might be noted that the nondailies in the least pluralistic communities were less likely than nondailies in more pluralistic communities to mention pressure from individuals and groups as among their "toughest" problems.

Organizational Constraints

The fourth hypothesis, that organizational problems would be more likely to be perceived in more pluralistic communities and in daily newspapers under outside ownership, is supported by the data (Table 8.3). None of the editors of nondailies in communities with low pluralism mentioned organizational problems. However, such problems were mentioned by 36% of the editors of dailies under out-of-state ownership in the more highly pluralistic communities. Pluralism again appears to be the primary variable, as can be seen from results of a hierarchical regression, with mention of organizational problems treated as a dichotomy. When pluralism is entered first as a fundamental variable, adding the next two variables makes only slight changes in the variance explained, .017 from publication frequency in the second step and .014 from ownership in the third step (Table 8.4). As with ranking of advertising and news-editorial concerns, ownership is a condition which appears to have relatively little additional impact on editor perceptions after community structure and daily vs. weekly publication are controlled.

Table 8.3 Percentage Mentioning Organizational Problems as One of the "Toughest" Editorial Decisions, According to Pluralism, Type of Newspaper and Ownership

	Low Pluralism				High Pluralism			
	Nondaily		Daily		Nondaily		Daily	
In-state ownership	0%	(34)*	0%	(8)	15%	(20)	23%	(39)
Out-of-state ownership	0%	(4)	29%	(7)	—		36%	(39)*

*Difference, chi-square test, $p < .01$.

Table 8.4 Hierarchical Regression, Mention of Organizational Problems as One of the "Toughest" Editorial Decisions, 152 Editors

Independent Variable	Simple Correlation	Multiple R Square	Change in R Square	Overall Significance
Step				
1. Pluralism	.31	.095	.095	.001
2. Publication frequency	.27	.112	.017	.001
3. Ownership	.26	.126	.014	.001

NOTE: The number of cases is reduced by three for this table because of missing data.

Conclusions

These results as a whole suggest that the basic value of information dissemination may be a characteristic of the journalism profession that transcends structural differences. Similarly, how to distinguish between personal loyalty to a person under accusation and journalistic obligation to report that accusation is a vexation for editors regardless of structure.

Perceptions of other constraints do vary by community structure. The higher ranking of advertising by small town editors does not necessarily suggest a more crass view of their community roles. Rather, because of their multiple roles as entrepreneurs and information gatekeepers, their concern with advertising income and profits is to be expected as part of their role definitions. Among editors of dailies, advertising and profit values exist as corporate reality, but are dealt with by specialists outside the news-editorial department.

Problems of organizational management are more likely to appear as strains in regional centers which constitute the more pluralistic communities in this study. A question which cannot be analyzed with these data is whether problems of organizational management are even more salient among editors of larger metro newspapers. If they are, it may well be that the tough organizational decisions of editors occur in precisely the same structures in which reporters are often most concerned about autonomy and professional fulfillment.

Another question is whether problems of negative news about individuals are as likely to be seen by editors of newspapers in larger metro centers, where there is not only greater separation from the citizen role but also greater dependence upon formal legal advice. Such questions suggest that further analysis of both internal and external structures, and how they impinge on values and organizational constraints, may be fruitful.

Notes

1. Ben Bagdikian, *The Media Monopoly* (Boston: Beacon Press, 1983); Robert M. Hutchins, *A Free and Responsible Press: A General Report on Mass Communication* (Chicago: University of Chicago Press, 1947).

2. Douglas Anderson, "How Managing Editors View and Deal With Ethical Issues," *Journalism Quarterly*, 64:341-345 (Summer/Fall, 1987). See also Deni Elliott, "All Is Not Relative: Essential Shared Values and the Press," *Journal of Mass Media Ethics*, 3:28-32 (1988) and David H. Weaver and G. Cleveland Wilhoit, *The American Journalist* (Bloomington: Indiana University Press, 1986). The Weaver and Wilhoit volume (pp. 127-145) concentrates particularly on perceptions of journalists about ethics of various reporting practices.

3. Anderson, *op. cit.*

4. John W. C. Johnstone, Edward J. Slawski and William M. Bowman, *The News People: A Sociological Portrait of American Journalists and Their Work* (Urbana: University of Illinois Press, 1976), pp. 149 ff.

5. Walter Gieber, "Across the Desk: A Study of 16 Telegraph Editors," *Journalism Quarterly*, 33:423-432 (1956).

6. D. Charles Whitney, "Information Overload in the Newsroom," *Journalism Quarterly*, 58:69-76, 161 (1981).

7. Johnstone, Bowman and Slawski, *op. cit.*

8. Warren Breed, "Social Control in the Newsroom," pp. 178-194 in Wilbur Schramm, ed., *Mass Communications* (Urbana: University of Illinois Press, 1960).

9. Rodney W. Stark, "Policy and the Pros: An Organizational Analysis of a Metropolitan Newspaper," *Berkeley Journal of Sociology*, Spring, 1962, pp. 11-31.

10. C. N. Olien, P. J. Tichenor and G. A. Donohue, "Relation Between Corporate Ownership and Editor Attitudes," *Journalism Quarterly*, 65:257-264 (1988).

11. Merrill Samuelson, "A Standardized Test to Measure Job Satisfaction in the Newsroom," *Journalism Quarterly*, 39:285-291, 1962; Johnstone, Bowman and Slawski, *op. cit.*

Organizing News

News as a Workplace Product

In contrast to the gatekeeping literature's emphasis on individual-level explanations for news, this section of the book examines the effect of a journalist's social setting. This level of analysis greatly downplays individual judgment, portraying it as constrained and shaped by the policies and imperatives of the news organization. The focus is not on journalists' decisions but rather the social forces that shape and constrain those decisions.

Warren Breed's 1955 "Social Control in the Newsroom" explores how an organization's news *policy* is maintained among journalists and identifies the conditions by which policy can be bypassed. Breed defines policy as a more-or-less consistent orientation shown by a paper (in editorials, news, and headlines), whereas *slanting* is the way that a story is managed to conform to policy. Breed develops his case by examining the intersection of organizational management and ethical journalistic norms, contrasting the interests of *executives* and *staffers*. For example, a publisher cannot openly tell a staffer which stories to cover or how to cover them. That act would violate journalists' norms regarding autonomy from the business side of a media organization.

Instead, policy is learned during on-the-job socialization, by "osmosis." Staffers then attain personal goals and avoid punishments by following the policy they have learned. Breed identifies six social factors that enforce policy, demonstrating how newswork cannot be done under the relatively isolated conditions depicted by the gatekeeping tradition.

Despite the prevalence of policy in the newsroom, five factors allow a reporter to bypass policy. Two overarching concepts are key. First, policy can be bypassed when a story departs from what is typically covered by policy. Second, a staffer's reputation may allow departure from policy, both in terms of originating stories and in the way that stories are developed.

Charles R. Bantz's "News Organizations: Conflict as a Crafted Cultural Norm" deals specifically with the clash between organizational demands and journalistic ideals, highlighting the conflict that regularly results. Surprisingly, Bantz portrays conflict as a normal, even necessary part of life in a news organization. Conflict, then, becomes part of a common system of symbolic organizational meaning by which expectations for appropriate actions are defined.

Bantz identifies five sites of organizational conflict, relating professional norms to the social environment both inside and outside a media organization. Because news is often cast within a frame of conflict, he argues, newsworkers see their own work world in the same terms. Furthermore, conflict is a more or less constant element across news organizations.

John Soloski's "News Reporting and Professionalism: Some Constraints on the Reporting of the News" also examines the clash between professional norms and organizational policy. Rather than casting professional norms as guides for news selection, however, norms become complementary tools by which media organizations control journalists and maintain adherence to policy. From this view of professionalism, media organizations must control their subsystems to survive in their external environment. Organizations that face relatively stable environments can manage their work processes through highly structured rule systems, but newswork does not present a stable environment. Thus, professionalism functions well because it "makes the use of discretion predictable."

Key among professional norms regulating journalists' behavior is the myth/ritual of objectivity, which journalists internalize and regularly enact to accomplish their work. As a result, news tends to represent organizational policy. Much like Bantz's argument about conflict, Soloski asserts that professionalism is a relatively constant control mechanism across news organizations. When professionalism combines with the organization's idiosyncratic policy, the two mechanisms allow little leeway for news staffers. Drawing on a case study that assesses these two forces, Soloski concludes that professionalism and policy implicitly support the existing political-economic order, further enhancing stability of the news organization as a social system.

Sharon Dunwoody's "Science Writers at Work" steps outside the news organization's boundaries to show how organizational production demands and the collective news judgment of beat reporters combined to affect coverage of a large national science conference. Writers who regularly covered that beat shared a system of meaning within an inner circle, so that stories could be produced efficiently with reasonably similar results. Competition among these journalists did not mean winning but simply keeping up with each other. These collective efforts helped reduce news selection uncertainty and ensured that reporters could succeed in meeting organizational expectations. Even though these reporters were competitors, they ultimately saw themselves as colleagues who faced their news organizations together.

In all, the chapters in this section depict individual judgment as only a small part of what shapes the news. A much greater effect on the news comes from news cultures and their interface with the social environment.

CHAPTER 9

Social Control in the Newsroom

A Functional Analysis

Warren Breed

Top leaders in formal organizations are makers of policy, but they must also secure and maintain conformity to that policy at lower levels. The situation of the newspaper publisher is a case in point. As owner or representative of ownership, he has the nominal right to set the paper's policy and see that staff activities are coordinated so that the policy is enforced. In actuality the problem of control is less simple, as the literature of "human relations" and informal group studies and of the professions[1] suggests.

Ideally, there would be no problem of either "control" or "policy" on the newspaper in a full democracy. The only controls would be the nature of the event and the reporter's effective ability to describe it. In practice, we find the publisher does set news policy, and this policy is usually followed by members of his staff. Conformity is *not* automatic, however, for three reasons: (1) the existence of ethical journalistic norms; (2) the fact that staff subordinates (reporters, etc.) tend to have more "liberal" attitudes (and therefore perceptions) than the publisher and could invoke the norms to justify anti-policy writing; and (3) the ethical taboo preventing the publisher from commanding subordinates to follow policy. How policy comes to be maintained, and where it is bypassed, is the subject of this article.

From *Social Forces*, 1955, Vol. 33, pp. 326-355.

Several definitions are required at this point. As to personnel, "newsmen" can be divided into two main categories. "Executives" include the publisher and his editors. "Staffers" are reporters, rewrite men, copy readers, etc. In between there may be occasional city editors or wire editors who occupy an interstitial status. "Policy" may be defined as the more or less consistent orientation shown by a paper, not only in its editorial but in its news columns and headlines as well, concerning selected issues and events. "Slanting" almost never means prevarication. Rather, it involves omission, differential selection, and preferential placement, such as "featuring" a pro-policy item, "burying" an anti-policy story in an inside page, etc. "Professional norms" are of two types: Technical norms deal with the operations of efficient news gathering, writing, and editing; ethical norms embrace the newsman's obligation to his readers and to his craft and include such ideals as responsibility, impartiality, accuracy, fair play, and objectivity.[2]

Every newspaper has a policy, admitted or not.[3] One paper's policy may be pro-Republican, cool to labor, antagonistic to the school board, etc. The principal areas of policy are politics, business, and labor; much of it stems from considerations of class. Policy is manifested in "slanting." Just what determines any publisher's policy is a large question and will not be discussed here. Certainly, however, the publisher has much say (often in veto form) in both long-term and immediate policy decisions (which party to support, whether to feature or bury a story of imminent labor trouble, how much free space to give "news" of advertisers' doings, etc.). Finally, policy is covert, due to the existence of ethical norms of journalism; policy often contravenes these norms. No executive is willing to risk embarrassment by being accused of open commands to slant a news story.

While policy is set by the executives, it is clear that they cannot personally gather and write the news by themselves. They must delegate these tasks to staffers, and at this point the attitudes or interests of staffers may—and often do—conflict with those of the executives.[4] Of 72 staffers interviewed, 42 showed that they held more liberal views than those contained in their publisher's policy; 27 held similar views, and only 3 were more conservative. Similarly, only 17 of 61 staffers said they were Republicans.[5] The discrepancy is more acute when age (and therefore years of newspaper experience) is held constant. Of the 46 staffers under 35 years of age, 34 showed more liberal orientations; older men had apparently "mellowed." It should be noted that data as to intensity of attitudes are lacking. Some staffers may disagree with policy so mildly that they conform and feel no strain. The present essay is pertinent only insofar as dissident newsmen are forced to make decisions from time to time about their relationship to policy.[6]

We will now examine more closely the workings of the newspaper staff. The central question will be: How is policy maintained, despite the fact that it often contravenes journalistic norms, that staffers often personally disagree with it, and that executives cannot legitimately command that it be followed? The frame of reference will be that of functional analysis, as embodied in Merton's paradigm.[7]

The present data come from the writer's newspaper experience and from intensive interviews with some 120 newsmen, mostly in the northeastern quarter of the country. The sample was not random and no claim is made for representativeness, but on the other hand no paper was selected or omitted purposely and in no case did a newsman refuse the request that he be interviewed. The newspapers were chosen to fit a "middle-sized" group, defined as those with 10,000 to 100,000 daily circulation. Interviews averaged well over an hour in duration.[8]

There is an "action" element inherent in the present subject—the practical democratic need for "a free and responsible press" to inform citizens about current issues. Much of the criticism of the press stems from the slanting induced by the bias of the publisher's policy.[9] This criticism is often directed at flagrant cases such as the Hearst press, the *Chicago Tribune,* and New York tabloids, but also applies, in lesser degree, to the more conventional press. The description of mechanisms of policy maintenance may suggest why this criticism is often fruitless, at least in the short-run sense.

How the Staffer Learns Policy

The first mechanism promoting conformity is the "socialization" of the staffer with regard to the norms of his job. When the new reporter starts work he is not told what policy is. Nor is he ever told. This may appear stranger, but interview after interview confirmed the condition. The standard remark was "Never, in my ___ years on this paper, have I ever been told how to slant a story." No paper in the survey had a "training" program for its new men; some issue a "style" book, but this deals with literary style, not policy. Further, newsmen are busy and have little time for recruit training. Yet all but the newest staffers know what policy is.[10] On being asked, they say they learn it "by osmosis." Sociologically, this means they become socialized and "learn the ropes" like a neophyte in any subculture. Basically, the learning of policy is a process by which the recruit discovers and internalizes the rights and obligations of his status and its norms and values. He learns to anticipate what is expected of him so as to win rewards and avoid punishments. Policy is an important element of the newsroom norms, and he learns it in much the following way.

The staffer reads his own paper every day; some papers *require* this. It is simple to diagnose the paper's characteristics. Unless the staffer is naive or unusually independent, he tends to fashion his own stories after others he sees in the paper. This is particularly true of the newcomer. The news columns and editorials are a guide to the local norms. Thus a southern reporter notes that Republicans are treated in a "different" way in his paper's news columns than Democrats. The news about whites and Negroes is also of a distinct sort. Should he then write about one of these groups, his story will tend to reflect what he has come to define as standard procedure.

Certain editorial actions taken by editors and older staffers also serve as controlling guides. "If things are blue-pencilled consistently," one reporter said, "you learn he [the editor] has a prejudice in that regard."[11] Similarly, an executive may occasionally reprimand a staffer for policy violation. From our evidence, the reprimand is frequently oblique, due to the covert nature of policy, but learning occurs nevertheless. One staffer learned much through a series of incidents:

> I heard [a union] was going out on strike, so I kept on it; then the boss said something about it, and well—I took the hint and we had less coverage of the strike forming. It was easier that way. We lost the story, but what can you do?

> We used a yarn on a firm that was coming to town, and I got dragged out of bed for that. The boss is interested in this industrial stuff—we have to clear it all through him. He's an official in the Chamber. So . . . after a few times, it's irritating, so I get fed up. I try to figure out what will work best. I learn to try and guess what the boss will want.

In fairness it should be noted that this particular publisher was one of the most dictatorial encountered in the study. The pattern of control through reprimand, however, was found consistently. Another staffer wrote, on his own initiative, a series about discrimination against Jews at hotel resorts.

> It was the old "Gentlemen's Agreement" stuff, documented locally. The boss called me in . . . didn't like the stuff . . . the series never appeared. You start to get the idea.

Note that the boss does not "command"; the direction is more subtle. Also, it seems that most policy indications from executives are negative. They veto by a nod of the head, as if to say, "Please don't rock the boat." Exceptions occur in the "campaign" story, which will be discussed later. It is also to be noted that punishment is implied if policy is not followed.

Staffers also obtain guidance from their knowledge of the characteristics, interests, and affiliations of their executives. This knowledge can be gained in several ways. One is gossip. A reporter said:

> Do we gossip about the editors? Several of us used to meet—somewhere off the beaten path—over a beer—and talk for an hour. We'd rake 'em over the coals.

Another point of contact with executives is the news conference (which on middle-sized papers is seldom *called* a news conference), wherein the staffer outlines his findings and executives discuss how to shape the story. The typical conference consists of two persons, the reporter and the city editor, and can amount to no more than a few words. (Reporter: "One hurt in auto accident uptown." City editor: "Okay, keep it short.") If policy is at stake, the conference may involve several executives and require hours of consideration. From such meetings, the staffer can gain insight through what is said and what is not said by executives. It is important to say here that policy is not stated explicitly in the news conference nor elsewhere, with few exceptions. The news conference actually deals mostly with journalistic matters, such as reliability of information, newsworthiness, possible "angles," and other news tactics.

Three other channels for learning about executives are house organs (printed for the staff by syndicates and larger papers), observing the executive as he meets various leaders, and hearing him voice an opinion. One staffer could not help but gain an enduring impression of his publisher's attitudes in this incident:

> I can remember [him] saying on election night [1948], when it looked like we had a Democratic majority in both houses, "My God, this means we'll have a labor government." (Q: How did he say it?) He had a real note of alarm in his voice; you couldn't miss the point that he'd prefer the Republicans.

It will be noted that in speaking of "how" the staffer learns policy, there are indications also as to "why" he follows it.

Reasons for Conforming to Policy

There is no one factor which creates conformity-mindedness, unless we resort to a summary term such as "institutionalized statuses" or "structural roles." Particular factors must be sought in particular cases. The staffer must be seen in terms of his status and aspirations, the structure of the newsroom organization and of the larger society. He also must be viewed with reference to the operations he performs through his workday, and their consequences for him. The following six reasons appear to stay the potentially intransigent staffer from acts of deviance—often, if not always.[12]

1. Institutional Authority and Sanctions

The publisher ordinarily owns the paper and from a purely business standpoint has the right to expect obedience of his employees. He has the power to fire or demote for transgressions. This power, however, is diminished markedly in actuality by three facts. First, the newspaper is not conceived as a purely business enterprise, due to the protection of the First Amendment and a tradition of professional public service. Second, firing is a rare phenomenon on newspapers. For example, one editor said he had fired two men in 12 years; another could recall four firings in his 15 years on that paper. Third, there are severance pay clauses in contracts with the American Newspaper Guild (CIO). The only effective causes for firing are excessive drunkenness, sexual dalliance, etc. Most newspaper unemployment apparently comes from occasional economy drives on large papers and from total suspensions of publication. Likewise, only one case of demotion was found in the survey. It is true, however, that staffers still fear punishment; the myth has the errant star reporter taken off murders and put on obituaries—"the Chinese torture chamber" of the newsroom. Fear of sanctions, rather than their invocation, is a reason for conformity, but not as potent a one as would seem at first glance.

Editors, for their part, can simply ignore stories which might create deviant actions, and when this is impossible, can assign the story to a "safe" staffer. In the infrequent case that an anti-policy story reaches the city desk, the story is changed; extraneous reasons, such as the pressure of time and space, are given for the change.[13] Finally, the editor may contribute to the durability of policy by insulating the publisher from policy discussions. He may reason that the publisher would be embarrassed to hear of conflict over policy and the resulting bias, and spare him the resulting uneasiness; thus the policy remains not only covert but undiscussed and therefore unchanged.[14]

2. Feelings of Obligation and Esteem for Superiors

The staffer may feel obliged to the paper for having hired him. Respect, admiration, and gratitude may be felt for certain editors who have perhaps schooled him, "stood up for him," or supplied favors of a more paternalistic sort. Older staffers who have served as models for newcomers or who have otherwise given aid and comfort are due return courtesies. Such obligations and warm personal sentiments toward superiors play a strategic role in the pull to conformity.

3. Mobility Aspirations

In response to a question about ambition, all the younger staffers showed wishes for status achievement. There was agreement that bucking policy constituted a serious bar to this goal. In practice, several respondents noted that a good tactic toward advancement was to get "big" stories on Page One; this automatically means no tampering with policy. Further, some staffers see newspapering as a "stepping stone" job to more lucrative work: public relations, advertising, free-lancing, etc. The reputation for troublemaking would inhibit such climbing.

A word is in order here about chances for upward mobility. Of 51 newsmen aged 35 or more, 32 were executives. Of 50 younger men, 6 had reached executive posts and others were on their way up with such jobs as wire editors, political reporters, etc. All but five of these young men were college graduates, as against just half of their elders. Thus there is no evidence of a "break in the skill hierarchy" among newsmen.

4. Absence of Conflicting Group Allegiance

The largest formal organization of staffers is the American Newspaper Guild. The guild, much as it might wish to, has not interfered with internal

matters such as policy. It has stressed business unionism and political interests external to the newsroom. As for informal groups, there is no evidence
available that a group of staffers has ever "ganged up" on policy.

5. The Pleasant Nature of the Activity

a. *In-groupness in the newsroom.* The staffer has a low formal status
vis-à-vis executives, but he is not treated as a "worker." Rather, he is a
co-worker with executives; the entire staff cooperates congenially on a job
they all like and respect: getting the news. The newsroom is a friendly,
first-namish place. Staffers discuss stories with editors on a give-and-take
basis. Top executives with their own offices sometimes come out and sit in
on newsroom discussions.[15]

b. *Required operations are interesting.* Newsmen like their work. Few
voiced complaints when given the opportunity to gripe during interviews.
The operations required—witnessing, interviewing, briefly mulling the
meanings of events, checking facts, writing—are not onerous.

c. *Nonfinancial perquisites.* These are numerous: the variety of experience, eye-witnessing significant and interesting events, being the first to
know, getting "the inside dope" denied laymen, meeting and sometimes
befriending notables and celebrities (who are well advised to treat newsmen
with deference). Newsmen are close to big decisions without having to make
them; they touch power without being responsible for its use. From talking
with newsmen and reading their books, one gets the impression that they
are proud of being newsmen.[16] There are tendencies to exclusiveness within
news ranks, and intimations that such near out-groups as radio newsmen
are entertainers, not real newsmen. Finally, there is the satisfaction of being
a member of a live-wire organization dealing with important matters. The
newspaper is an "institution" in the community. People talk about it and
quote it; its big trucks whiz through town; its columns carry the tidings from
big and faraway places, with pictures.

Thus, despite his relatively low pay, the staffer feels, for all these reasons,
an integral part of a going concern. His job morale is high. Many newsmen
could qualify for jobs paying more money in advertising and public relations,
but they remain with the newspaper.

6. News Becomes a Value

Newsmen define their job as producing a certain quantity of what is
called "news" every 24 hours. This is to be produced *even though nothing much
has happened.* News is a continuous challenge, and meeting this challenge is
the newsman's job. He is rewarded for fulfilling this, his manifest function.
A consequence of this focus on news as a central value is the shelving of a
strong interest in objectivity at the point of policy conflict. Instead of mobi-

lizing their efforts to establish objectivity over policy as the criterion for performance, their energies are channeled into getting more news. The demands of competition (in cities where there are two or more papers) and speed enhance this focus. Newsmen do talk about ethics, objectivity, and the relative worth of various papers, but not when there is news to get. News comes first, and there is always news to get.[17] They are not rewarded for analyzing the social structure, but for getting news. It would seem that this instrumental orientation diminishes their moral potential. A further consequence of this pattern is that the harmony between staffers and executives is cemented by their common interest in news. Any potential conflict between the two groups, such as slowdowns occurring among informal work groups in industry, would be dissipated to the extent that news is a positive value. The newsroom solidarity is thus reinforced.

The six factors promote policy conformity. To state more exactly how policy is maintained would be difficult in view of the many variables contained in the system. The process may be somewhat better understood, however, with the introduction of one further concept—the reference group.[18] The staffer, especially the new staffer, identifies himself through the existence of these six factors with the executives and veteran staffers. Although not yet one of them, he shares their norms, and thus his performance comes to resemble theirs. He conforms to the norms of policy rather than to whatever personal beliefs he brought to the job, or to ethical ideals. All six of these factors function to encourage reference group formation. Where the allegiance is directed toward legitimate authority, that authority has only to maintain the equilibrium within limits by the prudent distribution of rewards and punishments. The reference group itself, which has as its "magnet" element the elite of executives and old staffers, is unable to change policy to a marked degree because first, it is the group charged with carrying out policy, and second, because the policymaker, the publisher, is often insulated on the delicate issue of policy.

In its own way, each of the six factors contributes to the formation of reference group behavior. There is almost no firing, hence a steady expectation of continued employment. Subordinates tend to esteem their bosses, so a convenient model group is present. Mobility aspirations (when held within limits) are an obvious promoter of inter-status bonds as is the absence of conflicting group loyalties with their potential harvest of cross-pressures. The newsroom atmosphere is charged with the related factors of in-groupness and pleasing nature of the work. Finally, the agreement among newsmen that their job is to fasten upon the news, seeing it as a value in itself, forges a bond across status lines.

As to the six factors, five appear to be relatively constant, occurring on all papers studied. The varying factor is the second: obligation and esteem held by staffers for executive and older staffers. On some papers, this obligation-esteem entity was found to be larger than on others. Where it was large, the paper appeared to have two characteristics pertinent to this discussion. First, it did a good conventional job of news-getting and news-publishing, and second, it had little difficulty over policy. With staffers drawn toward both the membership and the reference groups, organization was efficient. Most papers are like this. On the few smaller papers where executives and older staffers are not respected, morale is spotty; staffers withhold enthusiasm from their stories, they cover their beats perfunctorily, they wish for a job on a better paper, and they are apathetic and sometimes hostile to policy. Thus the obligation-esteem factor seems to be the active variable in determining not only policy conformity, but morale and good news performance as well.

Situations Permitting Deviation

Thus far it would seem that the staffer enjoys little "freedom of the press." To show that this is an oversimplification, and more important, to suggest a kind of test for our hypothesis about the strength of policy, let us ask: "What happens when a staffer *does* submit an anti-policy story?" We know that this happens infrequently, but what follows in these cases?

The process of learning policy crystallizes into a process of social control, in which deviations are punished (usually gently) by reprimand, cutting one's story, the withholding of friendly comment by an executive, etc. For example, it is punishment for a staffer when the city editor waves a piece of his copy at him and says, "Joe, don't *do* that when you're writing about the mayor." In an actual case, a staffer acting as wire editor was demoted when he neglected to feature a story about a "sacred cow" politician on his paper. What can be concluded is that when an executive sees a clearly anti-policy item, he blue-pencils it, and this constitutes a lesson for the staffer. Rarely does the staffer persist in violating policy; no such case appeared in all the interviews. Indeed, the best-known cases of firing for policy reasons—Ted O. Thackrey and Leo Huberman—occurred on liberal New York City dailies, and Thackrey was an editor, not a staffer.

Now and then cases arise in which a staffer finds his anti-policy stories printed. There seems to be no consistent explanation for this, except to introduce two more specific subjects dealing first, with the staffer's career line, and second, with particular empirical conditions associated with the career line. We can distinguish three stages through which the staffer progresses. First, there is the cub stage, the first few months or years in which the new man learns techniques and policy. He writes short, nonpolicy stories, such as minor accidents, meeting activity, the weather, etc. The second, or "wiring-in" stage, sees the staffer continuing to assimilate the newsroom values and to cement informal relationships. Finally, there is the "star" or "veteran" stage, in which the staffer typically defines himself as a full, responsible member of the group, sees its goals as his, and can be counted on to handle policy sympathetically.[19]

To further specify the conformity-deviation problem, it must be understood that newspapering is a relatively complex activity. The newsman is responsible for a range of skills and judgments which are matched only in the professional and entrepreneurial fields. Oversimplifications about policy rigidity can be avoided if we ask, "*Under what conditions* can the staffer defy or bypass policy?" We have already seen that staffers are free to argue news decisions with executives in brief "news conferences," but the arguments generally revolve around points of "newsiness," rather than policy as such.[20] Five factors appear significant in the area of the reporter's power to bypass policy.

1. The norms of policy are not always entirely clear, just as many norms are vague and unstructured. Policy is covert by nature and has large scope. The paper may be Republican, but standing only lukewarm for Republican Candidate A who may be too "liberal" or no friend of the publisher. Policy, if worked out explicitly, would have to include motivations, reasons, alternatives, historical developments, and other complicating material. Thus a twilight zone permitting a range of deviation appears.[21]

2. Executives may be ignorant of particular facts, and staffers who do the leg (and telephone) work to gather news can use their superior knowledge to subvert policy. On grounds of both personal belief and professional codes, the staffer has the option of selection at many points. He can decide whom to interview and whom to ignore, what questions to ask, which quotations to note, and on writing the story which items to feature (with an eye toward the headline), which to bury, and in general what tone to give the several possible elements of the story.

3. In addition to the "squeeze" tactic exploiting executives' ignorance of minute facts, the "plant" may be employed. Although a paper's policy may proscribe a certain issue from becoming featured, a staffer, on getting a good story about that issue may "plant" it in another paper or wire service through a friendly staffer and submit it to his own editor, pleading the story is now too big to ignore.

4. It is possible to classify news into four types on the basis of source of origination. These are: the policy or campaign story, the assigned story, the beat story, and the story initiated by the staffer. The staffer's autonomy is larger with the latter than the former types. With the campaign story (build new hospital, throw rascals out, etc.), the staffer is working directly under executives and has little leeway. An assigned story is handed out by the city editor and thus will rarely hit policy head on, although the staffer has some leverage of selection. When we come to the beat story, however, it is clear that the function of the reporter changes. No editor comes between him and his beat (police department, city hall, etc.); thus the reporter gains the "editor" function. It is he who, to a marked degree, can select which stories to pursue, which to ignore. Several cases developed in interviews of beat men who smothered stories they knew would provide fuel for policy—policy they

personally disliked or thought injurious to the professional code. The cooperation of would-be competing reporters is essential, of course. The fourth
type of story is simply one which the staffer originates, independent of
assignment or beat. All respondents, executives and staffers, averred that any
employee was free to initiate stories. But equally regularly, they acknowledged that the opportunity was not often assumed. Staffers were already
overloaded with beats, assignments, and routine coverage, and besides,
rewards for initiated stories were meager or nonexistent unless the initiated
story confirmed policy. Yet this area promises much, should staffers pursue
their advantage. The outstanding case in the present study concerned a
well-educated, enthusiastic reporter on a conventional daily just north of the
Mason-Dixon line. Entirely on his own, he consistently initiated stories about
Negroes and Negro-white relations, "making" policy where only void had
existed. He worked overtime to document and polish the stories; his boss
said he didn't agree with the idea but insisted on the reporter's right to
publish them.

5. Staffers with "star" status can transgress policy more easily than cubs.
This differential privilege of status was encountered on several papers. An
example would be Walter Winchell during the Roosevelt administration,
who regularly praised the president while the policy of his boss, Mr. Hearst,
was strongly critical of the regime. A *New York Times* staffer said he doubted
that any copy reader on the paper would dare change a word of the copy of
Meyer Berger, the star feature writer.

These five factors indicate that given certain conditions, the controls
making for policy conformity can be bypassed. These conditions exist not
only within the newsroom and the news situation but within the staffer as
well; they will be exploited only if the staffer's attitudes permit. There are
some limitations, then, on the strength of the publisher's policy.

Before summarizing, three additional requirements of Merton's functional paradigm must be met. These are statements of the consequences of
the pattern, of available alternative modes of behavior, and a validation of
the analysis.

Consequences of the Pattern

To the extent that policy is maintained, the paper keeps publishing
smoothly as seen both from the newsroom and from the outside, which is no
mean feat if we visualize the country with no press at all. This is the most
general consequence. There are several special consequences. For the society
as a whole, the existing system of power relationships is maintained. Policy
usually protects property and class interests, and thus the strata and groups
holding these interests are better able to retain them. For the larger community, much news is printed objectively, allowing for opinions to form openly,

but policy news may be slanted or buried so that some important information is denied the citizenry. (This is the dysfunction widely scored by critics.) For the individual readers, the same is true. For the executives, their favorable statuses are maintained, with perhaps occasional touches of guilt over policy. For newsmen, the consequences are the same as for executives. For more independent, critical staffers, there can be several modes of adaptation. At the extremes, the pure conformist can deny the conflict, the confirmed deviate can quit the newspaper business. Otherwise, the adaptations seem to run in this way: (1) Keep on the job but blunt the sharp corners of policy where possible ("If I wasn't here the next guy would let *all* that crap go through."); (2) attempt to repress the conflict amorally and anti-intellectually ("What the hell, it's only a job; take your pay and forget it."); (3) attempt to compensate, by "taking it out" in other contexts: drinking, writing "the truth" for liberal publications, working with action programs, the guild and otherwise. All of these adjustments were found in the study. As has been suggested, one of the main compensations for all staffers is simply to find justification in adhering to "good news practice."

Possible Alternatives and Change

A functional analysis, designed to locate sources of persistence of a pattern, can also indicate points of strain at which a structural change may occur. For example, the popular recipe for eliminating bias at one time was to diminish advertisers' power over the news. This theory having proved unfruitful, critics more recently have fastened upon the publisher as the point at which change must be initiated. Our analysis suggests that this is a valid approach, but one requiring that leverage in turn be applied on the publisher from various sources. Perhaps the most significant of these are professional codes. Yet we have seen the weakness of these codes when policy decisions are made. Further leverage is contained in such sources as the professional direction being taken by some journalism schools, in the guild, and in sincere criticism.

Finally, newspaper readers possess potential power over press performance. Seen as a client of the press, the reader should be entitled to not only an interesting newspaper but one that furnishes significant news objectively presented. This is the basic problem of democracy: To what extent should the individual be treated as a member of a mass, and to what extent fashioned (through educative measures) as an active participant in public decisions? Readership studies show that readers prefer "interesting" news and "features" over penetrating analyses. It can be concluded that the citizen has not been sufficiently motivated by society (and its press) to demand and apply the information he needs, and to discriminate between worthwhile and spurious information, for the fulfillment of the citizen's role. These other forces—professional codes, journalism schools, the guild, critics and readers—could result in changing newspaper performance. It still remains, however, for the publisher to be changed first. He can be located at the apex of a T, the crucial point of decision making. Newsroom and professional forces form the base of the T; outside forces from community and society are the arms. It is for the publisher to decide which forces to propitiate.

Suggestions for Validation

The Merton paradigm requires a statement concerning validation of the analysis. Checks could be forthcoming both from social science researchers and from newsmen. If the latter, the newsman should explicitly state the basis for his discussion, especially as regards the types of papers, executives, and staffers he knows. A crucial case for detailed description would be the situation in which staffers actively defied authority on policy matters. Another important test would be a comparative description of two papers contrasted by their situation as regards the six factors promoting conformity, with particular reference to the variable of obligation and esteem held toward superiors, and the factors permitting deviation. In any event, the present exploratory study may serve as a point of departure.

A second type of validation may be suggested. This would focus on the utility of the paradigm itself. Previous studies have been based on functional theory but before the development of the paradigm.[22] Studies of diverse social systems also lend themselves to functional analysis, and such comparative research could function not only to build systematic theory but to test and suggest modifications of the paradigm. Situations characterized by conflict and competition for scarce goals seem particularly well suited to functional analysis. Several points made in the present essay might have been overlooked without the paradigm.[23]

Summary

The problem, which was suggested by the age-old charges of bias against the press, focused around the manner in which the publisher's policy came to be followed, despite three empirical conditions: (1) Policy sometimes contravenes journalistic norms; (2) staffers often personally disagree with it; and (3) executives cannot legitimately command that policy be followed. Interview and other data were used to explain policy maintenance. It is important to recall that the discussion is based primarily on study of papers of "middle" circulation range, and does not consider either nonpolicy stories or the original policy decision made by the publishers.

The mechanisms for learning policy on the part of the new staffer were given, together with suggestions as to the nature of social controls. Six factors, apparently the major variables producing policy maintenance, were described. The most significant of these variables, obligation and esteem for superiors, was deemed not only the most important but the most fluctuating variable from paper to paper. Its existence and its importance for conformity led to the subhypothesis that reference group behavior was playing a part in the pattern. To show, however, that policy is not iron-clad, five conditions were suggested in which staffers may bypass policy.

Thus we conclude that the publisher's policy, when established in a given subject area, is usually followed, and that a description of the dynamic sociocultural situation of the newsroom will suggest explanations for this conformity. The newsman's source of rewards is located not among the readers, who are manifestly his clients, but among his colleagues and supe-riors. Instead of adhering to societal and professional ideals, he redefines his values to the more pragmatic level of the newsroom group. He thereby gains not only status rewards but also acceptance in a solidary group engaged in interesting, varied, and sometimes important work. Thus the cultural pat-terns of the newsroom produce results insufficient for wider democratic needs. Any important change toward a more "free and responsible press" must stem from various possible pressures on the publisher, who epitomizes the policy-making and coordinating role.

Notes

1. See, for instance, F. J. Roethlisberger and William J. Dickson, *Management and the Worker* (Cambridge: Harvard University Press, 1947); and Logan Wilson, *The Academic Man* (New York: Oxford University Press, 1942).

2. The best-known formal code is The Canons of Journalism, of the American Society of Newspaper Editors. See Wilbur Schramm (ed.), *Mass Communications* (Urbana: Univer-sity of Illinois Press, 1949), pp. 236-238.

3. It is extremely difficult to measure the extent of objectivity or bias. One recent attempt is reported in Nathan B. Blumberg, *One-Party Press?* (Lincoln: University of Nebraska Press, 1954), which gives a news count for 35 papers' performance in the 1952 election campaign. He concluded that 18 of the papers showed "no evidence of partiality," 11 showed "no conclusive evidence of partiality," and 6 showed partiality. His interpreta-tions, however, are open to argument. A different interpretation could conclude that while about 16 showed little or no partiality, the rest did. It should be noted, too, that there are different areas of policy depending on local conditions. The chief difference occurs in the deep South, where frequently there is no "Republican" problem and no "union" problem over which the staff can be divided. Color becomes the focus of policy.

4. This condition, pointed out in a lecture by Paul F. Lazarsfeld, formed the starting point for the present study.

5. Similar findings were made about Washington correspondents in Leo C. Rosten, *The Washington Correspondents* (New York: Harcourt, Brace, 1937). Less ideological conflict was found in two other studies: Francis V. Prugger, "Social Composition and Training of the Milwaukee Journal News Staff," *Journalism Quarterly*, 18 (Sept. 1941), pp. 231-244, and Charles E. Swanson, *The Mid-City Daily* (Ph.D. dissertation, State University of Iowa, 1948). Possible reasons for the gap is that both papers studied were perhaps above average in objectivity; executives were included with staffers in computations; and some staffers were doubtless included who did not handle policy news.

6. It is not being argued that "liberalism" and objectivity are synonymous. A liberal paper (e.g., *PM*) can be biased, too, but it is clear that few liberal papers exist among the

many conservative ones. It should also be stressed that much news is not concerned with policy and is therefore probably unbiased.

7. Robert K. Merton, *Social Theory and Social Structure* (Glencoe: Free Press, 1949), esp. pp. 49-61. Merton's elements will not be explicitly referred to but his principal requirements are discussed at various points.

8. The data are taken from Warren Breed, *The Newspaperman, News and Society* (Ph.D. dissertation, Columbia University, 1952). Indebtedness is expressed to William L. Kolb and Robert C. Stone, who read the present manuscript and provided valuable criticisms and suggestions.

9. For a summary description of this criticism, see Commission on the Freedom of the Press, *A Free and Responsible Press* (Chicago: University of Chicago Press, 1947), chap. 4.

10. While the concept of policy is crucial to this analysis, it is not to be assumed that newsmen discuss it fully. Some do not even use the word in discussing how their paper is run. To this extent, policy is a latent phenomenon; either the staffer has no reason to contemplate policy or he chooses to avoid so doing. It may be that one strength of policy is that it has become no more manifest to the staffers who follow it.

11. Note that such executives' actions as blue-pencilling play not only the manifest function of preparing the story for publication but also the latent one of steering the future action of the staffer.

12. Two cautions are in order here. First, it will be recalled that we are discussing not all news, but only policy news. Second, we are discussing only staffers who are potential nonconformers. Some agree with policy; some have no views on policy matters; others do not write policy stories. Furthermore, there are strong forces in American society which cause many individuals to choose harmonious adjustment (conformity) in any situation, regardless of the imperatives. See Erich Fromm, *Escape From Freedom* (New York: Farrar and Rinehart, 1941), and David Reisman, *The Lonely Crowd* (New Haven: Yale, 1950).

13. Excellent illustration of this tactic is given in the novel by an experienced newspaperwoman: Margaret Long, *Affair of the Heart* (New York: Random House, 1953), chap. 10. This chapter describes the framing of a Negro for murder in a middle-sized southern city, and the attempt of a reporter to tell the story objectively.

14. The insulation of one individual or group from another is a good example of social (as distinguished from psychological) mechanisms to reduce the likelihood of conflict. Most of the factors inducing conformity could likewise be viewed as social mechanisms. See Talcott Parsons and Edward A. Shils, "Values, Motives and Systems of Action," in Parsons and Shils (eds.), *Toward a General Theory of Action* (Cambridge: Harvard University Press, 1951), pp. 223-230.

15. Further indication that the staffer-executive relationship is harmonious came from answers to the question, "Why do you think newspapermen are thought to be cynical?" Staffers regularly said that newsmen are cynical because they get close enough to stark reality to see the ills of their society, and the imperfections of its leaders and officials. Only 2, of 40 staffers, took the occasion to criticize their executives and the enforcement of policy. This displacement, or lack of strong feelings against executives, can be interpreted to bolster the hypothesis of staff solidarity. (It further suggests that newsmen tend to analyze their society in terms of personalities, rather than institutions comprising a social and cultural system.)

16. There is a sizable myth among newsmen about the attractiveness of their calling. For example, the story: "Girl: 'My, you newspapermen must have a fascinating life. You meet such interesting people.' Reporter: 'Yes, and most of them are newspapermen.' " For a further discussion, see Breed, *op. cit.*, chap. 17.

17. This is a variant of the process of "displacement of goals," newsmen turning to "getting news" rather than to seeking data which will enlighten and inform their readers. The dysfunction is implied in the nation's need not for more news but for better news—

quality rather than quantity. See Merton, *op. cit.*, "Bureaucratic Structure and Personality," pp. 154-155.

18. Whether group members acknowledge it or not, "if a person's attitudes are influenced by a set of norms which he assumes that he shares with other individuals, those individuals constitute for him a reference group." Theodore M. Newcomb, *Social Psychology* (New York: Dryden, 1950), p. 225. Williams states that reference group formation may segment large organizations; in the present case, the reverse is true, the loyalty of subordinates going to their "friendly" superiors and to the discharge of technical norms such as getting news. See Robin M. Williams, *American Society* (New York: Knopf, 1951), p. 476.

19. Does the new staffer, fresh from the ideals of college, really "change his attitudes"? It would seem that attitudes about socioeconomic affairs need not be fixed, but are capable of shifting with the situation. There are arguments for and against any opinion; in the atmosphere of the newsroom the arguments "for" policy decisions are made to sound adequate, especially as these are evoked by the significant others in the system.

20. The fullest treatment of editor-reporter conferences appears in Swanson, *op. cit.*

21. Related to the fact that policy is vague is the more general postulate that executives seek to avoid formal issues and the possibly damaging disputes arising therefrom. See Chester I. Barnard, *Functions of the Executive* (Cambridge: Harvard University Press, 1947).

22. References are cited in Merton, *Social Theory and Social Structure, op. cit.*, and also in the works of Talcott Parsons.

23. That the paradigm might serve best as a checklist or "insurance," or as a theoretical guide to fledgling scholars, is shown by the excellence of an article published before the paradigm—and quite similar to the present article in dealing with problems of policy maintenance in a formal organization: Edward A. Shils and Morris Janowitz, "Cohesion and Disintegration in the Wehrmacht in World War II," *Public Opinion Quarterly*, 12 (Summer 1948), pp. 280-315.

CHAPTER 10

News Organizations

Conflict as a Crafted Cultural Norm

Charles R. Bantz

Analyses of news organizations have engaged a variety of perspectives. This essay utilizes a cultural viewpoint identifying five factors that suggest the proposition that the organizational cultures in newswork, particularly in television news, should "normalize" the occurrence of conflict. That is, the incompatibilities of factors such as professional norms and business norms result in conflict becoming ordinary, routine, perhaps even valuable. In news organizations, conflict, disputes, disagreements are to be expected and defined as appropriate. Further, the interaction of these factors makes such a finding even more likely. The essay makes no claim as to the relative frequency of conflict in news organizations compared to other organizations; rather, it outlines the rationale for predicting that news organizational cultures make conflict acceptable within organizational norms. To present this rationale, the essay (1) briefly reviews the potential contribution of a cultural viewpoint in the study of media organizations, (2) outlines the viewpoint of organizational culture research, (3) presents the proposition and five factors suggesting it, and (4) considers the consequence of the factors.[1]

From *Communication*, 1985, Vol. 8, pp. 225-244. Used with permission of Gordon and Breach Science Publishers.

Potential Contribution of
Organizational Culture Viewpoint

The three major elements of a mediated communication system are the communicator organizations, the messages produced, and the audience which uses those messages. A full understanding of media necessitates examination of all three elements of the system. While media scholarship still emphasizes audiences, since the 1960s communicator organizations have drawn increasing attention. The study of communicator organizations contributes to understanding (1) the relationships among the elements of the system (audience, message, and communicator), (2) the relationship between the system and society, and (3) the process of message creation.

A variety of theoretical and methodological perspectives have guided the research on news organizations (cf. Gans, 1979; Tuchman, 1978; Turow, 1984). It is beyond the purview of the present work to chart the varying perspectives in prior research. Rather, in these pages my goal is to consider the analysis of news organizations through an alternative perspective—that of organizational culture. While the culture orientation has been infrequently applied to news organizations (an exception in Ewart, 1985), this perspective: (1) provides information essential for understanding the life world of the news organization; (2) permits analyzing how concepts central to other perspectives affect organizational culture (e.g., how the concept of power affects organizational culture); and (3) contributes to understanding how organizational culture may affect the applicability of concepts of other perspectives (e.g., how culture limits the applicability of the concept of power).

Each of these possibilities can be briefly illustrated. First, as is argued in detail below, when researchers understand the culture of an organization, they can understand the life world of its members. This would include knowing how newsworkers define words and actions, what they value and devalue, what constitutes a good reason and a bad reason for acting, how time and space are structured, and numerous other aspects of the newsworker's life in the organization. In a news organization, an understanding of culture will reveal, for that organization, the way news stories are defined, what constitutes a good or bad reporter, when a reporter is "doing right" in seeking a story, how deadlines are set, and how the physical "turf" of the newsroom is divided. Understanding the life world means understanding how the organizational member interprets and constitutes social reality (see Putnam & Pacanowsky, 1983).

Second, with an understanding of an organization's culture, a researcher can then consider how noncultural theories and concepts relate to organizational culture. For example, Turow (1984) argues that media organizations can be analyzed by using the concept of resource dependence. Resource dependence theory predicts that Media, Inc. will seek to increase Supplier, Inc.'s dependence on it for resources, while itself not becoming dependent on Supplier, Inc. (You become dependent on me, but I won't become dependent on you.) This concept can be used to understand patterns in an organization's culture. Thus resource dependence theory may help to explain a hypothetical finding that Supplier, Inc.'s culture developed a definition of Media, Inc. as exploitative.

Third, an understanding of an organization's culture provides the opportunity to consider how cultural factors can limit the applicability of noncultural theories and concepts. Such an analysis could focus on how cultural variations covary with theoretical and conceptual predictions. For example, Tuchman's (1978) oft-cited division of news stories into hard, soft, continuing, and developing stories is often assumed to be consistent across news organizations. However, Lester (1980) found a quite different definition of newsworthiness in her study of *The Interpreter* (a pseudonym), and she argues that newsworthiness is organizationally defined. An analysis of the organizational culture of *The Interpreter* and other news organizations may identify cultural factors that systematically contribute to variations in the constitution of newsworthiness. Thus, consideration of organizational cultures could contribute to refinancing both the domain and range of noncultural concepts.

Organizations as Cultures

There are numerous views of organizations as cultures and a number of excellent reviews of the concept (see Deal & Kennedy, 1982; Pacanowsky & Putnam, 1982; Putnam & Pacanowsky, 1983). Pettigrew's (1979) managerially situated discussion and Pacanowsky and O'Donnell-Trujillo's (1982) and Schall's (1983) communicatively situated discussions present useful extended descriptions of the perspective. The evolution of Bormann's fantasy theme analysis (1972) into symbolic convergence theory (1982, 1983) represents an approach to organizational culture founded in a symbolic interactionist tradition (see Bantz, 1983).

The fundamental assumption of the cultural approach is that organizations exist as symbolic realities. Cultures are symbolic constructions created by members of organizations that shape the symbolic realities of those members' organizations (cf. Putnam, 1983). Cultures function reflexively in organizations. Cultures are created and maintained by the members and they simultaneously influence how members understand the organization (cf. Pacanowsky & O'Donnell-Trujillo, 1982). For example, the members of a hightech organization may build a culture that highly values rapid change—organizational, technical, and competitive—but concurrently such a culture would limit the members' ability to create stability—say in personnel. The most popular metaphor for organizational culture is the one Geertz (1973, p. 5) borrowed from Weber: "that man is an animal suspended in webs of significance he himself has spun . . . culture [is] those webs." The metaphor emphasizes that culture is a human creation that both facilitates and constrains human action. The web of culture constitutes and organization permits it to act and ensnares its members. Tuchman's analysis of newswork

(1978) effectively uses a web metaphor to characterize the efficiency and limitation of routine newsgathering procedures.

To develop the concept of organizational culture, I postulate (following Johnson, 1977) that organizational cultures are systems of meanings that are continuously available to organizational members. Further, modifying Johnson (1977) and building on Schneider's description (1976) of the relationship of meaning and action, I propose that organizational cultures involve expectations that define accepted patterns of action. *Organizational cultures are, therefore, patterns of meanings that define appropriate action. Hence to understand an organizational culture one identifies the organization's patterns of meanings, the expectations that define appropriate action, and the relationship between meanings and expectations.* From the variety of possible patterns of expectation (see Bantz, 1981), this essay emphasizes *norms,* defined as "an idea in the minds of the members of a group, . . . specifying what the members or other [people] should do, ought to do, are expected to do, under given circumstances" (Homans, 1950, p. 123). *The presence of norms (i.e., normative expectations) is evidenced by consistent patterns of behavior defined as appropriate.*

From this perspective, a study of organizational culture necessarily involves generating material that permits identifying meanings and expectations of the culture. While there are a number of techniques that can be used for such research, the most typical is observation—participant or nonparticipant. (For discussions of various techniques see Bantz, 1983, ...) The researcher gathers messages generated by the organization through observing meetings, work, talk, and social conversations as well as reading memos, histories, and bulletin boards. How the researcher proceeds once the data are gathered varies greatly depending on the perspective of the analyst. For example, Pacanowsky and O'Donnell-Trujillo (1982) urge looking for constructs, rituals, fact, practices, vocabulary, metaphors, and stories. Deetz (1982) argues the analyst seeks understanding by describing the deep meaning structures in organizational texts, criticizing those texts, and forming new concepts for organizational members. Bantz (1981) argues the analyst first looks for the patterns of vocabulary, themes, architecture, and temporality before inferring the patterns of meanings and expectations in the culture.

Whatever the perspective, the goal of organizational culture analysis is to detail the symbolic patterns that constitute the world organization. The strength of this approach is that the product, a well-done analysis, will provide a richly textured description that makes the organization understandable to scholars. Rather than providing a structural description of factors influencing television news (e.g., Epstein, 1973), a cultural study provides a reader with vivid images of news people, the world in which they work, and the newsworkers' interpretation of that world. A complete description of organizational culture should make the meanings and expectations of the organization concrete, so that the logic of life in that organization is understandable.

Coser (1956), Kriesberg (1973), and other social theorists (e.g., Marx, 1964) argue that conflict is an integral aspect of social life. When one accepts that argument, it is assumed that conflict is an everyday occurrence in all realms of social life, including organizations. Yet, realizing that conflict will occur in organizations is *not* to argue that conflict will be defined as culturally acceptable in all organizations (e.g., managers telling subordinates to "Get on board," implying disagreement is not acceptable). Different organizations develop different cultural definitions and consequent norms of conflict. *The argument presented here, however, is that the culture of news organizations, particularly television news organizations, will define conflict as a routine, expected, and appropriate occurrence.* Not only will social conflict (i.e., disputes between persons or groups over goals; Kriesberg, 1973, p. 17) and interpersonal conflict (i.e., disputes between persons) be observed in news organizations, but their cultural meaning will be "ordinary," "routine," perhaps even "good" and "necessary." The concomitant cultural expectations will be that conflictive behavior is "appropriate," perhaps even "required" for organizational functioning. In other words, conflict is normalized, that is, defined as routine behavior in the culture of news organizations.

The proposition that television news organizations are cultures that normalize conflict is based on five major factors and the interaction of those factors: (1) newsworkers' distrust of and disputing of individuals who propagate a point of view; (2) conflicts between professional norms and business norms; (3) conflicts between professional norms and entertainment norms; (4) controlled competition among newsworkers and among news organizations; and (5) the structure of television news messages. Considered together these factors suggest that television news organizations are cultures where conflict is a pattern of expected behavior, and conflict is, therefore, ordinary, routine, and reasonable. In fact, the culture's normalization of conflict may even require accounts to justify cooperative behavior (cf. Tunstall, 1970, chap. 7, 1971, chap. 6). This pattern is simultaneously created and maintained by newsworkers and influences the newsworkers' definition of the culture. Thus these factors contribute to the normalization of conflict in the culture by organizational members and that culture in turn influences organizational members as they exist in and reconstitute that culture.

Newsworker Distrust and Dispute

Tuchman (1978) argues that the pattern of newsgathering typically leads to support for the status quo; Altheide (1984) argues there is a tendency for journalists to cast themselves in opposition to the focus of the status quo. It is not necessary to accept either position to find that newsworkers are characterized by a skepticism of sources in general, but are likely to be distrustful of persons obviously presenting a point of view. Johnstone, Slawski, and Bowman's (1976) newsworkers reported a commitment to public responsibility. When the intentions of sources become apparent and the source's intentions are seen by journalists as being inconsistent with their conception of public responsibility, newsworkers are likely to distrust and dispute the sources. For example, newsworkers are very aware and somewhat accepting that the news secretaries of political candidates attempt to present their candidate in a positive light. When, however, news secretaries appear to be deliberately deceiving and obfuscating to protect their candidates for what newsworkers deemed inappropriate reasons, newsworkers may become extraordinarily distrustful (e.g., the attacks on Richard Nixon's news secretary Ron Ziegler during Watergate; see Rather, 1978, chap. 11, 12, 13).

Journalists' expectations concerning interaction with news sources depends upon the meanings shared about the relationship between journalists and those sources. If the relationship developed as an open exchange with obvious motivations for interaction, the expectations for behavior are likely to be clear. For example, the reporters and news secretaries may develop detailed norms that regulate asking questions, answers and parries, follow-up, and leaks (see Sigal, 1973, chap. 3). The specific interaction norms will be influenced by many factors, including national and regional culture. Hence the norms are likely to vary from country to country (e.g., Israel vs. United States) and within country on a number of dimensions (e.g., community homogeneity; see Tichenor, Donohue, & Olien, 1980). In the U.S., one assumption guiding the interaction is that some incompatibility between the newsworkers' goals and the sources' goals is accepted, but that incompatibility is managed within mutually defined meanings and expectations. The range of those meanings (e.g., interaction as an agreement to disagree) and expectations (e.g., to be civil) is established over time. However, if one party to the exchange perceives a shift in the relationship that seems inconsistent with prior shared meanings and expectations (e.g., instead of the exchange being sport, it is war), then the level of dispute may escalate dramatically. For example, former U.S. Vice President Agnew's vitriolic attacks on the media seemed to alter the previous definition of media-administration relations and seemed to polarize journalists (see Schorr, 1977, chap. 3).

When sources and reporters have interacted for an extended period or where sources have great power over reporters, the interaction between sources and reporters may be routinized as a nonconflict interaction. This is often the case when reporters on beats build long-term relationships—e.g., the police reporter "goes native" or the political reporter becomes a political actor (see Sigal, 1973, chap. 3). Even in those cases, professional norms may support the assumption that there are circumstances where a more conflictive interaction is appropriate. That is, the newsworker can imagine a circumstance, where despite long-established nonconflict relationships, she or he would necessarily confront a source (e.g., a major crisis occurs when the reporter faces a deadline). In other words, newsworkers utilize a calculus that includes the legitimate value of disputing sources and conflict when balancing their relationship with sources and the demands for work. The calculus is only made more complex by factors of professionalism, isolation, and group norms, which are discussed below.

Professional Norms vs. Business Norms

News organizations employ a large number of individuals who work within a set of journalistic professional norms, even though not all employed by those organizations were trained as journalists (Johnstone et al., 1976, chap. 3). Professional norms affect the prevalence of organizational conflict in a number of ways. There may, for example, be an inconsistency between professional norms and other norms within a news organization (e.g., business norms or what Ritzer, 1977, chap. 5, refers to as bureaucratic norms). If the culture of a news organization includes a set of organizational meanings (e.g., quality means completeness) and consequent norms (e.g., workers should be very thorough) that are consistent with journalistic professional norms, there should be less incidence of endemic organizational conflict within the culture (see the characterization of *The Interpreter* in Lester, 1980). If, however, the news organization has built a set of organizational meanings (e.g., good work is efficient work) and consequent expectations (e.g., workers should work quickly and produce high volume) that are inconsistent with professional norms, then there should be greater incidence of endemic organizational conflict. In the television news organization studied by Bantz, McCorkle, and Baade (1980), we found "an organization that mechanizes [newsworkers'] work, emphasizes worker interchangeability, encourages rapidity in production, has high employee turnover and seldom offers qualitative evaluation of work" (p. 64). We found an organizational culture dominated by business norms, populated by newsworkers who appeared to follow professional norms, and characterized by conflict. (In contrast, Gans, 1979, found little conflict, while Stark, 1962, found much conflict, but the conflict was over newspaper policy and professional autonomy.)

The incompatibility of professional and business norms can produce a variety of effects: (1) Workers leave the workplace, seeking work in organizations that seem to have developed norms more consistent with their training, (2) workers may alter their meanings and expectations to become more consistent with the workplace they currently are in, or (3) workers may make the conflict between professional norms and existent organizational norms (e.g., business norms) itself an expected occurrence—i.e., make conflict a norm. Stark (1962) observed all three of these patterns. In the third pattern, workers may use the professional community as a reference group to provide input to their meanings and expectations for work and may characterize the newsworker's role as one of upholding professional norms in the face of competing normative pressures. The work on cosmopolitans and locals (Merton, 1968, chap. 12), as well as pressures toward group conformity (Festinger, 1950), and the development of group cultures (Bormann, 1975, chap. 10) detail these processes and the resulting consequences. Stark's (1962) use of the cosmopolitan (he calls them pros) and local distinction demonstrates how groups developed norms that produced conflict—as the pros looked to their professional peers for standards, felt mobile, and tried to finesse the system, while locals identified with the organization, felt a lack of mobility, and accepted the system. The incompatibility of these world views and group affiliations contributed both to intraorganizational conflict and intergroup conflict. Even if such an occurrence is an extreme, the inconsistency between professional norms of newsworkers and business norms of managers is likely to yield an organizational culture with less consistency and endemic conflict.

Professional Norms vs. Entertainment Norms

News organizational cultures must manage the conflict between entertainment norms and professional norms. That conflict is manifested in a number of ways. Three interrelated ways are developed here: (1) the source of information for decision making; (2) internal organizational inconsistency as to which set of norms is primary; and (3) differing definitions of performance.

Television news organizations particularly need to cope with a fundamental difference in source of information for decision making as defined by professional and entertainment norms. Professional norms place responsibility both for providing information and making decisions in the hands of professionals. For example, both physicians and reporters generate information as well as make decisions on the best way to interpret that information (although reporters are probably second-guessed more often—by editors, see Dunwoody, 1980; Sigal, 1973, chap. 3). Entertainment norms make the audience the principal source of information for decision making, with entertainment specialists taking major responsibility for interpretation and decision making. In entertainment norms (especially when connected to a business norm), no matter how much the decision maker likes a product, if the audience continues voting "no," sooner or later the decision makers' answer will also be "no." The contrast between professionals and entertainment decision-making norms is apparent in the frequency with which entertainment specialists ask audiences for judgments concerning programs and the infrequency of professionals asking the clients for their judgment (e.g., how often do surgeons ask patients their opinion of surgical techniques?). Different organizational cultures are likely to develop different weights for the professional and entertainment norms, and a study of how those different patterns develop could be extremely interesting. However, when the two sets of norms exist in one media organization the likelihood of endemic conflict is great.

The norms of entertainment and professionalism, which affect decision making in all news organizations, are most likely to collide in television news. Television has been dominated by entertainment norms in the majority of its schedule and throughout most of its history, while newspapers, taken as a whole—scandal sheets and newspapers of record—seem to have had a more balanced tension between entertainment and professional norms. As a result, television news organizations, as part of larger organizations (stations and groups of stations) that create and transmit programming, find themselves the representatives of professional norms in arenas of entertainment. The newsworkers are often professionally oriented; news directors tend to be professionally oriented; the organization as a whole tends to be entertainment and business oriented. The station's culture often exerts entertainment norms on the news organization; news departments are major profit centers of television stations, so management often utilizes business norms in judging news departments; newsworkers are likely, however, to be professionally oriented. As a consequence, newsworkers may define conflict as positive when it is used to defend professional norms from encroachment by entertainment and business norms (see Friendly, 1967, chap. 9).

This conflict of professional versus entertainment norms is most apparent in the paradox of the on-air newsworker—a paradox reflected in the various names given that person: reader, anchorperson, managing editor, or talent. The on-air person is often judged by entertainment standards: attractiveness, delivery style, dress, vocal quality, age, and timing. As a consequence of the application of entertainment standards a critical evaluative test of the on-air person is the *appearance of performance.* The appearance of performance is captured in the ability to be perfect (i.e., make no visible errors in pronunciation, delivery), to be in control, and to be durable. The audience's judgment of performance is one based on appearance while broadcasting, and the audience's judgment is to entertainment norms. Thus the on-air person is judged in the entertainment mode through the appearance of performance, a phrase that suggests both the elusive nature of performance per se and the value placed on appearance for the on-air person. Thus the on-air person, the most publicly visible member and in the most professionally prestigious position (in U.S. television news), is likely to be judged on entertainment norms. Yet the on-air person works in a news organization where professional norms are typically held. Thus the on-air person illustrates the ongoing conflict between the two sets of norms: Should she strive to meet professional norms and satisfy journalistic colleagues or strive to meet entertainment norms and satisfy management?

Controlled Competition

Competition in news is a managed form of conflict. There are pressures both toward competition and toward cooperation in newswork (see Dunwoody, 1980; Tunstall, 1971). The balancing of those pressures seems to produce a controlled competition with "rules" limiting both how intense competition may become and how close cooperation can become.

Both professional and business norms may stimulate the organization toward competition with other news organizations. The professional norms associated with getting the story before the other station or paper does (getting the scoop, getting a beat) generates competition between journalists and between their organizations. Research on negotiation and bargaining indicates that when negotiations are more competitive they are more conflictive (see

Kriesberg, 1972, chaps. 1, 2; Smith, 1972). Given an organizational demand to provide a more complete or a unique story, the relationship between news organizations can become win-lose. Further, given a limited number of rewards in newswork (positions, income) and given that performance (or the appearance of performance) may gain access to those rewards, reporters with mobility aspirations may become competitive with reporters within their own organization as well as with reporters in other organizations.

This conflict is intensified by business norms that often characterize the competition between organizations as warfare (the prevalence of military and war metaphors in organizations has often been commented on; see Pondy, 1983). In addition to the professional competition between reporters, news competition may escalate into interorganizational conflict where television stations compete for stories, newsworkers, prestige, and ratings as well as advertiser dollars. Commentators have often noted that editors and managers compare their product with their competitor's and criticize newsworkers who "miss" a story or story element (see Darnton, 1975; Dunwoody, 1980; Sigal, 1973).

What makes competition in newswork so intriguing is that it is controlled and its management may include collegial cooperation. Reporters often work well side-by-side and do collaborate (see Crouse, 1973; Darnton, 1975; Dunwoody, 1980; Sigal, 1973, chap. 3; Tiffen, 1978, chaps. 5, 6; Tunstall, 1970, chap. 7, 1971, chap. 6). Reporters seem to learn a set of expectations about how one manages the conflict between newsworkers—particularly when the newsworkers find themselves on a beat or in a confined situation (e.g., campaign coverage, war coverage, foreign correspondents—this latter circumstances is illustrated in the 1983 film *The Year of Living Dangerously*). In such situations, the reporters' reference group is likely to be the professional journalist rather than the business organization. Further, the professionals working together will develop a pattern of small group interaction and its concomitant norms (see Bormann, 1975). Both factors facilitate the newsworkers developing patterns to manage the competition between themselves. While different groups will develop different norms, the development of such group norms may permit reporters to provide competitors factual information (something publicly available and the withholding of which would be seen as petty) or even to delegate one member the task of gathering all the information for sharing (Darnton, 1975). At the same time, the reporters may subtly compete for additional details that will differentiate their story from their colleagues.

The competition between news organizations and between journalists means conflict is defined as *necessary* and *useful*. Defining conflict as such creates the expectation that newsworkers will seek to do better than their competitor-colleagues and their organizations. However, the newsworkers, particularly when spending time in groups, may elaborate the meaning and expectations of competition. By invoking professional norms and developing group norms, they define conflict as controlled and establish the expectation that the competition will be constrained by those professional and group norms. Working within the cultural definition of competition and conflict, the newsworkers thus reconstruct the pressures toward competition, thereby illustrating the reflexivity of organizational culture. It must be noted, however, that just as the norm of cooperation develops through interaction, the actions of individuals who violate the cooperative norms (e.g., seeking exclusives) and institutional action (e.g., rotation of beats) can weaken the pressures toward cooperation and intensify competitive pressures.

Structure of Television News Messages

The final factor contributing to a culture of conflict is the nature of the product. The product of the television journalist is a story. A "story" suggests that television news casts events in a dramatic format (see Epstein, 1973, chap. 5). In fact, Epstein quotes "NBC Evening News's" executive producer, Reuven Frank, as instructing his staff that news stories should have the structure of drama—including conflict (1973, pp. 4-5). Television news stories often present events that are conflicts by definition and frequently present nonconflict events in that social conflict (conflicts among social groups over ideas and goals) constitutes 35% of U.S. television news (Adoni, 1984). Further, the structural form of television newscasts often presents stories as dramatic conflicts between two or more parties (see Bantz, Robinson, & Ewbank, 1984).

The relevance of this pattern for television news organizations is highly speculative. However, within the skein of factors that normalize conflict within an organizational culture, it is quite likely that when newsworkers construct their daily product in a form that is predicated upon conflict, conflict's meaning is seen as *ordinary, everyday, routine,* and perhaps *essential to social life.* The daily creation of nonfiction drama, which is supposed to be the reconstitution of reality, utilizing a conflictive form is likely to encourage the newsworker to view the everyday world (including the world of the news organization) through the frame of conflict. In other words, newsworkers who constitute stories about extra-organizational events in conflict terms are likely to constitute stories about organizational events using a conflict form. The use of this form of storytelling by newsworkers to understand social life contributes to an organizational culture where conflict is a normal occurrence and a typical interpretive framework.

Interaction of the Five Factors

The five factors outlined contribute to the development of organizational cultures in newswork where conflict is normative, that is, defined as ordinary and viewed as appropriate. Organizational culture theory would argue that no matter what the factors, the cultures of similar organizations would *not* be the same; however, my argument is that systematic patterns associated with a type of organization make a particular cultural pattern likely. Individually, the five factors (newsworker distrust, professional norms vs. business norms, professional norms vs. entertainment norms, controlled competition, and the structure of televised news messages) contribute to news organization cultures where the meaning of conflict is *routine, everyday, necessary, valuable,* and *ordinary.* Consequently, conflictive behavior is defined as acceptable (i.e., normative) behavior. In addition, the interaction of the five factors increases the likelihood of a conflict culture. Three such possible interactions are suggested below.

First, as a result of the interaction of business norms and professional norms, newsworkers who are based in the organization itself and whose contact with newsworkers in competing organizations is limited in duration are likely to see their organization in competition with other organizations. Conversely, when newsworkers are based outside their organization, are not closely supervised, and are in close contact with workers from competing organizations, the development of professional group norms will hamper the interaction between business norms and professional norms. From these two we would predict (1) competition will operate within professional group constraints when newsworkers are physically separate from their news organization but close to their competitor-colleagues, and (2) conflict should be more unbridled when newsworkers are more closely tied to their organizations (Tiffen, 1978, chap. 4, contrasts different news organizations on the autonomy granted foreign correspondents; see also Dunwoody, 1980; Stark, 1962; Tunstall, 1970, 1971).

Second, the journalist tendency to distrust and dispute sources may be exaggerated when the reporter works in a medium that utilizes conflict as a structural form for its product—i.e., television news. Thus the television reporter may try to generate conflict, whether by confrontation or artful questioning, so the resultant story will contain the requisite elements of conflict. It probably is not coincidental that in the U.S. the reporters with the most combative reputations are television reporters (e.g., Dan Rather, Sam Donaldson, Mike Wallace).

Third, the entertainment norms embodied in television's appearance of performance notion should mesh with the business norms of profit in such a powerful way that newsworkers holding professional norms experience an ongoing conflict between entertaining and informing.

There is every reason to believe that meanings and expectations learned in one realm have the potential to affect other realms. The newsworker thus functions in and helps create an organization where conflict between news organizations is appropriate, where part of the newsworker's job is to be in conflict with those who wish to withhold information, where professional, entertainment, and business norms collide daily. All these experiences contribute to an organizational culture in which conflict is *necessary, ordinary, valuable, routine* and such expectations make conflict legitimate. In news organizations we can expect frequent disagreements and individuals are unlikely to be reprimanded for disagreeing as long as conflict is maintained within a "normal range." Similarly, the organizational culture of newsrooms is likely to be constituted by stories of conflict, though they will be typically heroic rather than tragic tales. Obviously, there are limits to these expectations—as the discussion of beat reporters indicates—but if my proposition is valid, conflict should be an integral part of the cultural fabric of news organizations.

Note

1. This essay is not typical of organizational culture research in that it does not report the gathering of culturally framed data on news organizations and that it presents a proposition of cultural consistency. Presenting a proposition seems appropriate in areas where much research has been done and a proposition may make a contribution to the ongoing theorizing about news organizations. The proposition that television news organizations are cultures that normalize conflict emerges in those circumstances.

References

Adoni, H. (1984, May). *The dimensions of social conflict in TV news.* Paper presented at the International Communication Association convention, San Francisco.

Altheide, D. (1984). Media hegemony: A failure of perspective. *Public Opinion Quarterly, 48,* 476-490.

Bantz, C. R. (1981, July). *Interpreting organizational cultures: A proposed procedure, criteria for evaluation, and consideration of research methods.* Paper presented at the SCA-ICA Summer Conference on Interpretive Approaches to the Study of Organizational Communication, Alta, UT.

Bantz, C. R. (1983). Naturalistic research traditions. In L. L. Putnam & M. E. Pacanowsky (Eds.), *Communication and organizations: An interpretive approach.* Beverly Hills, CA: Sage.

Bantz, C. R., McCorkle, S., & Baade, R. C. (1980). The news factory. *Communication Research, 7,* 45-68.

Bantz, C. R., Robinson, D. C., & Ewbank, A. (1984, May). *Social conflict on television news: Actors roles, and bias.* Paper presented at the International Communication Association convention, San Francisco.

Bormann, E. G. (1972). Fantasy and rhetorical vision: The rhetorical criticism of social reality. *Quarterly Journal of Speech, 58,* 396-407.

Bormann, E. G. (1975). *Discussion and group methods: Theory and practice* (2nd ed.). New York: Harper & Row.

Bormann, E. G. (1982). The symbolic convergence theory of communication: Applications and implications for teachers and consultants. *Journal of Applied Communication Research, 10,* 50-61.

Bormann, E. G. (1983). Symbolic convergence: Organizational communication and culture. In L. L. Putnam & M. E. Pacanowsky (Eds.), *Communication and organizations: An interpretive approach.* Beverly Hills, CA: Sage.

Coser, L. A. (1956). *The functions of social conflict.* New York: Free Press.

Crouse, T. (1973). *The boys on the bus.* New York: Random House.

Darnton, R. (1975). Writing news and telling stories. *Daedalus, 104,* 175-194.

Deal, T. E., & Kennedy, A. A. (1982). *Corporate cultures: The rites and rituals of corporate life.* Reading, MA: Addison-Wesley.

Deetz, S. A. (1982). Critical interpretive research in organizational communication. *Western Journal of Speech Communication, 46,* 131-149.

Dunwoody, S. (1981). The science writing inner club: A communication link between science and the lay public. In G. C. Wilholt & H. de Book (Eds.), *Mass communication review yearbook* (Vol. 2). Beverly Hills, CA: Sage. (Originally published 1980)

Epstein, E. J. (1973). *News from nowhere: Television and the news.* New York: Random House.

Ewart, J. (1985). *The dynamics of the organizational "engineering" of a newcomer to crew member: A descriptive analysis of the socialization process in local television news stations.* Ph.D. dissertation, University of Minnesota.

Festinger, L. (1950). Informal social communication. *Psychological Review, 57,* 271-282.

Friendly, F. W. (1967). *Due to circumstances beyond our control.* New York: Vintage/Random House.

Gans, H. J. (1979). *Deciding what's news: A study of "CBS Evening News, NBC Nightly News,"* Newsweek, *and* Time. New York: Pantheon.

Geertz, C. (1973). *The interpretation of cultures.* New York: Basic Books.

Homans, G. C. (1950). *The human group.* New York: Harcourt, Brace & World.

Johnson, B. McD. (1977). *Communication: The process of organizing.* Boston: Allyn & Bacon.

Johnstone, J. W. C., Slawski, E. J., & Bowman, W. W. (1976). *The news people: A sociological portrait of American journalists and their work.* Urbana: University of Illinois Press.

Kriesberg, L. (1973). *The sociology of social conflict.* Englewood Cliffs, NJ: Prentice Hall.

Lester, M. (1980). Generating newsworthiness: The interpretive construction of public events. *American Sociological Review, 45,* 984-994.

Marx, K. (1964). *Selected writings in sociology and social history* (T. B. Bottomore & M. Rubel, Eds.). New York: McGraw-Hill. (Originally published 1844-1873)

Merton, R. K. (1968). *Social theory and social structure* (1968 enlarged ed.). New York: Free Press.

Pacanowsky, M. E., & O'Donnell-Trujillo, N. (1982). Communications and organizational cultures. *Western Journal of Speech Communication, 46,* 115-130.

Pacanowsky, M. E., & Putnam, L. L. (1982). Special issue: Interpretative approaches to the study of organizational communications. *Western Journal of Speech Communication, 46.*

Pettigrew, A. M. (1979). On studying organizational cultures. *Administrative Science Quarterly, 22,* 580-581.

Pondy, L. R. (1983). The role of metaphors and myths in organizations and the facilitation of change. In L. R. Pondy, P. J. Frost, G. Morgan, & T. C. Dandridge (Eds.), *Organizational symbolism.* Greenwich, CT: JAI.

Putnam, L. L. (1983). The interpretative perspective: An alternative to functionalism. In L. L. Putnam & M. E. Pacanowsky (Eds.), *Communication and organizations: An interpretive approach.* Beverly Hills, CA: Sage.

Putnam, L. L., & Pacanowsky, M. E. (Eds.). (1983). *Communication and organizations: An interpretive approach.* Beverly Hills, CA: Sage.

Rather, D., with Herskowitz, M. (1978). *The camera never blinks: Adventures of a TV journalist.* New York: Ballantine. (Originally published 1977)

Ritzer, G. (1977). *Working: Conflict and change* (2nd ed.). Englewood Cliffs, NJ: Prentice Hall.

Schall, M. S. (1983). A communication-rules approach to organizational culture. *Administrative Science Quarterly, 28,* 557-581.

Schneider, D. M. (1976). Notes toward a theory of culture. In K. H. Basso & H. A. Selby (Eds.), *Meaning in anthropology.* Albuquerque: University of New Mexico Press.

Schorr, D. (1977). *Clearing the air.* Boston: Houghton Mifflin.

Sigel, L. V. (1973). *Reporters and officials: The organization and politics of newsmaking.* Lexington, MA: D. C. Heath.

Smith, D. H. (1972). *Applications of behavioral research to speech fundamentals: Applications from research on bargaining and negotiations.* Paper presented to the Central States Speech Association (April).

Stark, R. (1962). Policy and the pros: An organizational analysis of a metropolitan newspaper. *Berkeley Journal of Sociology, 7*, 11-31.

Tichenor, P. J., Donohue, G. A., & Olien, C. N. (1980). *Community conflict and the press.* Beverly Hills, CA: Sage.

Tiffen, R. (1978). *The news from Southeast Asia: The sociology of newsmaking.* Singapore: Institute of Southeast Asia Studies.

Tuchman, G. (1973). Making news by doing work: Routinizing the unexpected. *American Journal of Sociology, 79*, 110-131.

Tuchman, G. (1978). *Making news: A study in the construction of reality.* New York: Free Press.

Tunstall, J. (1970). *The Westminster lobby correspondents: A sociological study of national political journalism.* London: Routledge & Kegan Paul.

Tunstall, J. (1971). *Journalists at work: Specialist correspondents, their news organizations, news sources, and competitor-colleagues.* Beverly Hills, CA: Sage.

Turow, J. (1984). *Media industries: The production of news and entertainment.* News York: Longman.

CHAPTER **11**

News Reporting
and Professionalism

Some Constraints on the
Reporting of the News

John Soloski

The romantic vision of journalism is that of a crusading reporter who, much
to the consternation of a cantankerous but benevolent editor, takes on one of
the more villainous politicians in the city, and after some hard work and a
bit of luck, catches the politician "red-handed," helps to send him to jail and
betters the lives of the downtrodden and helpless. This myth has many
versions, some less grand but all of them more or less the same. Embedded
in these myths are many of the professional norms and values of journalism
as it is practiced in the United States. To fully understand the process by
which events are selected for presentation as news, it is necessary to examine
news professionalism. Much ink has been spilled over arguments about
whether journalism is a bona fide profession. Even more ink has been used
by scholars who have attempted to identify the criteria that make an occu-

From *Media, Culture & Society*, 1989, Vol. 11, pp. 207-228. Copyright © 1989 Sage
Publications, Ltd.

AUTHOR'S NOTE: The author would like to thank Michael Schudson, University of
California, San Diego, and Hanno Hardt, University of Iowa, for their comments on early
drafts of this essay.

pation a profession. But, as Hughes (1958: 45) points out, it is not important to argue about which occupations qualify as professions; what is important is to ask what it means for an occupation to claim it is a profession. With this as a jumping-off point, this essay will attempt to show how journalistic professionalism affects the gathering and reporting of the news. Specifically, the essay argues that professionalism is an efficient and economical method by which news organizations control the behavior of reporters and editors. But news organizations (or for that matter any business organization) cannot rely just on professional norms to control the behavior of their professional employees; to further limit the discretionary behavior of journalists, news organizations have developed rules—news policies. News organizations rely on the interplay of news professionalism and news policies to control the behavior of journalists. The second part of this essay reports the results of a participant-observation study that examined how one news organization enforces its news policies.[1]

Since U.S. journalists work within profit-making business organizations, news organizations need to develop techniques for controlling the behavior of their professional employees. If the news organization is conceptualized as an open system (Perrow, 1970; Thompson, 1967) composed of subsystems that are interrelated and interconnected with one another and with the larger organization, then the problem of control becomes clearer. Typically, subsystems of an organization exhibit the characteristics of both wholes and parts. That is, at one level the subsystem is a whole and its teleological behavior is not completely controlled by the larger organization; at another level the subsystem is part of the larger organization and is, to an extent, controlled by it. Subsystems of an organization may pursue a variety of goals simultaneously, and some of them may conflict with the goals of the organization. To ensure its long-term survival, management must develop techniques for controlling the behavior of its subsystems. The nature of these control procedures will be related to the environment in which an organization operates (Laurence and Lorsch, 1969). The more stable (predictable) the environment, the more structured (bureaucratic) an organization will be. Complex and unpredictable environments require an informal and flexible structure so that the various subsystems can better deal with rapid changes (Hall, 1968; Stinchcombe, 1959).

The news department as a subsystem of a news organization must deal with a highly unpredictable environment—news. Decisions about news coverage must be reached rapidly, with little time for discussion or group decision making. Thus the structure of the news department must be fluid enough to deal with a constantly changing news environment. Reporters and editors must have considerable autonomy in the selection and processing of the news. Controlling the behavior of its journalists could be a difficult problem for management of a news organization, especially since reporters spend most of their time outside of the newsroom and out of sight of supervisors. One method management could use to control its journalists would be to establish elaborate rules and regulations. This bureaucratic form of administration would not be very efficient because (1) the rules would have to cover all possible situations that journalists might encounter, including rules to deal with situations not covered by the rules; (2) elaborate rules are prescriptive and would limit a journalist's ability to deal with the unexpected, which is the essence of news; and (3) the news organization's management would have to establish an expensive and time-consuming system for teaching its journalists the rules and regulations. A more efficient method for controlling behavior in nonbureaucratic organizations, such as news organizations, is through professionalism. Professionalism *"makes the use of discretion predictable.* It relieves bureaucratic organizations of responsibility for devising their own mechanisms of control in the discretionary areas of work" (Larson, 1977: 168) (emphasis in original).

Ideology of Professionalism

The vast literature on professionalism is preoccupied with two major historical-sociological pursuits: (1) attempts to define what a profession is, usually based on a historical analysis of the rise of medicine and law; and (2) examinations of the relationships between professionals and bureaucratic business organizations that employ them. The first pursuit is the older of the two and is responsible for much of the literature on professionalism. The second approach recognizes the inadequacy of the model of professionalism that was built on the older, free professions like medicine and law, since the newer, dependent professions—such as engineering, accountancy and journalism—operate within profit-making business organizations. This second theme will be the primary concern of this essay.

For many scholars of professionalism, the goals and procedures of bureaucratic business organizations will inevitably lead to conflict with the goals and procedures of their professional employees. To put it simply, the professionals' allegiances to the norms of the profession will bring the professionals into conflict with the profit motive of the business organization (Kornhauser, 1963). These scholars assume that the ideology of capitalism and the ideology of professionalism are not compatible. On the surface, the ideology of professionalism has strong anti-profit and anti-market components which are manifested in the idea of service to society. Cost is not seen as being the determining factor in the delivery of professional services. Physicians, for example, provide a service that has come to be seen as a universal good that should be available to everyone regardless of a patient's ability to pay for the services (Elliot, 1972: Larson, 1977). Although most professionals are well paid, service to society and not financial reward is seen as being the primary reason for becoming a professional. But this altruistic and anti-profit nature of professionalism tends to obfuscate the close relationship between professionalism and capitalism. In an important work on the rise of professionalism, Larson (1977: 136-158) argues convincingly that professionalism and capitalism are closely related and share the same historical roots. The history of professionalism is marked by long and often bitter struggles by competing occupations to secure a monopoly in the professional marketplace. A profession cannot exist if two or more occupations lay claim to the cognitive base of the would-be profession (Larson, 1977: 14-15). The histories of law and medicine are replete with examples of how competing occupations attempted to capture the professions through legal, legislative and moral arguments (Elliot, 1972). For a profession to exist, it must secure control over the cognitive base of the profession. To do this a profession requires (1) that a body of esoteric and fairly stable knowledge about the professional task be mastered by all practitioners, and (2) that the public accepts the professionals as being the only individuals capable of delivering the professional services. By securing control over the cognitive base of the profession, the profession also establishes a monopoly in the professional marketplace. Competition between members of the same profession can occur, but there is no competition between professions for the right to provide the same professional services. If that were the case, then the cognitive base of the profession would be claimed by more than one occupation and the legitimacy of the services provided and the methods employed would be challenged.

The public's acceptance of a profession's monopoly in the marketplace is not difficult to achieve, mainly because the professions are seen as being highly democratic. Professions maintain a strong ideal of service to society and many of the professions' services have come to be seen as universal goods that are available to all in need of them. In the public's eyes, membership in the professions is not based on social class but on the innate abilities of would-be professionals. The success or failure of an individual to be a professional is determined by his or her intelligence, dedication and perseverance.

To facilitate their control over the cognitive base, and to standardize professional training, most professions control the professional education process through the establishment of accredited professional schools in colleges and universities.[2] These professional schools ensure (1) that future professionals have learned, mastered and accepted the prevailing cognitive base of the profession; (2) that the production of the producers of the professional services is standardized (Larson, 1977: 47); and (3) that the profession's ideals and goals are accepted by the new professionals. It is during their formal education that the professionals-in-training are socialized to their professions, learning professional norms and procedures. This means more than just learning correct professional technique; it means learning how to structure and live one's life as a professional (Johnson, 1972).

Control over professional education and monopolization of the professional marketplace cannot take place unless the ideology of professionalism is closely linked to the ideology of capitalism. Larson argues that the professionalization process helps to maintain and promulgate capitalism, especially when capitalism moved from its competitive phase into its monopoly phase. The rise of large corporations during monopoly capitalism minimized the uncontrolled competition built on the free marketplace model which threatened to bring about the collapse of capitalism (Baran and Sweezy, 1966). The relatively small number of large business organizations may have made competition more rational and predictable, but the problem of having to manage large numbers of people over large geographical areas became more acute. The problem of control within the large business organizations was solved by the rise of the manager. Larson argues that "the overall cognitive and normative legitimation for the rise of the manager" was science, especially as it was embodied in Taylorism (Larson, 1977: 142; Wiebe, 1967). Management's appeal to science for its legitimation meant that management was portrayed as being built on methods that were nonideological and thus outside of any class interest. Management's reliance on science—the mastering of esoteric knowledge and skills—is the same foundation on which the professionalization process rests. And the position of both manager and professional is further secured by the rise of large business organizations which became the source of new occupations and careers for the middle class (Larson, 1977: 145).

In monopoly capitalism, new professions arose that were unable to exercise as much control over the work situation as the free professions could. Engineering, accountancy and journalism depend on large business organizations for their employment. Work assignments and the choice of clients are, for the most part, out of the hands of these professionals. But these professionals have been able to achieve social status through financial compensation, upward mobility and distinctive work tasks that require special skills. To facilitate control in the workplace, management has come to rely on professionalism to control the behavior of its key employees. Professionalism, then, must be seen as an efficient and rational means of administering complex business organizations.

In summary, professionalism and the bureaucratic business organization cannot be conceived of as being opposite poles on a continuum of freedom and control. Both bureaucratic business organizations and professionalism "belong to the same historical matrix: they consolidated in the early twentieth century as distinct but nevertheless complementary modes of work organization" (Larson, 1977: 199). And the type of administration (bureaucratic or professionalism) used by an organization will depend on the work situation: The less stable the work environment, the greater the reliance on professionalism (Stinchcombe, 1959).

News Professionalism

News professionalism controls the behavior of journalists in two related ways: (1) It sets standards and norms of behavior, and (2) it determines the professional reward system.

Since news professionalism establishes norms of conduct for journalists, it is unnecessary for individual news organizations to arbitrarily establish elaborate rules and regulations for staff members. Also, there is no need for news organizations to establish expensive and time-consuming training programs for new journalists since all journalists come to the organization with a certain amount of professional training. But unlike engineering or accountancy, there are a number of educational paths that lead to careers in journalism (Johnstone et al., 1976: 35-37). Journalism, then, cannot rely just on controlling professional education to achieve cognitive standardization necessary for professionalism. It is through formal professional education, on-the-job professional training or, as is usually the case, a combination of these (Johnstone et al., 1976: 65) that journalists come to share the cognitive base of news professionalism. The norms of behavior that emanate from news professionalism constitute a *trans*organizational control mechanism. Since the behavior of journalists is rooted—to a great extent—in shared professional norms, this minimizes the problem of how news organizations are able to maintain control over journalists. But shared professional norms do not eliminate completely the problem of organizational control because (1) professionalism provides journalists with an independent power base that can be used to thwart heavy-handed interference by management in the professional activities of the news staff, and (2) professionalism provides too much freedom for journalists, and thus news organizations must adopt procedures that further limit the professional behavior of their journalists. By examining some professionalism norms, we can show how news professionalism guides the behavior of journalists.

Professional Norms

For journalists in the United States, objectivity is the most important professional norm, and from it flows more specific aspects of news professionalism such as news judgment, the selection of sources and the structure of news beats. Objectivity does not reside in news stories themselves; rather, it resides in the behavior of journalists (Roscho, 1975: 55). Journalists must act in ways that allow them to report the news objectively. For journalists, objectivity does not mean that they are impartial observers of events—as it does for the social scientist—but that they seek out the facts and report them as fairly and in as balanced a way as possible. As Phillips notes, by having journalists define objectivity as being the balanced reporting of the facts, the question of whether or not objectivity is possible in its scientific sense is neatly side-stepped. "By definition, then, journalists are turned into copying machines who simply record the world rather than evaluate it" (Phillips, 1977: 68). This makes it incumbent on the journalist to seek out the facts from all "legitimate" sides of an issue, and then to report the facts in an impartial and balanced way. It would be an oversimplification to suggest that the selection of issues to cover and the choice of sources to present to the public in news stories is politically motivated. While it is true that news legitimizes and supports the existing politico-economic system, it is not true that journalists' selection of news stories reflects a conscious desire on their part to report the news in such a way that the status quo is maintained.

Objectivity, as practiced by journalists, is an eminently practical—and apparently highly successful—way of dealing with the complex needs of journalists, news organizations and audiences. Events can be safely presented as a series of facts that require no explanation of their political significance. By presenting the news as a series of facts, news organizations are protected in at least two ways. The first and most obvious way is that since journalists need to rely on sources to provide them with the facts about events, sources and not journalists are responsible for the accuracy of the facts. To a limited degree this helps to insulate both journalists and their news organization from charges of bias and inaccurate reporting (Tuchman, 1972). Being duped by a news source is embarrassing to the news organization but, provided it does not happen often, the integrity of the news organization is not threatened. The news organization's position in the marketplace is directly linked to its ability to maintain the integrity of its news operation. And this brings us to the second advantage objectivity has for news organizations: It helps to secure their monopoly position in the marketplace.[3] If the news were to be reported in an overtly political or ideological manner, the market would be ripe for competition from news organizations that held opposing political or ideological points of view. By reporting the news objectively, reader loyalty to a newspaper is not a function of the ideology of that newspaper. It is rather based on the thoroughness of the news coverage, subscription costs, delivery services or some other tangible factor that a newspaper can control. Therefore, as long as news organizations report the news objectively, monopoly control of the marketplace will not be seen as being much of a problem by audiences, journalists, advertisers and media owners.

Journalists are nonideological in the sense that they do not report the news according to an ideological perspective that is consciously shared by the members of the profession. Therefore, the natural place to find newsworthy sources will be in the power structure of society because journalists see the current politico-economic system as a naturally occurring state of affairs (Gans, 1979; Tuchman, 1978). News sources, then, are drawn from the existing power structure; therefore, news tends to support the status quo. But journalists do not set out to consciously report the news so that the current politico-economic system is maintained. The selection of news events and news sources flows "naturally" from news professionalism. This does not mean that news judgments do not change, nor does it mean that journalists do not differ in their news judgments, but differences are worked out within a specific frame of reference, namely, that of the prevailing norms of news professionalism. Furthermore, news judgment requires that journalists share assumptions about what is normal in society, since an event's newsworthiness is related to its departure from what is considered to be normal. By concentrating on the deviant, the odd and the unusual, journalists implicitly support the norms and values of society. Like fables, news stories contain hidden morals.

While the selection and presentation of news events and sources are determined by news professionalism, the news organization for which a journalist works will also influence this process. For instance, in an effort to maximize its return on its economic investment, the news organization routinizes news coverage through the establishment of news beats (Tuchman, 1978: 44-45). The choice of beats results from the interplay of news professionalism and the resources of the news organization. News professionalism will determine the legitimacy and value of news beats, but the news organization, through its control over the news department's budget, will determine the number of beats that can be covered. News professionalism identifies more legitimate news beats than can be covered by journalists on the staff.

The Professional Ladder

In addition to specifying norms of behavior for journalists, news professionalism establishes a reward system for journalists. That is, journalists will look to their profession for recognition of professional success. However, a reward system that is determined by criteria outside direct management control would, on the surface, appear to be another source of conflict between professionals and business organizations (Goldner and Ritti, 1967). The assumption is that professional employees will look to the profession and not to their business organization for rewards. In other words, the ideals of the profession will be more of a concern to professionals than are the goals of the organization.

The dilemma, then, for management is how to reward professionals for outstanding professional performance even if that performance does not result in any significant benefits for the business organization. Kornhauser (1963) argues that to accommodate professional employees business organizations have been forced to develop two types of career ladders: the management ladder and the professional ladder. The management ladder is the traditional measure of success within business: Successful employees are rewarded by moving into the management hierarchy and become part of the decision-making team. The professional ladder was instituted to reward successful professionals by increasing their salaries and rank without having to increase their supervisory or managerial responsibilities. The professional ladder provides professionals with "advances in salary and status without taking on administrative duties. Instead of greater authority, they are rewarded with greater freedom to engage in their specialties" (Kornhauser, 1963: 205). Without the professional ladder, successful professionals could be forced to join the management ladder, which would deprive an organization of the services of its top professional employees.[4]

But the problem with the professional ladder, according to Goldner and Ritti, is that there is only a negligible increase in authority for the professional who moves up the professional ladder. The successful professional has little say in the decision-making processes of the organization. Goldner and Ritti argue that the professional ladder is actually a very effective method of "cooling out" professional employees who have been unable to advance within the management (power) hierarchy. This cooling-out process actually begins with the socialization of the individual to the profession, when the new professional learns what it means to be a professional (Goldner and Ritti, 1967: 497-501). Professional employees, who would otherwise be considered failures for not moving into management, are provided with an alternative definition of success by the professional ladder. The professional ladder enables a business organization to placate its dedicated professionals, who are necessary for the success of the organization, without having to provide opportunities on the management ladder.

Applying these observations to journalism, it appears that a professional ladder exists within news organizations. The structure of the news department permits management to promote successful journalists without having to bring them into the organization's decision-making process. As successful journalists move up the professional ladder in the news department, they have more individual freedom to pursue stories without carrying more responsibility for decisions concerning the allocation of scarce organizational resources. By providing opportunities for upward movement, the news organization is able to maintain the loyalty of key professionals without providing access to the actual power hierarchy of the organization. Although some journalists move onto the management ladder and into key management positions, most journalists use the professional ladder as their gauge of success, and movement on that ladder will be determined by professional norms. The viability of the professional ladder as a measure of success is the result of journalists' professional training, and it is part of the romantic lore of the profession. Journalism schools, stories about crusading journalists and journalists themselves have all contributed to making the professional ladder a means of measuring success.

Intraorganizational Controls

From the point of view of management, news professionalism is an efficient and effective means for both controlling and rewarding journalists. Although professionalism makes the use of discretion predictable, it does not dictate specific behavior for journalists; rather, professionalism establishes guidelines for behavior. Even so, professionalism provides journalists with more freedom in the selection, reporting and editing of news stories than most news organizations can permit. To further limit journalists' discretionary behavior, news organizations have established news policies. As Breed and others have shown, all news organizations have news policies, but the actual nature of news policies will vary from organization to organization (Breed, 1960; Darnton, 1975; Stark, 1962). Just as news professionalism can be seen as a transorganization control mechanism, the idiosyncratic news policies of individual news organizations can be seen as an *intra*organizational control mechanism. Together, these two control mechanisms direct the actions of journalists. Since the norms of news professionalism are shared by all journalists, the news organization needs only to concentrate on teaching journalists its own news policies, and needs only to develop techniques for ensuring that its journalists adhere to the policies. To examine how news policy works and how a news organization enforces its policies, I undertook a participant-observation study at a medium-sized daily.[5] The results of this study form the basis for the remainder of this essay.

Both news professionalism and news policy are used to minimize conflict within the news organization. That is, professional norms and a news organization's news policies are accepted by journalists, and only in rare instances are either professional norms or news policies a point of disagreement among the staff of the news organization. Like a game, professional norms and news policies are rules that everyone has learned to play by; only rarely are these rules made explicit, and only rarely are the rules called into question.

News professionalism is a double-edged sword. Since news professionalism is independent of any one news organization, it provides journalists with an independent power base that can be used in confrontations with a news organization's management because the tenets of news professionalism limit the ability of management to be directly involved in the news-making process. A publisher who continually intervenes in news coverage would run the risk of undercutting the professionalism of his or her journalists and, if the intervention resulted in biased reporting, would hurt the reputation of the newspaper and potentially damage the newspaper's position in the marketplace. News professionalism makes it taboo for management to continually interfere in the news-making process. Of course, this does have some benefits for management because it is a good argument to put off advertisers, politicians or others who may want management to intervene in news coverage.

To some extent, news professionalism shields journalists from the intervention of management by allowing journalists to deflect management's desires without jeopardizing their position in the news organization. For example, the publisher of the paper under study wanted the news department to follow up on a series of stories on drug trafficking in the city that had appeared in a newspaper published in a nearby city. Both the editor and the city editor[6] believed that there was nothing to the stories and that they did not warrant assigning a reporter to follow them up. During a meeting of the paper's editors, the city editor said, "We've gone through this before, doesn't he [the publisher] believe us when we tell him there is nothing there?" The editor responded, saying, "[The publisher] says that if the [other paper's] stories are not true that we've got to get the city manager, the mayor or [another civic leader] to say so." The editor decided not to assign a reporter to the story, saying that it was not worth following up the story just to satisfy the publisher. Later, when the publisher was interviewed about the amount of attention his story suggestions received from the editor, he said that he had talked to the editor a number of times about story ideas but he cannot get the editor to follow up on his ideas. The publisher went on to say that this has caused considerable friction between the editor and him. None of the journalists could recall any instance when the publisher bypassed the editor and ordered reporters to follow up his story ideas. The city editors summed it up by saying, "The publisher is an old newsman and wants to have some impact on the news operation. He doesn't have a great impact on the news operation. His story ideas do get attention, but I wouldn't go so far as to say that every one he gives he gets an immediate response to."

Within any business organization that employs professionals, there is at least one administrator between management and the professional employees. The underlying tension in this position is the need, on the one hand, to protect professional employees from interference by management and, on the other hand, to direct the work of the professional employees according to the goals and interest of the organization (Kornhauser, 1963: 60). In the news organization it is the editor who functions both as a professional and as a member of the news organization's management. Any examination of news policies must therefore focus on the editor as the executive in charge of the news operation. At the paper I studied, the editor uses a variety of methods to ensure that his journalists follow the paper's news policies. These included editorial meetings, story assignments, reprimands and supervision of the paper's production.

During the editorial meeting, the editor selects stories for the newspaper from news budgets prepared by the junior editors, and he tells the city editor which reporters to assign to various stories. He also uses the meeting to criticize the work of the news staff, which takes the form of marking up a copy of yesterday's paper, pointing out poor layout, reporting problems and the lack of editing poorly written stories. The criticisms are couched in terms of improving the professional competence of the news staff. Although the criticisms can be severe, the editor rarely criticizes a reporter directly, preferring to have the news editor pass on his criticisms to the reporter.

Also during the editorial meeting, the editor acts as arbiter of disputes among the junior editors. At this particular newspaper, the news editor, the city editor and the sports editor all have about equal authority in the news department, although technically the news editor ranks next in authority after the editor. In disputes among the junior editors, they attempt to gain the support of the editor. Instead of settling disagreements among themselves, the junior editors rely on the editor to decide the dispute. This procedure avoids open conflict in the news department and allows the junior editors to maintain a friendly work atmosphere in the newsroom. On the other hand, it provides the editor with an opportunity to arbitrate differences according to the paper's news policy. In effect, disputes among junior editors act as an early-warning system to potential policy violations.

The editorial meeting is also crucial for understanding how the editor controls the content of the newspaper because it is during these meetings that he decides which stories to cover or ignore. The editor is not heavy-handed in making story decisions, nor will he not assign a reporter to a story because it may have policy implications. But his involvement in the story selection process minimizes confrontations with reporters over policy issues. It is easier for the editor to control story assignments than to have to kill or tone down a story after it has been written. Reporters see story assignments as part of the editor's professional responsibilities, but they perceive heavy-handed editing as the editor's bowing to the interests of management. By controlling assignments, the editor ensures that the more important stories, which are more likely to have policy implications, are covered by the more trustworthy reporters.

Even so, quite a few stories deal with controversial issues that have policy implications. Although the editor is not involved in the day-to-day editing process, he does edit all stories that deal with controversial issues. During an interview, the editor said, "I like to see all sensitive stories and [potentially] libelous stuff especially. A lot of copy goes across my desk for approval. I like to keep my hands in the newsroom."

Reporters who have had their stories changed have strong feelings about the editor and why he changed their stories. Often they believe it is because the editor is bowing to pressure from management to keep the paper out of controversy, and not to upset important advertisers. In one instance a reporter had been assigned to a story involving the largest car dealership in the city. According to the reporter, the owner of the dealership was being sued by a lawyer whose new car broke down shortly after he had purchased it. The lawyer wanted the car replaced, but the dealer claimed that the purchase agreement required only that he repair the car. The reporter said, "When I wrote the story I had to give it to the editor to look at. He changed my story. He considerably toned it down. He did it because the car dealer is very powerful in the city."

Another reporter talking about the editing of controversial stories said, "This paper is very conservative. There's creative and degrading conservatism, and we are caught up in the degrading type. When I first signed on here I was told our editor was somewhat left of center. I find him to be very right of center now. Our editorial page, for example, is notorious for its lack of stance."

This reporter was involved in an incident that provides some insights into what happens when news policy is violated. The reporter wrote a story about a teenage girl who claimed that her father had molested her and was the father of her baby. In the story the reporter used the names of the father and daughter, and he relied primarily on the father's attorney for most of his information. In the absence of the editor, the city editor cleared the story for publication. According to the city editor and the reporter, when the editor read the story in the paper he became very angry and both were severely reprimanded. Later, during interviews, I asked all three about the incident. The reporter maintained that he had written the story objectively, relying on both the defense attorney and the assistant county attorney. The reporter thought that he had written a good story and that the editor had overreacted. The city editor said that at first he had thought that he had made the right decision, but after talking with the editor, he believed that he had made a professional error by not asking more questions about the story. The editor said that he had two major problems with the story. First, the paper has a policy of not publishing the names of rape victims, but the reporter had used the father's and daughter's names. Second, the reporter relied too heavily on the defense attorney, which biased the story by making the father appear to be the innocent victim of his lascivious daughter. To make matters worse, the editor said, the county attorney dropped all charges against the father after the daughter admitted that her boyfriend was the father of her baby. The editor said that the story had destroyed the daughter's life and had held the family up to public ridicule. According to the city editor, the paper ran a retraction saying that the original story had been run by mistake. He said that this incident had soured the relationship between the reporter and the editor, who no longer had any faith in the reporter's professional abilities. The editor told me that this reporter had no future at the newspaper. During my time at the newspaper, this reporter's stories received special attention by the copy desk and, as a copy editor, I was told to be especially watchful for biased and incomplete reporting.

Reprimands, or the threat of being reprimanded, offer yet another method of controlling the news staff. Although I witnessed only a few reprimands, the ones I did witness, and the ones staff members told me about, were severe. Usually just the fear of being reprimanded is enough to keep most staff members in line. Reprimands help to establish policy not only for the journalists who receive them but for those who witness or hear of them. In some cases the policy established by a reprimand may not actually be part of the newspaper's policy at all. For example, a junior editor had heard the editor reprimand another junior editor for using the word "Soviet" in a headline. The junior editor who had overheard the remark had interpreted it to mean that "Soviet" must not be used anywhere in the paper, and he would change "Soviet" to "Russian" in all stories he edited. When I asked the editor if I should change "Soviet" to "Russian" in stories I edited, he said that he had no objections to the word in stories but that it should not be used in headlines because it was not accurate. The junior editor had assumed that the newspaper had a policy that prohibited the use of the word.

The final control over the content of the newspaper lies in overseeing the production of the paper. The editor makes it a point to check all pages before they are removed from the production area, but he pays particularly close attention to the front page and the late page.[7] In fact, neither the front page nor the late page can be taken from the production area without the editor's permission, and even though it is difficult to change stories or headlines once copy is set and pasted on the pages, it was not uncommon for the editor to order some last-minute changes.

Junior editors were often irritated when the editor checked their work. One junior editor said, "When the editor is looking over your shoulder you always wonder what he is thinking about. In general his suggestions are good. And usually I don't mind his looking over my shoulder, but it has a tendency to be irritating." Another junior editor said that he was especially bothered by the editor's tendency not to explain why he ordered changes in stories or headlines. He said, "I go ahead and make the changes the editor wants, but I don't know why he ordered the changes." As a result, the junior editors defer even minor editing decisions to the editor. As one reporter put it, "The news desk is frustrated, overburdened and under the thumb of the editor. The desk doesn't take on much responsibility. They pass the buck and let the editor make all the decisions. The editors are not free to make policy decisions."

Although all of the journalists working for the newspaper had complaints about the editor, none said that the editor was professionally inept or that he had sold out to management. On the contrary, the journalists thought that the editor was in a no-win situation, being caught between management and the news department. And most of the journalists thought that the editor did a good job of protecting them from managerial interference. Yet the editor must walk a fine line between management and news professionalism. To be successful he must convince his staff that the newspaper's policies do not conflict with news professionalism. By examining two incidents involving policy, we can see that news policy has been incorporated into the news professionalism of the paper's journalists.

Part of the newspaper's news policy reflects management's decision to define the paper as a family newspaper. One aspect of this policy affects selection of photographs. A junior editor said, "The editor has a policy on pictures. No bloody photos like accidents are used. It's policy." Another junior editor said, "[The newspaper] is a family newspaper. Once in a while I get called on the carpet for doing something which management doesn't like. I consult with the editor whenever something is possibly upsetting. Nothing of bad taste—sex, immoral, bodies—gets in unless it is really necessary. We ran a picture of a student beating a hung [sic] body in Thailand once, but I consulted with the editor before using it."

When Pope Paul VI died, the Associated Press wirephoto service carried many pictures of the pope lying in state. The front page of the newspaper was "dummied" with a photo of the pope lying in state surrounded by his guards and church officials. Because the page contained a photo of a body, the junior editor brought the dummy to the editor for his approval, and he was turned down. The junior editor said, "We don't run pictures of bodies on the front page." In its place the paper used a photograph taken a month earlier of the pope blessing a crowd. But because the death was such a big news story, the paper did run photographs of the pope lying in state on some inside pages.

In the second incident a man convicted of murdering a 10-year-old girl had had his conviction overturned by the U.S. Supreme Court. A new trial was ordered and it was held in a nearby city. The newspaper did not send a reporter to cover the trial but relied on the Associated Press coverage. The defense rested its case on whether or not the accused had sexually assaulted the girl, and much of the wire stories about the trial dealt with the sexual assault. One day a junior editor showed me what he had edited out of the story. Almost every sentence that had contained the words "vagina," "rectum" or "sperm" had been deleted from the story. The junior editor said that he had given the story to the editor to check and he had cut even more out of the story. The junior editor said, "A lot of our readership don't care to see those words used in the paper. This is a family newspaper. I know that's how the editor thinks. On other papers I would have used it but not here in [this newspaper]." During an interview, the editor was asked about the editing of the trial stories. He said, "The reason parts of the stories were edited out is because I would not want to have to define the terms used in the stories to my 10-year-old son, if I had one. [This newspaper] is a family newspaper which goes into people's homes and youngsters read it. The editing of the stories did not do readers a disservice because the stuff edited out wasn't necessary to show [the man's] defense."

During interviews with the paper's journalists, they were asked about these and other incidents involving the paper's policy of not publishing potentially offensive material. None of them believed that the policy affected the ability of the newspaper to inform its readers. All of the journalists had accepted the policy, and it had become part of their professional task. A few of them provided examples of where they thought that the policy had gone too far and had affected the news that was reported. But when other journalists were asked about these examples, they tended to stress personality differences between a reporter and the editor, and not issues involving professional norms. Except for those involved in the incidents, most of the journalists believed that the editor had been right to reject or edit stories because the reporters had acted in an unprofessional manner. The journalists at this newspaper are convinced that the policy of protecting readers from potentially offensive material does not interfere with the norms of news professionalism, and they have come to accept the paper's news policy as a natural part of their jobs.

Conclusion

Drawing upon organizational theory and the literature of professionalism, this essay argues that news professionalism is an efficient and effective means for controlling the professional behavior of journalists. The essay attempts to show how the norms of news professionalism determine the legitimate arenas and sources of news in the United States. Although journalists do not set out to report the news so that the existing politico-economic system is maintained, their professional norms end up producing stories that implicitly support the existing order. In addition, the professional norms legitimize the existing order by making it appear to be a naturally occurring state of affairs. The tenets of news professionalism result in news coverage that does not threaten either the economic position of the individual news organization or the overall politico-economic system in which the news organization operates. Also, news professionalism produces news stories that permit news organizations to maximize audience size and to maintain firm control over the marketplace. In the final analysis, news professionalism biases news at a societal level.

Since news professionalism is independent of any one news organization, news professionalism provides journalists with an independent power base that can be used against management. To minimize the potential for conflict, management has established news policies that further limit the professional behavior of its journalists. Although the specific nature of these policies will vary from organization to organization, the purpose of the policies does not. News policies lessen the potential conflict between journalists and management, and there is no reason to assume that an organization's policies will be a source of tension between management and journalists (Sigelman, 1973). As long as news policy does not force journalists to violate the norms of news professionalism, there is no reason to assume that journalists will see news policy as a constraint on their work, even though it does limit the type of stories that can be reported.

The organizational nature of news is determined by the interplay between the transorganizational control mechanism represented by news professionalism and the intraorganizational control mechanisms represented by news policy. Together, these control mechanisms help to establish boundaries for the professional behavior of journalists. It would be wrong to assume that these boundaries dictate specific actions on the part of journalists; rather, these boundaries provide a framework for action. The boundaries are broad enough to permit journalists some creativity in the reporting, editing and presentation of news stories. On the other hand, the boundaries are narrow enough so that journalists can be trusted to act in the interest of the news organization.

Notes

1. Although most of the references in this essay are to the print medium, the arguments can be applied to the electronic media.

2. For an interesting discussion of the rise of schools of engineering, see Noble (1977).

3. The term "monopoly" is being used in its economic and ideological senses. For a discussion of monopoly in this context, see Owen (1975).

4. If only the management ladder existed, a professional who refused a promotion into management in order to continue his or her professional work would be defined as a failure. Without a professional ladder, professionals would reach the pinnacle of their corporate careers quite rapidly and would be blocked from any further advancement.

5. As a participant observer, I worked as an editor on the copy desk, which provided an exceptionally good vantage point to observe how news policies are enforced. Unlike nearly all of the so-called participant observer studies of the news-making process, I actually joined the staff of the paper with the specific purpose of studying its news operation. As a researcher/journalist, I was able to see and understand behavior that would have been unavailable to a researcher who relied on observing and interviewing.

6. The editor is the executive in charge of the news department. The other editors will be referred to as junior editors, or by their titles, in order to distinguish them from the editor.

7. The late page is the last news page to be produced. Late-breaking stories that do not warrant remaking the front page are placed on this page.

References

Baran, P. A. and P. M. Sweezy (1966) *Monopoly Capital: An Essay on the American Economic and Social Order*. New York: Monthly Review Press.

Breed, W. (1960) "Social Control in the News Room," in W. Schramm (ed.), *Mass Communication*. Urbana: University of Illinois Press.

Darnton, R. (1975) "Writing News and Telling Stories," *Daedalus* 104: 175-193.

Elliot, P. (1972) *The Sociology of the Professions*. New York: Herder & Herder.

Gans, H. J. (1979) *Deciding What's News*. New York: Pantheon.

Goldner, F. H. and R. R. Ritti (1967) "Professionalization as Career Immobility," *American Journal of Sociology* 72: 489-502.

Hall, R. E. (1968) "Professionalization and Bureaucratization," *American Sociological Review* 33: 92-104.

Hughes, E. C. (1958) *Men and Their Work*. Glencoe, IL: Free Press.

Johnson, T. J. (1972) *Professions and Power*. London: Macmillan.

Johnstone, J. W. C., E. J. Slawski and W. W. Bowman (1976) *The News People*. Urbana: University of Illinois Press.

Kornhauser, W. (1963) *Scientists in Industry: Conflict and Accommodation*. Berkeley: University of California Press.

Larson, M. S. (1977) *The Rise of Professionalism: A Sociological Analysis*. Berkeley: University of California Press.

Laurence, P. R. and J. W. Lorsch (1969) *Organization and Environment*. Homewood, IL: Richard D. Irwin.

Noble, D. (1977) *American by Design: Science, Technology and the Rise of Corporate Capitalism*. New York: Alfred A. Knopf.

Owen, B. (1975) *Economics and Freedom of Expression*. Cambridge, MA: Ballinger.

Perrow, C. (1970) *Organizational Analysis: A Sociological View*. Monterey, CA: Brooks/Cole.

Phillips, E. B. (1977) "Approaches to Objectivity: Journalistic vs. Social Science Perspectives," in P. M. Hirsch, P. V. Miller and F. G. Kline (eds.), *Strategies for Communication Research*. Beverly Hills, CA: Sage.

Roshco, B. (1975) *Newsmaking*. Chicago: University of Chicago Press.

Sigelman, L. (1973) "Reporting the News: An Organizational Analysis," *American Journal of Sociology* 79: 132-151.

Stark, R. W. (1962) "Policy and the Pros: An Organizational Analysis of a Metropolitan Newspaper," *Berkeley Journal of Sociology* 7: 11-31.

Stinchcombe, A. L. (1959) "Bureaucratic and Craft Administration of Production: A Comparative Study," *Administrative Science Quarterly* 4: 168-187.

Thompson, J. D. (1967) *Organizations in Action*. New York: McGraw-Hill.

Tuchman, G. (1972) "Objectivity as Strategic Ritual: An Examination of Newsmen's Notions of Objectivity," *American Journal of Sociology* 77: 660-679.

Tuchman, G. (1978) *Making News: A Study in the Construction of Reality*. New York: Free Press.

Wiebe, R. H. (1967) *The Search for Order: 1877-1920*. New York: Hill and Wang.

CHAPTER **12**

Science Writers at Work

Sharon Dunwoody

Attempts to single out criteria that define news have been going on for some time. But it is only within recent years that investigators have moved away from the search for "universal" criteria that presumably define news consistently across time and events and instead have intensified the examination of news selection *situationally*. One can no longer be satisfied with determining that certain variables may affect what becomes news in general. The problem arises in that what is elevated to "news status" in one social context may be ignored in another; a particular criterion may be crucial to one coverage event but irrelevant to the next.

The question of "what's news," then, requires a situation-specific answer. One must look for criteria relevant to specific journalists in specific coverage areas.

This study attempts to do just that by examining the effects of two factors on the news-selection behavior of a special group of journalists in a single situation. It gauges the effects of (1) newsroom production pressures and (2) degree of peer interaction on the news selections of science writers at the annual meeting of the American Association for the Advancement of Science (AAAS). The study does so by examining how these two factors affect individual journalists' dependence on AAAS for news-selection guidance.

From Research Report No. 7 of the Center for New Communications reports, School of Journalism, Indiana University, December 1978. Used by permission.

That "guidance" comes in the form of press conferences. One of the largest scientific meetings in the country, the AAAS annual meeting attracts from 300 to 600 science journalists every year. A main goal of AAAS is "to increase public understanding and appreciation of the importance and promise of the methods of science in human progress," [1] so the institution is interested in attracting as much coverage of its meeting by journalists as possible. Toward that end, AAAS sets up a series of press conferences that continue from the beginning of the six-day meeting to its end. The institution thus makes a conscious and sophisticated effort to determine what becomes news about its own meeting. And the goal of this research was to see how newsroom production pressures and peer status affected the extent to which AAAS actually could "control" news-selection decisions of the working press.

The Journalistic Setting

Why were newsroom production pressures and peer status selected from among many potential factors for study? One major reason is that the annual meeting situation provides an excellent "laboratory" for examining these two variables: It is a huge event that offers many stories with "hard news pegs," and it attracts a group of competing specialty writers who have formed some very strong professional and personal associations with one another. Let's define the two factors more clearly:

Newsroom production pressures. The selection of news may be governed by a host of constraints built into a journalist's job. Few reporters are free to cover what they please; among other things, they are limited by deadlines, by knowledge of what competing reporters are doing, and by the amount of equipment (cameras, tape recorders, technicians) needed to do their jobs. Investigators such as Epstein and Tuchman[2] argue that news is largely determined by such mechanical and organizational constraints.

Extent of peer interaction. A number of other researchers, among them Crouse, Tunstall, and Chibnall,[3] have found that specialty writers who cover the same news situations often develop intense interactive patterns that include sharing story ideas, notes, and information. Although the reporters may be in direct competition with one another, they form close bonds of friendship, and their behaviors in a news-gathering situation are predominantly cooperative.

This seems to be the case with a group of experienced science writers who work for the prestige newspapers, news magazines, and wire services in the United States. Since the heyday of the manned space program in the 1960s, these reporters often travel far from their city rooms to cover such national events as scientific meetings, space shuttle tests, and the Viking landings on Mars. While remaining autonomous of the newsroom back home, members of this science-writing "inner club" are constantly coming into contact with each other on the road. The question for this study was whether participation in this inner club affected a science writer's dependence on AAAS press conferences.

Findings in Brief

Analysis of interviews with science writers, observation of their behaviors at the meeting, and content analysis of the resulting stories led to these conclusions:

1. The "average" journalist in the study was highly dependent on press conferences, indicating that AAAS generally could control what became news about its meeting through the press conference structure.

2. Reporters operating under a greater number of newsroom constraints—principally deadlines—were *more dependent* on press conferences than were reporters with few constraints. Thus science writers who anticipated writing few or even no stories from the meeting were more independent of AAAS than were reporters who were expected (by their editors) to produce at least one story a day. Increases in other kinds of job constraints had the same effect. If a reporter felt he was in direct competition with other reporters, he depended more heavily on AAAS press conferences than did reporters who perceived less competition. And dependence on AAAS topic selections increased as the number of equipment constraints increased, making broadcast journalists more dependent on AAAS than print journalists.

3. Greater expertise in covering science conversely *decreased* a reporter's dependence on AAAS press conferences. The less a journalist knew about science, then, the more he or she was likely to depend on AAAS to tell him or her what was important.

4. When considered together, findings 2 and 3 meant that the experienced print science writer who came to the meeting with few deadlines was the most *independent* of AAAS, while the broadcast reporter who knew little about science but who had to produce daily stories was the most *dependent* on AAAS.

5. An informal organization—an "inner club"—seems to have evolved to help its "member" science journalists deal with their newsroom deadline and competitive pressures when they are away from the city room without sacrificing the potential benefits of cooperation among each other.

6. Membership in the science-writing inner club did not substantially alter a reporter's dependence on press conferences, but it did seem to increase the accuracy and ultimate quality of the stories produced by serving as a large pool of shared resources for members.

Description of the Study

Data for the study were collected in four phases during late 1976 and throughout 1977: (1) a group of inner club and non-inner club science writers was interviewed about their work; (2) the news-selection behaviors of the reporters were observed at the 1977 AAAS annual meeting; (3) all stories about the meeting published in daily newspapers and magazines were content analyzed; and (4) the group of science writers was reinterviewed after the meeting.

The science writers. Twenty-four science journalists were involved in all phases of the study. Of the 24, 17 were identified as inner club members (see Table 12.1) and 7 as nonmembers (see Table 12.2).[4] Because the inner club numbers no more than 25 to 30 altogether, the 17 represent the majority of members in the country and included all inner club members who attended the meeting. The seven non-inner club members were included to provide perspectives on the inner club from persons outside the group.[5]

Phase 1. Prior to the meeting, face-to-face interviews were conducted with the science journalists. The main purpose of the interviews was to obtain self-reports from journalists about criteria they use to select newsworthy information, particularly at an AAAS meeting. Additionally, during this phase the investigator interviewed two AAAS officials, one of whom is primarily responsible for organizing the annual meeting and the other for constructing the press conferences. They are, respectively, Arthur Herschman, head of the AAAS Meetings and Publications Division, and Carol Rogers, public information officer.

Phase 2. Four persons trained in observational techniques then attended the 1977 AAAS annual meeting, held February 21-25 in Denver, to observe the science writers on the job. Observers remained primarily in the press area, where most reporters attended the press conferences, wrote and filed their stories, and interacted with one another and with the press officials.

Phase 3. AAAS hires a clipping service to monitor coverage of the annual meeting in all daily newspapers and news magazines in the country.[6] All 772 stories identified by the service through May 1977 were collected and content analyzed with the story as the unit of analysis. Emphasis in the analysis was on the subject of each story, perceived sources of information, and on such characteristics of the newspapers and magazines as size and geographic location.[7]

Phase 4. Following the content analysis, all science journalists in the sample who had covered the meeting[8] were contacted by telephone and asked to discuss in detail their reasons for selecting topics and sources for each story.

Table 12.1 Inner Club Members Interviewed

Name	Title	Affiliation
George Alexander	Science writer	*Los Angeles Times*
Jerry Bishop	Staff reporter	*Wall Street Journal*
Bob Cooke	Science editor	*Boston Globe*
Ed Edelson	Science editor	*New York Daily News*
Peter Gwynne	Science editor	*Newsweek*
Don Kirkman	Science writer	Scripps-Howard Newspapers
Ron Kotulak	Science editor	*Chicago Tribune*
John Langone	Medical editor	*Boston Herald-American*
Tom O'Toole	Science editor	*Washington Post*
David Perlman	Science editor	*San Francisco Chronicle*
Judy Randal	Science writer	*New York Daily News*
Joann Rodgers	Medical writer	Hearst Newspapers/*Baltimore News-American*
Al Rossiter	Science editor	United Press International
Joel Shurkin	Science writer	*Philadelphia Inquirer*
Brian Sullivan	Science writer	Associated Press
Walter Sullivan	Science editor	*New York Times*
Pat Young*	Science writer	*The National Observer*

NOTE: $n = 17$.
*Since the demise of *The National Observer* in July 1977, Young has worked as a free-lance science writer in the Washington, D.C., area.

Table 12.2 Younger Journalists Interviewed

Name	Title	Affiliation
Ira Flatow	Science reporter	National Public Radio
Jon Franklin	Science writer	*Baltimore Sun*
Bob Gillette	Science writer	*Los Angeles Times*
Elizabeth Maggio	Science writer	*Arizona Daily Star*
Cristine Russell	Science/medical writer	*Washington Star*
David Salisbury	Science writer	*Christian Science Monitor*
Michael Woods	Science editor	*Toledo Blade*

NOTE: $n = 7$.

Detailed Findings

When covering the meeting, a science writer had four major information sources at his or her disposal: news conferences, symposia, individual interviews with scientists, and research papers. Heavy use of press conferences would indicate a high degree of dependence on AAAS for selection guidance, while use of the other three sources would indicate a selection process more independent of AAAS.

Table 12.3 The "Average" Journalist's Performance During the AAAS Meeting: Mean Values on a Number of Production/Source Variables

	Status			Constraints	
	All (n = 19)*	*Inner Club* (n = 14)	*Other* (n = 5)	*Many* (n = 14)	*Few* (n = 5)
Mean number of stories	6.5	6.5	6.4	7.6	3.4
Mean number of press conferences attended	6.4	6.5	6.0	7.7	2.6
Mean number of stories utilizing					
Press conference	2.8	2.8	3.0	3.4	1.2
Symposium	1.3	1.2	1.6	1.1	1.8
Paper	2.4	2.6	1.8	2.9	1.0
Interview	2.6	2.3	3.6	2.8	2.2
Single source	3.0	3.0	2.8	3.8	0.6
Two sources	2.5	2.6	2.2	2.8	1.8
Multiple sources	0.7	0.5	1.2	0.6	1.0

*ns indicate number of respondents in the respective subgroups.

Additionally, a science writer could vary the number of sources he or she would use for any single story. In this analysis stories will be classified as single-source, double-source, or multiple-source (three or more sources) stories.

The information-selection behaviors of the 19 journalists are first examined as a group. Then the writers are divided into those with daily deadlines (14 reporters) and those with few or no deadlines (5) to examine the constraints question, and into inner club members (14) and outsiders (5) to look for effects of peer status on news selections.

The "Composite" Science Writer

The average science writer in this study wrote more than one story a day during the 6-day meeting (see Table 12.3). He produced either single-source or two-source stories, and more of his stories utilized press conferences than any other source.

Stories utilizing more than two sources were rare; in fact, nearly half of all the stories written by the 19 respondents were single-source stories, while another 41 percent of the stories were produced from only two sources.

Of the single-source stories, press conferences accounted for 40 percent, more than any other single source.

In sum, the "average" journalist in this study managed to file at least one story a day by limiting the number of sources he used for each story to one or two and by utilizing the available press conferences more heavily than any other source.

Our composite journalist was quite prolific and indeed seemed to be dependent to some degree on press conferences as sources of information. But was that dependence related to either of the factors being examined in this study?

Newsroom Constraints

Number of constraints proved to be the best predictor of dependence on AAAS. Three types of constraints will be examined briefly here: number of deadlines, the pressures of competition, and equipment requirements.

Deadline Pressures

The more stories a reporter was expected to write, the more likely he was to rely on the press conferences as an efficient means of gathering information. In fact, there is startling difference between the number of press conferences attended by constrained reporters and the number attended by reporters with few constraints (see Table 12.3). Similarly, the "average" constrained science writer utilized press conferences as story sources far more often than any other source, while reporters with few or no deadlines were more likely to have gone to a meeting symposium or obtained an interview with the scientist.

The number of constraints under which the reporter operated also seems to have been the major factor governing the number of sources used for a story. More than 50 percent of the stories produced by reporters with daily deadlines were single-source stories, while the majority of stories written by the less constrained journalists used two sources. Constrained reporters did very few multiple-source stories, but less constrained reporters were more likely to write stories utilizing more than two sources than they were to do single-source stories.

Thus daily deadlines seemed to force reporters into a single-source or double-source story pattern that in turn mandated dependence on the press conference structure. When time was of the essence, press conferences offered an efficient means of gathering information in a large meeting setting. One respondent noted that "you'll find some people—myself sometimes included—who go to nothing but press conferences" because sitting through meeting symposia can "waste an awful lot of time. Press conferences are vital. If you've got to produce a story every day, that's the way you're going to get it."

Competitive Factors

Competition proved to be another constraint that increased dependence on press conferences. As members of the prestige press, inner club members particularly are each others' main competition. They know their editors are gauging the quality of their work on the basis of what the competition is doing, and if the *Boston Globe* and the *New York Times* science writers each write different stories on a given day, they leave themselves open to accusations from their city rooms that they somehow "missed" a story that the other reporter obtained.

Even editors on less prestigious newspapers will tend to define "good" coverage of scientific events on the basis of what comes over the AP or UPI wires: Thus the ultimate quality of a science writer's coverage (in the eyes of her newspaper) may be largely dependent on how closely she follows the leads of the wire service reporters.

Science writers can minimize complaints from their city rooms, then, not by doing different stories but by *duplicating* each other. And press conferences provide the best means of doing this. If all journalists cover the same event in the same room and write essentially the same story, there's no question about whether one "got" the story for that day. Reporters, using press conferences, have *created* the story for the day *en masse*. One inner club member explained the situation succinctly:

> I go to a press conference because I don't want to be surprised the next day by seeing that somebody else picked up a big story that I missed. I know what newspapers my editors watch, too. If [the competition] files a story. I want to be sure I don't get a call the next day [from the desk wondering] why I didn't write it. I know that they've seen the wires and I'm out there [at the meeting]. So there's a bit of self-protection.

Equipment Constraints

Observational data indicated that while the print reporters with few deadlines were most independent of AAAS, the broadcasting reporters, who were saddled not only with deadlines but also with equipment constraints, were most dependent on AAAS to tell them what to cover. Local television and radio reporters were frequently observed asking AAAS personnel to give them "a couple good ideas" for stories for the next day. If a broadcast reporter had isolated a story topic, then he or she often would ask AAAS to find an appropriate scientist to talk about it.

Peer Interaction

Inner club affiliation seemed to have little effect on a science writer's dependence on press conferences. Inner club members were under the same daily deadline constraints as were outsiders, and production of daily stories made them just as dependent on press conferences (see Table 12.3). The only difference in source usage seemed to be that inner club members, when writing single-source stories, were just as likely to use scientific papers as they were press conferences, while nonmembers relied primarily on press conferences and secondarily on interviews for their single-source stories.

So whether or not you were an inner club member made little difference in your dependence on AAAS for story-selection guidance, because everyone relied on the press conferences. Club membership did seem to have an effect, however, on the accuracy and overall quality of stories produced. For all practical purposes, the inner club at an event like the AAAS meeting serves its members as a large pool of resources. Inner club reporters can share information, provide each other with technical definitions, and can warn each other away from suspicious sources and unsubstantiated research reports.

In one instance at the meeting, for example, an inner club member came away from a press conference about the Martian moon Phobos with the idea that the tiny moon harbored huge reserves of oil. Other club members quickly checked out that possibility and warned their colleague that this conclusion was not substantiated by the research presented. The reporter subsequently downplayed the potentially misleading "little Saudi Arabia" theme in his story.

Thus access to the expertise of other science writers—one benefit of the inner club—may not have a substantial effect on a reporter's dependence on press conferences but may indeed affect his or her ability to be critical of the scientific information presented in those press conferences.

Extent of scientific knowledge did increase independence from AAAS selections, and this is best illustrated with broadcast reporters. Both local and national broadcast media covered the event, but AAAS personnel were able to exercise much greater control over local reporters than over the network and National Public Radio crews. Since equipment constraints for all broadcasters were similar, the major difference seemed to lie in scientific expertise. Few broadcast reporters in this country have extensive science knowledge, and those who do are likely to work for national media. Thus local radio and television reporters, who knew little about science and who had virtually no access to the opinions of science writers covering the meeting, were almost completely dependent on AAAS for topic suggestions. For this group, then, what's news was literally up to the institution itself.

Why Does the Inner Club Exist?

All journalists must deal with the kinds of newsroom pressures described above. But few find themselves in the conflicting positions of the experienced science writers in this study.

To cover their beats, science writers for the prestige publications must often leave their city rooms, fly to other parts of the country, and cover stories for days or weeks at a time. Under these conditions, their constant companions are science writers from other prestige newspapers. A reporter lives and writes in the lap of his or her main competitors.

Additionally, the reporters are faced with the task of translating difficult technical material into lay language and must deal with sources (scientists) who are wary, sometimes ill prepared to talk to journalists, and who are likely to be very critical of the journalistic product.

The result is that science writers band together on the road; a journalist's main competitor becomes his best friend. As one inner club member noted:

> We see more of each other because of going to these meetings, covering these stories. You're with each other for several days at a time, most of the day and most of the evening; you tend to go out and eat dinner together. So you get to be very good friends. You've got a common interest. . . . I have more in common with science writers from other papers than I do with reporters here on the _____, because we're covering the same stories, we interview the same people, and we see each other not just casually. So we all get to be pretty good friends.

The contradiction lies in that these "friends" must also respond to the organizational and competitive requirements of their own editors, who view competing science writers as opponents, not as friends.

The inner club seems to have evolved in part as a way of dealing with this opponent/friend contradiction. The group has its roots in the manned space program of the 1960s, when the reporters suddenly found themselves appointed science writers and were sent to Cape Canaveral and Houston to cover one of the most exciting stories of the decade.

One writer who places the genesis of the club with the space program described it in this way:

> At the height of it, they were making a major launch every three months, and you would be down there at the Cape for two and a half weeks at a time. The result was that it (the group of science writers) became your family. There were love affairs, there were hates and fights. . . . It became a traveling road show with the same people showing up time and time again, going to the same places and doing the same things. There was great cohesiveness.

The club serves as a means of accommodating the various conflicting pressures encountered by science writers away from the city room by promoting cooperation among members rather than competition. By sharing ideas and information, the science writers can more efficiently meet their deadline demands and at the same time can reduce the potential for being scooped.

Efficiency is increased because the journalists are working together, using each other as sounding boards for story ideas, sharing information from interviews at the writing stage, and helping one another with definitions and concepts.

The club reduces competitive tensions through the same sharing mechanisms. One neutralizes competition not by scooping one's colleagues but by duplicating news judgments. So the cooperative aspect of the club facilitates such duplication.

By turning what should be a highly competitive situation into a highly cooperative one, then, the club allows the science writer to meet the demands of his or her city room without sacrificing the strong personal and professional relationships that have developed among colleagues on the road.

Implications

This study was conducted primarily to examine criteria that control "what's news" about a large scientific meeting. The overwhelming answer seems to be: the institution itself. AAAS can dictate what becomes news about its own meetings to a great degree simply by offering particular topics in press-conference formats.

The reason *why* this is the case, however, should be of more immediate interest to practicing journalists. AAAS is successful because it caters to a set of selection criteria that dominates the information-selection process at the meeting: *newsroom production pressures*. The more deadlines, competitive pressures, and equipment restraints the journalist is saddled with, the greater the degree of "control" by AAAS over its own news coverage.

Additionally, the less a reporter knows about science, the more successfully AAAS can dictate what's news.

Thus the journalist in such a meeting situation seems to lose control over the information-selection process *as the number of traditional demands placed on him or her by the city room increase*. One way, then, of putting control back into the hands of the journalist would be to decrease those demands. Four recommendations would have that effect:

1. Many editors who allow their reporters to cover events away from the city room expect a return on their travel investment in terms of sheer numbers of stories. But by eliminating deadline pressures, editors may give their reporters room to make independent news judgments. Rather than expecting a story or two a day from an event like the AAAS annual meeting, editors could instruct their journalists to write a story when something worth writing about takes place and to spend the rest of the time gathering information and making contacts for future stories.

2. Competition is something of a sacred cow in journalism, but it becomes counterproductive when it reinforces the kind of "mass" coverage of the same events (press conferences) found at meetings. The newspaper science writer covers the same press conference and writes the same story as the AP science writer, for example, because he knows his editor is defining "good" coverage of the meeting in terms of what the wire services are producing.

One alternative would be to regard the presence of more than one reporter as a supplementary rather than competitive situation. This would work only if an editor stopped evaluating the quality of his reporter's choices on the basis of what others choose and instead assumed that his reporter can and will apply some reasonable criterion to the selection process. If the competing newspaper publishes a story on a different topic, then, the editor would not conclude that his reporter had "missed" a story but rather that there were many rational topic choices available at the meeting.

3. It is clear from this study that the more a reporter knows about the topic he is covering, the more control he will be able to exercise over the information-selection process in situations like the AAAS meeting. Such a finding argues for specialty writers in the mass media, for persons who can

maintain enough expertise in a content area to make independent news judgments possible. Broadcast operations have even fewer specialty report-ers than do print media, but if this study is any indication, this lack of specialists may cost them dearly in terms of their ability to control informa-tion selection in situations like the AAAS meeting.

4. The media have traditionally viewed cooperation between competing reporters rather negatively; the term "pack journalism," for example, is one negative label often applied to the concept. And to the extent that cooperative behavior promotes rampant homogeneity in story selections, criticism is warranted.

But when information in a field is highly technical, when one reporter simply cannot bring enough expertise to the job to perform effectively at all times, then cooperative behavior could be highly beneficial.

The science-writing inner club sanctions cooperative behavior, its mem-bers argue, precisely *because* scientific information is so difficult that report-ers can do their jobs better if given access to other reporters. Noted one inner club member:

> As a whole, science writers are less competitive than other kinds of
> writers. That's my assessment. . . . By and large I've always had a sense
> among my colleagues that we have more of a community interest in
> promoting science news accurately and fairly, if not uniformly.

If one can argue that cooperation indeed benefits science writers, then it would seem that such behavior could benefit other reporters as well. Tradi-tionally, journalists perceive themselves as loners, one individual against the competition. This study suggests that in a field where concepts are complex and where it is difficult for one individual to understand the entire subject field (in short, most fields), reporters and readers may gain much from cooperative behavior.

Notes

1. Margaret Mead, "Towards a Human Science," *Science* 191:903-909, 5 March 1976, p. 909.

2. Edward J. Epstein, "News From Nowhere," in Gaye Tuchman, ed., *The TV Estab-lishment: Programming for Power and Profit* (Englewood Cliffs, NJ: Prentice Hall, 1974), pp. 44-52; Gaye Tuchman, *Making News: A Study in the Construction of Reality* (New York: Free Press, in press).

3. Timothy Crouse, *The Boys on the Bus* (New York: Ballantine, 1973); Jeremy Tunstall, *Journalists at Work* (London: Constable, 1971); Steve Chibnall, *Law-and-Order News* (London: Tavistock, 1977).

4. To isolate those mass media science journalists who make up the inner club, three newspaper science writers who have held leadership positions in the National Association of Science Writers, Inc., and four public information persons who, through their work for large scientific institutions, come into regular contact with the inner club were asked to list

journalists who they felt were inner club members. Providing lists were David Perlman, then-science editor of the *San Francisco Chronicle:* Ed Edelson, science editor of the *New York Daily News;* Ron Kotulak, science editor of the *Chicago Tribune;* Don Phillips, American Hospital Association; Audrey Likely, director of public relations for the American Institute of Physics; Dorothy Smith, manager of the news service for the American Chemical Society; and Carol Rogers, AAAS public information officer. The lists were merged and the journalists ranked according to the number of times they were mentioned. Those named by four or more persons were considered the most likely candidates for inner club status, and interviews were obtained with all such individuals who indicated they were likely to attend the AAAS meeting.

5. The non-inner club respondents were ranked by three or fewer persons on the list; they too planned to attend the AAAS meeting, and most of them worked for media comparable in size and prestige to those employing inner club reporters.

6. AAAS subscribes to the Washington-based Press Intelligence, Inc.

7. These data are not discussed in this report. Details of the content analysis are available from the author upon request.

8. Of the 24 journalists in the sample, 5 did not attend the meeting for various reasons. They were David Perlman, *San Francisco Chronicle;* Joel Shurkin, *Philadelphia Inquirer;* Jerry Bishop, *Wall Street Journal;* Michael Woods, *Toledo Blade;* and Bob Gillette, *Los Angeles Times.*

Professionalizing News

News as Journalists'
Norms and Routines

The previous section built a sense of how a journalist's social world shapes what becomes news. This section draws on that context to examine how professional and newsroom cultures influence the way that journalists do their jobs. To begin, it becomes crucial to see journalists not as journalists, but as people who have to get their work done. Similarly, a news organization needs to be considered as simply another production facility with expectations for the quality and quantity of its workers' activities.

Seen this way, news becomes the outcome of strategic work routines that journalists apply to meet organizational expectations. To complete this perspective on news, news stories must be seen not as naturally defined entities, but as amorphous *occurrences* that journalists learn to see in certain ways to define them as predictable *events* that can then be covered through common work routines to process those raw materials.

In "Making News by Doing Work: Routinizing the Unexpected," Gaye Tuchman takes the position that people at work always have too much to do, so that a worker's main challenge is controlling the flow of work. In most work settings, the work flow is quite predictable both in its nature and its quantity. Journalism, though, is routinely required to process the unexpected: Occurrences must be turned into news stories. A key to journalists' management of work is learning to categorize raw materials—occurrences—and then to apply appropriate work routines.

Tuchman begins by describing the news categories that journalists regularly invoked during her interviews, using labels such as hard news, soft news, and spot news. She found, though, that journalists could not classify news consistently by this scheme in a way that helped manage their accomplishment of work. After further analysis, Tuchman discovered that journalists actually classified occurrences by the work rhythms involved. That is, they classify or "typify" news by the way that occurrences tend to unfold and by the usual work processes applied to report on them.

Tuchman makes the point that journalists sometimes make erroneous typifications, so that major unplanned alterations must be made to their work process. Interestingly, this misclassification only results in the application of yet another typification: the "what-a-story." This work rhythm is rarely invoked, though, because of its intense resource demands in the newsroom. In sum, Tuchman argues that journalists typify not only *what* has happened but the *way* it has happened to get their jobs done and successfully meet organizational expectations.

Harvey Molotch and Marilyn Lester's "News as Purposive Behaviour" also looks at different categories of news, but the emphasis is on the actors involved in a story and their interests in a story's outcome. As Tuchman also argued, people learn to see activities as "real and patterned happenings" in a way that helps make sense out of both the past and the future. Past news stories serve as references for identifying and interpreting future occurrences, helping journalists to order personal experiences and "carve up reality temporally."

Molotch and Lester depict news as the result of work news promoters who identify occurrences to the news media, by news assemblers who transform an occurrence into an event for public consumption, and by news consumers who use media content to order their sense of "public time." The work of news assemblers involves taking cues from news promoters to select which occurrences should be acknowledged as "really happening." When news is viewed this way, it becomes not an objective reality about discrete events but instead an effort to present one version of reality as news rather than another.

Mark Fishman's "News and Nonevents: Making the Visible Invisible" reconsiders an unspoken assumption of Molotch and Lester's work: If news represents the practical accomplishment of work, how do journalists first come to consider the events that news sources promote? Fishman's answer is that reporters' methods for seeing news follow largely from learning the interpretation schemes of agency officials on their news beats. A nonevent, then, is an occurrence with a poor fit to these schemes of interpretation. Even though a journalist might witness a certain happening, if it is not part of an event *phase structure*, it will not be even thought of as news. Phase structures are ways of seeing the beginning, middle, and end of occurrences; *bureaucratic* phase structures are the typical way that a story unfolds within a bureaucratic public institution.

Fishman carefully points out that this characterization of news differs from the notion of news selectivity, such as in the gatekeeping tradition. A nonevent is not selected-out news, but a "by-product" of an occurrence, something that is irrelevant to a beat reporter's scheme of interpretation. A small, but interesting point is that because television journalism relies less on beats than does newspaper journalism, television reporters do not learn bureaucratic schemes of interpretation as fully and must therefore turn to newspapers for learning which events will be newsworthy.

Nina Eliasoph's "Routines and the Making of Oppositional News" challenges the conclusions of the "routines theorists," arguing that work routines in themselves do not result in a single representation of reality. Several selections in this book have made the point that a single subversive reporter could not produce oppositional news that contradicts newsroom policy, but this study examines an entire organization of subversive reporters where traditional reporters become the outsiders.

Routines once again become a way of predictably accomplishing work to meet organizational expectations. But because newsroom policy is quite different, the organization's culture produces an oppositional slant. Routines thus become a kind of strategic insurance for producing this alternative reality. Through an observational case study, Eliasoph shows how traditional routines can be adapted to accommodate a different set of organizational expectations.

In the end, this study makes a clear case for the power of organizational policy and the newsroom culture, two forces that end up "scaring away" staffers who cannot "get the politics right" despite their adherence to conventional organizational procedures for accomplishing work.

CHAPTER 13

Making News by Doing Work

Routinizing the Unexpected

Gaye Tuchman

One theme dominant in the sociology of work is the "control" of work. Proponents of the structural and technological approach (Perrow 1967; Thompson 1967; March and Simon 1958) stress that organizations routinize tasks if possible, for routinization facilitates the control of work. As discussed by Hughes (1964) and others of the Chicago school (Becker, Geer, and Hughes 1961), persons at work always have too much work to do. To cope with this problem, they try to control the flow of work and the amount of work to be done.

Prompted, possibly, by a view of routine as negotiated process (Bucher 1970), members of the Chicago school extend the discussion of work to the handling of emergencies. For instance, Everett Hughes (1964, pp. 55-56) suggests that the professional's "struggle . . . to maintain control over [his or her] decisions of what work to do and over the disposition of [his or her] time and [his or her] routine of life" may be particularly acute for workers who "deal routinely with what are emergencies to the people who receive their

From *American Journal of Sociology,* 1973, Vol. 79, No. 1, pp. 110-131. Used by permission.

AUTHOR'S NOTE: Lewis A. Coser, Rose Laub Coser, Arlene K. Daniels, Robert Emerson, Carolyn Etheridge, Kenneth A. Feldman, Melvin Kohn, and Marilyn Lester were all kind enough to read earlier drafts, as were newsmen James Benet and Howard Epstein. I owe a special debt to Rue Bucher, Eliot Freidson, and Harvey Molotch, who criticized several drafts. The extent of my debt is indicated by the slight resemblance this version bears to earliest versions, discarded upon sound advice.

services." He speaks of this situation as introducing a "chronic tension" between worker and client, and, in an often-quoted passage, explains: "The person with the crisis feels that the other is trying to belittle his trouble. The physician plays one emergency off against the other; the reason he can't run right up to see Johnny who may have the measles is that he is, unfortunately right at that moment, treating a case of the black plague" (p. 55). Hughes's example suggests that, in handling some types of emergencies, specialists seek to impose priorities and routines upon them. It also implies that some workers, such as doctors, lawyers, and firemen, may profitably be viewed as specialists in handling *specific* kinds of emergencies.

Sociologists have paid scant attention to workers who routinely handle nonspecialized emergencies, ranging from fires and legal cases to medical problems. Yet some workers do precisely this task. Newsmen (and they are still overwhelmingly men) stand out as workers called upon to give accounts (for a discussion of accounts, see Scott and Lyman [1968]) of a wide variety of disasters—*unexpected* events—on a *routine* basis. News work thrives upon processing unexpected events, events that "burst to the surface in some disruptive, exceptional (and hence newsworthy)" manner (Noyes 1971). As Helen Hughes (1940) noted, "Quickening urgency" is the "essence of news" (p. 58).

That workers impose routines upon their work poses a problem concerning nonspecialized unexpected events: How can an organization routinize the processing of unexpected events? Specifically, how do newsmen[1] routinize the handling of a variety of unexpected events in order to process and to present accounts and explanations of them?[2] For, without some routine method of coping with unexpected events, news organizations, as rational enterprises, would flounder and fail.

To answer these questions, this article uses two ideas developed in the sociology of work. (1) Routinization is impeded by variability in raw material (an idea in the organizational literature [Perrow 1967]). (2) Persons categorize the objects of their work to control it (an idea in the literature on occupations and professions [Becker et al. 1961]). Together these ideas suggest that the way in which newsmen classify events-as-news decreases the variability of the raw material processed by news organizations and facilitates routinization.

The first part of this article explores the newsmen's classifications of events-as-news as definitional categories. It asks, How do newsmen define categories of news? What are the bases of their definitions? Are their categories sufficiently consistent to enable the routinization of news work? The answers indicate that this method of analyzing the classifications is inadequate.

The second section of the article approaches the same classifications as typifications. (By typifications, I mean classifications whose meanings are constituted in the situations of their use.) It asks, How are these classifications related to the practical organizational tasks confronting newsmen as they go about their work? How are they related to the contingencies of the situation that the newsmen are reporting? This analysis suggests that typifications enable the routinization of news work. More important, typifications arise out of and reflect the requirements of the organizational structure within which news stories are constructed. This structure and the exigencies of the way the story develops combine to define events as the raw material of news work. The last sections of the article explore the theoretical implications of this analysis.

Throughout this essay, I shall refer to events (happenings in the everyday world), to news (accounts and explanations of events presented by news organizations), and to events-as-news. Derived from the theoretical problem posed here, this last term indicates that newsmen categorize events not only as happenings in the everyday world but also as potentially newsworthy materials—as the raw material to be processed by news organizations.

A Note on Methods

The data presented here were gathered by participant observation at two sites. They were a local independent television station affiliated with a major network and a daily morning newspaper with a circulation of about 250,000. Both had substantial competition within their own medium and from other media. Both are located in the same city, a major television market. Research at these two sites lasted a little over two years. Informants knew me to be a sociologist engaged in research.

As part of the research, I observed work in the newsrooms, accompanied newsmen to news events, and then followed the course of their stories through the news process. I also conducted semiformal interviews on a regular basis. They were used to glean information concerning the initial choice of which event-as-news to cover and to ask questions about the handling of specific stories whose processing I had observed. In addition, I asked newsmen for definitions of the terms they were using. Specific hypotheses did not prompt the requests for definitions. Rather, to observe adequately, I had to know the meanings of the terms I heard used.

Most of the data discussed here are taken from the newspaper field notes. The local television station concentrated upon local stories, and so it was the newspapermen who were more likely to discuss stories of national scope. I have used national stories as extended examples, because they are more accessible to the sociological reader. However, the principles and definitions invoked by both the electronic and the ink-press newsmen were generally the same. Disagreements on these topics will be specified.

Newsmen on Categories of News

At work, newsmen use five terms to differentiate categories of news: hard news, soft news, spot news, developing news, and continuing news. Journalism texts and informants explain that these terms differentiate *kinds of news content* or the *subject* of events-as-news. Asked for definitions of their categories, newsmen fluster, for they take these categories so much for granted that they find them difficult to define. To specify definitions, newsmen offer examples of the stories that fall within a category. They tend to classify the same stories in the same manner, and some stories are cited with such frequency that they may be viewed as prototypes. This section reviews the prototypical cases mentioned by informants.

Hard News Versus Soft News

The informants' main distinction was between hard news and its antithesis, soft news. As they put it, hard news concerns events potentially available to analysis or interpretation and consists of "factual presentations" of events deemed newsworthy (for a discussion of "factual presentations" and analysis, see Tuchman [1972]). When pressed, informants indicated that hard news is "simply" the stuff news presentations are made of. For instance, asked for a definition of hard news, a television editor offered the following catalog of basic news stories: "Hard news is the gubernatorial message to the legislature, the State of the Union Address to Congress, the train-truck accident or the murder, the bank hold-up, the legislative proposal . . . and the fire tomorrow."

This editor and other informants voluntarily contrasted hard news with soft news, also known as the feature or human interest story. Some examples of soft news stories are: an item about a big-city bus driver who offers a cheery "good morning" to every passenger on his early morning run, a feature about a lonely female bear, a story about young adults who rent for a month a billboard proclaiming "Happy Anniversary Mom and Dad."

Newsmen distinguish between these two lists by saying that a hard news story is "interesting to human beings" and a soft news story is "interesting because it deals with the life of human beings" (Mott 1952, p. 58). Or, they state that hard news concerns information people should have to be informed citizens and soft news concerns human foibles and the "texture of our human life" (Mott 1952, p. 58). Finally, they may simply summarize, hard news concerns important matters and soft news, interesting matters.

Each of these separate yet similar attempts to distinguish between hard news and soft news presents the same classificatory problem. They are difficult to use in everyday practice, because the distinctions overlap. Take the last attempt to state the difference between the two lists: Frequently, it is difficult—if not impossible—to decide whether an event is interesting or important or is both interesting and important. Indeed, the same event may be treated as either a hard news or a soft news story. During the two-year period, the observed television station presented as feature stories some events that its primary television competition presented as hard news and vice versa.

Spot News and Developing News

Difficulties also appear in the newsmen's distinctions between spot news and developing news. The most important of these difficulties is that the newsmen partially abandon the statement that the categories are based upon the content or subject matter of events-as-news.

Asked to discuss spot news, newsmen replied that spot news is a type (subclassification) of hard news. Newsmen cited the fire as a prototypical example of spot news. (Occasionally, informants added a second example, either a robbery, murder, accident, tornado, or earthquake.) The subject matter of all examples was conflicts with nature, technology, or the penal code.

Asked about developing news (another subclassification of hard news), the newsmen cited the same examples. Asked, then, to distinguish between spot news and developing news, informants introduced a new element, the amount of information that they have about an event-as-news at a given point in time. When they learned of an unexpected event, it was classed "spot news." If it took a while to learn the "facts" associated with a "breaking story," it was "developing news." It remained "developing news" so long as "facts" were still emerging and being gathered. When I pressed by pointing to previous statements that the subject of the story determined that story's classification, the newsmen insisted that both statements were correct. In essence, they countered, the subject matter of certain kinds of events-as-news had a tendency to occur in specific ways (e.g., fires break out unexpectedly: Many demonstrations are preplanned). And so, newsmen happen to learn of them in certain ways.

Continuing News

Asked to define continuing news, informants reverted to discussing the subject matter of an event-as-news. As the newsmen put it, continuing news is a series of stories *on the same subject* based upon events occurring over a period of time. As a prototype, the newsmen cited the legislative bill. The passage of a bill, they explained, is a complicated process occurring over a period of time. Although news of the bill's progress through the legislative maze may vary from day to day, all stories about the bill deal with the same content—the bill's provisions and whether they will be enacted. In this sense, they said, the story about the legislative bill continues as news. (Other examples cited by informants included trials, politics, economics, diplomacy, and war. Almost all examples were confrontations within or among recognized institutions.)[3]

Then, once again, the newsmen partially modified their statements. Maintaining that certain kinds of news content tend to fall under the rubric "continuing news," they added that certain kinds of content (stories about legislative bills and trials, for example) "simply" tend to occur over an extended period of time.

From Category to Typification

Examination of the newsmen's definitions of their categories had been prompted by the notion that the categories would enable the routinization of work. To be sure, the definitions, prototypical examples, and lists of events decrease the variability of events as the raw material of news. Yet they are problematic: The newsmen state that their categories are based upon the subject matter of events-as-news. But it is difficult to apply consistently their distinctions between hard news and soft news. Also, discussing spot news, developing news, and continuing news, the informants introduced a *seemingly* extraneous element: The subject matter of certain kinds of events-as-news tends to happen in certain kinds of ways. And so, newsmen "just happen" to be alerted to the need to process them in different ways.

The newsmen's insistence that the way something happens is important to their classificatory system suggests a reconsideration of the relevance of classifications to the organization of work. The need for a reanalysis is supported by attempts to discuss events that become news (Boorstin 1964; Molotch and Lester 1971) and by research on disasters (Bucher 1957). For, like the newsmen, this research insists that the way an event happens influences accounts of it. For example, discussing a plane crash, Bucher (1957) argues that, faced with a disaster, persons try to locate the point in the process that "caused" the accident so they may prevent future accidents from happening in the same manner. Bucher's findings suggest that the way in which an event happens, the classifications used to describe the event, and the work done to prevent a recurrence are related. They prompt the proposal that newsmen do not categorize events-as-news by distinguishing between kinds of subject matter.[4] Rather, they typify events-as-news according to the way these happen and according to the requirements of the organizational structure within which news stories are constructed.

The theoretical distinction between "category" and "typification" is crucial, for "typification" implies a phenomenological perspective.[5] "Category" refers to classification of objects according to one or more relevant characteristics ruled salient by the classifiers, frequently by what anthropologists term a "formal analysis." (For a discussion of categories and formal analysis, see Tyler [1969, pp. 2, 194-342].) The use of "category" connotes a request for definitions from informants and a sorting of those definitions along dimensions specified by the researcher. "Typification" refers to classification in which the relevant characteristics are central to the solution of practical tasks or problems at hand and are constituted in and grounded in everyday activity. The use of "typification" connotes an attempt to place informants' classifications in their everyday context; typifications are embedded in and take their meaning from the settings in which they are used and the occasions that prompt their use.[6] (Anthropologists use "componential analysis" to discover meaning in context [see Tyler 1969, pp. 255-288, 396-432].)

Typifications of News

Because typifications are embedded in practical tasks in everyday life, they provide a key to understanding how newsmen decrease the variability

Table 13.1 Practical Issues in Typifying News*

Typification	How Is an Event Scheduled?	Is Dissemination Urgent?	Does Technology Affect Perception?	Are Future Predictions Facilitated?
Soft news	Nonscheduled	No	No	Yes
Hard news	Unscheduled and prescheduled	Yes	Sometimes	Sometimes
Spot news	Unscheduled	Yes	No	No
Developing news	Unscheduled	Yes	Yes	No
Continuing news	Prescheduled	Yes	No	Yes

*As McKinney and Bourque note (1972, p. 232), typifications are flexible and undergo continual transformation. Technically, then, as noted by Lindsay Churchill (personal communication), recording typifications in this manner transforms them into components of a typology.

of events as the raw material of news. This section argues that news organizations routinize the processing of seemingly[7] unexpected events by typifying them along dimensions that reflect practical tasks associated with their work. These tasks are related to both organizational structure and the manner in which an event occurs. As summarized in Table 13.1, newsmen's distinctions between hard news and soft news reflect questions of scheduling; the newsmen's distinctions between spot news and developing news pertain to the allocation of resources and vary in their application according to the technology being used; and the typification "continuing news" is based upon problems in predicting the course of events-as-news.

Hard News: The Flow of News Work and Scheduling

As previously noted, "quickening urgency" is the "essence of news." Because it is timely and urgent, hard news "demands" speed, especially in gathering "facts" and meeting deadlines. Both Breed (1955) and I (1972) have described these processes. We stressed that the need for speed is so overarching that it influences characteristics of news stories. If newsmen do not work quickly, the hard news story will be obsolete before it can be distributed in today's newscast or in the newspaper sold tomorrow.[8] As Park wrote (Park and Burgess 1967, p. 19), old news is "mere information."

In contrast, soft news stories do not need to be "timely." The Sunday newspaper is padded with feature stories about events that occurred earlier in the week. Because they are concerned with "timeliness," newsmen make fine distinctions. They explain that some kinds of content (hard news stories) become obsolete more quickly than others (soft news items). This distinction is based upon the distribution of nonscheduled, prescheduled, and unscheduled events as hard news and as soft news.

A *non*scheduled event-as-news is an event whose date of dissemination as news is determined by the newsmen. A *pre*scheduled event-as-news is an event announced for a future date by its conveners; news of the event is to be disseminated the day it occurs or the day after. An *un*scheduled event-as-news is an event that occurs unexpectedly; news of it is to be disseminated that day or the day after. *The type of scheduling characteristic of an event-as-news affects the organization of work.*

Most hard news stories concern prescheduled events (a debate on a legislative bill) or unscheduled events (a fire). Newsmen do not decide when stories about prescheduled and unscheduled events-as-news are to be disseminated. Newsmen do decide when to gather "facts" and to disseminate accounts and explanations of nonscheduled hard news stories. Nonscheduled hard news stories tend to involve investigative reporting. The publication of the Pentagon Papers by the *New York Times* is an example of a nonscheduled hard news story, for the *Times* held the papers three months before it published extracts, digests, and analyses of them. Processing nonscheduled stories, the news organization controls the timing and flow of work.

Members of the news enterprise almost always control the timing and flow of work required to process soft news stories. Few soft news stories concern unscheduled events, as indicated by the previous list of feature stories. Another example is "The Man in the News" series run by the *New York Times*. Like the obituaries of famous men and women, the "facts" can be gathered, written up, and edited in anticipation of future dissemination. Prescheduled soft news also includes such annual "February stories" as an item appropriate to Washington's birthday, another for Lincoln's birthday, and a third for Valentine's Day. A reporter may be assigned to these stories days in advance, and the specific information to be included in the story may be gathered, written, and edited days before its eventual dissemination.

Of course, there are exceptions to these rules. But news organizations handle those exceptions in a manner that conserves manpower and retains control of the flow of news work. For instance, "facts" to be used in a feature story about the atmosphere at an important trial cannot be gathered in advance. Nor can feature information about an unscheduled event, such as a fire, be gathered in advance. However, the impact of these events-as-feature stories upon the allocation of manpower is minimal. In the first case, a reporter may be assigned to write the "feature angle" of the trial several days in advance and his name stricken from the roster of reporters available to cover the fast-breaking news of the day. In the second case, the same person generally reports on both the hard news "fire" and its soft news angle, so that the news organization conserves manpower.

In general, the distinction between hard news and soft news as typifications reflects a practical task in news organizations: scheduling work in relation to both the way an event-as-story happens and the way in which a story is to be processed and disseminated.

Spot News: Allocating Resources
and Dealing With Technology[9]

Governing the flow of news work, like the organization of most work, involves more than scheduling. It also involves the allocation of resources and the control of work through prediction. To cope with these tasks, newsmen distinguish among spot news, developing news, and continuing news.

Spot news events are unscheduled; they appear suddenly and must be processed quickly. The examples of spot news offered by informants indicate that spot news is the *specifically unforeseen event-as-news*. For instance, although the newsmen may anticipate the probability of a fire, they cannot specifically predict where and when a fire will start. This inability to make a specific prediction concerning some events affects the flow of news work. If a three-alarm fire starts close to deadline, information must be gathered and edited more quickly than usual to meet that deadline. If a major fire starts 50 miles from the city room, transportation problems influence the time needed to gather and to process "facts" and so influences the allocation of resources to cover the fire.

Some events that newsmen nominate for membership in the typification "spot news" are of such importance that newsmen try to create a stable social arrangement to anticipate them. (For a discussion of the newsman's view of importance, see Tuchman [1969].) This takes place even if the probability that the event will occur is minute. For instance, the city desk of most major dailies is staffed around the clock in case a spot news event should occur. The *New York Times* London Bureau processes and relays international stories from far-flung regions of the world because the London time zone enables bureau members to get a jump on the schedules of people working in the New York time zone (Adler 1971). The president of the United States is covered 24 hours a day in case something should happen to him. Continually creating stable social arrangements such as these to cope with spot news requires both extended allocation of resources (assigning a staff member to sit at the city desk all night) and immediate reallocation of resources (pulling a reporter off another story if and as necessary).

As one might expect from findings that the organization of work is influenced by its technology (Hage and Aiken 1969; Perrow 1967; Thompson 1967), the allocation of resources in the newspaper newsroom was different from the allocation of resources in the television newsroom. At the newspaper, at least 3 of the 20-person staff of general reporters and rewrite men were in the city room from 8 a.m. until midnight. Usually, they covered minor stories by telephone, rewrote copy phoned to them by correspondents scattered in small towns around the state, and wrote obituaries. To some extent, this work is essential: The items produced fill small holes in the newspaper and are supposed to be of interest to some readers. To some extent, it is busywork to alleviate the boredom of sitting and waiting for a specifically unforeseen event to happen. If needed, though, this reserve personnel was available to cover spot news.

The television station had few reserve reporters and no reserve camera-men, except from 4 p.m. to 6 p.m. and from 9:30 p.m. until 11:00 p.m. At these times, reporters and cameramen, bringing their film to be processed, had generally returned from their assignments. They would wait either to cover a spot news story or to go off shift. Should a specifically unforeseen event occur at any other time of day, the station had to (1) pay overtime, (2) pull a reporter and a cameraman from a less important story they were already covering, (3) pull a cameraman from a "silent film story" he was covering by himself, (4) hire a free-lance cameraman, (5) pull a staff announcer from his routine duties, such as reading station identification, or (6) assign a news-writer to act as reporter after gaining permission from the appropriate unions. The alternative(s) chosen depended upon the specific situation.

Two points concerning these arrangements are of particular pertinence. First, newsmen stress that creating and recreating stable situations to cope with spot news is a continual, ongoing process. As they discuss it, it seems more like a battle. Second, the nature of those created situations depends upon the technology used by the medium.

Developing News: Technology and the Perception of Events

Practical problems of dealing with a technology are so important that they even affect the newsman's perception of a spot news story, especially whether he will apply the typification "developing news" to an event-as-story. In the case of developing news, technology provides a lens through which events-as-news are perceived.

Developing news concerns "emergent situations" (for a discussion of emergent situations, see Bucher [1957]), as indicated by the following proto-typical example. A plane crashes. Although this event is unexpected, there are, nonetheless, limitations upon the "facts" it can possibly contain. The newsmen would not expect to run a story stating that those reported dead have come to life. Nor would they expect to run a report of an official denial that a crash occurred. The "facts" of the news story are: A plane crashed at 2:00 p.m., in Ellen Park, when an engine caught fire and another went dead, damaging two houses, killing eight people and injuring an additional 15 persons. All else is amplification. Since the plane crash was specifically unexpected, reporters were not present to record "facts" "accurately." "Facts" must be reconstructed, and as more information becomes known, the "facts" will be more "accurate." Although the actual event remains the same, the account of the event changes, or as the newsmen put it, "the story develops." Ongoing changes of this sort are called "developing news." [10]

Most spot news stories are developing news. Since both present interre-lated work demands, the newspapermen tend to use the terms interchange-ably. Television newsmen use the term "developing news" in a more re-stricted manner: They identify some stories as spot news that newspapermen term "developing news." This variation occurs because of the differing technologies associated with the two media.[11] The process of covering the death of Martin Luther King—an event that raised different practical problems for the two local media—illustrates this variation.[12]

At the local newspaper, King's injury and subsequent death were labeled "developing news." A continual flow of updated copy needed editing and "demanded" constant revision of the planned format. The executive editor learned of the attempted assassination and plotted a format for the front page. King's condition was reported as "grave" by the wire services, and the editor drew another format, including stories about other topics above the fold on page one. A wire service bulletin reported King to be dead; all other stories were relegated below the fold. Every story on page 1 needed a new headline of a different size of type, and lead paragraphs of some stories had to be reset into smaller type. Inside pages were also affected.

The television network with which the observed local station is affiliated reported on King's condition as a developing story. Periodically, it interrupted programs to present bulletins. But this was a spot news story for the local television station's personnel. Obviously, the format of the 11 p.m. newscast was modified early in the evening. Because of the network's bulletins, the story about King (whatever it might have turned out to be) had to be the program's lead. At the newspaper, the production manager and compositors bemoaned the need to reset the front page three times, each reset accompanying a major development in the story. All production staff worked overtime. At the television station, readjustments in production plans meant less work, not more. By prearrangement, the network preempted the first few minutes of the late evening newscast to tell the story, just as it had preempted the same five minutes some months earlier to report the death of three astronauts.

The degree to which resources must be reallocated to meet practical exigencies and the way reallocation is accomplished depends upon both the event being processed and the medium processing it. The technology used by a specific medium does more than "merely" influence the ways in which resources are allocated. It influences the typification of event-as-news or how that news story is perceived and classified.

Continuing News: Controlling Work Through Prediction

Spot news and developing news are constituted in work arrangements intended to *cope* with the amount of information specifically predictable *before* an event occurs. This information is slight or nonexistent, because the events are unscheduled. In contrast, continuing news *facilitates* the control of work, for continuing news events are generally prescheduled. Prescheduling is implicit in the newsmen's definition of continuing news as a "series of stories on the same subject based upon events occurring over a period of time." [13] This definition implies the existence of prescheduled change. For instance, the account of the progress of a legislative bill through Congress is an account of a series of events following one another in a continual temporal sequence. An event occurring at any specific point in the sequence bears consequences for anticipated events.

Because they are prescheduled, continuing news stories help newsmen and news organizations to regulate their own activities; they free newsmen to deal with the exigencies of the specifically unforeseen. Take that legislative bill. It is to be channeled through the House, the Senate, and the executive office. To cover this series of events-as-news, the newsman must be familiar with the legislative process. Such familiarity may even be viewed as part of his "professional stock of knowledge at hand" (a term discussed by Schutz [1962, vol. 2, pp. 29 ff.]). He knows the ideas of pertinent committee members, as well as the distribution of power within the House committee, the Senate committee, and the Senate as a whole. In addition, he also knows the progress being made by other legislative bills. With this cumulative stock of knowledge at hand, he may not only predict the bill's eventual disposition, including the specific route through the legislative process (this bill will be bogged down in the House Ways and Means Committee), but also, he can weigh the need to cover this bill on any one day against the need to cover another bill for which he had comparable information. The newsman's "expert" or "professional" stock of knowledge at hand permits him, other newsmen, and his news organization to control work activities.

This matter of control is a key theme in the study of work, for there is always too much work to be done. In news work, no matter how many reporters from any one news organization may be assigned to a legislature or to work at a specific beat or bureau, newsmen (and news organizations) are inundated with more work than they can do. There are so many bills being introduced, so many committee hearings, so many minute yet potentially important readjustments in the distribution of power. In a sense, the newsmen make more work for themselves by choosing to cover several stories in a cursory manner rather than covering one story intensively. Certainly, such a practice is tempting, for the newsman wants to turn in as much copy as possible and this is accomplished more easily by skimming the surface of many stories than by digging down a potential "blind alley" to provide intensive coverage of one event-as-news. The latter alternative is made even less appealing by the possibility that the news desk will dismiss the story as "illegitimate," as frequently happens to stories about social movements. More important, the news desk, the beat reporters, and the news bureaus are increasingly inundated by larger and larger batches of news releases. Most of these can lay claim to being a legitimate hard news story. As I have discussed elsewhere (1972), hard news is "factual" and newsmen are leery of news analysis. As a result of this emphasis upon "facts," newsmen interpret the increasing piles of news releases as more and more stories for them to cover.

Being able to predict the future coverage of a continuing story (whether it concerns a bill, a trial, or a new economic policy) enables an editor, a bureau chief, and, ultimately, a newsman to decide where to go and what to do on any one crowded day. Also, the ability to predict helps the individual newsman to sort out which reportorial technique to use on various stories. For instance, drawing upon the collective professional stock of knowledge shared by newsmen, he can decide which of today's assignments require his presence at hearings, which can be covered by telephone, which can be reconstructed through interviews with key informants, and which "merely" require him to stick his head through a door to confirm that "everything" is as anticipated. The ability to predict enables the news organization in general and a reporter in particular to make choices and still accomplish such mundane but routinely necessary tasks as chatting with potential news sources.

The continuing news story is a boon to the newsman's ability to control his own work, to anticipate specifically and so to dissipate future problems by projecting events into a routine. The newsman's and the news organization's ability to process continuing stories routinely by predicting future outcomes enables the news organization to cope with unexpected events. At the very least, it enables an assignment editor to state, "Joe Smith will not be available to cover spot news stories a week from Tuesday, because he will be covering the X trial." In sum, continuing news typifies events as raw materials to be specifically planned for in advance, and this typification is constituted in practical tasks at work.

An Additional Issue: The Typification "What-a-Story!"

The discussion insistently suggests that newsmen typify events-as-news to transform the problematic events of the everyday world into raw material which can be subjected to routine processing and dissemination. As summarized in Table 13.1, typifications are constituted in practical problems posed by events-as-news. They impose order upon events as the raw material of news and thus reduce the variability of events as the raw material of news. Also, the process of typifying channels the newsmen's perceptions of the "everyday world as phenomenon." [14]

That typifications channel perceptions raises another issue. As indicated by recent research (Sudnow 1965; Cicourel 1968; McKinney and Bourque 1972), people and groups typify and take for granted background features in order to operate in everyday life. But those same background features can cause problems specifically because they are taken for granted. That is, a system of typification can never be all inclusive; it continually requires readjustment (Schutz 1962; Wilson 1970; McKinney and Bourque 1972). Typifications can even be seductive. For instance, faced with the need to predict and to plan, the newsmen may be seduced into applying what everyone knows, that is, what all newsmen collectively agree upon (see Tuchman 1972; Schutz 1962, vol. 1, p. 75). Having a collective stock of knowledge at hand and a system of typification partially based in the utility of known-in-detail prediction, newsmen may predict inaccurately. The Wilson-Heath and Dewey-Truman elections are classic examples of such "inaccurate prediction." [15]

Inaccurately predicted events-as-news require major unplanned alterations in work processes. Like spot news, they are unscheduled and specifically unforeseen. Like developing news, they are perceived through the lens
of a specific technology. Like continuing news, they involve both postdiction
and prediction of an event as a member of a chain of events. They challenge
knowledge and routines that newsmen take for granted.

Newsmen cope with the problems of inaccurately predicted events by
invoking a special typification—"what-a-story!" This typification is constituted in the unusual arrangements that are routinely made to cope with a
"what-a-story!" That newsmen typify these events emphasizes the centrality
of typification to their work and the degree to which typifications are
constituted in their work.

Symbolically, the degree to which this typification is itself routine is
captured by the almost stereotypical manner in which verbal and nonverbal
gestures accompany the pronunciation of "*What* a story!" "What" is emphasized. The speaker provides additional emphasis by speaking more slowly
than usual. The speaker adds yet more emphasis by nodding his head slowly,
while smiling and rubbing his hands together.

Stereotypically, Hollywood portrays the relatively rare "what-a-story"
as the routine of the "exciting world of news." The editor in chief rolls up his
sleeves and writes headlines; the copyboy gets his "big break" and is sent to
cover a major assignment; someone cries, "Stop the presses!"

Sociologically, the extent to which unusual arrangements are routinely
made to cope with a "what-a-story" is illustrated by the reaction of newspaper informants to President Johnson's speech of March 31, 1968. Learning of
Johnson's announcement that he would not run for reelection, the newsmen
immediately instituted taken-for-granted routines to handle the "what-a-
story" and referred to similar situations in the past.

Johnson's speech was prescheduled; the newspaper, like other news media,
had an advance copy of the text that omitted, of course, Johnson's "surprise
announcement" that he would not run for reelection. As Johnson spoke on
television of the de-escalation of American bombing, the men awaited compan-
ion stories concerning reactions of political leaders to the so-called bombing halt.
These were to be sent by the wire services. A preliminary format had been drawn
for page 1. The lead story about the military situation (the "bombing halt") had
been headlined and edited and was being set into type. Page 1 was also to include
a political story, not placed prominently, about the 1968 election. Several other
assessments of the political situation had already been set into type, including
columnists' analyses of the 1968 presidential election to be printed on the
editorial page and the page opposite the editorial page, a political cartoon
showing Johnson speaking on the telephone and saying "Yes, Bobby," and a
small story speculating whether Robert Kennedy would join Eugene McCarthy
in challenging the president as a candidate for the Democratic nomination. The
newspaper was in good shape for the first edition deadline, 11:00 p.m.

And then it happened: bedlam. A prescheduled announcement concerning the continuing "Vietnam problem" and warranting a limited amount of

political speculation turned into a major surprise of military, political, and diplomatic importance. An excited assistant city editor ran, shouting, into the city room from before the television set of the newspaper's entertainment critic. His action was perhaps more unprecedented than the president's announcement.[16] The telephone of the assistant managing editor rang. The managing editor was calling to discuss coverage of the speech. The assistant managing editor automatically said "Hello, Ted," before he had even heard the voice on the other end.[17]

It would be impossible to describe the amount of revision accomplished in a remarkably brief time as telephoned reporters, volunteering editors, and mounds of wire service copy poured into the newsroom. But the comments of editors and reporters are telling. Lifting their heads to answer telephones, bark orders, and clarify them, the editors periodically announced, "*What* a story! . . . the story of the century . . . what a night: what a night . . . who would have believed it . . . there's been nothing like it since Coolidge said, 'I will not run.' "

These remarks are telling. First, they reveal the extent to which typification is based upon taken-for-granted assumptions. For the newspaper's top political reporter, when covering the New Hampshire primary, had offered to bet anyone that Johnson would not run for reelection. Few had taken his bet, and they had taken it for only $1.00, because it would be like "taking money from a baby." [18]

Second, the remarks emphasize the degree to which work routines were routinely altered. Johnson's speech of March 31 was said to require reassessing the military situation in Vietnam, reassessing the diplomatic situation vis-à-vis Vietnam, especially the possibility of successful peace talks, and reassessing the political situation in the United States. The managing editor and the assistant managing editor specifically alerted the copyboys to watch the news services carefully for analyses of these topics. Without being notified (although notifications eventually came), they "knew to expect" analyses of these topics. In addition, handling the story required a substantive amount of revision and readjustment of the allocation of resources. Significantly, all the editors took for granted the nature of those readjustments. No discussion was required to decide which political reporters would come back to work. Only minor discussion was required to decide which of the general reporters would be asked to return to work from their homes.

Third, the analogy to Coolidge (the editor who mentioned Coolidge thought the others might be too young to remember him) alerted the staff to an unusual routine. That is, rules governing the coverage of a "what-a-story" were invoked by citing another "what-a-story." Indeed, the invocation of Coolidge involves an implicit call to reduce the variability of events as the raw material of news, for it states, this event-as-news is "like" that one from years ago.

Finally, the degree to which an individual "what-a-story" is typified and, thus, routine, is indicated by the assistant managing editor's reference to previous "what-a-story(s)." He rejected an offer to help from another editor, recalling that that editor had been more of a hindrance than a help in processing a previous "what-a-story." Some months later, trying to decide the size of type to be used in a headline about Robert Kennedy's death, he thought back to Christmas and explained, "What a year! What a year. . . . The Tet offensive, Johnson's speech, King's death . . . now this." [19]

The typification "what-a-story" affirms that newsmen typify events-as-news in ways that reflect practical issues of news work and that decrease the variability of events as the raw material processed by newsmen and news organizations. It also affirms the importance of typification, for newsmen invoke a special typification to cope with the "routinely nonroutine." Like the other typifications newsmen use, this typification is constituted in practical tasks—in work.

Conclusion

To answer the question of how an organization can process information about unexpected events, I have examined the categories newsmen use to describe events-as-news. Based upon distinctions between and among kinds of news content, the newsmen's categories neither significantly decrease the variability of events as the raw material of news, nor explain the newsmen's activities. However, viewed as typifications, the same classifications reduce the variability of the raw material of news. News organizations can process seemingly unexpected events, including emergencies and disasters, because they typify events-as-news by the manner in which they happen and in terms of the ramifications "this manner of happening" holds for the organization of work. Each of the typifications is anchored in a basic organizational issue concerning the control of work. Further, the newsmen's typifications reconstitute the everyday world. They construct and reconstruct social reality by establishing the context in which social phenomena are perceived and defined.

To some extent, the approach used here has roots in past research on news, particularly the work of Lang and Lang (1953, 1968). However, it provides an essential modification, for past research emphasizes the notion "distortion." As Shibutani (1966) implies in his seminal work on rumor, the concept "distortion" is alien to the discussion of socially constructed realities. Each socially constructed reality necessarily has meaning and significance (Berger and Luckmann 1967; Schutz 1962). Elsewhere (1973), I have argued that "distortion" is itself a socially constructed concept. The construction of reality through redefinition, reconsideration, and reaccounting is an ongoing process. The newsmen's typifications indicate that it might be valuable to think of news not as distorting, but rather as reconstituting the everyday world.

Second, the arguments presented here, when compared to the Molotch (1970) and Bucher (1957) findings, suggest a tantalizing possibility: Individuals, groups, and organizations not only react to and characterize events by typifying *what* has happened, but also they may typify events by stressing the *way* "things" happen. Of particular importance may be the way events may be practically managed, altered, or projected into the future. Recent work on deviance (Emerson and Messinger 1972) and the recent attempts of Molotch and Lester (1972) to analyze public events suggests that such an approach may cut across areas of sociological inquiry and so prove theoretically fruitful.

Notes

1. Throughout this essay, the terms "news organization" and "newsmen" are used as though they were interchangeable. In part, this is because one speaks with newsmen and observes them. The participant observer can neither interview nor observe an organizational rationale. However, there is also some theoretical justification for this usage. Zimmerman (1970, p. 237) concludes, "It appears that the 'competent use' of a given [organizational] rule or set of rules is founded upon members' practiced grasp of what particular actions are necessary on a given occasion to provide for the regular reproduction of a normal state of affairs." And this article asks how news organizations can process accounts of emergencies while continually reproducing a normal state of everyday affairs.

2. Some topics are necessarily excluded here. The most important is, how do newsmen distinguish between newsworthy and non-newsworthy events? For purposes of analysis, I assume that the events discussed have already been deemed newsworthy and that the newsmen must decide how to classify that event-as-news. In practice, the decision that an event is to be made into news and characterization of an event-as-news are mutually dependent. Frequently, they are inseparable procedures. For instance, arguing that a story should be written about an event, a reporter may state, "Of course that's news. . . . It's a good hard news story, similar to the one about [another event] that we ran last week."

3. One young reporter, classifiable as a "young turk," included a conflict between social movements and government among his examples. Characterization of social movements is presently being negotiated between younger and older newsmen and is frequently discussed in journalism reviews.

4. Strictly speaking, this statement is not accurate, for newsmen also use a parallel set of classifications seemingly based upon content, such as "education news," "political news," etc.

5. The phenomenological perspective is not alien to sociological thought. In recent years, researchers (Zimmerman 1970; Cicourel 1968; Emerson 1969; Emerson and Messinger 1971; Sudnow 1965) have discussed the relationship of typification to practical tasks in people-processing organizations. Examining the production of typifications has enabled labeling theorists to highlight the moral and occupational assumptions underpinning the treatment of deviants: It has enabled them to locate the *practical* considerations that police, judges, doctors, and social workers rely upon to label offenders and clients (for an extended discussion, see Emerson and Messinger [1972] and Freidson [1971]). As Schutz pointed out (1962), typifications help to routinize the world in which we live. They epitomize the routine grounds of everyday life; they enable us to make limited predictions (projections) and thus to plan and to act.

6. Schutz's (1962) use of the term "typification" is slightly different from that used here. In some contexts, Schutz uses the term "category" to apply to social science constructs. At other times, he refers to categories as a subtype of typification whose application depends upon the specificity of the phenomenon being typed. Another attempt to grapple with some of these issues may be found in McKinney (1970).

7. Inasmuch as unexpected events can be recognized as such, they must themselves be typified in some way. If they can be recognized and accordingly typified, they are not "completely" unexpected. So, one must speak of "seemingly" unexpected events.

8. Some events-as-stories, especially spot news, appear on newscasts before they reach the morning newspapers. However, I frequently observed television newswriters churning out a script while reading a newspaper. Morning newspapers also serve as sources of ideas for evening newscasts.

9. Some might argue that other organizational variables, such as size, interorganizational relationships, and market structure, influence the allocation of resources as much as or more than technology does. To be sure, markets are of some relevance. Television is primarily an entertainment medium. But, as indicated elsewhere (Tuchman 1969), technology appears to determine the size of the general-news organization, the work needed to process a story, and the relationship between a news organization and a more centralized news-processing agency. For instance, although both the newspaper and the television station subscribe to Associated Press reports, only the electronic medium has the capability of disseminating information at the same time as a more central news-processing agency, in its case, the network with which it is affiliated. Similarly, one need not have film of an event, such as a plane crash, to interrupt programming and announce this "newsworthy event."

10. Although newsmen only single out this type of news as being subject to ongoing change, phenomenological theories would insist that this process is ongoing for all kinds of news at all times. Suffice it to say that developing news provides a particularly clear example of indexicality (for an explication of indexicality, see Garfinkel [1967] and Wilson [1970]).

11. Howard Epstein (personal communication) notes an additional problem that developing news poses for newspapers, the point at which to "break" a story for successive editions. For instance, should one hold the mail edition for 15 minutes to include the start of a speech or should one hold the start of the speech for inclusion in the later home-delivery edition? Television competition makes this decision more difficult and somewhat "meaningless," for whatever the newspaper editors decide to do, the television newscast may carry the speech first.

12. I observed coverage of King's death at the newspaper. Activities at the television station are reconstructed from the television newsmen's subsequent accounts.

13. An issue beyond the scope of this essay arises: How do newsmen decide that two events are about the "same topic"?

14. Zimmerman and Pollner (1970) raise similar issues regarding the sociologist's treatment of the "everyday world as phenomenon," although Luckmann (1972) correctly points out that, technically, the everyday world is not a "phenomenon."

15. It is tempting to identify "inaccurate predictions" as mistakes. "Mistake" is a lay term (Hughes 1964). As Bucher and Stelling (1971) argue, this notion is cast aside in the course of professional socialization to be replaced by concepts emphasizing the process of doing work. Given evidence of inaccurate *collective* predictions, the newsmen essentially argue: We are specialists in knowing, gathering, and processing "general knowledge" (Kimball 1967). If and when our predictions are collective, they are necessarily accurate, for they are based upon shared expertise. The newsmen continue: Since our stock of knowledge is necessarily correct, the situation is in "error." That is, the situation changed in a way we could not anticipate. The post hoc explanation of Heath's "surprise victory" over Wilson, offered in the daily press, supports this interpretation: Confident of victory, Wilson did not campaign sufficiently. Scared by accounts he was the underdog, Heath made a special effort to win. A similar process, dependent upon knowledge in detail, might also explain Agnes's ability to con her doctors (Garfinkel 1967, pp. 116-185, 285-288). Given their stock of knowledge at hand, the doctors assumed it was impossible for a boy to self-administer the correct dosages of the correct hormones at just the right time to interfere with "normal" sexual development.

16. The newsmen were particularly proud of the quiet that dominated the newsroom. One editor, who had worked at the *New York Times*, claimed the news of D-Day spread through the *Times'* city room in whispers.

17. Neither this incident nor the previous one were witnessed. They were reported to me by five different newsmen as the evening progressed. After finishing dinner with his family, the managing editor routinely called the assistant managing editor each evening to check on how the newspaper was shaping up. He had already called before Johnson spoke.

18. This event-as-news is also discussed in Tuchman (1972), and similar stories concerning the assumptions about Johnson's candidacy made by newsmen based in Washington, D.C., have circulated in the mass media. A question asked by Kurt H. Wolff (personal communication) prompts me to note a more technical interpretation of the "what-a-story." One might say that the content of the "what-a-story" challenges the newsmen's taken-for-granted notions of the social world so much that it threatens their ability to maintain the "natural attitude." (Schutz [1962, vol. 1, pp. 208-229] provides an extensive explication of the "natural attitude.") The routines used to process a "what-a-story" may then be seen as the process through which newsmen work to reestablish the natural attitude. Another approach is also possible. The five typifications previously discussed enable the newsmen to process other people's emergencies. When faced with a "what-a-story," newsmen are themselves placed in a state of emergency. That they immediately invoke routines to handle the "what-a-story" again stresses the use of typification grounded in routine to accomplish practical tasks. In this case, the task might be simultaneously processing information and working one's way out of an organizational emergency.

19. King's death was retrospectively treated as a "what-a-story." At the time, newsmen greeted it with head shaking devoid of glee, and some quietly discussed the racism of other staff members. The extent to which a "what-a-story" is subject to routine is forcefully indicated by an incident at the television station on the day of Robert Kennedy's death. Most newsmen were called into work at 6:00 a.m. Several were not, so they would still be fresh for the 11:00 p.m. newscast. Coming to work in the midafternoon, one newsman asked an early morning arrival, "Did we gather the *usual* reaction?" (emphasis added). Then, he indicated his realization that this question would seem crass to an outsider by asking me not to include his question in my field notes.

References

Adler, Ruth. 1971. *A Day in the Life of the* New York Times. New York: Lippincott.

Becker, Howard, Blanche Geer, and Everett C. Hughes. 1961. *Boys in White*. Chicago: University of Chicago Press.

Berger, Peter, and Thomas Luckmann. 1967. *The Social Construction of Reality*. Garden City, N.J.: Anchor.

Boorstin, Daniel. 1964. *The Image: A Guide to Pseudo-Events in America*. New York: Harper & Row.

Breed, Warren. 1955. "Social Control in the Newsroom." *Social Forces* 33 (May): 326-335.

Bucher, Rue. 1957. "Blame and Hostility in Disaster." *American Journal of Sociology* 62 (March): 467-475.

———. 1970. "Social Processes and Power in a Medical School." In *Power in Organizations,* edited by Mayer Zald. Nashville, Tenn.: Vanderbilt University Press.

Bucher, Rue, and Joan Stelling. 1971. "Professional Socialization: The Acquisition of Vocabularies of Realism." Paper presented at the meeting of the Society for the Study of Social Problems, Denver.

Cicourel, Aaron. 1968. *The Social Organization of Juvenile Justice*. New York: John Wiley.

Emerson, Robert. 1969. *Judging Delinquents: Context and Process in Juvenile Court*. Chicago: Aldine.

Emerson, Robert, and Sheldon Messinger. 1972. "Deviance and Moral Enterprise." Paper presented at the meeting of the Society for the Study of Social Problems, New Orleans, August 28.

Freidson, Eliot. 1971. "Deviance as Diagnosis: Defiance, Deficiency, and Disability." Paper presented at the meeting of the American Sociological Association, Denver, September 1.

Garfinkel, Harold. 1967. *Studies in Ethnomethodology.* Englewood Cliffs, N.J.: Prentice Hall.

Hage, Jerald, and Michael Aiken. 1969. "Routine Technology, Social Structure and Organizational Goals." *Administrative Science Quarterly* 14 (3): 366-378.

Hughes, Everett C. 1964. *Men and Their Work.* Glencoe, Ill.: Free Press.

Hughes, Helen MacGill. 1940. *News and the Human Interest Story.* Chicago: University of Chicago Press.

Kimball, Penn. 1967. "Journalism: Art, Craft or Profession?" In *The Professions in America,* edited by Kenneth S. Lynn et al. Boston: Beacon.

Lang, Kurt, and Gladys Engel Lang. 1953. "The Unique Perspective of Television." *American Sociological Review* 18 (February): 3-12.

————. 1968. *Politics and Television.* New York: Quadrangle.

Luckmann, Thomas. 1972. Review of *Understanding Everyday Life. Contemporary Sociology* 1 (1): 30-32.

March, James, and Herbert Simon. 1958. *Organizations.* New York: John Wiley.

McKinney, John C. 1970. "Sociological Theory and the Process of Typification." In *Theoretical Sociology,* edited by John C. McKinney and Edward Tiryakian. New York: Appleton-Century-Crofts.

McKinney, John C., and Linda Brookover Bourque. 1972. "Further Comments on 'The Changing South': A Response to Sly and Weller." *American Sociological Review* 37 (April): 230-236.

Molotch, Harvey. 1970. "Oil in Santa Barbara and Power in America." *Sociological Inquiry* 40 (Winter): 131-144.

Molotch, Harvey, and Marilyn Lester. 1972. "Accidents, Scandals, and Routines: Resources for Conflict Methodology." Paper presented at the meeting of the American Sociological Association, New Orleans, August 30.

Mott, Frank Luther. 1952. *The News in America.* Cambridge, Mass.: Harvard University Press.

Noyes, Newbold. 1971. Extract from speech to the American Society of Newspaper Editors, Washington, D.C., April 14.

Park, Robert, and Ernest Burgess. 1967. *The City.* Chicago: University of Chicago Press.

Perrow, Charles. 1967. "A Framework for the Comparative Analysis of Organizations." *American Sociological Review* 32 (April): 194-208.

Schutz, Alfred. 1962. *Collected Papers.* 2 vols. The Hague: Nijhoff.

Scott, Marvin, and Stanford Lyman. 1968. "Accounts." *American Sociological Review* 33 (February): 46-62.

Shibutani, Tamotsu. 1966. *Improvised News: A Sociological Study of Rumor.* Indianapolis: Bobbs-Merrill.

Sudnow, David. 1965. "Normal Crimes: Sociological Features of the Penal Code in a Public Defender's Office." *Social Problems* 12 (Winter): 255-272.

Thompson, James. 1967. *Organizations in Action.* New York: McGraw-Hill.

Tuchman, Gaye. 1969. "News, the Newsman's Reality." Ph.D. dissertation, Brandeis University.

————. 1972. "Objectivity as Strategic Ritual: An Examination of Newsmen's Notions of Objectivity." *American Journal of Sociology* 77 (January): 660-670.

————. 1973. "The Technology of Objectivity." *Urban Life and Culture,* vol. 2 (April).

Tyler, Stephen A., ed. 1969. *Cognitive Anthropology.* New York: Holt, Rinehart & Winston.

Wilson, Thomas P. 1970. "Conceptions of Interaction and Forms of Sociological Explanation." *American Sociological Review* 35 (August): 697-710.

Zimmerman, Don H. 1970. "Record-keeping and the Intake Process in a Public Welfare Organization." In *On Record: Files and Dossiers in American Life,* edited by Stanton Wheeler. New York: Russell Sage.

Zimmerman, Don H., and Melvin Pollner. 1970. "The Everyday World as Phenomenon." In *People and Information,* edited by Harold B. Pepinsky. New York: Pergamon.

CHAPTER **14**

News as Purposive Behaviour

On the Strategic Use of Routine Events, Accidents and Scandals

Harvey Molotch
Marilyn Lester

Everyone needs news. In everyday life, news tells us what we do not experience directly and thus renders otherwise remote happenings observable and meaningful. Conversely, we fill each other with news. Although those who make their living at newswork (reporters, copy editors, publishers, typesetters, etc.) have additional needs for news, all individuals, by virtue of the ways they attend to and give accounts of what they believe to be a pregiven world, are daily newsmakers.

News is thus the result of this invariant need for accounts of the unobserved, this capacity for filling in others, and the production work of those in the media. This article seeks to understand the relationships between different kinds of news needs and how it is that news needs of people

From *American Sociological Review*, 1974, Vol. 39, pp. 101-112. Used by permission.

AUTHORS' NOTE: This article was originally published in the *American Sociological Review*, Vol. 39, February 1974. We would like to thank Aaron Cicourel, Mark Fishman, Lloyd Fitts, Richard Flacks, Eliot Freidson, Richard Kinane, Milton Mankoff, Hugh Mehan, Linda Molotch, Milton Olin, Charles Perrow, Michael Schwartz, David Street, Gaye Tuchman, John Weiler, Eugene Weinstein, and Don Zimmerman. Financial support was provided through a faculty senate grant, University of California, Santa Barbara.

differently situated vis-à-vis the organization of newswork produce the social and political "knowledge" of publics.[1]

Theoretical Groundings

Humans schedule and plan.[2] We learn from the experience of a sociologist-patient in a tuberculosis sanatorium[3] that whether, from the standpoint of the outside observer, anything is "really happening" and whether there is any "real reason" to create calendars, reckon time, or scheme a future, people nonetheless provide accounts of activities which make those activities observable as real and patterned happenings. In a manner analogous to the creation of a meaningful spatial world, those happenings are used as temporal points of reference for ordering a past and future.

Pasts and futures are constructed and reconstructed, as a continuous process of daily routines. In such constructions an infinite number of available activities are not attended to, and a certain few become created observables. These few become resources—available as practically needed—to break up, demarcate, and fashion lifetime, history, and a future.

Our conception is not of a finite set of things that "really happened out there" from which selection is made; our idea is not analogous to selective perception of the physical world. We propose (following Garfinkel[4] and others) that what is "really happening" is identical with what people attend to. Our conception thus follows Zimmerman and Pollner's description of the work of "assembling the occasioned corpus":

> By the use of the term occasioned corpus, we wish to emphasize that the features of socially organized activities are particular, contingent accomplishments of the production and recognition work of parties to the activity. . . . The occasioned corpus is a corpus with no regular elements; that is, it does not consist of a stable collection of elements. The work of assembling an occasioned corpus consists in the ongoing "corpusing and decorpusing" of elements rather than the situated retrieval or removal of a subset of elements from a larger set transcending any particular setting in which that work is done.[5]

Thus, pasts and futures are not accomplished once and for all, with new "additions" embellishing an established "whole." A new happening reinforms what every previous happening was; in turn each happening gets its sense from the context in which it is placed.

An *occurrence* is any cognized happening; it can be infinitely divided and elaborated into additional happenings and occurrences. "Important" occurrences are those which are especially useful in demarcating time in their individual lives. Americans conspicuously use such rites of passage as birthdays, anniversaries, employments, promotions, geographical moves, and deaths for this end. Depending upon the context, other occurrences may serve the same function (e.g., the date the house was painted, the time one's son was arrested, the year the crop failed). We will use the term "events" to refer to occurrences which are creatively used for such purposes. Once such use occurs, an occurrence becomes, to a degree, reified as an object in the social world[6] and thus available as a resource for constructing events in the future.

Doing Events

The everyday activities of constituting events are guided by one's purposes-at-hand. A much oversimplified analogy to fact-making about the physical world may be helpful here. Individuals "see" chairs when they enter a room because of the recurrent need to sit. Sociologists sometimes "see" religion as an explanatory variable in their data because it sometimes "works." The analogous process in creating temporal points of reference means that occurrences *become events* according to their usefulness to an individual who is attempting on a particular occasion to order her or his experience.[7] But the creation of temporal points of reference varies over time. Each time there is a need to carve up reality temporally, the reason for doing so constrains what kind of carving will be done. Events may thus, to a degree, persist, but they are not intrinsically durable. Any occurrence is a potential resource for constructing an event, and the event so constructed is continuously dependent on purposes-at-hand for its durability.

Collectivities of people—communities, klans, societies, civilizations—similarly appear to create (or have created for them) temporal demarcations which are assumed to be shared in common among those who are deemed and deem themselves to be competent individuals in the collectivity.[8] *Public Time* is the term which we will take to stand for that dimension of collective life through which human communities come to have what is assumed to be a patterned and perceptually shared past, present, and future. Just as the rudiments of an individual lifetime consist of private events, so public time is analogously constituted through public events. Thus, the content of an individual's conceptions of the history and the future of his or her collectivity comes to depend on the processes by which public events get constructed as resources for discourse in public matters. The work of historians, journalists, sociologists, and political scientists helps to accomplish this task for various publics by making available to citizens a range of occurrences from which to construct a sense of public time.

To the degree to which individuals or collectivities have differing purposes, rooted in diverse biographies, statuses, cultures, class origins, and specific situations, they will have differing and sometimes competing uses for occurrences. An *issue* arises when there are at least two such competing uses, involving at least two parties having access to event-creating mechanisms. For public issues, these mechanisms are the mass media.

Conflicting purposes-at-hand lead to competing accounts of what happened or, what is a variant of the same question, to dispute over whether anything significant happened at all. Under these circumstances an *issue* takes form. The thirtieth birthday, or the thirteenth birthday, or menopause, or the signing of a lease, will become an issue if there are competing interpretations of what really happened. That is, a struggle takes place over the nature of the occurrence, and embedded in that struggle are differing interests in an outcome. It is currently being disputed, for example, whether menopause is a "real" event. Women's liberationists assert that although it is in fact an occurrence, that is, it "simply" happens, it is not an event. It should not serve as a time-marking feature of the environment *through which certain consequences* (e.g., no woman should hold important responsibility) *should follow.* Others (usually men) assert the contrary, and in these differing accounts of the meaning of the occurrence (i.e., whether it is or is not an event) an issue resides.

In all public issues, analogous processes are at work. We debate, for example, whether the "My Lai massacre" "really" happened or whether it was "only" a routine search-and-destroy mission. That choice between accounts determines the nature of the occurrence, and at the same time, the degree to which it was special enough to be used to reorder past occurrences and events, change priorities, and make decisions. Any public issue involves a similar struggle over an occurrence and similar interests in the outcome: Did the ITT lobbyist send that memo as specified? Is the crime rate so high that now "you-can't-walk-the-streets"? The existence of an issue demonstrates that competing *event needs* exist with respect to a given occurrence. Sometimes, in fact, the issue itself can become an issue. For example, a politician might charge that his opponents have deliberately "cooked up" a "phony issue" to deflect voter attention from the "real issue." In such instances, the issue of the issue becomes an event.

The work of promoting occurrences to the status of public event springs from the event needs of those doing the promoting. Unlike the case of private events, it involves making experience for great numbers of people. This potential public impact means that the social multiplier effect of the work of those who do news for publics is much greater than the effect of people who do news for themselves and their face-to-face associates. Although analogous processes and distinctions exist for private and public events, this greater impact of the latter leads us to focus our discussion on public events.

Career Lines of Public Events

In the career pattern of a public event, an occurrence passes through a set of agencies (individuals or groups), each of which helps construct, through a distinctive set of organizational routines, what the event *will have turned out to be* using as resources the work of agencies who came before and anticipating what successive agencies "might make out of it."[9]

For simplicity, we view events as being constituted by three major agencies.[10] First, there are the *news promoters*—those individuals and their associates (e.g., Nixon, Nixon's secretary; Kuntsler, Kuntsler's spokesman; a-man-who-saw-a-flying-saucer) who identify (and thus render observable) an occurrence as special, on some ground, for some reason, for others. Second, there are the *news assemblers* (newsmen, editors, and rewritemen) who, working from the materials provided by the promoters, transform a perceived finite set of promoted occurrences into public events through publication or broadcast. Finally, there are the *news consumers* (e.g., readers) who analogously attend to certain occurrences made available as resources by the media and thereby create in their own minds a sense of public time. Each successive agency engages in essentially the same kind of constructing work, based on purposes-at-hand which determine given event needs. But the work accomplished at each point closes off or inhibits a great number of event-creating possibilities. In this closing off of possibilities lies the power of newswork and of all accounting activity. We now turn to a detailed examination of the newswork done by each agency in the newsmaking process and the power implications of that work.

1. Promoting

There are interests in promoting certain occurrences for public use, as well as interests in preventing certain occurrences from becoming public events. By "promoting" we merely mean that an actor, in attending to an occurrence, helps to make that occurrence available to still others. In some instances, the promoting may be direct, crass, and obvious—as in public relations work[11] or transparently political activity (e.g., a candidate's press conference). In others, promotion work is less crassly self-serving as when a citizen tries to publicize a health danger. Commonly, promotion work revolves around one's own activity, which like all social activity is accomplished with its prospective and retrospective potential uses in mind. Thus, the press conference is held for the benefits which its public impact are assumed to provide; a protest demonstration is, in the same way, geared for its selection as an event.[12] Similarly, a decision to bomb North Vietnam is conducted with what-will-be-made-of-it and what-it-really-was-all-along (e.g., its deniability) as two of its constituent features. In our language, then, doing and promoting are part of the same process; indeed, the career of the occurrence will, in the end, constitute what was "done." That is, if the bombing is not widely reported or is reported as "bombing selected military targets," the nature of the act itself, from the perspective of the agent (Nixon), will radically differ from the result of prominent and widespread coverage which stipulates "indiscriminate massive bombing." Thinking through these possible coverages is part of the work of a newsmaker and is essential to competent event creation.[13]

Although promoters often promote occurrences for which they themselves are responsible, they also have access (within limits) to promote the activities of others—including individuals whose purposes are opposed to their own. Thus, a political candidate can "expose" the corrupt occurrence work of a political rival or take credit for its beneficent consequences.

Similarly, Richard Nixon could promote letters from P.O.W. mothers which were written as private communications and perhaps not envisioned by their authors as public events. The richness and irony of political life is made up of a free-wheeling, skilled competition among people having access to the media, trying to mobilize occurrences as resources for their experience-building work.

2. Assembling

Media personnel form a second agency in the generation of public events. From their perspective, a finite number of things "really happen," of which the most special, interesting, or important are to be selected. Their task involves "checking a story out" for worthiness, a job which may involve months of research or a fleeting introspection or consultation with a colleague. The typical conception of the media's role, then, at least in Western, formally uncensored societies, is that the media stand as reporter-reflector-indicators of an objective reality "out there," consisting of knowably "important" events of the world. Armed with time and money, an expert with a "nose for news" will be led to occurrences which do, indeed, index that reality. Any departure from this ideal tends to be treated as "bias" or some other pathological circumstance.

To suggest the view that assemblers' own event needs help to constitute public events is also to imply the importance of the organizational activities through which news is generated. The nature of the media as formal organization, as routines for getting work done in newsrooms, as career mobility patterns for a group of professionals, and as profit-making institutions all become inextricably and reflexively tied to the content of published news.[14] The extent to which news organizations generate event needs among news assemblers that vary from those of occurrence promoters is the extent to which the media have an institutionally patterned independent role in newsmaking. How then does the construction work of the media coincide or conflict with the construction work of promoters? Assemblers' purposes-at-hand, as they contrast or coincide with the purposes-at-hand of different types of promoters, will determine the answers to such a question.

Powerful promoters may attempt to increase the correspondence between their event needs and those of assemblers by pressuring media into altering their work routines. The sanctions which the powerful exercise to control media routines may be direct and crude (e.g., threatening speeches, advertising boycotts, antitrust suits against broadcasters) or subtle (e.g., journalism awards and the encouragement, through regularized interviews, leaks, and press conferences, of newsroom patterns which inhibit follow-up, experimentation, and deviation). Thus, for example, all television networks have abandoned their habit of "instant analysis" of presidential speeches, as a response, we assume, to White House pressure. What may eventually evolve as a journalistic "professional canon" will have been historically grounded in an attempt by the institutionally powerful to sustain ideological hegemony. In this instance, the event needs of assemblers come to closely resemble those of promoters who affect journalistic work routines.

In societies having a formally controlled press, the substantive relationship between news promoters and assemblers is less obscured. In such societies, media are organized to serve a larger purpose (e.g., creating socialist man or maintaining a given regime). Validity thus tends to be equated with utility. Presumably, career advancement and survival depend on one's ability to mesh her or his "nose for news" with the bosses' conceptions of the general social purpose and thus of the utility of a given occurrence.

Because Western conceptions of news rely on the assumption that there is a reality out-there-to-be-described, the product of any system which denies this premise is termed "propaganda." Thus, in the Western mind, the distinction between news and propaganda lies in the premise seen to be embedded in the assemblers' work: Those with purposes produce propaganda; those whose only purpose is to reflect reality produce news.

As Tuchman[15] has argued, the assumption of an objective reality allows Western newsmakers at all levels to have an ever available account of their activities—that is, they report (or at least try their best to report) what is there. But this kind of self-definition by practitioners should not be allowed to obscure the purposiveness of media work. In fact, that self-definition as an account is itself part of the very organizational activities through which newswork gets done. By choosing to suspend belief in an ability to index "what really happened"[16] we make manifest the basic similarities between newsmaking in any social or political context.

In the West as in the East, parallels exist between the event needs of assemblers and promoters. These parallels do not necessarily result from plots, conspiracies, "selling out," or even ideological communalities.[17] While not ignoring these, we are intrigued by the possibility of news generated through the parallel needs of promoters and assemblers which arise for different reasons. Though perhaps unaware of the implications of one another's work, they somehow manage to produce a product which favours the event needs of certain social groups and disfavours those of others.

3. Consuming

Members of publics, glutted with the published and broadcast work of the media, engage in the same sort of constituting activity as news assemblers. A residue of biography, previous materials made available by media, and present context all shape the consumer's work of constructing events. Their newswork is procedurally identical with that of promoters and assemblers, but with two important differences: The stock of occurrences available as resources has been radically truncated through the newswork of other agencies, and, unlike assemblers, they ordinarily have no institutional base from which to broadcast their newswork.

A Typology of Public Events

Despite the overarching similarity of individuals' and organizations' methods of newsmaking, we find it useful to describe certain substantive differences in the ways in which occurrences are promoted to the status of public event.[18]

In using this typology, we are imposing ideal types on data. Consistent with that fact, any event which we may pull from a newspaper's front page for illustrative purposes may be seen to contain some features of each event type. Similarly, the category which any kind of event "fits" may similarly shift with changing features or schemes of interpretation, which may lead to a revision of what "really happened."

We distinguish between events by the circumstances of the promotion work which makes them available to publics. The answers to two questions which can be asked of any event provide the basis for our typology. First: Did the underlying happening come into being through intentional or unintentional human activity? And second: Does the party promoting the occurrence into an event appear to be the same as the party who initially accomplished the happening on which the event is based? The relevance of these questions will become clearer as each event type is described.

Routine Events

Routine events are distinguishable by the fact that the underlying happenings on which they are presumably based are purposive accomplishments and by the fact that the people who undertake the happening (whom we call "effectors") are identical with those who promote them into events. The prototypical routine event is the press conference statement, but the great majority of stories appearing in the daily press fall in this category; hence, on grounds of frequency, we term them "routine." [19]

Whether or not a given promoter is the "same" as the effector can be difficult to determine in some instances. It is clear, for example, that if Richard Nixon's press secretary promotes the president's trip to China or Russia, the effector (Nixon) and the promoter (press secretary) can be taken as identical for all intents and purposes. If, however, Nixon reads a letter on TV written to him by a P.O.W.'s wife, the degree of identity between Nixon, the promoter, and the P.O.W. wife, as effector, is less clear. To the extent to which it can be assumed that both parties' purposes are identical—e.g., to bring public attention to P.O.W.s and/or to mobilize support for the war—the promoter and agent can be deemed identical, and the written letter as a public event can be classified as routine. Of course, it may be that Nixon wants to bring attention to the P.O.W.s for other long-range ("ulterior") purposes not shared by the P.O.W. wife. In such a case, Nixon is not merely using his position to advance the effector's public event needs but is fostering a new occurrence of his own and promoting it as a public event. After noting that kind of constructing work, the "new" occurrence is analytically the same as any other.

While all routine events share certain features, elucidating those features does not tell us what makes for a successful routine event. Each day a multitude of activities is done with a view to creating routine events. But those intentions must complement the work done by news assemblers if a public event is to result. The success of a potential routine event is thus contingent on the assembler's definition of an occurrence as a "story." Put another way, those who seek to create public events by promoting their activities (occurrences) must have access to that second stage of event creation. With respect to this accessibility, various subtypes of routine events can be discussed:

a. Those where the event promoters have *habitual access* to news assemblers;
b. Those where the event promoters are seeking to *disrupt* the routine access of others to assemblers in order to make events of their own; and
c. Those where the access is afforded by the fact that the promoters and news assemblers are *identical.*

a. *Habitual access.* As the term implies, habitual access exists when an individual or group is so situated that its own event needs routinely coincide with the newsmaking activities of media personnel. Thus, for example, the president of the United States is always assumed to say "important" things. This "importance" is taken for granted, and a Washington reporter who acts on the opposite assumption will probably lose his job. Habitual access is likely limited in this country to high government officials, major corporate figures, and, to a lesser extent, certain glamour personalities.[20] Such people, especially those in political life, must be concerned with keeping their podia alive and organizing the news so that their goals do not suffer in the continuing competition to create publics. That competition may involve occasional struggles with other powerful figures, or, on the other hand, with insurgent groups seeking to provide a different set of public experiences. Intra- or intergroup competitions notwithstanding, habitual access is generally found among those with extreme wealth or other institutionally based sources of power. Indeed, this power is both a result of the habitual access and a continuing cause of such access. Routine access is one of the important sources and sustainers of existing power relationships.

The function of habitual access is illustrated by a routine event such as Richard Nixon's "inspection" of a Santa Barbara beach after the calamitous 1969 oil spill.[21] Nixon was depicted leaving his helicopter on a section of the sand, "inspecting" the beach beneath his feet. Needless to say, Nixon's talented assistants could have done the inspection for him; furthermore, Nixon is scientifically incompetent to "inspect" beaches. The activity was an attempt to generate an event so as to inform the American public that Richard Nixon was personally concerned about oil on beaches. His efforts and inspection were meant to instruct the public that the beaches were in fact clean. When Fidel Castro visits a hospital or Mao checks up on a generator, a similar dynamic is at work. When this type of occurrence becomes a successful public event, the results are seen as close to those first envisioned by the effector/promoter.

Although news assemblers commonly act upon the assumption that those with official authority are the most newsworthy,[22] other individuals and groups are occasionally in the position to generate events. Yet, whereas the U.S. president's access to the media continues across time and issue, the access of other groups—e.g., spokespeople for women's rights, civil rights, and youth—will ebb and flow over time and place.[23] For this reason, the ideal-typical routine event is taken to be the generating of a public experience by those in positions to have continual access to asserting the importance and factual status of "their" occurrences.

b. *Disruptive access.* Those lacking habitual access to event making, who wish to contribute to the public experience, often come to rely on disruption.[24] They must "make news," by somehow crashing through the ongoing arrangements of newsmaking, generating surprise, shock, or some more violent form of "trouble." Thus, the relatively powerless disrupt the social world to disrupt the habitual forms of event making. In extreme cases, multitudes are assembled in an inappropriate place to intervene in the daily schedule of occurrence and events. Such activities constitute, in a sense, "anti-routine" events. This "obvious" disruption of normal functioning and its challenge to the received social world prompts the coverage of the mass media.

The disruptive occurrence becomes an event because it is a problem for the relatively powerful. We would argue that a protest event—e.g., a student sit-in or a Jerry Rubin remark—receives media play precisely because it is thought to be an occurrence which "serious people" need to understand. What does a sit-in mean? Have students gone berserk? Will secretaries be raped? Is order in jeopardy? People interested in maintaining the ongoing process need to answer these questions before developing strategy and plans for restoration of order. The coverage which results typically speaks to these implications—not to the issues which raised the protest in the first place. Thus, to the extent that student protest activity continues as an issue, it does so because important parties disagree about what the protest means and how it should best be handled. Important liberals think it means that certain institutions need to be reformed (e.g., a particular war ended, stepped-up counselling in the dean's office, improved student-faculty ratios); important conservatives think it means that students are bums and should be coddled less. Issues exist through this disagreement on meaning-methods among parties with access. The focus is typically on how to handle dissidents and not on the points raised by the dissidents. That is why the leaders of campus revolts almost never find themselves quoted *substantively* in the press.[25]

We would argue that coverage of student protest fades as the event needs of one or the other important party decline. The mystery of the student protest declines as the scenario becomes increasingly typified through repetition: Buildings are taken—speeches made—administrations respond—cops are called—heads are cracked—ringleaders arrested—trials proceed. No rapes, little destruction, token reform (maybe). People can go back to their everyday activities; the strategic need to know is satisfied.

There is a second reason this type of routine event declines in usefulness to important people. The very reporting on the occurrence may come to be seen as precipitating the creation of more such occurrences. Thus, an interest develops in eliminating such events from the news—either by taking actions to prevent them (e.g., softening resistance to student demands) or by agreeing not to report them. Police, for example, may bar reporters from the sites of ghetto riots, and be supported in doing so by politicians, civic leaders, and publishers as well. Certain canons of the "responsibility of the press" are readily available to editors who choose to bypass anti-routine events. The purposiveness underlying all routine events can be selectively perceived at appropriate moments to justify cancelling a story because it is viewed as promoted precisely for its media effects.[26] When important people see a potential event as too costly, given their purposes-at-hand, there are various resources for eliminating it.

c. *Direct access.* Some news stories are generated by assemblers who go out and "dig up" the news. Feature stories are often of this sort, but many "straight news" articles can be of the same type. For example, assemblers in scrutinizing the police blotter may detect that "crime is rising" or may interview or poll a population for attitude shifts. This newswork is routine in that creating the occurrence (e.g., record checking, attitude polling) is a purposive activity promoted as a public event by the effector. It is distinctive, however, in that the promoter and the assembler are identical. When this identity is sufficiently transparent, the media involved may be castigated for lacking "objectivity" or for engaging in "muckraking" or "yellow journalism." A tenet of the "new journalism" is that such newsmaking is indeed appropriate. This controversy is, in our terms, a conflict over whether or not media personnel can legitimately engage in transparent news promotion, or whether they must continue to appear to be passively reporting that which objectively happens.[27]

Accidents

An accident differs from a routine event in two respects: (1) The underlying happening is not intentional, and (2) those who promote it as a public event are different from those whose activity brought the happening about. In the case of accidents, people engage in purposive activity which leads to unenvisioned happenings which are promoted by others into events. Accidents thus rest upon miscalculations which lead to a breakdown in the customary order.

Events such as the Santa Barbara oil spill, the Watergate arrests, the release of nerve gas at Dugway Proving Ground, and the inadvertent U.S. loss of hydrogen bombs over Spain all involve "foul ups" in which the strategic purpose of a given activity (e.g., oil production, political espionage, gas research, national defence) becomes unhinged from its consequences.

The accident tends to have results which are the opposite of routine events. Instead of being a deliberately planned contribution to a purposely developed social structure (or in the language of the literature, "decisional outcome"), it fosters revelations which are otherwise deliberately obfuscated by those with the resources to create routine events.

For people in everyday life, the accident is an important resource for learning about the routines of those who ordinarily possess the psychic and physical resources to shield their private lives from public view. The Ted Kennedy car accident gave the public access to that individual's private activities and dispositions. As argued elsewhere[28] an accident like the Santa Barbara oil spill provided the local public analogous insights into the everyday functioning of American political and economic institutions.

When accidents surface as public events, they do so in "error"; we can expect that unless the needs of powerful people differ, routine event-making procedures subsequently and increasingly come into play to define the accident out of public politics. But the suddenness of the accident and its unanticipated nature mean that event makers are initially not ready and thus the powerful could give uncoordinated, mutually contradictory accounts. This process of accidental disruption, followed by attempts to restore traditional meanings can, we have found, be observed empirically, and thus, *we take accidents to constitute a crucial resource for the empirical study of event-structuring processes.*[29]

In their realization as events, accidents are far less contingent than are routine events on the event needs of the powerful. Given the inherent drama, sensation, and atypicality of accidents, it is difficult to deny their existence, and typically nonimportant groups can more easily hold sway in the temporal demarcation process. Thus, the outflow of a small sea of oil on the beaches of California is for "anybody" a remarkable occurrence, and a reporter or newspaper which ignored it would, owing to the physical evidence widely available to direct experience, be obviously "managing the news." That is, if newsmaking results in published accounts considered by a multitude to differ from "what happened" as determined by their own event needs, the legitimacy of newsmaking as an objective enterprise is undermined. Of course, not all accidents become public events. Oil spills off the Gulf of Mexico, almost as large as the Santa Barbara spill, received far less coverage; similarly, the massive escape of nerve gas at Dugway Proving Ground[30] could easily be conceived as far more disastrous to the natural environment and to human life than any oil spill, yet again, relatively little coverage occurred.[31] All this attests to the fact that all events are socially constructed and their "newsworthiness" is not contained in their objective features.

Scandals

Scandals share features of both accidents and routine events but differ from both as well. A scandal involves an occurrence which becomes an event through the intentional activity of individuals (we call them "informers") who for one reason or another do not share the event-making strategies of the occurrence effectors. Like a routine event, the precipitating happening is intended and the event is promoted, but unlike a routine event, the promoting is not done by those who originally brought about the happening. In fact, the event's realization typically comes as a surprise to the original actors. Thus, Ronald Reagan deliberately paid no state income tax 1970-71, but did not expect, in so doing, to read about it in newspapers. Dita Beard did, we assume, write the notorious "ITT Memo," but again, did not envision it as a public event. (The ITT *issue* derives from an attempt by ITT to destroy the scandal by denying the precipitating occurrence.) A scandal requires the willing cooperation of at least one party having power and legitimacy which derive either from firsthand experience (the eyewitness) or position in the social structure (e.g., a "leaker" of memos or Pentagon papers). The more both circumstances are fulfilled, the greater the capacity to generate a scandal. Again, this capacity is disproportionately in the hands of élites, but their trusted hirelings are also strategically well situated. Like the accident, the scandal reveals normally hidden features of individual lives or institutional processes.

The My Lai massacre is one of the more dramatic examples of scandal. It is not a routine event in that those originally involved in making it happen—whether defined as the troops in the field or the president and generals—did not intend that the mass murder become a recorded phenomenon. The tortuous route the occurrence followed (it was twenty months becoming a public event) has been elucidated in some detail.[32] My Lai was originally reported as a successful, routine offensive against Viet Cong soldiers; only later was it transformed into a "massacre." In other scandals, high-status people "fink" on each other—as, for example, when political reformers expose "the machine," or when political leaders wage internecine war to eliminate opponents (e.g., the Fortas, Dodd, Goldfine scandals). Of course, scandals can also occur when statuses are more asymmetrical; it may have been a clerk who exposed Reagan; it was an Army corporal who exposed My Lai. Also, when the informer is of relatively low status and unsupported by a group with power, the scandal-making business can be quite arduous (e.g., My Lai) and often a complete failure. Frequently, an accident can stimulate a series of scandals, as in the instance of the Santa Barbara oil spill, and in the McCord and Dean testimony in the aftermath of the Watergate arrests.

Serendipity

A fourth type of event, the serendipity event, shares features of both the accident and the routine. The serendipity event has an underlying happening which is unplanned (as with accidents) but is promoted by the effector himself (as with routine events). Examples of the serendipitous event are hard to come by precisely because one of its features is that the effector/promoter

Table 14.1 Event Classificatory Scheme

	Happening Accomplished Intentionally	Happening Accomplished Not Intentionally
Promoted by effector	Routine	Serendipity
Promoted by informer	Scandal	Accident

disguises it to make it appear routine. Self-proclaimed heroes are perhaps a variant of those who effect serendipitous events: One inadvertently performs a given act which results in the accomplishment of some courageous and socially desired task. Thus, through self-promotion (or at least tacit approval), one converts an accident into a deliberate act.

Unlike the accident, the underlying happening in the serendipity event remains unobserved and perhaps unobservable for members of publics. Because the agent can transform the unintended happening into a routine event through his promotion activities, people are not given the kinds of information which accidents and scandals afford. Because serendipity events are difficult to differentiate from routine events, they are as irretrievable for sociological investigation as accidents are retrievable. They are the least sociologically useful of any event type.

By way of summary, Table 14.1 displays the four event types, distinguished by the degree to which their underlying happening is accomplished intentionally and by whether the occurrence effector or an informer does the promotion work.

Summary Discussion

Consistent with Gans's[33] urgings, we attempt a new departure for the study of news. We see media as reflecting not a world out there, but the practices of those having the power to determine the experience of others. Harold Garfinkel made a similar point about clinical records he investigated; rather than viewing an institution's records as standing ideally for something which happened, one can instead see in those records the organizational practices of people who make records routinely. Garfinkel concludes that there are "good organizational reasons" for bad clinical records. Following Garfinkel, our interest in their "badness" does not rest in spelling out the clinic's social organization.

We think that mass media should similarly be viewed as bad clinical records. Following Garfinkel, our interest in its "badness" does not rest in an opportunity for criticism and depiction of irony, but rather in the possibility of understanding how the product comes to look like it does, i.e., what the "good reasons" are. We advocate examining media for the event needs and the methods through which those with access come to determine the experience of publics. We can look for the methods through which ideological hegemony is accomplished by examining the records which are produced.

Seen in this way, one approach to mass media is to look not for reality, but for purposes which underlie the strategies of creating one reality instead of another. For the citizen to read the newspaper as a catalogue of the important happenings of the day, or for the social scientist to use the newspaper for uncritically selecting topics of study, is to accept as reality the political works by which events are constituted by those who happen to currently hold power. Only in the accident, and, secondarily, in the scandal, is that routine political work transcended to some significant degree, thereby allowing access to information which is directly hostile to those groups who typically manage public event making. Future research on media and on the dynamics of power would be strengthened by taking this "second face of power"[34] into consideration. More profoundly, sociologists who habitually take their research topics and conceptual constructs as they are made available through mass media and similar sources may wish to extricate their consciousnesses from the purposive activities of parties whose interests and event needs may differ from their own.

Notes

1. The term "public" throughout this essay is used in the sense John Dewey used it: a political grouping of individuals brought into being as a social unit through mutual recognition of common problems for which common solutions should be sought. Information thus does not merely *go to* publics, it *creates* them. See John Dewey, *The Public and Its Problems* (New York, Holt, Rinehart, 1927).

2. George Miller, Eugene Galanter, and Karl Pribram, *Plans and the Structure of Behavior* (New York, Holt, Rinehart & Winston, 1960).

3. Julius Roth, *Timetables: Structuring the Passage of Time in Hospital Treatment and Other Careers* (New York, Bobbs-Merrill, 1963).

4. Harold Garfinkel, *Studies in Ethnomethodology* (Englewood Cliffs, Prentice Hall, 1967).

5. Don Zimmerman and Melvin Pollner, "The Everyday World as Phenomenon," in Jack Douglas (ed.), *Understanding Everyday Life* (Chicago, Aldine, 1970), pp. 94-97.

6. Cf. Richard Appelbaum, "Social Mobility: A Study in the Reification of Sociological Concepts" (1973), Department of Sociology, University of California, Santa Barbara (mimeographed).

7. Schutz draws a similar parallel between the world of space and the world of time constituting the natural attitude of everyday life. Cf. Alfred Schutz, *Collected Papers*, Vol. I, Pt. III (The Hague, Martinus Nijhoff, 1966).

8. As we imply above, while members assume that meanings are shared, we view that sharedness as yet another accomplished feature of the process of creating events.

9. Aaron Cicourel makes an analogous argument with respect to the creation of a juvenile delinquent. A delinquent is constituted by a set of accounts produced by a series of law enforcement agencies motivated by the need to appear rational to others in the processing system. Any youth's activities will be made (through a course of accounting work) to tally with or violate some law. Thus, a delinquent is an accomplishment of a chain of processing agencies who need to do a "competent job for all practical purposes." That is, what the act, the person, (or event) "really is," is as it is attended to through members'

practical work. See his book, *The Social Organization of Juvenile Justice* (New York, Wiley, 1968). This view departs fundamentally from the gatekeeping theory of newswork, which sees the selfsame happening as acted upon by a series of newsworkers (cf. Tamotsu Shibutani, *Improvised News*, New York, Bobbs-Merrill, 1966). For a discussion of gatekeeping, see D. M. White, "The 'Gate Keeper': A Case Study in the Selection of News," and Walter Gieber, "News Is What Newspapermen Make It," in L. A. Dexter and D. M. White, *People, Society and Mass Communication* (New York, Free Press, 1964).

10. These agencies, as here presented, are generally consistent with Holsti's six "basic elements": source, encoding process, message, channel of transmission, recipient, decoding process. See Ole R. Holsti, *Content Analysis for the Social Sciences and Humanities* (Reading, Mass., Addison-Wesley, 1969), p. 24.

11. Cf. Daniel Boorstin, *The Image: A Guide to Pseudo-Events in America* (New York, Harper & Row, 1961).

12. Cf. Barbara Myerhoff, "The Revolution as a Trip: Symbol and Paradox," in Philip G. Altbach and Robert S. Laufer (eds.), *The New Pilgrims: Youth Protest in Transition* (New York, David McKay, 1972).

13. Our mention of policy statements by public figures raised the question of *lies* for readers of earlier drafts of this essay. Based on the principle that event creation universally stems from contextually constrained purposes, our schema does not make an objective distinction between telling a truth and telling a falsehood. For us, a lie is a meaning accomplished for purposes at hand, including those involved in having to deal with others. A lie to us is distinguishable by the fact that another party (observer) sees it as a deliberate move to effect a purpose done without respect for the conditions of an assumed, objective reality. This assumed lack of correspondence to reality is typically invoked when the second party has purposes contrary to the liar's. Lies, like any meanings, are thus created because they are "looked for" by the second party. When a liar is "caught"—that is, when he cannot persuade others that his promoted account corresponds to an objective reality—he attempts to handle the situation by (a) demonstrating that the second party was, in fact, looking for the lie, being "picky," or making a mountain out of a molehill; or (b) minimizing the effect of the objectivity assumption by selectively claiming inherent ambiguity in the present case, as expressed in the claims, "it all depends on how you look at it," or "if you knew what I knew at the time, you would see it as indeed corresponding to what is, to all intents and purposes, the truly relevant reality." A selective assertion of a subjective world thus become a resource like any other.

14. Breed, Gieber, and Tuchman have provided important insights into the assembling process. See Warren Breed, "Social Control in the Newsroom," *Social Forces* 33 (May 1955): 326-335; Gieber (1964) and "Across the Desk: A Study of 16 Telegraph Editors," *Journalism Quarterly* 43 (Fall 1956): 423-432; and Gaye Tuchman, "Objectivity as Strategic Ritual," *American Journal of Sociology* 77 (January 1972): 660-679, "News as Controlled Conflict and Controversy," New York, Department of Sociology, Queens College (mimeographed) (1972), and "Making News by Doing Work: Routinizing the Unexpected," *American Journal of Sociology* 79 (July 1973): 110-131.

15. Gaye Tuchman (1972), *op. cit.*

16. Cf. Thomas Wilson, "Conceptions of Interaction and Forms of Sociological Explanation," *American Sociological Review* 35 (August 1970): 697-710.

17. A. J. Liebling, in *Mink and Red Herring: The Wayward Pressman's Casebook* (Garden City, Doubleday, 1949), provides anecdotal illustrations of the occurrence of such plots and related chicanery. See also almost any issue of *Chicago Journalism Review* or *(More): A Journalism Review*, or Robert Cirino, *Don't Blame the People: How the News Media Use Bias, Distortion and Censorship to Manipulate Public Opinion* (Los Angeles, Diversity Press, 1970).

18. That is, following the ethnomethodological instruction, we have heretofore attempted to suspend our belief in a normative order. However, to extend our analysis to a

common-sensically useful approach to news, and to provide tools of concise description for mundane, practical work, we enter the "attitude of everyday life" in this section of the essay.

19. Roger Manela, in "The Classification of Events in Formal Organizations" (Ann Arbor: Institute of Labor and Industrial Relations, mimeographed, 1971), in an analogous typology of events, treats events as objective phenomena which are categorized in terms of how well they fit ongoing formal organization rules and routines.

20. Cf. Gaye Tuchman (1972), *op. cit.*

21. Cf. Harvey L. Molotch, "Oil in Santa Barbara and Power in America," *Sociological Inquiry* 40 (Winter 1970): 131-144.

22. Gaye Tuchman (1972),*op. cit.*

23. Cf. Harvey Molotch and Marilyn Lester, "Accidents, Scandals and Routines" (1972, presented at the American Sociological Association meetings, New Orleans).

24. Cf. Barbara Myerhoff (1972), *op. cit.*

25. Cf. Kirkpatrick Sale, "Myths as Eternal Truths" *(More): A Journalism Review* 3 (June 1973): 3-5. This situation eventually changed in reference to anti-war activity, because the position and event needs of the American press and a substantial portion of the élite became sympathetic with the movement. Thus, the event needs of a segment of the élite came to correspond to those of the protesters; accordingly, the war became the issue, not the protest itself.

26. In response to a complaint that his newspaper was holding back an important story, a reporter for the *Los Angeles Times* wrote Molotch the following defence: "We have not run an extensive story on _____ because of the judgment of my editors that because the _____ case has not become an issue of major proportions enveloping the campus community, we might be accused of creating an issue if we give it full-blown treatment at this point in time. It is not a case of holding back information, but the concern that my editors have for trying to avoid the situation where something becomes a major issue *because* a large daily newspaper has written about it at length" (personal communication to the author, January 8, 1971).

27. What is or is not a transparently nonobjective technique changes historically. Fishman (in Forthcoming, *News of the World: What Happened and Why*, unpublished doctoral dissertation, Department of Sociology, University of California, Santa Barbara) details how the use of interview in straight news came as a radical departure from objective news coverage. The technique was introduced as part of the yellow journalism movement and was denounced by the more traditional papers.

28. Harvey L. Molotch (1970), *op. cit.*

29. It is precisely these forms of events which tend to be excluded in community power research using the decisional technique (cf. Edward Banfield, *Political influence*, New York, Free Press, 1962). By uncritically accepting those stories which appear in newspapers over an extensive time period as corresponding to the basic local political conflicts, use of the decisional technique guarantees that only those matters on which the élites do internally disagree will emerge as study topics. Thus, pluralistic findings are guaranteed through the mode of case selection.

30. Seymour Hirsch, "On Uncovering the Great Nerve Gas Cover-Up," *Ramparts* 3 (July 1969): 12-18.

31. Marilyn Lester, "Toward a Sociology of Public Events" (1971, unpublished master's paper, University of California, Santa Barbara).

32. See *New York Times*, November 20, 1969; *The Times* (London), November 20, 1969.

33. Herbert Gans, "The Famine in American Mass Communications Research: Comments on Hirsch, Tuchman and Gecas," *American Journal of Sociology* 77 (January 1972): 697-705.

34. Cf. Peter Bachrach and Morton Baratz, "The Two Faces of Power," *American Political Science Review* 56 (Dec. 1962): 947-952; and Murray Edelman, *The Symbolic Uses of Politics* (Urbana, University of Illinois Press, 1964).

CHAPTER 15

News and Nonevents

Making the Visible Invisible

Mark Fishman

Some happenings in the world become public events. Others are condemned to obscurity as the personal experience of a handful of people. The mass media, and in particular news organizations, make all the difference. This study examines a crucial part of the newsmaking process—the routine work of beat reporters—that determines what becomes a public event and what becomes a nonevent. I will show that reporters' "sense of events," their methods for seeing the newsworthiness of occurrences, are based on schemes of interpretation originating from and used by agency officials within the institutions beat reporters cover. Nonevents are specific happenings that are seen as "out of character" within the institutional settings in which they occur. They are treated as "illegitimate occurrences" because they violate or challenge the procedural basis on which all routine business is transacted in the setting. To seriously entertain these occurrences as potential news events would force journalists to question their own methods for detecting news-worthy events. In short, what routine newswork systematically excludes from public view are just those occurrences that might challenge the legitimacy of the institutions reporters depend on for news.

From J. S. Ettema and D. C. Whitney (Eds.), *Individuals in Mass Media Organizations: Creativity and Constraint*, 1982, pp. 219-240. Copyright © 1982 Sage Publications, Inc.

Theoretical Background

Borrowing from ethnomethodological, phenomenological, and symbolic interactionist perspectives,[1] several studies within the past ten years have taken a fresh look at news and the work that produces it (Molotch and Lester, 1973, 1974; Lester, 1975, 1980; Tuchman, 1972, 1976, 1978b; Fishman, 1980). What sets these studies apart from earlier approaches is their primary focus on news as a practical accomplishment. The practical accomplishment perspective says that journalists' routine methods for producing news—that is, the very process of "newsgathering"—constructs an image of reality. In this view, news is neither a reflection nor a distortion of reality because either of these characterizations implies that news *can* record what is "out there." News stories, if they reflect anything, reflect the practices of the workers in the organizations that produce news.

Some time ago, Walter Gieber (1964) made the point that "news is what newspapermen make it." What he and most of the traditional literature argued was that journalists, operating under newsroom norms, professional standards, and the deadlines and story quotas of their news organization, make crucial decisions involving the selection of which events to cover and which stories to print (Breed, 1955; Gieber, 1956, 1964; White, 1964; Stark, 1962; Galtung and Ruge, 1973; Epstein, 1973; Sigelman, 1973).

But the idea that news is a practical accomplishment implies much more than this. In recent years, several studies have made the point that prior to any selection of events or stories, journalists must determine what constitutes an event, where events can be found, and how events can be told as stories (Molotch and Lester, 1974; Tuchman, 1978b; Fishman, 1980). All these matters, too, are accomplishments. Something must be done to see and to say that an event "happened" and that it was "timely" or "important." The world is not already organized into discrete events waiting to be noticed and selected by reporters. Nor do events have intrinsic qualities (such as "newsworthiness," "importance") that tell journalists how to deal with them (Lester, 1980).[2] Rather, events, and the qualities associated with them, are constituted in the process of their being noticed (Molotch and Lester, 1974). "What's going on here" or "what happened today" are things formed in the process of making an account (Tuchman, 1976; Fishman, 1980).

Molotch and Lester (1974) make the point that happenings in the world become potential events for the news only insofar as there is someone with an interest in noticing them, someone with a practical concern about telling a story. In this context, Molotch and Lester make a useful distinction between "mere occurrences" and "public events." Mere occurrences are happenings that participants or observers attend to during an ongoing activity. But they are not necessarily happenings about which one is interested in formulating an account for outsiders to the scene. Public events, however, are those occurrences about which accounts are constructed for the consumption of some wider public, the widest public of all being the audience of mass media news. The news media transform mere occurrences into public events, thereby making them "a resource for public discourse" (Molotch and Lester, 1975). The world outside an individual's firsthand experience is a "public reality" constructed by those who have the power to promote mere occurrences as public events. Occurrences not so promoted are lost to public consciousness: They remain either the "private troubles" of individuals powerless to make news or the little-known workings of the powerful who choose not to make certain things news.[3]

To be sure, events are formulated and accounts are made for strategic purposes. But Molotch and Lester's analysis passes over a fundamental question for the practical accomplishment perspective: How are journalists first able to perceive something as an event? Newsworkers must have ways of seeing meaningful chunks of activity in the happenings going on around them. They must have ways of delimiting the boundaries of events. How journalists routinely do these things is the subject of this study.

To examine the issue of how journalists see events, we must first consider what an event is. Events are interpreted phenomena, things organized in thought, talk, and action. People employ schemes of interpretation to carve events out of a stream of experience. Any scheme of interpretation, if it is to be useful in newswork, must allow reporters to pick events out of some ongoing activity and allow them to see events in relation to one another. That is, any scheme of interpretation that will be useful to a professional storyteller must enable that person to structure his or her experience in terms of a beginning, a middle, and an end. It must enable him or her to see a "chain of events"; that is, to see the overall action in terms of its phases with one phase leading into the next. Schemes of interpretation that do this will be called "phase structures."[4] Shortly, we will examine the specific phase structures that beat reporters use.

When we examine journalists' routine methods for perceiving news events, we also discover what they routinely do not or will not see as news events. In other words, nonevents are by-products of schemes of interpretation (or phase structures). By a nonevent, I do not simply mean any happening or "mere occurrence" that goes unpublicized. We can think of nonevents as a special class of mere occurrences, that is, those that are or could be conceived as events worthy of public attention.

Since events are interpreted phenomena, an event is always an event *for* somebody or some collectivity who has come to define a complex of activities as a meaningful entity. Because events are part of actors' definitions of the situation, and because these definitions are not always harmonious, all parties to some ongoing activity can differ considerably over "what's happening here"; that is, what are the "real events"? Nonevents are born in such a conflict.

Individuals or collectivities who do not share the same schemes of interpretation can see different events in the same displays of behavior. From one point of view, a behavioral display can be "obviously a significant event," while from another point of view it can either go unnoticed or be noticed but deemed "trivial" or "a fragment of something else." Moreover, one can notice that others who were present did not see an event; that is, for them it was a nonevent. The term nonevent, then, denotes that which cannot be seen under a certain scheme of interpretation, but can be seen under a different one. It is a relational concept referring to a discontinuity between perspectives.

The concept of nonevent should be distinguished from the notion of "news selectivity" that is frequently employed in the literature on news bias (Lang and Lang, 1953, 1958; White, 1964; Gieber, 1956, 1964; Oestgaard, 1965; Robinson, 1970) to explain why journalists do not report some events. While that too is my purpose, I part ways with the latter concept in its assumption that all events (both the reported and unreported) are objective, unformulated entities "out there" in the world and that they are given in perception and available to any competent, clear-headed observer. Consequently, most sociologists studying news bias have assumed that they (and perhaps a few other select social scientists) are objective enough to recognize all the "really real" events, against which they can measure the extent and pattern of selective reporting.

I am arguing that nonevents are not the "pure" events screened out by journalists. It makes no sense to speak of a "pure," unformulated event. Molotch and Lester (1973: 1) term the assumption that news can (or ought to) reflect some "pure" reality "out there" the *objectivity assumption*. As a methodological strategy Molotch and Lester (1974: 111) advocate dropping this assumption in order to study news not as a distortion of a reality that could be reflected but as a document that reflects the work of news promoters and journalists, those who have the power to construct reality for a public (see also Tuchman, 1978a). Following that strategy, this study examines the practices of beat reporters and the practices of those they depend on for their "raw data" for news stories. These practices are viewed as methods for constructing public accounts. These methods ought to tell us why journalists and news sources formulate some mere occurrences as news events, while other occurrences, although formulated by somebody as an event, become a nonevent.

Method

The data for this study come from research conducted in a small California city in 1973-1974. Two kinds of participant observation were done. First, I worked for seven months on an alternative weekly newspaper reporting about the affairs of city hall and county government. This, my first experience as a journalist, allowed me to observe beat reporters working for other media in the community. More important, my experiences as an apprentice journalist provided data that no veteran newsworker could have told me and that is only clear to the novice: the invisible background knowledge one has to know in the first place to determine "what's going on" in a setting in order to "see" news in it. Thus, my fieldnotes from that period were, in part, a kind of diary reflecting not only what I saw of the work of other beat reporters but also my observations of myself learning to report news.

The second phase of my research was conducted inside the city's major newspaper. Over a three-month period, I observed the daily work routines of three journalists who covered the city hall, county government, and police-court beats. I shadowed each of these reporters as they moved through their workdays, tape recording wherever possible their interactions with other reporters, editors, and news sources. Interviews were also conducted both before and after observations of their work.

Exposure to Occurrences: The News Net

To understand how nonevents arise in newswork, we must first examine just what part of the world journalists come in contact with, and then we must look at the schemes of interpretation newsworkers employ to identify newsworthy events.

Happenings that become news must first become objects of experience to journalists. Journalists do not look for news everywhere at all times, but follow routines of coverage that locate reporters spatially and temporally in a determinate pattern, what Tuchman (1976, 1977, 1978b) terms a "news net." News organizations favor coverage of occurrences taking place during weekday business hours, since that is when the media allocate the vast majority of their newsgathering resources (Tuchman, 1977: 46, 1978b). Moreover, they favor coverage of prescheduled activities (news conferences, trials, legislative sessions) because these allow news personnel more control over their work (Tunstall, 1971: 24-30; Bagdikian, 1971: 97; Epstein, 1973: 103-105; Tuchman, 1973: 123-124).

News organizations also spatially allocate their newsgathering resources according to a system of beats and bureaus that locates reporters almost exclusively in legitimated institutions of society (Sigal, 1973: 119-130; Roshco, 1975: 62; Fishman, 1980; Tuchman, 1978b). Elsewhere (Fishman, 1980: 27-53) I have shown that the beat system includes within it a routine round of coverage activities that routes reporters through a small number of governmental agencies. Inside these agencies, reporters follow a path that takes them to a few "key" locations that are seen as focal points of information (such as master files, press officers, and meetings). Thus, on the newspaper I studied this meant that crime was covered through the police and court bureaucracies. Local politics were covered through the meetings of the city council, county board of supervisors, and a host of other commissions, committees, and departments. Even nature was covered through a formally constituted organization (the U.S. Forestry Service). Whatever the sphere of human activities or natural occurrences (as long as it was covered through a beat) the newsworker knew it through officials and authorities, their files and their meetings. The round systematically exposed reporters to settings in which only formally organized transactions of official business appeared. Thus, the temporal and spatial organization of the news net is institutional-

ized in a beat round that steers reporters away from collectivities that are not
formally constituted or bureaucratically organized (Fishman, 1980: 32-46).
Community organizations and other informal groups, with members who
have other jobs during normal business hours, meet on evenings and weekends when most reporters are off work. Grassroots social movements who
lack the resources of press agentry, have few if any meetings, have no formal
leadership structure, and have no "headquarters" are virtually impossible to
cover according to standard news practices (Tuchman, 1977, 1978b; Gitlin,
1980).

Following the round ensures that reporters will be in a position of
exposure to occurrences on a beat. But it is quite another matter for reporters
to know what to make of the activities to which they are exposed. Things
going on right under a reporter's nose may not be noticed and thus not
become news because the reporter does not have the means to see them as
"something," as an event.

Seeing Events: Phase Structures

What kinds of schemes of interpretation do reporters employ on beats
to understand what is going on and to find events in complicated displays
of activities available in talk, gestures, and documents? My ethnographic
evidence indicates that journalists see events by using the same phase
structures that beat agency officials use to formulate their own and others'
activities as events.

Within organizational settings (whether or not there is a reporter covering them), complexes of activities are organized into events on the basis of a
few specific phase structures. When stepping into a new beat, the novice
reporter is confronted with an established domain of "typical events." For
example, on the police beat, which included the city and county police and
felony court, typical events were such things as "arrests," "sentencings,"
"preliminary hearings," "plea bargains," and "arraignments." These typifications were not encountered as a loose collection of event categories. They
were seen as interrelated in a highly structured scheme: Typical events were
organized along a timeline or career path. Thus, the police reporter saw crime
news events as organized around "legal cases," each of which progressed
through a fixed sequence of phases: "the arrest," "the preliminary hearing,"
"arraignment," "readiness and settlement hearing" (plea bargaining), "pro-
bation review," and finally "the sentencing." The entire sequence of events
is a phase structure, each phase defining a possible news event. A phase
structure portrays streams of interwoven activities as an object moving
through a series of stages, or as a case moving through a career.

This manner of picturing events and reporting on them is not restricted
to formally organized collectivities. In everyday conversation, one can present a complex of activities (e.g., "What I did on my summer vacation") in a
similar mode ("First, I went to Boston and saw some close friends, then I flew
to . . . "). The formulation of phase structures in everyday (nonbureaucratic)

settings tends to be open ended, something that can emerge in conversation. The names of each phase of action (the terminology of events) and the number of phases (how far back the chain of events begins, how recently it ends, and how much "detail" goes in between) can be formulated in a variety of ways, depending on the purposes of the speaker, what the speaker thinks hearers already know, the dynamics of the conversation, and a number of other contextual matters.

However, phase structures that reporters encounter in the agencies that they cover on their beat are formally fixed and prespecified. In these bureaucratic phase structures, the sequential order of phases, the number of phases, their names, where they begin and end, the duration of time between each phase—all these are standardized because they are *made to happen* by bureaucrats following "proper" agency procedures. Bureaucratic phase structures are organizationally produced and organizationally enforced. For agency workers, a bureaucratic phase structure is not merely a scheme of interpretation; it is used to produce the case and to move it through a sequence of stages. It is a scheme for doing as well as a scheme for seeing. It continually informs workers "what the case looks like when it is done right" and "what I have to do in order to make it look like I have done it right." A bureaucratic phase structure is employed like a road map to produce the proper career of a case, and it is used as a scheme of interpretation to see the results of that work as the proper career of the case it was supposed to have been all along.

Despite the power and authority of legitimated institutions to impose an official scheme of interpretation on the activities taking place within their jurisdiction, it is important to note that bureaucratic phase structures are but one perspective on the chain of events associated with any actual case. For example, an individual taken into the criminal justice system as a "suspect" would most certainly organize his or her own experiences differently than the way an agency official or a journalist would. Events for the "suspect" could include such matters as the betrayal to police by a friend-turned-informer, the whole gamut of experience in jail, the formulation of a legal defense with an attorney, and so on. These kinds of "personal" or nonbureaucratic phase structure have received considerable attention in the sociological literature on "careers," both deviant and nondeviant. Most notably, Goffman's studies of "moral careers" (1961, 1963) and Roth's work on "timetables" (1963) show the way in which clients, patients, and prisoners organize a set of experiences under institutional and noninstitutional conditions.

Although alternative formulations of activities may abound in the places reporters cover, the journalist's sense of events comes not from clients' oral histories (as it did for Goffman and Roth), but from official case histories. Journalists simply do not regularly expose themselves to "unofficial" interpretive schemes. For example, the police reporter steered clear of suspects, victims, and their families on his round. The only routine occasion in which the reporter was exposed to the suspect's version of events was during formal court hearings. But these are settings in which the suspect's version necessarily has been reformulated through an attorney to fit the legal-bureaucratic

definition of events. In general, reporters in courtrooms will seek out lawyers, not their clients, as news sources. Why, then, do newsworkers so readily
adopt a bureaucratic definition of events?

As already pointed out, beat reporters systematically and exclusively
expose themselves through their rounds to formally organized settings that
present them with bureaucratically packaged activities. Officials produce
these activities so that they are seen as events composing some larger
bureaucratic phase structure. Without reference to this intended phase structure, no observer could understand what agency personnel were doing at
any given moment of producing the case and its movement through a career.
Thus, reporters must learn bureaucratic phase structures when they learn
how to cover their beats. They employ these idealizations as schemes for
interpreting bureaucratic activities, just as the officials they observe employ
these idealizations to produce what the reporter sees. If the reporter does not
have cognizance of the specific phase structures of the beat, the reporter
cannot understand at the simplest level what is happening there, what
officials mean by what they are doing. Lack of understanding this basic could
be seen as serious journalistic incompetence. After a few stories betraying
this "ignorance," the reporter would be transferred off the beat. For the
journalist, bureaucratic phase structures are socially sanctioned schemes of
interpretation.

The Uses of Phase Structures

Bureaucratic phase structures are of much wider use to journalists than
the mere passive understanding of "what's going on" within the agencies
covered on a beat. In particular, bureaucratic phase structures enable newsworkers routinely to solve two practical problems in their work: (a) How is
the reporter to know when something "new" is happening? and, (b) how is
the reporter to distinguish "important" from "trivial" events? Let us consider
each of these.

Seeing "Newness"

News is considered a highly perishable commodity (Park, 1940: 676;
Tuchman, 1973: 118; Roshco, 1975: 10-11). One aspect of the newsworthiness
of stories is their timeliness. News must be published recently with respect
to the occurrence of an event. But what is meant by "the occurrence of an
event"? After all, most objects of news coverage are "occurring" all the time.
A defendant in the criminal justice system is an "active case" whether
standing before a judge, sitting in jail, or conferring with a lawyer. Antitrust
suits develop over a period of several years through a succession of investigations, private negotiations, and court hearings. Legislative issues can
continue over months and years of public debate, backroom agreements, and
official voting. Even so-called spot news events like floods, plane crashes, oil
spills, and nerve gas leaks can take months before a "full" account of what

took place surfaces. How does the journalist know at what points in time these continuing activities warrant a story?

Bureaucratic phase structures solve this problem because they provide the resource for reporters to sense when something "new" is happening. That is, an event "occurs" when a case crosses a boundary between phases, when it moves into a new phase of its bureaucratic career. This movement provides the occasion for writing a news story, although by no means does it guarantee that one will be written. When a case enters its next phase, a news story is warranted only in the sense that the case's official change in status justifies for reporters and their superiors the coverage of the story at that point in time. Consider this routine crime story which I saw formulated on the police beat:

Woman Pleads in Shootout Case

Martha Mungan pleaded guilty today to a charge stemming from a predawn shootout last December that left her wounded and her common-law husband dead from police bullets.

Mrs. Mungan pleaded guilty to one count of threatening and interfering with police officers, and a second count was dismissed.

Her sentencing was set for March 22 in the court of Superior Judge Lloyd Bennett.

Police were called to Mrs. Mungan's home at 410-B Oceano Ave. last December by Rodney Charles Harvey, her common-law husband, during a family fight. In the ensuing gunfight, Mrs. Mungan was wounded and Harvey was killed when he retrieved the pistols and shot at police.

The reporter who was to write this article had been sitting in a courtroom looking for news. He suddenly knew that the court proceedings he had been viewing constituted "an event" as soon as he recognized that the defendant was Martha Mungan,[5] that a plea bargain was being discussed, and that "this must be the Martha Mungan case in its next official phase" (the readiness and settlement hearing). On returning to the newsroom, he told his city editor what happened and said he preferred to wait until the sentencing in four weeks to write about the case. The city editor, however, told him to write about it now, because by doing a piece on her guilty plea the future story on her sentencing would be a "follow-up story."

The Martha Mungan case was only "an event" each time it resurfaced in the courts to enter a next phase in its judicial career. For all practical (journalistic) purposes, the case was invisible in between these resurfacings. Reporters will not write about a case at any point in time; they need a "news peg" or "news hook" to hang their story on (Crouse, 1974: 115, 240; but see Goldenberg, 1975). Bureaucratic phase structures provide these pegs and hooks. The agencies covered on a beat establish for journalists their very concept of timeliness.

Moreover, journalists can plan the reporting of future news stories around bureaucratically defined news pegs. With the publication of successive stories about a case, newsworkers establish for themselves and for their audience a sense of continuing news and follow-up stories. Bureaucratic phase structures create the possibility of continuing news and, at the same time, enable preplanned coverage.

Seeing "Importance"

Over and above the use of phase structures to occasion news stories, reporters employ these interpretive schemes in another important way. Once journalists have adopted a bureaucratic frame of reference, they possess a convenient means for spotting the highlights of events. That is, bureaucratic phase structures contain implicit *schemes of relevance*. A "scheme of relevance" is a scheme of interpretation that is used for deciding the relative importance of various perceived and interpreted objects. Two such schemes of relevance emerged from my observations of beat reporting in local government: the police, the courts, city hall, and county government. One scheme focused journalists' attention on the official dispositions of cases; the other focused their attention on policy (as opposed to administrative) deliberations among officials.

One of the striking features of bureaucratic phase structures is their consistent orientation toward "the disposition of the case." Each official phase of a case is procedurally organized around some decision to be made or action to be taken that "settles" the case for the time being; that usually means sending it to its next phase, if there is one. This disposition of the case is seen as the "key" or "central" activity within each phase. The reason for this is not hard to understand. Insofar as journalists (or bureaucrats) see something as a case moving through a phase structure, then their interest is bound to focus on the official outcome of the case since bureaucratic cases only exist so that they can be properly settled.

The Martha Mungan case illustrates this. After encountering the case in court, the police reporter told me he was "very interested in what would happen to her." His primary interest was couched in terms of her "ultimate" disposition in the court system, that is, the future sentencing. His immediate practical interest was defined by her most recent disposition in the plea-bargaining stage, that is, the results of the bargaining. In classic journalistic style, the lead sentence of the reporter's article stated, along with some background information, the "most important" aspect of the event, namely, its disposition. It was only at the end of the story that something other than the disposition of the case was mentioned.

The phenomenon of focusing on the dispositions of cases was not restricted to the police beat. On the city hall and county government beats, the key activities reported were the formal legislative dispositions of issues, which usually meant the results of voting in meetings. Pleading guilty to interfering with a police officer, getting sentenced to two years in prison, voting down a raise in the property tax, and passing a new loitering ordinance are all bureaucratically appropriate dispositions *and* they are the stuff of which routine news stories are made.

All other features of these kinds of events are of secondary importance. They become the "details" that are defined by and revolve around the "central" fact of the case's actual disposition. The bargaining process that produced the guilty plea, the judge's lecture to the sentenced prisoner, the defendant's reason for "interfering" with the police, the arguments for and against the legislative issue, the behind-the-scenes lobbying that arranged the voting—these are all "details" that embellish the "basic event." By focusing on bureaucratically appropriate dispositions in their everyday reports, journalists' stories leave invisible the agency procedures and social conditions that give rise to these dispositions. In this sense, routine news stories implicitly support the status quo by taking for granted these "background" factors. The report of Martha Mungan's guilty plea renders the procedure of plea bargaining unproblematic by obscuring it. Even less visible are the social conditions of Martha Mungan's life (as a ghetto resident) that surrounded the incident that made her into a judicial case in the first place.

The point is not that such "background" factors are never reported but that they are rarely given attention. When they are highlighted, they are not published as routine news but "human interest stories," "news analysis," and "editorial opinion." In short, what is written outside a bureaucratic scheme of relevance is "soft news," not "hard news." [6]

Besides the dispositional aspect of cases, there is another, equally important bureaucratically defined scheme of relevance based on an orientation toward "policy" versus "administrative" matters in bureaucratic work. The policy-administrative scheme of relevance derives from a fundamental "political division of labor" in governmental work: Legislative or executive bodies deal with ("ought to deal with") policy matters, while an administrative staff deals with ("ought to deal with") administrative matters. Policy matters are considered "political decisions" (matters of opinion) of widespread importance that provide guidelines for the conduct of bureaucrats in the form of work instructions and the conduct of citizens in the form of laws and taxes. Administrative matters are considered "technical decisions," matters of professional problem solving, which are made in the implementation of policy decisions.

Bureaucratic work is self-consciously organized in these terms. The policy-administrative distinction provides an orientation principle by which decision-making authority and bureaucratic work is distributed or delegated. As such, it provides participants in bureaucratic settings with procedures for organizing, displaying, and recognizing "proper" governmental work. These procedures include:

1. If the business before us is an administrative matter, and this is a policy-making setting, then "rubber-stamp" the matter.
2. If the business before us is a policy question, and this is an administrative setting, then refer the matter to a policy-making body.
3. Serious questions about administrative matters should be taken up outside policy-making settings.

The distinction between policy and administrative business is so well known around institutions of government that it is normally taken for granted. Both the individuals who produce formal governmental business, in files or in meetings, and the journalists who cover these files and meetings employ the distinction as a means for deciding what matters of business are "important" and what are "trivial." For example, on every formal agenda for city and county meetings there were items of business that reporters would know in advance to focus on as potential newsworthy policy matters, while other agenda items were known in advance to be "merely" administrative matters on the agenda for technical reasons. To distinguish the newsworthy from the trivial agenda matters, these reporters were relying on the bureaucratically defined policy-administrative distinction. The actual determination of whether any given agenda item was "policy" or "administrative" was an ad hoc decision for reporters, primarily depending on the way the item was presented in the agenda, any previous experience the reporter had with the matter, and the way local officials were talking about it prior to the formal meeting. Shortly, we shall see an example of how the policy versus administrative distinction can lead to nonevents.

Nonevents

Bureaucratic phase structures serve as schemes of interpretation and relevance that are definitive of news events. By implication, these schemes also define what activities within the reporter's beat territory are nonevents. To explicate the nature of journalistic nonevents, I will present two rather typical cases in which reporters "saw" no event, while others within the same setting were clearly trying to formulate such an event. Both cases reveal that nonevents are happenings that are seen as "out of character" in the social settings in which they occur. Reporters, and others familiar with the routine business transacted in a given setting, ignore a nonevent because if it were attended to as a reasonable occurrence, the nonevent would call into question the procedural basis on which all routine business is transacted and would make problematic reporters' routine methods for identifying "important" events. Because they disrupt the "normal" flow of business-as-usual, nonevents reveal the taken-for-granted background features of social settings that reporters depend on for their sense of events.

Illustration 1: The Invisible Crank

In the course of its annual budget hearings, the county board of supervisors was considering next year's budget for the Sheriff's Department. This agenda item followed a prescribed sequence of activities: First, the chief administrative officer and the auditor-controller read their recommendations, then the board questioned the two bureaucrats, then the floor was opened to opponents and proponents, and finally the supervisors debated and voted on the issue.

During the "public input" phase, the speeches focused on whether the administrator was justified in recommending fewer new deputy sheriff positions than the county sheriff had asked for. The Sheriff's Department argued for a larger force so as to keep up with population increases. A taxpayer's group argued that new positions were unnecessary if one correctly calculated a "service ratio," the number of officers per 1,000 inhabitants. Then a young woman took her turn at the public podium to say that she felt any consideration of funding the Sheriff's Department was "shameful." She recounted an incident in which she had been selling wares from a pushcart when a sheriff's car pulled up to her. Two deputies stepped out and asked what she was doing and if she had a license. She protested that she did not know she needed one.

At this point in the story, the chairman of the board of supervisors interrupted and told the woman to come to the point or give up the floor. She simply continued: The sheriff's deputies had ordered her into their patrol car, and when she refused she was handcuffed and pulled in. When she insisted on knowing why she was being accosted, she was subjected to verbal abuse. At the sheriff's station, she was bound hand and foot and left in a room for several hours. Once again, the chairman interrupted and asked the woman to please leave the podium. She ignored him and went on to say that the sheriffs finally released her with no explanation, but that they would not accept complaints she tried to lodge afterward. By this point in her presentation, the woman was upset and angry. Again, the chairman broke in, said that they had heard enough, and told her she would be removed from the room if she insisted on staying at the podium. The woman quietly left.

From the point of view of those present, the woman's talk was so out of character with the budget proceedings that her presentation could only be "bizarre." Throughout her speech, no one in the room maintained eye contact with her; some people demonstrably showed their uninvolvement by doodling, reading, or conversing with others, and others clearly indicated their impatience by rolling their eyes, smiling, or making jokes. At the press table, all the reporters acted as if the woman's talk signaled a "time out." Reporters stopped taking notes; soon one journalist left the room, while others started up conversations about unrelated matters. Attention to the meeting returned as soon as the woman left the podium.

The incident was not reported in any news medium. It was a nonevent, not in the sense that it was never seen, but in the sense that journalists considered it "not worth seeing." It never occurred to reporters that it could be a newsworthy event. It could only be an uncomfortable time out, a "snag" in the flow of the meeting. Why?

After all, the speaker was not incoherent, nor was her argument, taken on its own terms, senseless or irrelevant. But instead of speaking to the issues of "service ratios" and "tax cuts," the woman spoke of a corrupt law enforcement agency unworthy of any public support. What she proposed was "unreasonable" because it was not among the set of alternatives procedurally prescribed for the board to entertain in budget hearings. Moreover, the woman was not, and made no pretense to be, speaking from a structural position of interest: She represented no formally constituted group that fit into the constellation of interests appropriate to the issue. To entertain her talk as appropriate to the occasion, those present would have had to break the procedural bounds of the budget session in order to take on a wider political perspective from which one could render as problematic the issue of any funding for the Sheriff's Department.

Illustration 2: The Invisible Controversy

At a city council meeting, a "routine" agenda item came up, titled "Recommendation for contract award: Bid No. 943—one three-wheeled street sweeper, diesel powered, to lowest bidder, Boulder Beach Machine Company, in total amount of $17,623.20." The public works director had placed the item on the agenda. Matters of this sort, in which a department head requests approval to purchase equipment after competitive bidding, are normally rubber-stamped by the council.

A council member began by pointedly asking the public works director why he was replacing the old gasoline street sweeper with a more expensive diesel one. The director responded that the more expensive vehicle would last longer and consume less fuel. Two other council members joined with the first to press the original question. In doing so, they also seemed to be implying that the director's motives were suspect. Soon a controversy had taken shape, with three council members defending the director, three questioning him, and one refraining from the debate.

It was apparent to the four reporters at the press table and to others present that this was not merely a dispute over a street sweeper. One side was implying incompetence or venality on the director's part; the other side was asserting that the whole matter was overblown and that it was not the council's business to embroil itself in the details of staff operations. The longer the controversy was kept alive, the more the issue became a question of confidence in a department head. After 20 minutes of increasingly bitter debate, the council voted four to three that the director should return next week with more information.

During the debate, the four members of the press showed increasing signs of impatience with the proceedings. At first the reporters stopped taking notes, then they began to show disapproval to each other, and finally they made derisive jokes about the controversy. This was considered a "stupid debate" over a "trivial matter" unworthy of everyone's time and energy.

Although the incident did not go entirely unreported, one city hall reporter gave it only a brief mention. It was placed toward the end of a long story that cited several "miscellaneous" items of council business: "In other matters . . . the City Council voted 4-3 to continue until next week the recommendations of Public Works Director R. D. Dolan to purchase a diesel-powered street sweeper." This one-sentence report, the only mention of the incident in any news medium, rendered the controversy invisible.

Even though at the time of the incident I was sitting at the press table as a reporter making derisive comments about the "foolishness" of the council along with the other journalists, later it occurred to me how this controversy could be seen as an "important event" in city hall. The controversy explicitly dealt with whether it was appropriate for the council to embroil itself in the "details" of its staff's "administrative decisions." That is, *the controversy rendered problematic the policy-administrative scheme of relevance* discussed earlier. This was a debate over whether the council was going to abide by that traditional distinction. Three council members were challenging the underlying political analysis of government embodied in the policy-administrative scheme: that power is held by elected policymakers who, in turn, delegate authority to a professional staff to implement their decisions. Such an analysis contrasts with alternative views that power is held by an economic elite that manipulates official decision making, or that power is held by bureaucrats and technicians who form a technocracy that runs government. By reference to these alternative schemes, I could see the debate as "significant," "relevant," and "newsworthy."

But the controversy was a nonevent for the newsworkers at the press table. The incident was "a waste of time" because it was "an administrative matter" that "ought to have been rubber-stamped." It prevented other "more important policy matters" on the agenda from being considered. Thus, reporters could not see the controversy as a sign of the council's brewing dissatisfaction over who, in fact, was running city government (elected officials or technocrats). This was invisible because the means by which reporters oriented to the meeting in order to sort out the "important" from the "trivial" was also the very topic of the controversy. For the journalists to have taken that topic as a serious issue would have meant calling into question some of their basis procedures for interpreting routine governmental activities. Newsworkers do not readily part with their familiar methods of event interpretation—methods that make coverage of the beat territory possible in the first place.

Discussion

There is a good deal of similarity between the two cases I have described. In both nonevents, the reporters noticed things going on, but ignored them by taking a time out and pointedly showing their disapproval. Even though they literally "saw" something, all they saw was a moral character: These were occurrences that "did not deserve reporting." They were unnewsworthy in the strongest sense. The reporters never considered them as candidates for news. It is not that the journalists weighed their relative newsworthiness against other events, and then rejected the nonevents as not newsworthy enough. Rather, the two incidents were events that never had a chance. As soon as they were encountered, the reporters knew to cease paying attention to them as serious candidates for news. They were unpublishable because they were "illegitimate events" that did not belong as topics in the territory (setting) in which they occurred.[7] To publish an illegitimate event would be "unprofessional." If the city council becomes embroiled in a dispute over an administrative matter, it would be "misleading" to cover it "as if" it were another plausible argument in the debate. In short, to the reporter nonevents have the quality of being morally seen but professionally unnoticed.[8]

In both these nonevents, their morally seen and professionally unnoticed character derived from the fact that they were occurrences that stood outside the procedurally provided-for alternative courses of action possible in the bureaucratic setting. Bureaucratic procedures organize activities within formal settings. To follow these activities—to understand "what's happening" and "what's important"—reporters rely on these same procedures as schemes of interpretation and schemes of relevance. Incidents that defy, ignore, or question the procedural foundation of the setting, if taken seriously by journalists (i.e., entertained as potentially newsworthy events), would bring them to question the very methods they have come to rely on in doing their work. Nonevents are possible because, ironically, reporters are blinded by their own methods for seeing events.

Nonevents are violations of the bureaucratic procedures that organize beat settings. If, from a bureaucratic point of view, something is not a legitimate occurrence, then, from a journalistic point of view, it cannot be a genuine news event. News events and bureaucratic events are tightly bonded, and nonevents are the consequence of this union, the illegitimate offspring, as it were. Thus, nonevents are not primarily the result of reporters' personal biases, nor of their attempts to protect friendly bureaucratic sources, nor of their following orders from politically motivated editors. Rather, nonevents are a consequence of journalists' protecting their own methods of event detection—methods that are wedded to the bureaucrat's methods of formulating events.

Because this study has dealt with beat reporting on a single newspaper, the generality of the findings can be questioned. Moreover, it is not clear whether and to what extent this analysis of nonevents applies to news produced by reporters who do not cover a beat, such as general assignment reporters and most broadcast journalists. Further research on nonbeat reporting and on other news organizations is necessary.

Nevertheless, the available data dealing with whether American newspapers detect occurrences mainly through beats or through general assignment indicate that the beat system is the predominant mode of coverage. Sigal (1974: 119-130) found that on the *New York Times* and *Washington Post* reporters largely worked on beats, particularly in government institutions in Washington, and heavily relied on official channels for news. The news organization I studied, which was fairly typical of the smaller news organizations that make up the vast majority of American dailies, located most of its reporters on beats: 69 percent of the paper's reporting staff positions were devoted to full-time beats while 31 percent were full-time general assignment.

The situation is rather complex with regard to broadcast journalism. Few television reporters seem to cover beats in the same sense that their colleagues in the print media do (Epstein, 1973: 135-138). This does not mean, however, that most occurrences are detected and interpreted by general assignment reporters. TV news organizations, both network and local, heavily depend on the print media for their sense of newsworthy events (Epstein, 1973: 141-143; Fishman, 1978). Thus, newspaper reporters, who largely work beats, may indirectly determine what most of the newsworthy events are for television journalists.

Summary and Conclusions

A massive bureaucratic apparatus mediates between happenings in the world and reports of those happenings in the media, between mere occurrences and public events. Recent research on the news media shows that newsworkers detect occurrences primarily through legitimated institutions of the society, which is to say, through such bureaucratically organized agencies as police departments, mortuaries, welfare agencies, congressional committees, and the like. What is known and knowable by the media depends on the information-gathering and information-processing resources of these agencies. Moreover, since reporters mainly "see" events during city council meetings, at White House press conferences, in arrest reports, and through the announcements of public relations officers, news as a form of knowledge is shaped by the contexts in which agencies present and package occurrences for journalists.

Journalists do not simply detect happenings through bureaucracies. They also interpret what they are exposed to by means of schemes of interpretation and schemes of relevance. They employ, and need to employ, virtually the same schemes of interpretation and relevance used by agency officials. While this similarity of perspectives allows journalists to "see" some things as events, it also makes invisible a specific class of occurrences as newsworthy happenings. These become nonevents.

Nonevents are occurrences that cannot be seen as legitimate events under the interpretive schemes of agency officials. Nonevents are occurrences that pay no mind to the idealizations of "proper" bureaucratic procedure embodied in an agency's interpretive schemes. Because reporters adopt the schemes of interpretation and relevance employed within the agencies of their beat, they cannot and will not see as news things that might seriously challenge an agency's idealizations of "what's going on" and "what should be happening."

To a certain extent, newswork on a beat is "repair work." In the case of the invisible "crank" who was seen as sidetracking the normal progression of the budget hearings, both the county officials and the reporters at the press table worked to repair the situation, to restore it to "a right state of affairs," by getting rid of the crank. The same repair work was apparent in the case of the invisible controversy at city hall. Not reporting both matters was a way of discouraging these and other incidents like them. Beat reporters "clean up" and repair flawed bureaucratic proceedings. Making coherent news stories out of bureaucratic proceedings in this way renders matters that violate or challenge official idealizations invisible in newspapers. Anything outside the "proper" official treatment of the case tends to be ignored in bureaucratic settings and in routine news stories.

Repair work is designed to normalize activities in bureaucratic settings. Beat reporters do not show this repair work and the part they play in doing it because it is one of the methods by which they construct their accounts. Thus, the news story does not show the sense in which it is a repaired version of what happened. Routine news legitimates the existing political order by disseminating bureaucratic idealizations of the world and by filtering out troublesome perceptions of events. It leads the public to assume that the world outside their everyday experience is a proper sphere of bureaucratic (official) control; that everything falls within some agency's jurisdiction; that policymakers, indeed, make the important decisions while administrators merely implement those decisions; and that, with the exception of a few corrupt and incompetent officials, government institutions function smoothly according to rational-legal standards. What readers of routine news see is normalized bureaucratic work, nothing more or less than the orderly bureaucratic universe as it is meant to be and as it is continually trying to be.

Notes

1. The work of Garfinkel (1967), Goffman (1974), Smith (1974a, 1974b), and Zimmerman and Pollner (1970) have been major influences on the studies cited below.

2. For example, in the traditional literature "newsworthiness," "timeliness," or "importance" are sometimes thought to be characteristics in events that enable journalists to decide whether and how to cover them. More often, the assumption is that "newsworthiness," "timeliness," or "importance" are criteria of news selection that journalists apply to particular events. In the latter case, events are assumed to have other intrinsic characteristics (e.g., a certain duration, the participation of important persons, drama) that journalists directly translate into their "criteria" of news selection.

3. In a sense, mere occurrences in the collective life of a society are analogous to dreams in the conscious life of the individual: If we do not write, talk, or think about them on awakening, they are lost to us as meaningful experiences that can be reflected on and have some bearing on our wakeful existence.

4. The term "phase structure" is my own. However, the idea that schemes of interpretation allow people to see ongoing activities in terms of phases of action or chains of events is a theme that appears throughout the work of Alfred Schutz (1962, 1964, 1966). The concept of "phase structure" also has certain similarities to Tuchman's (1976) and Gitlin's (1980) concept of news as a "frame" (see also Goffman, 1974).

5. This and all other names of specific people, places, and organizations in the research setting are pseudonyms.

6. This distinction between hard and soft news differs from Tuchman's (1973). She claims that the distinguishing characteristic for journalists has to do with the scheduling aspect of the event; that is, an event that demands speedy coverage on the newsworker's part is hard news; an event that can be published at the newsworker's leisure is soft news.

However, events themselves cannot demand anything. Rather, it is the way journalists treat events that produces the sense of timeliness. Thus, Tuchman's distinction begs the question of how newsworkers know in the first place whether to treat something as demanding speed. Journalists distinguish hard news from soft news on the basis of whether it is to be written from the angle of its phase structure disposition or from some other nonbureau-cratically defined angle. The hardness and softness of news is not inherent in events themselves but in the decisions of newsworkers.

7. This illegitimate quality of nonevents is closely related to Goffman's (1963) notion of "spoiled" social identity. Like the stigmatized person, the stigmatized event is shunned because it possesses attributes that are out of character with the setting in which it is found.

8. This terminology ("morally seen but professionally unnoticed") is patterned after Garfinkel's (1967) characterization of certain essential features in common discourse as "seen but unnoticed" in everyday social settings.

References

Bagdikian, B. H. (1971) *The Information Machines*, New York: Harper and Row.

Breed, W. (1955) "Social control in the newsroom." *Social Forces* 33: 326-335.

Crouse, T. (1974) *The Boys on the Bus*. New York: Ballantine.

Epstein, E. J. (1973) *News From Nowhere*. New York: Random House.

Fishman, M. (1978) "Crime waves as ideology." *Social Problems* 25 (June): 531-543.

———. (1980) *Manufacturing the News*. Austin: University of Texas Press.

Galtung, J. and M. Ruge (1973) "Structuring and selecting news," in S. Cohen and J. Young (eds.), *The Manufacture of News*. Beverly Hills, CA: Sage.

Garfinkel, H. (1967) *Studies in Ethnomethodology*. Englewood Cliffs, NJ: Prentice Hall.

Gieber, W. (1956) "Across the desk: A study of 16 telegraph editors." *Journalism Quarterly* 33 (Fall): 423-432.

———. (1964) "News is what newspapermen make it," pp. 173-182 in L. A. Dexter and D. M. White (eds.), *People, Society and Mass Communications*. New York: Free Press.

Gitlin. T. (1980) *The Whole World Is Watching*. Berkeley: University of California Press.

Goffman, E. (1961) *Asylums*. Garden City, NY: Doubleday.

———. (1963) *Stigma*. Englewood Cliffs, NJ: Prentice Hall.

———. (1974) *Frame Analysis*. New York: Harper and Row.

Goldenberg, E. (1975) *Making the Papers*. Lexington, MA: D. C. Health.

Lang, K. and G. E. Lang (1953) "The unique perspective of television." *American Sociological Review* 18 (February): 2-12.

———. (1968) *Politics and Television*. New York: Quadrangle.

Lester, M. (1975) "News as practical accomplishment." Ph.D. dissertation, University of California, Santa Barbara.

———. (1980) "Generating newsworthiness: The interpretive construction of public events." *American Sociological Review* 45 (December): 984-994.

Molotch, H. and M. Lester (1973) "Accidents, scandals and routines." *The Insurgent Sociologist* 3 (Summer): 1-11.

———. (1974) "News as purposive behavior: The strategic use of routine events, accidents and scandals." *American Sociological Review* 39 (February): 101-112.

———. (1975) "Accidental news: The great oil spill." *American Journal of Sociology* 81 (September): 235-310.

Oestgaard, E. (1965) "Factors influencing the flow of news." *Journal of Peace Research* 2: 40-63.

Park, R. E. (1940) "News as a form of knowledge." *American Journal of Sociology* 45 (March): 669-686.

Robinson, G. J. (1970) "Foreign news selection is non-linear in Yugoslavia's Tanjug agency." *Journalism Quarterly* 47: 340-351.

Roshco, B. (1975) *Newsmaking*. Chicago: University of Chicago Press.

Roth, J. (1963) *Timetables*. Indianapolis: Bobbs-Merrill.

Schutz, A. (1962) *Collected Papers, Vol. I: The Problem of Social Reality*. The Hague: M. Nijhoff.

———. (1964) *Collected Papers, Vol. II: Studies in Social Theory*. The Hague: M. Nijhoff.

———. (1966) *Collected Papers, Vol. III: Studies in Phenomenological Philosophy*. The Hague: M. Nijhoff.

Sigal, L. V. (1973) *Reporters and Officials*. Lexington, MA: D. C. Heath.

Sigelman, L. (1973) "Reporting the news: An organizational analysis." *American Journal of Sociology* 79 (July): 132-151.

Smith, D. (1974a) "Theorizing as ideology," pp. 41-44 in R. Turner (ed.), *Ethnomethodology*. Baltimore: Penguin.

———. (1974b) "The social construction of documentary reality." *Sociological Inquiry* 44, 4: 257-267.

Stark, R. (1962) "Policy and the pros: An organizational analysis of a metropolitan newspaper." *Berkeley Journal of Sociology* 7: 11-31.

Tuchman, G. (1972) "Objectivity as strategic ritual." *American Journal of Sociology* 77 (January): 660-678.

———. (1973) "Making news by doing work: Routinizing the unexpected." *American Journal of Sociology* 79, 1: 110-131.

———. (1976) "Telling stories." *Journal of Communication* 26, 4: 93-97.

———. (1977) "The exception proves the rule: The study of routine news practices," pp. 43-62 in P. Hirsch, P. V. Miller, and F. G. Kline (eds.), *Strategies for Communication Research*. Beverly Hills, CA: Sage.

———. (1978a) "Television news and the metaphor of myth." *Studies in the Anthropology of Visual Communication* 5 (Fall): 56-62.

———. (1978b) *Making News: A Study in the Construction of Reality*. New York: Free Press.

———. (1978c) "The newspaper as a social movement's resource," pp. 186-215 in G. Tuchman, A. K. Daniels, and J. Benet (eds.), *Hearth and Home: Images of Women in the Media*. New York: Oxford University Press.

Tunstall, J. (1971) *Journalists at Work*. London: Constable.

White, D. M. (1964) "The gate-keeper: A case study in the selection of news," pp. 160-172 in L. A. Dexter and D. M. White (eds.), *People, Society and Mass Communications*. New York: Free Press.

Zimmerman, D. and M. Pollner (1970) "The everyday world as a phenomenon," pp. 80-103 in J. D. Douglas (ed.), *Understanding Everyday Life*. Chicago: Aldine.

CHAPTER **16**

Routines and the Making of Oppositional News

Nina Eliasoph

There is little official censorship in the United States,[1] and yet, as many media scholars and journalists point out, reporters usually tell stories in a way that does not seriously question the society's dominant way of seeing. I have been a participant observer at an oppositional news organization, in the hopes of sorting out the factors that lead normal reporters to portray the world according to dominant world views. This "deviant case study" challenges some of the most compelling scholarly explanations of the media's political complacency. Journalists and media theorists try to explain the puzzling media acquiescence in part by pointing to the literary conventions of news gathering and reporting. But I found that oppositional news reporters use the same literary conventions mainstream reporters are said to use and that the conventions are not a source of media complacency but an oppositional tool.[2]

Routines Theories

Some media sociologists argue that news routines operate in such a way that no matter who is making the news, as long as it is made in a news

From *Critical Studies in Mass Communication*, 1988, Vol. 5, pp. 313-334. Used by permission of the Speech Communication Association.

organization, it will be under the sway of these unspoken conventions. Michael Schudson (1982, p. 98), for example, argues that the literary conventions of news writing—providing a summary of the story at its beginning, focusing on a single event rather than a long-term happening, and others— "help make culturally consonant messages readable and culturally dissonant messages unsayable." Todd Gitlin (1980, pp. 122-123) finds that these literary conventions (*"cover the event, not the condition; the conflict, not the consensus; the fact that 'advances the story,' not the one that explains it"*) converged with the media's political predispositions to create distortions of the New Left in the 1960s. Edward J. Epstein (1973, p. 200) argues that the news makers' political persuasion does not matter very much, as long as they are subject to limitations imposed by the combined forces of the news organizations and the news form. Leon Sigal (1973, p. 66) states that "conventions, the customary ways of thinking about news and newsmaking, help to standardize newspaper content." Herbert Gans (1979, pp. 128-130) enumerates patterns reporters use to select sources and routinize writing. Sources, writes Gans, are judged legitimate if they have been used before, if they are "productive," "reliable," "trustworthy," "authoritative," and "articulate." Stories, in turn, should describe something that affects a large number of people or something out of the ordinary. This eternal quest for impact and novelty, Gans argues, causes reporters to ignore long-term social problems. Gans also points to the constraints on perspective caused by the reporters' class positions and career pressures to avoid offending powerful advertisers and owners.

Much of this literature shows organizational constraints, economic constraints, the journalists' own class positions, ideologies, career pressures, and general "values" in the news combining in unspecified proportions with literary constraints of the type Schudson describes, *all* seeming to predispose journalists toward dominant ideas. My questions in this article concern the relations between the organizational and economic factors, on the one hand, and the relations of these factors to the routines, on the other.

The "routines theorists," as I dub Gans, Gitlin, Schudson, and others, assert that for several reasons the ownership of the news outlet may not be crucial. They say that owners themselves rarely directly intervene in news gathering and news writing, reporters themselves usually do not have any reason to question fundamental assumptions about society, and the normal routines of the trade usually prevent such questioning. These theorists do acknowledge economic and organizational constraints on commercial news content: the corporate ownership of most news outlets, advertisers' interests, journalists' class positions and their social myopia which blurs the vision of issues that do not affect them, and the journalists' careerism which propels them to seek their superiors' approval and prevents them from being too outspoken or going out on a political limb. Yes, these are important factors in determining news content, the routines theorists acknowledge, but, they contend, the routines are crucial, tending to neutralize any truly oppositional news content even if a subversive reporter were to appear. The routines theorists argue against a perceived economism on the part of other left or liberal critiques of the media (such as Ben Bagdikian [1983] or the work of many Third World scholars or Marxists), which basically says that "freedom of the press" exists only for those who own one. Owner intervention, though it undeniably occurs, is not necessary to enforce the media's political complacency, the routines theorists say. They conclude that all of these factors— literary conventions, organizational pressures (including commercial ones), and the journalists' own ideologies—come together to create the news.

At the oppositional radio station, I found that the literary rules do not automatically constrain news content, since the rules themselves are, as ethnomethodologists would say, negotiated continuously, doing different work in different contexts depending on who is using them. More important, I found, is the interaction between two sets of pressures: that from within the news organization and that coming from the relations between the news organization and the rest of the political world. Of overwhelming importance in determining normal news content are the pressures from, on the one hand, normal reporters' careerism and the relation between reporters and their superiors (who have their own ideologies and are beholden to corporate advertisers) and the pressures coming, on the other hand, from reporters' and the station's ideology and their social positions and involvement with the audience and the social movements and institutions that are the subjects of news.

As Gaye Tuchman (1972, 1978) found in her investigation of a mainstream newspaper, most of the conventions can be bent sufficiently to be oppositional, as well as acquiescent, to the dominant ideological framing of questions. The "rules" provide a reified justification for reporters' work, both protecting them from potential disputes and legitimating their roles as professionals.[3] At the oppositional radio station I studied, the conventions serve other purposes for the organization and the reporters.

The literary form of news does not determine its political content at the oppositional news station. The conventions are open, and reporters manipulate them, choosing among a range of possible news routines and using them to explain things according to their own "common sense" and their own organizational needs. Reporters, including the oppositional ones, agree to the rules in the abstract. In practice, however, the rules are open enough to accommodate all kinds of implicit messages.

At the oppositional radio station, the same literary conventions that lead to conventional news in mainstream outfits lead to oppositional news. Where there is a choice among conventions, the oppositional reporter's approach is often informed by a conscious political decision, whereas a normal reporter's approach is informed by an unconscious political decision (Breed, 1955, p. 328; Gans, 1979, chap. 2, p. 199; Gitlin, 1980, p. 259).

In mainstream outfits, the routines both structure the news and act as an alibi for the hidden ideology. They make news appear to journalists and the audience alike as something automatic, professional, based on the decisions of experts who know what is important, the routines theories say. But the news at the oppositional station is not understood or intended in the way routines theorists say the news form requires. That is, it is not intended or taken as a neutral sum of the day's facts arrived at by technocratic news professionals.

In this study, I argue that the economic and organizational factors help determine the news content more than the routines. To ownership theories, I add the idea that the reporters' own ideologies are important as well as the relations among the station, the political actors about whom the station reports, and the listeners. That is, if tomorrow the government offered unconditional funding to all news organs, with no editorial caveats, the news content would probably not change as dramatically as the ownership theories imply. Dominant world views would still probably prevail. Within the context of the routines theories, I show that routines accomplish different things in different contexts.

A Sociologist in the News Room

None of the routines theorists compares *normal* news production with any *other* kind of news production. That makes it difficult to tell whether these conventions necessarily shape the news, as the routines theorists imply, or whether the news routines do not in themselves spell dominant ideology, as Tuchman and Carlin Romano (1986) imply.

Part of the reason scholars in the United States have not compared normal news routines to possible dissenting news routines may be that there are no major daily sources of oppositional print news in this country. I have worked for almost two years at KPFA-FM in Berkeley. The radio station is affiliated with four other Pacifica stations scattered across the country. Together, the Pacifica stations comprise the largest source of left-wing alternative daily news in the country; of these, KPFA is the oldest and, in fact, generally has been credited with inspiring and initiating the world's community radio movement since pacifists founded it in 1949 (Lewis, 1984). It is noncommercial, nongovernmental radio, funded solely by listeners. Bay Area leftists consider it a venerable old institution of oppositional politics.

The station is "oppositional" in the sense Ernesto Laclau and Chantal Mouffe (1982, p. 105) discuss, fostering "a plurality of democratic struggles, aiming to change the relation of forces at all levels of society." The loosely articulated "new social movements" such as the feminist, ecological, gay and lesbian, black, Chicano, tenants' and immigrants' rights, anti-intervention, and antinuclear organizations, as well as more traditional organizations like some unions, see KPFA as their ally. As members of such groups often told me while I was reporting on their events, they assume that KPFA will cover issues they consider important in a way more fair to them than the mainstream press' coverage. The station's training manual declares that KPFA's explicit purpose is to give "access to unique and often unpopular ideas generally absent from the commercial media" (Betserai & Salniker, 1983).

Participant observation has been my primary method of investigation. I have also interviewed past and present members of the volunteer news staff and several mainstream newspaper reporters and editors. To ascertain whether KPFA's news is different, I took an informal survey and did a short content analysis comparing KPFA's news both to other local outlets' news and to the standard news several other scholars have analyzed. I have been as much "participant" as "observer," seeing myself, to some extent, as a typical reporting and anchoring novice at KPFA. The process of socialization into the norms of the news enterprise is a crucial moment to capture: the movement when the budding reporter learns what news is and how to make it. KPFA's news director arranges a six-week evening class twice a year to train new volunteers. I took the class with 14 people and have conducted interviews on the process of learning news at least once a month with those who continued working at the station. I also attended a four-session class on "anchoring" for more advanced volunteers.

I worked as a reporter for a year, then as a morning news writer for a few months, and then for six months as coanchor or anchor one morning a week or on weekends. Reporters go out to press conferences or other events, on assignments given by the anchors of the evening news, producing one or two taped long stories for the hour-long evening news. Anchors are in charge of putting together the newscast, which also runs 10 minutes long in the morning, a half hour on weekend evenings: selecting stories, putting them in order, rewriting wire copy, editing stories which the evening anchors did not have time to air the night before, editing news writers' stories, occasionally producing taped stories based on phone interviews, and reading the news on the air. Coanchors do all the same things anchors do but, unlike anchors, do not have the final word on story selection or order. Writers usually just rewrite the wire copy anchors give them, unless the writers have strong initiative.

At the station, only about 20 people are paid for their work: The paid staff members are mostly engineers or support staff such as a fund raiser and the person who answers the main phone. In the news department, the only regularly paid people are the news director and codirector, who anchor weekday evening news every day, a full-time reporter, and an extremely part-time reporter. Now and then, volunteers are paid to substitute for paid staff members.

There may be a problem with comparing radio news production with print or television news production. However, I know of no other daily source of oppositional news in the country. Further, the questions I am asking about the importance of the different constraints posed by routines and economic and organizational factors would apply to all news. KPFA's hour-long weekday evening newscast is meant to be a listener's primary news source. A news director teaching my "new class" told us we should see ourselves as a primary news source like the *New York Times* or NPR's "All Things Considered" (National Public Radio's very thorough news program). More important for this project, the conventions KPFA reporters and normal reporters invoke are the same, and the time and space constraints are the same for both groups.

What It Means to Follow a Rule

What follows is a list of some of the literary conventions which the routines scholars say influence the ideological content of news. In each case, I discuss the routine, describing why the routines theorists say it leads to politically complacent news and showing how KPFA uses it for oppositional purposes.

Covering Events, Not Long-Term Conditions

According to routines theorists, the problem with the specific event orientation is that important trends often unfold gradually, with no specific events for news "pegs." Like mainstream journalists, those at KPFA have to say something "new" and often rely on events to do so. The rule concerning newness, however, can be overridden, and ongoing conditions can be *made* into timely news in a number of ways.

First of all, the Berkeley reporters, like normal ones, can override the rule favoring newness with the importance rule. Such was the case in the mainstream news with the repetitive stories of battles in Vietnam, argues Gans (1979, p. 326), or the case with the repetitive stories about the Persian Gulf War. KPFA journalists also, reluctantly, repeat stories about the Persian Gulf, saying to each other, "It's boring—just more of the same." The importance rule wins out. Also, on occasion, "really important" stories repeat points made previously. For instance, coverage within a week of two demonstrations concerning the destruction of the tropical rain forests repeated past points.

Reporters can develop a "new angle" on an old story. Such was the case in the continuing coverage of the United States-backed war in Nicaragua despite the fact that KPFA had covered it many times before. Discovering a new angle often depends, again, on ideology, knowledge, and social position. I tried to force the idea of newness into relief one day: Coming back from a demonstration, I complained that the demonstrators were not saying anything new, that it was a "cheerleading for the left type story." The news director, who was in a hurry, replied, "Yeah, I know." But an experienced reporter told me, "You *make* the story. You don't—well, you don't just make it *up*, but sometimes if the people *there* don't come up with an angle, you have to figure one out yourself." A fellow KPFA reporter gave me an angle on another demonstration I covered. The Salvadoran government often bombs villages, but the demonstration against this particular bombing was newsworthy in part because it involved a new *movement* of peasants who were leaving refugee camps to repopulate their bombed-out hamlets. A reporter not intimately involved in Salvadoran peasant movements would not have known this new angle, but the KPFA reporter was working in an organization which supported this movement in El Salvador.

Deciding something is new also often means relying on organizations to address the issue. Drug abuse is not an event, but the president's last speech about it is. World poverty is not an event, but the United Nations Children's Day drawing attention to impoverished children is. So, saying something new often means nothing more than going along with an important person or organization which certifies its "eventfulness." KPFA bases its suggestions for eventfulness on a different set of officials than normal news producers do, so it covers the United Nation's Children's Day celebration in San Francisco but not all of the president's antidrug speeches.

After I anchored the news one morning, I listened to NPR's morning news and found that it had covered a whole different set of stories than I had. A few weeks later, I asked the news director if I was wrong to have devoted so much of the newscast to reports of demonstrations. "There were big demonstrations all over the country, and NPR just had stuff about summit meetings that might not even happen!" I exclaimed. "Honduras, right?" he nodded, acknowledging the general divergence between KPFA's and other news organs' coverage of protests against Reagan's sending troops there. "NPR *never* does demonstrations. They don't like demonstrations," he said. Someone else added, "Unless they're in Poland."

Focusing on events is said to blind the news to structural, historical analysis. Using sources with no sense of history or structure, reporters make stories with no sense of history or structure. But given other sources, other kinds of stories are possible. Any number of things can be excuses for news: The *New York Times* (Halloran, 1986) ran a full-column article describing the childhood and home town of Eugene Hasenfus, the U.S. pilot caught running guns to the Contras. KPFA used the incident as a peg for an interview with John Stockwell, former CIA operative turned critic, about CIA covert tactics in all parts of the globe.

A "Wages for Housework" rally presented figures, generated for the United Nations Conference on Women of 1985, that showed what percentage of the world's work is done by women, how much it would be worth if wages were paid, and what percentage of the world's assets are controlled by women (1%).[4] That was "news" at KPFA because the women were saying it at the rally that day. The event provided a springboard hinting at a structural, historical approach to the problem of women's poverty. All that mattered was the sources KPFA used. And of course, if there is a peg, there is no need for an event that day. The conventions contradict each other and depend on choices made by the reporters. Similarly, as I show elsewhere (1986), reporters managed to find numerous pegs for stories on the 67 missing children in the United States in 1984-1985 but could not seem to find pegs for stories on the 5 children who were killed daily by their own parents. Both problems are equally "uneventful" in that they are by definition without responsible, yet uninvolved, witnesses, but the one fits more easily into typical reporters' ideology than the other. While most reporters would probably not say that missing children are more inherently newsworthy than those killed by their parents, those reporters' "common sense," not the routines of news gathering, makes them report more on the first kind of child than the second.

Reliance on Officials for Stories, Information, and Analysis

Like other news organs, KPFA relies on officials, but KPFA's officials often come from the Sierra Club, unions, or other oppositional organizations. In a small sample of four KPFA broadcasts, tape from oppositional officials accounted for over half of the taped interview minutes in the evening broadcasts. Compare this to Sigal's account (1973) that from 1949-1969 U.S. government officials alone provided 46.5% of all sources for stories in the *Washington Post* and the *New York Times*. (Since then, the amount of space devoted to U.S. government officials has probably declined but not so far as to equal the portion KPFA devotes to government sources.) Officials from other governments, many of whom may have been quite similar ideologically to U.S. officials, accounted for another 27.4% of all sources. The remaining 16.5% of the sources were nongovernmental, though not necessarily oppositional. Since the rules also call for balance, it is clear that KPFA's reliance on officials from all sides, and not just on government officials, is not a violation of any rule.

If the officials are speakers at the United Nations Children's Day celebration or leaders of the groups demonstrating against U.S. intervention in Central America, the oppositional reporters' sense of what makes something eventful, new, or important will be distinctive.[5] And even Bay Area government officials are often critical of the national government. Tape from the socialist mayor of Berkeley or a gay, socialist San Francisco city supervisor will more likely set a different agenda than a typical city official's offerings. If the government were more monolithic in ideology, relying on government officials, as the routines theorists say, would reinforce their power. But routines theorists neglect to consider that the government is not necessarily monolithic. If there are fewer oppositional forces in many reporters' districts, that is a problem with the public, not a result of media routines alone (Hallin & Mancini, 1985).

Producing a Regular Amount of News Every Day

Like other news organs, KPFA has to produce a regular amount of news every day. The time pressure at KPFA is probably, in fact, much greater than the pressure on normal reporters because of the station's ramshackle office and studio equipment. Sometimes the news room has only one or two working typewriters. Reporters always must recycle used audiotape themselves, an unheard-of practice for most radio stations. Many KPFA reporters have to take sluggish public transportation to events. In fact, many do not own a cassette recorder and have to pick up one at the station before covering live stories.

Media sociologists say the crush of time usually leads to beat reporting and stereotyping and that these lead to politically complacent reporting, but at KPFA they do not lead to such complacency:

1. *Beat reporting.* Scholars note that a reporter will find it convenient and time saving simply to check in with a source every day or so by phone or in person. If the source is a bureaucrat, the reporter will be guaranteed a regular stream of stories. In this way, beat reporters become intimately familiar with the workings and people of the institutions they cover. Reporters, the theorists say, thus often develop symbiotic relations with sources: Reporters get daily news, and sources get out the messages they desire. Further, the theorists say it is easier for reporters to extract information from sources by chatting informally with them than through formal interviews.

The notion of beats needs clarifying, in two ways. First, run-of-the-mill reporting does not divulge sources' secrets but simply covers already scheduled pseudoevents. While the informal chat is said to help reporters get the scoop on inside stories sometimes, most of the greatest inside stories of the century have not come from beat reporters: for example, the Bay of Pigs, Watergate, the Iran-Contra affair, and the connections between the U.S. government and some Latin American drug smugglers.[6] So, for big scoops, beats are not as useful as reporters and scholars think. For routine news, coverage of pseudoevents, any reporter keeping close track of the organization's workings will do, though the reporter at KPFA who has a beat with San Francisco city officials does say that it is not always easy to cover them. Pacifica reporters in Washington are probably not good friends with many governmental sources, but such friendship is not as necessary as researchers believe. There are other ways of finding information about powerful officials than by being friends with them. High government sources usually only divulge standard information, which does not require friendship to obtain. And for a good deal of reporting on covert or complicated military issues, left or liberal research institutes often provide KPFA with information the station considers reliable and steady. There is another problem with the concept of beats which KPFA's work makes clear. Deciding that something is important enough to require a beat reporter is in itself an ideological move. Some reporters at KPFA do have beats, but their focus is not the police or the White House but feminists or labor.

Sigal (1973, p. 54) states that reporters covering a powerful institution like the Pentagon have to cooperate with their sources, or the sources will find another reporter to reward with scoops. This is the model scholars use to describe the relation between reporters and beat sources. Yet there is a more complex power dimension buried in the whole notion of beats. While covering a campus demonstration, I noticed that other reporters, whom I recognized as campus beat reporters, often acted rude to the organizers. However, the organizers, unlike the Pentagon, can rarely afford to blacklist rude reporters; any coverage is welcome. Because a student newspaper and radio station and KPFA are the only daily news organs in the city of Berkeley, an organization would have a difficult time getting exposure if it refused coverage from KPFA. Reporters covering oppositional beats, then, can be much more critical of their sources than reporters on other beats.

In sum, KPFA does have some beats, like other news organizations, but beat reporting is not as necessary as scholars assume. Moreover, reporting on beats does not necessarily have to be uncritical, depending on the power relations between reporter and source.

2. *"Getting the news out every day"* also is said to exacerbate stereotyping. Like other news organs, KPFA stereotypes: "Go get some heartbreaking tape of a refugee," the anchor told me one morning. Still, the station perhaps does not stereotype as much as normal news organs, since its stories are not as culturally consonant.

A few former Pacifica reporters I interviewed criticized the current KPFA news, saying that it was too formulaic. It is certainly not as prone to formula as the mainstream media, they said, but "our media should ask interesting questions, not supply pat answers." They said, however, that KPFA's news has *not always* been so susceptible to formula. The mainstream obviously does not have a monopoly on low-quality news. As it does for sonnets, symphonies, and mystery novels, formulaic composition may make news easier to produce, understand, and enjoy. There may be a built-in bias toward stereotyping in the news form and in all others as well. As some of us at the station joked, one of KPFA's molds goes: "X happened today. Why? Corporate or Government Official A thinks this (tape from Official A). But So-and-So, from the leftist, feminist, Third World, antinuclear, environmentalist, gay and lesbian task force union, has another side of the story (tape from So-and-So). Her group plans on taking the issue further."

People cannot think without categorizing, stereotyping. The problem seems to be a matter of degree and of the nature of the stereotype. It could be argued that the normal news does not produce enough stereotypes of the right kind. The news seems a high speed jumble of car accidents, coups, and new consumer goods, category-less, wandering around in the limbo of quasi-meaning, immobilizing the listener. Another routine, say something new and unusual, too often gets in the way, especially in the less elite media.

Yet, when assigned that day to get "heartbreaking tape from refugees," I decided that showing refugees always expressing emotions and never analyzing was racist and instead taped a refugee making a clear analytic speech. That did not take any more time. Mindlessness is not an inevitable result of the press of time. Stereotyping, in fact, often runs against another news convention, namely, the convention which mandates newness.

Showing Balance or Conflict

KPFA usually tries to balance stories, as do normal news agencies. The fulcrum at KPFA is often at a different point in the social debate. A dispute about proliferation of air traffic over the Grand Canyon led KPFA to focus on environmentalist concerns about whether the regulations drawn up that day were strong enough. The wire copy, however, situated the debate in terms of whether or not there should be regulations at all. Though the regulations had already been decreed, an Arizona senator stated that they should be repealed, a fact mentioned in KPFA's coverage. The station's decision over where to place the fulcrum differed from the standard, then, but the "pro" and "con" "balance" format was the same.

At normal stations, there are certain "crusades" which do not require balance. Nobody, for example, was in favor of pollution, hunger, or poverty in the television station Epstein (1973) examined in the late 1960s. In the late 1980s, normal reporters are not expected to balance their antidrug stories with interviews from addicts and dealers justifying such work or habits, and, until recently, reporters were not expected to interview Palestinians on their side of the story, since they were almost always treated as "terrorists." Two mainstream reporters from a small city paper told me that their paper decided that a mayoral candidate was racist because he was anti-Zionist. The journalists made sure the candidate's purported racism was apparent in their reports and eventually blacked out coverage of him altogether. KPFA's crusades are rare, since it would be glaringly unbalanced to have, for example, a story about U.S. intervention in Central America without having the pro-intervention side. The range of debate in the larger society would preclude such a topic from becoming a legitimate one-sided crusade, even though everyone at the station is in agreement against U.S. attempts to support the Salvadoran government or the Contras who are trying to overthrow the government of Nicaragua.

Most KPFA reporters are insistent on balancing stories. Several reporters organized a series of evening meetings for the volunteer staff to critique each other's stories. At one of these meetings, a reporter played her story about California offshore oil drilling. On the tape, a U.S. Interior Department official argued that if Californians want to keep driving along their beautiful coast, they will soon need their oil and gas from offshore rigs. Another reporter at the meeting criticized the story for not finding good refutations of this idea. He said, "We have to be telling people what's true." But all 10 other reporters at the meeting agreed that it is important to "show the opponents in the most favorable light" so that listeners can "know their enemy." I often hear KPFA reporters say they do not just want "to preach to the converted."

KPFA reporters agree that listeners should know informed arguments supporting their viewpoints and assume that, once the facts are all in, people will support the right side. In the offshore oil drilling case, everyone at the meeting assumed that there were good refutations of the Interior Department official's ideas, but no one present knew what they were (though a few days later, another reporter working on a story about the drilling found a source who gave convincing arguments against the Interior Department's).

KPFAers assume that many stories are too complex to have just one right and wrong side, but when writing a story with a clear right and wrong side, it is ideal to get tape from the wrong side first. That gives the right side a chance to refute the incorrect facts and analysis. Unfortunately, it is rarely possible to schedule interviews in such a controlled sequence.

While normal news outlets use balance to avoid sounding involved, to sound professionally detached, KPFA uses the same routine for different ends. The intention of KPFA reporters in using this routine is to give listeners the knowledge necessary to arrive at, and argue in favor of, their own conclusions. But the KPFA reporters will try to find someone who can give what the reporters consider a good analysis, even if it means putting the fulcrum of the debate in a different place than the mainstream media puts it.

Starting With the Most Important Facts First

Schudson (1982) states that this story structure makes the reporter structure the event for the readers and is based on the assumption that readers are too ignorant to be able to pick out the most important ideas. He observes that the form itself tends to make the expert, nonpartisan reporter seem like the only one capable of discerning what is important. Like normal news, KPFA's stories start out with the facts the reporters consider to be the most important ones.

The summary lead can appear to be technocratic truth only if the experts agree. At KPFA, summary leads have different content than the summary leads of standard news agencies, but they are still summaries of what the reporters deem the main issues to be. The crucial difference is, KPFA's is clearly one possible interpretation among many, since anyone can look at a normal newspaper for a different summary. In this deviant case, the summary lead helps bring partisan passion back into politics.

Refraining From Editorializing

KPFA reporters learn early that it is unnecessary to add their own opinions to pieces, since they can find sources to do the analysis for them. KPFA reporters are aware of their own political agenda. Where a normal journalist, as Gans points out, would unconsciously use words like "hordes" and "gangs," KPFAers have to sift that jargon out of the wire service copy they rewrite. KPFA subscribes to AP, Reuters, the *New York Times*, the *San Francisco Chronicle*, the *Tribune* of Oakland, some other papers, and a good number of magazines; every novice's very first, and constantly repeated, lesson is to "watch for wire copyisms": "regime," when describing a government the United States does not like; "terrorists," when describing other factions the U.S. government does not like; "the worst student demonstrations in 20 years," when describing a successful student revolt; "reclassification," when a corporation wants to rename workers' job titles and halve their pay; and so on.

Reporters at mainstream papers whom I interviewed on the linguistic bias of news could not justify it. On the difference between "terrorist" and "rebel," or "detention" and "imprisonment without trial" in South Africa, all the mainstream reporters questioned came to the conclusion that the distinctions were vague, if discernible at all.

KPFA reporters do not see the screening of wire copyisms as editorializing. Rather, it seems to them that the wires editorialize and the KPFA reporters correct them. On the one hand, they clearly believe that their version of the story is *right*, not just a special perspective. On the other hand, they do not want to feed the audience dogmatic understandings of events.

Manipulating Literary Forms

In general, KPFA reporters learn to look for sources that will give analyses that the reporters find reasonable. At a meeting, a few reporters analyzing a strike situation agreed that the strike was going to come on hard times unless the workers ended it soon since both union officials and the county's central labor council had said the unionists should return to work, and almost half of the union's members agreed. A reporter asked, "Know any retired members of the working class? We need someone who can give us the true story without feeling like they're betraying their class." That is, the reporters themselves could not make this analysis, but they could find a source to say it. It was also pointed out that reporters should not "froth at the mouth" about the Iran-Contra affair ("It's bad for the mikes," someone quipped), but they should certainly find sources who will froth for them.

Nevertheless, there are limits drawn on the manipulation allowable by oppositional organization sources. In the news class, the director said that if no one is saying that the solution to homelessness is free housing for the homeless, even if reporters think that is the solution, they cannot make that a big part of their story. Thus, for example, I called six environmentalist organizations to find someone to interview on a newly published report that implied that the Environmental Protection Agency (EPA) was slacking off in protecting endangered species from pesticide poisoning. To me, it seemed clear that the EPA was not doing its job, but the environmentalist I reached for an interview did not say that. I kept trying to find an organization that would say so, but it was the afternoon before the Labor Day weekend, and all the other ecology organizations' offices were closed. Finally, an anchor took me aside and said that, since I had already spoken with someone from a trustworthy organization, I should just use the tape from him. She said, "What's wrong with them? You can't just mold a story to how you think it should go. I'm sure if you listen to it again you'll find him saying some stronger things than you thought." I did, and did not find him saying anything stronger, but used the tape anyway. A few days later, another reporter mentioned to me that she had heard my story and asked why I did not get tape that said more clearly the EPA was not doing its job. She said I should have called her sister, an environmentalist who specializes in pesticide research.

At KPFA, reporters often explicitly read into the literary debate a political agenda, while in normal news organizations, according to routines theorists, reporters are almost never consciously aware that their political ideology influences their stories. KPFA reporters have something to say but have to follow the standard routines.

There is a tension between the station's roles as political advocate and news station. Like normal journalists, those at KPFA, interestingly enough, almost never discuss politics while doing news. Even in meetings to discuss editorial policy, theoretical political reasoning remains tacit. When the news department discussed coverage of the Iran-Contra affair, the whole discussion hinged on how, not why, to cover it one way or another. KPFA reporters are self-described "politics junkies," much more opinionated than Epstein (1973) found normal journalists to be. When I have gone out for dancing, dinner, or demonstrations with KPFAers, we have inevitably "talked politics." While *doing* news, though, we hardly ever have deep political discussions.

One reporter at the station was sometimes dismissed as an "ideologue," since he seemed not to understand the news form. This reporter congratulated another for "rooting for the Palestinian cause" in her story of the day. The reporter he congratulated later told me, "All I did was let the Palestinian guy *talk*. I let the Israeli guy talk, too." At a meeting, the same ideologue complained that he often disagreed with things he heard on the station's news, and everyone laughed. "That's how it should be," one person exclaimed. The ideologue quickly tried to repair the damage. "What I meant," he said, "was that we don't always present things in their correct relations to the development of the historical progression of the lines of contradiction, if I can paraphrase Mao. . . . " "Well, *that's* a problem," one person chortled. "Why don't we just read *Das Kapital* on the air?" another chuckled. The problem is not so much his political position but that he does not understand that he should have spoken his criticism through the literary code of journalism. Since KPFA reporters are supposed to use the literary routines of normal journalism, the reporter should have known to couch what he said in those terms.

One novice reporter was extremely knowledgeable, but she thought it was important to call people in her stories "fascists" too often for the liking of the news directors, who prefer a very narrow, technical definition of the term. They are adamantly opposed to what they call "leftist jargon," which they see as a leftist equivalent to the wire copyisms they deplore. The knowledgeable novice quickly left the station.

Conflicts do arise about *how* to manipulate the literary conventions to express the correct political points of view. An argument at the station in 1986 revolved around using "rebel" to describe the Nicaraguan Contras. Some said the Contras identified themselves as rebels but thought "terrorist" would better describe them. Others said "the United States-backed mercenaries who are trying to overthrow the elected government of Nicaragua" would be better, while still others said KPFA listeners know who the Contras are without having it spelled out for them each time. They could not agree on a suitably neutral and succinct term for them. In this case, the station opted for brevity and conformity, usually calling them "rebels," but no one was satisfied. In another case, a coanchor and I decided that I should peg a story about men's violence against their lovers and spouses on an incident in which a high school boy killed his girlfriend at the school. After reading the news on the air, the other anchor came into the news room fuming, "That wasn't a story! It was just a 'men are bad' story. There wasn't anything *new* in it!" He seemed to think that the peg was not sturdy enough, though others disagreed. He never once said that it was not an important enough issue, though another reporter there told me later that she though that the anchor simply was not a feminist and therefore not that interested in the issue of domestic violence. Like a normal news director, the KPFA anchor couched his critique completely in news-literary terms.

So, the news routines per se do not *determine* coverage. What does determine content, I think, is the interaction between two sets of forces that push normal news in a culturally consonant direction. The one set of forces revolves around relations within the normal news organizations, around the interaction between managers and careerist reporters. The other set of forces comes from the station's position in the world: the station's and reporters' ideologies and social positions and the relations among the station, reporters, audience, and the social movements and institutions reporters cover.

The News Organization

Owners of news organizations may rarely intervene directly in the news process, but they hire directors they like, respect, and understand, and journalists wanting to get ahead will not risk antagonizing their directors. Directors, as Peter Dreier (1982) shows, are inextricably knitted into the corporate elite of the country. They are, themselves, often owners of large corporations. Bagdikian states that by April 1987, 29 corporations owned almost all the daily newspapers, magazines, broadcasting, and book and movie production in the country (down from 50 in 1982) and that the parent corporations often do exert editorial control over their broadcast subsidiaries.[7] Further, the news organs are often beholden to advertisers, who may be potential subjects of critical stories. Powerful advertisers can launch campaigns against journalists whom they particularly resent for unfavorable coverage (Bagdikian, 1983, pp. 61-67).

The pressures from above come in two ways. First, most often they come indirectly. As Gitlin (1980, p. 259) states, managers try to avoid overt invasions of the reporters' professional territory. Rather, they opt for a more delicate approach:

> To avoid a reputation for having an ax to grind, the top media managers endow their news operations with the appearance, and a considerable actuality, of autonomy; their form of social control must be indirect, subtle, and not at all necessarily conscious. Their standards flow through the processes of recruitment and promotion, through policy, reward, and the sort of social osmosis that flows overwhelmingly in one direction: downward.

Second, less often media heads sometimes *do* pressure reporters directly, if clumsily, when covert intervention fails. Though this kind of pressure is rare, it must have considerable effect, since the career-hungry reporters are, as Epstein (1973) describes, basically apathetic and are just trying to be successful technocrats at their jobs. A good deal of Gitlin's book describes just such managerial intervention (Schudson, 1981, p. 37). That is, the managers and politicians Gitlin studied *often did* directly invade the reporters' domain in the 1960s, as soon as the reporters' political views began to differ from the views of their superiors, corporate sponsors, and powerful politicians.

So, normal reporters are under pressure to conform to the social and political controls of the news organization if they want to get ahead professionally. They absorb the knowledge that jabbing at corporate sponsors or even offending general corporate ideology is not the route to professional success. At KPFA, there is no wealthy proprietor and no corporate or government sponsor. As a weekend news anchor quipped when asked for a tape measure or a ruler, "We have no ruler here. This is a nonhierarchical organization!" Of course, there is hierarchy, but there is no career ladder, since hardly anyone is paid for work at the station. (A footstool, with one, very low step perhaps would be a more accurate image for KPFA.) Social control in the news room is not absent, though. Even without careers at stake, KPFA reporters have reasons for conforming to the general KPFA approach.

The news directors at KPFA have an enormous effect on the news. Reporters are often novices or, in any case, do not want to displease the people with whom they are working. One reporter told me that she attended a press conference and found out when she returned to the station that she "had asked all the wrong questions." The anchor told her he did not agree with her choice of frames for the story. For the novice reporter at KPFA, the news·director's political beliefs and knowledge matter. In a normal news organization, a reporter who wants a promotion or to stay employed will not diverge too drastically from the director's tacit views. At KPFA, reporters who are just learning look to the anchors for the "frame," ask them for the important questions to ask sources. Soon, reporters learn to consult sources for these frames: the news department rolodex and reference notebooks are like tour guides of America's new social movements. Reporters who stay at the station for any length of time learn of dozens of oppositional resources on which to rely for analysis. As in a normal news organization, the reporters leave who cannot learn how to determine these questions themselves, who can never learn which are the sources KPFA deems reliable or what types of analyses sound convincing, or who persist in framing stories incorrectly.

For example, many of the recruits in my news class left after repeated unsuccessful efforts to figure out what were the basic issues in the stories they were assigned. Another faithful reporter often clashed with the news directors on his reporting, saying that KPFA was not interested in his science stories because he did not find a bad guy in them. To translate this into the language of literary rules, he was annoyed that the station was requiring balance, making him show conflict, when he just wanted to use the form acceptable for human interest stories (i.e., the kind of story that does not require balance, like zoo animals' obituaries). He took a leave from the station in part because of this disagreement. KPFA, like a normal news agency, has a self-selecting process.

Though the reporter's superiors at the station itself may exert eccentric political pressure, there are also pressures from outside KPFA per se to standardize the news form. Some of the unpaid staff members hope to gather resumé tape of their best stories to use for future applications for jobs in media.[8] Resumé tape cannot be in a form unsuitable to other media, and this is one reason why KPFA's literary routines are not different from the standard ones.

Reporters at KPFA, however, would not stay if they had to write mainstream stories. A person primarily devoted to finding a career in broadcasting would go for training at a better-equipped news station. The news writers at KPFA are oppositional activists who decide radio is a good way of "getting the truth out," not reporters who become leftists. There are precious few paying jobs for oppositional journalists in this country, so most at KPFA assume they will make their living outside of journalism. Since the reporters are not paid and most make their living outside of journalism, institutional forces do not exert as much pressure as in a normal news outlet.

When a reporter and the news anchors disagree over the importance of a story, the anchors cannot force the reporter to produce a story because the anchors do not hold the reporter's livelihood in their hands. They, however, do control the reporter's access to the airwaves, and to the extent that this access shapes the news content, it pushes coverage in the direction of the station's principles. So, while subtle social controls in normal news rooms serve to dull social critique, the subtle controls at KPFA work mainly to sharpen critique.

The World of Politics

Mainstream journalists are supposed to be politically uninvolved, and Epstein (1973) concludes that they generally are. Their social distance from the movements they cover leads them to miss stories or miss aspects of stories KPFA would consider important. A *New York Times* reporter in 1965, for example, did not notice the unprecedented racial mix at an antiwar demonstration, probably because the reporter "was not close enough to the radical movement to notice that there was anything extraordinary about the racial composition" (Gitlin, 1980, p. 55).

All reporters use informal networks to find stories. Since most reporters at KPFA are active in oppositional politics or friends with politically active people, the reporters sometimes find ideas for stories in their political commitments or from activist friends, who call them at home to tell them about events. One source to whom I was directed for information on the beginnings of Berkeley's anti-apartheid movement was an old KPFA reporter. A blind reporter at KPFA, active in furthering the rights of the disabled, called a Pacifica stringer near Detroit to suggest covering a demonstration by disabled people in that city. People refer to their peers. In a normal news organization, reporters typically find ideas by talking with their elite peers and simply by living the life of an affluent professional, as many scholars note. For example, normal reporters will find the "revitalization" of an inner city to be news, though they have not found the inner city's problems to be news for a decade. Most KPFA reporters work at part-time, fringe jobs: two night-shift typesetters, a part-time legal secretary, a part-time printer, a doctor who works in a clinic three days a month, a lawyer who quit law, a fund raiser for a local peace group, many unemployed people, a student, a number of free-lance reporters. KPFA reporters generally do not subscribe to the "enduring news values" Gans (1979) describes: KPFA reporters do not adhere to the idea that our government's leaders and the capitalist system are generally benevolent. At KPFA, it is assumed that reporters have a kind of oppositional background knowledge. As one reporter said of a government bombing in El Salvador, "It makes sense, considering what else is happening. It sounds like something that could be going on there." When this same wisdom is applied in a normal news situation, it does not make sense. One KPFA reporter was a journalism student, often accused in her classes of "having an ax to grind." At a station news department meeting discussing recruiting, I offered to make an announcement to a media class at the University of California, which I described as "full of corporate-drones-in-training." A news anchor quelled any fears that such recruits would change news standards. "Don't worry," she laughed, "we'll scare 'em away!" Most media organizations "scare away" radicals and others with strong, conscious political beliefs. KPFA scares away those whose beliefs are normal by placing a great deal of emphasis on "getting the politics right."

Normal news writers live in a world distant from their audiences. At KPFA, most staff members are part of the general movement which includes not only the station but many of the station's news sources and audience members. Mattelart and Piemme (1980, p. 322), in a report to the Belgian Congress, distinguish between institutional media and social movements. European "free radio," they point out, is a social movement rather than an institution; it is as irregular, portable, and transitory as the movements of which it is part and which it covers. KPFA is not as thoroughly tied to a single movement as these antinuclear "pirate" stations seem to be; nevertheless, the social lines between the reporter and the reported on, between the reporter and the reported to, are barely drawn at the station. The station has fund-raiser dances, holiday fairs, and picnics to which "the KPFA community" is invited. Like any noncommercial, listener-sponsored radio, KPFA requests donations from listeners; this makes them "members." Listeners and sources many times have praised KPFA's work, telling me that they are members.

"Who pays?" is a different question for reporters and managers at KPFA than at other news agencies. KPFA's source of funds is a segment of the audience which distinguishes itself by its political orientation. Crucial here is not just the fact that KPFA's audience is ideologically eccentric but that there is a different *relationship* here between listeners and producers. Mainstream news producers see the audience as "consumers," but at KPFA the audience is seen as a "constituency," mobilized, active, needing information in order to act. Giving instructions to the anchoring class on how to write headlines, the news director told us to "pay attention to the different constituencies in our audience—which include, but are not limited to, people working on AIDS, South Africa, Central America, gay and lesbian issues, labor, environment." Whenever possible, the director said, headlines should address issues on which activists are working.

In the same anchoring class, a couple of reporters pressed the news director on why KPFA routinely skips stories about some far-away wars. By way of example, I chimed in with a story about one morning when the anchor and I decided not to run a story about a war in Uganda, since neither of us knew what the issues were. All we knew was what the wire copy said, which we assumed could not be trusted for analysis. The director responded with a general rule for news writing at KPFA: "You want to be able to put it in a context and say how their own country is involved. That's the bottom line, right?" He paused, as if it was obvious what he meant, then continued, developing the idea: "You want to be able to tell people what's going on so they can do something about it. . . . People think KPFA is plenty internationalist—it's easy to rewrite wire copy from Indonesia, but what about the Oakland City Council?"

Why does KPFA use these routines? In typical news organizations, the routines help quell reporters' anxieties about a distant audience. Gitlin describes in *Inside Prime Time* (1984) a process that may also be applicable to journalists. Prime-time programmers, he states, are filled with anxiety about who their audience is. They live in a world apart from their audience. The result is that they try to routinize their work, repeating what they think were the successful elements of past shows and recombining them with elements from other shows. Rules for how to produce a successful show are clearly rituals designed to make it easier for programmers to reject shows they do not feel will be popular and to relieve producers' anxieties over the invisible audience. They are alibis for ideology.

The KPFA staff does not have the same anxiety. It could afford less than religious fervor about the capacity of the rules to filter out ideology. There are other reasons for using the routines than alleviation of anxiety over a distant audience. Career goals outside the station proper is a relatively minor reason. Another reason is that the routines help smooth over political divisions within the left and within the station. As another researcher observing KPFA some years back wrote:

> These and other strains and stresses tended to be addressed for the most part in private conversation rather than in public. As Ginny Berson [then head of the station's Women's Department] remarked, the station contained within it lesbians, homophobes, liberals, anarchists, marxists, Zionists and anti-Zionists. Public debates around these subjects, while unlikely to resolve them, could have split the whole project into multiple

factions and destroyed the broadly based coalition it represented. Feminists were not alone in thinking that at least in KPFA you could talk to people individually about these things, and that in this respect it was much better than in the outside world. (Downing, 1984, p. 91)

Reporters understand the audience to be divided along similar lines. Furthermore, all agree that the station should equip the audience with a variety of viewpoints, not just the "correct line," and should include a correct analysis if anyone involved is advocating one. The audience is said to want respect and to resent being "fed a line." To act effectively, the KPFA audience needs to know a range of views and arguments for and against them.

But Is It Oppositional?

In this article, I have argued that there would be nothing in the news form itself to prevent the propagation of oppositional interpretations of the world if news organizations could exist which were not so beholden to corporate and commercial interests, *and* which employed noncareerist reporters with different ideologies themselves, *and* which had different relations both to their audiences and the social movements on which they reported. The routines themselves do not preclude oppositional news when they operate in oppositional organizations. The cultural forms of the day, which most leftists share with everyone else, are not completely immune to oppositional messages. The cultural forms are open.

But what if, for all its good intentions, KPFA is not doing such oppositional news after all? What if producers and listeners of the station's news are all mistaken in seeing it as oppositional? KPFA news does share a great deal with standard news. Though KPFA and its audience situate themselves in opposition to the dominant ideology, they are still part of this society. For example, everyone who works at the station agrees that stories should be as short and as fast-paced as possible. They should be colorful, using interesting atmospheric sounds.

An extreme reading of the routines-centered approach to news might say that even KPFA's news conveys an ideologically dominant message embedded in the form itself, and there would be some good arguments for that view: Walter Benjamin (1955, p. 158) stated in the 1930s that news is an unassimilable compilation of disjointed information that echoes the incomprehensible speed of modern cities and crowds, modern life itself, with its excess of surface clutter. Private contemplation, felt experience, the quiet weight of tradition all remain "issueless" in the face of so much disembodied information. This is the "anti-lyric" attitude that propels today's postmodern world. Regular, on-time, on-the-hour, up-to-the-minute, the news dovetails with dominant notions of time, scheduling, and novelty (Gitlin, 1980, p. 266), just as the literary form of the novel dovetailed with the social world of early capitalism in a way that the recited epic poem did not. Another argument for the idea that KPFA's news is not as oppositional as it tries to be is that there is no such thing as a neutral observer, yet the news routines cover the tracks left by the reporter's ideology, leaving a falsely pristine landscape. And the daily diet of disembodied facts allows for, and even can perpetuate, a collective amnesia which makes analysis difficult. If all normal news forms point the journalist down the road of dominant ideological content, then clearly "oppositional news" is an oxymoron, and the leftist reporters at KPFA would do better to spend their time on other political projects.

The problem with discarding news completely is that news has become one of society's predominant political and cultural forms. Dismissing the news as a form which obstructs real social understanding leaves the scholar and journalist painted into a corner: All news is dominant ideology, yet the news is the major form of distributing political information in our society. As a shared cultural form, news can bring people together, potentially giving strangers a common ground of conversation. The fact that political debate is generally taboo in polite company is not the fault of the news but of the larger political culture.

Probably no one would argue that it is useless for listeners to know about revolutions, wars, and strikes around the globe. If the news were really to report on issues that demand immediate social action, the entire newscast would be overwhelmed with true-life horror stories about pending nuclear war and jeremiads about the ongoing ecological destruction of the planet (Rosen, 1988). But then what would be the proper forum for publicizing less global issues, like revolutions, unionization drives, uprisings, and invasions? If audiences need to know more about the issues that deserve action, they can read books.

If the news form is bloodless and disembodied, it also can make possible a sense of connection daily with global events. It allows for a continuously decentered sense of the world, a feeling that one's own home is not the center of the universe. This could lead to a stronger feeling for the global scale of politics, not an entirely negative outcome. What is missing is the means of connecting the far-away dots of scattered events so that they fit together in a coherent picture.

News should be seen as part of a whole range of communication (Carey, 1986). The fact that many people only pay attention to the most surface layers available does not mean that surface layers themselves are useless. They make sense when placed in a theoretical, historical context, but this cannot be done by the journalists themselves. Sectarian left papers, for example, may try their best to do so, decrying the forces of capitalism in every other sentence, without attempting to make this seem like anything "new," like an "advance in the story." This kind of reporting is usually simplistic because news stories are not long enough for deep historical analysis or development of carefully reasoned theories. Reporters can only evoke historical or theoretical understandings already present in the audience, so that the listeners can think, along with the KPFA reporter, "That makes sense considering what else I know about how that system works."

To be oppositional, a form needs an audience.[9] Even KPFA's audience, probably some of the most politically concerned in the United States, in an area of the country with one of the highest concentrations of oppositional political activists, is more interested in the daily diet of facts than the longer analytical pieces, radio dramas, or weird musical or spiritual programs that try to challenge Western ideas about art, space, and time. Listeners tune in the news more than any other program at the station.

Their reasons for tuning in are different from those of mainstream news listeners. In a study, viewers of mainstream news found in it a "reassurance that the world both near and far was safe and secure and demanded no immediate action on their part" (Levy cited in Gitlin, 1980, p. 267). In letters to KPFA, on the other hand, listeners often say that KPFA news inspires them to act in the world. I asked some discussion sections of a class of undergraduates to listen to KPFA's news, and many of those who liked and could follow KPFA news said that it had a distinctly unsettling effect on them, opposite from the effect Levy described. It made them want to "go out and do something." KPFA tries not to preach to the converted, yet, for other students in the discussion sections I surveyed and interviewed, KPFA's news was pitched "too high" and assumed too much political involvement. They said KPFA's news had too much information, that the production was not slick enough, and that they could not follow the stories concerning places and people about which they had never heard. Some, for example, did not know which side the United States was on in Nicaragua or what apartheid was. One of the people who dropped out of my KPFA news class did not know that "unions" and "management" are two different entities and could not tell that KPFA's news was trying to be oppositional. He had no conceptual category for oppositional politics. Politics was a blur to him, so the news was too.

Oppositional news only makes sense when the audience already has some inkling of a theory with which to interpret the scattered daily crises. The problem is not that there is news; the problem is that there is little else in the empty American public sphere.

Notes

1. Though a June 1987 Pacifica production, "Hear No Evil: Free Speech, Censorship, and Broadcasting," shows that the amount of official censorship should not be underestimated.

2. I thank Ann Swidler, Michael Schudson, Todd Gitlin, and Michael Burawoy for their generous and thoughtful assistance and encouragement. Thanks also to the members of my study group on American culture and politics, the Culture Club: Lyn Spillman, Rich Kaplan, Arlene Stein, and, above all, Paul Lichterman.

3. Carlin Romano's theoretical work (1986, p. 76) draws on Ludwig Wittgenstein's ideas and makes an argument similar to my own.

4. An implication of this finding, which could be useful for activists who are trying to bring a broader range of views into the media's eye, is that supplying normal news

organizations with alternative or oppositional sources' telephone numbers might help bring these views into the spotlight. Media activists in San Francisco are trying this strategy, sending to normal news desks rolodex cards already filled out with such groups' numbers.

5. Perhaps an extreme version of the routines-centered theory would assert that by focusing on leaders and not undistinguished participants, even KPFA's news could give the "ordinary person" the feeling that her or his involvement is peripheral, that the "experts" have everything under control. However, the coverage also can provide a sociological, analytical perspective that would be impossible to reach if reporters were simply to interview random individuals. Gitlin (1980) points out that the media's need to "certify leaders," even New Left ones, was damaging in any case. His point is not that leadership is a universally bad thing but that a group should not tailor itself to the needs of the media. The need for leaders is firmly embedded in our society, media or no media; the media here only have a deleterious effect when they create leaders where leaders have not been picked.

6. The planning of the Bay of Pigs invasion was reported first in the *Nation* (Sigal, 1973, p. 81). Woodward and Bernstein, the famed sleuths who uncovered the Watergate scandal, were not White House beat reporters but police reporters who were sent to investigate a common break-in (Epstein, 1973, p. 197). The Iran-Contra affair began to unravel when a Syrian newspaper talked to divergent factions of the Iranian leadership. Many connections between U.S. officials and Latin American drug smugglers were exposed on Pacifica's airwaves, in the *Nation* magazine, and by the Christic Institute long before they had been revealed by the major papers or their Latin America beat reporters.

7. Interview taped for KPFA, aired June 20, 1987; data to be published in his forthcoming update of his 1983 book, *The Media Monopoly*. He said that by June 1987; after his update had gone to the printers, the figure had fallen even further, to 26. Conversely, Bagdikian continues, reporting, and reporters, can become an integral part of political power brokerage, as when politicians say, and believe, that NBC reporters report unfavorably on politicians who are not generous with military contracts to General Electric, NBC's parent company.

8. This was not always so. For example, someone played me a recording of KPFA reports on People's Park from the 1960s. They were formally outrageous and, in fact, unintelligible to my 1980s ears.

9. An alternative has been explored in art and film. In film, for example, a radical genre set out to show that reality does not come in the narrative forms acceptable to the Broadway style. The result was films like Chantal Ackerman's *Jeanne Diehlmann*, a three-hour piece with very little plot or emotional display in which the camera almost never moves. While this may be truly oppositional, it is not very appetizing to many people.

References

Bagdikian, B. (1983). *The media monopoly.* Boston: Beacon.

Benjamin, W. (1955). On some motives in Baudelaire. In H. Arendt (Ed.), *Illuminations* (pp. 155-200). New York: Shocken.

Betserai, T., & Salniker, D. (1983). *KPFA training manual* [pamphlet].

Breed, W. (1955). Social control in the newsroom: A functional analysis. *Social Forces, 33,* 326-333.

Carey, J. (1986). The dark continent of American journalism. In K. R. Manoff & M. Schudson (Eds.), *Reading the news* (pp. 143-199). New York: Pantheon.

Downing, J. (1984). *Radical media: The political experience of alternative communication.* Boston: South End.

Dreier, P. (1982). The position of the press in the U.S. power structure. *Social Problems, 29,* 298-310.

Eliasoph, N. (1986). Drive-in morality, child abuse, and the media. *Socialist Review, 16*(6), 7-32.

Epstein, E. J. (1973). *News from nowhere.* New York: Vintage.

Gans, H. (1979). *Deciding what's news.* New York: Vintage.

Gitlin, T. (1980). *The whole world is watching.* Berkeley: University of California Press.

Gitlin, T. (1984). *Inside prime time.* Berkeley: University of California Press.

Hallin, D., & Mancini, P. (1985). Speaking of the president: Political structure and representational form in U.S. and Italian television news. *Theory and Society, 13,* 829-850.

Halloran, R. (1986, October 8). American is captured after plane is downed in Nicaragua territory. *New York Times,* pp. A1, A8.

Laclau, E., & Mouffe, C. (1982). Recasting Marxism: Hegemony and new political movements. *Socialist Review, 12*(6), 91-113.

Lewis, P. (1984). Community radio: The Montreal conference and after. *Media, Culture & Society, 6,* 137-151.

Levy, M. (1978). The audience experience with television news. *Journalism Monographs, 55.*

Mattelart, A., & Piemme, J.-M. (1980). New means of communication: New questions for the left. *Media, Culture & Society, 2,* 321-338.

Romano, C. (1986). Grisly truths about bare facts. In R. K. Manoff & M. Schudson (Eds.), *Reading the news* (pp. 39-77). New York: Pantheon.

Rosen, J. (1988). *The problem of the public in the nuclear age.* Unpublished manuscript, New York University, Center for War, Peace, and the News Media.

Schudson, M. (1981, April 4). Starring SDS. *New Republic,* pp. 36-38.

Schudson, M. (1982). The politics of narrative form: The emergence of news conventions in print and television. *Daedalus, 11,* 97-112.

Sigal, L. V. (1973). *Reporters and officials: The organization and politics of newsmaking.* Lexington, MA: D. C. Heath.

Tuchman, G. (1972). Objectivity as strategic ritual: An examination of newsmen's notions of objectivity. *American Journal of Sociology, 77,* 660-679.

Tuchman, G. (1978). *Making news: A study in the construction of reality.* New York: Free Press.

Selling News

News as Economic Entity

This section moves toward a level of analysis beyond the journalist and the news organization to consider how financial arrangements of the U.S. press system affect the nature of newswork and news organizations. Both political-economic and culturological approaches are introduced within this section's readings.

"Boundaries of Journalistic Autonomy," an excerpt from J. Herbert Altschull's *Agents of Power*, sets the scene for thinking about news as a commodity, contending that news content reflects the interests of those who pay the bills, what Altschull calls "paymasters." Journalists are referred to as "the pipers" who are paid to play tunes composed by the paymasters. Within American media, the *commercial* pattern of media financing centers on the effect of advertisers and their commercial allies, including media owners and publishers. Key to understanding the economic influence on news is the idea that an organization must keep its content within the bounds of acceptability to its financiers. Altschull points out the irony that although the job of journalists is to pay close attention to society, journalists tend to overlook the role of financiers.

Altschull highlights three factors that contribute to the absence of challenge to the commercial pattern. First, journalism education performs the role of ideological trainer, helping journalists-to-be adopt the system's goals and values as their own. Second, the mass media hiring system weeds out applicants who do not seem to be properly "educated." Finally, as Eliasoph demonstrated in Chapter 16, pressures within news organizations ensure that journalists conform to policy.

If news is indeed a commercial product, then the site of production can be considered as "The News Factory," where Charles R. Bantz, Suzanne

McCorkle, and Roberta C. Baade explore product manufacturing techniques in local television news. After delineating five factors that encourage work routinization (staffing, technology, consultants, profit, and product), the authors describe key aspects of a news assembly line that breaks down tasks into smaller chunks. Five key steps are involved in this news assembly line, starting with story ideation and ending with product distribution in the newscast.

A case study based on observation at a television station then demonstrates how the factory model brings four negative consequences. One consequence is that the lack of production flexibility requires a high degree of routinization and limits responsiveness to the news environment. In addition, television newsworkers tend to be generalists, which reduces their stake in work outcomes. An organization's productivity expectations, both in terms of deadlines and quantity of stories, provide another disincentive to go beyond minimum product quality. In sum, Bantz, McCorkle, and Baade argue that because local television news is a profit center, newswork is organized to produce a uniform product in a limited time period. The result is a constrained, routinized approach to news.

An excerpt from John H. McManus's *Market-Driven Journalism*, "The First Stage of News Production: Learning What's Happening," also considers the economic effect of news production. Ideally, creating a successful commodity requires that production costs are kept low while market demand remains high. However, this "economic logic" runs counter to journalistic logic that depicts news media as society's watchdogs—active surveillance brings a much more expensive mode of news discovery. McManus offers three models for the way that journalists discover news, each based on the degree to which discovery is a passive or active process. He then suggests three theoretical expectations for the relationship between a television station's profit orientation and its dominant mode of news discovery.

Through case studies based on observation at medium, large, and very large television news departments, McManus concludes that market pressures were served better than the public, with passive discovery of news being most common. At the largest station, the one with the greatest resources, a greater proportion of story discovery was found, but this proportion was attributed mainly to the increased financial stakes of a competitive media market.

Matthew C. Ehrlich's "The Competitive Ethos in Television Newswork" addresses competition as its central focus, but the emphasis is on the "power of the idea of winning," rather than on the actual competition that exists in a media market. *Competitive ethos*, as Ehrlich defines it, refers to a set of norms and values about competitiveness that pervades both newswork and American culture. To demonstrate the nature of the competitive ethos, he draws on all three research thrusts discussed by Schudson in Chapter 1: *political-economic, sociology of organizations*, and *culturological*.

In addressing political-economic concerns, Ehrlich applies McManus's concept of "market logic," concluding that rather than making news better, competition helps make more money for the news organization. From a sociological perspective, journalists socially construct their newsroom realities by enacting beliefs about competition: Running a competitive race becomes an organizational ritual that encourages producing the same news as competitors.

From a culturological approach, the competitive ethos builds and maintains what Zelizer has called an interpretive community within the newsroom. However, this community emphasizes individual competition, so that the competitive ethos becomes an oppressive cultural force that negatively affects the nature of the news product.

In all, a marketplace view of news represents yet another plausible vantage point for viewing the news hologram. Compared with the individual and organizational vantage points, the marketplace approach requires standing further back to look at the media not only as part of a social system but also as part of political and economic systems. What appears from this view is that market pressures tend to serve the profit interests of media organizations more than they do the information of the society in which they are embedded.

CHAPTER **17**

Boundaries of Journalistic Autonomy

J. Herbert Altschull

The content of the news media inevitably reflects the interests of those who pay the bills. The argument, in other words, is that the financiers—or the paymasters, as we can call them—or the group they represent will not allow their media to publish material that frustrates their vital interests. This form of control is often subtle, and we will develop this thesis in some detail later. For now, it is useful to note four basic patterns of relationships between the paymasters and the content of the news. We will call these relationships official, commercial, interest, and informal. Rarely is the relationship a pure one; overlapping is quite common. So are exceptions. Still, the four basic patterns are clear enough.

In the *official* pattern, the content of the newspaper, magazine, or broadcasting outlet is determined by government rules, regulations, and decrees. Some news media may be themselves state enterprises, some may be directed through government regulations, and some may be controlled under a network of licensing arrangements. All dictatorships, whether run by one person or by a group, follow the official pattern. No nation is free of official controls; the variations come in the degree of autonomy permitted. In the *commercial* pattern,

From "Freedom of the Press" and "The Lords of the Global Village," chapters in *Agents of Power*, 2nd edition, by J. Herbert Altschull. Copyright © 1995 by J. Herbert Altschull. Reprinted by permission of Longman Publishers.

the content reflects the views of advertisers and their commercial allies, who are usually found among the owners and publishers. The means of control are advertising and public relations. Even under planned economies, commercial influences can be detected, although for the most part these are exerted only indirectly. In the *interest* pattern, the content of the medium echoes the concerns of the financing enterprise—a political party, a trade union, a religious organization, or any other body pursuing specific ends. In the *informal* pattern, media content mirrors the goals of relatives, friends, acquaintances, or lobbying groups who supply money directly or who exercise their influence to ensure that the desired reports are circulated. The less heavily industrialized a country, the more apparent the impact of informal patterns will be.

We must be careful not to stumble into the trap here. We must not force the press into a classification system that is national in nature. Freedom House and other organizations that rate the press of one country as free and the press of another as controlled are simplifying highly complex patterns. To be sure, we can set forth plausible arguments, as Freedom House has done, that the press has a greater degree of political autonomy in some places than in others, but there are forms of control that are not purely political. Equally controlling are economic or religious or cultural factors. Rating systems establish the fiction that the press of one country is a monolith. The newspapers and magazines within the borders of a nation are not identical.

No newspaper, magazine, or broadcasting outlet exceeds the boundaries of autonomy acceptable to those who meet the costs that enable them to survive. These boundaries, it must be remembered, are not carved in stone. They are very flexible, and in every place on earth, the boundaries have changed over time. Measuring sticks that seek to classify the dynamic are necessarily flawed, as are those that place national labels on the measuring sticks. The imperfect best we can do is deal in degrees. For example, we can say with some confidence that the political system in a country derives from the economic power structure and that the press of that country by and large will reflect the ends of those who manage the economy. Those ends may be openly stated, or they may be concealed. When the ends are openly stated, the press is likely to be subjected to a large measure of official control. When they are concealed, the press is likely to be directed through either commercial channels or informal arrangements. In all cases, for whatever their purpose, interest groups (both those that support the objectives of power and the dissidents who oppose those ends) make use of media, sometimes the mass media, and sometimes in forms that we can speak of as minimedia. . . .

* * *

Among the most remarkable aspects of the folklore of the press is the absence of references to money. The mythology casts the press as Athena, sprung full-born from the brow of the people. The authors of *Four Theories of the Press* mention the financing of the press only in passing and ignore the question of profit.[1] In the reports of the Hutchins Commission and the British Royal Commission, money took the form of an ominous cloud threatening to divert the press from the duty assigned it by the people, who are perhaps the representatives of Zeus. Even more startling is the cavalier treatment accorded by working journalists to the influence of money on their livelihood. To be sure, they are concerned about their own incomes and expense accounts and are cognizant of the costs of publishing and broadcasting. Yet, until quite recently, little attention has been given to the connection between those details of financing and the news product they deliver. It is as if journalists, whose daily lives are dedicated to close observation, have blinded their senses to the realities of their calling. Advertisers are often held in contempt; they and their kind are not welcome in the newsroom, and many reporters and editors would cheerfully go to prison rather than allow their news judgment to be influenced by the crass commercial world of advertisers. Journalists are willing—more than willing—to let it go at that. Beyond the surface of reality many journalists are not prepared to go. Or, rather, beyond the surface of reality journalists do not permit themselves to go—for in the shadows beyond lies the fear that the truth would surely explode the comforting folklore of press independence.

Such, at least, is the pattern of journalistic life in the United States and, in varying degree, throughout the capitalist world. In the former Soviet Union, the financing of the press was a matter of no greater concern among socialist journalists. The part of Zeus in the Soviet Union was taken not by the people but by the Communist party serving as vanguard of the people. If pressures were brought on Soviet journalists, they came not from the sellers of commercial notices but from party functionaries. In other words, the press mythology in the lands of the Superpowers (and their allies as well) held and continues to hold that it is from politicians the pressure for conformity comes, not from the moneyed interests.

The reality, on the other hand, is that the content of the press is directly correlated with the interests of those who finance the press. The press is the piper, and the tune the piper plays is composed by those who pay him or her. This is so even though the identity of the paymaster is not always known: In fact, it is in the paymaster's interests to maintain the lowest sort of profile, for to do so contributes to the maintenance of the folklore.

The image of the press as piper is a perfectly natural one. It occurred to Johann Amos Komensky, a Moravian churchman and educator, as early as the first years of the seventeenth century, only a short time after newspapers made their appearance in Europe. Komensky—or Comenius, as he called himself—was one of the most distinguished writers of his era, although his work has received only limited attention outside eastern Europe and Western educational circles.[2] Complete translations of Comenius's writings are rare. His *Labyrinth of the World*, for instance, is best known in English in a 1901 translation by Count Lützow.[3] The *Labyrinth*, which appeared in 1623, bears some resemblance to John Bunyan's *Pilgrim's Progress*, and indeed Comenius sent his Pilgrim into the world to study workers and their behavior. Chapter 22 found the Pilgrim in the company of journalists. Count Lützow, recognizing how primitive was the state of journalism at the time, used the word *newsmen*, but Vladimír Hudec, dean of the journalism school at the University of Prague, spoke of the workers as journalists.[4] In the marketplace of a city, the Pilgrim noticed these journalists piping melodies into the ears of bystanders. When the piping was pleasing, the audience rejoiced, and when it was doleful, the people were sad. The pipes were provided by "vendors" whom Comenius did not otherwise describe: From our vantage point three and a half centuries later, we can identify them as paymasters. Comenius was intrigued by the fact that those who heard the piper could be exulted by the sound or plunged into terrible grief, as "men allowed themselves to be deceived by every gust of wind." Even back in the seventeenth century, he perceived with rare prescience an important fact of life in the universe of the press: To be a journalist is risky business. From all sides, the Pilgrim observed, the journalists found accusations falling on their shoulders, especially from those who did not listen carefully to what was being piped around them. "I see here . . . that it was not safe for all to use these whistles. For as these sounds appeared different to different ears, disputes and scuffles arose," the Pilgrim concluded; the victims of these scuffles were most likely to be the journalists themselves.[5] Many writers, Shakespeare among them, have called attention to the danger of being the bearer of unwelcome news. It was a situation that distressed MacBride as well.

The tolerance of the paymaster for behavior he or she considers unsuitable is inevitably limited, as was that of William Congreve's character Sir Sampson Legend, who introduced the piper-paying metaphor into the English language in *Love for Love*. Sir Sampson announces that as a father he possesses both authority and arbitrary power and will cut off his son without money in retaliation for the son's lack of subservience to the father's wishes and his offensive behavior. "I warrant you," Sir Sampson says, "if he danced till Doomsday, he thought I was to pay the Piper." [6] That, in 1695, was the promise of an early paymaster. The threat of punishment for offenses has not been modified over the past 300 years. Such is the case despite the fact that the faces of both piper and paymaster have changed drastically in that time frame. Few pipers work for a single paymaster any longer. Among journalists, the employer today is likely to be a syndicate or conglomerate.

The relationship between the piper and the paymaster, as noted earlier, takes four different forms: official, commercial, interest, and informal. The press cannot, however, be forced into a national classification system; there is too much overlapping for that. The degree of political autonomy differs from one publication to another. The mistake is to equate levels of political autonomy with freedom. No newspaper, magazine, or broadcasting outlet exceeds the boundaries of autonomy acceptable to the paymasters. The boundaries are not carved in stone; rather, they are flexible, and in every place on earth the boundaries have changed over time. Models that quantify the dynamic are inevitably flawed, as are those that tag the measuring sticks with national labels. The imperfect best we can do is to deal in degrees. The political system in a country derives from the economic power structure. Its press reflects at any given time the ends of those who manage the economy.

Those ends may be openly stated or may be concealed. When the ends are openly stated, the press is likely to be subjected to a large measure of official control, and when they are concealed, the press is likely to be directed through either commercial channels or informal arrangements. In all cases, interest groups, those that support the objectives of power, and the dissidents who oppose those ends use the press for their own differing purposes.

In the former Soviet Union, the identity of the paymaster was supremely clear: The Communist party made the ultimate decisions about how money was spent. No doubt existed in any mind that newspapers, magazines, and broadcasting outlets were required to operate within the boundaries fixed by the party. Journalism students in the Soviet orbit were instructed to present information "objectively" and work for the benefit of society. To present contrary information was to serve reactionary interests and was thus unacceptable. The piper carried out the goals of the paymaster, the tunes played in the interests of the paymaster. Not surprisingly, Marxist schools of journalism failed to examine the financing of the Soviet press but taught that capitalist journalists served the interests of their paymasters. They dismissed Western notions of fairness and balance as mere pretenses and held that objectivity was possible only under the banner of Marxism-Leninism.

Statistical data on the financing of the Soviet press were difficult if not impossible to obtain. Very likely no one knew the cost of conducting the Soviet press system. Take, for example, the case of *Pravda*, the official party newspaper that collapsed financially as soon as the Soviet Union fell apart. The word may ring strangely in this context, but, according to Soviet authorities, *Pravda* operated at a profit. With a circulation of 11 million, the newspaper sold for 3 kopecks, or about 5 U.S. cents. Soviet officials said newsprint for the six-page paper ran to less than 1 kopeck per issue. With a staff of only 200 to be paid, subscriptions produced more revenue than it cost to publish the paper. According to Soviet estimates, any newspaper with a circulation in excess of 10,000 was a profit-making venture. In line with these estimates, Soviet officials said they had to subsidize only the tiniest of papers. Radio and television were fully subsidized since they were operated by civil servants. No one listed newspapers and magazines as state-run enterprises. Missing from this curious financial accounting were all capital expenses. The cost of equipment was simply not counted, nor were the costs of the buildings housing the newspapers or the costs of maintenance of equipment and buildings. Even distribution costs were budgeted under other headings. By these standards, almost every newspaper on earth would be a profitable enterprise. The most agonizing challenge for those news organizations in the post-Soviet world has been to build up a new network of paymasters.

The Soviet accounting system, of course, was not designed especially for newspapers. Capital costs were not included in any budget reckonings. The vertical system was highly compartmentalized; work units did not communicate with one another, only with authorities above. Whatever the cost of producing newspapers, when they appeared on the streets their content was not displeasing to the managers of the papers or to their superiors in the

Kremlin, who footed the bill for the capital outlays under whatever budget heading they were hidden.

The party was not the only paymaster in the Soviet Union. *Izvestia*, with a circulation equal to that of *Pravda*, was financed by the Council of Ministers, *Trud* by the trade unions, and *The Literary Gazette* by cultural organizations. Various interest groups were prominent as financiers of the pipers whose tunes were sung in the pages of the papers. In the tightly controlled Soviet society, the identity of the paymasters was not publicized; still, they profited personally from their positions in money as well as power. To this extent, they were financing a kind of commercial venture. Informal arrangements also existed. For a long time, for instance, the son-in-law of Party Chairman Nikita Khrushchev held the position of *Pravda's* chief editor. Thus, in one form or another, all the patterns of relationships between piper and paymaster could be found in the Soviet Union. The same is true in the United States, although the emphases are different. While the most obvious relationship in the former Soviet Union was official, in the United States the commercial pattern is most evident. Exceptions are permitted—a modest dissident press has continued to persist with limited resources and power—but the overriding concern of U.S. press paymasters is with profit, and the measure of profit is revenue from commercial notices. As in the Soviet Union, it is extraordinarily difficult to find out how much it costs to produce a newspaper. It is impossible to determine the extent of profits, but some inferences can be drawn.

Eighty percent of the income of U.S. dailies comes from advertising, which occupies somewhat more than 60 percent of the space. Despite the ups and downs of the economy, revenue from advertising has been steadily increasing and even with declining readership, investment in the news media remains a sound business venture. When profits decline, the newspapers or broadcasting outlets can still be sold for financial gain to the rising number of combines and conglomerates in the field. Although profit is the goal of the industry, it is always represented as a means and not as an end. The phrase "a sound financial basis" often appears as a euphemism for profit because it suggests a more altruistic purpose than the acquisition of money.[7]

Massive infusions of money from advertisers are mandatory if the news media are to maintain a viable economic posture. The vital interests of both publishers and advertisers lie in healthy, profitable print and broadcast media. While completely accurate figures are not available, it is clear the rate of profitability of both television and newspapers is much higher than that of industry as a whole; some analysts say it is more than twice as high. At a conservative estimate, before-tax profits were running at more than 20 percent per year for both newspapers and television. Clearly, the interests of advertisers coincide with those of the owners of the print and broadcast media. Whatever furthers the goals and values of the system that provides profit to both is good, and whatever puts that system at risk is bad. This same simple truth underlies the structure of the commercial mass-media system and ideology.

As the content of the Soviet press reflected *official* goals and values, so the content of the U.S. press reflects *commercial* goals and values. Censorship is unnecessary in either case. Only in the rarest of circumstances are challenges raised to basic goals and values. Three factors contribute to the absence of challenges in the United States. First, there is the *educational system* under which the journalists learn to adopt those goals and values as their own. Second, the *hiring process* weeds out nearly all those who might be likely to raise challenges. Finally, those rebels who make it through the first two screening processes undergo *pressure to conform*—either from their colleagues or from their own wish to rise up the ladder. Desirable assignments and promotions go to those who make the minimum of waves. A few independent thinkers survive, tolerated as illustrations of the "true independence" of the media. Others give up the battle and move into different professions, as statistical evidence demonstrates.

Most journalists in the United States, China, Nigeria, and everywhere else are true believers. If they are the products of the journalism schools in market or socialist systems, they tend to endorse and promote the goals and values they have learned. If they are from the advancing nations, they are more likely to be dissidents, free thinkers, or perhaps learned supporters of either market or communitarian goals and values. Third World journalists continually experience conflicts between their cultural heritage and the modern educational systems they encounter. In their puzzlement, they are often more inclined to search than merely to accept. Moreover, peer pressures in the more fluid places of work in the advancing countries are less persistent than those in news offices in the industrialized world. In the newer nation-states, informal and interest patterns of relationships are more prevalent than official or commercial ones.

In the revolutionary period in the Third World, groups committed to overthrowing the colonial powers discovered they had a most excellent tool at hand. The press, especially in Africa, followed the U.S. model—the pages of many colonial papers became rallying points for opposition to British rule and later to active support for rebellion. The African revolutionaries represented a particular interest group. The financial resources they poured into their newspapers were meant to bring specific results: the end of colonial rule and their own ascent to power. Once entrenched in power, they anticipated that a press no longer under their direct control would still continue to support their goals and values. However, when these leaders ceased to be the paymasters, the pipers no longer played the tunes they expected. The repression that followed was inevitable. Another avenue beyond repression was open to them, however. It was a far more fruitful road to travel than repression, because journalists everywhere react with hostility to censorship, rigid official directives, and direct pressures from commercial forces. The approach that many of the advancing-world leaders adopted was an informal one enormously effective and difficult to trace. It was the hidden subsidy. Such subsidies have been common throughout the history of the press. In many cases, subsidies have represented the difference between profit and loss for owners of publications. As an example, the withdrawal of special low-cost mailing privileges to U.S. magazines in the 1970s forced so many closures and mergers that the face of the magazine industry was permanently altered. Printing subsidies still represent major sources of revenue in U.S. newspapers. Those designated to publish official notices can be assured of guaranteed advertising revenue that is denied to those without such designations. Usually the nature of the subsidies has been masked, like the profit-and-loss statements of newspaper owners.

Public-disclosure laws in the capitalist countries forced newspaper owners to use their imaginations to cloud their statements; they lumped some of their profits into other categories, such as reinvestment in new equipment or, increasingly, as newspapers have expanded into other financial activities, into diversified enterprises. Many have found their way into giant multimedia conglomerates.

Before World War II, most newspaper enterprises were family owned, and publishers refused to report information about their profitability. They said the public was not interested; however, at the same time, they demanded public disclosure of the financial activities of the government and other corporations. With the decline of competition and the growth of chain ownership, many newspapers went public and began offering shares on the stock exchanges. The 432,000-member workforce employed in the newspaper industry in 1992 was the largest among those in manufacturing industries in the United States. By 1993, circulation of the newspapers owned by the six leading chains totaled 20 million, or 40 percent of the total daily circulation in the country.[8] The Hutchins Commission expressed concern about the concentration of press ownership as early as 1947. By 1994, no fewer than 130 chains were active in the newspaper industry. All told, three of five daily newspapers were owned by conglomerates, four of five television stations, and more than a third of radio stations. At the start of the 1990s, the Gannett chain, the largest in the field and publisher of USA Today, owned 83 daily newspapers, more than 50 weeklies or other nondaily publications, 10 television stations, and 15 radio properties in major markets, as well as the largest outdoor advertising group in North America, the Lou Harris polling organization, satellites, and motion-picture production units.[9] In 1993, for the first time, USA Today operated at a profit, although Gannett declined to provide figures for its separate units. Gannett itself made a net profit of $398 million in 1993, double its profits of the previous year. Circulation of Gannett dailies was well over 6 million. USA Today accounted for nearly 2 million of that total. The mere existence of chains and conglomerates does not necessarily mean a decline in diversity of opinion. All along, the news media have tended to support the basic values of the political and economic system and have reflected the ideology of the paymasters.

No one knows exactly how profitable newspapers are, and though the newspaper industry in the United States has been shrinking, the newspapers that survive are doing very well.[10] E. F. Hutton, the market analyst, offered newspapers as one of the most lucrative investment opportunities available, noting the chief reason was that they sold access. "Advertisers buy access to potential purchasers of their products, providing newspapers with 70 to 80 percent of their revenues," a spokesperson observed. "Readers pay for access to news, information, advertising, and entertainment arranged in a convenient, predictable, and cheap package." [11] Since no new purveyors of access other than cable TV arrived in the consumer capitalist society, advertising rates rose steadily for both newspapers and broadcasters. They rendered themselves even more attractive by becoming diversified communication complexes.

The direct relationship between advertising and the viability of newspapers that marks the U.S. press scene is not the usual pattern in the Third World. There, the usual pattern of relationships between the piper and the paymaster is often informal; families and friends play an important part. Only those persons with substantial resources have been able to purchase controlling or total interest in newspapers, and those persons have inevitably had powerful friends or relatives in high positions in government. Even with initial capital, these owners have continued to need some form of subsidy to remain afloat, and they have naturally turned to their friends and relatives for help. The scenario frequently runs something like the following.

The brother-in-law of Publisher A in a certain country has held sway in the capital as finance minister. Because newsprint allotments were fixed by the finance ministry, the brother-in-law could count on regular shipments so long as his relative remained in power. Thus, it was no surprise his newspaper served as an unofficial voice for the government and its financial interests. The content of his paper reflected the goals and values of the government. The position of power over information held by the government in this situation was unassailable. Not only was it able to ensure favorable news reports in the brother-in-law's paper, but it could bring other owners either into line or into bankruptcy by assigning or withholding shipments of newsprint. None of these transactions was reduced to writing, so there was no way to check up. The head of government himself might not be aware of the newsprint arrangements, and the finance minister, if he himself sought power, could use his control of newsprint as a device to help him gain public support for a bid to overthrow the head of government. Informal arrangements exist in all nations, always operating to the end of ensuring the content of newspapers and broadcasting outlets does not stray far beyond the boundaries acceptable to those of the paymasters. This truth does not reflect on the integrity of the overwhelming majority of pipers. The point is that the interests of the pipers and those of their paymasters are generally in harmony.

Despite the high profitability of newspapers in the United States and among some allies, it grew increasingly difficult in most places to operate newspapers without government subsidies. For a number of years, Sweden has provided direct government support to its press. In other capitalist countries, the support has been less direct. In Africa, subventions were mandatory if a newspaper was to survive. In relatively prosperous Nigeria, it cost nearly 20 kobo (about 55 U.S. cents) to publish each copy of *The Daily Times* of Lagos, the country's most efficient newspaper. In order merely to break even, the paper required a subsidy of nearly 5 kobo (14 cents) per copy. The other Nigerian papers needed far greater subsidies, perhaps as much as 2 naira (a little over $5) a copy. Press freedom exists officially in Nigeria, but as Segun Osoba, general manager of *The Sketch* in Ibadan, commented: "Once you ask for subventions, you are controlled." *The Sketch* was operating in the 1980s without subsidies but was steadily losing money and had to go to interest groups for support. To provide sound information to Nigeria's millions, Osoba said, the country needed another 40 newspapers, but "anyone would be crazy to start a paper today." [12] The remark might be amended to add, "unless one could be assured of adequate subsidies." For along with the rising cost of salaries were even larger increases in the cost of raw materials, ink, and newsprint.

Notes

1. Fred S. Siebert, Theodore Peterson, and Wilbur Schramm, *Four Theories of the Press* (Urbana: University of Illinois Press, 1956).

2. In 1956, Unesco, recognizing the internationalism in Comenius's vision, decided to publish a volume of excerpts of his work and commissioned Jean Piaget, the Swiss educator, to write a preface. See Piaget's *On Education* (New York: Teachers College Press, Columbia University, 1957).

3. Count Lützow, *The Labyrinth of the World and the Paradise of the Heart* (London: Swan Sonnenschein, 1901).

4. Vladimír Hudec, *Journalism, Substance, Social Functions, Development* (Prague: International Organization of Journalists, 1978). Hudec used the English word *piper* as translation of Comenius's term: Count Lützow seemed unsettled as to whether the key word should be *piper* or *whistler*, but the effect is the same.

5. Since Comenius believed, as Piaget wrote, that educators should "teach all things to all men and from all points of view" (*On Education*, 7), he qualifies as a kind of patron saint of this book. Comenius was born in 1592 and died in 1670; it was in his lifetime that a press first appeared in Europe.

6. William Congreve, *Complete Plays*, ed. Hubert Davis (Chicago: University of Chicago Press, n.d.). The passage from the play originally performed in 1695 is from Act 2, Scene 1.

7. Newspaper Association of America, *Facts, 1982,* spoke of newspapers as serving as a watchdog, "a beacon in a murky world as a marketing voice for goods and services, as a source of entertainment, as a flagger of the important and the unpredictable—and as a source of the common knowledge that fashions common interests. To do that job newspapers must remain strong and independently free institutions—not only by exercising their right to express diverse views freely and openly but also by maintaining a viable economic posture." In the 1992 edition of *Facts*, the NAA dropped references to economic viability, stating that as the world and newspapers were changing, its goal was "to ensure that newspapers are just as vibrant and compelling today and tomorrow as they have always been, to inject vision and energy into an industry that continues to be a pillar of democracy and a force for change."

8. These figures were provided by the research bureau of the *American Journalism Review*, February 2, 1994.

9. *Wall Street Journal,* January 28, 1994.

10. Patrick O'Donnell, "The Business of Newspapers: An Essay for Investors," *Institutional Industry Review,* February 12, 1982.

11. O'Donnell.

12. Segun Osoba, interview with the author, Ibadan, Nigeria, April 14, 1980.

CHAPTER 18

The News Factory

Charles R. Bantz
Suzanne McCorkle
Roberta C. Baade

In the winter and spring of 1977, a research team of three members with diverse backgrounds spent 14 weeks observing a western metropolis television newsroom.[1] After using methods of participant observation research,[2] we were able to synthesize the team's various experience and observations into several characterizations of a television news organization's communicative environment. This essay includes a historic overview of factors that constrain the typical *local* television news organization and a descriptive characterization of the organizational nature of WEST-TV news.[3]

From *Communication Research*, 1980, Vol. 7, No. 1, pp. 45-68. Copyright © 1980 Sage Publications, Inc.

AUTHORS' NOTE: An earlier version of this article was presented at the meeting of the Western Speech Communication Association, Los Angeles, February 1979. Steven Chaffee's comments on that occasion and those of anonymous *Communication Research* reviewer were essential to our revision of this article.

The Routinization of Newswork: An Overview

While the popular conceptions of television news usually encompass some image of the glamorous on-the-air news personality, television has an underlying structure little different from any other organization that markets a product (see Hirsch, 1977). Like other organizations, television news is affected by myriad historic, technological, and "chance" factors that constrain the realm of possibilities within the organization.

We believe, as do others, the world of television news contains organizational and environmental pressures that have fostered a trend toward the "routinization" of newswork (see Altheide & Rasmussen, 1976; Tuchman, 1973a, 1977; see also Perrow, 1967). At WEST and other news organizations, five factors appear to have encouraged newswork routinization: (1) the nature of news staffs, (2) technological developments, (3) the impact of news consultants, (4) considerations of profit, and (5) constraints on the organization's product. Each of these factors has received considerable comment from observers of local television news. Here we demonstrate how these interdependent factors have combined to circumscribe the independent activity of reporters and photographers.

The News Staff

A principal characteristic of television news staffs is their mobility. Broadcast journalists change jobs throughout their careers, holding more jobs and receiving more job offers than print journalists (Johnstone et al., 1976). When these changes involve on-the-air talent, the moves are as visible as they are frequent.[4] A pattern of continuous personnel turnover compounds the need for news organizations to develop uniform structures and routine methods of work to facilitate the assimilation of new staff persons into working "team" members.

In recent years, news departments have experienced an increase in size (Barrett, 1978) and supervisory and managerial positions. The emergence of the producer on most television news staffs is the most visible example of a new supervisory position. As the title suggests, the "producer's" speciality is the presentation or appearance of the news show. In the early days of television news, the news director or anchorperson was responsible for overseeing the newscast. Gradually, the position of producer was adopted in many local operations. As supervision of the newscast was assigned to a producer, other organizational members also shifted into more specialized roles. For example, in some news organizations, the anchorperson now has little responsibility in preparing or coordinating the news show, often becoming a "talent" specialist whose job is to read copy. Similarly, the news director often became more of an administrator—hiring personnel, setting policy, and managing budgets. In Boulding's (1953) terms, local television news organizations have undergone not only simple growth (more personnel) but also structural growth (with more supervisory personnel and more specialized tasks for other personnel). The structural growth produces more specialized responsibility for the newscast, personnel, budgets, presentation, and so forth, producing greater control and routinization of the news organization.

Technology

As in all organizations, the development of technology altered the nature of news departments (Thompson, 1967; Tuchman, 1972, 1973b). In television news, the most important recent technological developments are portable video equipment and the subsequent introduction of microwave relays.

Traditionally, news programs used film in their productions. Film, however, takes time to photograph, process, and edit, and the cost of film constitutes a substantial expense for the organization.

The emergent video technology—portable video cameras and videotape machines—offered news departments faster production (instant playback capabilities) and lower expense (reusability of tape). One can, in theory, quickly edit the tape and be ready to broadcast. However, tape has limitations that encourage the organization to restrict its use. The equipment is more complex than film and requires constant maintenance. On an even more basic level, the effective use of video equipment in the field may require the presence of an additional person to carry the videotape recorder. In the absence of the extra person, the reporter and photographer must cope with the problems involved in physical manipulation of too much equipment. Unless the reporter helps carry the equipment, the team does not have the physical mobility to attain the desired visuals; if the reporter helps, he or she is inhibited in covering the story. Finally, the editing of videotape is time-consuming and requires an expensive editing machine. Hence, there are few machines and a great demand for them. Technology has increased the need for role specialists and coordinative activities in the newsroom. If this need is not met, long delays can result as equipment breaks down, tape does not get edited, and ultimately the news show is affected adversely.

The most recent technological development in television news, microwave transmission, has brought live, on-the-spot reporting into reality. However, new technology introduces new constraints. The skill and planning required for effective, quality broadcasts are immense. The technical limitations of microwave's line-of-sight transmission means the crew, including a new specialist in microwave technology, must locate the equipment to avoid buildings and mountains. Further, many stations have only one microwave unit, so its use is planned carefully to maximize its value to the news department.[5] The microwave technology represents a financial investment that necessitates scheduling and planning to maximize the everyday use of the equipment. Unfortunately, rigid scheduling minimizes the equipment's availability for "instant coverage." Thus, economic and scheduling factors may constrain the organization's ability to meet its goals.

Consultants

One of the most debated trends in local television news programs is the use of news consultants (see Powers, 1977; Whitehead, 1978). The pervasive impact of consultants, such as Frank Magid Associates or McHugh Hoffman, was reflected in the claim (made by a WEST-TV staff member) that one could identify a station's consulting firm simply by watching the newscast. For example, KSTP in Minneapolis-St. Paul and KOA in Denver have shared a visual style promoted by Magid, while KMGH in Denver and WCCO in Minneapolis-St. Paul have shared a style promoted by McHugh Hoffman. Overlooked in comments about visual style, however, are the organizational consequences of consultant recommendations, for example, encouraging stories of certain lengths or certain numbers of stories per newscast, stressing highly visual newscasts, and/or promoting reporter "involvement" in stories (Diamond, 1975; Eden, 1977). We observed an operative rule that news stories ran from 75 to 105 seconds. Not surprisingly, the activities or reporters and photographers produced only enough film and copy to fill that time. The system offered little reason to invest time and film in developing a longer story, as it would have a minimal chance of being aired. The only exceptions we observed were commissioned stories that would be split into several segments broadcast on different days, lead stories, and some feature stories. Whether the time limits had been set by consultant suggestion or were the by-products of other constraints (time and money), the effect at WEST was a functional law limiting the length of most stories.

Consultants almost uniformly have urged the use of more visuals in news (Diamond, 1975; Eden, 1977; Powers, 1977). Newsworkers are expected to provide usable film tape for virtually every story. At WEST, a lack of "appropriate" visuals often meant an assigned story was no longer desirable and was dropped from the show. Hence, newsworkers avoided any story without good visuals and/or invested a substantial amount of time pondering how to "visualize" a story (see Altheide, 1976; Crouse, 1974).

Finally, consultants also have played a role in the high mobility of news personnel by facilitating movement of newsworkers among stations. Carmody's (1977) and our observations indicate consultants will provide their clients with videotapes of newsworkers, enabling the client to view a wide range of potential employees quickly and easily.

Profit

In the not-too-distant past, local television stations treated their news operations as a necessary evil—necessary to demonstrate the station was serving the public as required by law, evil because news cost money and returned little profit. Today, local news programs are an integral part of the profit making of stations (Altheide, 1976; Diamond, 1975). As a result, upper management in most stations takes a strong interest in the news programs' ratings, sales, format, and talent.[6] At WEST, the level of management involvement was indicated by the fact the news consultants reported to the station's manager.

Product

The demands of profit, consultants, producers, and technology combine to constrain the type of product a news organization produces. The emphasis is on technically uniform, visually sophisticated, easy-to-understand, fast-paced, people-oriented stories that are produced in a minimum amount of time (see Rosenfield et al., 1976). These requirements mean the organization depends on a well-defined task structure, role specialization, speed, interchangeability of personnel, and commonly held conceptions of what the product should be.[7]

The manner in which news staffs, technology, consultants, and profit combine within an organization to yield a uniform product suggests functionalism's principle of equifinality may be in operation (see Stinchcombe, 1968). These factors and the description developed below reflect an organization structuring itself to yield a uniform product in the face of variable events, resources, and time. The attempt to routinize newswork is an attempt to regulate organizational activity so the organization not only meets the deadline but also produces a news show that the organization defines (with the help of consultants and ratings) as *good*.

WEST as a Television News Factory

The constraints described above are common to most local television news organizations, but are significant in their synergistic operation—as they build to increase routinization. In this section, we present a characterization of how organizational constraints manifested themselves at WEST. We argue that, descriptively, a *factory model*[8] is a heuristic metaphor for how work was accomplished within WEST's television news department. Before that description, however, several cautions are necessary.

First, the generalizability of our observations may be limited. While WEST typified the national trends discussed above, a high level of organizational and interpersonal conflict may make it atypical of local news departments, and our case study approach lacks the comparative data necessary to judge the impact of the conflict on our observations. Second, the present study is not a long-term longitudinal study, thus precluding us from reporting historical developments. The reader should note, therefore, any claims presented below about historical developments reflect the *perceptions of the newsworkers*, not the researcher's long-term observations. Third, our use of the factory model in the discussion below is analogical, rather than literal. As an analogy, we feel the factory model provides insight into television news organizations that is obscured from other viewpoints.

The News Factory Model

The factory metaphor for the newsroom is not a precise duplication of the traditional factory.[9] It follows the form of an assembly line factory—breaking tasks into smaller "chunks," but it has the chunks being performed by newsworkers with varying degrees of skill who employ complex technology. The news factory divides tasks into larger pieces (hence chunks) and for different reasons than a typical assembly line does. The size of the piece is related directly to the skill of the worker, rather than the amount of time necessary to perform the task (an auto assembly line may break tasks into one-minute pieces so the line can produce 60 autos per hour). A reporter who is experienced and/or educated has a larger chunk of the process than does a film editor.[10] Therefore, the news factory is a mixed assembly line, with varying amounts of responsibilities among employees.

WEST's news department is modeled as an assembly line in Figure 18.1. The elements of a newscast segment[11] flow through the factory, being processed step by step, with the amount of processing related to the complexity of each segment. The systematic flow of the elements through the assembly line leading to a newscast consists of five steps: story ideation, task assignment, gathering and structuring materials, assembling materials, and presenting the newscast. The operation of the news factory model is best explained by detailing each step in the assembly line.[12]

Step One: Story Ideation

Enacting story ideas, the first step in the assembly line at WEST, involved two related activities.[13] First, individual newsworkers assessed the information flowing into the newsroom from various sources: press releases, general mail, newspapers, magazines, reporter ideas, police-fire-FBI radios, wire services, phone calls, and so on. The principal person performing this assessment was the assignment editor, who received the bulk of information (see Kasindorf, 1972). At WEST, however, the producer took major responsibility for the wire service stories and on some occasions other newsworkers (e.g., news director, executive producer, or secretary) evaluated the information. The assessment involved rapid processing of information and enactment of those items deemed potential stories. Such items were either filed for future reference or prepared for immediate news factory processing.

Second, story ideas were enacted collectively in the daily story meeting, which functioned in conjunction with the individual assessment of information described above. At this daily meeting, the assignment person, news director, early evening producer, and executive producer discussed a variety of topics, but directed most of their attention to that day's early evening newscast. The assignment editor usually had a list of assignments sketched out by the meeting time; the list formed the basis of the discussions. The story meeting functioned to modify, expand, and approve the tentative plan of assignments for the day. It is notable that the story meeting, while open to

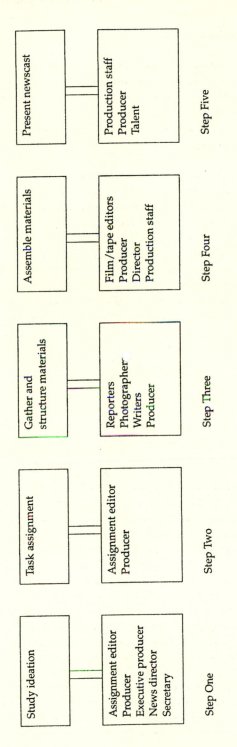

Figure 18.1. The News Factory Model

Study ideation	Task assignment	Gather and structure materials	Assemble materials	Present newscast
Assignment editor Producer Executive producer News director Secretary	Assignment editor Producer	Reporters Photographer Writers Producer	Film/tape editors Producer Director Production staff	Production staff Producer Talent
Step One	Step Two	Step Three	Step Four	Step Five

reporters and photographers, functioned as a meeting of management and supervisors to approve the day's work schedule.[14] The meeting narrowed the range of news inputs by committing the bulk of reporters' time, thus limiting their ability to generate additional items, and by emphasizing the ideation of a few individuals who enacted story concepts from a limited range of sources (see Tuchman, 1978).

Step Two: Task Assignment

Immediately after the story meeting, the assignment editor began his or her supervisory function, assigning tasks to the newsworkers as they arrived in the newsroom. The tasks often were assigned directly, with the assignment person informing (sometimes by two-way radio) the personnel involved of their duties. In addition, the assignment editor usually wrote the schedule of assignments on a large wallboard listing the story by title, reporter, photographer, completion time, type of equipment, and type of segment required. Like the "big board" in manufacturing plants, the story board functioned to inform personnel of their tasks for that day. As reporters and photographers moved in and out of the newsroom, they checked the board to monitor their duties and to evaluate the newsday. In a smoothly functioning television news factory, reporters and photographers would flow into the newsroom, receive a story assignment, move quickly to complete the task, and be ready for reassignment.

Some task assignments were made by the producers, who would either ask a writer to rewrite wire copy for broadcast or assign the task to themselves. Similarly, the producers would often assign themselves the task of selecting items from the network's morning or afternoon news feeds and write any copy necessary for the items.

Step Three: Gather and Structure Materials

Once a story was assigned, the newsworkers set out to gather and almost simultaneously structure the materials into a story. We observed, as have others, an interdependence of the gathering and structuring processes (gathering and structuring may occur simultaneously or either process may precede the other), which is why we join them here (see Altheide, 1976; Epstein, 1973; Roshco, 1975; Tuchman, 1972, 1973b).

In its most simplistic form, this involved nothing more than taking a wire story, writing it for the newscast, and requesting appropriate available visuals. More often, however, this process involved five related tasks: (1) obtaining any information the assigner had (news release, newspaper clippings), (2) talking to someone on the phone or in person, (3) going somewhere to gather material, (4) shooting film tape, and (5) writing copy.

Although the reporters and photographers often worked together during this process, each person also performed specialized tasks. Reporters sought information, wrote material to read, and coordinated the field work.

Photographers had a creative technical task requiring specific skills—an ability to handle equipment and a good visual sense—combined with frugality. Reporter and photographer worked together, but the different skills and differing levels of power and authority meant their rolls were clearly differentiated.[15] The division of labor was most pronounced when a photographer was sent into the field to shoot film tape on order—"get 30 seconds of air pollution"—while the reporter or writer remained in the newsroom to write the story.

The structuring of materials was formalized in the "shot sheet," which informed the film/tape editor what parts of the film/tape should be selected, what sound elements should be used, and in what order they should be assembled. The vast majority of times this sheet was made out before the reporter even saw the processed film or the videotape. Questions about the length of a segment were sometimes raised as the shot sheet was prepared; however, the manner in which the materials were gathered would have prohibited structuring a long (e.g., five-minute) segment, even if the producer desired one.

Step Four: Assemble Materials

The assembly of materials involved two activities: constructing individual segments and assembling the segments into the newscast. While the two activities are to some extent sequential, a segment's assembly is affected by and affects the show's assembly.

The assembly of a segment was performed by a film/tape editor, who edited the film/tape according to the instructions on the shot sheet. If the editor saw alternative modes for editing the film/tape, he or she could have altered the sequences, sometimes with or sometimes without the reporter's knowledge. The assembly of a segment was a technical operation, which could be time-consuming—particularly when editing tape.

The assembly process brought together the various elements of a newscast (except the newscasters) and prepared them for use during the program. The producer and director oversaw the assembly process, spending the last hour before airtime going over the script, adjusting times, and planning while the other newsworkers completed their own work.

Step Five: Present Newscast

Shortly before airtime, the parts of the newscast—script, film, tape—were turned over to the production staff, who were responsible for the broadcast itself. The production staff performed the technical coordination of the visual and oral elements during the newscast.

The producer remained involved with the news product throughout the telecast. He or she oversaw the progress of the program—watching the time, dropping stories if necessary, informing the newscasters of any new information. News personnel were involved in the production by reading copy and presenting the weather and sports.

The Assembly Line

While there are links between these five steps and some personnel are involved in several stages, a newscast is nonetheless a product of a series of activities that are performed separately. The idea for a segment seldom came from a reporter or photographer (except in the rare case when a reporter or photographer was assigned a permanent beat). Idea selection at WEST occurred at higher levels in the organization: news director, executive producer, producer, and assignment editors.

The assignment editor had the most direct influence on story ideation and was the supervisor of the newsroom, with the assignment desk being the focal spot in the flow of information to the reporters and photographers. The assignment editor's work was circumscribed, however, once an assignment was made.

Reporter responsibilities were to gather and structure materials, with occasional responsibility for assembly and presentation. The regular on-the-air talent for the weekday evening newscast were not active reporters. The photographers' principal responsibilities were gathering materials, but they also often functioned as film/tape editors. The film/tape editors assembled stories, with little or no feedback to the reporter, and had no role in any other processes. The news writers wrote copy and often filled other roles in the organization where they performed additional tasks (e.g., noon producer, assistant producer, editorial writer).

Of all the members of the organization, the producer was most likely to be found performing tasks in each step. The producer was an active supervisor, who coordinated the flow of segments and structured the entire show. The producer worked within the constraints of time, visuals available, segments prepared, show format, newsworkers' availability, and technical limitations to prepare a show that met product requirements. The division of labor was pronounced and likely would have been even more pronounced if WEST was a union shop, with contracts limiting movement across job descriptions.

The only persons immediately responsible for the entire product—the newscast—were the producer and director—the former for the content and the latter for the coordination of the technical elements. Thus, the reporter, who from the outside is often seen as the central figure in news organizations, was responsible—at best—for a segment or two in the telecast and those segments could be altered or dropped completely without the reporter's knowledge. While the reporter had freedom to leave the place of work (unlike a typical factory worker) and some ability to identify his or her contribution to the company's product, the broadcast reporter had no lasting control over his or her own work and no control whatsoever over the remainder of the newscast (Argyris, 1974, discusses the former problem in print organizations). Despite arguments for newsworkers' professionalism, the task distribution of the television news organization we observed shared more characteristics of a factory than it did the characteristics of a professional organization (see Ritzer, 1977; Tuchman, 1978; Tunstall, 1971).

Organizational Consequences of Factory News

The development of a factory news model, with its assembly line approach, in conjunction with the trends toward routinization appear to have at least four organizational consequences: (1) The news factory lacks flexibility, (2) there is a lack of personal investment in the news product, (3) newswork becomes evaluated in productivity terms, and (4) goal incongruence emerges between newsworkers' job expectations and job reality. Significantly, throughout our observations, newsworkers negatively characterized specific instances of these consequences.

Lack of Flexibility

Scene 1. It is 2:30 in the afternoon. One of the two videotape editing machines is not working. There are 15 videotape segments to be edited before the evening telecast. One segment has been waiting to be edited since 12:30. An argument ensues about the impossibility of editing all 15 segments by newstime. Several stories are dropped. Several tape segments are modified and partially edited. During the newscast, the director improvises as some tapes are incomplete. After the show, the producer sarcastically comments: "Isn't television exciting?" A meeting about the problem produces a suggestion that editing time be scheduled.

Scene 2. A mild snowstorm turns into a major blizzard. Both the assignment editor and news secretary leave early to beat the blizzard home, creating a gap in the normal flow of information through the newsroom. The news director, producer, and executive producer decide a live remote is necessary to cover the storm. The only reporter in the newsroom is told to do the remote on overtime. The microwave van operator is told about the live remote and angrily responds: "It wasn't planned!"

These two scenes are illustrative of the lack of flexibility in a factory production system. As Figure 18.1 shows, it is necessary for each story idea to pass sequentially through three steps before it is ready to be a segment on the newscast. A breakdown at any point requires adjustments to continue production. The lack of flexibility means the factory finds itself increasingly incapable of coping with such breakdowns and yet meeting self-imposed standards of production.

The technology involved in Steps Three, Four, and Five is critical. If, as in Scene 1, the assembling technology breaks down or even slows down, the progress of the story through the assembly line is impaired and the product must be modified. Organizational evaluation of system breakdowns produced plans to prevent the need for such last-minute improvisation in the future—that is, to make the task accomplishment more routine (see Altheide & Rasmussen, 1976).

The newsworkers do exhibit, at times, a clock-punching syndrome. Scene 2 illustrates this with the remote operator being angered by a change in plans. Further, there are examples of newsworkers "working to contract," with a reluctance or even resistance to being assigned tasks not designated as their own. (Remember, WEST was *non*union.) For example, on several occasions the reporter who did investigative reports was angered when taken from his semi-autonomous work to do general reporting. The emergence of work rules, both institutionalized (several work rule memos appeared during our observations) and self-imposed, is indicative of routinization.

The combination of increasing technology, task specialization, and adherence to work rules encourages more rigidity in the news factory. When rigidity merges with the demands of consultants and the requirements of a sophisticated product, the time required to assemble the product is increased, while the tolerance for error is decreased. This encourages the system to take a more carefully prescribed approach to gathering, structuring, and assembling the news. At WEST, these requirements were spelled out in detailed memos, instructing the staff on exactly how segments were to be prepared. The goal is not to simply meet the deadline, but to do so with a sophisticated, visual product (which is defined as necessary for a good show).

The television news factory, given the trends in television news and the operation we observed, appears to lose flexibility as it attempts to cope with technology and other requirements. The frustration this produces was bitterly summed up by the executive producer after the news the night of Scene 2: "This place doesn't respond to anything but a real disaster."

Personal Investment

The factory system reduces a newsworker's personal investment both in the segment he or she helps produce and in the entire newscast. This is a consequence of the interchangeability of newsworkers[16] and the newsworkers' lack of control over the final product. While a number of reporters have specialities, the assumption was any WEST reporter could be assigned to any topic and expected to produce a story (see Epstein, 1973; Tuchman, 1978). Similarly, photographers are expected to handle any assignment even though some are credited with being better with certain types of photography—such as sports or features.

Interchangeability means not only that any reporter could be assigned any story but also that any pairing of reporter and photographer is possible. The news factory assumption is that any type A part (reporter) can be paired with any type B part (photographer) to make a product C (story). While the wise assignment editor may avoid certain pairings because of past conflicts, personal strengths, or differences in work style, if necessary any pairing of personnel will be, and is, used.

The newsworkers' lack of control over the final product is apparent in the model. Neither the photographer nor the reporter can claim complete responsibility for a segment—each contributes to the material gathering and structuring. The assembly of the segment may be performed by a third person with constraints introduced by a fourth (the producer). Finally, the appearance of the segment is under the control of the producer and director, rather than the photographers or reporters.

The consequence of this system, with its interchangeability of personnel and lack of control, was a demonstrated lack of personal involvement. Several newsworkers admitted they simply wanted to get a story done on time and be done with work. We rarely observed a reporter or photographer ripping a breaking story off the newswire. Several reporters admitted they seldom watched the newscast. These patterns indicate a lack of involvement with the news product and the station. Further, the public job hunting of several persons demonstrated this lack of involvement with others in the newsroom.

This consequence of the general factory operation was highlighted by the contrast provided by a reporter and photographer who were treated as a team, assigned a regular feature slot, and granted much autonomy and control over their work. These two followed through the first four steps of the process: They generated ideas, gathered material, structured it, assembled most material, and sometimes even participated in presenting it. Not surprisingly, their work was distinctly different than their colleagues', and the team treated it differently, often promoting it for network syndication.

Productivity

The emergence of a factory model of news—combined with the demands for a high story count, for profit, and for cost-efficient use of sophisticated equipment—has directed the news organization toward evaluating newswork in productivity terms. Specifically, productivity is defined as doing one's assignment and doing it on time.

Under this measure of newswork, good workers are ones who get their work done on time; bad workers do not (with the consequences that the producer has to alter the show's rundown and perhaps the script, which in turn requires the director to change his or her plans for the telecast). The importance of this measure of productivity appeared in the supervisor's hostile response to the announcement that a story would be late and in the sharp criticism slow reporters and photographers received from faster newsworkers (who would have to produce more work to make up for the slower workers).

The productivity measure is significant for what it does not consider—any evaluation of quality, whether in the eyes of management, the reporters, or the outside journalistic establishment. With the exception of one series, we observed little discussion among newsworkers of "good" or "bad" newswork.

The popular guideline for WEST newsroom could read (1) only do the assignments given, (2) only attempt to complete them, and (3) meet the time deadline. The effect of the productivity measure is epitomized in the "quick and dirty," a story which would be treated simply, gathered and structured quickly, and evoke little personal investment from the newsworkers because they did not understand the purpose of the assignment.[17]

Expectations and the Factory

A fundamental problem of the mechanization of newswork is that newsworkers were not told newswork is factory work (see Johnstone et al., 1976). It may seem overdrawn, but we suspect (and Johnstone et al.'s 1976 data indicate) newspeople—like much of the public—have images of newswork similar to the popularized values portrayed in Bernstein and Woodward's (1974) *All the President's Men* and the personalized glamour of the network superstars or local anchorpersons.

In addition to these expectations, newsworkers are affected by the recognition television provides. On-the-air reporters are recognized on the street and invited to charity affairs and other public activities. In the era of eyewitness news, reporters are aware they are often hired not simply for reporting skills but also because they *look* good. Without the aid of comparative data on self-evaluation, we cannot support a claim that newsworkers have higher levels of self-value than other workers. We would note, however, several reporters commented that the television news business is full of people with large egos. Based on our observations, we would hazard the claim that newsworkers' self-valuation exceeds that of most workers in factory settings.

These circumstances produce a straightforward problem for the news factory. The factory newsworker values public service, autonomy, and freedom from supervision (Johnstone et al., 1976) and appears to have a strong sense of self-value. These same workers are in an organization that mechanizes their work, emphasizes worker interchangeability, encourages rapidity in production, has high employee turnover, and seldom offers qualitative evaluation of work. Thus, newsworkers concerned about being professional (Johnstone et al., 1976) find themselves in a climate in which work must be completed quickly within only minimum standards—no matter what complications develop—and then must relinquish the work to a factory assembly line (see Waters, 1978).

Conclusion

It is clear a newsroom is not an assembly line as most persons conceive of one. However, newswork is accomplished within steps of organizing that are designed to use nearly identical reporters and photographers to produce a uniform product within a limited period of time. The trends in television news—the turnover of newsworkers, the influence of consultants, the producer supervision, the increased technical sophistication, increasing organizational size, and the emergence of the news as a profit center—have contributed to local television news' development of a highly constrained, routinized approach to news.

The consequences of mechanizing newswork in television are a lack of flexibility, lack of personal investment in the product, an evaluation of newswork in productivity terms, and a mismatch between newsworkers' expectations and the factory in which they work. Throughout our observations, specific instances of these consequences were labeled negatively by newsworkers. Both supervisors and reporters would criticize the lack of flexibility for causing disagreements and as being "stupid." Instances of lack of personal involvement would appear as supervisors criticized newsworkers for not "following through" and some newsworkers criticized others for being "lazy." Some newsworkers complained that management's emphasis on productivity prevented them from doing a complete job. There were confrontations between newsworkers who sought autonomy and supervisors who demanded adherence to work routines. In their words and through their behavior, many newsworkers defined these four consequences as negative. The implications of the consequences for the viewing public remain to be evaluated.

Notes

1. Members of the team varied in age, credentials, media knowledge, and personal style, providing for a wider range of possible experiences and observations within the organization.

2. The organization's members were aware of the team's identity and purpose. Techniques varied from unobtrusive observation to near participation in work activities. Because of the team's composition and the wealth of different experiences afforded to each researcher, factors that similarly emerged from our individual field notes were considered significant and comprised the basis for the development of this report.

3. WEST-TV is a pseudonym. Please note we are restricting our comments to local news organizations. There is reason to believe the operation of network news differs from the argument we present below.

4. Barbara Walters and Harry Reasoner are two highly visible network examples; David Schoumacher and Connie Chung exemplify the moves from network to local operations; we suspect most readers can provide examples of station switching within one's own local market.

5. As we observed, maximation of value can have different meanings for different members of the organization. For some it is to save film expense, for some to show off the station's new toy, for some it is to get the news fast, and for others merely being sure the microwave unit is used at least once a day.

6. This interest can produce serious conflict between management and the news department, as illustrated in the highly publicized conflict at WCCO-TV, Minneapolis-St. Paul (Demick, 1978).

7. Role specialization and interchangeability are complimentary processes. Even as role specialization develops, workers are expected to be able to do the work of any person within their work class. Thus, a legislative reporter can be assigned a nonlegislative story. Reporters are assumed capable of reporting any story (see Tuchman, 1978). Photographers are assumed capable of filming any story. As technical specialization increases, the work class narrows and the interchangeability is limited. Thus, not all photographers are assumed capable of running microwave equipment even though it is a subspeciality of photography. Thus, role specialization and technology interact making the functioning of the news organization more fragile.

8. The traditional factory model was born in the Industrial Revolution and is epitomized by the assembly line, where tasks are broken into tiny bits, with each worker adding his or her piece to the ever-growing product (see Kranzberg & Gies, 1975).

9. See Tunstall (1971), who argues journalists are part of a nonroutine bureaucracy. While we would not dispute television workers must deal with exceptional cases, comparing our observations and others (Altheide, 1976; Altheide & Rasmussen, 1976) with studies examining print news (Tuchman, 1978, emphasizes print) suggests television news is more routine than print news and seeks to increase its routinization for the reasons discussed above.

10. This relationship was illustrated when an experienced film editor was dealing with an inexperienced reporter. In those cases, the editor assumed greater control over the assembly of the segment, while the reporter lost some of his or her control.

11. A segment would be wire copy written for reading with or without visuals, film or videotape to be shown with the copy being read (a voice-over), a film or tape package (incorporating all the visual and oral elements of a story, except the introduction), a live remote, and in-studio material (e.g., the weather).

12. In explicating the model, we will focus on the news component of a telecast (as opposed to sports and weather). The sports and weather segments are produced by the sports and weather persons, who operate semi-independently of the assembly line process; however, if they choose to use the resources of the factory (e.g., a photographer), the sports or weather segment becomes part of the assembly line process.

13. The terms *enacting* and *enactment* are used to suggest the active, meaning-creating nature of story ideation (Weick, 1969)—in contrast with the "story sorting" concept that dominates gatekeeper studies (e.g., White, 1950).

14. Wire stories were rewritten for broadcast as they came in and were not a regular feature on the story meeting agenda.

15. There were examples of open reporter-photographer conflict at WEST. In some cases, this appeared to be the result of one exerting dominance over the other.

16. "Ford established the final proposition of the theory of industrial manufacture—not only that the parts of the finished product be interchangeable, but that the men who build the products be themselves interchangeable parts" (Doctorow, 1975, p. 113).

17. There were newsworkers who sought to do more than meet a deadline; however, the system made productivity its primary measure of work.

References

Altheide, D. L. (1976). *Creating reality: How TV news distorts events.* Beverly Hills, CA: Sage.
Altheide, D. L., & Rasmussen, P. K. (1976). Becoming news: A study of two newsrooms. *Sociology of Work and Occupations, 3,* 223-246.
Argyris, C. (1974). *Behind the front page: Organizational self-renewal in a metropolitan newspaper.* San Francisco: Jossey-Bass.
Barrett, M. (1978). *Rich news, poor news.* New York. Crowell.
Bernstein, C., & Woodward, B. (1974). *All the president's men.* New York: Simon & Schuster.
Boulding, K. E. (1953). Toward a general theory of growth. *Canadian Journal of Economics and Political Science, 19,* 326-340.
Carmody, J. (1977, April 10). "Cosmetic" or "overrated," consultants do influence TV. *Denver Post,* pp. 27-28.
Crouse, T. (1974). *The boys on the bus.* New York, Ballantine.
Demick, B. (1978, January). News victory WCCO boss resigns, wanted happy talk. *[More], 8,* 10-11.
Diamond, E. (1975). *The tin kazoo: Television, politics, and the news.* Cambridge: MIT Press.

Doctorow, E. L. (1975). *Ragtime.* New York. Random House.

Eden, D. (1977, December 30). "News doctor" orders "happy talk." *Minneapolis Star,* pp. 1C, 12C.

Epstein, E. J. (1973). *News from nowhere: Television and the news.* New York: Random House.

Hirsch, P. M. (1977). Occupational, organizational, and institutional models in mass media research: Toward an integrated framework. In P. M. Hirsch et al. (Eds.), *Strategies for communication research* (pp. 13-42). Beverly Hills, CA: Sage.

Johnstone, J. W. C., Slawski, E. J., & Bowman, W. W. (1976). *The news people: A sociological portrait of American journalists and their work.* Urbana: University of Illinois Press.

Kasindorf, J. (1972, July 1). Spending a day on the hot seat. *TV Guide, 20,* 6-8.

Kranzberg, M., & Gies, J. (1975). *By the sweat of thy brow: Work in the Western world.* New York: Putnam.

Perrow, C. (1967). A framework for the comparative analysis of organizations. *American Sociological Review, 32,* 194-208.

Powers, R. (1977). *The newscasters.* New York: St. Martin's.

Ritzer, G. (1977). *Working: Conflict and change.* Englewood Cliffs, NJ: Prentice Hall.

Rosenfield, W. W., Hayes, L. S., & Frentz, T. S. (1976). *The communicative experience.* Boston: Allyn and Bacon.

Roshco, B. (1975). *Newsmaking.* Chicago: University of Chicago Press.

Stinchcombe, A. L. (1968). *Constructing social theories.* New York: Harcourt Brace Jovanovich.

Thompson, J. D. (1967). *Organizations in action: Social science basis of administrative theory.* New York: McGraw-Hill.

Tuchman, G. (1972). Objectivity as strategic ritual: An examination of newsmen's notions of objectivity. *American Journal of Sociology, 77,* 660-679.

Tuchman, G. (1973a). Making news by doing work: Routinizing the unexpected. *American Journal of Sociology, 79,* 110-131.

Tuchman, G. (1973b, April). The technology of objectivity: Doing objective TV news film. *Urban Life and Culture, 2,* 3-26.

Tuchman, G. (1977). The exception proves the rule: The study of routine news practices. In P. M. Hirsch et al. (Eds.), *Strategies for communication research* (pp. 43-62). Beverly Hills, CA: Sage.

Tuchman, G. (1978). *Making news: A study in the construction of reality.* New York: Macmillan.

Tunstall, J. (1971). *Journalists at work: Specialist correspondents, their news organizations, news sources, and competitor-colleagues.* Beverly Hills, CA: Sage.

Waters, H. F. (1978, January 16). The local-news blues. *Newsweek,* pp. 82-83.

Weick, K. E. (1969). *The social psychology of organizing.* Reading, MA: Addison-Wesley.

White, D. M. (1950). The "gate keeper": A case study in the selection of news. *Journalism Quarterly, 27,* 383-390.

Whitehead, R., Jr. (1978, March/April). Show news. *Columbia Journalism Review,* pp. 58-59.

CHAPTER **19**

The First Stage of News Production

Learning What's Happening

John H. McManus

The discovery phase of news selection, in which journalists learn of events and issues that might be covered, is extremely important because it predicates all other decisions within the newsroom. No matter how artistic the photographers, how brilliant or tough minded the reporters, or how careful the editors, their talents have no effect on issues and events of which the newsroom is not aware. If unreported elsewhere, such events may fail to exist in the public mind. Their exclusion may lead at a minimum to uninformed public decision making. More threatening are cases in which critical information hidden from the public encouraged serious social and governmental blunders.[1]

Active scrutiny of society, particularly government, is a fundamental obligation of journalism, as Ralph Barney noted:

> A first reason for journalists to exist is the gathering and distributing of information, most particularly information that others are taking pains to keep from being distributed. It is that type of information that . . . would prove most valuable to society.[2]

A Market Model of News Discovery

If the news is a commodity only, the production of news narratives should follow market logic. Given scarce resources of time and capital, rational media firms should provide the least expensive mix of content that is hospitable to advertisers and investors and generates the largest audience those advertisers want to reach. It is reasonable to assume that passive discovery of events—when television journalists read about them in local and regional newspapers or wire services or in press releases—is less expensive than more active means, such as hiring and deploying reporters or field producers (personnel who set up stories but do not appear on camera) throughout the signal area to cultivate sources and learn what might be newsworthy. This is because subscriptions to newspapers, wire services, and "feeds" from network sources are substantially less costly than reporter or field producer salaries. So if a station acts rationally, a business model would predict largely passive discovery, or at least as passive as competing stations permit.

A Journalistic Model of News Discovery

If news has a public service component in addition to being a product sold for profit, journalistic norms should influence the business rationale described above. To maximize public understanding of its environment, the fundamental mission of journalism, news departments must actively and independently scrutinize their environments. Even if more viewers could be attracted by selecting inexpensively discovered emotionally charged stories from wire and network sources than from choosing less arousing stories learned from covering local government and business, the journalistic model would require an orientation toward the latter. A journalistic model would predict largely active discovery, or at least as active a discovery process as the station could afford.

Method

To measure how active news discovery is at a particular station, you can examine how the newsroom is organized. For example, who is tasked with learning of events? How do they go about it, and how much time do they spend? It is also useful to classify the numbers of stories actually broadcast by the circumstances of their origination. If stations act rationally, selection priorities should match discovery priorities; a station deploys its resources where it expects to find what it considers most newsworthy.

To evaluate both the journalistic and cost implications of various means of discovery, three categories were created based on the level of observed and reported effort on the part of newsworkers. Two assumptions underlie these classifications: (1) In general, the more active the means of learning of issues and events outside the newsroom, the more completely journalistic norms of independent and objective surveillance of the environment are met; and (2) by and large, the more active the means of such discovery, the greater the cost to the news department, principally in terms of staff size and time.

The categories were conservatively designed. Classification rules were not based on rigorous standards of independent journalism. In fact, they permit a station to be rated "highly active" without ever undertaking investigative reporting—where the station tries to establish evidence of socially significant incompetence or wrongdoing. Stories were classified by asking the person who originated the story how it was discovered. The respondent, most often the assignment editor, checked 1 of 11 boxes on a questionnaire corresponding to categories ranging from "from wire services," to "a question to which I wanted to find the answer." [3]

Minimally Active Discovery

Minimally active discovery includes events or issues that can be learned from promoters or other media firms without leaving or phoning outside the typical newsroom, other than to contact emergency service dispatchers. Such means include monitoring paper, telephonic, or video press releases; newspapers, radio, and television competitors; wire services; video feeds provided by networks[4] or mailed from independent producers of generic news materials; and scanning police and fire emergency radio channels. Discovering events from these sources is largely passive. An outside organization, for its own purposes, has revealed the event.

Stations incur two costs for stories discovered with minimal activity: (1) staff time spent scanning these sources; and (2) subscription fees for newspapers, wire services, syndicated materials, and satellite feeds. Compared to more active means, such as deploying journalists to walk the halls of government, these costs are minimal. At all three stations, scanning incoming channels of information was primarily performed by news assistants earning the lowest wages in the newsroom. The annual budget for all subscriptions from outside news services was less than the average reporter's salary at each station.

Moderately Active Discovery

Moderately active discovery includes events or issues that either originate from the news department through enterprise or previous reporting, or are communicated to the newsroom but require outside checking to ascertain newsworthiness. Examples are anonymous tips, follow-up stories, and enterprise reporting. These require greater effort than scanning events and issues already certified as news by an outside organization. Enterprise stories, in which a reporter or editor originates a question the story answers, require keeping up with news events and issues so as to notice what has not been addressed or what might tie together a series of events. Story leads based on earlier reporting require reporters to think and gather information more broadly than they might if completing only the assigned story. Listening to a phoned-in tip costs practically nothing, but verifying the information enough to proceed with a story may require a number of phone calls.

Highly Active Discovery

The third category—highly active discovery—required newsworkers to contact sources outside the newsroom. Issues and events reporters learned of while sitting through government, business, or social meetings belong in this category. Covering the bulk of a meeting requires a substantial time commitment. Only a fraction of the proceeding may be immediately newsworthy. Events discovered by conversing with sources the reporter has cultivated also fit in this category because of the time required to develop trust. Also events or patterns of events discovered in searches of government or business records or documents belong here because of the time they require. All investigations of government or corporate wrongdoing as well as systematic polls conducted or funded by the station were included in this category. Even if an investigation began with an anonymous tip, it was classified here because illegal or unethical behavior is often hidden and therefore requires diligence to uncover. Likewise, even though most polls begin as enterprise stories, they were placed here because framing the study questions and delineating the population to be surveyed may require considerable effort and background knowledge.

To assess whether these categories made sense, three veteran television journalists whose stations were not included in the study were asked to sort means of discovery into the three levels of increasing station effort. There was substantial agreement among the newsmen with the coding scheme.[5]

Although it creates only an ordinal measure—one category is higher than another but not by a set amount—the classification scheme has advantages over more precise methods considered. For example, putting a stopwatch on the discovery process for a particular story can be misleading. Suppose a reporter learned of a story within the first 2 minutes of a chat with a source she or he had spent weeks cultivating. If clocked by story, the discovery cost is 2 minutes. The real cost, however, should reflect all the visits during which the reporter was establishing rapport.[6]

Theoretical Expectations

All else held equal, *if a station seeks to maximize profit*, the newsroom will be organized to allocate greater resources to more passive means of discovery than either of the two more active categories. The proportion of airtime consumed by stories originating from minimally active means of discovery will be greater than the proportion originating from the moderately active, which in turn will be greater than the proportion originating from highly active means.

If a station compromises between market and journalistic norms, the news-room will be organized to allocate roughly equal resources to active and passive means of discovery. One of two conditions should prevail: (1) Airtime will be relatively equally distributed among categories; or (2) more airtime will be found in the middle-effort category than either of the others.

Finally, *if a station follows journalistic norms,* the newsroom will be organized to allocate greater resources to highly active discovery than to moderately or minimally active means. Airtime consumed by stories originating from highly active means of discovery will be greater than that originating from stories moderately actively discovered, which in turn will be greater than airtime consumed by stories classified minimally active.

How the Study Was Conducted

Each of the three stations participating in this part of the research was visited 3 days per week, for a total of 12 days over the course of a month. Visits were concentrated on Tuesdays, Wednesdays, and Thursdays to avoid lower staffing and atypical news availability of Mondays and Fridays. Weekend newscasts were excluded for the same reason.[7] On four of those days, one chosen randomly from each week (except in one case when the newsroom was so exhausted an alternate date was selected), I distributed questionnaires analyzing every story on the premier evening newscast. At all three stations the newscast that commanded the greatest newsroom resources was broadcast in the early evening and lasted one hour. Sports, weather, and commercial segments were outside the scope of the study. A total of 239 questionnaires—one per story—were returned of 274 distributed, a response rate of 87%.

In addition, I conducted a series of case studies shadowing reporters throughout their day. At the midsized station, my sample included all reporters. At the two larger stations, however, there was not time to accompany all reporters. Those management and peers considered most able were selected in order to give newsrooms a chance to show their highest quality journalism.

Results

At the Midsized Station

Case Studies

The discovery function was almost exclusively the task of the assignment editor and two assistants. The description of their behavior that opened this chapter typified their daily routine during the period of study.

Most reporters at KMID were assigned beats—areas to search for news, such as city government, police, or the environment. However, with an average demand of three stories per day, no reporter said he or she could spend more than a few minutes a day looking for newsworthy events. As the reporter assigned to cover the environment put it: "It's like a joke." A poll of all eight KMID news reporters indicated that they originated only 2% of the stories covered.

There was one incident of investigative reporting at KMID during the period of study, an "exposé" of alleged drug use at a large federal office complex. That report, however, named no officials nor departments of the federal agency. Despite that incident, seven of KMID's eight reporters expressed skepticism that the station would investigate suspected official wrongdoing. The eighth gave a neutral response. Most reporters also mentioned the timidity of the station during the local newspaper's investigation of the core city's mayor.

Reporters were observed covering 16 stories. Of those, 5 were discovered in the newspaper, 4 were submitted by public relations agents, 3 were reported by the wire service, and 3 were suggested by reporters and editors. Of the 16, only the 3 enterprise stories could be classified as a moderately active means of discovery. None involved such active and time-consuming processes as developing sources or searching documents, or sitting through government meetings. Taken as a whole, the case studies describe a minimal commitment to actively examining the doings of local government and business. The business model of news discovery prevailed.

Quantitative Findings

The data from KMID are summarized in Figure 19.1. Frequencies were computed for each category of effort in two ways: The first was a straight count of stories; the second weighted those stories by the amount of time they consumed in the newscast. The second measure is a fairer representation of reality than the first, because it assigns greater value to the longer, major stories. The bar graph shows airtime for 93 stories. There is little probability that this pattern is due to chance alone.[8]

Regardless of measure, three quarters of the news portion of the broadcast was passively discovered; one fifth came from moderately active discovery methods and less than 5% from highly active means. The market model overwhelmed the journalistic.

At the Large Station

Case Studies

As at KMID, the discovery function was primarily the task of the assignment editor and his assistants. Also like KMID, KLRG learned of news from public relations agents seeking coverage, morning phone calls to police

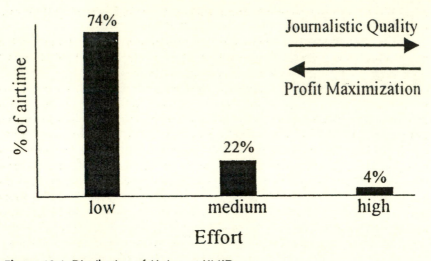

Figure 19.1. Distribution of Airtime at KMID

and fire dispatchers, monitoring emergency radio, and from other local media firms—primarily the local and regional newspapers. Network and regional feeds of video and the Associated Press broadcast wire were also received. Like KMID, KLRG also bought generic medical news features. Unlike KMID, KLRG operated a two-reporter bureau in another city within the signal area. News discovery at the bureau, however, also depended largely on secondhand news, particularly the newspaper, and assignments were made from the main newsroom.

Again reporters were assigned beats. Unlike KMID, reporters covered stories within their beats. A poll of 9 of KLRG's 14 news reporters estimated that they originated the ideas for one out of four stories covered, although observation of the assignment desk showed a lower level of reporter initiative. Reporters were supposed to receive one day per week to build rapport with sources and uncover news on their beats, but that day was routinely reclaimed by the assignment editor for a pressing story.

The nine reporters who responded to the survey said they spent one hour per day, on average, looking for newsworthy events and information. During the month of my visit, however, I observed only one reporter searching for future news stories. She relied solely on low and moderately active means of discovery. Charged with covering education in two major cities, several counties, and the state board of education, as well as several state universities within the station's signal area, she expressed frustration. On her desk were a stack of regional newspapers "I haven't had time to read," she said. "It's too much!" Her solution to the overload was to call the public relations officers of the larger school districts and ask, "What's controversial?" The strategy was not particularly effective, she conceded, because public information officers disclose information selectively, usually showing their employers only in a positive light.

Despite its location in a large city, KLRG employed no city hall reporter. "We routinely miss what goes on in city hall, except for the really big things," the assignment editor explained. "And we read newspapers to get that."

Like KMID, KLRG appeared to investigate government and corporations very infrequently. Polled reporters said the station was unwilling to commit resources to investigations. Two stories challenged this perception, however. Both were multipart series prepared for the following month, a "sweeps" month when the station's audience would be measured. The stories both involved weeklong trips to Latin American nations, to El Salvador and Nicaragua. The stories were commissioned immediately after a competing station aired stories from a similar foreign visit. The reporters responsible for writing KLRG's stories both complained of pressure from the news director to depoliticize their reporting—emphasize the suffering but censor references to its causes, particularly criticism of U.S. policy. The news director later explained that both stories were "lose-lose" propositions for the station because in his view the audience was deeply polarized on U.S. involvement in Central America. If the coverage appeared to favor either side, he said, partisans on the other side might switch channels. Such reasoning is the antithesis of investigative reporting—which seeks to reveal the truth regardless of the message's popularity.

I directly observed seven complete stories. Of those, three were suggested by public relations agents, one was taken from the newspaper, and one story's origin was unclear. In the two remaining cases, moderately active modes of discovery were observed; one story originated from checking out a phoned-in tip and another was the idea of a reporter. No observed stories originated from cultivated sources, document searches, or attending government meetings.

Although more attention was paid to news discovery at KLRG than KMID, the station still relied more on inexpensive outside sources to learn of newsworthy events than on its own staff. More tellingly, when the station did exercise initiative in learning of news, it suppressed reporters' findings when they collided with the economic interest in maximizing audience (and, perhaps, when they might have offended advertisers or the parent corporation and its investors).

Quantitative Findings

The quantitative analysis graphed in Figure 19.2 tells a similar story. Stories discovered with minimal effort consumed about 60% of the news portion of the broadcasts, and moderate-activity discovery takes the rest, except for 1% that is highly active. The graph shows airtime for 56 stories. (The count is lower than at KMID or KVLG because I grouped a set of stories about a teacher's strike together into one larger story. Thus, effort that went into any part of the coverage was weighted for the whole. Every benefit of the doubt goes to the station.) Again, the pattern is so distinct there is little probability it can be explained by chance.

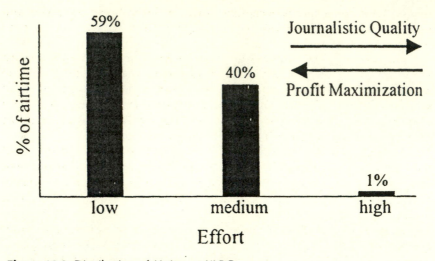

Figure 19.2. Distribution of Airtime at KLRG

At the Very Large Station

Case Studies

Between 7 a.m. and 4 p.m., KVLG employed five persons at its main newsroom to discover newsworthy events within the major metropolitan area the station's signal encompassed. Three editorial assistants listened to emergency scanner radios and an all-news radio station. The assistants also scanned stories sent to the station by the Associated Press and a local news wire service. The assignment editor read the area's four major newspapers and several minor daily papers, monitored the wire services, and kept an ear on the scanners. Last, a planner reviewed press releases and clipped stories from newspapers and national news magazines.

The station also maintained a four-person bureau in the area's second largest city, a two-person bureau (since eliminated) in the state capital, and a one-person bureau in the third largest city in the area. KVLG also partially sponsored a bureau in Washington, D.C. The bureaus discovered news in the same manner as the home newsroom—relying on the scanner radio and local newspapers, with an occasional story developed by reporters. All assignments were made from the central newsroom.

Only 4—of 19 news reporters and field producers working for the early evening newscast—were assigned to specific beats. The remainder were on general assignment. With 19 journalists to cover an area home to several million persons, a beat system would be a charade, the news director explained. Eleven of the 19 reporters and field producers who responded to questionnaires said they spent an average of 2 hours daily searching for news. The average here is deceptive, however. Several field producers and reporters accounted for most of the discovery time. They belonged to an investigative projects team.

Most reporters interviewed felt discovery was not their responsibility. In a signal area with three large cities and scores of medium-sized cities, one reporter still managed to complain, "The problem is there's not enough local news sometimes. It produces 'licking the spoon' journalism. There's not much there so you have to lick the spoon." Such a passive attitude suggests an unfamiliarity with enterprise reporting or investigation.

As at the smaller stations, most reporters interviewed and observed tended to rely on public relations officers and top bureaucrats to warn them about news even though they acknowledged that such officials are unlikely to call public attention to controversies that might show their agency in a negative light.

There were several exceptions to the pattern of passive discovery, however. On one occasion, KVLG joined with a local newspaper in sponsoring a comprehensive political poll in the region's major city. Such discovery is expensive. The most impressive exception was investigative reporting. KVLG was one of the few television stations in the nation to have an investigative team and a special projects producer. That producer drew on the 19 newsworkers allotted to the evening newscast. The investigative team comprised four field producers who dug up and reported stories but did not appear on camera. The team's efforts, however, were not a daily part of the newscast. Instead, the team concentrated on series of stories that ran periodically. One series ran during the month of observation, and the investigative team produced one other story during the observation period and assisted on at least one more. The investigative and special projects work of KVLG reporters accounted for many of the nearly 300 television journalism prizes decorating the newsroom walls.

Because reporters often spent a day on each story, only seven stories could be followed from start to finish within the observation period. Of those seven, three came from minimally active means of discovery—one each from the newspaper, the scanner radio, and the news wire. Three showed moderate activity. They were developed through enterprise—reporters or editors pursuing their own questions. One story—the only Category 3 method observed at all three stations—was generated from a reporter who had developed a relationship with a source.

News discovery at KVLG described a compromise between the market model and the journalistic. It was the only station of those studied to commit significant resources to highly active scrutiny of its environment.

Quantitative Findings

The quantitative analysis of story origination summarized in Figure 19.3 supports the observational study. Although the percentage of time spent in minimally active discovery is nearly twice that spent in highly active, the

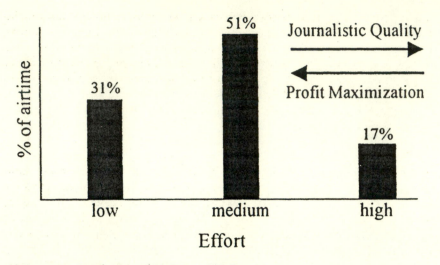

Figure 19.3. Distribution of Airtime at KVLG

majority of stories falls in the middle category. The graph shows airtime for 90 stories. Again, the pattern is unlikely to be explained by chance.[10]

Discussion

In all but the sample from the largest station, minimally active—essentially passive—news discovery prevailed. However, station size did make a difference in discovery effort that cannot be explained by chance. The greater the station's resources, the more active the discovery.[11]

A simple explanation might be that the larger the market, the more the station can afford to discover news actively. But this explanation is too simple, partly because each of the stations visited made enough profit to afford a much more active discovery profile. A fuller explanation arises from the analysis of how markets work.

That analysis suggests that the market model and the normative model of journalism overlap somewhat more in larger than smaller markets. This occurs because as market size increases, the number of consumers who demand informative news reaches a minimum economic threshold—enough people to attract advertisers. If news executives wish to compete for such viewers—many of whom may be middle-class or higher income—they may need to spend more to learn what's going on.

To some extent, market reasoning even supports the presence of an investigative team at KVLG: In a market as big and as competitive as the one KVLG served, enough highly educated and motivated consumers live to render the occasional investigative report valuable in differentiating the station somewhat from its competitors. On the other hand, a station maintaining a permanent investigative team pays a high price for a competitive edge. Other strategies for expanding upscale audience may be more cost-effective. At this point in the study, it seems more reasonable to classify KVLG's investigative team as evidence of normative rather than market journalism.

Conclusion

Taken as a whole, these results indicate that when market logic and journalism logic conflicted at the first stage of news production, market logic won most of the time. Even at KVLG with its investigative team, almost twice as much airtime was consumed by stories discovered relatively passively as by highly active means. Across the three stations, the market was served better than the public.

Society enjoys some benefit even when a station merely repeats news reported by other sources—particularly the part of society that does not read newspapers. But journalism demands more. At the least, it requires independent scrutiny of the environment in the expectation that the more agencies seeking answers the better for the public's perception of reality. Also, from the time of John Stuart Mill in England and Thomas Jefferson in the United States, a primary social value of news media has arisen from their role as a check on the power of government, and now business as well.[12] In fact, it is the "watchdog" role ascribed to news gathering that justifies its special protection under the First Amendment.[13] Reliance on passive means of discovering the environment abdicates this role.

Finally, passive discovery tends to surrender control over the public information stream to powerful interests in government, large corporations, and among the wealthy.[14] By reducing the cost of discovery of events and views flattering to themselves, these special interests can take advantage of cost-conscious media to influence what the public learns.[15] The proliferation of public relations efforts suggests that these special interests are eager to assume such influence.[16]

While passive discovery has civic costs, active discovery may have corporate costs. Hiring additional personnel to look for stories might reduce profit margins if larger audiences were not attracted to a more independent newscast. Even were more active news discovery to trim profits, however, there is still room for stations to do well by doing good. Figures compiled by the National Association of Broadcasters for 1985, the year before this study began, showed a median pretax profit on gross revenues of 15.8% for stations of KMID's size and type, 30% for KLRG, and 39% for KVLG. Compare these figures to the national manufacturing average of 9%. Even with some diminishment in network affiliate audiences since this research was conducted, it appears that local television news could afford to do considerably better.

Notes

1. Herman and Chomsky (1988).
2. Barney (1987, p. 15).
3. The assignment editor, producer, reporters, and writers were asked the following questions in separate questionnaires. Producers normally selected nonlocal news; assignment editors chose local news. For local stories the responses of reporters, writers, and assignment editors were cross-checked. In the few cases of discrepancies, further questioning led to an assignment of the story to the appropriate category.

I. Minimally active discovery

Did the story idea originate primarily from:
☐ A press release/announcement, or phone call from a PIO?
☐ Material provided by another news organization—wire service, network or other feed, newspaper, magazine, radio, other television station?
☐ Emergency frequency scanner radio?
☐ Routine checks with police/emergency dispatchers?

II. Moderately active discovery

Did the story idea originate primarily from:
☐ A news conference?
☐ A phoned-in tip from an unofficial source?
☐ A question to which I wanted to find the answer?
☐ Reporter/writer enterprise, that is, a story idea suggested by a reporter or writer?
☐ A follow-up from a previously reported story?

III. Highly active discovery

Did the story idea originate primarily from:
☐ Talking to sources I have developed?
☐ Attending a meeting or perusing documents of an institution, either governmental or private?
☐ All investigative stories and those relying on systematic polls conducted by the station were also included here, regardless of where the story idea originated. An investigative story was one where a journalist through his/her enterprise uncovered allegations of governmental or business wrongdoing.

4. Because local news programming at each station was immediately followed or preceded by national network news, stories taken from network sources were seen within the three newsrooms as "filler."
5. A coefficient of intercoder reliability, Cronbach's alpha, was .87. The lowest correlation between my placement of sources and those of a coder was .73 (Spearman's rho).
6. The author welcomes suggestions for more precise measures.
7. Because weekend newscasts at each station tended to depend more heavily on wire stories and other nonlocally originated news, this sample makes the stations appear somewhat more active than they were.
8. Chi-square goodness-of-fit test. Chi-square statistic = 73.4, with 2 degrees of freedom, $p < .001$. Response rate = 94%.
9. Chi-square goodness-of-fit test. Chi-square statistic = 29.4, with 2 degrees of freedom; $p < .001$. Response rate = 75%.
10. Chi-square goodness-of-fit test. Chi-square statistic = 16, with 2 degrees of freedom; $p < .001$. Response rate = 90%
11. A 3×3 chi-square test of association between station size and level of activity shows a significant correlation; chi-square = 40.3, $df = 4$, $p < .001$.

12. Siebert, Peterson, and Schramm (1956).
13. Meiklejohn (1948), cited in Blasi (1977).
14. Boorstin (1961).
15. Gandy (1982).
16. Boorstin (1961).

References

Barney, R. D. (1987). Responsibilities of the journalist: An ethical construct. *Mass Comm Review, 14*(3), 14-22.

Blasi, V. (1977). The checking value in First Amendment theory. *American Bar Foundation Research Journal*, pp. 521-649.

Boorstin, D. (1961). *The image: A guide to pseudo-events in America*. New York: Atheneum.

Gandy, O. H. (1982). *Beyond agenda setting: Information subsidies and public policy*. Norwood, NJ: Ablex.

Herman, E., & Chomsky, N. (1988). *Manufacturing consent*. New York: Pantheon.

Meiklejohn, A. (1948). *Free speech and its relation to self-government*. New York: Harper.

Siebert, F., Peterson, T., & Schramm, W. L. (1956). *Four theories of the press*. Urbana: University of Illinois Press.

CHAPTER **20**

The Competitive Ethos
in Television Newswork

Matthew C. Ehrlich

Competition is central to the way that many, if not most, of us think about
mass communication. It is at the heart of the libertarian ideal of the marketplace of goods and ideas in which, to paraphrase Milton, truth and falsehood
can be left to grapple and finally make themselves apparent in the eyes of
the citizenry (Siebert, 1956). And it traditionally has been at the heart of the
way in which many journalists view their work, as they try to "scoop" each
other and as their organizations try to build ratings and circulation at the
expense of their rivals.

This article seeks to contribute to a broad-based critical understanding
of competition within one particular sphere of journalism—television news.
Such a study seems especially timely as observers express increasing concern
about the negative impact of the competition for ratings and news stories in
television journalism (e.g., "Bad News," 1993). Central to my argument is the
notion of a *competitive ethos* (Morgan, 1986, p. 137), a powerful, taken-for-
granted set of norms within the community of television newsworkers. This
competitive ethos pervades not only television news but American culture.
I will argue that studying competition as a practice and value system com-
plements and extends the critical study of the political and economic struc-

From *Critical Studies in Mass Communication*, 1995, Vol. 12, pp. 196-212. Used by permission
of the Speech Communication Association.

ture of the news industry. That is, it contributes to a sociology of news production that simultaneously incorporates political economic, social organizational, and "culturological" approaches (Schudson, 1991).

I will begin with a brief overview of how some mass communication scholars have conceptualized competition in economic terms, and then draw upon ethnographic studies of two local television newsrooms in arguing that competition also must be understood as a social and cultural phenomenon that is continually enacted via newswork. I will conclude with a short discussion of the implications of this competitive ethos for communication policy and media education.

Competition and Political Economy

Many researchers who have studied media economics and policy have viewed competition as a positive goal. In studying television news, some have asked whether competition (as measured by factors like station ownership, the number of competing newscasts in a market, and relative audience shares) does what it is presumably supposed to do according to the libertarian view of the marketplace—promote diversity of content, greater investment in news coverage, and so forth (e.g., Busterna, 1980, 1988; Atwater, 1984; Lacy, Atwater, Qin, and Powers, 1988; Lacy, Atwater, and Qin, 1989; Lacy and Bernstein, 1992). Based on their reading of these studies, Lacy and Bernstein (1992, p. 46) argue that "increasing competition should be a goal of any regulatory system."

But many critical mass communication scholars disagree. In adopting a political economy perspective, these scholars refute the notion that competition and the "marketplace" can address whatever ills might affect television and the rest of the media (e.g., Murdock and Golding, 1977; Streeter, 1983; Glasser, 1984; Meehan, 1984, 1990; Bagdikian, 1992). McManus (1994) provides an especially sharp critique of the "market logic" underlying the television news business, arguing that the drive to minimize costs and maximize profits has produced trivial, superficial, and often inaccurate reporting. In short, the political economy perspective argues that competition in television news aims not to produce better or more diverse coverage, but as Gitlin (1993, p. 24) says, "to make more money—more than the other guy, more than you used to make, more than you feared you might make."

But even acknowledging the value of this perspective and the extraordinary importance of the profit motive, is competition in television news *solely* a battle over money? Anecdotal evidence and scholarly research suggest otherwise. For example, Boyer (1988) and Auletta (1992) note that corporate efforts in the 1980s to maximize profits in network television news triggered bitter resistance within the news divisions, which protested that massive layoffs and budget cuts were hurting their ability to cover the news competitively. This is consistent with Gans's (1979, chap. 7) argument that journalists tend to be wary of the business side of the news industry; it also coincides with Bantz's

(1985) suggestion that business norms and professional journalistic norms routinely clash within television news organizations.

Beyond that, however, is the power of the very idea of *winning* in television news, a power that extends well beyond corporate goals of efficiency and profit maximization. Gitlin (1993, p. 24) makes special note of this power, contrasting it to "the weakness of other passions in American culture" and describing its effect on a friend and a former student who both worked in television news—both on the "fast track," with no time for critical reflection for fear that the "thousands of wannabes" wanting a "chance to go for the gold" might gain on them. Indeed, a book explicitly aimed at those "wannabes" lists "competitiveness" as one of the key traits for succeeding in television news: "Good journalists want to win. They want to be the best. They hate getting beat on a story. . . . In fact, good newspeople not only want to cover the biggest story of the day, they want to handle it so well that their competition *cries*" (Filoreto and Setzer, 1993, pp. 136, 138). A good scoop actually can produce tears of *joy*, even for those at the top of the business; Tom Brokaw reportedly cried happily after NBC broke the news in 1988 that George Bush had selected Dan Quayle as a running mate—beating the other networks by barely half an hour (Moore, 1988).

This "power of the idea of winning" needs to be examined critically alongside the study of the political economy of television news. I will describe it as a competitive ethos. The term is borrowed from Gareth Morgan (1986), who argues (p. 119) that American corporate culture is heavily influenced by an "ethic of competitive individualism" and that this culture "develops as an *ethos* [emphasis added] . . . created and sustained by social processes, images, symbols, and rituals" (p. 123). He adds (p. 137) that "environments are enacted by hosts of individuals and organizations each acting on the basis of their interpretations of a world that is in effect mutually defined. A *competitive ethos produces competitive environments*" [emphasis added]. The task, then, is to study how individual and organizational rituals and routines may help sustain a "competitive ethos" and competitive environment in television news, and if such a competitive ethos and environment exist, how they in turn appear to serve or hinder the dominant political and economic interests in the television industry. To that end, I turn from political economy to what Schudson (1991, pp. 147-151) calls the study of the social organization of news—that is, the study of *newswork*.

Competition and Newswork

Newswork studies are well attuned to examining how symbolic processes sustain an occupational ethos; as Schudson (1991, pp. 147-151) describes, such studies assume that reality is to a large extent socially constructed. From this perspective, journalists (or "newsworkers") are social actors working within various organizational and institutional constraints, particularly those dictating that news organizations produce a fresh batch of news daily for mass consumption. Hence, newsworkers adopt certain rituals and routines to help them manage their work, relying heavily on "legitimate" official sources. In doing so, they produce news accounts which construct a version of reality that rarely challenges the existing political and economic power structure, and in fact actively serves to legitimate it (e.g., Molotch and Lester, 1974; Altheide, 1976; Schlesinger, 1978; Tuchman, 1978; Fishman, 1980). These studies, with their emphasis on the social construction of reality, have much in common with the concept of *enactment* to which Morgan (1986, p. 137) alludes; according to this concept, organizational actors actively construct the environment which they share (Weick, 1979, chap. 6; Smircich and Stubbart, 1985; Bantz, 1990).

How might television newsworkers and organizations regularly enact and reenact a shared competitive environment by drawing upon a shared "ethic of competitive individualism"—that is, a competitive ethos? A passage from a television news trade publication offers some insight: "News is competition. From deadlines and budgets to ratings and shares, every day we run the race that determines who's the best. It takes skill and experience to win" (Radio-Television News Directors Association, 1988, p. 11).

This passage (part of a pitch aimed at attracting news directors to an annual convention) again indicates the power that money plays in television news, with its explicit reference to budgets and ratings and shares. But there is more at stake here. The very essence of television news is boiled down to competition: "News *is* competition." This competition is enacted via a "race that determines who's the best"—a race against *deadlines* in which news-workers try to beat the clock, a race for *news* in which newsworkers compete for stories (and, as in the examples cited above, try to make each other "cry"), and, of course, a race for *ratings and shares* in which newsworkers and organizations attempt to curry audience favor. The race is run "every day"; it is built into regular organizational rituals and routines. And it never ends—newsworkers literally find themselves caught on a "fast track" (Gitlin, 1993, p. 24), always trying to win, to prove themselves the "best," never able to stop and think for fear that someone may be gaining on them. Yet for whatever fear might underlie this race, there is also a shared pride in running it and in developing the "skill and experience" it takes to win.

Thus, we can understand television news competition in terms of news-workers and their organizations consistently measuring their performance against that of selected other newsworkers and news organizations (Sherif, 1976, p. 19). While economic imperatives fuel competition, so do powerful *social and cultural* imperatives. At least, that is implied by television insiders who assert that "good journalists want to *win*" and that "every day we run the race that determines who's the *best*." Furthermore, if previous critical studies of news-work (e.g., Tuchman, 1978) are any indication, this social and cultural competi-tion—ritualized and enacted in routine news practices—may have ideological ramifications (Ehrlich, 1992). That is, newsworkers engaging in such practices may inadvertently serve corporate interests and legitimate the status quo.

In order to see whether in fact this was the case, I observed and interviewed newsworkers over a six-month period in a medium-sized market television newsroom. In keeping with the methods of previous newswork studies, I watched newsworkers produce newscasts and edit stories, and I accompanied them outside the station on assignments. In addition, I conducted taped interviews with newsroom supervisors as well as with several reporters and producers. For purposes of comparison, I also visited a newsroom in a top-20 market, conducting similar observations and interviews. And I studied tapes of stories and newscasts from both newsrooms. Throughout the study, I drew upon my own professional background in broadcast news to help me interpret what I saw and heard.

Competition for News

The primary organization in this study—the medium-market station—historically had been number one in its market. This was largely due to the success of its ownership in manipulating the political and economic environment to hinder severely, if not cripple, its competition. It had gone on the air in the early 1950s as the only commercial VHF station in the area. It then defeated FCC efforts in the late 1950s and early 1960s to take away its VHF channel and put it on a more equal footing with the other commercial stations in the market, which were all UHF. Thanks to this giant competitive advantage, the station's owner earned enough profits to acquire other television stations across the country; eventually, he would be listed as one of the 400 richest persons in America, with a fortune estimated at $200 million. And his original station continued to dominate the ratings in local news, finishing first in at least 40 consecutive ratings periods prior to the time of the study, often by huge margins.

Because of this dominance, one newsroom manager told me he was worried that some of the station's newsworkers were too complacent; they did not take the competing news operations seriously. But my observations suggested the opposite to be true. I usually arrived in the newsroom in the late afternoon when preparations for the early evening newscast were in full swing, and stayed through the late evening newscast several hours later. At night, the person in charge was the late evening newscast producer. He was in his mid-20s, a graduate of a broadcast journalism program who had begun at the station as an intern a few years before. In general, he was free to assign stories, edit copy, and arrange the newscast however he saw fit.

It soon became clear that the producer and others in the newsroom consistently measured their work against that of the three other television news operations in the market. The most obvious manifestation was the presence of four television monitors in the newsroom, each tuned to a different station. Once, giving an impromptu tour of the newsroom to a group of visitors, a reporter pointed to the monitors and said: "We monitor the opposition. We don't want them to have anything we don't." And indeed, during newscasts or during "newsbreaks" when upcoming newscasts were being promoted, newsroom staffers would routinely position themselves in front of the monitors. They would turn up the volume of each in turn to make sure their station was not getting "scooped," and more often than not make derogatory remarks about the other stations' anchor teams and stories. ("Stale," the producer would mutter while watching the opposing stations, or: "You can't air *that*, partner!")

The producer also routinely monitored what rival stations' news crews were doing by quizzing his reporters. For example, when a reporter returned from the scene of the crash of a small plane, the producer immediately asked her whether a competing station had been at the scene first, and then responded with an oath when he heard the answer. (The reporter, meanwhile, called the rival station's reporter a "bitch" for shoving her as the two scrambled to get the story.) Other newsworkers proved that they, too, were concerned about the opposition, especially when they had some sort of "exclusive" story, no matter what the subject. One reporter was determined to air a story about a five-legged dog before "the whole world" found out about it (she was even unhappy that I, as an outsider, knew of the story). And one night when the station was airing the network telecast of a baseball playoff game that threatened to go into extra innings, the sportscaster said he hoped the game would go just long enough "so my competition can't show highlights" (i.e., so that the other stations' sportscasts would end before the game did).

The thrill-of-victory, agony-of-defeat competitive culture of the newsroom perhaps can be best illustrated by two incidents which took place on consecutive nights. In the first, a reporter and photographer responded to a call on the newsroom police scanner about a collision between a car and a municipal bus. The pair returned a short time later, loudly and exultantly. They had *great* video, they said—it had been a *bad* accident. (The video showed a woman pinned in her car by a sign pole which had smashed through the windshield.) Best of all, no other station was at the scene. "They weren't even there!" shouted the photographer. "We *scooped their butt!*" For the next several minutes, the reporter and photographer sat in the newsroom happily teasing each other over their respective roles in getting the exclusive story with the great video, the reporter saying words to the effect that covering accidents was more interesting than covering the dull government meetings that usually took place at night. The evening news producer, meanwhile, took the opportunity to boast during a phone call to his news director about both the accident story ("Boy, it's a dandy!") and another story concerning a local school official accepting a new job ("No one else has it").

The second incident, however, was not a happy occasion for the newsroom. The producer had received a phone tip about storm damage to a school in a small town several miles from the station. He dispatched a crew to the scene in a "live truck," only to learn that the truck did not have the proper equipment to transmit video directly back to the station. At the same time, his crew informed him that a rival station had arrived at the scene with its own live truck. So in response, the producer sent a *second* truck to the scene. "*God*, I want to pull this one off," he muttered. "I do not want [the other station] to get off a live shot when I don't have one. That would piss me off like you wouldn't believe. The competition has begun!" As it turned out, the producer's second live truck *also* could not transmit a live signal directly from the scene, while the rival station's truck could. The producer was livid: "We got fuckin' *smoked* on that story."

What these observations suggest is that competition is indeed "ritualized" and built into the norms and routines of everyday newswork. For example, "monitoring the opposition" serves as a "strategic ritual" similar to that of objectivity. That is, Tuchman (1972) argues that the rituals associated with "objective" journalism (such as getting "both sides" of a story) do not guarantee fair and balanced coverage, but they do help journalists protect themselves from potential criticism (e.g., charges of bias) and hence reduce the anxieties of newswork. Similarly, television newsworkers strategically and ritualistically monitor other stations in order to reassure themselves that they are not getting beaten on stories and to protect themselves from those who might ask why they *did* get beaten (see also Gans, 1979, pp. 180-181).

Furthermore, the competitive environment of television news does in fact appear to be *enacted* in the sense suggested by Morgan (1986, p. 137), when he notes that organizational "environments are enacted by hosts of individuals and organizations each acting on the basis of their interpretations of a world that is in effect mutually defined." In the live trucks incident, the arrival of one station's truck was interpreted as a competitive challenge by the other station and was met accordingly, thus magnifying the importance of the story. (This same phenomenon can be seen on a larger scale in "pack journalism" and in so-called feeding frenzies; see Bantz, 1990, pp. 139-140; Sabato, 1991, pp. 55-61.) In such ways, competitive norms and routines sustain themselves and a competitive organizational environment is continually constructed and reconstructed.

Competition for news in television thus is not merely a product of corporate coercion or economic constraints. The newsworkers at this particular station may have made a deliberate, rational decision to compete in order to maintain their first-place position and their economic advantage over their rivals, or station management may have pressured them to compete. But something deeper and more unconscious seemed to be at work. For example, the producer alone decided to send the second live truck to the storm damage scene. Nothing he said at the time or later seemed to indicate that he did so simply to conform to policy set by management intent on staying "number one." Nor did there seem to be any sort of economic incentive compelling him to do it, no obvious payoff in terms of higher ratings or more advertising revenue (in fact, the producer admitted later, his decision probably had cost the station money, because it had to pay overtime to the driver of the second truck). Instead, the producer's stated reason for sending the extra truck was very simple:

Producer: Well, I don't like having [the other station] being able to get a live shot out of [the storm scene] if I can't. (Laughs) It's just sheer competition. I just don't like it.

Author: What's the [big] deal there?

Producer: Well, they're my *competition*. And if they can go live from the parking lot [of the school], they've got me *beat*. That's the bottom line.

In short, the producer saw his job not in terms of dollars but in terms of avoiding defeat at the hands of the competition. He clearly understood the "competition" to be the three other television news operations in the area— *not* cable, independent stations, or others competing for the viewers of network affiliates within the broader political and economic environment. The fact that ratings data indicated that the station had little to fear from the other three stations was of little concern to the producer. He simply took it for granted that he was supposed to try to win, or least try not to lose—that was "the bottom line," an obvious and unquestioned fact of life. And if he occasionally did get "smoked" on a story, that was part of the game; the nights when he and his staff "scooped the butts" of the other stations and celebrated their victories more than made up for such defeats. They all had been socialized via their experiences in television newswork into a shared, commonsensical cultural system (Geertz, 1983, chap. 4) that said it was normal, right, and proper to compete.

Competition for Ratings

If the competition for news stories in television is at least as much a product of social and cultural pressures as it is of direct economic pressures, the competition to be first in the ratings is much more explicitly tied to a battle for profits. The ratings system is central in maintaining stability and predictability in the television industry in that it helps regulate and routinize relations among stations, networks, advertisers, and ratings firms (Streeter, 1989; Meehan, 1984, 1990; Larson, 1992). Within this system, an enormous amount of money is at stake, particularly during the "sweeps" ratings periods which help determine advertising rates for stations nationwide. One estimate says the loss of a single ratings point during the sweeps can cost a large-market station as much as $2 million (Vierria, 1994). And because of this, many newsrooms resort to tabloid-like "special reports" full of crime, sex, and fluff to try to boost ratings during sweeps, especially in the larger markets (Moritz, 1989).

The top-20 market station I visited for this study was no exception. It was number one in the news ratings, but faced a strong challenge from the second-place station. In response, it aired reports during one sweeps on topics ranging from "criminal clergy" to X-rated videos, pulling many of its reporters off everyday news coverage to produce the special reports. The newsroom managers did not apologize for doing what they believed was absolutely necessary. "Our job is to sell eyeballs [i.e., deliver audiences to advertisers]," one executive producer told me. "And without them, we're out of business."

Not everyone in the newsroom agreed with this philosophy. Some complained openly about having to do "sleazy" stories. And one reporter told me that while the station in the past had "kicked butt" in its daily news coverage, it now seemed to be "floundering." In other words, journalistic norms (centered around matching or bettering the news stories of the competition) clashed with business norms (centered around beating the competition in the ratings; see Bantz, 1985). But such were the monetary stakes at this station that business norms inevitably won; as McManus (1994, p. 203) writes, newsworkers at stations like this one who put journalistic interests ahead of market interests "may be tolerated about as long as a counter clerk at McDonald's who refuses to sell fried food." (In fact, the reporter quoted above soon left the station.)

That said, it should be added that social and cultural pressures do play significant roles in the competition for ratings. Bogart (1988, p. 15) notes that outside their offices, media managers can accept the fact that "ratings aren't all that matters," but once back in their workplaces, they "have to make believe that the numbers really make sense and deserve to be taken seriously." Indeed, for many, following the numbers becomes a "strategic ritual" similar to that of monitoring the opposition's newscasts; the managers at the top-20 station reviewed overnight ratings data each day to reassure themselves that they were not losing ground to the opposition (see also Auletta, 1992, p. 466). If the race for ratings is ritualized in this way, it is also "enacted" in that it is mutually constructed by individuals and organizations that program and counter-program their airwaves in continual reaction to what their competitors do. Through this ongoing competition, media managers form "social and cultural bonds" (Streeter, 1989, p. 10) built upon the shared, commonsensical understanding that the ratings are supremely important.

In many ways, the social and cultural influences connected to sweeps and the competition for ratings were even more pronounced in the medium-market newsroom that was the focal point of this study. Unlike its top-20 counterpart, the smaller newsroom felt much less economic pressure to compete for viewers, again because it always had dominated the ratings. Newsroom managers told me that the "special reports" they produced for sweeps made little difference in the numbers; they knew they would win the ratings race easily even without airing such stories. Nevertheless, they continued to produce these sorts of reports (on topics that were much less "sleazy" than at the top-20 station), because as one manager told me: "It's habit. I mean, we've *done* it. . . . We've done [sweeps reports] forever, and it's hard to break that mold." Creating special material for ratings periods thus had become a routine, ordinary part of the newsroom culture, despite having little to do with maximizing audiences and profits.

One other factor contributed to the emphasis on sweeps at the medium-market station. Some reporters saw the ratings periods as an opportunity to produce material that would enhance their resume tapes and help them "climb the market ladder," that is, compete for better and higher-paying jobs in larger markets. In that sense, sweeps was a competitive ritual aimed more toward furthering reporters' individual ambitions than toward making more money for the station.

The Competitive Ethos and Corporate Interests

The competitive ethos, continually ritualized and enacted via routine newsroom practices, helps give newsworkers a certain degree of control over their work (Gallagher, 1982). That is, they are socialized into "knowing" that they are supposed to act competitively. And that commonsense knowledge helps them understand their jobs and gives them a basis for action. They "know" that they have to keep track of the other station's newscasts, try to win in the ratings, and so forth.

But whatever degree of control the competitive ethos affords newsworkers is decidedly limited. As Tuchman (1978) and other critical scholars argue, newswork is necessarily ideological and legitimates existing power relations. Newsworkers do *not* do this intentionally; rather, newswork is a *means not to know*. According to sociologist Dorothy E. Smith (quoted in Tuchman, 1978, p. 179), a "means not to know" is "a practice which has the effect of making the fundamental features of our own society mysterious because it prevents us from recognizing them as problematic. . . . What ought to be explained is treated as fact or as assumption." Newsworkers typically take for granted the routine practices and norms of their work and thus do not attempt to explain or question how that work may serve corporate interests. Yet the competitive ethos in television newswork does appear to serve those interests in several ways:

Cheap and viewer-friendly news. First, competitive norms and practices contribute to trivial and superficial news coverage by encouraging the pursuit of stories like the car-bus collision that was discussed earlier. These sorts of stories produce clear "winners" and "losers," with the winners being those who get the story first (Schudson, 1986; Nelson, 1993), but in the long run they are of little importance to the audience. Yet they feature the kind of action and good visuals which television favors and which presumably are most attractive to audiences (Epstein, 1974; Altheide, 1976; McManus, 1994). In this way, journalistic standards again are subordinated to business and entertainment interests. These kinds of stories also can be "manufactured" cheaply and quickly within a highly routinized production system (Tuchman, 1973; Schlesinger, 1977, 1978, chap. 4; Bantz, McCorkle, and Baade, 1980; Fishman, 1980; Berkowitz, 1992a, 1992b). That means news organizations can extract more output from individual newsworkers—as many as three or more stories per reporter each day (Dracos, 1989). And this emphasis on "quick and dirty" news coverage discourages efforts at more thoughtful, in-depth reporting which at least potentially could be more critical of corporate interests and the status quo.

Homogenization of the news. Competitive norms and practices strongly appear to help *homogenize* the news rather than *diversify* it (Gans, 1979, p. 177; Glasser, 1987; Bagdikian, 1992, pp. 239-252). That is, competition does precisely the opposite of what it is supposed to do according to the libertarian view of the marketplace. Rituals like "monitoring the opposition" are aimed more toward *not getting beaten* on stories than they are toward producing genuinely original, unique news. In the words of two television news professionals (Filoreto and Setzer, 1993, p. 45): "Never underestimate the lack of originality and creativity in the news business. Unless you've got an amazing exclusive, you want to have the same lead story as every other station in your market." Even when story selection differs, competing stations still adopt highly similar news formats (with "anchor teams," sports and weather segments, and so forth). Such homogeneity appears to serve corporate interests in that, as Turow (1985, pp. 223-224) suggests, media companies that target large audiences tend to produce "highly predictable, highly patterned mass media content" (see also Owen, 1978; Bagdikian, 1992, pp. 132-133; McManus, 1994). They also rely heavily on "track-record talent" that has been socialized into standard occupational practices and values (like the "competitive ethos").

Control of labor costs. The competitive ethos helps preserve a system in which television stations are able to demand long hours from their employees and, especially in the case of entry-level workers, pay them little in return. Those just entering the business are told that "you'll probably make much less money than you expect. *Much* less" (Filoreto and Setzer, 1993, p. 91). And so newsworkers not only compete for news against other stations in the market, but also compete among themselves for higher-paying jobs in *larger* markets; as discussed earlier, they try to advance their careers by "climbing the market ladder." This too is part of the taken-for-granted shared understanding among television newsworkers—that you start low, take what you can get in terms of salary and hours, and then fight your way up. And in turn television organizations, especially in smaller markets, benefit from a constant, ready supply of cheap labor.

Perpetuation of the ratings system. Finally, as already argued, the ratings system serves the interests of all the key corporate players in the television industry, and the race for ratings in television news is explicitly tied to profit maximization. When newsroom managers define their jobs and their professional success in terms of beating the opposition in the numbers—for example, by making a daily ritual of reviewing overnight ratings data—they confirm the importance of the ratings system and help perpetuate it. Even the medium-market newsroom helped legitimate the ratings system by routinely preparing special reports to air during sweeps, despite there being no compelling economic reason to do so.

Thus, the irony of the competitive ethos is that the ferocious social and cultural competition for news and ratings ultimately serves the interests of the corporate oligopoly that controls most of the media industry—an oligopoly that by its very nature discourages competition in the political economic sphere.

Competition, Culture, and Community

If a newswork perspective helps illuminate television news competition as a social and cultural phenomenon while at the same time it helps clarify the links between newsroom competition and institutional power, Schudson (1991, pp. 151-155) reminds us that this perspective does have its limitations. He argues that news cannot be explained solely as a product of organizational routines, rituals, and ideologies any more than it can be seen solely as a product of political economic relations. As a complementary perspective, Schudson outlines what he calls a "culturological approach" to the sociology of news production (p. 155). In his view, there is "a specifically journalistic cultural air tied to the occupational practices of journalists," one that transcends organizational boundaries. The culturological perspective helps us view the competitive ethos in a broader journalistic and cultural context. In particular, it demonstrates how competition fosters a sense of *community* inside and outside of journalism, while at the same time it provides the starting point for a critique of that notion of "community."

For example, Zelizer (1993) views journalists as "*interpretive* communities," specific cultures united by shared discourses and interpretations. This concept may help explain why reporters from rival news organizations— ostensibly competitors—often cooperate in determining what is newsworthy and what their stories should say. In fact, studies of "specialist correspondents" like political and science reporters have found this to be the case (Tunstall, 1971; Crouse, 1974; Dunwoody, 1981). Such reporters begin to identify strongly with the community of other reporters on their particular beats, perhaps even more strongly than they identify with their respective news organizations.

The concept of journalistic interpretive communities also is useful in examining television news competition. Zelizer (1993, p. 223) notes that journalists use channels like "professional and trade reviews" and "professional meetings" in creating "a community through discourse." Trade publications which tell news directors that "news is competition" (Radio-Television News Directors Association, 1988, p. 11) are clearly targeted at a community of television news managers from different organizations who share common interpretations of a competitive world. The "insider's guide" which says "good journalists want to win" (Filoreto and Setzer, 1993, p. 138) and which urges prospective young newsworkers to start low and then work up the market ladder is socializing newcomers into the values of that same interpretive community. That this is a community of *rivals* who are in constant competition with each other should not be surprising, according to psychologist Stuart Walker (1986, pp. 3-4):

In few activities other than competition can a participant find a similar opportunity to assert his [sic] unique significance and simultaneously attain approval from the people he most respects. For his competitors become the people who mean the most to him. Their shared respect for the game and for the significance of involvement in it make them the most valued judges of his accomplishments. He wants both the opportunity they provide him to display his competence and their approval.

From this perspective, there is indeed community in competition. Those on the "fast track" who run a daily "race that determines who's the best" judge their progress according to the progress of their fellow runners in the lanes next to them, all of them joined by their "shared respect for the game." The competitive ethos becomes part of the glue that helps hold together the interpretive community of television newsworkers, even as they move from one organization to another.

But it is not just television newsworkers who draw upon competitive norms in this way. Many if not most of us feel the pressure to *win* in our professional lives and to measure our performance against that of others; we too are affected by the "ethic of competitive individualism" of which Gareth Morgan (1986, p. 119) writes. Schudson (1991) warns against reducing all such shared cultural values to the level of ideology or hegemony; still, we can avoid doing so without sacrificing the critical perspective that allows us to examine these shared values for their potentially negative consequences.

For example, Alfie Kohn (1986, p. 1) asserts that competition is the taken-for-granted and unquestioned "common denominator of American life." He goes on to argue that this way of life is fundamentally destructive and should be challenged on all fronts. Competition is not something that is biologically wired into human beings or mandated by the laws of nature; both "nature" and many non-Western cultures show that cooperative norms can be learned just as easily as competitive norms (see also Augros and Stanciu, 1991). Similarly, Eisler and Combs (1991) suggest that competitive norms are rooted in patriarchy and a "dominator myth," and should be replaced by a culture based on "gylany," or a cooperative, equal partnership between women and men.

These studies thus debunk the notion that the community to be found in competition is the best and truest form of community; in fact, they deny that competition fosters any sort of genuine community at all. Christians, Ferre, and Fackler (1993) make much the same argument in their study of social ethics and the press. They argue that the principles of Enlightenment individualism (which of course also gave birth to the libertarian ideal of the marketplace of competing goods and ideas) no longer are adequate in an age in which an increasingly small number of multinational corporations control the media and the routines of newswork mesh so completely with those of powerful, legitimated institutions. In such an age, an interpretive community of journalism centered around a competitive, individualistic ethos becomes an oppressive cultural force, one that Christians, Ferre, and Fackler assert should be countered with a genuinely "communitarian" media ethics based on principles of mutuality and civic transformation—principles which (much as Kohn [1986] and others argue) should apply to the rest of our culture as well.

Conclusion

A favorite topic of discussion among media critics is why so much of American television news is as poor as it is (e.g., "Bad News," 1993). I have suggested here that one answer to that question is competition—not just competition for profits (although that is a vitally important factor), but also a social and cultural competition within and among news organizations and within the broader community of television newsworkers. This is a competition centered around an ethos which holds that it is right and inevitable to measure one's performance consistently against that of others and that one should thrill in victory and agonize in defeat. The competitive ethos helps newsworkers understand and control their work, but it also contributes to shallow journalism and acts to homogenize rather than diversify the news. And it helps perpetuate corporate control of the media and block efforts, in journalism as well as in the rest of our culture, to build a more humane and cooperative world.

This analysis implies that if one is to counter the negative consequences of the competitive ethos, one must do so both in the political economic sphere and in the cultural sphere. In terms of communication policy, one must continue to resist the notion that all we need is more competition. Blumler (1991, p. 213) argues that the "ingrained free market ethos of the American culture fosters a presumption that all consequences of increased competition in the television marketplace will be beneficial," whereas in fact such consequences are likely to include an even greater emphasis on that which "has most immediate and arresting appeal." Instead, significant structural reform of the television and media industry is needed, producing what Blumler (p. 214) describes as "a principled and an amply and securely funded public sector" that would be relatively free of corporate control and commercial pressures.

In terms of culture, media educators in the classroom should call attention to and actively seek to counteract the competitive ethos. Such an ethos is merely one version of the "occupational ethos" which Blanchard and Christ (1993, chap. 4) strongly argue should *not* be reproduced by media education (see also Shoemaker, 1993). Helping to instill the principles of the "New Professionalism" which Blanchard and Christ advocate can help students exert more control and self-direction in their work. However, such educational efforts must be accompanied by genuine structural changes within the television news industry in order for students to play a significant role in improving current news practice (McManus, 1994, p. 203).

At the very least, additional research is needed on the social and cultural aspects of media competition. We should examine further the circumstances under which different kinds of media workers and organizations compete or do not compete (Bantz, 1985, pp. 237-239) and compare how others compete in different contexts like sports and business. In these ways, we can gain a broader culturological perspective on how competition is enacted in American life, and we can form the basis of a broader-based critique of the false sense of community which competition produces. Most important, the unquestioned and taken-for-granted competitive norms within mass media occupations ought to be critically examined, questioned, and challenged. It is suggested here that teachers of mass communication, through their contacts with both present and future generations of professional communicators, are in a unique position to undertake that challenge.

References

Altheide, D. L. (1976). *Creating reality: How TV news distorts events.* Beverly Hills, CA: Sage.

Atwater, T. (1984). Product differentiation in local TV news. *Journalism Quarterly, 61*(4): 757-762.

Augros, R., & Stanciu, G. (1991). Competition and the enculturation of science. *World Futures, 31*(2-4): 85-94.

Auletta, K. (1992). *Three blind mice: How the TV networks lost their way.* New York: Vintage [orig. pub. 1991].

Bad news. (1993, September). *American Journalism Review, 15,* pp. 18-27.

Bagdikian, B. H. (1992). *The media monopoly* (4th ed.). Boston: Beacon.

Bantz, C. R. (1985). News organizations: Conflict as a crafted cultural norm. *Communication, 8*(2): 225-244.

Bantz, C. R. (1990). Organizing and enactment: Karl Weick and the production of news. In S. R. Corman, S. P. Banks, C. R. Bantz, & M. E. Mayer (Eds.), *Foundations of organizational communication: A reader* (pp. 133-141). New York: Longman.

Bantz, C. R., McCorkle, S., & Baade, R. C. (1980). The news factory. *Communication Research, 7*(1): 45-68.

Berkowitz, D. (1992a). Non-routine news and newswork: Exploring a what-a-story. *Journal of Communication, 42*(1): 82-94.

Berkowitz, D. (1992b). Routine newswork and the what-a-story: A case study of organizational adaptation. *Journal of Broadcasting & Electronic Media, 36*(1): 45-60.

Blanchard, R. O., & Christ, W. G. (1993). *Media education and the liberal arts: A blueprint for the new professionalism.* Hillsdale, NJ: Lawrence Erlbaum.

Blumler, J. (1991). The new television marketplace: Imperatives, implications, issues. In J. Curran & M. Gurevitch (Eds.), *Mass media and society* (pp. 194-215). London: Edward Arnold.

Bogart, L. (1988). Research as an instrument of power. *Gannett Center Journal, 2*(3): 2-16.

Boyer, P. J. (1988). *Who killed CBS? The undoing of America's number one news network.* New York: Random House.

Busterna, J. C. (1980). Ownership, CATV and expenditures for local television news. *Journalism Quarterly, 57*(2): 287-291.

Busterna, J. C. (1988). Television ownership effects on programming and idea diversity: Baseline data. *Journal of Media Economics, 1*(2): 63-74.

Christians, C. G., Ferre, J. P., & Fackler, P. M. (1993). *Good news: Social ethics and the press.* New York: Oxford University Press.

Crouse, T. (1974). *The boys on the bus.* New York: Ballantine [orig. pub. 1973].

Dracos, T. (1989, September). News directors are lousy managers. *Washington Journalism Review, 11,* 39-41.

Dunwoody, S. (1981). The science writing inner club: A communication link between science and the lay public. In G. C. Wilhoit & H. deBock (Eds.), *Mass communication review yearbook* (Vol. 2, pp. 351-359). Beverly Hills, CA: Sage.

Ehrlich, M. C. (1992). Competition in local television news: Ritual, enactment, and ideology. *Mass Comm Review, 19*(1-2): 21-26.

Eisler, R., & Combs, A. (1991). Cooperation, competition, and gylany: Cultural evolution from a new dynamic perspective. *World Futures, 31*(2-4): 169-179.

Epstein, E. J. (1974). *News from nowhere.* New York: Vintage [orig. pub. 1973].

Filoreto, C., & Setzer, L. (1993). *Working in TV news: The insider's guide.* Memphis, TN: Mustang.

Fishman, M. (1980). *Manufacturing the news.* Austin: University of Texas Press.

Gallagher, M. (1982). Negotiation of control in media organizations and occupations. In M. Gurevitch, T. Bennett, J. Curran, & J. Woollacott (Eds.), *Culture, society, and the media* (pp. 151-173). London: Routledge.

Gans, H. (1979). *Deciding what's news.* New York: Random House.

Geertz, C. (1983). *Local knowledge.* New York: Basic Books.

Gitlin, T. (1993, September). Money talks. *American Journalism Review, 15,* 24.

Glasser, T. (1984). Competition and diversity among radio formats: Legal and structural issues. *Journal of Broadcasting, 28*(2): 127-142.

Glasser, T. (1987, April). Intramural contests. *Twin Cities,* pp. 119-120.

Kohn, A. (1986). *No contest: The case against competition.* Boston: Houghton Mifflin.

Lacy, S., Atwater, T., & Qin, X. (1989). Competition and the allocation of resources for local television news. *Journal of Media Economics, 2*(1): 3-13.

Lacy, S., Atwater, T., Qin, X., & Powers, A. (1988). Cost and competition in the adoption of satellite news gathering technology. *Journal of Media Economics, 1*(1): 51-59.

Lacy, S., & Bernstein, J. (1992). The impact of competition and market size on the assembly cost of local television news. *Mass Comm Review, 19*(1-2): 41-48.

Larson, E. (1992, March). Watching Americans watch TV. *Atlantic Monthly,* pp. 66-80.

McManus, J. H. (1994). *Market-driven journalism: Let the citizen beware?* Thousand Oaks, CA: Sage.

Meehan, E. R. (1984). Ratings and the institutional approach: A third answer to the commodity question. *Critical Studies in Mass Communication, 1*(2): 216-225.

Meehan, E. R. (1990). Why we don't count: The commodity audience. In P. Mellencamp (Ed.), *Logics of television: Essays in cultural criticism* (pp. 117-137). Bloomington: Indiana University Press.

Molotch, H., & Lester, M. (1974). News as purposive behavior: On the strategic use of routine events, accidents, and scandals. *American Sociological Review, 39*(1): 101-112.

Moore, A. (1988, October). For NBC: A fine frenzy, a big scoop and a good cry. *Washington Journalism Review, 10,* 9.

Morgan, G. (1986). *Images of organization.* Beverly Hills, CA: Sage.

Moritz, M. (1989). The ratings "sweeps" and how they make news. In G. Burns & R. J. Thompson (Eds.), *Television studies: Textual analysis* (pp. 121-136). New York: Praeger.

Murdock, G., & Golding, P. (1977). Capitalism, communication and class relations. In J. Curran, M. Gurevitch, & J. Woollacott (Eds.), *Mass communication and society* (pp. 12-43). London: Edward Arnold.

Nelson, W. D. (1993, May). Head-to-head. *Quill, 81,* 29-33.

Owen, B. M. (1978). Diversity in broadcasting: The economic view of programming. *Journal of Communication, 28*(2): 43-47.

Radio-Television News Directors Association. (1988, July). 43rd annual international conference and exhibition. *Communicator, 42,* 11.

Sabato, L. J. (1991). *Feeding frenzy: How attack journalism has transformed American politics.* New York: Free Press.

Schlesinger, P. (1977). Newsmen and their time-machine. *British Journal of Sociology, 28*(3): 336-350.

Schlesinger, P. (1978). *Putting "reality" together: BBC news.* London: Constable.

Schudson, M. (1986). Deadlines, datelines, and history. In R. K. Manhoff & M. Schudson (Eds.), *Reading the news* (pp. 79-108). New York: Pantheon.

Schudson, M. (1991). The sociology of news production revisited. In J. Curran & M. Gurevitch (Eds.), *Mass media and society* (pp. 141-159). London: Edward Arnold.

Sherif, C. W. (1976). The social context of competition. In D. M. Landers (Ed.), *Social problems in athletics: Essays in the sociology of sport* (pp. 18-36). Urbana: University of Illinois Press.

Shoemaker, P. J. (1993). Critical thinking for mass communications students. *Critical Studies in Mass Communication, 10*(1): 99-111.

Siebert, F. S. (1956). The libertarian theory of the press. In F. S. Siebert, T. Peterson, & W. Schramm, *Four theories of the press* (pp. 39-71). Urbana: University of Illinois Press.

Smircich, L., & Stubbart, C. (1985). Strategic management in an enacted world. *Academy of Management Review, 10*(4): 724-736.

Streeter, T. (1983). Policy discourse and broadcast practice: The FCC, the U.S. broadcast networks and the discourse of the marketplace. *Media, Culture & Society, 5*(3-4): 247-262.

Streeter, T. (1989). Beyond the free market: The corporate liberal character of U.S. commercial broadcasting. *Wide Angle, 11*(1): 4-17.

Tuchman, G. (1972). Objectivity as strategic ritual: An examination of newsmen's notions of objectivity. *American Journal of Sociology, 77*(4): 660-679.

Tuchman, G. (1973). Making news by doing work: Routinizing the unexpected. *American Journal of Sociology, 79*(1): 110-131.

Tuchman, G. (1978). *Making news: A study in the construction of reality.* New York: Free Press.

Tunstall, J. (1971). *Journalists at work.* Beverly Hills, CA: Sage.

Turow, J. (1985). Learning to portray institutional power: The socialization of creators in mass media organizations. In R. D. McPhee & P. K. Tompkins (Eds.), *Organizational communication: Themes and new directions* (pp. 211-234). Beverly Hills, CA: Sage.

Vierria, D. (1994, December 3). The ratings game. *Sacramento Bee,* p. 7G.

Walker, S. H. (1986). *Winning: The psychology of competition.* New York: Norton.

Weick, K. E. (1979). *The social psychology of organizing* (2nd ed.). Reading, MA: Addison-Wesley.

Zelizer, B. (1993). Journalists as interpretive communities. *Critical Studies in Mass Communication, 10*(3): 219-237.

PART III: News as Text

Telling News

News as Familiar Story

This section of the book marks a transition from studying the social processes by which news is produced to examining the outcomes of those processes. The reason for considering news as story might not be intuitively obvious, because the conventions of news writing are supposed to lead toward treating each story uniquely through an emphasis on objectivity, inverted pyramids, and direct quotes from social actors. Below the surface, though, news stories from the past turn out to have a lot in common with those in the present.

In Chapter 2, Zelizer's "Has Communication Explained Journalism?" depicted news as stories told and retold within shared social and cultural meanings. That is, although specific details of a day's occurrences might be unique to that day, the way that journalists observe and report those occurrences has a lot to do with how similar occurrences have been observed and reported in the past.

Thus, if reporting the news involves strategic processes that enable the predictable accomplishment of work, then when journalists typify an occurrence to expedite the reporting effort, they must decide on the general narrative structure that best applies. That narrative structure provides a basic story line as well as guidance on the appropriate actors and social institutions that should be involved.

In "Mythic Elements in Television News," Robert Rutherford Smith takes this news-as-story perspective to analyze local television news content, asking whether television news might be structured from a relatively limited number of recurring narratives and social actors. Through literary criticism techniques, Smith identifies common themes, institutions, and actors and creates a chart called a *mythograph* that highlights structural elements of the most common narratives he identified. Smith concludes that television news is indeed a medium used for the transmission and reinforcement of society's myths.

S. Elizabeth Bird and Robert W. Dardenne, in "Myth, Chronicle, and Story: Exploring the Narrative Qualities of News," add conceptual refinement to Smith's basic argument. From a journalist's point of view, they explain that if six reporters were sent to cover a trial for six hours and they each produced rather similar stories, this outcome might be used to validate the existence of objective reporting. From the perspective of news as story, though, this outcome becomes a clear indicator of the prevalence of common narrative structures in the news. News, the authors argue, is a symbolic system that presents stories "about reality" rather than presenting reality itself. News therefore represents an ongoing human narrative, with specific news stories contributing to the telling of the larger ongoing one.

Like Tuchman and other authors, Bird and Dardenne argue that the hard news-soft news dichotomy hides the real nature of the news. Here, though, the argument is based on narrative forms rather than on work rhythms. Occurrences are not naturally hard news or soft news, Bird and Dardenne explain, but rather certain occurrences tend to be told and retold in traditional narrative forms that cast them that way. Hard news becomes "chronicle," a straightforward narrative structure describing the "facts" about how an event unfolded. Soft news becomes more of a "story," where the telling allows for greater interpretation by the journalist.

For either category of story, though, the authors make a case for the value of seeing news as myth—not myth as fiction, but myth as a form of folklore. Media audiences come to recognize narrative forms as familiar in a way that helps put new occurrences into a comforting perspective. Through this same familiarity, journalists use myths as "a skeleton on which to hang the flesh of the new story," casting new occurrences around the frameworks they have learned in the past.

The next three selections offer case study examples of how narratives shape the news. "When Technology Fails: The Drama of Airline Crashes in Network Television News," by Richard C. Vincent, Bryan K. Crow, and Dennis K. Davis, offers an example of how news is woven from common recurring narrative structures. After explicating three narrative theory perspectives, the authors examine network coverage of several airline crashes. As theory would predict, journalists tended to tell plane crash stories in similar forms that followed regular themes based on journalists' information discovery processes.

"Non-routine News and Newswork: Exploring a What-a-Story" applies ideas from Vincent, Crow, and Davis and from Tuchman to an observational study of local television journalists reporting on the crash of a military jet into a hotel. Although the terms here are somewhat different, this study shows how narrative structures facilitated coverage of a highly unexpected occurrence. As journalists typified the occurrence, they called on a "mental catalog" of story themes and actors to streamline both the cognitive and work processes of reporting. Once done, reporters could accomplish their reporting through familiar work routines. Furthermore, by monitoring local competing television stations, these journalists made sure they were getting the narrative "right."

An irony appears in this study, because the story that journalists told came closer to their typified narrative than to the realities they observed. More specifically, the story of a hotel fire started by an air crash was told using the framework of an air crash story rather than that of a hotel fire.

Jack Lule's "The Rape of Mike Tyson: Race, the Press and Symbolic Types" studies how coverage of race both draws on and propagates social stereotypes. In this case study, two main cultural myths about African Americans seemed to frame most of the coverage. One challenge of reading this piece is to view the notion of *stereotype* not as normative value judgment but as another way of expressing how myths facilitate and constrain the telling of social narratives. Stereotyping is not necessarily a conscious act, Lule explains, but the result of schemas that journalists apply to categorize and store information, recall it, and then cast their news reports in an ideologically resonant form.

In all, this section takes the innocent notion of the journalistic reporting process as neutral conveyer of reality and recasts it as the reteller of current occurrences through the aid of enduring social folklore.

CHAPTER **21**

Mythic Elements
in Television News

Robert Rutherford Smith

Is television news structured, consciously or unconsciously, on the basis of
a limited repertoire of consistent, predictable narratives? If television news
reports an unstructured series of events or narratives, we should find them
in random variety. If, on the other hand, television is a structuring agent, we
may expect to find certain kinds of narratives reported more often than
others. If television news is structured as a matter of policy, we should expect
to find certain networks, stations, or groups emphasizing certain kinds of
narratives. We expect, then, that it is possible to describe the narrative
structures of news events and that certain narratives will recur more frequently than others.

The most obvious method for answering questions about the content of
a television program is to count: numbers of males, females, and so on.
However, questions concerning the measurement of content are different in

From *Journal of Communication*, 1979, Vol. 29, pp. 75-82. Used by permission of Oxford
University Press.

AUTHOR'S NOTE: The author wrote this article while he was Chairman of the Department
of Broadcasting and Film at Boston University. He is indebted to Ms. Janet Meyer, a
graduate student in communication at Boston University, for her assistance in the design
of the research instrument, data gathering, and data analysis.

Table 21.1 Events

	N	%
Comment on preplanned events	120	38.1
Preplanned events	101	31.8
Spontaneous events	63	19.8
Comment on spontaneous events	33	10.3
Total	317	100.0

kind from questions concerning the meaning of content. The first deal with static phenomena while the second concern the integrated meaning of a series of interrelated events. The first is a problem of measurement, the second of interpretation. Thus, we began with an analysis of the content of twenty 30-minute newscasts and, in addition, we attempted to relate the news narratives to traditional narrative categories taken in part from literary criticism and in part from the literature of psychiatry.

Twenty newscasts, all weekday evening newscasts broadcast February 28-March 3 and March 6, 1978 (Tuesday through Friday, plus Monday), were analyzed. The sample included both the ABC and NBC 7:00 p.m. network news, the WCVB-TV, Boston (ABC affiliate) 11:00 p.m. news, and the WGBH-TV, Boston (public television) 10:00 p.m. news. A total of 317 separate news "stories" were analyzed. Sports[1] and weather reports were not included.

In an attempt to discover whether the news responds to spontaneous events or to preplanned events, we divided all stories into four categories: spontaneous events (floods, accidents); comment upon or analyses of spontaneous events; preplanned events (press conferences, opening nights); and comment upon or analyses of preplanned events. As shown in Table 21.1, preplanned events and comments upon them constituted almost 70 percent of all events reported. This goes along with Boorstin's complaint that the media give an inappropriate emphasis to "pseudo-events," that is, to events that (a) are not spontaneous, (b) are planned for the purpose of being reported, (c) have an ambiguous relation to "underlying reality," and (d) involve a self-fulfilling prophecy, for example, saying that a state of emergency exists creates a state of emergency (Boorstin, 1962, p. 11). In light of our analysis, this emphasis on preplanned events illustrates that the television news producers do have control over a major portion of what is chosen as news and how it is reported.

Looking at Table 21.2, if we note that appearances by leaders and most items concerning foreign news are also related to government activities, government-related stories accounted for 45.4 percent of the stories. Some health stories were also government oriented. If we include all of these, governments (city, state, and federal) are the subjects of more than half of the stories in our sample. What is striking is the absence of reports concerning the private sectors: corporations, families, clubs, and so on.

Table 21.2 Story Subjects

	N	%
Government investigations	72	22.7
Panama, foreign	50	15.8
Crime, wrecks, floods	49	15.5
Feature	37	11.7
Health, education, culture	31	9.8
Coal strike	27	8.5
Leaders (president, mayors)	22	6.9
Economy	19	6.0
Nature, ecology	9	2.8
Other	1	0.3
Total	317	100.0

Table 21.3 Actors

	N	%
Government	105	33.0
Males, age 46+	54	17.0
Voluntary groups	45	14.8
Males, age 31-45	41	12.8
Corporations	26	8.2
Other	11	3.2
Train, plane	10	3.2
Union	7	2.2
Females, age 19-30	5	1.6
Females, age 31-45	5	1.6
Males, age 19-30	3	0.9
Family	3	0.9
Males, age 1-18	1	0.3
Females, age 1-18	1	0.3
Total	317	100.0

We next asked what happens in these stories: Who acts? Whom do they act upon? As shown in Table 21.3, the individual actors in the news items with which we are concerned were primarily males. Voluntary groups (consumer groups, trade groups, school groups) accounted for 14 percent of all "actors," and government agencies accounted for slightly more than one-third. Impersonal forces, such as airplanes, flooding rivers, or trains, accounted for less than 4 percent of all actors. Despite the number of stories reported concerning the nationwide coal strike, only 2.2 percent of the total news items described the union as the actor.

Table 21.4 Acted Upon

	N	%
Government	123	38.8
Voluntary groups	101	31.9
Corporations	25	7.9
Union	16	5.0
Family	15	4.7
Other or none	14	4.5
Males, age 31-45	10	3.2
Males, age 46+	7	2.2
Train, plane	3	0.9
Females, age 19-30	2	0.6
Females, age 1-18	1	0.3
Total	317	100.0

We used similar categories to record the persons or institutions who were "acted upon" in the news stories (see Table 21.4). Again, individuals are seldom identified as the party acted upon in the narrative. Men are identified slightly more often than women, but individuals were identified in a total of only 7.3 percent of the stories analyzed.

Males acted more often than they were acted upon (5.82); voluntary groups were acted upon more often than acted (1.45); the government was also more often acted upon than acted (.85); corporations acted only slightly more often than they were acted upon (1.04). The United Mine Workers, despite having precipitated a crisis by striking, were depicted as being acted upon more often than acting (.44). It should be noted that many of the male actors were government leaders.

Television news, during the evenings studied, presented a narrative in which government was the dominant subject, the primary actor, and the primary acted-upon. Voluntary groups were more often acted upon. Men acted more often than they were acted upon, and women were represented infrequently in any role.

In an attempt to determine what kinds of stories were told, we categorized the narratives according to Jungian categories as shown in Table 21.5. Although our method is empirical, we have chosen those narratives Jung found to be the common stuff of his patients' experiences as a way to relate our data to the general human experience. Those narratives, derived from the wealth of his clinical observations, have "been absorbed into the wider presentation of those common denominators of psychic experience, the archetypes" (Jung, 1958, p. xxv). The most common archetypes identified by Jung (Narcissus, Dionysos, Christ, the child) have not been used and speculative interpretations (e.g., Barbara Walters as an animus figure) have been omitted. We have selected only those with prima facie application to the stories in the news.

Table 21.5 Narratives

	N	%
Man decides	110	34.8
Suffering	86	27.1
Villain caught	66	20.8
Trickster	19	6.0
Wise man	13	4.1
Rescue, escape	12	3.8
Nature	4	1.3
Woman nurtures	3	0.9
Woman liberated	3	0.9
Other	1	0.3
Total	317	100.0

Table 21.6 Themes

	N	%
Helpless, injustice	43	13.6
Corruption	42	13.2
Test of strength	41	12.9
Progress, cooperation	37	11.7
Law and justice	36	11.4
Armageddon	31	9.8
Hero rescues	17	5.4
Sacredness of life	14	4.4
Brotherhood	13	4.1
Other	12	3.9
Nature, destructive	9	2.8
Innocence	9	2.8
Progress, scientific	7	2.2
Nature, benign	3	0.9
Patriotism	3	0.9
Total	317	100.0

Television news reported primarily stories about decision making and suffering. The suffering was characterized by the imprisonment of two former legislators, the victims of a flood in California, and so on. Decision making included President Carter deciding to invoke the Taft-Hartley Act, decisions by miners to remain on strike, and so on.

We also looked for the thematic content of the news stories. As shown in Table 21.6, corruption, injustice, and law and justice were the themes of some 38 percent of the stories. This is consistent with the emphasis noted earlier upon government actions.

Table 21.7 Symbols

	N	%
None	98	31.0
Governmental activity	40	12.6
Judging, testifying	34	10.7
Wreck	28	8.8
Public speaking	26	8.2
Public building	22	6.9
Gun, tool	20	6.3
Commercial activity	19	6.0
Fighting, competing	17	5.4
Cooperating	13	4.1
Total	317	100.0

What we have termed themes are the general stories of which the narratives are special illustrations. One may think of the narrative as a response to the question "what happened?" and the theme as a response to the question "what was the story about?"

Finally, we looked at specific symbols identified visually in the news report (see Table 21.7). In some cases, these were flashed on a screen behind the news reader. In others—for instance, standing before the White House— the symbol provided a setting for the story. The most surprising aspect of this analysis is that one-third of all stories did not contain any identifiable visual symbol. Judging, testifying, and governmental activities were the most frequent symbols.

There are some clues in the data which suggest how specific stories were constructed (see Figure 21.1). We have provided an analysis of the stories in the analysis related to the three major actors: government leaders, males, and voluntary groups. Unfortunately, our sample is too small to allow us to perform a contingency analysis or describe the typical story from each category. The data do suggest, however, that regularities exist and that certain stories are repeated much more often than others.

Not only are the stories regular, but the actors are "licensed," in Lévi-Strauss's phrase, by newsreaders who set the terms of the actor's authority. For instance, we might view the male actor as one armature, the government and voluntary groups as two others. The narratives (injustice, test of strength, etc.) are codes which relate the armatures to the myths (see Moore, n.d., pp. 35-38).

The meaning of the pattern we have detected depends upon the framework in which we cast it. Let me point to a definition of myth devised by Paul Olson (1968, p. 4): "Myth is any narrative which explains or renders in fictive or anthropomorphic terms perceptions of physical nature of social life." Television news, to the extent that it is a medium for the communication

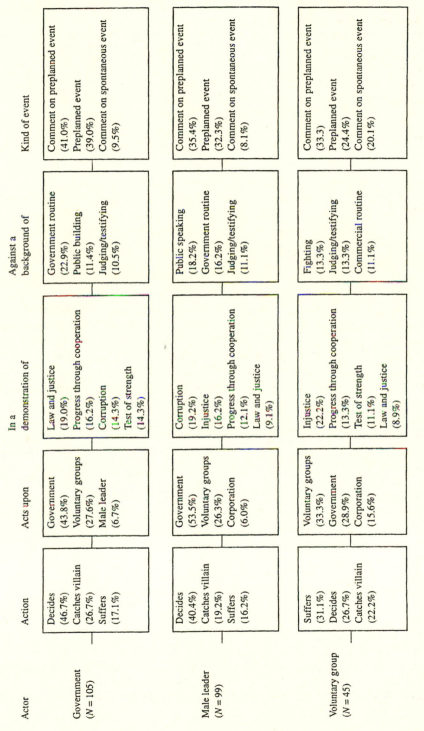

Figure 21.1. A Mythograph of the Evening Network News

NOTE: Percentages in each row are based upon the *N* at the beginning of the row.

of myths, can be understood, in this sense, as a narrative that "explains" or "renders" in fictive terms perceptions of our social environment.

What is the story of these myths of male actors, government bureaucracies, and voluntary groups who suffer, decide, and catch villains?

1. Television reports social reality by creating stories in which males are the primary individual actors. Most of these males occupy positions in government.
2. The government is the actor more frequently than any other group.
3. The government is also the group most frequently acted upon.
4. Women neither act nor are acted upon. They are part of the chorus.
5. These actors engage in prolonged decision making, suffering (usually portrayed by discomfort rather than pain), and occasionally catch villains.
6. These stories are concerned with injustice, corruption, and testing of the strength of the actor against the acted-upon, with a lesser emphasis upon progress through cooperation.

It is difficult to make a claim that television news is used for the creation of myths. We cannot stand outside our own culture and describe its features dispassionately. It is likely, though, that television is one of the media used for the transmission and reinforcement of the myths of our time.

Television news is cast in traditional mythic forms less often than expected, if our sample is a useful index.[2] In the place of sirens, demons, sensations of flying or falling, we have a new narrative: political leaders as an omnipotent elite, beyond both marketplace and law, struggling with each other to determine the rules under which the rest of us must live. The Greek gods on Mount Olympus were no less remote and only slightly more powerful.

Notes

1. Sports would have been included if they were part of the regular news (not narrated by a sports reporter), but no such stories occurred.
2. Preliminary analysis of a one-month sample of TV news broadcasts yielded similar results.

References

Boorstin, Daniel J. *The Image*. New York: Atheneum, 1962.
Jung, C. G. *Psyche and Symbol* edited by Violet S. de Laszlo. Garden City, N.Y.: Doubleday, 1958.
Moore, Tim. *Claude Lévi-Strauss and the Cultural Sciences*. Birmingham, England: Centre for Contemporary Cultural Studies, Occasional Paper No. 4, n.d.
Olson, Paul A. (Ed.) *The Uses of Myth*. Champaign, Ill.: National Council of Teachers of English, 1968.

CHAPTER 22

Myth, Chronicle and Story

Exploring the Narrative Qualities of News

S. Elizabeth Bird
Robert W. Dardenne

Although news accounts are traditionally known as *stories*, which are by definition culturally constructed narratives, little serious study has been made of the narrative qualities of news, and what constructing "stories" actually means. Many journalists continue "to think in terms of freedom of the press, objectivity, fairness, impartiality, balance, the reflection of reality, true representation, readily accepting a clear distinction between fact and opinion, and so on" (Halloran, 1974, pp. 14-15), treating discussion of the relationship between news and story with suspicion. "Scandals," such as the Janet Cooke affair or the more recent revelations that *New Yorker* writer Alastair Reid used fictional devices in his factual accounts, result in recriminations and "back-to-basics" appeals (see Murphy, 1985).

The pretense is maintained that every news story springs anew from the facts of the event being recorded. If it is true that "you can put six reporters in a court and they can sit through six hours of court verbiage and they'll come out with the same story" (Chibnall, 1981, p. 86), journalists prefer to see this as a vindication of objective reporting rather than the triumph of formulaic narrative construction. Rhetorical and structural devices are seen simply as methods to convey information accurately and effectively, and the

From J. W. Carey (Ed.), *Media, Myths, and Narratives: Television and the Press*, 1988, pp. 67-86.
Copyright © 1988 Sage Publications, Inc.

perceived gulf between fact and fiction is defended ever more vociferously. "It is very simple. . . . The writer of fiction must invent. The journalist must not invent" (Hersey, 1981, p. 25).

In other disciplines, meanwhile, the study of narrative and story is becoming increasingly important, as emphasis focuses on texts as cultural constructions. Cultural anthropologists have not only rediscovered narrative as an important element in the cultures they examine but have also begun reflexively to rethink their ethnographic narratives—their news stories— which had long been treated as objective accounts of reality (Marcus, 1982). As Bruner (1984) warns:

> There may be a correspondence between a life as lived, a life as experi-
> enced, and a life as told, but the anthropologist should never assume
> the correspondence nor fail to make the distinction. (p. 7)

Even in such an apparently "objective" discipline as physical anthropology, questions are being raised about the cultural conventions that shape such narratives as the scientific account of human evolution (Landau, 1984).

Historians have always debated the difference between events and stories about events: "Objective" history is now largely seen as naive—"a failure to take into consideration the initial distinction between a physical event which simply occurs, and an event which has already received its historical status from the fact that it has been recounted in chronicles, in legendary stories, in memories etc." (Ricoeur, 1981, p. 276). Like news, history and anthropology narrate real events, and their practitioners are finding that to understand their narratives, they must examine how they are constructed, including the story-telling devices that are an integral part of that construction.

In this interdisciplinary discussion, we consider the news genre as a particular kind of symbolic system. We aim to explore some of the questions arising from the serious consideration of news as narrative and story, and hence the troubled relationship between "reality" and "stories about reality." Media scholars are already studying the narrative paradigm in order to understand the nature of news (e.g., Bennett & Edelman, 1985). We aim to advance that discussion by drawing together converging ideas from several fields of inquiry and relating them to this growing communications literature. We believe that from this may come a clearer understanding of the context in which journalists construct news stories, and how these stories relate to the culture of which they are both a reflection and a representation.

Approaches to the Study of News

Running through most American writing on news is the assumption that there are two kinds of news, variously called "hard" versus "soft," "important" versus "interesting" (Gans, 1979), "news" versus "human interest" (Hughes, 1968), and "information" versus "story" (Schudson, 1978). Hughes, for example, claims that news articles either edify or entertain, and this either/or split has become a taken-for-granted, if constantly qualified, assumption in American journalism.

This assumption has held back productive discussion of the narrative qualities of news in two ways. First, it has hindered us from seeing news as a unified body that exhibits clear themes and patterns that have little to do with important/interesting splits. It leaves us viewing news within a traditional "transmission model"—essentially from the point of view of the professionals who created this dichotomy. There is little to suggest that audiences experience the world as so neatly divided.

Second, this assumption blinds us to the structural qualities of individual stories. It is accepted that hard news is informative and factual, while soft news is diverting. In ideal terms, this split is supposed to be dictated by content—certain types of news simply "are" hard, others soft. These qualities are intrinsic in the events being narrated. This perception blinds us to the way narrative devices are used in all news writing, maintaining the illusion that the structural devices used in hard news are merely neutral techniques that act as a conduit for events to become information, rather than ways in which a particular kind of narrative text is created.

We believe that to understand what news as narrative is and does, we must put aside the important/interesting dichotomy and look at news stories as a whole—both as a body of work that is a continuing story of human activity, and as individual stories that contribute to that continuing one. Considering news as narrative does not negate the value of considering news as corresponding with outside reality, as affecting or being affected by society, as being a product of journalists or of bureaucratic organization, but it does introduce another dimension to news, one in which the stories of news transcend their traditional functions of informing and explaining. The news as narrative approach does not deny that news informs; of course readers learn from the news. However, much of what they learn may have little to do with the "facts," "names," and "figures" that journalists try to present so accurately. These details—both significant and insignificant—all contribute to the larger symbolic system of news. The facts, names, and details change almost daily, but the framework into which they fit—the symbolic system—is more enduring. And it could be argued that the totality of news as an enduring symbolic system "teaches" audiences more than any of its component parts, no matter whether these parts are intended to inform, irritate, or entertain.

News as Mythological Narrative

News is part of an age-old cultural practice, narrative and story-telling, that seems to be universal (Rayfield, 1972; Scholes, 1982; Turner, 1982). As narrative, news is orienting (Park, 1944), communal (Dewey, 1927), and ritualistic (Carey, 1975). The orderings and creations in narrative are cultural, not natural; news, like history, endows past events with artificial boundaries, "constructing meaningful totalities out of scattered events" (Ricoeur, 1981, p. 278). So, rather than considering the "accuracy" of facts and their correspondence with an outside reality, we can consider them as contributing to the narrative, as elements in a human ordering of elements.

One of the most productive ways to see news is to consider it as myth, a standpoint that dissolves the distinction between entertainment and information. By this we do not mean to say that individual news stories are like individual myths, but that as a communication process, news can act like myth and folklore (Bird, 1987). Bascom (1954), in a classic statement on the functions of folklore, writes that it serves as education, as a validation of culture, as wish fulfillment, and as a force for conformity, while Malinowski (1974) considered myth to be a "charter" for human culture. Through myth and folklore, members of a culture learn values, definitions of right and wrong, and sometimes can experience vicarious thrills—not all through individual tales, but through a body of lore. As Drummond (1984) writes:

> Myth is primarily a metaphorical device for telling people about themselves, about other people, and about the complex world of natural *and* mechanical objects which they inhabit. (p. 27)

Myth reassures by telling tales that explain baffling or frightening phenomena and provide acceptable answers; myth does not necessarily reflect an objective reality, but builds a world of its own (Frye, 1957).

The mythical qualities of news, particularly television news, have been remarked on (Hartley, 1982; Knight & Dean, 1982; Smith, 1979). For news, too, is a way in which people create order out of disorder, transforming knowing into telling. News offers more than fact—it offers reassurance and familiarity in shared community experiences (Mead, 1925-1926); it provides credible answers to baffling questions and ready explanations of complex phenomena such as unemployment and inflation (Jensen, 1977). Consuming the news has been compared to religion (Gerbner, 1977), ritual activity (Carey, 1975), celebration (Capo, 1985), and play (Glasser, 1982; Stephenson, 1964). For through the ritualistic narrating of tales (including news), myths are acted out, transformed, and re-created in a "ritual process" (Turner, 1969). As a symbolic system, myth and news act both as a model of and as a model for a culture (Geertz, 1973).

For example, myth outlines the boundaries of acceptable behavior by telling stories, such as the Apache moral narratives that criticize social delinquents, "thereby impressing such individuals with the undesirability of improper behavior and alerting them to the punitive consequences of further misconduct" (Basso, 1984, p. 34). As Drummond (1984) notes, "Of the several boundary conditions, or cultural continuums, that define human identity, the one that holds our interest longest and last is what makes us like and unlike others" (p. 21).

So all news media report crime and deviant behavior, and not primarily as a duty to inform; the average reader does not require the quantities of information offered on crime. While it is possible to argue that readers need to know about crime in order to guard against it, or to bemoan the amount of crime news while saying it is what the "morbidly curious" public demand (Haskins, 1984), a central meaning of crime news is symbolic:

> Such news is a main source of information about the normative contours of a society. It informs us about right and wrong, about the parameters beyond which one should not venture and about the shapes that the devil can assume. A gallery of folk types—heroes and saints, as well as fools, villains and devils—is publicized not just in oral tradition and face-to-face contact, but to much larger audiences and with much greater dramatic resources. (Cohen & Young, 1981, p. 431)

Each individual crime story is written against a backdrop of other crime stories, drawing from them and adding to them. Readers rarely remember details of crime stories, and they do not "use" the information in their daily lives (Graber, 1984). Instead, the stories become part of a larger "story" or myth about crime and values. Graber (1984) and Roshier (1981) both point out that media do not reflect actual crime rates. If information were the only purpose of crime reporting, it would make sense to report all major crimes, such as burglaries and car thefts, so that readers could be on their guard. Instead, 26% of all news-reported crimes in Chicago are murders (Graber, 1984). Graber and Roshier show, however, that readers' estimates of actual crime rates are much closer to reality. Readers do not only consume news as a reflection of reality, but as a symbolic text that defines murder as more noteworthy than car thefts. News stories, like myths, do not "tell it like it is," but rather, "tell it like it means." Thus news is a particular kind of mythological narrative with its own symbolic codes that are recognized by its audience. We know, when we read or hear a news story, that we are in a particular "narrative situation" (Barthes, 1982) that requires a particular kind of stance to be understood.

Telling the Story

But how, in terms of individual news accounts, are the myths—the continuing stories—actually narrated? Myth has meaning only in the telling; cultural themes and values exist only if they are communicated. Obviously, there is no single myth or narrative that is merely repeated, yet to continue to have power, myths must be constantly retold. Rather, themes are rearticulated and reinterpreted over time, themes that are derived from culture and that feed back into it. Stories are not reinvented every time the need arises; instead, "you constantly draw on the inventory of discourse which [has] been established over time" (Hall, 1984, p. 6).

Folklorists discuss the oral tradition in terms of an ideal "story," an archetype that does not exist but that is re-created in individual tellings. Thus we have a "story" of Cinderella, of which there is no definitive version, but that we recognize as the same "story" regardless of variation. At a broader level, we know a "Cinderella" story when we hear one—"Cinderella" is a heavily encoded term in our culture. Every so often the story is retold, restructuring diffuse images "all of which will be organized, integrated or apprehended as a specific 'set' of events only in and through the very act by which we narrate them as such" (Herrnstein Smith, 1981, p. 225).

In a news context, Darnton (1975) recalls writing crime stories that while recording actual events, were rooted in conventional, larger stories, such as "the bereavement story":

> When I needed such quotes, I used to make them up, as did some of the others . . . for we knew what the "bereaved mother" and the "mourning father" should have said and possibly even heard them speak what was in our minds rather than what was in theirs. (p. 190)

Cohen (1981) makes a similar point in assessing how the British media defined the 1960s "mods and rockers" as "folk devils," describing interviews with them as not necessarily faked but as "influenced by the reporter's (or sub-editor's) conception of how anyone labelled as a thug or a hooligan *should* speak, dress and act" (p. 275).

Much of the mythical quality of news derives from such "resonance"—the feeling that we have written or read the same stories over and over again. The principle of consonance (Galtung & Ruge, 1965) ensures that events that may actually be different are encoded into frameworks that are already understood and anticipated. News "conveys an impression of endlessly repeated drama whose themes are familiar and well-understood" (Rock, 1981, p. 68). Frayn (1981) neatly satirizes this process in his "demonstration that in theory a digital computer could be programmed to produce a perfectly satisfactory daily newspaper with all the variety and news sense of the old hand-made article" (p. 71). Frayn's point is that such is the formulization of news that we need draw only on the existing body of news to create new configurations constantly.

So, as Lévi-Strauss (1972) notes, "we define myth as consisting of all its versions" (p. 217), or, to put it the opposite way, each version feeds from and nourishes the totality of the myth itself. As Frye (1957) comments, "Poetry can only be made out of other poems; novels out of other novels. Literature shapes itself" (p. 287).

Journalists, however, resist the view that news also shapes itself:

> Because of our tendency to see immediate events rather than long-term processes, we were blind to the archaic element in journalism. But our very conception of "news" resulted from ancient ways of telling stories. (Darnton, 1975, p. 191)

Indeed, "news values," which journalists often imply are something intrinsic in events, to be deduced using "news sense," are culturally specific story-telling codes. These values, summarized by Chibnall (1981) as "rules stressing the relevancy of: The Present, The Unusual, The Dramatic, Simplicity, Actions, Personalization and Results," are just those values that any storyteller uses in creating a tale. Stories never "reflect reality" and tell of mundane, everyday events. They are about the different and the particular, which yet represent something universal—just as is news.

In practical terms, news values, rules, and formulas are essential for journalists to do their jobs. Reporters may have to write many stories in a week, or they may have to move to a different community and start writing about it immediately. They can comfortably do this with all the story-telling tools at their disposal, giving them a skeleton on which to hang the flesh of the new story. It is the same skill as that of the Yugoslav epic poet described by Lord (1971):

> He can hear a song once and repeat it immediately afterwards—not word for word, of course—but he can tell the same story again in his own words. (p. 26)

The oral poet uses a "common stock of formulas" that give "the traditional songs a homogeneity" and create "the impression that all singers know all the same formulas" (Lord, p. 49), much as "most stories are simply minor updates of previous news or new examples of old themes" (Graber, 1984, p. 61). More than any other kind of story-telling, the time frame of the daily newspaper resembles oral narrative. The six crime reporters who leave the courtroom with the same story may be writing about reality, but their "story" emerges as much from the stories that have gone before as from the facts of the case on court.

Chronicle

While the "story-telling" aspect of news is clearly important, however, much of news can hardly be called "story" in any accepted sense—the daily background of routine stories in terse, inverted pyramid style, recording accidents, unremarkable crimes, day-to-day local or national government business. At the extreme local level, the small town weekly lists the visitors to the town and who left for vacation, while at the national level, Washington correspondents detail the arrival and departure of foreign dignitaries at the White House. Exactly how people read this kind of news is unclear, although it seems that they scan it for general patterns, and forget details (Graber, 1984).

These accounts are not "stories" designed to engage the mind, but "chronicles" provided as a record that something noteworthy has happened (White, 1981). This is not to imply that, unlike stories, chronicles simply record reality, although this seems to be how they have come to be perceived by news professionals. In fact, they are a vital element in the continuing mythological process. They provide us with the backdrop of events that tell us the world is still going on and that things we value still matter. The interminable (to the outsider) bulletin board of neighborhood comings and goings tell us that the local social structure endures, while the White House bulletin tell us that the government is continuing reliably.

Chronicles are not stories, but are still vital, myth-repairing narratives. And the recognition of qualitative differences between chronicle and story are not peculiar to our culture. In predominantly oral cultures, important events may be narrated as chronicle, in listing of wars, genealogies, and so forth. In some sense, they are akin to what historians once called "objective" history. For instance, the African Ndembu distinguish clearly between *nsang'u* (chronicle) and *kaheka* (story). Turner (1982) describes how a sequence of events involving Ndembu royalty may be told in either narrative style:

> This sequence may be told by a chief of putative Lunda origin in his court . . . as an *nsang'u*, a chronicle, perhaps to justify his title to his office. But episodes from this chronicle may be transformed into *tuheka*, "stories" and told by old women to groups of children huddled near the kitchen fire during the cold season. (p. 67)

When told as "story," the accounts are embellished with rhetorical flourishes, songs, and personal touches, and it is through stories that the people "really" understand the events in human terms. Turner emphasizes that the difference between chronicle and story lies not in the quality of the events, but in how they are narrated. "As in other cultures, the same events may be framed as chronicle or story. . . . It all depends where and when and by whom they are told" (p. 68). He stresses the more ritualized aspect of the chronicle, which involves a kind of roll call of events deemed newsworthy. Through chronicle, the overall structure of the myth is emphasized, although individual "stories" are not.

The parallels between this and news narratives are clear. News does a great deal of chronicling, recording newsworthy events in a routine fashion—"the routinization of the unexpected" (Tuchman, 1974). Judgments of what deserves to be chronicled change over time—simply tracing the changes in news chronicles can tell us a great deal about a culture and its dominant values.

The narrative form of chronicle essentially derives from the discursive form *logos*, which the Socratic philosophers distinguished from *mythos*, or story (Fisher, 1985) and became identified as "objective," in all forms of narrative, be they history, news, or social science. The perception developed that the chronicle was the real way to inform, while the story merely entertained, and within journalism the two became distinguished in both form and content in the hard/soft dichotomy (Bird & Dardenne, 1986; Schiller, 1981; Schudson, 1978). Chronicle is no more a reflection of reality in all its aspects than story is. Just as the Ndembu king chronicles events to make a point, historical chroniclers and news writers select whom and what is newsworthy. The "great man" syndrome in traditional history is mirrored in news chronicles.

Implications

Where does an appreciation of the narrative qualities of news take us? First, anthropologists use the study of narrative to find an entrance point into a culture, arguing that texts, like rituals, art, games, and other symbolic configurations, are cultural "models" that encode values and guides for behavior (Colby, 1966, 1975). If we study these models, of which news narratives are a type, we can learn about the values and symbols that have meaning in a given culture.

Like Colby, Rice (1980) drew on earlier work by Bartlett (1932), which showed that members of different cultures retell stories in different, culturally determined ways. Rice found that Americans, when asked to retell Eskimo tales, did so in predictable ways, adjusting the tales to the American "story schema":

> The suggestion here is that cultural schemata are . . . responsible for a sort of "selective perception" of the world which is common to members of a given culture and which has the effect of imparting a characteristic interpretation to the phenomena under consideration. (Rice, 1980, pp. 161-162)

So just as Americans "mend holes" in Eskimo tales, journalists are likely to do the same in their stories of real events, and they will do so in culturally prescribed ways. In other words, journalists, as members of a particular culture, are bound by the "culture grammar" (Colby, 1975) that defines rules of narrative construction, a realization that changes the notion of an "objective" transposing of reality. Seeing news as narrative representing culture thus allows us to study it as a symbolic model of cultural values (Corrigan, 1984), in an attempt to uncover the particular configurations characteristic of a given culture's news. We tend to assume that news media in different cultures have different aims and emphases, but we are not very clear on what these might be. It will also be valuable to examine how and why the narrative genre of news has changed over time as culture changes (e.g., Smith, 1975).

At the same time, journalists, while obviously part of a culture and bound by its narrative grammars, are also specialists trained in particular narrative techniques that may sometimes be at odds with the overriding cultural conventions, and a closer examination of the variety of narrative techniques used by journalists may be in order.

The narrative devices used in news writing are widely seen as ways to organize information clearly and effectively, with story-telling as such tending to be reserved for events deemed "soft" or human interest. The inverted pyramid form, using lead, frequent attribution, and so on, is at its most stylized in the newspaper staples of accident, crime, and other routine accounts—the type of story that "writes itself" for the experienced journalists—but it is used in more elaborate ways for much "hard news." The most striking feature of this style is that it is very different from traditional story form (Scholes, 1982). The lead comes first, dispensing with suspense, while explanation, rather than developing through the story, may follow the "result" of the events described. While still contributing to the continuing myth, it is chronicle, not story, and as such has significant narrative consequences.

For while the inverted pyramid is an efficient device for the writer, it may be a disaster for the reader. Readers ignore much of a newspaper because the subject does not interest them, but they may also ignore a great deal because the narrative form repels them. The inverted pyramid style encourages partial reading (Graber, 1984), and it may help ensure that readers forget much of what they do read. As Scholes (1982) writes, to become a "story," a narrative must be ordered in a particular way, usually presenting cause-and-effect relationships in a logical progression; Ricoeur notes that in order for readers to follow a story, "explanations must . . . be woven into the narrative tissue" (1981, p. 278). Stories must have "narrativity"—be recognizable as stories—if readers are to understand them properly:

> It may even be that no long form of discourse can be received by a
> reader . . . unless it allows and encourages a certain amount of narrativ-
> ity in its audiences. (Scholes, 1982, p. 64)

Increasingly, work on narrative reveals that readers respond to information presented in "story" form, regardless of content. Donahew (1983, 1984) conducted an experiment to measure the physical response of readers to news accounts of the Jonestown mass suicides, containing the same facts but structured differently. His conclusion:

> Messages written in narrative style generated significantly greater
> arousal and mood change responses than those presented in the tradi-
> tional newspaper style. (1984, p. 155)

The common assumption that readers prefer "human interest" stories only because the content is more interesting overlooks that these are the same stories that are usually written in traditional story form. Roshier (1981) stresses the interdependence of form and content when he discusses the readers of the *News of the World*, a British "sensational" Sunday paper. These readers have an unusually high recall of the "titillating" crime stories they enjoy, and while this memorability is obviously inherent in the subject matter, in addition,

> it is achieved by the use of relatively long reports with a literary style
> that often unfolds the plot like a novelette, with headlines which are
> suggestive without giving much away. (Roshier, 1981, p. 48)

Likewise, Robins and Cohen (1981) offer an explanation for the unlikely popularity of Kung Fu films among British working-class youth:

> There is an objective correspondence between *some* oral traditions in working-class culture and some genres produced by the media. It is a correspondence of form rather than content, and where it doesn't exist, the impact of the mass media on working-class consciousness is entirely negligible. (p. 484)

So people respond to and process accurately information presented in story form. Much of the information in newspapers and broadcast news is thus difficult to process, and may actually be perceived as barely comprehensible (Rayfield, 1972). La Baschin (1986) discusses studies that show the average television news viewer recalls only 1 in 19 of the stories presented in a news program. As Benjamin wrote much earlier this century, "Every morning brings us the news of the globe, and yet we are poor in noteworthy stories" (1969, p. 39).

This is not to say that some news is not efficiently communicated in stylized, chronicle structure. Much routine news performs the chronicling function, and, while details may not be recalled, the overall symbolic pattern is strengthened. Thus "crime is understood as a permanent and recurrent phenomenon and hence much of it is surveyed in the media in an equally routinized manner" (Hall et al., 1981, p. 352).

Journalists know, however, that the stylized account often will not do the job. They feel the need to "humanize" events—which, though rarely expressed as such, is the need to write a story. In order to explain, journalists are constantly reverting to the story form—attributed quotes take on the nature of dialogue, a point of view develops, details are added that turn a statistic into an unemployed miner or a bereaved parent. Whether in history or in news, the demands of narrativity ensure that events are most completely understood when they are transformed into story. Certain types of news (like unroutine crime) and certain types of audiences (particularly working class) are given the full story treatment, while most "serious" news is not. And while undoubtedly many readers have learned the particular narrative code of objective reporting, the majority of readers show a marked inability to process political news in anything but the broadest of terms (Graber, 1984).

Journalists find themselves poised uneasily between what they see as two impossible ideals—the demands of "reality," which they see as reachable through objective strategies, and the demands of narrativity. They face a paradox: The more "objective" they are, the more unreadable they become; while the better storytellers they are, the more readers will respond, and the more they fear they are betraying their ideals. So journalists do some chronicling, some story-telling, and a lot that is something of both. Every so often something comes along (like Janet Cooke or Alastair Reid) that makes them try to redraw the line, which invariably becomes instantly smudged once again.

Whose Story?

Perhaps most significant, the consideration of the narrative qualities of news enables us to look more critically at whose values are encoded in news—whose stories are being told? If anthropologists Colby and Peacock (1973) are right, the study of narrative should be at the center of any consideration of news in its cultural context:

> The subtle and undercover techniques of narrative as art, which do not obviously aim to control, may seduce people into letting their guard down. . . . The rise of the mass media, which lend themselves more to stories than sermons, strengthens the position of expressive culture. Expressive forms, including narrative forms, might well assume increasingly important roles in social control. Should this occur, the study of narrative will become increasingly relevant to the student of society. (p. 633)

American cultural studies have tended to adopt a consensual framework; Carey (1983) has commented on the "frequent and telling criticism that cultural studies in the United States, undercut as it is by the cheery optimism of pragmatism, inescapably fails to consider power, dominance, subordination, and ideology as central issues" (p. 313). The consensual approach accepts that news is part of and not apart from the rest of culture, but fails to appreciate that, as a mediated symbolic system, news does not stand in an identical position in culture as, say, oral tradition.

Even in the few discussions of news as story or myth, analysis rarely goes beyond saying that news tells stories about cultural values. Thus Barkin (1984) notes that journalists play a role in "affirming and maintaining the social order" (p. 32), tacitly assuming that there is indeed a recognized set of values to which all members of a culture subscribe.

Certainly, the story-telling or news values Barkin notes are culturally shared:

> There must be villains and heroes in every paper, and the storylines must conform to the usage of suspense, conflict, the defeat of evil, and the triumph of good that have guided the good sense and artistry of past storytellers and controlled their audience's ability to respond. (Barkin, 1984, p. 30)

The journalist-storyteller is indeed using culturally embedded story values, taking them from the culture and re-presenting them to the culture, and is thus akin to the folk storyteller who operates in a "communal matrix" vis-à-vis the audience (Cawelti, 1978).

A journalist, however, is also creating stories out of events that audiences are unfamiliar with, where they do not have their own experiences in which to place those events. In this case, newspapers and other media are much closer to the "mythological matrix," where although "the genres are a communal possession rather than individual creations," nevertheless

> the creator-performer is given a special authority, he is somewhat distanced from the audience and tends to become more so as the culture develops, to the degree that many versions of the mythological matrix develop a separate caste of creator-performers who are specialists in the performance of mythology. (Cawelti, 1978, p. 298)

In the mythological matrix, the audience tends to put faith in those "specialists" who have access to the "truth," at least in those areas that are unfamiliar. Myth, like news, rests on its authority as "truth." Television news, with its presenters seen in person by its audiences, has co-opted the storyteller/mythmaker role so effectively that it is now regarded as the most authoritative and hence "truthful" source of news (Sperry, 1976).

In newsmaking, journalists do not merely use culturally determined definitions, they also have to fit new situations into old definitions. It is in their power to place people and events into the existing categories of hero, villain, good and bad, and thus to invest their stories with the authority of mythological truth. Thus Hall (1975) agrees that news writing is a "social transaction" that picks up on existing cultural conventions, just as Eason (1981, p. 27) calls it an "interactive process." Nevertheless,

> at the same time, the producers hold a powerful position vis-à-vis their audiences, and they must play the primary role in shaping expectations and tastes. (Hall, 1975, p. 22)

Sperry (1976) argues that this process is in no way ideological. She maintains that in producing news stories, "if the story form you have chosen is a heroic tale, then there must be a protagonist and an antagonist. It is not political favoritism but simply a formulaic understanding of how the world operates" (p. 137). This view, however, begs the question of how these assignments are made; who is hero and who villain is not a question of random selection to fit existing formulas. As Schudson (1982) argues, "The power of the media lies not only (and not even primarily) in its power to declare things to be true, but in its power to provide the forms in which the declarations will appear."

Increasingly, it is up to the media to "place" such groups as strikers (Glasgow University Media Group, 1976, 1980), peace demonstrators and other protesters (Gitlin, 1980; Halloran et al., 1970), feminists (Tuchman, 1978), drug users (Young, 1981), and homosexuals (Pearce, 1981). Hartmann and Husband (1971) found that white children who had little contact with black people were more ready to see race relations in terms of conflict (as the issue was usually defined in the media, in accordance with news/story values) than were those with personal experience of black neighbors. For the media, using existing narrative conventions and "maps of meaning" (Hall et al., 1981), construct reality to conform to those maps and assign meanings to new realities. It is here that the "ideological effect" (Hall, 1977) is perceived:

> Ideology is not a collection of discrete falsehoods, but a matrix of thought firmly grounded in the forms of our social life and organised within a set of interdependent categories, which constitute a network of established "given" meanings embedded in the "assignment" of events to the "relevant" contexts within these pre-established cultural "maps of meaning." (Morley, 1981, p. 371)

Journalists have to make these "assignments" or "news judgments" quickly, and inevitably resort to existing frameworks. "Normality" is good, difference bad or deviant (or amusing). The media ultimately tend to "legitimize the American system by the deference they pay to its structures, its values, and its elected and appointed officials" (Graber, 1984, p. 207). The assignments reflect the interests of the status quo, whether the form chosen for the account is story or chronicle. The result is that the prevailing maps of meaning have come to be perceived as "natural" and "common sense," blinding us to the fact that even common sense is culturally derived (Geertz, 1983):

> This confusion of authority and legitimacy with objectivity makes the news an active agent in the construction of a narrow but compelling version of reality—a version that is communicated so broadly and filled with such familiar symbolism that other versions seem biased or distorted. (Bennett et al., 1985, p. 51)

So, in tracing the story-telling patterns in news, we must be aware that journalists are not only drawing on those patterns, they are also actively reshaping them, constantly "repairing the paradigm" (Bennett et al., 1985). It is a process that is more complex than either a consensual model or a manipulative model, which assigns all the control to the media and sees media as somehow outside of, yet affecting, culture. Rather, media are very much part of culture, but with a particular kind of privileged status within it. The media's narrative reshaping will be most successful when this can present new information in such a way that it accords with readers' existing narrative conventions and can be accommodated within them. The media cannot create mythology out of nothing, but it is more than the "passive transmitter" of myth that has been suggested (Gans, 1979, p. 294). Such media-shaped perceptions may then become part of the common cultural framework, to be drawn on again by journalists in a continuing dialectical process.

Conclusions

It is important to begin looking more critically at the narrative qualities of news. While news is not fiction, it is a story about reality, not reality itself.

Yet because of its privileged status as reality and truth, the seductive powers of its narratives are particularly significant. As Johnson (1983) writes, narrative forms are more than literary constructions; they give people a schema for viewing the world and for living their lives. "Human beings live, love, suffer bereavement and go off and fight and die by them" (p. 32).

News has the function of chronicling, and it does so in the backdrop of narratives recounting "newsworthy" events, written so that no one need read beyond the lead. Chronicling repairs the myth on a day-to-day basis, assuring us of continued order and normality while plotting the parameters of this normality. Yet it cannot fully explain and make things seem "real," because it lacks comprehensible narrativity.

Thus journalists know that events seem more real to readers when they are reported in story form: When they do this they find themselves slipping into the mire of "fiction" and hauling out the lifebelts of objectivity and fact. For the "best" and most readable and convincing stories are those constructed most tightly, so that sides are clearly delineated—stories make a point. Thus, according to White (1981), "narrativity, certainly in factual storytelling . . . is intimately related to, if not a function of, the impulse to moralize reality" (p. 14).

Journalists' training, steeped in the ideology of objective reality, leads them to speak in one narrative voice. Within the existing news paradigm, they frame the problem of "the impulse to moralize reality" in terms of fact/fiction or true/false dichotomies, and fall back on the technique of chronicling. Rather than constantly trying to redraw lines, however, we might do better to consider Tuchman's observation that being a reporter who deals in facts and "being a storyteller who produces tales are not antithetical activities" (1976, p. 96). We might think how journalists could learn to create stories that can be processed by their readers, but that speak in other narrative voices. Journalists do tend to tell the same stories in similar ways; the telling of one story by nature excludes all the other stories that are never told.

References

Barkin, S. M. (1984). The journalist as storyteller: An interdisciplinary perspective. *American Journalism, 1*(2), 27-33.

Barthes, R. (1982). Introduction to the structural analysis of narratives. In S. Sontag (Ed.), *Barthes: Selected writings* (pp. 251-295). London: Fontana-Collins.

Bartlett, F. C. (1932). *Remembering*. Cambridge: Cambridge University Press.

Bascom, W. R. (1954). Four functions of folklore. *Journal of American Folklore, 67*, 333-349.

Basso, K. H. (1984). Stalking with stories: Names, places, and moral narratives among the Apache. In E. M. Bruner (Ed.), *Text, play and story: The construction and reconstruction of self and society* (pp. 19-55). Washington, DC: American Ethnological Society.

Benjamin, W. (1969). The storyteller: Reflections on the work of Nikolai Leskov. In H. Arendt (Ed.), H. Zohn (Trans.), *Illuminations* (pp. 83-109). New York: Schocken.

Bennett, W. L., & Edelman, M. (1985). Toward a new political narrative. *Journal of Communication, 35*, 156-171.

Bennett, W. L., Gressett, L. A., & Haltom, W. (1985). Repairing the news: A case study of the news paradigm. *Journal of Communication, 35*, 50-68.

Bird, S. E. (1987). Folklore and media as intertextual communication processes: John F. Kennedy and the supermarket tabloids. In M. L. McLaughlin (Ed.), *Communication yearbook: Vol. 10*. Newbury Park, CA: Sage.

Bird, S. E., & Dardenne, R. W. (1986). *News and storytelling: Reevaluating the sensational dimension*. Paper presented at the Sensationalism and the Media Conference, Ann Arbor, MI.

Bruner, E. M. (1984). The opening up of anthropology. In E. M. Bruner (Ed.), *Text, play, and story: The construction and reconstruction of self and society* (pp. 1-16). Washington, DC: American Ethnological Society.

Carey, J. W. (1975). A cultural approach to communication. *Communication, 2*, 1-22.

Carey, J. W. (1983). The origins of the radical discourse in cultural studies in the United States. *Journal of Communication, 33*(3), 311-313.

Capo, J. A. (1985). Some normative issues for news as cultural celebration. *Journal of Communication Inquiry, 9*(2), 16-32.

Cawelti, J. G. (1978). The concept of artistic matrices. *Communication Research, 5*(3), 283-305.

Chibnall, S. (1981). The production of knowledge by crime reporters. In S. Cohen & J. Young (Eds.), *The manufacture of news: Social problems, deviance and the mass media* (pp. 75-97). London: Constable.

Cohen, S. (1981). Mods and rockers: The inventory of manufactured news. In S. Cohen & J. Young (Eds.), *The manufacture of news: Social problems, deviance and the mass media* (pp. 263-279). London: Constable.

Cohen, S., & Young, J. (Eds.). (1981). *The manufacture of news: Social problems, deviance and the mass media*. London: Constable.

Colby, B. N. (1966). Cultural patterns in narrative. *Science, 151*, 793-798.

Colby, B. N. (1975). Culture grammars. *Science, 187*, 913-919.

Colby, B. N., & Peacock, J. L. (1973). Narrative. In J. J. Honigman (Ed.), *Handbook of social and cultural anthropology* (pp. 613-636). Chicago: Rand McNally.

Corrigan, D. (1984). Valuation and presentation conventions in news communications: A formula for measurement. *Journal of Communication Inquiry, 8*(2), 29-45.

Darnton, R. (1975). Writing news and telling stories. *Daedalus, 104*, 175-194.

Dewey, J. (1927). *The public and its problems*. Chicago: Swallow.

Donahew, L. (1983). Newswriting styles: What arouses the reader? *Newspaper Research Journal, 3*(2), 3-6.

Donahew, L. (1984). Why we expose ourselves to morbid news. *Proceedings of symposium on morbid curiosity and the news* (pp. 154-191). Knoxville, TN.

Drummond, L. (1984). Movies and myth: Theoretical skirmishes. *American Journal of Semiotics, 3*(2), 1-32.

Eason, D. L. (1981). Telling stories and making sense. *Journal of Popular Culture, 15*(2), 125-129.

Fisher, W. R. (1985). The narrative paradigm: In the beginning. *Journal of Communication, 35*, 74-89.

Frayn, M. (1981). The complete stylisation of news. In S. Cohen & J. Young (Eds.), *The manufacture of news: Social problems, deviance and the mass media* (pp. 71-74). London: Constable.

Frye, N. (1957). *Anatomy of criticism*. Princeton, NJ: Princeton University Press.

Galtung, J., & Ruge, M. H. (1965). The structure of foreign news. *Journal of International Peace Research, 1*, 64-90.

Gans, H. (1979). *Deciding what's news*. New York: Pantheon.

Geertz, C. (1973). *The interpretation of cultures.* New York: Basic Books.

Geertz, C. (1983). Common sense as a cultural system. In *Local knowledge: Further essays in interpretive anthropology* (pp. 73-93). New York: Basic Books.

Gerbner, G. (1977, June). Television: The new state religion? *Et Cetera,* pp. 145-150.

Gitlin, T. (1980). *The whole world is watching.* Berkeley: University of California Press.

Glasgow University Media Group. (1976). *Bad news.* London: Routledge & Kegan Paul.

Glasgow University Media Group. (1980). *More bad news.* London: Routledge & Kegan Paul.

Glasser, T. L. (1982). Play, pleasure and the value of newsreading. *Communication Quarterly, 30*(2), 101-107.

Graber, D. A. (1984). *Processing the news: How people tame the information tide.* New York: Longman.

Hall, S. (1975). Introduction. In A. C. H. Smith (Ed.), *Paper voices: The popular press and social change 1935-1965* (pp. 1-24). London: Chatto & Windus.

Hall, S. (1977). Culture, the media and the "ideological" effect. In J. Curran, M. Gurevitch, & J. Woollacott (Eds.), *Mass communication and society* (pp. 315-348). London: Edward Arnold.

Hall, S. (1984). The narrative construction of reality: An interview with Stuart Hall. *Southern Review, 17*(1), 3-17.

Hall, S., Critcher, C., Jefferson, T., Clarke, J., & Roberts, B. (1981). The social production of news: Mugging in the media. In S. Cohen & J. Young (Eds.), *The manufacture of news: Social problems, deviance and the mass media* (pp. 335-367). London: Constable.

Halloran, J. D. (1974). *Mass media and society: The challenge of research.* Leicester: Leicester University Press.

Halloran, J. D., Elliott, P., & Murdock, G. (1970). *Demonstration and communication: A case study.* Harmondsworth: Penguin.

Hartley, J. (1982). *Understanding news.* London: Methuen.

Hartmann, P., & Husband, C. (1971). The mass media and racial conflict. *Race, 12*(3), 268-282.

Haskins, J. (1984). Morbid curiosity and the mass media: A synergistic relationship. *Symposium on morbid curiosity and the news* (pp. 1-50). Knoxville, TN.

Herrnstein Smith, B. (1981). Narrative versions, narrative theories. In W. J. T. Mitchell (Ed.), *On narrative* (pp. 209-232). Chicago: Chicago University Press.

Hersey, J. (1981). The legend on the license. *Yale Review, 70*(1), 1-25.

Hughes, H. M. (1968). *News and the human interest story.* New York: Greenwood.

Jensen, M. C. (1977). *The sorry state of news reporting and why it won't be changed.* (Speech to New York State Publishers Association, Rochester, NY).

Johnson, R. (1983). *What is cultural studies anyway?* Birmingham: Birmingham University, Centre for Contemporary Cultural Studies.

Knight, G., & Dean, T. (1982). Myth and the structure of news. *Journal of Communication, 32,* 144-161.

La Baschin, S. J. (1986). The ritual of newswatching: Why more news isn't better. *Et Cetera, 43*(1), 27-32.

Landau, M. (1984). Human evolution as narrative. *American Scientist, 72,* 262-267.

Lévi-Strauss, C. (1972). *Structural anthropology.* Harmondsworth: Penguin.

Lord, A. B. (1971). *The singer of tales.* Cambridge, MA: Harvard University Press.

Malinowski, B. (1974). *Myth in primitive psychology.* New York: Negro Universities Press.

Marcus, G. E. (1982). Rhetoric and the ethnographic genre in anthropological research. In J. Ruby (Ed.), *A crack in the mirror: Reflexive perspectives in anthropology* (pp. 163-172). Philadelphia: University of Pennsylvania Press.

Mead, G. H. (1925-1926). The nature of aesthetic experience. *International Journal of Ethics, 36,* 382-393.

Morley, D. (1981). Industrial conflict and the mass media. In S. Cohen & J. Young (Eds.), *The manufacture of news: Social problems, deviance and the mass media* (pp. 368-392). London: Constable.

Murphy, J. E. (1985). Rattling the journalistic cage: New journalism in old newsrooms. *Journal of Communication Inquiry, 8*(2), 8-15.

Park, R. (1944). News as a form of knowledge. *American Journal of Sociology, 45,* 669-686.

Pearce, F. (1981). The British and the "placing" of homosexuality. In S. Cohen & J. Young (Eds.), *The manufacture of news: Social problems, deviance and the mass media* (pp. 303-316). London: Constable.

Rayfield, J. R. (1972). What is a story? *American Anthropologist, 74,* 1085-1106.

Rice, G. E. (1980). On cultural schemata. *American Ethnologist, 2,* 152-171.

Ricoeur, P. (1981). The narrative function. In J. B. Thompson (Ed.), *Paul Ricoeur: Hermeneutics and the human sciences* (pp. 274-296). New York: Cambridge University Press.

Robins, D., & Cohen, P. (1981). Enter the dragon. In S. Cohen & J. Young (Eds.), *The manufacture of news: Social problems, deviance and the mass media* (pp. 480-488). London: Constable.

Rock, P. (1981). News as eternal recurrence. In S. Cohen & J. Young (Eds.). *The manufacture of news: Social problems, deviance and the mass media* (pp. 64-70). London: Constable.

Roshier, B. (1981). The selection of crime news by the press. In S. Cohen & J. Young (Eds.), *The manufacture of news: Social problems, deviance and the mass media* (pp. 40-51). London: Constable.

Schiller, D. (1981). *Objectivity: The public and the rise of commercial journalism.* Philadelphia: University of Pennsylvania Press.

Scholes, R. (1982). *Semiotics and interpretation.* New Haven, CT: Yale University Press.

Schudson, M. (1978). *Discovering the news: A social history of American newspapers.* New York: Basic Books.

Schudson, M. (1982). The politics of narrative form: The emergence of news conventions in print and television. *Daedalus, 111*(4), 97-112.

Smith, A. C. H. (1975). *Paper voices: The popular press and social change 1935-1965.* London: Chatto & Windus.

Smith, R. R. (1979). Mythic elements in television news. *Journal of Communication, 29,* 75-82.

Sperry, S. L. (1976). Television news as narrative. In R. Adler & D. Cater (Eds.), *Television as a cultural force* (pp. 129-146). New York: Praeger.

Stephenson, W. (1964). The ludenic theory of newsreading. *Journalism Quarterly, 41,* 367-374.

Tuchman, G. (1974). Making news by doing work: Routinizing the unexpected. *American Journal of Sociology, 79,* 110-131.

Tuchman, G. (1976). Telling stories. *Journal of Communication, 26*(4), 93-97.

Tuchman, G. (1978). *Making news: A study in the construction of reality.* New York: Free Press.

Turner, V. (1969). *The ritual process: Structure and anti-structure.* Chicago: Aldine.

Turner, V. (1982). Social dramas and stories about them. In *From ritual to theatre: The human seriousness of play* (pp. 61-88). New York: Performing Arts Journal Publications.

White, H. (1981). The value of narrativity in the representation of reality. In W. J. T. Mitchell (Ed.), *On narrative* (pp. 1-23). Chicago: Chicago University Press.

Young, J. (1981). The myth of drugtakers in the mass media. In S. Cohen & J. Young (Eds.), *The manufacture of news: Social problems, deviance and the mass media* (pp. 326-334). London: Constable.

CHAPTER **23**

When Technology Fails

The Drama of Airline Crashes in Network Television News

Richard C. Vincent
Bryan K. Crow
Dennis K. Davis

It was the worst air disaster in this nation's history. There were no survivors.

Few network news leads can match the compelling and dramatic horror of this one. The viewer, most likely unrelated to any of the victims, nevertheless feels drawn to the news coverage of the accident, from the initial day's shocking news and search for information to subsequent days' recovery and cleanup efforts and investigations into possible causes. The crash of a major commercial airliner is inevitably given extensive network news coverage for several days after the crash. But why can such extensive coverage be taken for granted? Is it because of the news value of the event? If so, what does the news communicate to the viewer? Is it that DC-10s are unsafe, that one should not fly in a snowstorm or rainstorm, that Federal Aviation Administration (FAA) regulations should be more strict, that flying in general is dangerous, or something else entirely? Is the coverage a reflection of news

From *Journalism Monographs*, 1989, No. 117, pp. 1-6, 21-26, published by the Association for Education in Journalism and Mass Communication. Used by permission.

AUTHORS' NOTE: An earlier version of this monograph was presented at the International Communication Association annual meeting in Honolulu in May 1985.

directors' knowledge that millions of people will turn to television news if they hear that there has been a major air disaster? Or, in addition to news value and commodity value, is the extensive coverage perhaps an indication that air disasters allow TV news to do what it does best: tell a compelling story, making full use of dramatic visual and narrative devices?

A variety of studies have concentrated on television news structure (Fishman, 1980; Gans, 1979; Gitlin, 1980; Glasgow Media Group, 1976, 1980, 1982; Hall, Critcher, Jefferson, Clarke, and Roberts, 1978; Tuchman, 1978), yet each uses a different mode of analysis. More recently, Nimmo and Combs (1985) have done a rhetorically based analysis of disaster news on television networks (including one plane crash story). They summarize the task of news reporting as "a literary act, a continuous search for 'story lines' that goes so far as to incorporate the metaphors and plots of novels, folk traditions, and myths" (p. 16). Hence the authors embark on an analysis of network television news narratives as they contribute "to the emergence of symbolic reality . . . [which] Walter Fisher calls 'rhetorical visions' " (1970, p. 18). Such sentiments seem to be echoed in recent works by van Dijk (1983, 1985, 1988), Carey (1988), and Barkin and Gurevitch (1987). In the latter, the authors make an observation similar to Nimmo and Combs's when they label news as a "storyteller" and propose that it must rely on various narrative frameworks to provide unity and develop plot. It is their examination of unemployment news on television which acknowledges narrative theory as a useful tool for examining such texts.

In this monograph, we also draw upon narrative theory as we analyze television journalists' accounts of major airline crashes. The molecular nature of narrative theory analysis lends itself to such event-oriented news studies. We intend to gain new insights into the influence and function of these stories through an examination of the narrative structure and dramatic content of such disaster stories. We also seek to further assess the utility for news analysis by incorporating three different, yet representative, perspectives on stories and storytelling developed by Fisher (1985), Bormann (1985), and Bennett and Edelman (1985).

Narrative Theory

Although narrative theory's origins are in literary theory and rhetorical analysis, it has been receiving increased attention lately from scholars in a variety of fields in both the humanities and the social sciences (Fisher, 1984). As might be expected, these scholars do not share a common theory. They do begin with a common assumption, though. That assumption is that storytelling is an important human activity, and through an informal knowledge of the narrative process, people interpret the indistinct information found in society.

The intriguing characteristic of a social world created by a narrative is the integral link among its components: the who, what, where, why, how, and when that gives acts and events a narrative frame. A choice among alternative settings or among origins of a political development also determines who are virtuous, who are threats to the good life, and which courses of action are effective solutions (Bennett and Edelman, 1985, p. 159).

In other words, say Barkin and Gurevitch, "narrative becomes . . . a means of understanding the social world" (p. 5). It recognizes that human beings are storytellers and, as such, acknowledges that we can better understand ourselves and our social environment by examining the manner in which we construct our stories. It is generally believed that our ability to interpret the world increases as we master the various narratives and begin to employ them (Davis and Robinson, 1989).

Yet theorists differ widely in their assessment of the specific purposes and consequences of narrative inquiry. We have chosen three perspectives which view stories as having quite different purposes and consequences. Our examination of the air crash stories permits assessment of the relative value of each perspective in viewing television news from a narrative standpoint.

Fisher (1985) has argued that "the world is a set of stories which must be chosen among to live the good life in a process of continual recreation" (p. 75). He believes that individuals construct their personal stories by choosing among the stories told in the world at large. They use an innate sense of "narrative fidelity" to judge the validity and personal utility of each story by comparing it against their personal experiences.

Bormann (1985) has focused on a particular type of story, the fantasy, which he believes is especially useful to groups as they seek orientation. He defines fantasy as "the creative and imaginative shared interpretation of events that fulfills a group psychological or rhetorical need. Rhetorical fantasies are the result of homo narrans in collectives sharing narratives that account for their experiences and their hopes and fears" (p. 130). According to Bormann, stories derive their power and popularity from the needs which they serve. Individuals can be expected to learn from and use content from stories which fulfill group needs.

Bennett and Edelman (1985) categorize stories as one of several "situation defining forms" which include metaphors, theories, and ideologies. They differentiate between constructive stories which provide new and useful insights into social life and recurring or stereotypical stories which "elicit powerful responses of belief or disbelief in distant audiences without bringing those audiences any closer to practical solutions for the problems that occasioned the stories in the first place" (p. 156). Their concern is that mass media contain too few constructive stories and too many stereotypical stories.

Each of these authors asserts that stories have the power to guide social construction of reality, but each views the role of storytelling in this process differently. Fisher is an optimistic humanist who sees individuals engaging in a personal search for true and meaningful stories on which they can base their experience. He has great faith in the ability of individuals to test the "narrative fidelity" of stories against their personal experience and then reject false or potentially misleading stories. Stories become the means by which the individual constructs a meaningful interpretation of existence. Such a perspective is interesting, but proves least relevant for the current analysis.

Bormann's thesis assumes that storytelling is essentially a group-controlled enterprise which ultimately serves group objectives, not individual concerns. He points out that groups may routinely create false or misleading stories which nevertheless serve group needs. Such stories may be widely understood and accepted as true by group members even when disconfirming information is readily available. If individuals do possess a sense of "narrative fidelity," this ability must be strongly influenced or even controlled by groups in cases where groups are able to effectively disseminate false or misleading stories.

Bennett and Edelman are concerned that in our society, story production and distribution are dominated by elites. Drawing upon assertions first developed by neo-Marxist theorists, they argue that elites can effectively maintain their positions of power by disseminating routinized stories which present no new information or insights. Such stories are consistent with a hegemonic ideology. While such stories may address important social problems, they do not offer alternative solutions. Instead, they tend to imply that current elites are doing the best they can to cope with a problem which has no apparent solution. Thus, stories may simply serve to enforce existing views of social reality.

Air Crash Stories

Our choice of air crash stories as the basis for this analysis has several advantages. First, air crashes are sufficiently important that lengthy narratives are constructed by television journalists to report them. Many routine events do not receive such coverage. Second, air crash stories report a clear disruption of social reality and suggest the need for reassessing the safety of flying. A crash provides unambiguous, incontrovertible evidence that a serious problem exists (as coverage of the 1986 crash of the space shuttle Challenger illustrated). Journalists are forced to provide an assessment of the problem. Third, the events which surround air crashes typically are inherently dramatic, involving life and death situations, heroic actions, fatal and fateful decisions, and unforgettable visual images. There is much raw material here for talented journalists to weave into compelling stories which will attract the attention of viewers.

Fourth, it is likely that air crash stories could provide material for the construction of modern myths. Air crashes involve events and actions which can be reconstructed by journalists so that they encourage reflection about the nature of the world and the role of human beings. Air crashes represent a direct threat to popular conceptions of the social order and how individuals fit that order. They are also highly ambiguous events which can be seen as isolated, seemingly random occurrences due to freak failures in technology or highly unusual weather conditions. Or they can be seen as signaling a more general breakdown in modern technology and the social bureaucracies which are responsible for regulating and operating this technology. The treatment of the dead and the survivors and family members following a crash can imply much about the value which this social order places on human life and the degree to which it supports persons who experience tragedy. The concern which many viewers are likely to have is one of self-interest—should they fear the possibility of being involved in a similar crash? If they died in a crash, would their death be treated with dignity and appropriately mourned? As Radway (1984) suggests in his study of romance fiction, "deep-seated" needs may exist to see ideal scenarios acted out in our narratives. The norm of objectivity, however, limits the ability of journalists to acknowledge such concerns and explicitly develop their stories to address them. It is the use of narrative devices that permits journalists rather effectively to tell stories which appear to be well-suited to addressing such fears.

Journalists as Storytellers

Our analysis of air crash stories is grounded in a view of journalism derived from recent studies of news organizations and the constraints under which they operate (Gans, 1979; Fishman, 1980; Tuchman, 1978). Television journalists are engaged in a highly competitive enterprise which places a premium on constructing visually attractive and verbally accurate reports of a wide range of events. It is essential that these stories attract large numbers of viewers on a continuing basis. It also is important that journalists retain the cooperation of elite news sources and that they abide by codes of professional ethics.

Journalists have developed a variety of strategies for creating stories which meet the constraints described above. Tuchman (1978) has discussed these strategies in some detail. Reporters seek to focus their reports on events which can be videotaped. They rely upon statements from eyewitnesses, widely recognized experts, or political authorities to provide descriptions of happenings which cannot be videotaped and call upon these same persons to speculate about causes or consequences. If more than one interpretation of an event exists, persons who offer differing interpretations will be sought out and quoted. These strategies ensure that objectivity of news reports can be easily defended. But they also result in the construction of stories which, Tuchman argues, serve to reinforce the status quo.

An air crash presents journalists with the opportunity to report an event which will necessarily attract a large and highly interested audience. It is an event which challenges the skills of reporters as they rush to the accident scene and attempt to gather an accurate and useful body of information and pictures which can be assembled into a report. We argue that this task is greatly aided by the use of particular narrative devices and story construction strategies which permit the creation of "realistic," immediate, dramatic accounts. While these accounts are quite acceptable to journalists and their audiences, their consequences for reality construction are open to question. As Barkin and Gurevitch conclude, "Television news presents . . . [tragic] events as stories, relying on a narrative framework that adheres to the requisites of dramatic unity and plot development" (p. 4).

Procedure

In selecting the news events to be covered, we limited our analysis to recent plane crashes which occurred in the continental United States. This eliminated events like the 1977 Canary Islands and 1985 Newfoundland tragedies. Thus we guaranteed stories to which the U.S. media would have fairly easy access. We settled on four plane crashes prior to 1985 which commanded major attention in this country—San Diego (September 25, 1978), Chicago (May 25, 1979), Washington, D.C. (January 13, 1982), and New Orleans (July 9, 1982). Three of these merit attention simply in terms of sheer life loss; Chicago (273 dead), New Orleans (153 dead), and San Diego (144 dead) were three of the four most serious air crashes to date in U.S. aviation history (the second most serious now is the Detroit crash [156 dead] which occurred in 1987). The other crash (Washington) merits attention not only because it occurred in a major news center but also because of the highly dramatic rescue efforts which followed the event (with 78 fatalities, it ranks seventh in terms of life-loss for domestic airline crashes of the last 12 years; others are: No. 1—Chicago, 1979; No. 2—Detroit, 1987; No. 3—New Orleans, 1982; No. 4—San Diego, 1978; No. 5—Fort Worth, 1985; and No. 6—Sioux City, 1989). We suspect, however, that although these incidents attracted considerable television news coverage, the manner in which they were reported would not be markedly different from air disasters with fewer fatalities.

Videotapes were obtained from the Vanderbilt Television News Archive. Until recently, network weekend reports were not uniformly collected and stored. For consistency, then, we decided to study at least the three weekday reports following each crash. If a weekend intervened, additional coverage was included. This was done to allow enough time for the story to develop. Working with the archive index, we found that after the third or fourth day, the story quickly lost its prominence as the newscast's lead story. One of the few exceptions was the Chicago story, which did not lose importance but was replaced by the related story of the DC-10 groundings.

To study the stories, we made transcriptions of all verbal material collected using the method developed by conversation analysts and set forth by Schenkein (1978). This technique offers a form of transcription designed to make audible sounds more comprehensible when converted to print. . . . General visual information was also transcribed. Besides the audio/video text, information on network, date, and time placement within the newscast was noted. Almost four hours of videotape was transcribed, producing a text of 113 pages for analysis. . . .

Discussion

Our three narrative theories all agree on media's power to help guide the social construction of reality. They differ, though, in the way each conceptualizes the narrative-building process. By applying these perspectives to the storytelling found in these air crash stories, we gain a better understanding of how exactly such reporting takes place.

Our analysis of air disaster stories has revealed that the stories provide compelling accounts of highly dramatic events. Three overall themes can be identified: (a) tragic intervention of fate into everyday life, (b) the mystery of what caused the crash, and (c) the work of legitimate authority to restore normalcy. Each of these themes is developed over a period of several days. Initial coverage develops the first theme, which is the most dramatic of the three and one which can readily be supported by the often diverse story elements found in proximity to the crash. This theme derives from the oral storytelling tradition and enables apparently random, discrete bits of evidence to be quickly woven into a narrative suitable to the gravity of the event. This is most like the narrative described by Bennett and Edelman. The story situation simply is being defined. Basic facts are relayed. Little more is transmitted as the journalist as storyteller is caught off-guard by the event. He or she rushes to the scene to graphically convey to us the experience of being present as a modern tragedy unfolds. With this first theme, stories fail to go beyond this most basic descriptive stage. The stories elicit powerful audience responses but are filled with stereotypic images. There are powerful images depicting the stark realities of the tragedy. The camera grinds away as it records one harsh scene after another. Powerful emotional reactions are evoked as we see shots of twisted, burning aircraft wreckage; stunned friends, relatives, and observers; and low-level officials desperately trying to cope with the confusion.

By the second day, the pieces of the event have begun to be sorted into thematic categories and its overall sequence has been identified. The disaster had been foretold but predictions were ignored. On the day of the crash, everything was proceeding routinely until suddenly fate intervened, causing a sudden break in normalcy. A heroic struggle ensued in which some were saved but most died. It is this notion of randomness that often recurs at this level, and when it does, it fits the storytelling paradigm described by Fisher. Such irrational explanations of phenomena apparently work because people want them to work. An explanation is sought to help explain the unexplainable. We have accepted technology as a way to make our lives safer and more comfortable. We now need an explanation so we can continue to subscribe to the myth.

Also at this level, we see family, friends, and neighbors gather to express their shock and grief. Religious rituals serve to structure expressions of grief and bring closure to this theme. Yet whether it be the memorial services, the haunting airport shots, or people grieving, community needs are satisfied, too, as the nation is ushered through this period of grief and confusion. Concrete answers are not supplied at this level, but viewers are at least pacified. The process is similar to that which Bormann (1985) discusses in his storytelling for group purposes.

The second theme requires more time to develop and is much more limited in the elements which can be used to develop it. The mystery of the crash is probed by examining alternate plausible causes. Again we find Bormann's narrative typology at work. Only those causes deemed by the reporter to be highly probable are mentioned, even though some of these may later prove false or misleading. Typically, these are causes which government investigators or aircraft technology experts have suggested. Mechanical failure and weather conditions are favored causes. Both can readily be supported by the types of evidence found at crash sites. After weighing available evidence, a probable cause can be declared with appropriate reservations.

The third theme is one of restoration of normalcy. Of the three themes, it is the least dramatic, but its very banality provides reassurances. Within hours, government bureaucrats from appropriate federal agencies are at the crash site to take control. They are shown supervising the cleanup and holding press conferences to calm fears. These experts almost always are government and industry elites, lending to the retention of power Bennett and Edelman describe. These elites dominate the medium with well-constructed, press release-type accounts of the tragedy. Earlier coverage, of course, only utilized low-level personnel like policemen, rescue workers, and airline ticket counter employees. In reporting probable causes, the television journalist satisfies an audience need to know what happened while also giving credence to the explanations offered by elites.

Airport scenes show the restoration of normalcy as airline employees deal with troubled passengers while planes routinely land and depart. Passengers are shown boarding the flight with the same number as the one that crashed on the previous day. This theme is developed through repeated coverage of routine activity, and again we see the satisfaction of certain group needs. This type of coverage is notable because television news typically avoids showing ordinary occurrences. Its inclusion serves as a balance to the highly emotion-arousing scenes of disaster and grief. The camera dwells upon FAA officials as they calmly discuss the crash and offer explanations or accept blame. These scenes also may help us rationalize other tragedies of life. Hence they work to provide behavior scenarios for other personal tragedies which might befall us.

News as a Vehicle for Status Quo Public Culture

Stories communicate at both rational and emotional levels. By fitting story elements into traditional oral narratives, journalists increase the likelihood that viewers will attend to and learn from their descriptions. Information learned will calm fears. Use of the traditional structure should offer subtle reassurance that though a disaster has occurred, it was a "typical" disaster. Thus it was an isolated, random instance of fate intervening in daily life and not evidence of a systematic spreading breakdown in technology (or society, or nature) which is likely to tragically disrupt the lives of average viewers. The story ends with a resolution of grief, a solution to the mystery, and fades to a reassuring glimpse of planes flying safely once more.

Several researchers have developed notions of news and of public culture which provide further insight into the social role of such stories. Tuchman (1978) has argued that news serves as a social resource which average persons use to construct their interpretations of the social world, especially those parts of the world which are remote from their everyday lives. In her view, the most crucial feature of news is that it limits social change by propagating status quo conceptions of even very disturbing or disruptive events. Events which might serve to mobilize public outcry or produce pressure for reform are portrayed by journalists to be remarkable only as atypical deviations from an otherwise acceptable status quo.

As we have seen, typical coverage of plane crashes is unlikely to spark any public outcry against the airline industry or create a panic in which flying is avoided. The three themes offer reassurance. They bring closure to events on both rational and emotional levels. In doing so, some story angles may go unaddressed and some plausible explanations may be overlooked. Angry relatives may not be filmed. Witnesses offering "irrational" explanations may be dismissed as too likely to alarm average viewers. Journalists may seek to be responsible by allowing government officials to "speak for themselves" and offer explanations which journalists do not evaluate. Although news sources should be used to offer explanations, note Barkin and Gurevitch, few news stories actually contain explanations (p. 10).

Gans (1979, p. 54) has also argued that news coverage of disorder tends to focus on themes which reassure viewers. Fishman (1980) advanced a similar argument after analyzing news coverage of a "crime wave" in New York City. He found that this coverage was dominated by what he called "news promotion." Officials effectively manipulated reporters to obtain the coverage they wanted by offering leads to stories which they could in turn explain in ways that served their interests. Fishman concludes that "routine news advances a definite interest: it legitimates the existing political order by disseminating bureaucratic idealizations of the world and by filtering out troublesome perceptions of events. The public is led to assume that the world outside their everyday experience is a proper sphere of official [bureaucratic] control; that everything falls within some agency's jurisdiction" (p. 154). Similar views have been proposed by Davidson (1974) in his conflict resolution research where he analyzes news messages coming from leaders, and the Glasgow Media Group (1982) where they put forth the view of "media as agencies of ideological manipulation and domination."

This argument is quite relevant to air crash stories. As we have noted, government officials are central to the third theme in which order is being restored. It is government which must determine air safety and take the lead in solving the mystery of the crash. At the time of the crash, journalists appear to be unusually willing to allow government officials to exercise control over the event and provide the interpretations which are presented to the public as the most plausible explanations.

Our analysis of air crash stories suggests that these stories are well suited to develop and sustain simple, consensual notions about the social order. There is little in such stories which would provoke questioning of the social order. The three dominant themes imply that though a deviant event of some magnitude has occurred, we can rest assured that it was an isolated event which had a specific natural cause and which has been (or is being) adequately dealt with by authorities. Therefore there is no need to worry about flying. One need not fear that irresponsible airline companies or incompetent pilots will endanger one's life. If the FAA has made an error in its enforcement of regulations, the error was inadvertent and is being corrected. People in authority are doing all they can to protect the lives of air travelers. We are reminded of an observation by Blumler, Gurevitch, and Katz (1985) on the relationship between a reader and a text where they note that "readers will be socially constrained in how they approach texts and that texts will be constrained in the readings they make available" (p. 264). Such a symbiotic relationship appears to be in effect between certain societal norms and the "messages" these television news stories are delivering to viewers.

News about air crashes may serve to perpetuate naive beliefs about the safety of air travel. Evidence which contradicts such beliefs is either ignored or subordinated to themes which emphasize that crashes are highly deviant events. This handling of air crash stories can be viewed as quite responsible. Journalists might alarm millions of viewers needlessly if they exaggerated the importance of inconsistent details about an accident. The average viewer probably seeks to have his or her confidence in air travel restored. The stories are structured to do this quite effectively. Viewers most likely do not want nor do they expect a detailed, critical analysis of the elites who control air travel. They simply want to be assured that these elites can continue to be trusted. The stories provide such assurance.

References

Barkin, S. M., & Gurevitch, M. (1987). Out of work and on the air: Television news and unemployment. *Critical Studies in Mass Communication, 4*(4), 1-20.

Bennett, W. L., & Edelman, M. (1985). Toward a new political narrative. *Journal of Communication, 35*(4), 156-171.

Blumler, J. G., Gurevitch, M., & Katz, E. (1985). Reaching out: A future for gratifications research. In K. E. Rosengren, L. A. Wenner, & P. Palmgreen (Eds.), *Media gratifications research.* Beverly Hills, CA: Sage.

Bormann, E. G. (1985). Symbolic convergence theory: A communication formulation. *Journal of Communication, 35*(4), 128-138.

Bradac, J., Bowers, J., & Courtright, J. (1980). Lexical variations in intensity, immediacy, and diversity: An axiomatic theory and causal model. In R. St. Clair & H. Giles (Eds.), *The social and psychological contexts of language.* Hillsdale, NJ: Lawrence Erlbaum.

Carey, J. W. (Ed.). (1988). *Media, myths, and narratives: Television and the press.* Newbury Park, CA: Sage.

Davidson, W. P. (1974). *Mass communication and conflict resolution.* New York: Praeger.

Davis, D., & Baran, S. (1981). *Mass communication and everyday life.* Belmont, CA: Wadsworth.

Davis, D. K., & Robinson, J. P. (1989). Newsflow and democratic society in an age of electronic media. In G. Comstock (Ed.), *Public communication and behavior* (Vol. 2). New York: Academic Press.

Epstein, E. J. (1973). *News from nowhere.* New York: Random House.

Fisher, W. R. (1984). Narration as a human communication paradigm: The case of public moral argument. *Communication Monographs, 51,* 1-22.

Fisher, W. R. (1985). The narrative paradigm: In the beginning. *Journal of Communication, 35*(4), 74-89.

Fishman, M. (1980). *Manufacturing the news.* Austin: University of Texas Press.

Forgas, J. (1982). Episode cognition: Internal representations of interaction routines. In L. Berkowitz (Ed.), *Advances in experimental social psychology.* New York: Academic Press.

Gans, H. (1979). *Deciding what's news.* New York: Pantheon.

Gitlin, T. (1980). *The whole world is watching.* Berkeley: University of California Press.

Glasgow University Media Group. (1976). *Bad news.* London: Routledge & Kegan Paul.

Glasgow University Media Group. (1980). *More bad news.* London: Routledge & Kegan Paul.

Glasgow University Media Group. (1982). *Really bad news.* London: Writers and Readers.

Goffman, E. (1981). *Forms of talk.* Philadelphia: University of Pennsylvania Press.

Hall, S., Critcher, C., Jefferson, T., Clarke, J., & Roberts, B. (1978). *Policing the crisis: Mugging, the state and law and order.* London: Macmillan.

Nimmo, D., & Combs, J. E. (1985). *Nightly horrors.* Knoxville: University of Tennessee Press.

Radway, J. (1984). Interpretive communities and variable literacies: The functions of romantic reading. *Daedalus, 113,* 49-71.

Schenkein, J. (Ed.). (1978). *Studies in the organization of conversational interaction.* New York: Academic Press.

Tuchman, G. (1976). Telling stories. *Journal of Communication, 26*(4), 93-97.

Tuchman, G. (1978). *Making news.* New York: Free Press.

van Dijk, T. A. (1983). Discourse analysis: Its development and application to the structure of news. *Journal of Communication, 33*(2), 20-43.

van Dijk, T. A. (Ed.). (1985). *Discourse and communication: New approaches to the analysis of mass media discourse and communication.* Berlin and New York: Walter de Gruyter.

van Dijk, T. A. (1988). *News as discourse.* Hillsdale, NJ: Lawrence Erlbaum.

CHAPTER 24

Non-Routine News and Newswork

Exploring a What-a-Story

Dan Berkowitz

The everyday work of gathering information and creating the news is often described as a routinized process (Altheide, 1976; Epstein, 1973; Fishman, 1980; Frayn, 1981). Routinizing newswork makes outcomes more predictable, increasing the chances that newsworkers will meet their organizational expectations. It takes amorphous public occurrences and turns them into discrete manageable chunks.

But what happens when newsworkers are suddenly confronted with a non-routine occurrence, one that cannot be accommodated by everyday work practices? The first part of this article develops and broadens the discussion of non-routine newswork beyond its scant treatment in existing literature. The second part presents a case study involving a military jet that crashed into an airport area hotel, and focuses on how newsworkers at one local television station accomplished their coverage.

My central point is this: Even when dealing with highly unusual, highly unexpected stories, newsworkers try to find routine ways of dealing with the

From *Journal of Communication*, 1992, Vol. 42, pp. 82-94. Used by permission of Oxford University Press.

AUTHOR'S NOTE: The author thanks the many people who commented on evolving drafts of this study.

non-routine. Key to their success is the ability to typify the scope of news situations, as well as to predict the resources required to report specific news items. Non-routine newswork, then, does not rely on procedures entirely different from routine coverage. Instead, it depends on adapting strategies from everyday work routines. Negotiation and improvisation are present in non-routine newswork, but these aspects are used mainly to guide the application of various routine practices.

The element of time is key to the accomplishment of newswork. Newspapers allocate a certain amount of space for news, and their news must be gathered and packaged within organizationally prescribed time frames (Tuchman, 1978). For local television, time is even more crucial. In contrast to producing one daily newspaper, newsworkers at television stations have to produce multiple newscasts (Altheide, 1976; Berkowitz, 1990).

Newsworkers in both newspapers and television attempt to meet their deadlines by anticipating or "typifying" the work rhythms required to gather information and produce a story. Spot news unfolds in a short period, and the basic frame and boundaries of a story can be quickly decided. Developing news takes longer to be framed, yet the "facts" involved remain relatively predictable. Continuing news involves a series of stories related to an occurrence and unfolding in predictable phases.

Typification also takes place in another way. In this case, typification depends on a view of news as "eternal recurrence" (Bird & Dardenne, 1988; Chibnall, 1981; Rock, 1981). Through experience and interaction with others in the news organization, newsworkers develop a mental catalogue of news story themes, including how the "plot" will actually unravel and who the key actors are likely to be. These thematic typifications serve as cognitive shortcuts that streamline the news decision-making process; that is, what has taken place in the past helps evaluate the predictability of a present occurrence (Stocking & Gross, 1989).

Sometimes, though, an occurrence is startlingly unexpected, either defying prediction or unfolding in a radically different way than anticipated. In this non-routine news situation, newsworkers have little sense of how long it will take to pull the story together, although journalists can often tell that the story will require an intensely concentrated effort. Newsworkers must, therefore, greatly redistribute their resources to rein in the facts and produce the news. Doing this, however, leads them to virtually ignore what would have otherwise been "the news" of the day.

Tuchman (1978) offers two small examples of what happens when newsworkers become aware that they are facing a highly unexpected news event. She calls these instances a "what-a-story." For Tuchman, a what-a-story is generally signified in the newsroom in two different ways. Most visibly, newsworkers label the story through their pronouncement, "What a story!" and by the excited gestures and conversations they reserve for this kind of occasion. A somewhat less obvious signification of what-a-story is the drastic change from the everyday work rhythm to a pull-out-the-stops, call-in-the-troops mode. Without this change in work rhythm, the story simply could not be covered within the organizational time structure for producing the news.

Although Tuchman, through different examples (Lyndon Johnson's un-expected announcement in 1968 that he would not run for a second term and the assassination of Robert Kennedy) operationally defined what-a-story based on newsworkers' responses in their "emergency routine," she did not fully develop the concept. Similar to Tuchman's what-a-story is Romano's (1986) "Holy-shit!" story. According to Romano, a wire story headlined "Guest Drowns at Party for 100 Lifeguards" was considered a Holy-shit! story because "it recounted an event too unusual, too unbelievable, to be true. It exposed the extreme and sometimes cruel irony of life, a matter American newspaper editors find difficult to ignore" (Romano, 1986, p. 45). For these reasons, "Guest Drowns" probably received more prominent placement and a better headline than typical wire pieces of its size and importance, although covering the story did not require a major change in the work routine.

In sum, it is possible to identify three elements of non-routine news. First, newsworkers are surprised and acknowledge it. Second, newsworkers de-cide to give non-routine news better play than most routine stories receive. Third, newsworkers become willing—and see a need—to stretch resources in terms of news space (or time), personnel, and equipment to give the story special treatment.

Beyond the elements that operationally define non-routine news, there is a need to further develop this concept as it pertains to certain contextual considerations. The Johnson speech example serves as a good counterpoint for this discussion. The characteristics of newswork in local television are more complex than suggested by this example.

First, the Johnson example focused on newsworkers at one newspaper, with analysis based at the individual- and organizational-level within that newsroom (see Hirsch, 1977, and Whitney, 1982, for more on news organiza-tional factors). For newspapers, the organizational level of analysis seems adequate, because most cities have only one major newspaper. Local televi-sion, however, is a highly competitive business where three or more stations compete with each other for an audience (Berkowitz, 1991b; Carroll, 1989; Smith & Becker, 1989). Decisions must therefore consider interorganiza-tional-level factors related to gaining top market ratings. The actual role of competition, thus, is ideological as well as real, and becomes part of the journalistic culture, shaping the way local television journalists perceive their work (Erlich, 1991).

Second, newspapers emphasize words, while television places a much higher value on visual elements. For the Johnson speech, a newspaper could cover the story over the telephone and through wire service reports and photographs. Most of the copy could be produced from inside the newsroom. Little of local television news, however, can be produced without a visual component. Crews must go to the story scene, shoot videotape, and either hand-deliver it to the station or beam it back electronically. Then a story must be written, the video edited, and the reporter's audio track recorded.

Third, unlike most newspapers, local television does not produce just one main "edition," but instead presents newsworkers with multiple deadlines throughout the day. Most stations offer a morning newscast (sometimes sandwiched within a national program), a midday program, an early evening newscast, and a night program. News managers must therefore allocate resources to provide anchors, reporters, and photographers for each program, even though personnel sometimes overlap. Further, television sometimes produces extra "editions" by cutting into regular programming with a short special report. Overall, the multiple programs and schedules of local television require a constant juggling of resources, so that more resources must be allocated to a what-a-story than for similar coverage by newspapers.

Thus, non-routine newswork is a highly strategic activity. For local television the need for strategic work practices is even greater because of the higher economic stakes, as well as the greater technical and temporal demands of the medium.

Creating a What-a-Story

The what-a-story discussed here began when an Air Force fighter jet crashed into the lobby of a hotel near the airport. At 31,000 feet, the jet's engine had failed and the pilot was forced to try an unpowered landing. When that failed, the pilot set the jet on a course toward a vacant field and ejected at 800 feet. The force of the ejection charges lowered the jet's nose, however, so that instead of crashing in the field, it bounced off the roof of a small, single-story bank branch and slammed into the second floor of an adjacent hotel. The jet then burst into flames, setting the hotel on fire. Rescue workers arrived within minutes, but by then, nine people were already dead and a tenth was in extremely critical condition.

The Research Site

For six weeks before, during, and after the crash-fire, I carried out field observations and interviews in the newsroom of a large-market network-affiliate television station in the midwest. I attended the daily morning (about 8:30 a.m.) story conferences where initial lineups were built by a group of producers, editors, news directors, and a few key reporters. Observation continued throughout the day and ended with production of two evening newscasts at 6:30 p.m. The plane crash occurred during the morning story conference on Tuesday of the third week. Newsroom observation then continued for a total of four weeks. This timing allowed me to put the what-a-story into the context of the station's everyday routine. It also helped highlight the transition back to everyday newswork, a transition guided by newsworkers' negotiations over a period of several days.

Of the station's two evening newscasts, the one at 5 p.m. lasted one hour and was designed to cover news from the central part of the state. The 6 p.m.

newscast lasted one-half hour and focused mainly on the city where the station was located. Each newscast used a different studio set and different pair of anchors. Newscasts at noon and 11 p.m. shared reporters and anchors with the 5 p.m. and 6 p.m. programs, and often aired a similar group of news stories.

Building a newscast, at least initially, amounted to choosing from a list of items (the news budget) provided by news sources, taking advantage of what has been called "information subsidy" (Berkowitz & Adams, 1990; Gandy, 1982). These items were the easiest to detect and the most predictable to report on. Newsworkers favored subsidized information from official, organizationally affiliated sources over information from individual citizens. Events scheduled for a certain time were preferred to occurrences such as all-day conferences that could not be discretely observed and capsulized. Pseudo-events that contained strong visual imagery were favored over routine public meetings. Few news items were gathered through reporter enterprise. The tendency was to fill out the skeleton of a newscast so that organizational requirements could be met (Berkowitz, 1990, 1991a). Breaking stories would then be worked in as they became apparent. While stories were being juggled into newscasts, newsworkers discussed how a story was likely to "go" in order to streamline their negotiation over newscast lineups.

By typifying stories under consideration, newsworkers could also evaluate the amount of payoff they would gain by covering the story. At least, journalists wanted assurance that their efforts would produce some kind of story. For newsworkers, the highest payoff would be to produce an award-winning story, one that would bring both individual and organizational prestige. Estimated payoff was important because of time, resource, and ratings considerations. An item that did not correspond to newsworkers' typifications would likely be bypassed for another one that would be easier to gather and package—it was too much of a long shot. If a typified item was thought to be too similar to other recently broadcast stories, however, it would not be used because it would make a newscast appear stale—it was one that appeared too easy to get.

Beginning the What-a-Story Process

First word of the what-a-story came over a scanner radio at the news desk during the morning story conference, and seemed to indicate that a big fire was under way. However, the location and the magnitude of the fire were not clear. Whatever was happening did not yet meet the criteria for a what-a-story; fire stories were commonplace. Indeed, unless there were raging flames, TV journalists barely considered a fire to be news at all. This was evident during the previous week when the station had covered a local fire live during its noon newscast. As newsworkers watched that story on the newsroom monitor, they made fun of the coverage. "Where are the flames?" they kidded each other, indicating that they thought this story did not merit air time.

A better indication of a possible what-a-story came when a scanner report made it clear that a plane was involved. This would not necessarily be a what-a-story either. The coverage of a small private plane that crashed carrying two people would not require a major change of work routine, and it would not be a particularly surprising event. Had this single-seat Air Force jet missed the hotel, it would not have been that great a departure from everyday newswork, but instead a story fairly similar to the private plane crashing into a cornfield.

On the other hand, an airliner crash would likely be considered non-routine, because it would present a dramatic event that required a large staff to cover. What made this a what-a-story was the combination of occurrences: Planes rarely, if ever, crash into hotels. The burning hotel, in fact, could act as a surrogate for an airliner because the hotel guests would serve the roles of airline passengers. Some would be killed, others saved. There would be heroic rescue efforts, community grief, and finally an officially guided return to the status quo (Vincent, Crow, & Davis, 1989). The typified story elements could proceed from there.

Once newsworkers realized that the story involved both an airplane and a hotel, everybody in the conference room immediately stopped discussing routine news items and headed for the news desk that served as their command post. So swift and calculated was this migration that they left their filled coffee cups and lit cigarettes behind. They expected it might take a substantial effort to cover this story. Once in the newsroom, though, newsworkers began to have second thoughts about the story's non-routine nature. First, they learned that the plane that crashed had been a small military jet, not a commercial airliner. Then, the pilot was said to have ejected safely into a field. For a moment, the newsroom commotion died down. But by then, another local television station broke into regular programming to report the story. From what was broadcast, the newsworkers concluded that, this was a big story after all. "Get the truck ready, plan a cut-in," the chief photographer called out to the newsroom. All journalists who had the day off were brought in to help. All of the station's remote production trucks for live reporting prepared to rush to the scene. The newsroom was no longer following its everyday routine.

Early Coverage: Live From the Scene

Competitive pressures, whether real or based on professional ideologies, had certified that this was a what-a-story. Competition also was key in shaping early decisions about coverage. The station had not been the first to cover the story and the general manager upstairs knew this from watching the three television sets in his office. In an unusual act, he headed for the newsroom to get the coverage started. Most of the time, there was a clear separation between personnel from the news and business sides of the station, and newsworkers strongly believed that news and business should not blatantly mix. The general manager's presence triggered another unusual action: The news director, rarely present in the newsroom, took the assignment editor's seat at the news desk and began to direct the coverage. If the news department was in trouble, it seemed, their leader (the news director) should assist them.

As newsworkers faced this pressure to get on the air, they also faced a conflict with their journalistic norms. Getting quickly on the air meant broadcasting from what was judged to be a poor location on the scene. Getting a better location for live reports would delay coverage. Under pressure from management, they opted for getting on sooner. The station's first report was based on wire copy read by a frazzled anchor at a small set in the newsroom. The bustling newsroom on camera in the background would at least convey some sense of immediacy. Reading wire copy for a major story was unusual, though. Usually wire stories served as unimportant fillers that could be dropped or added to adjust the timing of a newscast. Newsworkers expected major local stories to be covered by the station's own reporters.

In a note accompanying videotapes provided for this study, the assistant news director described the early jockeying for position at the scene:

> Most of our crews and news managers were attending a morning story conference where we decide what assignments to hand out for the day. Within two minutes we determined from scanner that a traffic plane had hit the hotel. We dispatched three news crews from the station and one microwave truck. It's a 20-minute drive from our newsroom to the airport. Our first news crew managed to get in front of the hotel right before police closed off the area. By the time our live truck arrived on the scene he was denied access to the front of the building and had to park on the airport expressway several hundred yards from the hotel. Cable had to be strung up a hill and through a fence in order to get a signal from our news crew back to the station.

The first live report from the scene clearly appeared as the compromise that it was. Rather than standing in front of the hotel where the plane had hit and the fire was raging, the reporter was only able to reach the rear of the hotel, completely on the wrong side of the action. Yet newsworkers knew that this kind of story called for live coverage at the scene, and for now, the back of the hotel was better than no coverage at all. So the reporter stood with the rear of the hotel behind him and described to viewers what they would be seeing if only he had been able to get to the right place. Overall, these early reports looked like a satirical spoof from a late-night comedy program, as the reporter gestured toward a small amount of smoke and what appeared to be an undamaged building. Although the reporter was offering viewers live coverage, this coverage was barely at the actual scene. As a result of competitive pressures, then, the first coverage was a compromise that created the spirit of early what-a-story news, even if the correct form and content were lacking.

After several disjointed live reports based only on observations and the constantly changing information, reporters finally were able to broadcast from the preferred side of the hotel. However, because they were unable to rely on their regular news sources and subsidized information, they needed to typify a list of news sources and then begin interviewing them. They first turned to eyewitnesses to reconstruct the occurrence, and while these people spoke, images of a smoking building being hosed by fire fighters appeared on the screen. Officials and grieving family members appeared in later news bulletins. As actors in the story, their role was to confirm that a tragedy had indeed taken place. A reporter interviewing the city's mayor asked him to put the story into perspective. "It's one of the biggest tragedies of this sort in our city in modern times," the mayor replied, likening the occurrence to an explosion that had occurred during an ice show 24 years earlier, once again signifying the story's what-a-story typification.

By this point late in the morning, the pull-out-the-stops effort stemming from the what-a-story typification had produced its desired effect, and newsworkers were able to produce special bulletins from the scene. What was now striking, though, was that their typifications of the story had begun to shape news reports. Newsworkers were routinely referring to this occurrence as a plane crash, which was ironic because only a small plane had crashed with no passengers on board. The real disaster was a hotel fire, but in the hierarchy of news occurrences, it seemed that a hotel fire did not rank as high as a plane crash. In any case, this typification allowed newsworkers to develop a strategy for successfully gathering and packaging non-routine news in a more or less routine fashion.

Confronting the Evening Newscasts

Back in the newsroom, it was an unusual scene. By midmorning, reporters and photographers should have been preparing to head out for their stories based on the ideas provided by news sources. Producers should have been writing a tentative rundown of stories on the newsroom's ancient Apple II computer. And the assignment editor should have been eagerly answering the phones to learn of fresh-breaking stories. With the what-a-story, though, what would have been news at most other times, no longer was. "It's all gone to hell with the plane crash," the six o'clock producer replied, when asked about the line-up of stories he had built earlier that morning.

During everyday newswork, information about story slugs, reporters, and photographers would be written on a huge assignment board behind the news desk. Now, however, the board was blank well into the morning. When the assignment editor answered the phones, he first told callers about the plane crash and did not respond to any information that was not directly related to the accident.

Overall, the huge effort required to cover the what-a-story determined the work process during those first few hours. Newsworkers seemed to show no real interest in the newscasts to come—usually their main passion—

instead they were directing all the resources toward covering the unfolding plane crash story. The competitive ideology in the newsroom was also an influential factor. When a competing station showed a particular graphic, producers asked if the art department could create a similar one. When a competitor showed an aerial view from a helicopter, they scurried to rent a helicopter and air a similar shot. At one point, the news director—busy running the news desk—turned to a student intern. "You doing anything right now?" he asked her. "Go into my office and see what kind of crap these guys [at a competing station] are putting out."

The assistant news director also defied the usual working conventions to help his station cover the story. In most situations, the station showed loyalty to an independent cooperative of stations that shared satellite news-gathering capabilities. The major national network this station was affiliated with, though, usually got less cooperation. As a result, the station would often produce live reports for the satellite cooperative, but only send a videotape to the network by air carrier. When the producer who coordinated the station's satellite coverage was asked for advice, the assistant news director quickly snapped back, "Fuck the damn [satellite] setup, we have our own station to worry about."

Finally, though, newsworkers turned to what usually was their main task: producing the evening newscasts. This signaled another change in what-a-story newswork. Rather than just provide some kind of coverage for a few minutes during live reports, they now had to create and package discrete chunks of information into stories for a newscast, just what the everyday work routine was designed to accomplish. The problem here was that there were no lists of source-subsidized stories to choose from.

At a 12:30 p.m. meeting, newsworkers attempted to typify likely story themes by creating lists of news items and then negotiating which items they would use, much as in their everyday routine. The meeting also reflected a tension that usually did not surface at this station. In most cases so far, newsworkers had been open about their activities, but now they asked me to come back after their closed-door meeting. The reason for the secrecy was not clear at the time. Later, I was told that considerable conflict had arisen from their slow response to the story, which had brought the general manager down into the newsroom. Several weeks later, I discovered that newsworkers had each been assigned what they called a "term paper" to discuss how they could better detect and respond to a major non-routine story, were another one to occur.[1]

As newsworkers exited the meeting, a list of possible stories remained on the dry-erase board. They were now closer to everyday newswork, but typification still took on a greater role by necessity, because the work they usually accomplished in a full day now had to be done in half that time. With resources stretched to the limit, newsworkers had to make sure that whatever they planned would bring a payoff for the newscast. Their typifications of story themes helped guide them toward stories that would likely be "out there," stories that could be built upon predictable images and familiar, easily located news sources. They could then take a rather amorphous occurrence—a story involving a plane crash and a hotel fire—and turn it into a group of discrete components that could be assigned, produced, and aired sequentially as a newscast.

Newsworkers developed stories that would depict the chaos, such as images of flames, debris, and dead bodies. There were stories based on firsthand experience, where both witnesses and the injured would recount what it had been like. There was also the official side, where experts and officials would appear at scheduled news conferences to tell what "really" had happened—the "objectivity" to balance eyewitnesses' emotionality and untrained observations.

Because of the non-routine work process, though, these newscasts did not look like everyday newscasts. Everyday newscasts were tightly paced and slickly produced. Just as the morning cut-ins had been rough and erratic, the evening newscasts suffered because of the day's additional demands. Although the occurrence was in itself typified by newsworkers as hard news, it was presented in the newscast through a series of human-interest items that provided a set of discrete pieces that could be gathered and packaged within the time frame and work rhythms of local television newswork.

Negotiating the Return to Everyday Routine

The newsroom did not return to normal even on the following day. Things were similar, yet different. There was still a need to turn an amorphous large occurrence into several smaller elements that could then be assigned, packaged, and scheduled. Yet the huge number of deadlines created by news bulletins and special reports was gone, and newsworkers could focus on their regular newscasts. Competitive ideology was also no longer the driving force it had been on the day before, since this story was no longer typified as breaking news. Instead, the story had become a huge tangle of elements that needed to be unraveled.

As the morning story conference began, newsworkers were caught between covering the routine news they had missed the previous day and covering the what-a-story. The plane crash brought excitement for some, but for others it had only brought extra demands. Producers and other news managers, after being immersed in an entire day of reactive efforts, were especially eager to move on to more routine situations. For reporters, though, the plane crash was the kind of thing that they lived for, and more general assignment reporters than usual attended the morning story conference.

The morning's prepared news budget was built largely from items such as government liability, "curses" on the hotel, and heroes. Early discussions were not about the news budget, however, because newsworkers still had to negotiate the scope of the day's what-a-story coverage. A reporter brought up a murder that had occurred the previous night, but was interrupted by a news anchor who talked about guests returning to the hotel for their belongings. The managing editor questioned the idea, but the five o'clock producer saw it as an opportunity for early closure of the what-a-story. "I think that's the only story we should do on it," he told the others, and at that point it seemed as if the plane crash story was going to be negotiated away.

However, newsworkers decided that what-a-story coverage was not over and began to bounce around ideas. Some ideas were discarded as "too insensitive," such as the one about the burned hotel's insurance coverage. The managing editor urged that they look at "a lot of irony stories," such as those about employees who had missed work the day that the plane hit the hotel. This was clearly their typified view of how coverage should proceed.

Once newsworkers had decided to continue with the what-a-story, they evaluated other stories based on an item's relation to it. About covering a challenging mayoral candidate's news conference: "He'll probably blame the crash on the mayor." As they discussed a drawn-out murder investigation, newsworkers suggested that the plane crash might finally make the murder story die away.

Overall, "Day II" (as it had been dubbed by the newsworkers), while still not easily routinized, was not difficult to plan for. Typifications provided a number of customary stories that could be framed in predictable ways. News conferences would also provide easily accessible information. A few everyday news stories would then round out the newscasts and provide a transition back toward the usual newswork mode.

A conversation between the two evening producers reflected the reduced effort required for planning this day's newscasts. "God, Jim, do you know how easy this day's going to be?" the five o'clock producer remarked to the six o'clock producer. "Yeah, after yesterday," the six o'clock producer replied. Despite how it had started out—in a tenuous balance between the non-routine and the routine—Day II saw a resolution back toward everyday life in the newsroom. Reporters, producers, and other newsworkers moved at a pace closer to normal. They now had time to reflect on the work to be done and could spend more time with it.

Everyday Routine Reestablished

Two days after the what-a-story, the work process was nearly back to the "normal" routine. Unlike the previous day, the third day's news budget looked like any other. Only one item concerned the plane crash, a memorial service to be led by the city's mayor. Discussion of what-a-story items did not even begin until several other unrelated stories had first been discussed. The main discussion centered on whether to cover several funeral services of victims or only the memorial service. The memorial service won out, because attending one event would be simpler than attending several. Further, the memorial service would allow the possibility of dramatic imagery, as well as additional interviews that could enhance the story.

With the close of the evening newscasts, the what-a-story had resolved into routine newswork. Closure was accomplished largely by a dramatic story about the church memorial service that signified to both viewers and newsworkers that the what-a-story had ended, even though the story of a jet crashing into a hotel had not. Over the next few days, tidbits about the plane crash continued to appear, but by then it had ceased to be the major, all-absorbing story it once was.

Routinizing the Very Unexpected

My observations regarding the coverage of a major non-routine story from the newsroom before, during, and after it unfolded suggests that even when faced with non-routine news, newsworkers were able to accomplish their work in a more or less routine fashion. Improvisation and negotiation were important in this instance, but those elements mainly shaped the choice of overall work modes—everyday newswork versus a what-a-story—rather than creating new ways to accomplish the coverage. Negotiations led toward a consensus of what could and should be done within the rhythms and demands of work in the news organization; improvisation helped adapt work routines to the particulars of the news situation.

Work routines, then, served two key purposes for this what-a-story. First, these routines served as a guide for organizational behavior: By electing to follow a modified version of an everyday news routine, newsworkers could quickly know the appropriate procedures for creating their news product. Second, these routines guided the evaluation of journalistic performance. If newsworkers knew the approximate product that should result from a particular routine, then the actual product they created could be compared to those expectations. For the what-a-story, the technical and logistical difficulties of accomplishing work routines often led to a product that was somewhat less than desired. Both the rough newscasts and the reactions of management made this point clear.

Typification became an important strategy in what-a-story newswork largely because subsidized information from regular news sources was unavailable. The need to rely on story typification to meet organizational demands led newsworkers to see a plane crash rather than a hotel fire, and the way that newsworkers subsequently covered the story was in line with their plane crash typification. By doing so, they could typify both story ideas and news sources, and the amorphous happening would turn into discrete units of news that could be processed through an adaptation of their everyday newswork routines. This strategy was very difficult to implement shortly after the what-a-story typification was agreed upon, but became easier over a relatively short period of time.

Once the initial emergency was under control, newsworkers continued to negotiate their typification of the occurrence between everyday news and a what-a-story. Initial reliance on work routines allowed only a relatively crude approximation of the usual news product, mostly because the situation was not a close match for the routines they employed. Each subsequent newscast, however, appeared a bit more like their everyday news product, as the routines helped create something much more similar to what was expected. In addition, the increased effectiveness of these work routines over time allowed the initial concentration of resources on the what-a-story to shift back toward everyday resource allocations for gathering and producing news.

Note

1. This what-a-story, combined with other incidents, actually led to the "term paper" assignment. Most apparent among the other incidents was a story about a highway worker who had been hit by a car while on the job. Although the other two network affiliates in the market led their newscasts with the highway accident, this station missed it completely. That led to considerable tension and conflict during the story conference on the following morning, when the news director began to question newsworkers' abilities to detect major stories.

References

Altheide, D. (1976). *Creating reality: How TV news distorts events.* Beverly Hills, CA: Sage.

Berkowitz, D. (1990). Refining the gatekeeping metaphor for local television. *Journal of Broadcasting & Electronic Media, 34,* 55-68.

Berkowitz, D. (1991a). Assessing forces in the selection of local television news. *Journal of Broadcasting & Electronic Media, 35,* 245-251.

Berkowitz, D. (1991b, August). *Journalists' perceptions of news selection in local television: A Q-methodology study.* Paper presented at the meeting of the Association for Education in Journalism and Mass Communication, Boston.

Berkowitz, D., & Adams, D. B. (1990). Agenda building and information subsidy in local television news. *Journalism Quarterly, 67,* 723-731.

Bird, S. E., & Dardenne, R. W. (1988). Myth, chronicle, and story: Exploring the narrative qualities of news. In J. W. Carey (Ed.), *Media, myths, and narratives: Television and the press* (pp. 67-86). Newbury Park, CA: Sage.

Carroll, R. L. (1989). Market size and TV news values. *Journalism Quarterly, 66,* 49-56.

Chibnall, S. (1981). The production of knowledge by crime reporters. In S. Cohen & J. Young (Eds.), *The manufacture of news: Social problems, deviance and the mass media* (pp. 75-97). Beverly Hills, CA: Sage.

Epstein, E. J. (1973). *News from nowhere: Television and the news.* New York: McGraw-Hill.

Erlich, M. (1991, August). *Competition in local TV news: Ritual, enactment, and ideology.* Paper presented at the meeting of the Association for Education in Journalism and Mass Communication, Boston.

Fishman, M. (1980). *Manufacturing the news.* Austin: University of Texas Press.

Frayn, M. (1981). The complete stylization of news. In S. Cohen & J. Young (Eds.), *The manufacture of news: Social problems, deviance and the mass media* (pp. 71-74). Beverly Hills, CA: Sage.

Gandy, O. H. (1982). *Beyond agenda setting: Information subsidies and public policy.* Norwood, NJ: Ablex.

Hirsch, P. M. (1977). Occupational, organizational, and institutional models in mass media research: Toward an integrated framework. In P. M. Hirsch, P. V. Miller, & F. G. Kline (Eds.), *Strategies for communication research* (pp. 13-42). Beverly Hills, CA: Sage.

Rock, P. (1981). News as eternal recurrence. In S. Cohen & J. Young (Eds.), *The manufacture of news: Social problems, deviance and the mass media* (pp. 64-70). Beverly Hills, CA: Sage.

Romano, C. (1986). What? The grisly truth about bare facts. In R. K. Manoff & M. Schudson (Eds.), *Reading the news* (pp. 38-78). New York: Pantheon.

Smith, C., & Becker, L. B. (1989). Comparison of journalistic values of television reporters and producers. *Journalism Quarterly, 66,* 793-800.

Stocking, S. H., & Gross, P. H. (1989). *How do journalists think? A proposal for the study of cognitive bias in newsmaking.* Bloomington, IN: ERIC Clearinghouse on Reading and Communication Skills.

Tuchman, G. (1978). *Making news: A study in the construction of reality.* Beverly Hills, CA: Sage.

Vincent, R. C., Crow, B. K., & Davis, D. K. (1989). When technology fails: The drama of airline crashes in network television news. *Journalism Monographs,* No. 117.

Whitney, D. C. (1982). Mass communication studies: Similarity, difference, and level of analysis. In J. S. Ettema & D. C. Whitney (Eds.), *Individuals in mass media organizations: Creativity and constraint* (pp. 241-254). Beverly Hills, CA: Sage.

CHAPTER **25**

The Rape of Mike Tyson

Race, the Press, and Symbolic Types

Jack Lule

The rape trial of former heavyweight boxing champion Mike Tyson was one of the more prominent, perhaps notorious, news stories of 1992. A dramatic and sensational spectacle, the trial pitted the celebrity boxer against a contestant in the Miss Black America pageant. It daily offered lurid testimony, legal machinations by prosecuting and defense attorneys, and various ongoing side-stories, including a fatal fire at the jurors' hotel and charges that Baptist ministers attempted to bribe the accuser. After two weeks of testimony and ten hours of deliberation, the jury found Tyson guilty of rape and he was sentenced to six years in prison.

From the start of the trial, questions were raised about press coverage. Some called the coverage sensational and overblown, comparing the hoopla and hype to reporting on a prize fight (McNulty, 1992). For others, the coverage was inadequate and insensitive; they pointed out it was most often covered by sportswriters and placed on the sports pages, "next to show-dog pictures" (Paley, 1992), as if rape was just another exotic sport (Witosky, 1992a).

Study of press coverage of the Tyson trial, however, may evoke larger issues. Caught up in an incendiary drama in which the African-American champion of a sport dominated by African Americans was accused of rape by an African-American woman, the Tyson trial press coverage unavoidably became embroiled in racial politics. The coverage may yield provocative

From *Critical Studies in Mass Communication*, 1995, Vol. 12, pp. 176-195. Used by permission of the Speech Communication Association.

insights into the press' troubled and troubling reporting on race. Tyson's trial also proved to be a site for more generalized political and cultural tensions—including gender relations, sexuality, class, and caste—tensions accentuated in this case through their admixture with race. As will be later shown, many press observers found substantial, if conflicting, meanings in Tyson's story. Press coverage of Tyson thus can also yield insights into the ways in which the media are enmeshed in ongoing social struggles. Through an analysis of press coverage of the Tyson trial, this article reflects on the reporting of race, particularly the symbolic types through which the press portrays people of color.

Scholars from a variety of disciplines continue to chart racist representations in the news media and express dissatisfaction with attempts to confront the problems race poses to the newsroom (Dates and Barlow, 1990; Entman, 1990, 1992; Martindale, 1985, 1986, 1990a, 1990b). Although instances of overt racism appear to be few, these writers say, press coverage of the Charles Stuart murder case in Boston, the Clarence Thomas confirmation hearings, the 1992 Los Angeles riots following the Rodney King verdict, the O.J. Simpson murder trial, and other events does suggest that reductive, degrading conceptions of race are firmly entrenched in press portrayals.

Such degrading portrayals, I will argue, may result in part from the press' limited and limiting cast of symbolic types—reified, constricting, culturally entrenched. I will look closely at the depictions of Tyson and suggest that the large drama of his degradation shaped and was shaped by American press mythologies about African Americans. Indeed, I will argue that press portrayals drew from and added to powerful symbolic types or stereotypes—defined here as prefigured patterns that influence and shape understandings and portrayals of the present. Specifically, this article will attempt to demonstrate through an extensive textual analysis that the many press portrayals of Mike Tyson during his trial actually drew from just two, crude, dehumanizing and—paradoxically—opposing archetypes for African Americans: the animal savage and the helpless, hapless victim. Though press portrayals are complex and subject to multiple interpretations, textual criticism can be valuable in pointing out *how* stereotypical depictions are invoked through the language and conventions of the press.

Yet the article will also demonstrate the complexities of modern racism—a term for the transformation of "old-fashioned," open bigotry to more subtle racist attitudes (McConahay, 1986, p. 92).[1] Modern racism will be shown to be an elusive phenomenon of abstraction, denial, and symbolic expression. "Racism, as defined by modern racists, is consistent only with the tenets and practices of old-fashioned racism," such as emphatic support for segregation and acts of open discrimination, says McConahay. "Thus, those endorsing the ideology of modern racism do not define their own beliefs and attitudes as racist" (p. 92). As the article will show, one hallmark of modern racism is that overtly racist rhetoric often is absent while muted racist beliefs are proffered in shadows and shades of expression (Sears, 1988, p. 57). Tyson's press coverage, I will argue, may offer a powerful illustration of the media's implication in modern racism.

The article will first review study of press reporting and race. After discussing in more detail events surrounding the Tyson case, I will take up an analysis of press coverage of the trial. Five newspapers will be analyzed. Selected for status and influence, as well as some geographical diversity, the newspapers studied were the *Chicago Tribune, Los Angeles Times, New York Times, USA Today,* and the *Washington Post.* The period examined was July 20, 1991—the day that police were notified of the rape—to April 9, 1992, when Tyson's petition to remain out on bail during appeal was denied. All news articles, editorials, and commentaries devoted to the Tyson case were examined. Editorials and commentaries were included because the study sought to capture the extent of coverage in each paper. More than 500 news items eventually were examined. Through an analysis of this coverage, I want to demonstrate that the reporting on the Tyson trial did invoke a larger drama around the boxer, a drama indeed structured by demeaning and racist cultural archetypes. The press coverage of Tyson then will be used to consider the entrenchment of racist reporting in the news media and the implication of the media in modern racism.

"The rape of Mike Tyson," of course, offers two, quite different meanings. The boxer's attack of Desiree Washington, I will attempt to show, provided a site for the press to proffer its own attack of the boxer. The charge here is that press reporting violated and debased Tyson. The charge takes on larger significance because, I will argue, the press resorted to the reproduction of crude and racist stereotypes in its debasement of Tyson. And these racist images were cast up large, daily, on the vast scale afforded a high-profile media event.

I wish to anticipate here an objection already raised by some colleagues and friends: Tyson's rape trial may seem an unlikely subject for press criticism. The crime was revolting; Tyson's actions and attitudes toward women—long before the rape conviction—have been unconscionable. In this view, Tyson was found guilty of rape and the disapprobation of the press was deserved. Not a defense of Tyson, this essay nevertheless will argue that the press' response to Tyson was ugly and flawed by its reliance upon racist imagery. Should Tyson be condemned for his crime? Yes. Should Tyson be condemned with degrading depictions? I start from the assumption that the press must find other means to depict such sordid lives, means that owe nothing to racist archetypes and images. Indeed, on a larger level, I hope to suggest that the perpetuation of racist types, particularly in such high-profile cases as Tyson's, can be especially debilitating to a press that struggles daily with its representation of people of color.

Race and the Press

Lippmann's classic discussion of stereotypes remains an excellent starting point for studies of race and the press. As part of his dissection of the press in *Public Opinion,* Lippmann (1922, pp. 79-156) devoted five chapters to examining public and press reliance on stereotypes. He argued that the stereotype is a form of perception that "imposes" ways of seeing. "For the most part we do not first see, and then define, we define first and then see," he wrote (p. 81). The stereotype "precedes reason" and thus unavoidably shapes the story of the story-teller.

Since Lippmann's times, a long literature on race and the media has affirmed that the press represents African Americans in narrowly defined, stereotypical roles (Corea, 1990; Diamond, 1991, pp. 101-122; Entman, 1990, 1992; Fisher and Lowenstein, 1967; Lule, 1993; MacDonald, 1992; Martindale, 1985, 1986, 1990a, 1990b; Pease, 1989; *Report of the National Advisory Commission on Civil Disorders*, 1968; Rivers et al., 1980; Signorielli, 1985; Wilson and Gutierrez, 1985). More than 70 years since Lippmann so carefully traced the problem (if not the solution), scholars continue to find that the news still casts up the experiences of people of color—in particular, African Americans—in ways that create and maintain racist stereotypes.

Also of interest to this study is research that has focused on stereotyped portrayals of African-American athletes. Perhaps the most visible members of their race, these athletes can receive intense press coverage; some critics have charged that this coverage is marred by racist depictions (Edwards, 1973; Koppett, 1981; Scott, 1971, pp. 80-88). Some writers have even suggested that boxing—in particular black heavyweight champions, such as Jack Johnson, Joe Louis, and Muhammad Ali—has had its own proscribed depictions. The high status of the *heavyweight champion of the world* must be acknowledged. Unlike many other sports, such as baseball, football, and basketball, boxing is exceedingly individualistic; the champion rises or falls alone. And boxing does truly crown a champion of the *world*. Boxers from many nations compete for the heavyweight title in matches held around the globe. At various times, the heavyweight champion is the most recognizable athlete on the planet. Some writers have suggested that the U.S. press has sought to deflate African Americans who attain such status (Carter, 1992; Gilmore, 1975, pp. 133-154; Hoberman, 1984, pp. 16-19, 166-174; Oates, 1992; Sammons, 1988).

The social science literature on modern racism is of particular interest to this study. Social scientists have begun from the assumption that traditional or old-fashioned racism, marked by open bigotry and opposition to equal opportunity, has been replaced by an updated "anti-black affect" (Sears, 1988, p. 55). Tenets of modern racism include beliefs that discrimination is a thing of the past, that blacks push too hard and too fast, that black demands for opportunity are unfair, and that recent gains by blacks are undeserved (McConahay, 1986, pp. 92-93). Modern racists disavow traditional racism and "do not define their own beliefs and attitudes as racist" (p. 93). Stereotypes are a key aspect of modern racism. The modern racist clusters blacks into a limited number of categories with negative characteristics and gives symbolic expression to beliefs through the use of stereotypes (McConahay, 1986, p. 95).

Press stereotypes have been implicated in the phenomenon of modern racism. Entman (1990, 1992) found that portrayals of blacks on local TV news supported components of modern racism. "Local news implicitly traces the symbolic boundaries of the community," Entman argued, and "in day-to-day news coverage, blacks are largely cast outside those boundaries" (1990, p. 343). Elsewhere, Entman (1992, p. 346) affirmed that "the typical images of blacks on local TV news may reinforce stereotyping that feeds modern racism."

Even such a brief review of the voluminous literature demonstrates that the study of press portrayals of African Americans remains a significant, even compelling, area of press criticism. In *Black Looks: Race and Representation*, bell hooks (1992, p. 6) puts the question eloquently. She asks, "If we, black people, have learned to cherish hateful images of ourselves, then what process of looking allows us to counter the seduction of images that threatens to dehumanize and colonize?" Her answer: "Clearly, it is that way of seeing which makes possible an integrity of being that can subvert the power of the colonizing image." Although the issue, as hooks knows, is more complex than renaming or re-representing the world, the interrogation of racist stereotypes is an essential starting point for press criticism of race and representation.

Background: The Tyson Trial

On July 17, 1991, former heavyweight boxing champion Mike Tyson arrived in Indianapolis for an appearance at the Miss Black America pageant sponsored by Indiana Black Expo. Although he had lost the heavyweight title the year before in Tokyo, Tyson still retained the high-profile, celebrity status for such appearances, based on his former domination of boxing, his well-publicized divorce from actress Robin Givens, and his run-ins with the law.

Three days after Tyson's arrival in Indiana, police received a call from a pageant contestant, Desiree Washington, who said Tyson had raped her in his hotel room the night before. Through August, a grand jury convened to hear the charges. On September 9, Tyson was indicted. A trial was set for January, 1992 in Indianapolis.

For those in Tyson's boxing circle, an immediate concern was the long-awaited bout between Tyson and current champion Evander Holyfield. Revenues from the lucrative pay-per-view screening of the fight were estimated at more than $50 million. No fight occurred, however. Tyson suffered injuries while training and then his trial began on January 27.

In Tyson's legal circle, another concern was the William Kennedy Smith trial, a high-profile date-rape case, held shortly before the Tyson trial. Smith had been found not guilty, a verdict that led to much protest. Tyson's lawyers suggested that public pressure against a second date-rape acquittal would be an important factor in the trial.

Tyson's trial lasted less than three weeks and was interrupted briefly by a fire in the hotel where the jurors were staying. On February 10, after ten hours of deliberation, the jury found Tyson guilty of rape. The judge sentenced him to six years in prison. After the conviction, the case still made news. Reports of a bribe offered by Baptist ministers to the accuser were investigated. Donald Trump, an acquaintance of Tyson and owner of a casino that sponsors boxing matches, suggested that Tyson be allowed to donate millions of dollars to rape counseling centers rather than serve time in prison. Tyson's attorneys asked the court that Tyson be allowed out on bail while his appeal was heard. The request was denied and Tyson was imprisoned.

The Press and the Tyson Trial: Preliminaries

The first striking fact to emerge from an analysis of the Tyson coverage is the sheer amount. Apparently, the combination of the sports celebrity's public persona, the nature of the charges, and the dramatic unfolding of the trial proved irresistible to the press. The five newspapers published more than 500 stories on Tyson during the nine-month period. Daily coverage was offered by all papers during February, 1992, the month of the trial. Coverage was also heavy by all papers during August and September, 1991 when the rape charges confounded the championship fight between Tyson and Holyfield.

Also of some interest was the placement of the stories. The papers largely covered the trial on the sports pages. Although significant moments of the trial, especially the indictment, conviction, and appeal, achieved front-page status, most news reports on the Tyson case appeared in the sports section. Of the 568 stories on Tyson, 458 (81 percent) were placed on sports pages. This figure does not reflect stories that began on the front page and jumped to the sports section, and so coverage in the sports section was actually somewhat greater.

This decision to cover the Tyson trial on the sports pages was bitterly criticized (Witosky, 1992a, 1992b). Readers complained that placing a rape trial on a sport page demeaned the issue. McNulty (1992, p. 5), reader representative of the *Hartford Courant*, noted that readers "argued that to put the story in the sports section trivialized it. Several people, not without bitterness, asked whether the *Courant* was suggesting that rape is a kind of sport."

The Rape of Mike Tyson

Although the amount and placement of Tyson trial coverage is of interest, the primary focus of this study was the nature of the reporting. An important aspect of the coverage was the unanimity and uniformity of portrayals.

Just two portraits of Tyson emerged. He was either a crude, sex-obsessed, violent savage who could barely control his animal instincts or he was a victim of terrible social circumstances, almost saved from the streets by a kindly overseer, but who finally faltered and fell to the connivance of others.

Both these portraits demean and debase Tyson, depicting him as a creature helpless either to base instincts or the machinations of others. Both portraits depict a man without self-control or determination, paradoxical for a former world champion.[2]

As will be shown in detail below, these portrayals affirm previous literature on stereotypes; the press reproduced two racist types in its reporting on Tyson. The coverage will also be shown to illustrate the subtle workings of modern racism; the press proffered racially charged stereotypes that might feed modern racism, but without resort to explicitly bigoted rhetoric. Yet the portrayals also will demonstrate the complexity of studying racist imagery in the press. Coverage of Tyson was conflicted by cultural and political tensions other than race—particularly those surrounding gender and class. The following sections will show how the press used the Tyson rape trial as a site on which to enact a convoluted drama that daily affirmed and confirmed racist symbolic types.

The Savage

The first predominant portrayal of Tyson in the press depicted him as a savage or decidedly inhuman beast. Tyson was a brute, an animal, unfit for civilized society. Rejecting notions that Tyson's problems were linked to race or his background, this portrayal included lengthy accounts of his previous problems with women and the law, and anticipated his punishment by authorities, and the possibility of his humiliation, even death, by his time in prison.

This depiction often was accomplished in the press through direct characterizations of Tyson as a savage or animal. One report in the *New York Times* was headlined "The 'Animal' in Mike Tyson" and said, "What Mike Tyson has never understood was that only until he stopped acting like an animal outside the ring would he be fine" (Berkow, 1992a). A column in the *Chicago Tribune* (Verdi, 1992a) said none of Tyson's advisers "ever could tame the animal within." A *Los Angeles Times* article (Gustkey, 1991) quoted a boxing historian who said Tyson's indictment "reinforces the belief that Mike Tyson is an animal." Numerous reports noted the accuser's testimony that Tyson "changed completely from a sweet, nice person into an animal, like a demon. In seconds" (Berkow, 1992b). One column on the conviction said, "Sentencing is March 6. The monster has been captured" (Verdi, 1992a).

Tyson was a danger to society, said some reports. One column called him "a dangerous man, filled with anger toward women" and said "it might take a stun gun and a platoon of armed guards and round-the-clock therapists to break through to the chaotic inner world of Mike Tyson" (Vecsey, 1991). Jim Murray (1991) of the *Los Angeles Times* said "Mike Tyson comes into public focus as a combination Jack the Ripper and Bluebeard." The *Chicago Tribune* stated that "fighters are like attack dogs, trained to be vicious and rewarded for it, but unfit to be around innocent people" (Lincicome, 1991).

The portrayal was aided and shaped by the controversial defense strategy of Vince Fuller, Tyson's attorney. Fuller portrayed his client as a vulgar, sex-obsessed athlete whose actions were so crude and intentions so obvious in Indianapolis that any woman who ended up with him should have known what she would get.[3]

Press reports simply extended Tyson's defense. For example, one report noted that "the defense in the rape trial took the position that their man was a lecher, a jerk, a grabber, a callous, out-for-one-thing thug" (Berkow, 1992a). Another said, "His lawyers sought to portray the former world heavyweight champion as a vile creature" (Kass, 1992b). The *Chicago Tribune* wrote, "His own lawyers argued Tyson was so obviously such a rutting beast that anyone who found herself alone with him got what she deserved" (Lincicome, 1992).

Reports pilloried the notion of Tyson as role model. The *New York Times* called Tyson "a role model in reverse" (Berkow, 1991a). Defending boxing, George Vecsey (1991) said the sport had "more decent people than ominous slobs like Tyson." The *Chicago Tribune* said, "Tyson is our savage side, not our role model" (Lincicome, 1991). Anna Quindlen (1992), a *New York Times* syndicated columnist, asked, "Why in the world should Mike Tyson, a man who apparently can't pass a ladies room without grabbing the doorknob, be a role model?" *USA Today* commentator DeWayne Wickham (1992), said, "Any minister who thinks Mike Tyson is a hero probably believes Sodom and Gomorrah got a bad rap, too."

Another part of the portrayal of Tyson as a savage was the inclusion of "biographies" or "highlights" of Tyson's life, which organized and emphasized his past problems with the law, highlighting any acts of violence. Such "biographies" could be understood as proof for a contention that Tyson was a creature barely in control of his great strength, a creature who needed to be restrained and imprisoned.

For example, after his conviction, the *New York Times* printed a 35-item chronology, "The Tyson Years" (1992), that began with his professional boxing debut and included entries such as, "May 8: Dents his $183,000 silver Bentley convertible when he sideswipes another car in Lower Manhattan." The *Los Angeles Times* offered a 57-date "Mike Tyson Chronology" (1992) and included dates of speeding tickets. A *USA Today* report, "Tracing Major Events of Heavyweight's Life" (1991), included "Tyson and friend thrown out of a department store." A column in the *Washington Post* (Boswell, 1991) began with details of Tyson's legal troubles and concluded, "So, all in all, Tyson's indictment for rape on Monday was not a surprise. What took so long?"

Press portrayals of the savage also rejected protests that Tyson was the victim of racism. For example, Royko (1992) dismissed the "view by some blacks that Tyson is the victim of some sort of white conspiracy to bring down successful black men." An editorial in the *Washington Post* ("The Mike Tyson Verdict," 1992) took issue with the paper's own reporting and said, "The somewhat sympathetic portrait now being painted of Mike Tyson as 'an undereducated, financially unsophisticated gladiator who frittered away much of his earnings on high living, legal entanglements and fees to managers and promoters' (as carried in one story yesterday) may be accurate. But it doesn't go far enough. There is no warrant in law or custom that gave Mike Tyson the prerogative of forcing himself upon a woman without her consent." A column in the *Los Angeles Times* (Gustkey, 1992) said, "And please, don't blame it on the ghetto. No, not this time. Evander Holyfield grew up in a ghetto, too. And it wasn't him standing before the judge Monday night. It was Michael Gerard Tyson." A commentary in the *Washington Post* from a reporter in France (Wilbon, 1992) rejected the notion of racism in particularly strong terms:

> I'm sick of Mike Tyson and his sleaze, even 4,200 miles away. . . . I'm sickened by those who want to absolve Tyson of any responsibility for his behavior because he was once impoverished and orphaned. I'm sickened by the people who want to make Tyson the victim of a racist conspiracy even though virtually any black woman who walks within arm's reach of him does so at risk.

Another key aspect of the portrayal of Tyson as savage was the enactment of his humiliation and demise. At his conviction and sentencing, reports painted Tyson's discomfort in the greatest detail, as if enjoying the spectacle of his pain. The *Chicago Tribune* described his wait for the verdict: "Tyson's eyes flitted everywhere. When the jurors came in, they would not look at him. He stood up, grabbing at the tie around his throat. He put his hands to his sides and tried to keep them still, but his fingers fluttered, grabbing at the edges of his gray suit. His eyes stared somewhere into the corners of the room" (Kass, 1992c). *USA Today* founder Al Neuharth (1992) offered satisfaction that "the overgrown brat who literally got away with everything but murder in his native New York ran into the realities of lifestyles in the heartland of the USA."

Vivid descriptions of him after the sentencing also detailed his humiliation. "There was a half-grin frozen on his face, and in a mocking gesture, he rattled the chains on his handcuffs," said the *Chicago Tribune* (Kass, 1992e). "Seconds earlier, police had proved to him how much freedom he'd lost. They pushed him up against a wall, his palms flat against the cinder block. They went through his pockets and he hung his head." The *Washington Post* (Muscatine, 1992b) said, "He would exchange his suit and tie for the standard prison attire of white T-shirt and blue jeans and would undergo a strip search, de-lousing and a shower before being assigned to a two-man cell." Aiding these descriptions were front-page photographs of Tyson in handcuffs and being led away by sheriffs ("Law Enforcement Officials Escort Mike Tyson," 1992; "Mike Tyson Leaving Court Yesterday After the Verdict," 1992). One photo in the *Washington Post* was captioned, "In Former Heavyweight Champion Mike Tyson's New Entourage There Are a Lot of People Wearing Badges" (1992).

Finally, perhaps the most disturbing aspect of the portrayal of Tyson as a beast was the anticipation by some reports of the punishment and humiliation that Tyson might receive in prison. Reports anticipated his subjugation to authorities, possible brawls and knife-fights with other inmates, sexual attacks, AIDS, even death.

Before his conviction, reports anticipated his demise. A column in the *New York Times* said, "Tyson is destined for jail or a bullet or a knife or an auto wreck" (Vecsey, 1991). The *Chicago Tribune* (Mitchell, 1992), in "Tyson Could Become a Marked Man in Prison," led with the thoughts of an anonymous Indianapolis cab driver. " 'I've got a lot of buddies who are prison guards in Indiana, and they said the prisoners can't wait for Mike Tyson to arrive. They're drawing straws.... Can you imagine the prestige those guys in prison would have if they could say they whipped Mike Tyson?' said the cabbie."

A Dave Anderson (1992b) column in the *New York Times* seemed to take particular pleasure in Tyson's hard fate, and his comments will be treated at length. "The Humiliation of No. 922335 Mike Tyson" states that "life for Mike Tyson as a jailhouse celebrity will be hard and humiliating." It then offers a litany of trouble, suggesting, even anticipating, the pain that awaits Tyson, beginning with attacks by prison guards as well as other prisoners.

> Most prisoners will welcome him, but sooner or later somebody will challenge him. The gunslinger syndrome. In every prison there's always somebody who thinks he's the toughest guy on the block, the cell block.
>
> If that somebody is tougher, at least in a prison brawl, he's really the boss of the prisoners now. But even if Mike Tyson is tougher the first time, that somebody might try to get even with a knife or a razor or a gun. Weapons have been known to be smuggled to prisoners, for a price.

Anderson sets up the scenario of a prison attack on Tyson and provides an alternate scenario in the event Tyson wins the brawl—vengeance by the knife, razor, or gun of another inmate. He then conjures up the daily humiliations that Tyson will face, including the possibility that Tyson himself will be raped:

> When it's time for Tyson to be assigned to a prison job, look for him to be put behind the kitchen counter wearing a little white jacket. The champ serving other inmates three times a day. Humiliating.
>
> Being constantly counted by the guards is constantly humiliating. Counted in his cell. Counted to and from work or meals. Counted to and from the yard. Counted as much as 20 or 30 times a day. . . .
>
> Homosexual attacks are a fact of prison life, but according to James Scott [an imprisoned boxer], that threat has decreased because of the fear of AIDS. . . .
>
> More than anything else, Mike Tyson must now cope with the loneliness of prison. Especially at night in the solitude of his cell.

The Anderson column exemplifies press portrayals of Tyson as an inhuman beast who finally was getting the punishment he deserved. These reports almost bitterly rejected previous notions of Tyson as a role model and anticipated his punishment and humiliation.

The Victim

The second primary depiction of Tyson in the press portrayed a victim. Emphasizing the hard poverty of his childhood in Brooklyn, this portrayal recounted Tyson's orphaned life on the streets, his lengthy childhood criminal record, and his tenure at an upstate reform school. Reports placed particular emphasis on Tyson's surrogate father, Cus D'Amato, an aging boxing trainer who died before he finished "building" his young protege. Other reports, while not absolving Tyson of culpability, placed blame for Tyson's fall on a larger system of entitlement that society grants to athletes, and perhaps, even more broadly, on dark wishes and fantasies that people harbored about Tyson.

The depiction of the victim was often founded upon establishing the crippling effects of an impoverished social life. The coverage is indicative then of how cultural and political struggles—other than race but accentuated by race—became part of the reporting on Tyson. The reporting has links to traditional narratives and tales in which lower-class people, granted sudden wealth, find they cannot escape their caste or past.

Often the depiction of Tyson as victim was done directly, appealing to the difficulties inherent in Tyson's rise from the lowest class of his childhood on the streets to the highest class of celebrity and wealth. "The Tyson trial reveals the stories of two victims," said the *Chicago Tribune* (Page, 1992), "one of rape, the other of circumstances." William Raspberry (1992) said, "In many ways, Tyson really is a victim—of a bad childhood, of bad advice, of bad choices." A report in the *Washington Post* said, "Tyson is portrayed by members of his entourage as a victim, not a victimizer" (Brubaker, 1991b). Some accounts said plainly that Tyson could not escape his past. *USA Today* (Saraceno, 1991b) used a biography of Tyson for a story on the "Boxer as Victim." According to the report, the book showed Tyson as a "pathetic, love-starved man-child worthy of reconsideration. He is a victim, not a victimizer." *Washington Post* columnist Tom Boswell (1991) wrote, "American sports may never offer a sadder story than Tyson's. His childhood was such a nightmare that, at one level, the basic human reaction is to say, 'There but for the grace of God go I.' "

Another part of the portrayal of Tyson as victim found especial tragedy in the death of his trainer Cus D'Amato. Tyson was depicted as an "unfinished" work who may not have strayed had the old white man lived. Bob Verdi (1992a) said, "D'Amato discovered Tyson but died too soon to save him." The *Chicago Tribune* (Page, 1992) noted D'Amato's influence and asked, "How different might Tyson's life have been if only someone had taken him under wing to rebuild his life, not just his career." Arthur Ashe (1991), in the

Washington Post, wrote, "Tyson has had no authority figure since D'Amato who could look him in the eye and say, 'You ought to be ashamed of yourself.' " Another writer said that "when D'Amato died, so did Tyson's beacon and discipline" (Page, 1992). Tom Boswell (1991) stated D'Amato "built" Tyson into a teenager and asked, "What if, like Tyson, your role model dies at just the wrong moment and makes the whole ordeal seem like a cosmic joke?" Murray (1992) in the *Los Angeles Times* used similar language and said, "D'Amato wanted to remake the person as well as the fighter."

New York Times columnist Robert Lipsyte (1991b) recognized the implications of the portrayal. He quoted an exchange between himself and Tyson's biographer Jose Torres:

> "Cus D'Amato didn't finish the job . . . Cus was in such a hurry to make
> a heavy-weight champion that he didn't make a human being. When
> D'Amato died, Mike was not a finished person."
> "That sounds like Dr. Frankenstein and his monster," I said.
> "Exactly," said Torres.

Some reports suggested Tyson was the victim of racism (Steptoe, 1992). Gildea (1992) of the *Washington Post* built a sympathetic portrait of Tyson around supporters convinced he was victimized. Gildea quoted World Boxing Council President Jose Sulaiman about the conviction: "I am starting to think it is true that what certain people here say, that it was a dinner of blacks by white cannibals." The *Chicago Tribune* too at times depicted Tyson through the eyes of supporters convinced the trial was racist: "They said that he had been railroaded, that he was a victim" (Kass, 1992c).

Another part of the portrayal of Tyson as victim was to cast the boxer as just another athlete caught up in a system of entitlement. Again, reports confronted complex intersections of class and privilege as they considered the relatively recent acquisition of wealth and power by modern-day athletes. A lengthy, 4,000-word report in the *Los Angeles Times* (Cart, 1992) suggested aberrant sexual conduct by athletes may be the "result of lifelong coddling" and said "what society has fostered is a segment of the population—elite athletes—that has learned from an early age that they are special. Often they form the idea that rules don't apply to them." Lipsyte (1991a), of the *New York Times*, wrote, "This is what it's about. Naked power. What you can get away with because you're a big boy, because too many people are afraid of you and dependent on you and hooked on a system of male entitlement that tolerates, if not encourages, a man forcing his way."

Other reports took up the entanglement of gender and race and tentatively offered the viewpoint of some in the black community that Tyson was a victim of a more subtle battle—a struggle for power between black men and women. *USA Today* (Malveaux, 1992) noted simply that "men and women, especially in the African-American community, are divided on whether boxer Mike Tyson should have been convicted of rape." *USA Today* commentator Barbara Reynolds (1992) took up the issue of Tyson's support from ministers and stated that "throughout history, black ministers often have stepped forward to replace whites as oppressors rather than liberators of black women" and that often, "black women echo those traditional views, even against their own self-interest." One commentator in the *Chicago Tribune* (Johnson, 1992) addressed the tensions that the Tyson trial caused for African Americans. "Those issues—protecting a man perceived as a hero for blacks and the strained relationship between black men and women—echo another celebrated case involving an African-American male and female: Clarence Thomas and Anita Hill." He continued, "The cases have stunned the black community like a one-two punch. In both, two points were clear: Vocal segments of the black population took the side of a black male against his black female accuser, and as a result, the woman was vilified." Another commentator (Page, 1992) also perceived that Tyson was embroiled in larger tensions between African-American men and women. He too noted the vilification of the black woman and called it "the Rasheeda Moore Syndrome," for the woman who took part in the FBI cocaine arrest of former District of Columbia Mayor Marion Barry. Page wrote: " 'The bitch set me up,' moaned Barry. The quote soon appeared on T-shirts that sold briskly outside his trial, adding weight to an old stereotype about the alleged treachery of black women."

The *Washington Post* (Rosenfeld, 1992) gave over the front page of its Style section to a lengthy report that showed black women saw Tyson as a victim and showed little sympathy for Tyson's accuser.

> In interviews on two college campuses, and in listener calls to local radio stations, the refrain from a number of young black women has been: She asked for it, she got it, and it's not fair to "cry rape." They may find Tyson's general attitude toward women repugnant—he seems to be well known as the crude propositioner he portrayed himself as during the trial—but there is little sympathy for her.

Some reflective columns offered the subtle perspective that Tyson was a victim of others' fears. *New York Times* columnist Robert Lipsyte (1991b) stated that with the rape charge, Tyson had managed "to transcend boxing, to join Jack Johnson, Joe Louis and Muhammad Ali as a social as well as a pugilistic symbol." He wrote, "Suddenly, even as Freddy Kreuger appears in his last 'Nightmare on Elm Street,' Mike Tyson has cracked into our subconscious: He is what we are afraid of, and we created him." The *Los Angeles Times* (Penner, 1992) said:

> We shake our heads, we cluck our tongues, we wag our fingers, we use words like "criminal" and "shameful" and "reprehensible." We are talking about Mike Tyson, but we are missing the point. The point can be found with one glance into the mirror. A sports champion is charged with rape, and then convicted, and we are simultaneously disgusted and intrigued, appalled and enthralled.

Such reports subtly add to the portrayal of Tyson as a victim of circumstances outside his control, demeaning him as they symbolically disempower him. The portrayal is complex and conflicted by numerous, salient, cultural and political issues. Yet the reports are founded upon a racially charged, symbolic type—a powerless African-American man, helpless against his background, his society, the women of his race, and other people's fantasies and fears.

The Press and Symbolic Types: Race and Representation

Grounded in the analysis of the Tyson trial press coverage, this section will first consider the implications of that coverage in the context of the literature on press stereotypes. From this perspective, I then will reflect on press representations of race, particularly its use of symbolic types. Finally, I will consider the ways in which press coverage of Tyson supports the notion of modern racism, in which racist images are re-presented and re-produced in the absence of overtly racist rhetoric.

Examination of press coverage of the Tyson trial has indeed shown that portrayals of the boxer were drawn from degrading, dehumanizing stereotypes. Cast as an animal savage or hapless dupe, Tyson was debased by press coverage that used his troubles to enact larger dramas about him. Despite the intensity of the coverage and the nine-month duration of the judicial and journalistic process, little insight was provided into the boxer and his life. None of the elite, influential papers studied here offered more than superficial storylines and crude stereotypes. Even those enraged at the cruelty of Tyson's acts must be dismayed at such portrayals.

The findings certainly support those who criticized press coverage of Tyson's trial (Gildea, 1992; Jordan, 1992; Reynolds, 1992). The implications in terms of the trial, however, are unclear; the influence of press coverage on jury members is not a question to be addressed by textual analysis. But with the trial jury sequestered, the influence of coverage would not appear great, except perhaps from images offered in pretrial coverage. The broader question of the relationship between the press coverage and people's understanding of Tyson and the trial is also unclear. News accounts are always open to multiple interpretations by readers and the ways in which news might shape or be shaped by cultural context is still to be understood. But the uniformity and unanimity of the press portraits here certainly are troubling to those concerned about press representations of Tyson.

The results of this study perhaps are most discouraging in the context of the long body of press criticism that has continued to demonstrate racist stereotyping in the news. More than 70 years since Lippmann's analyses of stereotypes, more than 25 years after the Kerner Commission, the press still draws upon racist stereotypes. This study's results complement the previous literature by pointing out *how* stereotypes are invoked subtly but inexorably through the language, conventions, and narrative forms of the press. Findings from the Tyson trial coverage highlight in particular the cruel process of *reduction* that lies at the heart of stereotyping. In fact, the critical tension surrounding the Tyson trial coverage can be conceived not only in terms of representation but also in terms of reduction.

The problem was not only that Tyson was depicted with racist stereotypes, though that was part of it. The problem was that over nine months, five newspapers, and 500 articles, the press confined itself to two depictions, drawn from a small well of racist types for African Americans. Press portrayals might have offered varied, complex depictions of Tyson. Instead, a complicated, compelling issue was starkly reduced to a few of the most offensive representations of race: Did the black, savage, sex-driven, former heavyweight champion use his animal strength to rape the virginal black princess who stupidly left herself alone with him? Or did the dumb, innocent but well-hung black boxer get manipulated again, this time by a promiscuous, black gold digger who had knowingly thrown herself at him only to be hurt by the size of his organ and his crude, rude approach to sex? These were the sparse choices echoed and extended by the press, choices that affirmed delimiting, dehumanizing, and degrading portrayals of African Americans. Perhaps future press criticism can consider in more depth how the unsaid and the unprinted can subvert representations of race in the press. That is, subversion may derive from a dearth of types, a lack of complex depictions, a reliance on a few degrading narratives, and an overwhelming paucity of portrayals.

If we accept seriously the thesis that members of the press are not overtly racist, yet still produce racist depictions, then critical attention must be directed to the language contributing to such depictions. Identification of the subtle, unovert expression of racist stereotypes leads finally then to a consideration of modern racism. Specifically: The study's findings of stereotyped portrayals of Tyson might be seen as an illustration of modern racism in the press.

As we have seen, scholars of modern racism affirm that traditional racism has been transformed. Bigoted terms, support for segregation, and open discrimination are no longer condoned or much espoused (McConahay, 1986, p. 93). Yet racism remains. Grounded in beliefs that discrimination no longer exists, that the history of segregation casts no shadow today, and that the problems facing the black community can be attributed to individual faults, modern racism offers "explanations" for black life in the post-civil-rights era. The use of stereotypes is the key to formulating and expressing such explanations (Dovidio, Evans, and Tyler, 1986; Hamilton and Trolier, 1986). Stereotypes help organize negative beliefs about blacks, and the espousal of stereotypes gives somewhat masked expression to those negative beliefs.

The news media are an important part of the process, one of the means by which "mass cultural institutions may promote negative stereotypes that are congruent with modern racism" (Entman, 1992, p. 346). Consistent with modern racism, however, the media's racial stereotypes are subtle. "Rather than the grossly demeaning distortions of yesterday, stereotyping of blacks now allows abstraction from and denial of the racial component" (Entman, 1992, p. 345).

From this perspective, then, press reports of Tyson can be seen as congruent with and supportive of modern racism. The articles overall cannot be judged as explicitly bigoted depictions or "grossly demeaning distortions." Yet as they reported on Tyson and his troubles, press reports clearly represented and reproduced racist stereotypes. The subtleties of Tyson's portrayals are such that some defenders of the press still might argue that much of what was said about the boxer was "true." It is important to be clear: Tyson is not an animal or monster or helpless man-child or passive victim. He is a man convicted of a heinous crime. The depictions may appear to have the aura of truth—may appear to explain—precisely because they draw from familiar, stereotyped categories for blacks.

Why did the press portray Tyson with such offensive stereotypes? Or more broadly: Why does the press continue to cast up the experience of African Americans in racist imagery? No firm answers are forthcoming, of course, but in the research on cognitive structures in stereotyping, social scientists suggest that people quite naturally process and store information through use of categories or schemas; categorizing others comes easily to humankind (Hamilton and Trolier, 1986; Tajfel, Sheikh, and Gardner, 1964; Wilder, 1978). Culture, economics, and politics apparently affect these schemas; certain outgroups are categorized and victimized with negative terms.

As members of an American social, cultural, and political matrix that has produced generations of racial conflict, journalists cannot expect that their cognitive categorizing will be free of stereotypes. In an oft-quoted passage, Lippmann said (1922, p. 81), "In the great blooming, buzzing confusion of the outer world we pick out what our culture has already defined for us, and we tend to perceive that which we have picked out in the form stereotyped for us by our culture."

The process may well be an unconscious one. As Hall (1982, p. 88) noted in a broader discussion of ideology in broadcast media, ideological distortions do not occur "at the level of the conscious intentions and biases of the broadcaster." He argued instead, "The ideology has 'worked' in such a case because the discourse has spoken itself through him/her." Similarly, Entman suggests, "Because old-fashioned racist images are socially undesirable, stereotypes are now more subtle, and stereotyped thinking is reinforced at levels likely to remain below conscious awareness" (1992, p. 345).

Stereotypes may also be embedded in narrative conventions and journalistic canon (Darnton, 1975; Eason, 1981; Schudson, 1982). As Lippmann made clear, stereotypes offer a system for selecting information. "For when a system of stereotypes is well fixed," Lippmann said (1922, p. 119), "our attention is called to those facts which support it, and diverted from those which contradict it." News stories thus can be formed before they are gathered. These story forms take root—"unquestioned and unnoticed conventions of narration" (Schudson, 1982, p. 98)—and probably assist in the reproduction and perpetuation of stereotypes in the press.

The implications of such inquiry for press criticism are large. Confronting racism in society and journalism is a formidable, imposing task. One place to begin, this essay has affirmed, is the language of the press. Support is offered by hooks (1992, p. 4). She appeals for a change first in our discourse. She writes that "the issue of race and representation is not just a question of critiquing the *status quo*. It is also about transforming the image, creating alternatives, and asking ourselves questions—about what types of images subvert, pose critical alternatives, and transform our worldviews." These are goals worthy of press criticism and worthy of a humane, just journalism.

Notes

1. Distinctions are made in the social science literature between modern racism and the similarly focused symbolic racism; see McConahay (1986, pp. 96-97) and Sears (1988). These distinctions have been brought to studies of media representations of race by Entman (1990, 1992). Also see Bell (1992) and Hacker (1992).

2. Both press portraits are based on racist types with roots in white American mythology of African Americans (Bogle, 1973; Brown, 1972; Colle, 1968; Dates and Barlow, 1990).

3. Fuller attempted to inject another stereotype into the trial; he requested that an expert testify about the size of Tyson's genitalia as a possible explanation for injuries to the accuser (Shipp, 1992a). The request was denied but became the basis for a raucous "Saturday Night Live" television comedy skit.

References

Abcarian, R. (1992, April 3). Mike Tyson's fans just don't get the message. *Los Angeles Times*, p. 1E.
Anderson, D. (1992a, March 27). 10 years, 10 years, 10 years. *New York Times*, p. 7B.
Anderson, D. (1992b, March 29). The humiliation of No. 922335 Mike Tyson. *New York Times*, sec. 8, p. 4.
Ashe, A. (1991, September 15). Heroes: Thomas vs. Tyson. *Washington Post*, p. 2C.
Bell, D. (1992). *Faces at the bottom of the well: The permanence of racism*. New York: Basic Books.
Berkow, I. (1991a, August 11). Tyson is a role model in reverse. *New York Times*, sec. 8. p. 2.
Berkow, I. (1992a, February 11). The "animal" in Mike Tyson. *New York Times*, p. 11B.
Berkow, I. (1992b, February 25). A champ named Desiree. *New York Times*, p. 9B.
Bogle, D. (1973). *Toms, coons, mulattoes, mammies and bucks: An interpretive history of blacks in American films*. New York: Viking.
Boswell, T. (1991, September 11). A one-sided bout against trouble. *Washington Post*, p. IG.
Brown, S. (1972). *The Negro in American fiction* (2nd ed.). New York: Atheneum.
Brubaker, B. (1991a, September 10). Tyson indicted on rape, 3 other counts in Indiana. *Washington Post*, p. 1A.
Brubaker, B. (1991b, September 15). Tyson maintains innocence, lifestyle. *Washington Post*, p. 1D.
Cart, J. (1992, February 2). Sports heroes, social villains. *Los Angeles Times*, p. 3C.
Carter, S. (1992, May). Boxing: The underground sport. *Z Magazine*, pp. 30-35.

Colle, R. D. (1968). Negro image in the mass media: A case study in social change. *Journalism Quarterly, 45*(1), 55-60.

Corea, A. (1990). Racism and the American way of life. In J. Downing (Ed.), *Questioning the media* (pp. 255-266). Newbury Park, CA: Sage.

Darnton, R. (1975). Writing news and telling stories. *Daedalus, 104*(2), 175-194.

Dates, J., & Barlow, W. (1990). *Split image: African Americans in the mass media*. Washington, DC: Howard University Press.

Diamond, E. (1991). *The media show: The changing face of the news, 1985-1990*. Cambridge: MIT Press.

Dovidio, J. F., Evans, N., & Tyler, R. B. (1986). Racial stereotypes: The contents of their cognitive representations. *Journal of Experimental Social Psychology, 22*(1), 22-37.

Eason, D. (1981). Telling stories and making sense. *Journal of Popular Culture, 15*(2), 125-129.

Edwards, H. (1973). *Sociology of sport*. Homewood, IL: Dorsey.

Entman, R. (1990). Modern racism and the images of blacks in local television news. *Critical Studies in Mass Communication, 7*(4), 332-345.

Entman, R. (1992). Blacks in the news: Television, modern racism and cultural change. *Journalism Quarterly, 69*(2), 341-361.

Fisher, P., & Lowenstein, R. (1967). *Race and the news media*. New York: Praeger.

Gildea, W. (1992, March 27). Many expect Tyson's return. *Washington Post*, p. 1D.

Gilmore, A. T. (1975). *Bad nigger: The national impact of Jack Johnson*. London: Kennikat.

Gustkey, E. (1991, September 10). Bad image is good box office. *Los Angeles Times*, p. 1C.

Gustkey, E. (1992, February 11). Don't blame boxing, don't blame ghetto—blame him. *Los Angeles Times*, p. 1C.

Hacker, A. (1992). *Two nations: Black and white, separate, hostile, unequal*. New York: Scribner.

Hall, S. (1982). The rediscovery of "ideology": Return of the repressed in media studies. In M. Gurevitch, T. Bennett, J. Curran, & J. Woollacott (Eds.), *Culture, society and the media* (pp. 56-90). London: Methuen.

Hamilton, D., & Trolier, T. (1986). Stereotypes and stereotyping: An overview of the cognitive approach. In J. Dovidio & S. Gaertner (Eds.), *Prejudice, discrimination and racism* (pp. 91-125). Orlando, FL: Academic Press.

Hoberman, J. (1984). *Sport and political ideology*. Austin: University of Texas Press.

hooks, b. (1992). *Black looks: Race and representation*. Boston: South End.

In former heavyweight champion Mike Tyson's new entourage there are a lot of people wearing badges. (1992, February 12). *Washington Post*, p. 1B.

Johnson, A. (1992, March 29). Tyson rape case strikes a nerve among blacks. *Chicago Tribune*, p. 1C.

Jordan, J. (1992, April). Requiem for the champ. *Progressive*, pp. 15-16.

Kass, J. (1992a, February 4). Defense paints Tyson as insatiable. *Chicago Tribune*, p. 1C.

Kass, J. (1992b, February 7). Defense depicts Tyson accuser as gold digger. *Chicago Tribune*, p. 1C.

Kass, J. (1992c, February 11). Ex-champ Tyson convicted of rape. *Chicago Tribune*, p. 1A.

Kass, J. (1992d, March 26). Tyson's sentencing: Circus time again. *Chicago Tribune*, p. 1C.

Kass, J. (1992e, March 27). Tyson exchanges his gloves for cuffs—for at least 3 years. *Chicago Tribune*, p. 1A.

Koppett, L. (1981). *Sports illusion, sports reality*. Boston: Houghton Mifflin.

Law enforcement officials escort Mike Tyson. (1992, February 11). *Chicago Tribune*, p. 1A.

Lippmann, W. (1922). *Public opinion*. New York: Harcourt, Brace.

Lincicome, B. (1991, August 13). Tyson a brute? So what's new? *Chicago Tribune*, p. 1C.

Lincicome, B. (1992, February 12). Olympic stars can learn from Tyson. *Chicago Tribune*, p. 1C.

Lipsyte, R. (1976). *Sportsworld: An American dreamland*. New York: Quadrangle.

Lipsyte, R. (1991a, August 4). The manly art of self-delusion. *New York Times*, sec. 8, p. 1.

Lipsyte, R. (1991b, September 13). Who is Tyson, and what may happen next? *New York Times*, p. 11B.

Lule, J. (1993). News strategies and the death of Huey Newton. *Journalism Quarterly, 70*(2), 287-299.

MacDonald, J. F. (1992). *Blacks and white TV*. Chicago: Nelson-Hall.

Malveaux, J. (1992, February 12). Women, men and Tyson. *USA Today*, p. 6A.

Martindale, C. (1985). Coverage of black Americans in five newspapers since 1950. *Journalism Quarterly, 62*(2), 321-328, 438.

Martindale, C. (1986). *The white press and black America*. Westport, CT: Greenwood.

Martindale, C. (1990a). Changes in newspaper images of black Americans. *Newspaper Research Journal, 11*(1), 40-50.

Martindale, C. (1990b). Coverage of black Americans in four major newspapers. *Newspaper Research Journal, 11*(3), 96-112.

McConahay, J. B. (1986). Modern racism, ambivalence, and the modern racism scale. In J. Dovidio & S. Gaertner (Eds.), *Prejudice, discrimination and racism* (pp. 91-125). Orlando, FL: Academic Press.

McNulty, H. (1992, February 29). Did the Tyson trial belong in the sports section? *Editor & Publisher*, pp. 5, 34.

Mike Tyson chronology. (1992, February 11). *Los Angeles Times*, p. 1C.

Mike Tyson leaving court yesterday after the verdict. (1992, February 11). *New York Times*, p. 1A.

The Mike Tyson verdict. (1992, February 13). *Washington Post*, p. 22A.

Ministers circulate petitions to keep Tyson out of prison. (1992, February 18). *Chicago Tribune*, p. 2A.

Mitchell, F. (1992, March 27). Tyson could become a marked man in prison. *Chicago Tribune*, p. 9C.

Murray, J. (1991, September 12). Boxing's soiled image suffers another blow. *Los Angeles Times*, p. 1C.

Murray, J. (1992, February 13). Patterson heard Cus teach class. *Los Angeles Times*, p. 1C.

Muscatine, A. (1992a, February 2). As Tyson defense waits, prosecution faring well. *Washington Post*, p. 1B.

Muscatine, A. (1992b, March 27). Tyson gets 6 years in prison for rape. *Washington Post*, p. 1A.

Neuharth, A. (1992, February 14). A heartland lesson for New York brat. *USA Today*, p. 7A.

Oates, J. C. (1992, February 24). Rape and the boxing ring. *Newsweek*, pp. 60-61.

Page, C. (1992, February 12). Blaming "Jezebel" ignores the violent truth about Tyson. *Chicago Tribune*, p. 17C.

Paley, A. M. (1992, March 15). Tyson's trial isn't sports news [Letter to the editor]. *New York Times*, p. 9H.

Pease, E. (1989). Kerner plus 20: Minority news coverage in the *Columbus Dispatch*. *Newspaper Research Journal, 10*(3), 17-38.

Penner, M. (1992, February 12). Boxing, the public are not blameless. *Los Angeles Times*, p. 1C.

Quindlen, A. (1992, February 9). Public & private: Tyson is not Magic. *New York Times*, sec. 4, p. 17.

Raspberry, W. (1992, February 14). The real victim in Indianapolis. *Washington Post*, p. 25A.

Report of the National Advisory Commission on Civil Disorders. (1968). Washington, DC: Government Printing Office.

Reynolds, B. (1992, February 21). In battle of good vs. evil, ministers choose Tyson. *USA Today*, p. 7A.

Rivers, W., Schramm, W., & Christians, C. (1980). *Responsibility in mass communication* (3rd ed.). New York: Harper & Row.

Rosenfeld, M. (1992, February 13). After the verdict, the doubts; Black women show little sympathy for Tyson's accuser. *Washington Post,* p. 1D.

Royko, M. (1992, February 13). Race has nothing to do with Tyson. *Chicago Tribune,* p. 3A.

Sammons, J. (1988). *Beyond the ring: The role of boxing in American society.* Urbana: University of Illinois Press.

Saraceno, J. (1991a, September 10). Ex-champ barrels ahead with lifestyle. *USA Today,* p. 1C.

Saraceno, J. (1991b, September 10). Tyson book paints boxer as victim. *USA Today,* p. 1C.

Saraceno, J. (1992a, January 27). Tyson on Tyson: "I'm no bad guy." *USA Today,* p. 1A.

Saraceno, J. (1992b, February 12). Some place downfall before King's arrival. *USA Today,* p. 3C.

Schudson, M. (1982). The politics of narrative form: The emergence of news conventions in print and television. *Daedalus, 111*(1), 97-112.

Scott, J. (1971). *The athletic revolution.* New York: Free Press.

Sears, D. O. (1988). Symbolic racism. In P. A. Katz & D. A. Taylor (Eds.), *Eliminating racism* (pp. 53-84). New York: Plenum.

Shipp, E. R. (1992a, January 26). With Tyson's arrival, a day of departures. *New York Times,* sec. 8, p. 10.

Shipp, E. R. (1992b, February 8). Tyson, on stand, denies that he raped woman. *New York Times,* sec. 1, p. 29.

Shipp, E. R. (1992c, March 27). Tyson gets 6-year prison term for rape conviction in Indiana. *New York Times,* pp. 1A, 12B.

Signorielli, N. (1985). *Role portrayal and stereotyping on television.* Westport, CT: Greenwood.

Stein, M. L. (1991, October 26). Female sportswriters and sexual harassment. *Editor & Publisher,* pp. 8, 40.

Steptoe, S. (1992, February 24). A damnable defense. *Sports Illustrated,* p. 92.

Tajfel, H., Sheikh, A. A., & Gardner, R. C. (1964). Content of stereotypes and the inference of similarity between members of stereotyped groups. *Acta Psychologica, 22*(2), 191-201.

Tracing major events of heavyweight's life. (1991, September 1991). *USA Today,* p. 8C.

The Tyson years. (1992, February 11). *New York Times,* p. B15.

Vecsey, G. (1991, September 12). Don't blame boxing for Tyson. *New York Times,* p. 15B.

Verdi, B. (1992a, February 13). Tyson need not look far for blame. *Chicago Tribune,* p. 1C.

Verdi, B. (1992b, February 15). Laws? What laws? They're sports "heroes" and you're not. *Chicago Tribune,* p. 1C.

Wickham, D. (1992, February 20). If Tyson is a hero, we need no more. *USA Today,* p. 7A.

Wilbon, M. (1992, February 12). Entitled to everything he got. *Washington Post,* p. 1B.

Wilder, D. A. (1978). Perceiving persons as a group: Effects on attributions of causality and beliefs. *Social Psychology, 1*(1), 13-23.

Wilson, C., & Gutierrez, F. (1985). *Minorities and the media: Diversity and the end of mass communication.* Beverly Hills, CA: Sage.

Witosky, T. (1992a, March 4). Tyson trial belonged on sports pages [Letter to the editor]. *New York Times,* p. 22A.

Witosky, T. (1992b). Beyond the games. *Nieman Reports,* pp. 25-28, 37.

Ideology and News
News as Social Power

Most of the previous readings made clear that news is far from objective and that news does indeed reflect many biases inherent in its socially shaped production process. For example, economic forces from a market-driven press system lead journalistic work in specific directions. Yet the press system that leads to these work practices is rarely challenged or questioned, even though it leads to class and power biases in the news. For journalists, these biases become an implicit part of a taken-for-granted social reality.

The readings in this section of the book make the implicit explicit by considering the relationship between news content and the building and rebuilding of *ideology*—a subconscious set of values and interpretations that stem from the dominant power base in a culture. Journalists are still at the core of this focus because they are the ones who evoke ideological interpretations of situations during the act of observing and reporting the news.

Two threads run through the readings in this section. In the first thread, journalism appears as a shared culture among those who practice it—a professional ideology. Journalists look to each other to learn how the news is "supposed to go" and they unconsciously police the instances where news and newswork practices stray from the ideological mold of the profession. A second thread here is that the news media, as social institutions, are facilitators of an ongoing social dialogue that maintains the social status quo. To do so, journalists learn to draw from socially legitimated sources who can frame and debate issues in ideologically resonant ways. Thus, the final section of this book considers the broader nature of how news is shaped by its cultural context.

Barbie Zelizer's "Journalists as Interpretive Communities" takes a culturological approach to adapt concepts about professionalism, organiza-

tional cultures, and news narratives. Zelizer argues that examining journalism as a profession skims over the real nature of doing journalistic work. A
more productive approach is to look at how an "interpretive community" is
built and maintained through a common discourse among journalists, a
discourse that teaches appropriate narratives and behaviors for the interpretation of occurrences. Zelizer's discussion goes beyond pointing out the
existence of news narratives to actually place news narratives within the
cultural context of journalistic practice.

Journalists work in "double time," Zelizer explains, drawing on the
profession's actions as well as media framing of key events from the past to
guide journalistic behavior and framing for new occurrences. This practice
considers both a "local mode of interpretation" that comes from the specific
news and newswork context and a "durational mode of interpretation" that
emerges from a broader, historical sense of the journalistic community's
culture. Through these two modes, the past is used to interpret the present,
but the present also serves to reinterpret the past.

Stephen D. Reese's "The News Paradigm and the Ideology of Objectivity: A Socialist at the *Wall Street Journal*" considers the nexus of the dominant
social ideology with that of "occupational ideology." A good way to understand the occupational ideology of journalism, he explains, is to identify
situations that expose weaknesses in that ideology's core beliefs. Objectivity
becomes a paradigm here—a way of seeing and interpreting that follows
from a set of internalized, unconscious beliefs and values.

Reese presents a case study where the news paradigm's assumptions
come under fire after an established journalist was found to have violated
objectivity norms. In this case, a long-time *Wall Street Journal* reporter had
been writing regularly for socialist publications while he was reporting for
a newspaper entrenched in society's dominant coalition. Objectivity requires
that journalists avoid developing strong personal values outside the mainstream. Therefore, the media *institution* needed to show that this reporter's
behavior was an anomaly.

Reese's analysis strategy does not assess the objectivity of the reporter's
stories, however—that would only reinforce the legitimacy of the very
paradigm the author is critiquing. Instead, the focus turns to the cultural site
where the paradigm repair took place to examine the media institution's
discourse surrounding the incident.

The next three readings offer examples of how ideology appears in media
accounts of socially marginalized groups: women, minorities, and environmentalists. Marian Meyers's "News of Battering" draws on the concepts of myths
and stereotypes, but these concepts are placed within a critical studies perspective about social power and social class. As Meyers explains, issues of crime and
deviance are key sites for embedding the dominant ideology into the news. Here,
textual analysis looks at how common social myths about battering reinforced
dominant social ideology through news reports.

Meyers develops a feminist critique through analysis of two news items
about a murder-suicide. Part of this is accomplished by highlighting news

narrative techniques used to tell the story from a perspective that favors the ideologically dominant male point of view. In these stories, the woman is "acted on" much as Smith's mythograph demonstrated in Chapter 21. The man who murdered her is portrayed as the victim, as unresponsible for his own behavior. In addition, the blame shifts to the actual victim—the murdered woman—who "made" her husband kill her.

James Stewart Ettema's "Press Rites and Race Relations: A Study of Mass-Mediated Ritual" depicts social issues as "a performance" by the media and other institutions. By facilitating a ritual for how certain types of issues are "supposed to go," press rites become a site of social struggle. Thus, even though press rites are both shaped by and draw on dominant ideology, these acts do not guarantee social stability will be maintained. This study takes a cultural approach to demonstrate the media's agenda-setting power—that the media shape how society "thinks about" issues—and then goes a step further by arguing that the media provide guidance for how social issues should be acted out.

Finally, Cynthia-Lou Coleman's "Science, Technology and Risk Coverage of a Community Conflict" discusses how two opposing "ideological lenses" were used to frame discourse about issues, actors, and values in an environmental issue. *Scientific rationality* asserts that facts rather than values are the central criteria of risk assessment. *Cultural rationality* contrasts sharply, arguing that values are crucial to risk communication within its cultural context. Of the two, scientific rationality follows most closely from the dominant ideology, and it was indeed drawn on by the dominant social institutions in this case study.

By reporting on ideologically legitimated news sources in the controversy, news content defined the limits of issue discourse in an ideologically resonant way. In media accounts, officials defined the decision as value free—"we do not care which outcome the facts support"—even though that judgment itself represents a certain set of cultural values.

The study simultaneously functions at two conceptual planes. At the microsocial level, the issue becomes a decision about a new mine. At a macrosocial level, though, the debate represents the ideological clash between scientific and cultural rationalities. At both levels, this case study shows how the news media tend to dichotomize the news into an ideological battle between dominant social institutions and the outsiders who challenge those institutions.

CHAPTER 26

Journalists as Interpretive Communities

Barbie Zelizer

What does it take to make a community? Since American journalists were first identified as an upwardly mobile group, the academy has looked upon reporters as members of a profession or professional collective. Seeing journalism as a profession, however, may have restricted our understanding of journalistic practice, causing us to examine only those dimensions of journalism emphasized by the frame through which we have chosen to view them.

This article suggests an additional way to conceptualize community other than through "the profession." The relevance of journalistic discourse in determining what reporters do, informal contacts among them, and the centrality of narrative and storytelling are all dimensions of journalistic practice that are not addressed in general discussions of professions yet help unite reporters. This article thereby suggests an additional frame through which to examine journalism, one that accounts for alternative dimensions of journalists' practice. It suggests that we consider journalism not only as a

From *Critical Studies in Mass Communication*, 1993, Vol. 10, pp. 219-237. Used by permission of the Speech Communication Association.

AUTHOR'S NOTE: The author thanks her anonymous reviewers and Michael Schudson for their comments.

profession but as an interpretive community, united through its shared discourse and collective interpretations of key public events.

This view calls for examining the proliferation of journalistic discourse around key events in the history of news gathering, as a means of understanding the shared past through which journalists make their professional lives meaningful and unite themselves. The article applies the frame of the interpretive community to our understanding of two events central to American journalists—Watergate and McCarthyism. In considering how reporters have collectively made sense of both events, it suggests that they not only use discourse to generate meaning about journalism, but they do so to address elements of practice overlooked by the formalized cues of the profession.

The Dominant Frame: Journalists as Professionals

Seeing journalism as a profession has long helped us understand how it works. Sociologists view an occupational group as "professional" when it shows certain combinations of skill, autonomy, training and education, testing of competence, organization, codes of conduct, licensing, and service orientation (e.g., Moore, 1970). "The profession" also provides a body of knowledge that instructs individuals what to do and avoid in any given circumstance (Larson, 1977; Freidson, 1986; Gouldner, 1979). Journalists thereby gain status through their work by acting "professionally" and exhibiting certain predefined traits of a "professional" community. This generates an ideological orientation toward the production of journalistic work that is necessary for journalism to maintain its communal boundaries (Freidson, 1986; Larson, 1977; Johnson, 1977; Janowitz, 1975). As such, the commonality of journalists is determined by a shared frame of reference for doing work.

How does journalism benefit from being called a profession? Since the early 1900s, when a scattered and disorganized group of writers was able to consolidate via agreed-upon standards of action (Schiller, 1981; Schudson, 1978), the profession has given reporters a sense of control over work conditions, wages, and tasks. Journalists' ability to decide what is news has constituted the expertise that distinguishes them from nonreporters. Already by the 1920s, "media professionals had themselves adopted the notion that professionals are more qualified than their audience to determine the audience's own interests and needs" (Tuchman, 1978b, p. 108).

While this idea has been used within media organizations to safeguard against change, loss of control, and possible rebellion (Soloski, 1989), the ideological orientation behind determining such expertise has nonetheless remained the foundation for recognizing journalism as a profession. Being professional has not only generated an aura of authoritativeness based on a specific attitude toward accomplishing work but has suggested that reporters ought to approach reporting in certain ways—as objective, neutral, balanced chroniclers (Schiller, 1979, 1981). Adopting such an attitude has helped offset the dangers inherent in the subjectivity of reporting at the same time as it has allowed journalists to call themselves professionals (Schudson, 1978).

Although contemporary academics tend to evaluate journalism through the frame of the profession, it is in fact unevenly realized in practice. Various dimensions of journalistic practice, for example, are not addressed in most formal discussions of journalism as a profession. For instance, practicing reporters rarely admit their *usage of constructions of reality*, seen among critical observers as a common way of presenting the news (Goldstein, 1985; Tuchman, 1978a; Schiller, 1979). They instead stress their adherence to notions of objectivity and balance, both of which are suggested by professional codes (Gans, 1979). This raises questions about how and why journalists use professionalism as a way to conceal the constructed nature of their activities. How does "being professional" become a codeword for hiding the elaborate mechanisms by which reality is constructed? The failure to address this common part of newswork has allowed it to flourish uncritically, creating a need for an alternative explanatory frame.

The *informal networking* among reporters has been similarly overlooked in formal discussions of journalism as a profession. Sociologists have found that journalists work via a distinct sense of their own collectivity (Gans, 1979; Tuchman, 1978b; Fishman, 1980; Roshco, 1975; Tunstall, 1971; Roeh et al., 1980), favoring horizontal over vertical management, and collegial over hierarchical authority (Blau & Meyer, 1956; Tuchman, 1978a; Fishman, 1980; Gans, 1979). Such informal networking may be as responsible for consolidating journalists into communities as the highly standardized cues of association and interaction that tend to be emphasized in formal analyses. Yet acting in ways that build upon such informal collectivity does not figure in discussions of journalism as a profession. An alternative frame is needed to address the relevance and function of so-called pack journalism, media pools, briefings, membership in social clubs, and other ways that reporters absorb rules, boundaries, and a sense of appropriateness about their actions without ever actually being informed of them by superiors. How, for instance, does journalistic community emerge through cultural discussion? How do journalists accomplish work by negotiating, discussing, and challenging other journalists? What role does checking regularly with one's colleagues about story ideas or modes of presentation play? How do journalists benefit by recycling stories across media? An alternative frame might address this shared collectivity, by which reporters engage in cultural discussion and argumentation across news organizations.

Practices of *narrative and storytelling* among reporters have been similarly overlooked. While journalists have long discussed among themselves issues connected with narrative and storytelling—questions about "how to tell a news story," distinctions between fact and fiction, stylistic and generic determinants and specific conventions of news presentation (Evans, 1991; "Be It Resolved," 1989-1990; Berryhill, 1983)[1]—admitting to nonreporters a dependence on narrative practice seems to imply a lack of professionalism.

Ignoring narrative in discussions of journalism as a profession has generated an ambivalence over narrative practice that has in turn produced scandals around the fact-fiction distinction, such as the Janet Cooke scandal in the early 1980s.[2] Journalists' awkwardness in dealing with discussions of fakery suggests that existing frames for understanding journalism have not accounted for storytelling practices. An alternative approach might address questions relevant to the centrality of narrative—how journalists have ascribed to themselves the power of interpretation, how certain favored narratives of events are adopted across news organizations, and how narrative has helped reporters neutralize less powerful or cohesive narratives of the same event. A narrative's repetition in the news may have as much to do with connecting journalists with each other as it does with audience comprehension or message relay.

And, finally, journalism simply does not require all the *trappings of professionalism*. Unlike classically defined professions like medicine or law, where professionals legitimate their actions via socially recognized paths of training, education, and licensing, these trappings have had only limited relevance for practitioners. Journalists tend to avoid journalism textbooks (Becker et al., 1987), journalism schools and training programs (Johnstone et al., 1976; Weaver and Wilhoit, 1986), and codes of journalistic behavior. Training is considered instead a "combination of osmosis and fiat," with largely irrelevant codes of ethics and a routine rejection of licensing procedures (Goldstein, 1985, p. 165). Reporters prefer instead the limited credentials issued by the police department, which, in Halberstam's view, function like a "social credit card" (quoted in Rubin, 1978, p. 16). Journalists also are unattracted to professional associations, with the largest—the Society of Professional Journalists, Sigma Delta Chi—claiming only 17 percent membership of American journalists (Weaver & Wilhoit, 1986). This suggests that the trappings of professionalism have not generated a coherent picture of journalism as a profession. Yet we know that journalists function as a community, even if they do not organize solely along lines of the profession.

When viewed through the frame of the profession, the journalistic community does not appear professional. In some cases, in tending to ignore, downplay, or at best remain ambivalent about its trappings, reporters run the risk of being labeled "unsuccessful professionals" and are faulted for promoting "trained incapacity" (Tuchman, 1978b, p. 111). As one research team suggested, "The modern journalist is *of* a profession but not *in* one. . . . The institutional forms of professionalism likely will always elude the journalist" (Weaver & Wilhoit, 1986, p. 145). Existing discussions of journalism as a profession thereby offer a restrictive way of explaining journalistic practice and community, with the organization of journalists into professional collectives providing an incomplete picture of how and why journalism works.

This does not mean that the collectivity represented by the profession does not exist among journalists. We can easily recall phrases like "the boys in the bus," "pack journalism," or in the recent view of one woman journalist, "the eyes in the gallery"—all of which signal some shared frame of reference. It does suggest, however, that we need another approach to account for practices other than those offered by formalized views of journalism as a profession. We need a frame that might explain journalism by focusing on how journalists shape meaning about themselves.

The Alternative Frame:
Journalists as an Interpretive Community

An alternative way of conceptualizing journalistic community can be found by looking beyond journalism and media studies to anthropology, folklore, and literary studies, to the idea of the "interpretive community." Hymes (1980, p. 2) defines the interpretive community as a group united by its shared interpretations of reality. For Fish (1980, p. 171) in literary studies, interpretive communities produce texts and "determine the shape of what is read." Interpretive communities display certain patterns of authority, communication, and memory in their dealings with each other (Degh, 1972). They establish conventions that are largely tacit and negotiable as to how community members can "recognize, create, experience, and talk about texts" (Coyle & Lindlof, 1988, p. 2). In some cases, they act as "communities of memory," groups that use shared interpretations over time (Bellah et al., 1985). These views suggest that communities arise less through rigid indicators of training or education—as indicated by the frame of the profession— and more through the informal associations that build up around shared interpretations.

While the idea of the interpretive community has been most avidly invoked in audience studies, where local understandings of a given text are arrived at differently by different communities (Lindlof, 1987; Morley, 1980; Radway, 1984), communicators themselves can be examined as an interpretive community (Zelizer, 1992b). Such a dependence by journalists on their collective character has its own place in scholarship on journalism. Park's (1940) view of news as a form of knowledge, Carey's (1975) definition of communication as ritual and a shared frame for understanding, O'Brien's (1983) ideas about news as a pseudo-environment, and Schudson's (1988, 1992) studies of how journalists construct knowledge about themselves all suggest the importance of generating meaning through discourse. Journalists as an interpretive community are united through their collective interpretations of key public events. The shared discourse that they produce is thus a marker of how they see themselves as journalists.

Examining journalists as an interpretive community addresses their legitimation through channels other than the cues provided by "the profession." Journalists, in this view, come together by creating stories about their past that they routinely and informally circulate to each other—stories that contain certain constructions of reality, certain kinds of narratives, and certain definitions of appropriate practice. Through channels like informal talks, professional and trade reviews, professional meetings, autobiographies and memoirs, interviews on talk shows, and media retrospectives, they create a community through discourse. Viewing journalism as an interpretive community differs substantially from the professional framework and addresses elements of journalistic practice that are central to journalists themselves.

The shared past through which journalists discursively set up and negotiate preferred standards of action hinges on the recycling of stories about certain key events. Journalists become involved in an ongoing process by which they create a repertoire of past events that is used as a standard for judging contemporary action. By relying on shared interpretations, they build authority for practices not emphasized by traditional views of journalism.

While journalists consolidate themselves as an interpretive community when discussing everyday work—such as covering politics, the police, or stories of conflict of interest—the value of the interpretive community as an analytical frame can best be seen by examining journalistic discourse about key incidents in the annals of journalism. Such targets of interpretation, through which journalists have marked their ascent as professionals, are "hot moments" (Lévi-Strauss, 1966, p. 259), phenomena or events through which a society or culture assesses its own significance. These incidents do not necessarily exist "objectively," but, following de Certeau (1978), are projections of the individuals and groups who give them meaning in discourse. When employed discursively, critical incidents are chosen by people to air, challenge, and negotiate their own boundaries of practice. For instance, contemporary wartime reportage, as seen with the Gulf War, is judged against the experiences of reporting World War II and Vietnam ("Reporting a New Kind of War," 1991; Valeriani, 1991; Williams, 1991; Zelizer, 1992a). Discourse about critical incidents offers a way of attending to concerns at issue for the journalistic community, and professional consciousness emerges at least in part around ruptures where the borders of appropriate practice need renegotiation. For contemporary reporters, such discourse creates standards of professional behavior against which to evaluate daily newswork.

Discourse tends to proliferate when addressing unresolved dimensions of everyday newswork. One such set of practices surrounds the journalist's relation to time. Journalists are constituted (or need to be) in what might be called "double-time" (Bhabha, 1990, p. 297). Journalists constitute themselves not only as the objects of the accounts they give but as the subjects of other accounts that elaborate on their earlier reportage. Thus, while traditional scholarship has examined journalists largely on the basis of their original reportage and not its recollection years later, viewing journalism as an interpretive community accommodates double-time positioning as a necessary given. It offers a way to analyze journalists' authority for events through simultaneous accommodation of two temporal positions, thereby enlarging the boundaries of their collective authority and the community this engenders. These narrativized interpretations of double-time have primarily a local and a durational mode.

Local Mode of Interpretation

Reporters establish themselves as qualified to discuss a certain critical incident through what I call the local mode of interpretation. Here reporters discuss the importance of one target of interpretation from a localized, particularistic viewpoint. This mode is critical for providing reporters with discursive markers that uphold their own professional ideology. Journalists' authority is assumed to derive from their presence at events, from the ideology of eyewitness authenticity. In producing metaphors like "eyewitnessing," "watch-dogs," "being there," practices of discovery, or "being on the spot," reporters establish markers that not only set up their presence but also uphold its ideological importance. To borrow from Bhabha (1990, p. 297), reporters assume the role of "pedagogical objects"—"giving the discourse an authority that is based on the pre-given historical event."

The local mode of discourse can be either positive or negative. Although journalists might and do discuss initially the pros and cons of any given change in their standards of practice, they quickly reach consensus about the meaning of such change. Already at the time of occurrence, then, the event is filtered for its value in setting up and maintaining standards of action. Discourse is highly emulatory in cases of professional accomplishment. In a sense, reporters acquiesce to the critical incident making headlines. They discuss the incident in a variety of news formats, claim to copy the practice it embodies, and emulate the reporters responsible for publicizing the practice: Awards and prizes abound. References to the critical incident appear in trade magazines and become the topic of professional meetings. Journalists become highly strategic about setting themselves up in conjunction with the event and in consolidating their own association. In cases of professional failure, the local mode of discourse displays less of these imitative practices and there are no prizes or awards. But this does not mean the incident is ignored. Rather, reporters set themselves up in a mitigated association with the event—sometimes emphasizing how they observed what was going on but did not participate, or referencing other journalists who were involved, or simply marking out their own membership in the community. The incident is discussed at professional meetings and trade reviews, but not as a marker of positive accomplishment.

Regardless of how positively the event is initially encoded, the local mode of discourse displays an initial tightness of the interpretive community. Because it is predictable and in keeping with journalists' explicit claims about practice, the local mode of discourse helps consolidate the boundaries of journalists as an interpretive community. Association, presence, and "being there" are instrumental in making larger authoritative claims that stretch across time. For this reason, change—as embodied by the event—is either embraced and accepted, or denied and rejected, but it is treated discursively in a unitary fashion. As events happen, journalists tend to interpret them unidimensionally because they see them collectively moving the community in one way or another. This underscores the instrumentality of discourse in maintaining collective boundaries.

Durational Mode of Interpretation

What is not yet explicit is how reporters use the authority of local discourse to transport themselves to a second interpretive mode—the durational. Reporters establish a second kind of cultural authority that allows them to compensate for not being there. In assessing events that occurred many years preceding their incorporation into discourse, journalists position the critical incident within a larger temporal continuum. Here we see reporters as recollectors, as historians. Often reporters use the authority culled from their local placement within the event to expound on its more general significance. Reporters create their own history of journalism by making each critical incident representative of some greater journalistic dilemma or practice.

In this view, the reporting of Vietnam becomes part of a larger discourse about war reportage. Covering the Kennedy assassination becomes representative of problems associated with live televised journalism. Reporters use durational discourse to generate a continuum of contemporary reportorial work against which they can situate themselves. They discuss a given incident as a marker in this continuum by connecting it to other incidents that both preceded and followed it. The reporter becomes, to use Bhabha's (1990) terminology, a performative subject engaging in a process of signification that uses the past as data to generate more contemporary accounts. *Washington Post* reporter David Broder (1987, p. 15), for instance, defined his journalistic career as stretching from "the Watergate case, which banished the President from government, to the Janet Cooke case, which tarnished the reputation of journalism's highest prize." James Reston (1991, p. ix) talked about a stretch of time—"from Pearl Harbor in 1941 to the Gulf War in 1991"—as years that for him "didn't always make sense but always made news."

Because reporters are involved in making their own history and construct such a continuum in books, films, or talk shows, the incident marks the discussion about journalism. Reporter Sam Donaldson (1987, p. 68) framed his book on TV news around the Vietnam War and Watergate, because "these two events . . . convinced many of us that we should adopt a new way of looking at our responsibilities." At issue here is the larger durational continuum into which reporters place these incidents and against which the whole of journalism is appraised. Starting one's overview of reporting with the Teapot Dome scandal or with Vietnam suggests highly different views of what is relevant to the journalistic community in determining contemporary standards of action.

Reporters in durational discourse tend to differentially associate themselves with the event, facilitating a loosening of the tight interpretations initially accorded it. If journalists initially praised the event, some continue to do so but through different technological lenses. Television reporters might interpret either Vietnam or the Kennedy assassination differently than do radio reporters. Some journalists begin to dissociate from the practices being emulated. At this point the "healthy" critique begins, as the critical incident makes its way into a more durational mode of appraisal. In cases of professional failure, reporters begin to show differential association by appreciating their pedagogical value even if at the time they occurred reporters found them problematic. These broad subcultures of interpretation within the larger community—subcultures that allow for the systematic tailoring of a key event over time—suggest that it may not be right to speak of a unitary interpretive community after a period of time. Rather, interpretation as it unfolds becomes an index of a wider networking of forces, interests, and capabilities. Yet it is only by examining discourse that its complexity presents itself for analysis. The traditional view of journalism has highlighted the local mode of discourse at the expense of the durational. The uncritical way in which the latter has flourished raises important questions about its role in maintaining community for journalists.

Watergate and McCarthyism

The interplay between these two modes of interpretation plays itself out systematically in events that are negative and positive markers of journalistic accomplishment. Watergate and McCarthyism offer two examples whose interpretations have collectively changed over time, and in both cases such change has enabled journalists to shape their recollections of these events for addressing larger discourses about the state of American journalism.

We can consider Watergate first. From a local perspective, Watergate appeared to be a glaring success, one that reporter Peter Arnett called "a glorious chapter in American journalism," alongside one of the "darkest in American history" ("Newsmen," 1973, p. 28). It was a "Watergate honeymoon" (Adamo, 1973, p. 152). Professional forums, like the Associated Press's Freedom of Information Committee, vigorously debated the issue made most relevant for journalists by Watergate's coverage, that is, how to protect sources (Ayres, 1972, p. 42). Guidelines appeared on how best to use the unidentified source (Pincus, 1973), and journalists hailed what appeared to be a marked rise in the use of anonymous sources ("Newsmen," 1973). Various news organizations started programs that sprang from extensive sourcing techniques. ABC News's "Closeup," for instance, began in September of 1973, and major news organizations permanently expanded their investigative staffs that same year (Sesser, 1973). It was, in reporter Mary McGrory's (1973, p. 437) view, a "time not to be away."

Reporters motivated the enthusiasm for Watergate that characterized this local discourse. As numerous prizes and other awards marked what seemed to be a turning point in American journalism—earning the *Washington Post* a Pulitzer Prize and Daniel Schorr three Emmy awards—reporters attempted to address Watergate in professional meetings, press columns, and other routes of association. Yet it was the *Washington Post*'s Carl Bernstein and Bob Woodward whose names won the spotlight. As Dan Rather commented, no one "in journalism can applaud themselves [for their coverage] but Woodward and Bernstein" (cited in Sesser, 1973, p. 15).

In 1973 Woodward and Bernstein earned nearly every award available to journalists, including the Sigma Delta Chi Award, the Worth Bingham Prize, the Newspaper Guild's Heyman Broun Award, the Drew Pearson Prize, and the George Polk Memorial Award ("Other Awards," 1973). Already that year Bernstein earned his own listing in the periodical guides under the entry "journalists," and one trade story on Walter Cronkite introduced the piece by apologizing "with all due respect to the *Washington Post*'s Bob Woodward and Carl Bernstein" (Powers, 1973, p. 1). CBS executive William Small predicted that the story as Woodward and Bernstein had reported it would turn out to be "the story of the decade," and he applauded the rare circumstances that had propelled the two reporters "so clearly ahead of the rest of us in covering that story" (cited in Bernstein, 1973, p. 45).

Yet Woodward and Bernstein's names persisted beyond the local interpretive mode; by the late 1970s they had written two best-selling books on Watergate (Woodward & Bernstein, 1974, 1976) and had appeared as the focus of a popular movie, *All the President's Men*. Collective persistence in remembering Woodward and Bernstein thus became linked with the emergence of a durational mode of interpretation surrounding Watergate that often bore little resemblance to the event as it had unfolded.

Of all the reporters available for the durational discourse around this event, Woodward and Bernstein fit best. They offered distinct markers that moved the story of Watergate from a particularistic discussion of sourcing techniques to discourse about a broader continuum of journalistic practice that pivoted on investigative reporting. By the mid-1970s, in some accounts the story of the journalistic coup began to displace the story of the nation's electoral and judicial processes, as in one commemoration titled "All the President's Men—and Two of Journalism's Finest" (1976). Investigative journalism became defined as a craft with "Watergate popularity" (Behrens, 1977, p. xix), and articles on investigative journalism began with anecdotes about Deep Throat and *All the President's Men* a full decade later (Leslie, 1986; Mauro, 1987). Even in cases where Watergate's effect on practice was questionable, editors and reporters altered the narrative to fit the recollection. Schudson (1992, p. 110) relayed how the *Atlantic Monthly* framed an article about journalism education as upholding the Watergate myth, even though the article's author had not intended the connection. By 1977, many of the articles concerning Watergate focused on the reporters who covered it.[3] Stories about reporting Watergate became a regular part of stories about Watergate itself. One recent retrospective of Watergate, the political scandal, was accompanied by a smaller piece about Watergate, the journalistic story. Significantly, the latter piece detailed how journalists had learned the wrong lessons in covering the event (Martz, 1992).

From a durational perspective, then, the event was reframed so as to acknowledge a broader perspective on journalism. Reporters saw Watergate not only as suggesting new practices of sourcing or news gathering but as instrumental in a larger way—in setting up standards of investigative reporting (Armstrong, 1990; Banker, 1991; Langley & Levine, 1988; Rather with

Herskowitz, 1977, pp. 238-296). Within that view, it was called "the most crucial event in the rise of investigative reporting" (Broder, 1987, p. 141); the "most intense story I've ever covered" (Donaldson, 1987, p. 61); and a marker of a "new degree of respectability" for the anonymous source (Schorr, 1977, p. 179). Dan Rather (1977, p. 340) said that the "the heroics of Woodward and Bernstein" turned journalism into a "glamour profession." All of this has made it easy to claim that Watergate remained a "proud moment in the history of American journalism" (Broder, 1987, p. 365), even though evidence now suggests it was Vietnam, not Watergate, that pushed reporters to be more aggressive in their reporting (Schudson, 1992).

In their more critical discourse about this event, journalists wondered whether Watergate actually changed journalism or just highlighted the atypicality of Woodward and Bernstein (Schudson, 1992). While early warnings to that effect had been relegated to sidebars—as in one reader's letter that called *The Quill*'s adulation of Watergate "excessive" ("Watergate," 1973, p. 6)—reporters began increasingly to question the immobilization of the general press by the Watergate scandal (Sesser, 1973). As time passed, journalists were criticized for uncovering very little without the aid of nonreporters (Epstein, 1974). Articles appeared that questioned the value of Watergate's input on journalism, exemplified by an *Esquire* article entitled "Gagging on Deep Throat" (Branch, 1976). Dan Rather (1977, p. 296), who devoted some 50 pages of his autobiography to the topic, argued that Watergate was in effect a story of the televised hearings—hearings that "said volumes about the Congress. And about television. Both systems worked." By the late 1980s, even Bernstein admitted that Watergate did not have the hoped-for effect on journalism (cited in Schudson, 1992, p. 121).

Implicit here were concerns as to whether the incident possessed effective standards of action for generally acting as reporters. One ASNE *Bulletin* ("The Press," 1974, p. 9) in late 1974 predicted that Watergate would demonstrate that "the American press oversold itself on its adversary role." That same year the *Columbia Journalism Review* warned that the press would overreach

> in the pride, or even arrogance, that may come with power. In the self-congratulation about Watergate, there has been perhaps too much assertion that only journalists know what is best for journalists. ("Press and Watergate," 1974, p. 1)

David Broder (1987) complained that reporters at Washington briefings adopted an overly prosecutorial style to their questions. The inability to meet the so-called Watergate standards involved renegotiating the boundaries of investigative journalism within the more general parameters of "good" reporting. Journalists failed to meet these standards in covering "Billygate," the name affixed to the ties between then-presidential sibling Billy Carter and Libya (Broder, 1987, pp. 112-113), "Irangate," referring to the Iran-Contra affair, or "Iraqgate" (Baker, 1993). As one trade headline proclaimed in 1990,

"Iran-Contra: Was the Press Any Match for All the President's Men?" (Armstrong, 1990, p. 27). Regardless of how positively they appraised it, reporters were able to evaluate the broader impact of Watergate on practice. These kinds of evaluation considerably expanded the unidimensional surge of interest in Watergate at the time it was taking place.

These patterns of recollection suggest that years after the event reporters were better able to appraise Watergate in a critical fashion, both positively and negatively. In doing so, they could position Watergate within a continuum of journalistic practice that made it, regardless of its accountability to real-life events, a representative incident of the quandaries surrounding investigative reporting. This was not accomplished through a local mode of interpretation, but required a more durational mode to set the shape of Watergate reportage in place.

Do similar distinctions between local and durational discourse exist surrounding a negative critical event, that is, McCarthyism? In 1986, the *Columbia Journalism Review* defined coverage of McCarthy as a "journalistic failure" because journalists had remained more "accomplice than adversary" (Boylan, 1986, p. 31). It was, recalled David Broder (1987, p. 137), a time when reporters felt "personally and professionally debauched by the experience."

How did local discourse about this event look? At first, reporters almost seemed to humor McCarthy and his cronies. Headlines like "Busy Man" (1951, p. 26) or "Dipsy-Doodle Ball" (1951, p. 21) suggested that they did not take him as seriously as they could have. But once the event became more than just a humorous sidebar, reporters generally wanted no part of it and agreed it was a nonstory. From the first days, it was framed as a "battle of the files" rather than a battle with the press, with the only exception a near fist fight between McCarthy and Drew Pearson that won coverage in 1950 ("Battle," 1950, p. 16). There were no prizes, no awards, no excess of the practices used to cover the Wisconsin senator. Rather, the event served to mark the vulnerability of objective reporting. As Ronald May of the *New Republic* wrote in 1953, "For decades the American press has worshiped the god of objectivity. This seemed to keep voters informed until the invention . . . of the big lie [which by current reportorial standards] . . . will be reported straight" (May, 1953, pp. 10-12). Almost no mention was made of McCarthy in the professional and trade literature, and one of the first indications that he had become a force in journalism came at the end of 1951, when the ASNE *Bulletin* ("Should Tass," 1951) debated whether Tass reporters in the United States should be curbed. Even more telling, in 1955 the ASNE voted McCarthy the second most overplayed story of 1954 ("Second Guessing," 1955, p. 1). All of this suggests that journalists were slow to recognize the impact this story would have on American journalism.

This is curious given the debates about interpretive reporting that proliferated at the time. In numerous trade columns and professional meetings, reporters fell on both sides of the fence, preaching "objectivity" or "interpretation" to each other (Christopherson, 1953; Hamilton, 1954; Lindstrom, 1953). Oddly enough, McCarthy was not initially mentioned in this discourse; only one article obliquely referenced him as "Senator McThing" (Markel, 1953, p. 1). Instead, much of the value of interpretive reporting was linked to reporting the Korean War. And while journalists did address the event—as in Edward R. Murrow's exposés in 1954, Drew Pearson's increasingly biting columns, or Herblock's cartoons—their voices joined the fray too infrequently and too late to have a lasting influence. As James Reston (1991, p. 227) recalled, "It wasn't until 1954 . . . that I was able, along with many other colleagues in the press, to take a stiffer line." Few journalists made the event a story about journalism, at least not at the time.

This changed, however, in durational discourse, where journalism became a fundamental part of the McCarthy story. There, reporters embedded tales of McCarthyism within a larger discourse about interpretive reporting. Within that discourse, reporters underscored the value of having experienced the event, even if they had not personally done so. Their comments often came in the form of apologetic statements, as in: "No journalistic memoir would be complete without an attempt to explain, however painful, the role of the press during McCarthy's anti-Communist crusade" (Reston, 1991, p. 222). Reston said that the McCarthy era gave him his "first test as an editor," a test that he "didn't handle well." Choosing the "best congressional reporter we had" to keep a careful record on McCarthy, Reston had been stunned when McCarthy attacked the *Times* for its coverage, screaming in the Senate that the *Times* had chosen as its reporter a former member of the Young Communist League. Reston repaired the damage by suggesting that the reporter be moved from Washington to New York. In his words, "The reporter [was ordered] back to New York, where he did excellent work until he retired" (Reston, 1991, pp. 225-226). It was no accident that Reston turned his narrative recounting of that incident into an event with a moral lesson for the larger community, for the damage inflicted by McCarthy in this case was mitigated by the larger threat to the continuity of journalism.

In durational discourse, journalists did not view the reporting of McCarthy positively. The journalistic community needed to frame the event in a way that would allow for a change demanded not by journalistic triumph but by journalistic failure. So in marking their link years later, reporters often chose to mitigate their association with the event, quoting other reporters rather than referencing their own presence in the event, positioning themselves as representative of whole cadres of reporters, emphasizing the event's instructional value regardless of its negative impact at the time. David Broder (1987, p. 138) quoted UPI correspondent John Steele as saying "there was very little opportunity in those days to break out of the role of being a recording device for Joe." Broder (1987, p. 138) also quoted Charles Seib of the *Washington Star* as saying "he felt trapped by our techniques. If [McCarthy] said it, we wrote it." Reston (1991, p. 228) admitted the press corps felt "intimidated much of the time." He said "with the exception of Ed Murrow everybody came out of the McCarthy period feeling vaguely guilty" (p. 227). Richard Rovere (1984, p. 100) was one of the few reporters who admitted he was "one of the first writers in Washington to discover what in time became known as McCarthyism." Durational discourse, then, was differentiated by the type and degree of mitigated associations it displayed. The associations central here were propelled not only by connecting oneself with the event as a reporter, but by connecting as a more distanced and less-knowing observer, as a colleague to the entrapped, as simply a journalist born from the experience but not of it. This occurred because it was interpretive reporting that rose following the McCarthy era, not the kind of objective recounting that got reporters into trouble in covering McCarthy (Bayley, 1981, p. 219). McCarthyism provided an example of what *not* to do as a reporter. Its value, then, by definition needed to emerge in discourse—not at the time of the event's unfolding but at the time of its retelling.

Journalists reframed the event within a continuum of journalistic practice that stressed the value of interpretive reporting. Broder (1987, pp. 137-139) held McCarthy responsible for setting up the limits of so-called objective reporting and starting an era of interpretive reporting. Another former journalist claimed that "covering McCarthy [had] produced lasting changes in journalism," in that it took "a performance [that] spectacular . . . to move the guardians of objectivity to admit that the meaning of an event is as important as the facts" (Bayley, 1981, p. 85). Others saw the event through other technological lenses: Daniel Schorr (1977, p. 2) claimed the event taught him about television's impact; Eric Sevareid complained that covering McCarthy's "exposés" of American Communists revealed the insufficiency of "our flat, one dimensional handling of news" (quoted in Broder, 1987, p. 138). McCarthy, in a word, forced the "leading journalists of the time . . . and their colleagues to reexamine how they were operating, the codes that guided their work" (Broder, 1987, p. 139). Here again, journalists utilized the event as a marker in durational discourse that often had little to do with the initial discussion of what happened. Moreover, it often obscured journalists' own susceptibility to McCarthy, exacerbated by considerable participation in the anti-Communist Cold War consensus (Bayley, 1981). In a sense, then, the value of the event increased over time, fulfilling a pedagogic function for journalists who invoked it in their discourse years later. It was transformed from an uncomfortable experience into a lesson well learned, again regardless of its accountability to real-life events.

What does this suggest? Thanks to the two modes of interpretation, journalists are able to consolidate authoritative evaluations of events that valorize them regardless of how problematic they might have been initially. As Schudson (1992) has demonstrated in his study of Watergate, the event's impact has more to do with the carrying power of the recollection than with the definitive changes it brings about in practice. In the best of cases, reporters can celebrate events because they uphold their own professional ideology of eyewitnessing. But when events do not meet expectations at the local mode of interpretation, journalists have a second chance at making things meaningful. They are able to employ a historical perspective in evaluating events differently from how they first transpired. This second chance at interpretation suggests a function for journalistic discourse that extends the authority of the journalistic community beyond that suggested by the frame of the profession. Through durational discourse, reporters are able to compensate for their own dual temporal positioning, despite the fact that their professional ideology accounts for their presence only at the time of the event. In establishing authoritative views of an event long after it took place, they generate contemporary standards of action for other members of the interpretive community.

The forcefulness of these two interpretive modes surrounding journalists' relation to time raises disturbing questions about the far-reaching ability of reporters to establish themselves as interpretive authorities for events, both past and present. It points to the possibility that journalists exercise similar license in building authority for other practices not accounted for by traditional views of journalism. Equally bothersome, it underscores our own bias in understanding journalism only in certain, preconstructed ways. For without a frame that validates the examination of discourse unfolding over time—in memoirs, news clippings, social clubs, and the proceedings of professional forums—we have no reason to examine it. In limiting our evaluations of journalism to the time of an event's initial reportage, we have little understanding of the ways in which journalists create community. Yet these pages suggest that they do so through a discourse that structures recollection of events according to evolving agendas and sets up ever-changing standards of action by which reporters conduct themselves in the present era.

Discourse and the Interpretive Community

The proliferation of discourse about each of these incidents suggests that reporters regularly use their own conversations to generate meaning about journalistic work. Through discourse, they set standards of evaluation to appraise more general journalistic coverage. Thus, during the first years following each incident, reporters displayed an excess of the practices that each incident represented. Yet as the employment of different practices leveled out over time, discourse about the incidents behind them came to be used as an effective standard for evaluating daily coverage.

It is a well-known truism among reporters that "journalism is but a first rough draft of history." That assumption, largely supported by existing understanding of journalism, suggests that journalism ends where history begins, and that as time passes reporters yield to historians in taking over authority for the message. But this examination of journalists' discourse suggests that in fact reporters do not necessarily yield their interpretive authority to historians, and that journalists use both kinds of discourse to maintain themselves in double-time. Double-time, in turn, allows them to claim historical authority on the basis of the recognized parameters of their so-called journalistic authority. If they miss the first time around, then, reporters can always cash in on the rebound.

What does this suggest about journalistic community? The swells of journalistic discourse around each target of interpretation underscore the centrality
of discourse for journalists. Reporters use discourse to discuss, consider, and at
times challenge the reigning consensus surrounding journalistic practice, facilitating their adaptation to changing technologies, changing circumstances, and
the changing stature of newswork. While these are not the only critical incidents
relevant to American reporters—and reporters from other eras would certainly
cite events like the Teapot Dome scandal, the Civil War, and the Spanish
American War—their usage of discourse points to the consolidation of journalists not only into a profession but also into an interpretive community. They
come together not only through training sessions, university curricula, or formal
meetings, but through stories that are informally repeated and altered as circumstances facing the community change. The collective discourse on which such a
community emerges may thus be as important in understanding journalism as
the formalized cues through which journalists have traditionally been appraised. This does not mean that other professional communities, such as
doctors or lawyers, do not do the same. Nor does it mean that the journalistic
community is not concerned with professional codes, only that it activates much
of its concern through its collective discourse.

Reporter Daniel Schorr (1977, p. vii) once offered the view that reporting is
"not only a livelihood, but a frame of mind." This discussion has addressed how
that frame of mind is set and kept in place. Recognizing journalists as an
interpretive community depends on the proliferation of discourse about events
that are instrumental in helping reporters determine appropriate practice. This
view suggests that journalism does not need to be coded as overly "folkish" or
unprofessional. Rather, it is "the profession" as a dominating frame that makes
it appear so. By viewing journalists also as an interpretive community, such
"folkishness" might be coded as much as a tool of empowerment as an indicator
of untrained incapacity. And understanding that empowerment may help us
better understand how and why journalists create their own history of journalism, and how and why they use that history in the relay of news.

Notes

1. Some academics have begun to examine these issues. See Darnton (1975), Carey
(1986), Schudson (1982), Campbell (1987), and Manoff and Schudson (1986).
2. Janet Cooke was a *Washington Post* reporter who received a Pulitzer Prize for her
fictionalized account of an eight-year-old drug abuser (Eason, 1986).
3. Of the 21 listings on the Watergate case in the *Reader's Guide to Periodical Literature*
for the period from March 1976 to February 1977, half concerned Woodward and Bernstein.

References

Adamo, S. J. (1973, September 8). Watergate honeymoon. *America*, p. 152.

All the president's men—and two of journalism's finest. (1976, January 13). *Senior Scholastic*, pp. 14-17.

Armstrong, S. (1990, May/June). Iran-Contra: Was the press any match for all the president's men? *Columbia Journalism Review*, pp. 27-35.

Ayres, D. (1972, November 20). Editors' parley focuses on concern for the reporter's freedom to protect sources. *New York Times*, p. 42.

Baker, R. W. (1993, March/April). Iraqgate: The big one that (almost) got away. *Columbia Journalism Review*, pp. 48-54.

Banker, S. (1991, June). In Bob we trust. *Washington Journalism Review*, p. 33.

Battle of the files. (1950, March 20). *Time*, p. 16.

Bayley, E. R. (1981). *Joe McCarthy and the press*. Madison: University of Wisconsin Press.

Be it resolved. (1989-1990, December/January). *The Quill*, pp. 46-48.

Becker, L., et al. (1987). *The training and hiring of journalists*. Norwood, NJ: Ablex.

Behrens, J. C. (1977). *The typewriter guerrillas*. Chicago: Nelson-Hall.

Bellah, R., Madsen, R., Sullivan, W., Swidler, A., & Tipton, S. (1985). *Habits of the heart: Individualism and commitment in American life*. Berkeley: University of California Press.

Bernstein, C. (1973, June). Watergate: Tracking it down. *The Quill*, pp. 45-48.

Berryhill, M. (1983, March). The lede and the swan. *The Quill*, 13-16.

Bhabha, H. K. (1990). DissemiNation: Time, narrative and the margins of the modern nation. In H. K. Bhabha, *Nation and narration* (pp. 291-322). London: Routledge.

Blau, P., & Meyer, M. (1956). *Bureaucracy in modern society*. New York: Random House.

Boylan, J. (1986, November/December). In our time: The changing world of American journalism. *Columbia Journalism Review* [Special anniversary issue], pp. 11-45.

Branch, T. (1976, November). Gagging on deep throat. *Esquire*, pp. 10-12, 62.

Broder, D. S. (1987). *Behind the front page*. New York: Touchstone.

Busy man. (1951, October 8). *Time*, p. 26.

Campbell, R. (1987). Securing the middle ground: Reporter formulas in *60 Minutes*. *Critical Studies in Mass Communication*, 4(4), 325-350.

Carey, J. (1975). A cultural approach to communication. *Communication*, 2(1), 1-22.

Carey, J. (1986). The dark continent of American journalism. In R. K. Manoff & M. Schudson (Eds.), *Reading the news* (pp. 146-195). New York: Pantheon.

Christopherson, F. (1953, January 1). Are we being objective in reporting the Cold War? ASNE *Bulletin*, p. 1.

Coyle, K., & Lindlof, T. (1988, May). *Exploring the universe of science fiction: Interpretive communities and reader genres*. Paper presented at the International Communications Association conference, New Orleans.

Darnton, R. (1975). Writing news and telling stories. *Daedalus*, 120(2), 175-194.

Degh, L. (1972). Folk narrative. In R. M. Dorson (Ed.), *Folklore and folklife* (pp. 53-83). Chicago: University of Chicago Press.

de Certeau, M. (1978). *The writing of history*. New York: Columbia University Press.

Dipsy-doodle ball. (1951, August 13). *Time*, p. 21.

Donaldson, S. (1987). *Hold on, Mr. President*. New York: Fawcett Crest.

Eason, D. (1986). On journalistic authority: The Janet Cooke scandal. *Critical Studies in Mass Communication*, 3(4), 429-447.

Epstein, E. (1974, July). Did the press uncover Watergate? *Commentary*, pp. 21-24.

Evans, H. (1991, March). Who has the last word? *The Quill*, pp. 28-29.

Fish, S. (1980). *Is there a text in this class?* Cambridge, MA: Harvard University Press.

Fishman, M. (1980). *Manufacturing the news*. Austin: University of Texas Press.

Freidson, E. (1986). *Professional powers*. Chicago: University of Chicago Press.

Gans, H. (1979). *Deciding what's news*. New York: Pantheon.

Goldstein, T. (1985). *The news at any cost: How journalists compromise their ethics to shape the news*. New York: Simon & Schuster.

Gouldner, A. (1979). *The future of the intellectuals and the rise of the new class.* London: Macmillan.

Hamilton, C. H. (1954, September 1). Call it objective, interpretive or 3-D reporting. ASNE *Bulletin*, pp. 6-7.

Hymes, D. H. (1980). Functions of speech. In D. H. Hymes, *Language in education* (pp. 1-18). Washington, DC: Center for Applied Linguistics.

Janowitz, M. (1975). Professional models in journalism: The gatekeeper and the advocate. *Journalism Quarterly, 52*(4), 618-626.

Johnson, T. (1977). *Professions and power.* London: Macmillan.

Johnstone, J., Slawski, E., & Bowman, W. (1976). *The news people.* Urbana: University of Illinois Press.

Langley, M., & Levine, L. (1988, July/August). Broken promises. *Columbia Journalism Review*, pp. 21-24.

Larson, M. S. (1977). *The rise of professionalism.* Berkeley: University of California Press.

Leslie, J. (1986, September). The anonymous source: Second thoughts on "Deep Throat." *Washington Journalism Review*, pp. 33-35.

Lévi-Strauss, C. (1966). *The savage mind.* Chicago: University of Chicago Press.

Lindlof, T. (Ed.). (1987). *Natural audiences.* Norwood, NJ: Ablex.

Lindstrom, C. (1953, January 1). By what right do we interpret or explain? [Address to APME, Boston]. Reprinted in ASNE *Bulletin*, pp. 2-3.

Manoff, R. K., & Schudson, M. (Eds.). (1986). *Reading the news.* New York: Pantheon.

Markel, L. (1953, April 1). The case for "interpretation." ASNE *Bulletin*, pp. 1-2.

Martz, L. (1992, June 22). For the media, a Pyrrhic victory. *Newsweek*, p. 32.

Mauro, T. (1987, September). The name of the source. *Washington Journalism Review*, pp. 36-38.

May, R. (1953, April 20). Is the press unfair to McCarthy? *New Republic, 128*, 10-12.

McGrory, M. (1973, December 8). A time not to be away. *America*, p. 437.

Moore, W. (1970). *The professions: Roles and rules.* New York: Russell Sage.

Morley, D. (1980). Texts, readers, subjects. In S. Hall, D. Hobson, A. Lowe, & P. Willis (Eds.), *Culture, media, language* (pp. 163-173). London: Hutchinson.

Newsmen hailed over Watergate. (1973, May 1). *New York Times*, p. 28.

O'Brien, D. (1983). The news as environment. *Journalism Monographs*, p. 85.

Other awards in journalism. (1973, June). *The Quill*, pp. 27-30.

Park, R. E. (1940). News as a form of knowledge. *American Journal of Sociology, 45*, 669-686.

Pincus, W. (1973, October 20). Unidentified news sources and their motives: The usable press. *New Republic*, pp. 17-18.

Powers, R. (1973, June). The essential Cronkite. *The Quill*, pp. 32-36.

The press after Nixon. (1974, November/December). ASNE *Bulletin*, pp. 6-11.

Press and Watergate: Intervening in history [Views of the editors]. (1974, September/October). *Columbia Journalism Review*, p. 1.

Radway, J. (1984). *Reading the romance.* Chapel Hill: University of North Carolina Press.

Rather, D., with M. Herskowitz (1977). *The camera never blinks.* New York: Ballantine.

Reporting a new kind of war. (1991, March). *Washington Journalism Review*, pp. 12-33.

Reston, J. (1991). *Deadline.* New York: Random House.

Roeh, I., Katz, E., Cohen, A. A., & Zelizer, B. (1980). *Almost midnight: Reforming the late-night news.* Beverly Hills, CA: Sage.

Roshco, B. (1975). *Newsmaking.* Chicago: University of Chicago Press.

Rovere, R. (1984). *Final reports.* Middletown, CT: Wesleyan University Press.

Rubin, B. (1978). *Questioning media ethics.* New York: Praeger.

Schiller, D. (1979). An historical approach to objectivity and professionalism in American news-gathering. *Journal of Communication, 29*(4), 46-57.

Schiller, D. (1981). *Objectivity and the news.* Philadelphia: University of Pennsylvania Press.

Schorr, D. (1977). *Clearing the air.* Boston: Houghton Mifflin.

Schudson, M. (1978). *Discovering the news.* New York: Basic Books.

Schudson, M. (1982). The politics of narrative form: The emergence of news conventions in print and television. *Daedalus, 3*(4), 97-112.

Schudson, M. (1988). What is a reporter? The private face of public journalism. In J. W. Carey (Ed.), *Media, myths, and narratives: Television and the press* (pp. 228-245). Newbury Park, CA: Sage.

Schudson, M. (1992). *Watergate in American memory: How we remember, forget and reconstruct the past.* New York: Basic Books.

Second-guessing. (1955, January 1). ASNE *Bulletin,* pp. 1-2.

Sesser, S. N. (1973, December). The press after Watergate. *Chicago Journalism Review,* pp. 14-20.

Should Tass reporters be curbed? (1951, October 1). ASNE *Bulletin,* pp. 1-2.

Soloski, J. (1989). News reporting and professionalism: Some constraints on the reporting of the news. *Media, Culture & Society, 11*(2), 207-228.

Tuchman, G. (1978a). *Making news.* Glencoe, IL: Free Press.

Tuchman, G. (1978b). Professionalism as an agent of legitimation. *Journal of Communication, 28*(2), 106-113.

Tunstall, J. (1971). *Journalists at work.* Beverly Hills, CA: Sage.

Valeriani, R. (1991, March/April). Covering the Gulf War: Talking back to the tube. *Columbia Journalism Review,* pp. 24-28.

Watergate bacchanal: Letter to editor. (1973, September). *The Quill,* p. 6.

Weaver, D., & Wilhoit, G. C. (1986). *The American journalist: A portrait of U.S. news people and their work.* Bloomington: Indiana University Press.

Williams, F. (1991, September). The shape of news to come. *The Quill,* pp. 15-17.

Woodward, B., & Bernstein, C. (1974). *All the president's men.* New York: Simon & Schuster.

Woodward, B., & Bernstein, C. (1976). *The final days.* New York: Avon.

Zelizer, B. (1992a). CNN, the Gulf War, and journalistic practice. *Journal of Communication, 42*(1), 68-81.

Zelizer, B. (1992b). *Covering the body: The Kennedy assassination, the media, and the shaping of collective memory.* Chicago: University of Chicago Press.

CHAPTER 27

The News Paradigm and the Ideology of Objectivity

A Socialist at the Wall Street Journal

Stephen D. Reese

On the evening of March 4, 1983, Cecil Andrews set himself on fire in a deserted Alabama town square, in what he called an act of protest against unemployment. The event was recorded by a local TV news camera crew, alerted by Andrews, who conveniently waited for them to arrive and set up. The national controversy following the event centered not on the jobless protestor but on the behavior of the news media. Would the man have ignited himself had the camera not been present? Probably not. Should the camera crew have tried to stop the man rather than filming his efforts for 37 seconds? Yes. The troubling story violated the journalistic norm that reporters record reality, not create it.

In their analysis of the Andrews episode and the commentary it provoked, Bennett, Gressett, and Haltom (1985) observe that the story was an "anomaly," a troubling story that did not fit comfortably into journalistic routines yet presented enough routine features to fall within what Tuchman

From *Critical Studies in Mass Communication*, 1990, Vol. 7, pp. 390-409. Used by permission of the Speech Communication Association.

AUTHOR'S NOTE: An earlier version of this article was presented to the Qualitative Studies Division of the Association for Education in Journalism and Mass Communication, Washington, D.C., 1989.

(1978) calls the "news net." The camera crew arrived to record what they thought would be authorities subduing the man. When police were delayed, however, the "script" was so strong that the news crew proceeded anyway, thus, in effect, triggering the event rather than responding to it. Bennett et al. contend that such anomalies bring the internal logic of news gathering into sharp focus and provide an excellent opportunity to study the limits of the journalistic paradigm.

In describing scientific inquiry, Kuhn (1962, p. 23) defined a paradigm as "an accepted model or pattern" that guides those engaged in complex information-producing tasks; it focuses attention on some problems and necessarily excludes others that cannot be as easily stated using the tools supplied by the paradigm. To make sense of the world, journalists, like scientists, rely on a paradigm, which remains of value so long as it provides a useful practical guide for them and they share its underlying assumptions.

Bennett et al. (1985, p. 55) note that like all paradigms, the news model faces the problem of "anomalous or troublesome cases that fall partly within the defining logic of the paradigm, yet fail to conform to other defining characteristics of the paradigm." These cases threaten the paradigm by calling into question its limitations and biases and, therefore, must be "repaired." They argue that the journalistic community repaired the Andrews case by retrospectively defining the core event as unnewsworthy, by introducing official sources as the story developed, and by blaming the event on methodological error rather than any blind spots in the professional guidelines. Bennett et al. note that "no single anomalous case can reveal the logic of an entire paradigm" (p. 56) but that a series of distinct cases can help develop a more complete understanding.

This study examines another such anomaly to probe the principle of objectivity and locates it within a larger ideological framework. Here I address what Becker (1984, p. 73) calls one of the key questions in critical media studies: How is the dominant ideology linked up to the norms and practices, or "occupational ideology," of media workers? Similarly, Murdock and Golding (1979) fault traditional studies of the sociology of media occupational practice for emphasizing pure description and failing to locate these occupations in the larger social order. They argue for "linking the general set of values and frame within which culture is set to the particular norms of occupational practice; in a phrase, linking the ruling ideology to occupational ideologies" (p. 35).

In this article, I examine these links by exploring the journalistic "occupational ideology" through the notion of paradigm, relating it to occupational practices and considering its larger ideological function. The following discussion analyzes a troublesome case for the news paradigm involving not a specific story but an individual reporter.

After a long career reporting for the *Wall Street Journal* and the *Los Angeles Times*, A. Kent MacDougall revealed that he had been a socialist throughout that time and had written for radical publications while employed at the *Journal*. The controversy within the journalistic community over his revelations helps shed light on unwritten paradigmatic assumptions, particularly regarding objectivity. I will review the commentary that was generated by his actions, particularly from within the profession, and show how paradigmatic assumptions and routines were reaffirmed and strengthened. If Mac-Dougall violated a central tenet, we should find evidence of paradigm maintenance—attempts to "repair" his apparent violation of those rules and normalize the case. The steps taken to address the anomaly help explain the nature and limits of the paradigm.

MacDougall's actions as a reporter direct attention toward that major part of mainstream press content that purports to be straight, objective news. Many journalists, of course, are expected to voice their opinions—albeit within a fairly narrow range—through newspaper columns and editorials or in broadcast commentary. Confining such opinions to clearly designated locations, such as the editorial pages, however, creates the illusion that other news content is delivered "straight," free of journalists' values. Indeed, by not appearing openly ideological, mainstream press reporting becomes all the more ideologically effective.

The fact that MacDougall reported for the *Wall Street Journal* makes his case especially intriguing for a study of values and objectivity. The *Journal*, more than any other paper, is associated with the inner core of U.S. capitalism. It is heavily relied on by the financial elite and is part of a larger corporate enterprise, Dow Jones. All of this, one might expect, would make it particularly sensitive to the values expressed by MacDougall. At the same time, the *Journal*'s reporting has had a long-standing reputation for credibility and factual accuracy (e.g., Kwitny, 1984), while sharing a faith in objectivity with the rest of the mainstream press.

As this case will show, the process of paradigm repair ultimately must be understood within the larger ideological context. Journalistic practice has its own autonomy yet stands in a structured relationship with powerful institutions. This is not to say that media practices are dictated automatically by ruling-class interests or the modes of production, but the paradigm must be negotiated and renegotiated in view of these forces. The meaning of objectivity itself is not fixed but continually contested in an ideological struggle.

Paradigms, Repair, and Hegemony

Paradigms

The notion of paradigm directs our attention, as Scholle (1988, p. 36) advocates, away from the ideological content of texts to an "analysis of the forms of knowledge, norms, and models that make particular forms of experience historically possible." Knowledge is produced as a consequence of the practices that constitute the news paradigm (Hall, 1985), or what Foucault (1980, p. 132) calls the "ensemble of rules according to which the true and the false are separated."

A paradigm exerts powerful influence by restricting the range of questions deemed appropriate for study. According to Kuhn (1962), paradigms provide examples rather than explicit rules. Thus, one learns the paradigm by engaging in the discipline, and the paradigm's effectiveness is not inhibited because it may be unwritten or even inarticulable by its practitioners.

The journalistic paradigm defines what becomes part of our secondhand reality received through the news media, and thus it is every bit as important as scientific paradigms. Both science and journalism are empirical information-gathering activities that have developed learnable routines for their practitioners. Both scientists and journalists are presumed to be dispassionate observers of the world, guided primarily by their observations (although scientists are perhaps given a broader mission to explain, in addition to describing, the physical world). Both science and journalism are guided by a positivist faith in empiricism, the belief that the external world can be successfully perceived and understood.

Unlike physical scientists, however, journalists observe phenomena that can fight back, dispute the way they are described, and set the rules for their observation. Scientists have theories to guide them, while journalists are supposed to be guided by the reality of events. In the absence of well-defined theoretical guideposts, journalists rely more heavily than scientists on routines as a basis and justification for descriptions of reality. Tuchman (1972), for example, notes that these routine practices represent a "strategic ritual" that helps protect against the risks of the trade, including such pressures as deadlines, libel suits, and reprimands from superiors. A violation of routines, then, threatens the news paradigm itself; conversely, routines can be invoked, particularly by those within the profession, as a defense against an alleged paradigm violation. Indeed, we should expect routines to be invoked as the defense of last resort (see Forrest, 1989).

Gans (1979, p. 183) argues that both scientific and journalistic methods are validated by consensus. The consensual nature of news gathering supports the notion of a guiding news paradigm, the mainstream press being particularly single-minded in its shared values and assumptions (see, e.g., Reese & Danielian, 1989). Lacking an objective standard for evaluating what are often highly ambiguous situations, journalists find it useful to agree among themselves. As Sigal (1973, pp. 180-181) found:

> Newsmaking is a consensual process. The forming of consensus takes place within a context of shared values—conventions about news as well as conceptions of the newsman's role. . . . So long as newsmen follow the same routines, espousing the same professional values and using each other as their standards of comparison, newsmaking will tend to be insular and self-reinforcing. But that insularity is precisely what newsmen need. It provides them with a modicum of certitude that enables them to act in an otherwise uncertain environment.

As the professionalization of newswork has increased, the paradigm perhaps has grown more entrenched but less obvious.[1]

Thus, the news paradigm may be seen as a model of information gathering, embedded in journalistic practices, and centered on ways of determining the newsworthiness of events and the way they are to be transmitted to an audience. The ideal of objectivity is central to this model.

Objectivity

Objectivity has been called "the emblem" of American journalism (Schudson, 1978, p. 9). In recent years, journalists have found it increasingly hard to maintain that they are wholly "objective" and have fallen back on more defensible standards, like "accuracy," "balance," and "fairness." The underlying principles of objectivity nonetheless remain firmly entrenched. The ideal of objectivity holds that facts can be separated from values or opinions and that journalists act as neutral transmitters who pass along events to an audience (Hackett, 1984). Therefore, the intrusion of value into a recitation of facts threatens objectivity, and a reporter with strongly held values threatens the smooth operation of the system.

As Hackett (1984, p. 251) observes, traditional studies of objectivity and bias in news accounts assume that "news can and ought to be objective, balanced and a reflection of social reality" and that "the political attitudes of journalists or editorial decision-makers are a major determinant of news bias." He argues that the practical objectivity criteria of *balance* and *nondistortion* are epistemologically incompatible. Both criteria, however, require that journalists' values be kept out of reporting.

For example, Hackett (1984) observes that news stories often balance competing truth claims that rest on incompatible worldviews by implying that the truth lies somewhere in between, but this relativist assumption requires that the news organization itself not take a position, letting the truth emerge from a plurality of perspectives. He also argues that the goal of nondistortion in objectivity rests on an assumption that "the facts" are ultimately knowable; the journalist is a detached observer, separate from the reality being reported, and capable of transmitting a truthful account of "what's out there." Thus, in this case too, the journalist must be value free so as to not keep "the real facts" from getting through.

In this study, I treat objectivity as part of the news paradigm. Doing so focuses analysis on the kind of knowledge made possible by this "ensemble of rules" and rejects the notion of an external reality, open to distortion through biased, nonobjective reporting.

Paradigms and Hegemony

The news media play an essential role in maintaining the authority of the political system. Thus, the news paradigm can be seen as operating within this larger ideological sphere, particularly in relation to hegemonic processes. Hegemony may be defined as the "systematic (but not necessarily or even usually deliberate) engineering of mass consent to the established order" (Gitlin, 1980, p. 253). By not appearing openly coercive, this control is all the more effective. The concept of hegemony, as developed by Gramsci, entails moral, political, and intellectual leadership within a social system; the ruling group does not simply impose a class ideology on others but rather provides the articulating principle by which diverse ideological elements are unified into a worldview. As Mouffe (1981) puts it, complex ideological ensembles existing at a given moment are the result of a constant process of transformation.

The media function in this process to "certify the limits within which all competing definitions of reality will contend" (Gitlin, 1980, p. 254). Media reproduce a consistent ideology without being instructed directly by the state. This leads Hall (1985, p. 101) to ask, "How is it that they are driven again and again, to such a limited repertoire within the ideological field?" The answer, in large part, is that they accept the frames imposed on events by officials and marginalize and delegitimate voices that fall outside the dominant elite circles. By perpetuating as commonsensical notions of who ought to be treated as authoritative, these routines help the system maintain control without sacrificing legitimacy. Despite journalism's stated goal of depicting reality, the news media—tightly interlocked at the top levels with other powerful institutions—have an interest in preserving the larger liberal, capitalist system by helping maintain the boundaries of acceptable political discourse. The media establish what is normal and deviant by the way they portray people and ideas. Journalists may frequently conflict with representatives of government and business, but this is a reformist antagonism that does not threaten underlying hegemonic principles (e.g., Dreier, 1982; Parenti, 1978).

The journalistic paradigm, therefore, has been developed, sustained, interpreted, and modified within this larger hegemonic context. Elements of the paradigm may contest the dominant ideology, but this tension is part of the hegemonic process and must be negotiated on an ideological field articulated by ruling interests. As self-perceived professional truth tellers who objectively cover events, journalists naturally resist being overtly manipulated by sources or their own managers. The paradigm provides them with enough latitude to satisfy their professional objectives without treading on core societal values (e.g., the desirability of private property, democracy).

Indeed, the self-policing character of the news paradigm is essential for its hegemonic effectiveness. Values that pose a threat cannot be suppressed directly by ruling interests; doing so would contradict the commonsensical notion that the media are free to report from within their own autonomous position. Instead, the media enforce their own boundaries by insisting that reporters with nonmainstream values keep them out of news accounts and through the natural workings of their own routines. For example, by relying heavily on official statements made through routine channels (Sigal, 1973), journalists give these sources the power, by default, to frame much of their reality. This helps solve the key problem of defining news: News is what authorities and other institutional elites say it is. Official and corporate sources make themselves even more attractive to journalists by "subsidizing" the media's cost of gathering information about them (Gandy, 1982). By making it easier to be covered, through predictable and prearranged packaged pronouncements, these sources can crowd out less strategically advantaged voices. The media benefit by being assured of efficient channels through which to get an acceptable raw information product.

The logic of the news paradigm must take into account and help justify this state of affairs. The notion of objectivity rests on assumptions that are eminently compatible with hegemonic requirements. Hackett (1984, p. 242) observes that the rules of impartiality not only *disguise* ideological messages in the media but are an essential *part of* their ideological functioning. Prevailing definitions of situations are reinforced, while viewpoints outside the consensus are rendered irrational and illegitimate. Thus, while journalists are being "objective" when they let prominent sources dictate the news, if they use their own expertise to draw conclusions they are considered biased. Giving serious attention to nonofficial sources is discouraged as "unnewsworthy." The press, for example, largely treated Ronald Reagan uncritically during his first term, because no opposing elites were able or willing to mount an effective challenge and thus make themselves available as oppositional media voices (Hertsgaard, 1988).

By accepting valueless reporting as the norm, the media accept and reinforce the boundaries, values, and ideological "rules of the game" established and interpreted by elite sources. Journalists threaten the paradigm when they express values openly, particularly values outside the societal mainstream. (Normally, radical writers can be dismissed as falling clearly outside the mainstream paradigm, but MacDougall could not, having worked in the mainstream press for almost 25 years.)

The editing process is particularly compatible with hegemonic requirements. Editors rise to their positions only after fully internalizing the norms of the journalistic paradigm (e.g., Breed, 1955). Although reporters are presumably in closer contact with the reality of their stories, editors are considered less apt to succumb to bias than reporters, who may get "wrapped up" in a story and be blinded to the "big picture." High-ranking editors, particularly at major papers, are also more directly in touch with the values of official and other elite sources and are reluctant to exceed these boundaries. In the early 1960s, for example, David Halberstam was a highly knowledgeable reporter in Vietnam, yet he often had difficulty getting his stateside editors to accept his pessimistic version of the war. The editors had received a more optimistic version from Pentagon and administration officials and were reluctant to contradict it (Sheehan, 1988).

If the individual political views of the communicator are the chief barrier to fully objective reporting of "the facts," it follows that mainstream journalists should not find strongly held values to be occupationally useful. Indeed, Gans (1979) found few journalists in the national media who would admit to consciously held values. He did locate those at *Time* and *Newsweek* who were identified as house radicals and house conservatives. These were the rarities, however, and served primarily to identify boundary markers and help the other journalists feel free of ideology. (Important from a hegemonic perspective is his finding that the house radicals eventually tired of political differences and quit, while the conservatives remained.) In MacDougall's experience, most Left journalists have found mainstream journalism uncomfortable; he cited Chomsky's observation that he knows of no socialists in the strikingly uniform media (MacDougall, 1988a, p. 15). MacDougall also noted the reaction of *Los Angeles Times* publisher Otis Chandler when asked in 1977 about *Times* staffer Robert Scheer, former editor of the leftist publication *Ramparts:* "A radical? If that were true he wouldn't be here" (MacDougall, 1988b, p. 12).

Of course, journalists hold many values that aren't obvious because they are safely within the range of core societal values. Sources notice journalists' values only when those values differ markedly from their own. MacDougall (1988a), for example, said that sources he spoke with while at the *Wall Street Journal* were more candid because they assumed he was as soft on business as the writers for the editorial pages. Referring to the Columbia University School of Journalism, for example, MacDougall noted (p. 16) that this "trade school" gives reporters the mind set needed to thrive in the mainstream press, during the 1950s this mind set included vigorous anti-communism (in addition to valueless reporting).

Anomalies and Evidence of Repair

The MacDougall case can be treated as an anomaly in need of repair, although with some important differences from a conventional "story." Unlike the "man on fire" anomaly, here repair work cannot be traced over time as different facts and frames are introduced into a running story. The MacDougall case does not present a specific story but rather an individual, his statements about what he did, and the resulting commentary. I examine this material for evidence of paradigm violation and repair. The body of work produced by MacDougall is examined only indirectly through references to it by him and others. Thus, I do not focus on the "texts" of MacDougall's articles but rather on the larger discourses surrounding the case and the practices that it called into question. The alleged bias in his stories is less at issue than the assessments by the journalistic community of paradigm violations.[2] A strategy of normalization is examined through references to existing standards of journalistic practice.

First, I look for indications that the MacDougall case represents an anomaly by seeking evidence of its ambiguity. If the case is problematic for the paradigm, journalists should have difficulty coming to grips with it. If it is problematic, particularly regarding objectivity, we should be able to observe repair work centering on the role of reporters' values as the paradigm is defended and reaffirmed. Because routines are central to the news paradigm, I expect repair work within the media to resort to them as a major way of normalizing the anomaly.

The Case of A. Kent MacDougall

A. Kent MacDougall, who is now on the faculty at the Graduate School of Journalism at the University of California at Berkeley, began his award-winning mainstream press career[3] in 1956 at the *Herald-News*, Passaic, New Jersey. Between 1961 and 1972, he worked at the *Wall Street Journal;* beginning in 1977 he spent ten years at the *Los Angeles Times*. His two-part memoirs, "Boring From Within the Bourgeois Press," published in November and December 1988 in the socialist *Monthly Review* (1988a, 1988b), set off a storm of controversy in journalistic circles (see also MacDougall, 1989a). In the article, he said he had written under an alias for radical publications while at the *Wall Street Journal*[4] and had selected story topics based on his radical beliefs. For example, at the *Wall Street Journal* he profiled I. F. Stone and wrote other articles surveying radical economists and historians; at the *Los Angeles Times* he profiled other radical economists and the left-leaning magazine *Mother Jones*.

The case generated a strong response, including articles and columns in the mainstream press as well as in industry publications. I conducted a thorough search, including the use of DIALOG, Nexis, and VuText[5] database services, for all relevant published mentions of the MacDougall case. The resulting materials referenced in this study represent as thorough and comprehensive a list as possible.

The Case as Problematic for the Paradigm

The ostensible violation of the journalistic paradigm appeared to center on the uneasy relationship between reporter values and objectivity. The first serious attention from inside the media came from former *Journal* reporter Dean Rotbart, who wrote a lengthy review of the case in early January 1989 in a business journalism newsletter, *TJFR: The Journalist & Financial Reporting*. He called MacDougall's career "exemplary" but questioned his professionalism, particularly the practice of seeking out sources supportive of a thesis and of having preconceived sympathies or antagonisms toward subjects (Rotbart, 1989a; rewritten as 1989b). Dow Jones & Company, Inc., parent company of the *Wall Street Journal*, issued the most vociferous reaction a few days later through its corporate relations department, although it declined to mention MacDougall by name or publish a story or editorial in the paper itself. This statement was issued for attribution to a spokesperson for the *Journal:*

> We are offended and outraged that a former *Wall Street Journal* reporter now claims he tried to pursue a hidden ideological agenda within the pages of the *Journal*.
> However, this reporter left the *Journal* more than 15 years ago and his importance at the *Journal* or in journalism seems somewhat greater in his own mind these days than it was in fact.

> We have reviewed articles he wrote while at the *Journal* and we believe our editing process succeeded in making sure that what appeared in print under his byline met *Journal* standards of accuracy, newsworthiness and fairness.
>
> Finally, we find it bizarre and troubling that any man who brags of having sought to push a personal political agenda on unsuspecting editors and readers should be teaching journalism at a respected university. (Austin, 1989)

I also obtained a form letter from Dow Jones (March 29, 1989) sent to those complaining about the matter, which does name MacDougall and makes the same points, referring in the opening paragraph to a "hidden ideological agenda." *TJFR* framed the issue in much the same way, as striking at perhaps the most sensitive nerve—journalistic credibility: How vulnerable is a paper to reporters manipulating the news in pursuing their personal agenda? ("Recent Revelations," 1989). MacDougall's more recent media employer, the *Los Angeles Times*, refused to make a statement officially, but it did so in a backhanded manner. A spokesperson said *Times* policy prohibited comments about ex-employees, adding, "it can give them more credibility" ("Recent Revelations," 1989, p. 8)—implying, "more credibility than is warranted."

The violation also may be seen in the amount of publicity surrounding the case and the way it was characterized. For example, a nationally distributed *Los Angeles Times* story said that MacDougall's memoirs had "sparked a contretemps in the mainstream journalistic community" (Shaw, 1989a, p. 1; reprinted as Shaw, 1989b). In a follow-up reaction piece to its first article, *TJFR* noted that the incident has sparked "heated debates" in journalistic circles ("Recent Revelations," 1989, p. 1). An article in the newspaper trade publication *Editor & Publisher* said that MacDougall had "created a media furor with his revelations" (Stein, 1989, p. 10). Considering how long it had been since MacDougall worked for the *Journal*, the case received more publicity than might have been expected. Indeed, the case continued to draw interest at least six months after MacDougall's initial revelations in November (Walljasper, 1989). The problematic nature of the story gave it staying power.

Unlike the Andrews case, this story was not carried by the supreme arbiter of newsworthiness, the *New York Times*—although it almost was. *Times* correspondent Albert Scardino was assigned the story the first week in January, but he could not find an angle acceptable to his editors. He says his first story was rejected for failing to define an ethical issue or to present a compelling case that MacDougall had done anything wrong. A revised story asked whether reporters have points of view and whether, if they do, it is helpful or harmful. Scardino says he declined to simplify an issue that he saw as complex but that his editors saw as black and white—that is, reporters should be apolitical (personal communication, August 2, 1989).[6] Exactly why the *Times* declined to run the story is unclear, but the reporter's difficulty in finding an acceptable angle itself suggests that the story was problematic.[7]

The case also presented ample overt evidence of being problematic. The *TJFR* follow-up article said that the case provided a rare glimpse of the fuzzy lines between right and wrong in journalism, where there is often no rule book or final arbiter ("Recent Revelations," 1989, p. 1). The same article noted that journalists like to present a united front to the outside world even though they vary in their beliefs and behavior (p. 1). MacDougall himself acknowledged the ambiguousness of the paradigm and used the uneasy relationship between routines and values to his advantage. He learned that "editors would support a reporter against charges by a news source, special-interest group, or reader that the reporter's story was biased or had some other major defect as long as the reporter had gotten all the minor facts right" (MacDougall, 1988a, p. 19).

Knowing that reporters must speak through sources, he said, "I made sure to seek out experts whose opinions I knew in advance would support my thesis. . . . Conversely, I sought out mainstream authorities to confer recognition and respectability on radical views I sought to popularize" (MacDougall, 1988a, p. 23). He paid his dues by cranking out routine business stories, playing within the established rules of the *Wall Street Journal*. Thus, he was given latitude to pick feature topics and report in depth. His writing included enough attributes of the paradigm to be acceptable— although not without provoking the occasional angry audience response: "Are you a communist?" said one reader in reaction to his *Mother Jones* piece (MacDougall, 1988b, p. 14). A forestry industry group, critical of his series for the *Los Angeles Times*, "The Vanishing Forests," suggested he was fostering an "anti-private-enterprise view" (Benneth, 1989).

MacDougall said that his stories contained enough "significance, controversy, color and surprise to satisfy commercial journalistic standards for relevance and readability" and that his "calm, matter-of-fact, non-polemical tone fit the formula" (MacDougall, 1988a, p. 24). He said that the *Los Angeles Times* permitted its reporters wide latitude, valuing diversity as an attention getter as long as the reporter "adheres to the readily assimilated professional code of objectivity and impartiality and doesn't violate canons against being shrill and propagandistic or stating a personal opinion" (MacDougall, 1988b, p. 13). One columnist felt that MacDougall had "got away with" slanting by being factually accurate and avoiding leftist clichés (Morris, 1989).

The ambiguity of the case is also revealed through editors' reactions to MacDougall's work at the time. At the *Los Angeles Times,* one editor liked a series on economic inequality enough to write a glowing Pulitzer Prize nomination statement, which noted that MacDougall had backed up his research with "interviews with scores of economists, historians, sociologists, and anthropologists"; the page-one feature editor downplayed the series, choosing not to run it on consecutive days (as was the custom) and to not run one of the four stories on page one (MacDougall, 1988b, p. 19).

The notion that MacDougall fell outside the hegemonic boundaries maintained by the news paradigm is supported by the language used to describe him. Throughout the case, the rhetoric includes terms that set limits.

MacDougall himself said: "What I was—and wasn't—able to report in two of the nation's most enlightened dailies indicates the limits within which socially conscious journalists can practice their craft in mainstream media" (MacDougall, 1988a, p. 14). His success, he said, suggests that the "limits of the permissible are wider than many radicals would suppose" (p. 15) (but perhaps not as wide as they might like). He admitted that he had been "pushing against the limits set by the *Wall Street Journal*'s standardized news formula" (p. 24).

The predictable attack from the conservatives zeroed in on this idea of violated boundaries (e.g., Irvine, 1989). Kincaid (1989, p. 7) noted that Accuracy in Media had started a letter-writing campaign to media heads, asking, for example, if NBC "has adequate safeguards against similar abuses by other media moles." Kincaid (1988, p. 4) said that the case raised concern "about the ability of Marxist agents to penetrate the mainstream media" and would make it harder for the *Wall Street Journal* to defend itself against charges of liberal bias. Columnists referred to MacDougall's "subterranean antics" (Cheshire, 1989) as a "clandestine Marxist" (Morris, 1989). MacDougall himself entitled his *Monthly Review* piece "Boring from Within" (1988a, 1988b).

The Normalization Process

I have argued that the news paradigm helps justify the maintenance of ideological boundaries. If the radical socialist values represented by MacDougall and expressed in his memoirs fall outside these boundaries (and this should be apparent from the rhetorical descriptions and the known range of hegemonic acceptability), then repair work would be in order. The stories MacDougall wrote were beyond "repair," but several post hoc repair strategies were possible: (a) disengaging and distancing these threatening values from the reporter's work, (b) reasserting the ability of journalistic routines to prevent threatening values from "distorting" the news, and (c) marginalizing the man and his message, making both appear ineffective. The press takes an active role in the normalization process and, indeed, carried out the repair work in this case without any help from other institutions. And to a large extent MacDougall, too, engaged in this normalization process.

Disengage Threatening Values

In response to the attack on him, MacDougall mounted a vigorous defense, reaffirming the distinction between values and his professional work, contending that he was "a journalist first and a radical second throughout my career. . . . I stuck to accepted standards of newsworthiness, accuracy and fairness" (Shaw, 1989a, p. 15) and adding that his remarks were misconstrued. He makes it a point to assert that he keeps ideology out of the classroom at Berkeley, choosing to train aspiring journalists in the routines. He says that he never criticizes business in class (because it is all a student can do to get the facts right) ("Recent Revelations," 1989, p. 9). MacDougall does not banish values completely, however. He maintains that his "emergence from the ideological closet" is serving a useful purpose in encouraging debate over whether journalists' having unpopular views interferes with their job performance. In his case, he claims, it made him a better reporter (e.g., MacDougall, 1989b).

Others also reaffirmed the distinction between values and reporting (albeit uneasily), claiming that reporters should not seek to promote their own agenda. Tom Goldstein, Dean of the Graduate School of Journalism at Berkeley and a former *Journal* reporter, praised MacDougall's teaching, saying, "We have no ideological litmus test at this school," and adding that MacDougall's personal beliefs were his own, "not ours, and he scrupulously keeps ideology out of the classroom" (Shaw, 1989a, p. 16). An unsigned editorial in the *Columbia Journalism Review* sums up this disengagement repair, asking if there is a place for socialist reporters in the capitalist media. It contends that a reporter should "be judged not on the basis of his political beliefs but by the integrity of his work," and maintains that MacDougall's work did have integrity ("Comment," 1989, p. 16). The article goes on to argue that mainstream journalists ought not to have only one set of mainstream values, supporting MacDougall's contention that a variety of perspectives can benefit journalism (p. 17).

The repair work using the disengagement approach was not completely successful, nor could it have been. The counterparadigmatic yet appealing notion of free expression of diverse opinion kept intruding. One columnist criticized MacDougall for "promoting radical causes" yet praised MacDougall's radical father, a long-time Northwestern University journalism professor, for being outspoken. He concluded that it is wrong when a man admits his "professional life was a masquerade and is allowed to teach others the craft" (Cheshire, 1989). He does not explain why MacDougall is accused of masquerading even though values are ideally to be kept out of reporting. (Ironically, this apparently conservative columnist made the same argument as leftist Alexander Cockburn—that MacDougall should have promoted his views forthrightly.) *Wall Street Journal* and *Los Angeles Times* editors also said they valued diversity. Frederick Taylor, *Journal* managing editor during MacDougall's last two years there, accepted that MacDougall would choose some stories over others because of his views, as would others with more conservative values (Taylor, 1989). A *Seattle Times* ombudsman's column similarly argued that reporters with differing views "can help broaden and enrich" political discussion, while of course being held to the same "rigorous standards of fairness" MacDougall followed (Wetzel, 1989).

Reassert Journalistic Routines

The primary defense within the journalistic community was to reaffirm the ability of the editing routine to handle the anomaly, to wring out any potential bias. As the *Columbia Journalism Review* senior editor told a reporter:

"The safeguards worked, the editing system is in place" (Vick, 1989).[8] The Dow Jones letter made the same point: "We believe our editing process succeeded" (Austin, 1989). If that was true, why was Dow Jones so upset? Indeed, journalistic consensus was not perfect.

The common reaction among editors responding to the story, however, was that bias would have been dealt with in the editing process. *Los Angeles Times* editor at the time, John Lawrence, explicitly stated that he edited out any hints of MacDougall's bias (Shaw, 1989a, p. 16). In another article Lawrence expressed ambivalence about MacDougall's reporting: "Being a Marxist doesn't necessarily have to detract from his journalistic integrity. Every reporter comes to a story with some level of bias. The question is: Are they capable of rising above that bias to write a fair story?" Lawrence concluded that MacDougall was capable, and went on to support his contention that radicals might be more objective than conservatives and therefore might be better journalists ("Recent Revelations," 1989, p. 8). Yet he said he would not have allowed MacDougall to write about a Marxist economist if he had known he was "as strong a proponent . . . as he now claims to have been" (Shaw, 1989a, p. 16). This uneasiness suggests that Lawrence thought reporters are able to rise above their bias but that it is better not to tempt them.

MacDougall received general support from his former editors;[9] of course, they were the ones who had approved his stories. Michael Gartner, now head of NBC News and MacDougall's editor at the *Wall Street Journal*, said that he had assumed MacDougall was liberal but that it didn't affect his reporting: "I judge journalists by one thing—whether they are fair, thorough and accurate" (Shaw, 1989a, p. 15). Gartner agreed that the strict *Wall Street Journal* editing process would have filtered out any bias before it got into print ("Recent Revelations," 1989, p. 8). William F. Thomas, editor of the *Los Angeles Times* until January 1, 1989, affirmed the ability of a reporter to keep values separate from professional duties. He said that he knew MacDougall was left of center but that he "met every journalistic standard. He was a professional" (Shaw, 1989a, p. 15).

Columnist Donald Morris (1989) also reaffirmed the effectiveness of the editing process, saying that editors would simply "spike" or edit out bias, or not hire reporters prone to such slanting in the first place. (Note the emphasis on recruitment in maintaining the paradigm.) In addition, Morris claimed that slanting a story is hard to do, given the simple factual nature of most stories (but this avoids the issue of selectivity). *Time* magazine's article concluded with an uneasy paradigmatic tension between bias and diversity. The editing process would have prevented MacDougall from "pursuing any hidden agenda," said the article, yet it noted editor Gartner's belief that having a socialist on the staff added a diversity that benefited readers (Zuckerman, 1989).

Minimize the Man and His Message

The third repair technique used to neutralize the paradigmatic threat was to minimize MacDougall and his message. This included, as in the Dow

Jones letter quoted above, questioning his participation in carrying on the paradigm through his teaching function. In the first apparent media mention of the case and official response, on December 15 the *New York Post* carried a blurb quoting *Journal* corporate relations spokesperson Charles Stabler, who adopted the minimization strategy: "He said in the story that he spent his weekends writing about CIA dirty tricks and restrictive immigration laws. If he had been doing that for us, he'd have had a more successful career." He added that "no one cared" that MacDougall was using the *Journal* to spread his ideology because "he wasn't taken that seriously" ("Radical Doings," 1988). Others continued this theme. Morris (1989) quoted an anonymous *Los Angeles Times* editor saying, "If he slipped any messages through, they were so oblique that nobody got it" and concluding that there are easier ways to get messages across than being a closet Marxist.

Others attempted to marginalize MacDougall, and de-emphasize his contribution, by referring to him in derogatory terms.[10] *Times* editor William Thomas said that the name "Walter Mitty" came to mind (Gomes, 1989). Paul Steiger, deputy managing editor of the *Journal*, said that MacDougall was "more a secret agent in his own mind" (Shaw, 1989a, p. 15). *Los Angeles Times* editor Tim Rutten explained, "You know, there's something concocted about this. I catch the odor of rationalization for personal dissatisfaction with his life. . . . I don't find any politics in this man's pieces" (quoted in Cockburn, 1989). Frederick Taylor, *Journal* editor, also took this tack (having also supported the diversity value), saying that he was "madder than hell. I think it is gutless of him to confess now. He's like a lot of liberals. They want their cake and to eat it too. Why didn't he say so up front if he believes it so strongly?" ("Recent Revelations," 1989, p. 8). Taylor said he would not have fired MacDougall for being a socialist but would have had he known of his extracurricular writing.[11] He said he was especially upset about defending MacDougall against conservative attack and then finding he was a leftist after all (p. 9).

Three columns labeled MacDougall a "Marxist" (Cheshire, 1989; McCarthy, 1989; Morris, 1989), a term he did not use to describe himself and one with more negative connotations than "socialist." One of these writers found it disturbing that MacDougall "abused that position of trust," adding that he not only "insinuated his flaky politics into news stories" but unethically contributed to radical publications under a nom de plume. The same writer disparaged MacDougall's father, describing his arrival at an editorial writers conference, "shambling and snarling along, attended by a handful of admirers" (Cheshire, 1989). One article used a loaded term in saying, inaccurately, that MacDougall claimed to have worked to popularize "Marxist dogma" (Vick, 1989). The *Time* article termed MacDougall's career "shadowy"[12] and featured a picture of Karl Marx with the caption, "his favorite newsman." (In his two-piece *Monthly Review* contribution, MacDougall had called Marx his favorite journalist— the only mention in the 27 pages.)

Discussion

I have used this case to illustrate an important theoretical intersection of hegemony, a Kuhnian paradigm, and journalistic practice. Tracing the epistemological roots of objectivity as it relates to the news paradigm directs attention toward the type of knowledge made possible by this model of information gathering and its ideological implications—and away from the traditional news research question of whether that knowledge represents some distortion of an actual external reality. I have discussed this news paradigm in an ideological context in order to link it to the larger hegemonic process. We can learn much about the limits of the paradigm by observing such nonroutine cases and by examining the discourse surrounding the anomaly as repair work is engaged. The journalistic community must undertake this repair if the model is to remain effective, and the ongoing repair project must function within a hegemonic framework, articulated by the dominant ideology.

Although the limited commentary on the MacDougall incident restricted the materials available for analysis, that lack itself suggests the mainstream press's difficulty in dealing with the issue. However, repair work can be discerned in the case. This repair necessarily focused on MacDougall himself and the issues he raised rather than on his stories, which had been written long ago and could not be spiked or re-edited.

It could be argued that the lack of coverage indicates that the case was not problematic, or was less so than other cases. Janet Cooke's fabricated story for the *Washington Post*, for example, generated much more commentary. Perhaps her Pulitzer Prize gave her a higher profile. More likely, fabricating stories outright represents a more direct threat to the paradigm than using values to guide reporting.

As in the "man on fire" case, here repair work relied largely on the assertion that readily available and reliable professional routines constitute a reliable news paradigm; the editing process was asserted to have worked to perfection. Three strategies of repair were employed: (a) disengaging the reporter's values from the news; (b) reaffirming journalistic routines, especially the editing process; and (c) marginalizing and minimizing the man and the effectiveness of his message.

Different people within the media engage in different kinds of repair work. Certainly, MacDougall's immediate editors had less problem with his work than did the *Journal*'s top editor, Taylor, and its corporate office, which issued the denunciatory letter. These higher levels in the media system are more concerned with protecting the paradigm at the institutional level. And editors at the lower echelon could not easily attack MacDougall's stories, given that they had personally approved them. Future studies may want to probe the different forms of paradigm repair performed at different levels of media systems.

The repair process helps us understand how the paradigm reinforces and justifies hegemonic boundaries. By crossing the lines of hegemonic acceptability, the case required that the paradigm be reaffirmed. Of particular note is that MacDougall prompted greater attack from the Right than from the Left, perhaps not surprising given his value system. The discovery of a conservative at the *Wall Street Journal* surely would have caused no rush to defend journalistic routines. This differential attention to violations of the leftward border shows the importance of interpreting the news paradigm within its hegemonic context.

The most strongly worded media industry complaint was from Dow Jones.[13] Perhaps, as MacDougall suggested, the company wanted to avoid offending its conservative subscriber base ("Recent Revelations," 1989, p. 9). He notes that the Dow Jones reaction escalated from Charles Stabler's negative but mild comment ("He wasn't taken that seriously") in December to the "offended and outraged" letter in January, with the intervening event being the right-wing December 24 attack in *Human Events* (personal communication, June 5, 1989).[14] That article charged that the *Journal* sheltered other "left-wing" reporters, including Jonathan Kwitny (Kincaid, 1988).

Herman and Chomsky (1988) would characterize this as successful "flak"—negative responses to the media that include complaints, threats, petitions, letters, and articles. In their view, flak originates mostly from the Right—including foundations, think tanks, and media monitors like Accuracy in Media—and is designed to harass, intimidate, discipline, and generally keep the media from straying too far from acceptable elite viewpoints. Certainly, mainstream journalism gives more attention to attacks from the Right than from the Left. One could argue that Dow Jones was obliged to respond to right-wing flak. Alternatively, flak may be considered a paradigm maintenance device. Clearly, judging from the frequency of attacks from conservatives, the paradigm is showing signs of wear on its right flank and may have to be shored up there in particular.

The Left stance finds value in being apart from "the system," while the Right finds journalists outside the "system" to be necessarily inimicable to it. In both cases, the usually invisible "system" comes into view; the objectivity framework becomes shakier as one moves toward either end of the political spectrum. An Accuracy in Media Report (quoted in "Comment," 1989, p. 16) noted that the MacDougall case "explodes the myth that our media have effective safeguards to screen out propaganda hostile to our country and our system." On the other hand, MacDougall found support in a *Washington Post* column: Coleman McCarthy (1989) criticized writers and reporters for often being glorified dictationists, thereby supporting MacDougall's assertion that journalists improve their vantage point by stepping outside the system—and further indicating the inherent tension embedded in the news paradigm.

Conservative press critics recognize more than media insiders that story selection is a form of bias. The growing right-wing industry of press criticism (Accuracy in Media, MediaWatch, etc.) has at least called into question the prevailing news paradigm, pointing out the power of selectivity as a way of bypassing the filters of "objectifying" routines. Kincaid (1989, p. 7), for example, quotes Joe Farah, editor of *Between the Lines*, who notes that many Left journalists "got into the media . . . because they saw it as a way of changing the world. And you can do that by choosing to write certain stories." Conservative critics must elevate the power of the individual journalist over the objectifying structural routines or else render moot their frequent "liberal journalist" charge.

The case also points out the paradigmatic dilemma faced by journalists on the Left. On the one hand, they can speak out forthrightly (as Alexander Cockburn recommends) and be relegated to small-circulation publications like *The Nation*, where their impact is minimal. On the other hand, they can choose mainstream journalism and reach a wider audience. There, though, they will be frustrated and constrained by the mainstream news paradigm and perhaps criticized for "selling out" or, as MacDougall was, for "masquerading." For example, MacDougall's editor made him introduce a conservative spokesperson to balance a story about inequality: "Even though I knew he was wrong, I quoted Gilder as saying that the growing gap between rich and poor was almost entirely demographic" (MacDougall, 1988b, p. 18). Another example of paradigmatic limits is seen in MacDougall's editor's allowing him to mention Marx but only if introduced in a humorous way. MacDougall agreed in order to get the story in print (MacDougall, 1988b, p. 17).

When MacDougall came under attack, he fell back on a strongly paradigmatic defense: that he had followed the guidelines of "accuracy, fairness and newsworthiness." [15] He made another important point in his defense, however: that radical journalists may be even more objective than "bourgeois" journalists, who are often not conscious of the presuppositions that they bring to their reporting on capitalist institutions (MacDougall, 1988b, p. 22, 1989b). By taking the "system" itself as problematic, radical journalists may be better equipped to address the structural causes for social ills. The *Columbia Journalism Review* article supported this claim that socialist perspectives can contribute to robust journalism, hearkening back to the muckraking socialist journalists at the turn of the century who called the country's attention to the Beef Trust, child labor, and urban poverty ("Comment," 1989).

Like ideology, a paradigm is not static but continually negotiated. Like ideology, the news paradigm contains self-contradictory oppositional values, such as a diversity of views in the newsroom versus objective, value-free reporting. These values must be managed and adapted to the ideological requirements of the large society. In this article, I have explored from an ideological perspective the nature of the news paradigm and some of its constitutive norms and practices. The MacDougall case helps illustrate the power of the news paradigm, as an occupational ideology, in enforcing boundaries within the mainstream press, and the way this power functions within the large hegemonic process.

Notes

1. The news paradigm has been remarkably resilient over the years. During the 1960s, the Left mounted an attack with some success, particularly following the observation

of discrepancies between the reality of social upheavals (Vietnam, campus unrest, civil rights marches) and mainstream press coverage of them. More recently, the Right has seized the momentum and has been more successful in keeping the media on the defensive.

2. My focus in this article is not on reading off ideological codes from news texts or in evaluating them against some yardstick of bias, but on the news paradigm itself and what the contesting interpretations of the case tell us about that paradigm. The "meta-commentary" I examined did not center on an evaluation of specific articles, but rather on the reliability of news practices and whether strongly held beliefs should influence a journalist's work.

3. His newspaper career included four Pulitzer Prize nominations and a Professional Journalism Fellowship at Stanford University (1969-1970). In addition, he edited one book (1972) and wrote another (1981), both published by Dow Jones.

4. Most of MacDougall's writing for the Left press was done on the side during his five years at the *Herald-News*. He stopped the practice after six months at the *Wall Street Journal* (MacDougall, 1988a, pp. 17-18).

5. I wish to thank Gale Wiley of the University of Texas Department of Journalism for help with accessing the VuText database.

6. Scardino says the second story was set to run at the end of January or first of February and was to have coincided with a review of a new book by journalist Carl Bernstein, *Loyalties: A Son's Memoir*, about growing up with his left-wing parents. As it happened, the *Times* review was negative, and according to Scardino editors were reluctant to peg a story to a panned book (although one wonders why that should have made any difference). Scardino says reaction in his second story divided along generational lines. Younger editors tended to want passionate reporters, not just processors of data, while older editors hewed closer to the wire-service, "just the facts ma'am" model. Certainly, changing generations provide a major source of evolution in the news paradigm.

7. MacDougall says that *The Nation* also apparently ordered up a major story but declined to run it (personal communication, June 5, 1989).

8. This line recalls the Watergate case, in which it was said that "the system worked" by successfully rooting out political wrongdoing. In this sense, Watergate became not a threat to the system but an opportunity to reaffirm it. When successfully repaired, anomalous cases can have the same effect.

9. The exception may be Warren Phillips, first of four managing editors MacDougall served under and now chairman of Dow Jones. MacDougall contends that Phillips is principally responsible for the denunciatory January letter (personal communication, June 5, 1989).

10. Even a seemingly natural ally, *Journal* op-ed contributor Alexander Cockburn, got into the act. Cockburn, whom ironically MacDougall praised as a "sophisticated, stylish leftist critic" (MacDougall, 1988b, p. 23), attacked MacDougall for not making his views forthrightly. He minimized MacDougall in one such column using phrases like "a man called Kent MacDougall," and "revealed with schoolboyish glee," later calling him "Walter Mittyish."

11. The *Wall Street Journal* does not appear to have a firm policy on its staff members writing for outside publications, and many writers do so, although I was told by a corporate relations spokesperson (March 29, 1989) that they would not want such work to reflect unfavorably on the paper.

12. MacDougall says that the writer later apologized to him for that term, claiming that an editor had inserted it over his objection (personal communication, June 5, 1989).

13. MacDougall considers it an important distinction that the attack on him originated from Dow Jones (the January 6 statement came from Dan Austin, Dow Jones Director of Corporate Relations) and not the *Journal*, (personal communication, June 5, 1989). I have observed that distinction in this article.

14. *TJFR: The Journalist & Financial Reporting*, however, ran its first story, a lengthy front-page feature, in the first week of January, just before the Dow Jones letter. One can speculate whether the letter responded more to the conservative attack or to publicity *TJFR* gave the case among business journalism insiders.

15. In my initial telephone interview with MacDougall (March 21, 1989), he resisted the notion that his story would make a good case study on objectivity because he had not violated any of the rules. After obtaining an initial draft of this article, he sent along several articles that I had missed as well as several pages of comments, which clearly demonstrated his penchant for meticulous reporting and helped me improve the accuracy of this article.

References

Austin, D. (1989, January 6). [Corporate relations statement]. Dow Jones & Company, Inc.

Becker, S. (1984). Marxist approaches to media studies: The British experience. *Critical Studies in Mass Communication, 1*, 66-80.

Benneth, J. E. (1989, March 7). [Letter to the editor]. *Wall Street Journal*, p. A-21.

Bennett, W. L., Gressett, L. A., & Haltom, W. (1985). Repairing the news: A case study of the news paradigm. *Journal of Communication, 35*(2), 50-68.

Breed, W. (1955). Social control in the newsroom: A functional analysis. *Social Forces, 33*, 326-335.

Cheshire, W. P. (1989, February 5). Kent MacDougall: The journalist who came in from the cold (column). *Arizona Republic*, p. C-4.

Cockburn, A. (1989, February 9). Secret life of radical journalist pure milquetoast [Column]. *Wall Street Journal*, p. A-19.

Comment: The case of the closet socialist. (1989, March/April). *Columbia Journalism Review*, pp. 16-17.

Dreier, P. (1982). The position of the press in the U.S. power structure. *Social Problems, 29*, 298-310.

Forrest, D. (1989). *Journalism reporting on itself: Paradigm maintenance in the R. Budd Dwyer and Gary Hart cases.* Unpublished master's thesis, University of Texas, Austin.

Foucault, M. (1980). *Power/knowledge.* New York: Pantheon.

Gandy, O., Jr. (1982). *Beyond agenda setting: Information subsidies and public policy.* Norwood, NJ: Ablex.

Gans, H. (1979). *Deciding what's news.* New York: Random House.

Gitlin, T. (1980). *The whole world is watching.* Berkeley: University of California Press.

Gomes, L. (1989, March 27). When a radical comes out of the closet [Business profile]. *Tribune* [Oakland, CA], p. B-8.

Hackett, R. A. (1984). Decline of a paradigm? Bias and objectivity in news media studies. *Critical Studies in Mass Communication, 1*, 229-259.

Hall, S. (1985). Signification, representation, ideology: Althusser and the post-structuralist debates. *Critical Studies in Mass Communication, 2*, 91-114.

Herman, E., & Chomsky, N. (1988). *Manufacturing consent: The political economy of the mass media.* New York: Pantheon.

Hertsgaard, M. (1988). *On bended knee: The press and the Reagan presidency.* New York: Farrar, Straus, Giroux.

Irvine, R. (1989, February 15). [Letter to the editor]. *Los Angeles Times*, p. 6.

Kincaid, C. (1988, December 24). The *Wall Street Journal's* "closet socialist." *Human Events*, pp. 4-6.

Kincaid, C. (1989, March 4). How many media moles are out there? *Human Events*, pp. 6-7.

Kuhn, T. S. (1962). *The structure of scientific revolutions.* Chicago: University of Chicago Press.

Kwitny, J. (1984). *Endless enemies: The making of an unfriendly world.* New York: St. Martin's.

MacDougall, A. K. (Ed.). (1972). *The press: A critical look from the inside.* New York: Dow Jones.

MacDougall, A. K. (1981). *Ninety seconds to tell it all: Big business and the news media.* New York: Dow Jones.

MacDougall, A. K. (1988a). Boring from within the bourgeois press: Part one. *Monthly Review, 40*(7), 13-24.

MacDougall, A. K. (1988b). Boring from within the bourgeois press: Part two. *Monthly Review, 40*(8), 10-24.

MacDougall, A. K. (1989a, March/April). Memoirs of a radical in the mainstream press. *Columbia Journalism Review,* pp. 36-41.

MacDougall, A. K. (1989b, March 7). Closet case: Leftists in the news room [Letter to the editor]. *Wall Street Journal,* p. A-21.

McCarthy, C. (1989, February 25). Confessions of a Marxist newsman [Column]. *Washington Post,* p. A-23.

Mouffe, C. (1981). Hegemony and ideology in Gramsci. In T. Bennett et al. (Eds.), *Culture, ideology and social process* (pp. 219-234). London: Open University Press.

Morris, D. R. (1989, March 2). Marxist slanted his stories, but few got the message [Column]. *Houston Post,* p. A-29.

Murdock, G., & Golding, P. (1979). Capitalism, communication and class relations. In J. Curran, M. Gurevitch, & J. Woollacott (Eds.), *Mass communication and society* (pp. 12-43). Beverly Hills, CA: Sage.

Parenti, M. (1986). *Inventing reality: Politics and the mass media.* New York: St. Martin's.

Radical doings at Wall St. Journal. (1988, December 15). *New York Post,* p. 6.

Recent revelations of a "closet" socialist stir strong emotions among journalists. (1989, January). *TJFR: The Journalist & Financial Reporting, 3*(2), 1, 8-9.

Reese, S., & Danielian, L. (1989). Intermedia influence and the drug issue: Converging on cocaine. In P. Shoemaker (Ed.), *Communication campaigns about drugs: Government, media, and the public* (pp. 29-46). Hillsdale, NJ: Lawrence Erlbaum.

Rotbart, D. (1989a, January). A socialist in the capitalist press. *TJFR: The Journalist & Financial Reporting, 3*(1), 1, 11-14.

Rotbart, D. (1989b, March). A hidden agenda. *Fame,* pp. 16, 18, 20.

Scholle, D. (1988). Critical studies: From the theory of ideology to power/knowledge. *Critical Studies in Mass Communication, 5,* 16-41.

Schudson, M. (1978). *Discovering the news.* New York: Basic Books.

Shaw, D. (1989a, January 31). A "closet socialist" stirs furor over news stories: Ex-reporter tells of radical ideas. *Los Angeles Times,* pp. 1, 15-16.

Shaw, D. (1989b, February 3). Leftist reporter's boast raises a ruckus [Syndicated reprint of Shaw, 1989a]. *San Francisco Chronicle.*

Sheehan, N. (1988). *A bright shining lie: John Paul Vann and America in Vietnam.* New York: Random House.

Sigal, L. V. (1973). *Reporters and officials.* Lexington, MA: D. C. Health.

Stein, M. L. (1989, March 18). Radical defends his revelation. *Editor & Publisher,* pp. 10, 11.

Taylor, M. (1989, February 3). What's all the fuss? The writer asks [Sidebar to Shaw, 1989b]. *San Francisco Chronicle,* p. 16.

Tuchman, G. (1972). Objectivity as strategic ritual: An examination of newsmen's notions of objectivity. *American Sociological Review, 77,* 660-679.

Tuchman, G. (1978). *Making news: A study in the construction of reality.* New York: Free Press.

Vick, K. (1989, March 5). Reporter's hidden agenda gives fuel to media critics. *St. Petersburg Times.*

Walljasper, J. (1989, May/June). Is there any hope for the mainstream press? *Utne Reader,* pp. 126-127.

Wetzel, F. (1989, March 12). Journalism needs divergent points of view [Ombudsman column]. *Seattle Times,* p. 25.

Zuckerman, L. (1989, February 6). Confessions of a closet leftist: A veteran reporter reveals his 24-year undercover career. *Time, 133*(6), 58.

CHAPTER **28**

News of Battering

Marian Meyers

In 1974, Erin Pizzey published *Scream Quietly or the Neighbors Will Hear*, the first book about battered wives. Released in England, this pioneering effort helped ignite the battered women's movement on both sides of the Atlantic by increasing awareness of the problem as well as efforts to establish shelters for battered women and their children.

Two decades later, an estimated 3 to 4 million American women are battered by their husbands and boyfriends each year (Stark et al., 1981). Some estimate that as many as 50% of all women will be battered at some point in their lives (Mahoney, 1991, p. 3; Walker, 1979, p. ix). Among all female victims of murders in 1989, the FBI (1990) reports, 28% were believed slain by husbands or boyfriends (p. 12). However, getting out of an abusive relationship is often more dangerous than remaining inside one. Separated or divorced women were 14 times more likely than married women to report having been a victim of violence by a spouse or ex-spouse, accounting for 75% of reported spousal violence (Harlow, 1991, p. 5).

From *Journal of Communication*, 1994, Vol. 44, No. 2, pp. 47-63. Used by permission of Oxford University Press.

AUTHOR'S NOTE: The author wishes to thank Cassandra Amesley and Mary Ellen Brown for helpful comments on an earlier draft of this article, and Dick Bathrick and Gus Kaufman for their valuable insights about news coverage of Wanda Walters's murder.

Given the epidemic proportions of the problem, one may well ask how the news media have represented battering in the years since Pizzey named wife abuse as a serious social problem.[1] Unfortunately, the answer would have to be that very little research has been done in this area. With one exception (Finn, 1989-1990), researchers have largely ignored news coverage of battering.

The goals of this study were to (1) expand on current understandings of news representations and social construction by exploring an area of coverage previously neglected by news scholars; and (2) explore linkages between social constructions of gender, race, and class in the signification of sexist violence. To do this, I focused on news representations of battering, the batterer, and the battered woman.

The findings indicate that news coverage of battering is socially distorted, rooted in assumptions, myths, and stereotypes that link it to individual and family pathology rather than to social structures and gendered patterns of domination and control. The analysis also suggests that previous theorizing about crime reporting ignored the victimization of women and therefore may be applicable only when the victim is male. In addition, this study demonstrates the necessity of applying feminist theory to established communication theory as a way to check communication theory for gender-related biases.

Deviance and Battering

Most media scholars concur that the news, by and large, supports the status quo by primarily representing the interests of a ruling elite.[2] Those working within British cultural studies (Brunsdon & Morley, 1978; Hall, 1977, 1982; Hall, Connell, & Curti, 1977; Hartley, 1982) and other critical perspectives (Gitlin, 1980; Molotch & Lester, 1974) have emphasized that the news works ideologically to support the dominant power structure by creating a consensus that appears grounded in everyday reality. This consensus, produced through language and symbolization, legitimizes the hegemony of the ruling social formation by manufacturing the consent of the governed (Gramsci, 1971, 1983).

Critical researchers claim this consent is produced partly by the media, which portray crime and deviance as ripping at the social fabric of community and family values (Cohen & Young, 1973; Ericson, Baranek, & Chan, 1987; Hall, Critcher, Jefferson, Clarke, & Roberts, 1978). The ensuing moral panic created by the media is then used by the ruling classes to justify the imposition of a law-and-order society. Based on this argument, one might expect crimes of violence against women to be the target of a law-and-order campaign directed at eradicating this threat to family and society. However, the crime-as-deviance theorists failed to recognize the gendered nature of violence and so never examined violence specifically directed against women by men.

The theoretical framework for understanding battering appears similar to the framework for understanding rape. Stoltenberg (1989) notes that "the ethics of male sexual identity are essentially rapist" (p. 19) and are promulgated by social myths: "Women want to be raped, women deserve to be raped, women provoke rape, women need to be raped, and women enjoy being raped" (p. 20). The same is said about battering. Pagelow (1981) emphasizes that myths and stereotypes about battered women are pervasive and serve "to victimize the victim(s) further by stigmatizing them or helping to keep them locked in their violent relationships" (p. 88). She noted that the primary myths about battering are: (1) Those involved are pathological—the woman is masochistic, the batterer is "sick"; (2) the woman provoked him; (3) the woman must have had a reason for staying; (4) battered women never press charges; and (5) battering is restricted to the "lower classes" (p. 54).

This mythology reinforces the dominant social context and structure by obscuring the relationship of male supremacy to anti-women violence. Battering then appears unconnected to the

> historical development of the isolated nuclear family in a capitalist society, to division of the public and private/domestic domains, to specialization of "appropriate" male and female family roles, and to the current position of wives as legally and morally bound to husbands. (Bograd, 1988, pp. 14-15)

Dobash and Dobash (1979) also trace the origin of anti-woman violence to the structure of the patriarchal family. They point out that battering is a form of male control and domination within a social hierarchy. Dworkin (1981) places this hierarchy within the context of the "seven tenets of male supremacy." The second tenet is that "men are physically stronger than women and, for that reason, have dominion over them" (p. 14). Along with that dominion, she adds, is the capacity to terrorize a whole class of persons (the third tenet) and the right to own women (tenet five) (pp. 14-19). Pharr (1988) credits the interaction between economics, violence, and homophobia with keeping patriarchy in place. She emphasizes that violence against women is misogynistic, related to the condition of women in society:

> Men physically and emotionally abuse women because they can, because they live in a world that gives them permission. Male violence is fed by their sense of their right to dominate and control, and their sense of superiority over a group of people who, because of gender, they consider inferior to them. (p. 14)

The result of this systemic misogyny is that the battering of women is a "predictable and common dimension of normal family life" (Bograd, 1988, p. 14). The brutalization of women by men is seen as neither accidental nor random, but intentional, goal oriented, and calculated, "the heritage of a patriarchal society" (Fortune, 1990, p. 1).

Traditional sociologists and psychologists, however, tend to see battering not as the practice of male supremacy but as the result of family dysfunction. Their approaches are concerned with patterns of relationships among families or couples, as well as the culture, norms, and values guiding behavior, and violence is seen as a response by both sexes to structural and situational stimuli. Most psychodynamic explanations also minimize anti-woman abuse by reinterpreting it as an ineffectual attempt to meet a normal human need, such as intimacy or mastery (Avis, 1991, p. 10). Thus, "the majority of nonfeminist clinicians and researchers approach various forms of domestic violence . . . as symptomatic of distinct family dynamics, psychopathology and stress" (Stark & Flitcraft, 1988, p. 294). For example, systems theory focuses on "the processes that occur and the interrelationships between events, people, or other elements of the system" (Giles-Sims, 1983, p. 18). In a system consisting of a woman and a man, systems theory asks what circumstances precipitated battering: Was it something the woman said or did?

Feminists reject this traditional approach as an example of blaming the victim. They argue that male violence against women differs from other forms of domination "because it converges with broader patterns of discrimination" (Stark & Flitcraft, 1988, p. 294). And they seek answers to the question of anti-woman violence at the group or social level, not the individual level, by attempting to understand the role of this abuse within a given society during a specific, historical juncture (Bograd, 1988, p. 13).

According to Pharr (1988), the division between traditional and feminist perspectives is reflected in the battered women's movement, which was begun by women with a more radical agenda than generally exists within the movement today. As social workers have replaced feminist activists at shelters seeking more legitimacy and funding, the movement has been pressured "to provide services only, without analysis of the causes of violence against women and strategies for ending it" (p. 24).

Feminist scholars also have found this lack of analysis within the news, which they claim is the product of a male perspective that perpetuates stereotypes and myths while ridiculing or minimizing women's concerns (Mills, 1988; Molotch, 1978; Sanders & Rock, 1988; Tuchman, 1978; Tuchman, Daniels, & Benet, 1978). Yet, despite their general critique of the news as serving the interests of male supremacy, they have largely ignored the question of how the news covers an issue central to the perpetuation of male domination and control—that of battering. Indeed, Finn's (1989-1990) research is unique in having examined news coverage of *domestic terrorism*—a term she uses to include child abuse and rape, as well as battering. Finn concluded that the state and the media collude to exonerate male perpetrators of these crimes and that the inequalities of social relations "encourage and condone" violence against women and children (p. 381).

For the most part, though, a feminist critique of news coverage of battering has been left to activists within the battered women's movement. For example, Fortune (1988), the founder and executive director of the Center for the Prevention of Sexual and Domestic Violence in Seattle, Washington, says, "One of the primary blocks to justice for all women is the serious distortion of our experience which comes to us from many directions, but particularly comes to us through the media" (p. 9). Peck (1987), who has worked with the London Rape Crisis Center, observes: "Over and over comes the message: men can't help it, and even if they could, women deserve it anyway" (p. 103).

Activists also have pointed to the interconnections between sexist violence and racism, as well as the media's role in perpetuating both. Adams (1990), writing in the newsletter of Seattle's Center for the Prevention of Sexual and Domestic Violence, notes that racism and sexism work together to promote the myth that "the villains are those who are 'others' in our society" rather than suburban husbands (p. 2). She points to the Stuart case in Boston, in which a white suburbanite claimed a black man killed his pregnant wife, as evidence of the media's willingness to believe and perpetuate that myth.[3]

Although the coverage of battering remains to be studied by communication scholars, research on rape coverage may be applicable. Studies that compared crime statistics with rape coverage indicate that the news downplays the extent of the crime through underreporting and distorts what is reported through the omission of significant details (Lemert, 1989). Schwengels and Lemert (1986) found that rape coverage was highly selective and "portrayed a 'reality' that differed from police reports" (p. 42). Based on news reports, they stated, potential victims could wrongly conclude from the news that rape only occurs in dangerous parts of town and not at home. Heath, Gordon, and LeBailly (1981) noted that rape stories had fewer details than stories about murder or assault. And Gordon and Riger (1989) concluded that rape coverage "enhances women's fears and leaves misleading impressions of both the crime and how it might be dealt with" (p. 132). More responsible treatment by the press, they suggest, could dispel myths about the victim, location of the assault, and the victim's relationship with her assailant (p. 134).

While the notion of gender as a semiotic system of meaning is not new among feminists (DeLauretis, 1987; Mulvey, 1975), few have attempted to examine women as signs within the masculine discourse of news; fewer still have explored the signification of anti-women violence within the news. Among the exceptions are Rakow and Kranich (1991), who studied women sources as signs within the news. They found that women are used to illustrate the private consequences of public events and actions, as spokespersons for organizations and institutions, and as "unusual signs" or feminists. They also found that "only white women were allowed to signify as 'women,' " so that "the meaning of the sign 'woman,' bound up as it is with the assumption of whiteness, is critical to the construction of both a gender system and a race system" (p. 19).

Bumiller's (1990) and Chancer's (1987) analyses of the rape trial of six Portuguese men in New Bedford, Massachusetts, took a semiotic approach to the coverage of violence against a woman. Bumiller concluded that news coverage may have reinforced dominant preconceptions about women, men, and sexual violence. By satisfying the "internal logic of the legal system" (p. 140)—which is itself a masculine discourse[4]—the trial and press coverage of it may have actually "narrowed the interpretive framework for understanding the crime" (p. 130). Chancer, on the other hand, explored how media portrayals helped exonerate the rapists while focusing the anger of New Bedford's Portuguese community at the rape victim.

Unlike Chancer's and Bumiller's research, the focus of this study is not on rape, but the murder of a battered woman as represented within the news. The analysis presented here is an attempt to broaden the interpretive framework for understanding news coverage of violence against women by including battering.

Examining the Text

My study is based on a close textual analysis of two articles in the *Atlanta Journal-Constitution* about the murder of Wanda Walters by her husband, Dennis. The first article, written by Katie Long, appeared in the morning *Atlanta Constitution* on August 11, 1990. The second, written by Gary Pomerantz, appeared in the Sunday *Atlanta Journal-Constitution* on September 9, 1990. No other articles about the murder appeared in the Atlanta newspapers.

The *Atlanta Journal-Constitution*—consisting of the morning *Constitution*, the afternoon *Journal*, and the combined Sunday edition, the *Atlanta Journal-Constitution*—is owned by Cox Enterprises. The Sunday circulation of 700,739 (Gale, 1993) makes it one of the largest circulation newspapers in the South. Gary Moore (1992) contends that under the leadership of editor Ron Martin, who helped bring out *USA Today* for Gannett, the *Atlanta Journal-Constitution* in recent years has adopted a *USA Today* approach and has settled for complacency rather than striving for journalistic excellence. This is not to say that the *Atlanta Journal-Constitution* is a bad newspaper; it is simply unremarkable when compared to papers such as the considerably smaller *Louisville Courier-Journal*, which has won the highest number of Pulitzer Prizes in the South.

In using textual analysis as a methodology to disclose underlying meanings, this study acknowledges both the polysemia of the text—that is, its inability to close off meanings—and the reader's individual decoding strategies, which are related to the reader's understandings, background, and experiences (Morley 1980, 1985). Any number of interpretations are possible, although Eco (1990) cautions that all interpretations are contextually bound. In the case of this study, the reading is informed by a feminist analysis of battering derived from feminist theory and, in particular, the battered women's movement. By applying feminist theory to an analysis of the text, then, this study is explicitly a feminist analysis of the news coverage of Wanda Walters's murder.

On the night of August 9, 1990, Wanda, who had previously moved out of the couple's suburban Atlanta home, returned to pick up her remaining possessions. Dennis shot Wanda four times in the back and then shot himself in the head. She died on the driveway, where she was shot; he died 24 hours later in a hospital.

News coverage of Wanda's murder was chosen for this study because it was extensive and in-depth—the result of Dennis's high profile as director of the city's Cyclorama, a popular tourist attraction that depicts the Civil War's Battle of Atlanta. Because social prominence is directly related to access to the news media (Gans, 1980; Sigal, 1973), it is reasonable to assume that the murders of women who are poor and black are less likely to receive extensive coverage (or any coverage) than are the murders of women who are white, middle- and upper-class. The more socially prominent the people involved—that is, the higher their "social ranking" (Roshco, 1975)—the more extensive and prominent the coverage.

A good deal of Dennis's job-related high profile was the result of Dennis having fought, and won, a reverse discrimination lawsuit against the city for the Cyclorama position. In addition, the in-depth coverage may have been a result of the unusual circumstances of the relationship between Wanda and Dennis, who was 23 years her senior. According to the articles, they became sexually involved when Wanda was 14 years old and Dennis was married to his third wife. Dennis and his wife then adopted Wanda, and Dennis later divorced his wife, signed away his adoption rights, and married Wanda.

The two articles about the murder of Wanda Walters were prominently displayed—particularly the follow-up. The first story began on the front page of the metropolitan-state news section of the newspaper. Its jump[5] contained two photos—one a head shot of Dennis Walters, which noted he "sued city to get Cyclorama job," and the other of the suburban home that was the "crime scene."

The second story was an in-depth feature that attempted to explain how the murder came about. It began at the top of the front page of the Sunday paper, where it covered five of the newspaper's six columns and included a photo of Dennis and Wanda in 1986 "as father and daughter." The jump took up almost a full page and contained four more pictures. A small insert of the couple "as man and wife" was in the middle of the page, and two photos of Dennis in a professional capacity were at the bottom. The representations of Wanda and Dennis in the photos in both stories emphasize her dependence on him for definition and his independence through his work. There are no photos of Wanda other than those defining her role as wife to Dennis's man (not husband) or as daughter to his father.

The largest and most prominent photo, at the top of the jump page, was of Wanda's mother, Louvale Westbrooks—slouched in a torn reclining chair, overweight and barefoot, a grandchild at her feet. In this photo, a floor lamp with neither bulb nor shade is near a porch door propped open by what appears to be a ceiling light fixture. The cinderblock wall behind the door appears dirty. The cutline, echoing a theme within the story, informs the reader that she "caught Dennis Walters and her 14-year-old daughter having sex." The convergence of class, gender, and race in this photo and cutline signify Wanda's mother not simply as a poor, white woman, but as a poor, white woman unable or unwilling to care about her appearance or to exert moral control over her young daughter. Within the historically distinct race, class, and gender consciousness of the South, she is made to signify what many Southerners, black and white, disdain as "white trash." [6] In this way, Wanda is defined not only by her relationship to Dennis, but by her relationship to her mother. If her mother is trash, so, then, is she.

Pathology as Excuse

In the stories, Dennis's mental state is used to explain why he killed Wanda and then himself. The first story merely quotes a police officer's opinion that Dennis Walters apparently "was having an extremely difficult time dealing with" his separation from Wanda. However, from the first sentence of the second article—"Dennis Walters was a man of obsessions"— his emotional and mental health are framed as obsessive and are represented as the cause of his actions: Dennis "used a blue-steel Colt revolver to fight his personal obsession"; Wanda's first attempt to leave him "fell prey to Dennis Walters's obsession" when he broke down the door to her apartment, beat her, and took her home with him.

Dennis also "brooded" over the impending divorce and Wanda's new boyfriend, and he "fumed" about her staying out late—or all night—in the months prior to their separation. His brother is quoted as saying he believed Dennis "ultimately was broken by the notion of having lost his wife to another man" and that he "was not of sound mind" six weeks before the murder when he wrote a will that alluded to what was to come and requested a double funeral. Drawing on a deposition from the reverse discrimination lawsuit against the city, the article even quotes then Mayor Andrew Young calling Dennis "a nut." Dennis's mental condition on the night of the murder is of particular concern: Dennis had been drinking, heated words were exchanged, and "something snapped," causing Dennis to go into the house for a gun with which to shoot Wanda and then himself.

The notion that "something snapped" implies a spontaneous reaction, a spur-of-the-moment, uncontrollable response. (This belies the fact that Wanda's murder appears to have been planned at least six weeks earlier, when Dennis wrote his will.) The representation of Dennis as obsessed or out of control offers both a rationale and an excuse for his actions. As a pathological individual, a victim of his own obsession, he is not responsible for his behavior. Even the statement that Dennis "apparently had planned the tragedy"—not the murder, but the "tragedy"—denies his responsibility. Tragedy does not happen to the perpetrators of crimes. To characterize what happened as a tragedy is to represent Dennis Walters as a victim, just as Wanda was.

As yet another indication of his mental state, as well as what the newspaper characterized as Dennis's ability to be "headstrong," the feature story notes that Dennis "had played Russian roulette with Wanda, pointing a gun at her head and clicking the trigger." Wanda's brother explains Dennis's actions by recounting what Dennis told him: There was a dud bullet in the gun, and Dennis was merely testing Wanda's "toughness." However, the term "Russian roulette" generally assumes a voluntary "game" of reciprocal bravado in which participants spin a gun with one cartridge in it on its side until it points to a person who then puts the gun to her or his own head and pulls the trigger. There is no indication that Wanda agreed to have a gun put to her head, nor that Dennis participated in the game as Wanda's target. By referring to Dennis's actions as "playing" Russian roulette, the article denies the seriousness of what was essentially an act of terrorization and domination.

Blaming the Victim

In addition, by representing Dennis's obsession as the reason for his actions, Wanda becomes the only one who is in control of the situation. If she let it get out of hand, then, she has no one but herself to blame. This blaming of the victim "diverts attention from the true abuser or the cause of the victimization" (Pharr, 1988, p. 60) and becomes a primary barrier to social change (Ryan, 1971).

The news codes of *objectivity* and *balance*—of getting both sides of the story—also negate the seriousness of the crime and represent Wanda as at least partly at fault. The first article notes the conditions surrounding the shooting: Dennis "had been drinking" when Wanda stopped by for her belongings and an "argument erupted." While this implicates alcohol and, by extension, Dennis, it also exonerates him because he was, presumably, under the influence. Besides, it is not clear from the article who started the argument.

But the follow-up article is quite specific in pointing to provocations by Wanda, who, like Dennis, is characterized as "headstrong and prone to jealousy." After detailing how Dennis would "test" Wanda's toughness with Russian roulette, the article attempts to achieve balance by noting that Wanda "could test her husband's toughness in other ways." She wore "the fancy dresses her husband had purchased for their social events" when she "left alone for the evening for an unannounced destination" from which she returned after midnight. Occasionally, the article added, Wanda even "stopped at her husband's home at 6 a.m. to shower" before going to work. She also is reported to have "playfully" suggested to her estranged husband that perhaps they could begin to date again after the divorce. And she was "wearing his mother's diamond-studded necklace" when she arrived to pick up her belongings the night she was murdered. Wanda's choice of clothing and jewelry is presented as equivalent to Dennis's pointing a gun to her head and pulling the trigger. Both actions are represented as ways they tested each other's toughness, although Wanda's also is signified as provocation.

Behind the representation of Wanda's attire as attempts to provoke Dennis is the notion that he had a right to determine what she wore, that he was entitled to control Wanda's choice of clothing and, by extension, her body. The signification of women's clothing and bodies as provocation is central to the belief that a woman causes her own victimization by what she wears, how she sits, where and when she goes out.

Wanda's background is offered as a plausible explanation for why a 14-year-old would become sexually involved with a married man and threaten to disown her mother if she didn't consent to her adoption by him. Wanda is represented as using Dennis as her way out of the poverty into which she was born. Indeed, the only explanation for why Wanda stayed and what she got out of the relationship is in the lengthy treatment of her background and family. Wanda was, the article states, "the 12th of 14 children from a broken family . . . that long has remained in the grips of poverty."

Details about Louvale Westbrooks's past and current home situation—no telephone, no running water for the first six months of the year, 5 of 14 children taken by the state in 1957—reinforce the white trash stereotype. The notion of Wanda as being, or coming from, white trash is supported with the anecdote that, during arguments, Dennis would offer to build her a "little white-trash room" where, he would tell her, she could go when she wanted to act like her family. The contrast between Wanda's background and Dennis's "solidly middle class family" also is reinforced in the feature by interviews with her siblings—who recall their parents in soup lines and asking for food, money, and clothing at churches—as well as by the prominently displayed photo of her mother. In this way, the symbolic representations of class, race, and gender within the newspaper's photos work intertextually with the stories.

Neither of the articles mentions Wanda's feelings for or about Dennis at any time during their years together, although the second story goes to great lengths to emphasize Dennis's love/obsession for Wanda. The message that Dennis murdered Wanda out of love was a constant refrain throughout the second article. The feature story headline was "Walters Family Affair: A Fatal Attraction." A subordinate headline, or deck, quoted Dennis as saying, "I never loved anybody like that girl. . . . Never like this." This quote was from the story in which Dennis's brother recalls Dennis telling him, " 'I've never loved anybody like that girl. I thought I'd been in love before, but never like this.' " The banner headline on the jump page was more explicit: "Walters: in the end, his love consumed them both."

But Dennis Walters was not just a victim of his obsession and love for Wanda. The first two paragraphs of the feature indicate that Dennis was *Wanda's* victim: "Nothing owned his spirit like the Civil War and his fourth wife, Wanda. The first was the vehicle for his rise, the latter for his fall." She was, it seems, the cause of his demise, responsible for his death as well as her own.

Although Wanda is represented as (at least partly) responsible for her own death and Dennis's, she remains symbolically unimportant. Throughout both stories, Wanda has been silenced. The headline of the first article— "Cyclorama chief tries to end life of battles"—does not even hint at his having murdered Wanda. Instead, the headline tells us Dennis Walters and his actions are what's important. It is not until the fourth paragraph of the story—after learning that Dennis Walters "fought for years to gain his lifelong dream—the directorship of the popular Civil War tourist attraction"—that the reader learns "Mr. Walters shot his wife four times in the back and then shot himself in the head" in the driveway of their suburban home. The headline on the jump for the first story, "Walters: shoots wife, then himself," similarly denies Wanda's importance. It does not say, "Walters: Murdered by husband," which would make her the subject, rather than the object, of the story. The headline also equalizes Dennis's actions—he did to her what he did to himself. She suffered no more than he. Or, as the article suggests, he may have suffered more. He was the victim of his obsessions, devastated by Wanda's leaving. She, on the other hand, had plans to remarry.

The articles signify Wanda's murder as an aberration, as the product of individual pathology rather than the logical result of the systematic oppression of women. This representation is similar in content to the underlying assumptions of traditional sociological studies which "not only obscure the actual history of violence against women, but by disregarding the feminist critique of patriarchy, they effectively discourage analysis of family violence from a context of both societal and male supremacy" (DeLauretis, 1987, p. 34).

Pagelow (1981) equates male domination and control of women in the home with the notion of "women as property requiring varying degrees of control, much like children, domesticated animals and pets" (p. 63). As with children and pets, a certain amount of control is deemed not just justifiable but necessary. The question then becomes not whether Wanda's murder was justified, for that would place responsibility squarely on the shoulders of her murderer, but whether she brought it on herself. At the very least, the articles suggest her death is equivalent to Dennis's; they are represented as the same tragedy, the result of Dennis's obsessive love over which he had no control. At most, Wanda provoked Dennis and got what she deserves.

An analogy can be made with Dworkin's (1981) contention that women are seen as holding sexual power over men when, in fact, men have the power of sex:

> The argument is that women have sexual power because erection is involuntary; a woman is the presumed cause; therefore, the man is helpless; the woman is powerful. The male reacts to a stimulation for which he is not responsible; it is his very nature to do so; whatever he does he does because of a provocation that inheres in the female. (p. 22)

From a Feminist Framework

The representation of Dennis as a victim and of Wanda's murder as obsession gone awry is incompatible with a feminist perspective that views their relationship as one of male control and female subordination and as characterized by victimization, incest, misogyny, abuse of power, domination, battering, and ultimately, murder. The newspaper coverage denies that Dennis sought to control and, in fact, own Wanda—first through adoption, and then, when she was old enough, through marriage. It even denies that Wanda was a battered woman (the terms *battered* or *battered woman* are never used) despite stating that Dennis beat her in her apartment and pointed a gun to her head. To acknowledge Wanda as a battered woman would have changed the context of the story and signified Dennis as an aggressor, rather than as obsessed or headstrong, and Wanda as *his* victim. As Finn (1989-1990) points out, white, middle-class men who batter and/or kill their wives are "constructed in state and media discourses as the victims of provocation or personal stress, more deserving of mercy and compassion than condemnation and constraint" (p. 381).

An alternative framing of Wanda's murder would recognize that the victimization of women is sanctioned by society, that misogyny and the oppression of women are the real reason men like Dennis Walters believe they have the right to control women and, when they fear they are losing control, to murder them. That Dennis Walters also killed himself should not deflect attention from this issue. Despite the newspaper's characterization of Wanda's death and Dennis's suicide as the same "tragedy," they are separate and differently motivated. Wanda did not choose to die; Dennis made that choice for her and, then, for himself. Dennis's suicide also should not be viewed as evidence of his not being responsible for his actions. Although his reasons for taking his own life are less clear than his reasons for murdering Wanda, he well may have viewed suicide as preferable to jail. What is clear is that there is no evidence Wanda remained in an abusive relationship because she was somehow using Dennis. She did, after all, attempt to leave before and was beaten by Dennis and taken home. According to Martin (1976), women remain in abusive relationships because (1) they fear what their partners might do to them if they left and were caught; (2) societal pressure to remain in a marriage is intense; and (3) they do not have the financial resources to leave. Stanko (1985) adds that women remain in abusive relationships "because of the real conditions of their lives within a male-dominated world. Men's power is not an individual, but a collective one. Women's lives are bounded by it" (p. 57).

The representation of Wanda as guilty of both her own murder and Dennis's suicide is reflective of what Martin (1976) has called "society's almost tangible contempt for female victims of violence" (p. 6). The coverage also provides evidence of an ethical double standard. Besides murder, Dennis is guilty of incest, adultery, and statutory rape. This is not the sort of man one would expect to receive sympathetic news coverage. And yet, Dennis's actions are excused while Wanda is blamed for her own murder (and Dennis's death) because of what she wore, how late she stayed out, and her family's background. In this way, the discursive representation of gender, race, and class converged in a multiplicity of oppression which marked Wanda as guilty.

Violence against women must be understood within a complexity of oppression that victimizes women not simply because of their sex, but because the symbolic representation of gender is inextricably tied to issues of race and class. As Bartky (1990) explains, "each mode of oppression with the system has its own part to play, but each serves to support and maintain the others" (p. 32).

In Wanda's case, race and class were conflated in the signifier white trash. For a middle-class black woman—or any other woman—gender, race, and class are no less intertwined. However, "the interlocking character of the modes of oppression" (Bartky, p. 32) is not limited to sexism, racism, and classism, but includes ageism, heterosexism, and any number of other signifiers of domination and exclusion.

In applying feminist theory to the textual analysis of news coverage of Wanda Walters's murder, this study disclosed the underlying assumptions, myths, and stereotypes that shaped that coverage. The news, socially constructed, represents the values of the dominant social order (Gans, 1980; Roshco, 1975). And when that order is steeped in an ethic of male supremacy, the news reflects it. By perpetuating the idea that violence against women is a problem of individual pathology, the news disguises the social roots of battering while reinforcing stereotypes and myths which blame women. In this way, the news sustains and reproduces male supremacy.

The findings also suggest that previous studies of crime news, by ignoring the gendered nature of violence, may not apply to the victimization of women. Crime-as-deviance research conducted by Hall et al. (1978) and others (Cohen & Young, 1973; Ericson et al., 1987) on the social construction and effects of crime reporting appears fatally flawed in its conclusion that the news portrays criminals as deviants who are deserving of society's censure. The news stories about Wanda's murder did not condemn Dennis. Instead, by presenting him as a victim of provocation and obsession, it is Wanda who appears deserving of condemnation.

While no argument can be made for the representativeness of this study, the findings nevertheless make a case for the re-examination of crime-as-deviance theory from a feminist perspective and for a broadening of the traditional understandings of the social construction of news to include issues of gender, race, and class. The findings also expand the interpretive framework for understanding news coverage of violence against women by showing how the news frames an issue of male domination and control to support, sustain, and reproduce male supremacy. Last, this study suggests that other areas of communication research might well benefit from the application of feminist theory to explore the social inequities of gender, race, and class. For if crime-as-deviance theory was developed without a consideration of women as victims, one may well ask where else women have been left out.

Notes

1. Terms such as *family violence* and *domestic violence* obscure the relationship between gender and power by failing to define the perpetrators and victims. Although Bograd (1988) prefers *wife abuse*, this ignores violence in dating, which may be as prevalent as in marriage

(Cate, Henton, Koval, Christopher, & Lloyd, 1982; Makepeace, 1981). Pharr (1991) suggests *sexist violence* because it indicates "that it has societal roots, and is not just any violence or hatred that occurs" (p. 2).

2. Although this is the dominant perspective within sociological studies of the news (Gans, 1980; Gitlin, 1980; Molotch & Lester, 1974; Roshco, 1975; Sigal, 1973), a relatively small but vocal minority, led by S. Robert Lichter, Linda Lichter, and Stanley Rothman (Lichter, Rothman, & Lichter, 1986), insists that the news reflects the biases of a liberal media elite.

3. When evidence surfaced that Carol Stuart was murdered by her husband, Charles, he committed suicide.

4. U.S. law was passed down from English common law, which considered women the property of men. For this reason, laws concerning rape and battering have historically put women at a disadvantage compared to the victims of other crimes. It is only within the past 20 years that reformers have worked to change these laws.

5. A jump is the continuation of a story on a different page.

6. The *Encyclopedia of Southern Culture* (Wilson & Ferris, 1989) notes that the term "poor white" has "connotations of moral as well as material impoverishment and even degeneracy" and, in the antebellum period, was used to describe "the character of a people, rather than strictly being a term of economic classification" (p. 1405). The myth of "poor, white trash" characterized poor Appalachians as "backward hillbillies who were inclined toward incest, fundamentalist religion, laziness and irresponsibility" (p. 1138).

References

Adams, C. J. (1990). What we choose to believe. *Working Together, 10*(2), 2, 5.

Avis, J. M. (1991, May). *Current trends in feminist thought and therapy: Perspectives on sexual abuse and violence within the family.* Paper presented at the International Colloquium of Women in Family Therapy, Copenhagen.

Bartky, S. L. (1990). *Femininity and domination.* New York: Routledge.

Bograd, M. (1988). Feminist perspectives on wife abuse. In K. Yllo & M. Bograd (Eds.), *Feminist perspectives on wife abuse* (pp. 11-26). Newbury Park, CA: Sage.

Brunsdon, C., & Morley, D. (1978). *Everyday television: "Nationwide."* London: BFI.

Bumiller, K. (1990). Fallen angels: The representation of violence against women in legal culture. *International Journal of the Sociology of Law, 18,* 125-142.

Cate, R. M., Henton, J. M., Koval, J., Christopher, F. S., & Lloyd, S. (1982). Premarital abuse: A social psychological perspective. *Journal of Family Issues, 3,* 79-90.

Chancer, L. S. (1987). New Bedford. Massachusetts, March 6, 1983-March 22, 1984: The "before" and "after" of a group rape. *Gender & Society, 1*(3), 239-260.

Cohen, S., & Young, J. (1973). *The manufacture of news: Deviance, social problems and the mass media.* London: Constable.

DeLauretis, T. (1987). *Technologies of gender.* Bloomington: Indiana University Press.

Dobash, R. E., & Dobash, R. (1979). *Violence against wives.* New York: Free Press.

Dworkin, A. (1981). *Pornography: Men possessing women.* New York: Perigee.

Eco, U. (1990). *The limits of interpretation.* Bloomington: Indiana University Press.

Ericson, R. V., Baranek, P. M., & Chan, J. B. (1987). *Visualizing deviance.* Toronto: University of Toronto Press.

Federal Bureau of Investigation (FBI). (1990). *Crime in the United States: Uniform crime reports for the United States, 1989.* Washington, DC: Author.

Finn, G. (1989-1990). Taking gender into account in the "theatre of terror": Violence, media and the maintenance of male dominance. *Canadian Journal of Women and the Law. 3*(2), 375-394.

Fortune, M. (1988, August). A feminist vision of justice. *The Exchange, 2*(3), 7-9.

Fortune, M. (1990). A response to the massacre of women students at the University of Montreal. *Working Together, 10*(2), 1.

Gale Research, Inc. (1993). *Gale directory of publications and broadcast media.* Detroit, MI: Author.

Gans, H. J. (1980). *Deciding what's news.* New York: Vintage.

Giles-Sims, J. (1983). *Wife battering: A systems theory approach.* New York: Guilford.

Gitlin, T. (1980). *The whole world is watching.* Berkeley: University of California Press.

Gordon, M. T., & Riger, S. (1989). *The female fear.* New York: Free Press.

Gramsci, A. (1971). *Selections from the prison notebooks.* London: Lawrence and Wishart.

Gramsci, A. (1983). *The modern prince and other writings.* New York: International.

Hall, S. (1977). Culture, the media and the "ideological" effect. In J. Curran, M. Gurevitch, & J. Woollacott (Eds.), *Mass communication and society* (pp. 315-348). Beverly Hills, CA: Sage.

Hall, S. (1982). The rediscovery of "ideology": Return of the repressed in media studies. In M. Gurevitch, T. Bennett, J. Curran, & J. Woollacott (Eds.), *Culture, society and the media* (pp. 56-90). London: Methuen.

Hall, S., Connell, I., & Curti, L. (1977). The "unity" of current affairs television. *Working Papers in Cultural Studies, 9,* 51-93.

Hall, S., Critcher, C., Jefferson, T., Clarke, J., & Roberts, B. (1978). *Policing the crisis: Mugging, the state and law-and-order.* New York: Holmes and Meier.

Harlow, C. W. (1991). *Female victims of violent crime.* Washington, DC: U.S. Department of Justice, Bureau of Justice Statistics.

Hartley, J. (1982). *Understanding news.* London: Methuen.

Heath, L., Gordon, M. T., & LeBailly, R. (1981). What newspapers tell us (and don't tell us) about rape. *Newspaper Research Journal, 2,* 48-55.

Lemert, J. B. (1989). *Criticizing the media: Empirical approaches.* Newbury Park, CA: Sage.

Lichter, S. R., Rothman, S., & Lichter, L. S. (1986). *The media elite: America's new power brokers.* Bethesda, MD: Adler and Adler.

Long, K. (1990, August 11). Cyclorama chief tries to end life of battles. *Atlanta Constitution,* pp. D-1, 6.

Mahoney, M. R. (1991). Legal images of battered women: Redefining the issue of separation. *Michigan Law Review, 90*(1), 1-94.

Makepeace, J. (1981). Courtship violence among college students. *Family Relations, 30,* 97-102.

Martin, D. (1976). *Battered wives.* New York: Pocket Books.

Mills, K. (1988). *A place in the news: From women's pages to the front page.* New York: Dodd, Mead.

Molotch, H. L. (1978). The news of women and the work of men. In G. Tuchman, A. K. Daniels, & J. Benet (Eds.), *Hearth and home: Images of women in the mass media* (pp. 176-185). New York: Oxford University Press.

Molotch, H., & Lester, M. (1974). News as purposive behavior: On the strategic use of routine events, accidents and scandals. *American Sociological Review, 39*(1), 101-112.

Moore, G. (1992, January/February). Southern journalism: Gone with the wind? Seems like nobody's left to name names and kick ass. *Columbia Journalism Review,* pp. 30-34.

Morley, D. (1980). *The "Nationwide" audience: Structure and decoding.* London: Methuen.

Morley, D. (1985). Cultural transformations: The politics of resistance. In M. Gurevitch & M. Levy (Eds.), *Mass communication review yearbook* (pp. 237-250). Beverly Hills, CA: Sage.

Mulvey, L. (1975). Visual pleasure and narrative cinema. *Screen, 16*(3), 6-18.

Pagelow, M. D. (1981). *Woman-battering: Victims and their experiences.* Beverly Hills, CA: Sage.

Peck, J. (1987). Violence against women. In K. Davies, J. Dickey, & T. Stratford (Eds.), *Out of focus: Writings on women and the media* (pp. 96-103). London: Women's Press.

Pharr. S. (1988). *Homophobia: A weapon of sexism.* Inverness, CA: Chardon.

Pharr, S. (1991). Redefining hate violence. *Transformations, 6*(2), 1-2+. (Little Rock, AR: Women's Project)

Pizzey, E. (1974). *Scream quietly or the neighbors will hear.* London: If Books.

Pomerantz, G. (1990, September 9). Walters family affair: A fatal attraction. *Atlanta Journal-Constitution,* pp. A-1, 8.

Rakow, L., & Kranich, K. (1991). Woman as sign in television news. *Journal of Communication, 41*(1), 8-23.

Roshco, B. (1975). *Newsmaking.* Chicago: University of Chicago Press.

Ryan, W. (1971). *Blaming the victim.* New York: Pantheon.

Sanders, M., & Rock, M. (1988). *Waiting for prime time.* New York: Harper and Row.

Schwengels, M., & Lemert, J. B. (1986, Spring). Fair warning: A comparison of police and newspaper reports of rape. *Newspaper Research Journal, 7*(3), 35-42.

Sigal, L. (1973). *Reporters and officials: The organization of politics and newsmaking.* Lexington, MA: D. C. Heath.

Stanko, E. A. (1985). *Intimate intrusions: Women's experience of male violence.* London: Routledge & Kegan Paul.

Stark, E., & Flitcraft, A. (1988). Violence among intimates: An epidemiological review. In V. B. Hasselt, R. L. Morrison, A. S. Bellack, & M. Hersen (Eds.), *Handbook of family violence* (pp. 293-317). New York: Plenum.

Stark, E., Flitcraft, A., Zuckerman, D., Grey, A., Robison, J., & Frazier, W. (1981). *Wife abuse in the medical setting: An introduction for health personnel.* Monograph No. 7. Office of Domestic Violence. Washington, DC: Government Printing Office.

Stoltenberg, J. (1989). *Refusing to be a man: Essays on sex and justice.* Portland, OR: Breitenbush.

Tuchman, G. (1978). *Making news: A study in the construction of reality.* New York: Free Press.

Tuchman, G., Daniels, A. K., & Benet, J. (Eds.). (1978). *Hearth and home: Images of women in the mass media.* New York: Oxford University Press.

Walker, L. E. (1979). *The battered woman.* New York: Perennial Library.

Wilson, C. R., & Ferris, W. (Eds.). (1989). *Encyclopedia of southern culture.* Chapel Hill: University of North Carolina Press.

CHAPTER **29**

Press Rites and Race Relations

A Study of Mass-Mediated Ritual

James Stewart Ettema

In some of the most elegant and influential lines ever written in our field, James Carey brought together several traditions of thought about communication and society in a cultural approach to the study of communication, an approach that highlighted the concept of ritual: "A ritual view of communication is not directed toward the extension of messages in space but the maintenance of society in time; not the act of imparting information but the representation of shared beliefs," he wrote (1975, p. 6). "It does not see the original or highest manifestation of communication in the transmission of intelligent information but in the construction and maintenance of an ordered, meaningful cultural world which can serve as a control and container for human action." In this view, the archetypal communicative act is "the sacred ceremony which draws persons together in fellowship and commonality."

While this "ritual view" has captured the imagination of many in media studies, Carey's essay actually said rather little about the nature of mass-mediated ritual itself. In his only, brief example, he claimed that newspaper

From *Critical Studies in Mass Communication*, 1990, Vol. 7, pp. 309-331. Used by permission of the Speech Communication Association.

AUTHOR'S NOTE: This research was supported by the Chicago Community Trust Human Relations Task Force and the Institute for Modern Communications of Northwestern University. A draft of this article was presented to the annual meeting of the International Communication Association, Dublin, May 1990.

reading is a ritual because, like the Mass, it is "a situation in which nothing new is learned but in which a particular view of the world is portrayed and confirmed" (1975, p. 8). News is a drama of "the contending forces in the world"—Germany and Japan, for instance, now arrayed against the United States on the battlefield of international trade—and the reader is "an observer at a play." This little example was, as always, elegantly presented, but it was in fact at odds with the theoretical position that presumably generated it.

While news reading is, no doubt, often experienced in just this way, the emphasis on the experiences of readers rather than on the actions of those "contending forces in the world" suggested, ironically, a transmission view of ritual. In this characterization of ritual, there was still a one-way flow of messages from sender to receiver, but a flow of "drama" instead of "information." There was still an atomized mass audience, but that audience was "enjoying" a dramatic experience instead of "learning" about current events. And, of course, there was a psychological effect, but that effect was the affirmation of myth instead of change in opinion. Following Geertz, Carey acknowledged human thought to be an essentially public and social activity occurring "primarily on blackboards, in dances, and recited poems" (1975, p. 15); nevertheless, this particular example of ritual emphasized private consumption over public interaction and social stasis over political process.

Ritual as Politics

The concept of ritual may include those situations in which a mass audience passively receives the transmission of a consensus-affirming story, but it also must include situations in which individuals or institutions actively engage each other—often to further their own ends—in a stylized public *event*—a "public enactment," in Douglas's (1975) phrase, or a "cultural performance," in Turner's (1984). Ritual, of course, may "express a common vision of society," as Douglas (1975, p. 71) wrote in the tradition of Durkheim, and, therefore, it may provide "a control and container for human action" that ensures the "maintenance of society in time," as Carey wrote in the same tradition. But at the same time, according to Douglas, ritual affords "scope for using the situation to manipulate other people" (p. 61). Although rituals express a cosmology that controls action and maintains society, Douglas knew that people are "living in the middle of their cosmology, down in amongst it; they are energetically manipulating it, evading its implications in their own lives if they can, but using it for hitting each other and forcing one another to conform to something they have in mind."

The concept of ritual is, then, complex, even contradictory. "That ritual performances can contribute powerfully to the maintenance of society—a crucial insight of functionalist and structural-functionalist theoreticians—remains an accepted truism," noted Lincoln (1989, p. 53), "and others who write from a Marxist position have advanced powerful arguments in support of the view that ritual is both intrinsically and categorically conservative in nature." But, like Douglas, Lincoln saw tension between ritual and the social order. The Newala ritual of the Swazi culture in southeastern Africa provides a spectacular example. That ritual ostensibly affirmed the right of the king to rule by symbolically banishing his rivals, but during the colonial period it also came to affirm the right of the Swazi Nation to exist by symbolically banishing the Europeans as well. Thus, enactment of the ritual was at once maintenance of the Swazi king's legitimacy and resistance to colonial rule. "To be sure, this may be described as the ritual maintenance of established (if temporarily eclipsed) social patterns," concluded Lincoln (p. 74), "but even should one adopt this grudgingly minimalist view, it must still be acknowledged that the maintenance in question is hardly something simple, passive, or reactionary." In the same vein, Kertzer argued that rituals are not "simply a blind product of communal existence; rather, they serve certain political interests and undermine others" (1988, p. 87). "The political elite employ ritual to legitimate their authority, but rebels battle back with rites of delegitimation" (p. 2). Thus, as Slack argued in her critique of Carey's essay, "a theory of ritual would have somehow to be explicable in terms of cultural contradiction and discontinuity as well as in terms of unity and continuity" (1989, p. 7).

Ritual's simultaneous embrace of both stability and change is nowhere more richly explicated than in Turner's treatment of "social drama" (1969, 1974, 1980-1981, 1984). Such dramas, according to Turner, exhibit four characteristic phases: *breach*, in which some norm, law, or custom is violated in a public setting and in a way that challenges entrenched authority; *crisis*, in which antagonisms become visible and factions form along enduring social fault lines; *redress*, in which adjustive mechanisms ranging from personal advice to formal juridical procedures to rituals of sacrifice are invoked; and *reintegration or separation*, in which the attempts at redress are seen either to succeed or fail and ceremonies may be enacted to mark reconciliation or else permanent cleavage. These phases are not themselves rituals, but each phase may contain a number of different rituals that comprise a "repertoire . . . of motifs" for inauguration, transition, and conclusion of the drama (1980-1981, p. 149).

Together, the phases form a "processual structure" or "paradigm" for social action, particularly the action of social leaders. Leaders—or "star groupers," as Turner called them—"are the ones who develop to an art the rhetoric of persuasion and influence, who know how and when to apply pressure and force, and who are most sensitive to the factors of legitimacy" (1980-1981, p. 148). For example, in the redress phase, "it is the star groupers who manipulate the machinery of redress, the law courts, the procedures of divination and ritual, and impose sanctions on those adjudged to have precipitated crisis, just as it may well be disgruntled or dissident star groupers who lead rebellions and provoke the initial breach." But throughout all phases, "genres of cultural performance" (p. 154) are spun out and woven together into what Kenneth Burke called "dramas of living"—dramas with real and enduring consequences for social life.

Returning to our own intellectual domain of media studies, Elliot (1982) elaborated the idea of "press rites" in a way that captured the idea of "enactment" or "performance" involving more than simply stories told by the media and consumed by the audience. To qualify as a press rite, according to Elliot, press coverage must not only *portray* powerful individuals and institutions but must *interact* with them. "The media do not act alone in the performance of political ritual but in concert with other political and social institutions," he argued (p. 606). "Concert suggests harmony and this appears to be the more usual case but discordant press reporting may also be one of the instigators of ritual performance by other institutions." For example, the media may uncover a scandal. In response, officials express outrage and appoint a commission to investigate. In turn, the media report and comment upon the findings. Eventually, officials attempt to "put the issue behind them." Throughout the drama, the media provide the enactment with its particular symbolic form—its imagery and plotline—and they assemble an audience to witness, and perhaps become involved in, the performance.

In case studies of press response to clashes between the Irish Republican Army and British authorities, Elliot found two different genres of the rite: *affirmation* of "we-ness," and *cauterization* of social wounds. According to Elliot, the import of these (and all other) rituals for secular, class-structured societies is, of course, ideological. "If we read the rite as ideology, then one account would concentrate on the way in which the agents of the state were shown to be effective and the hierarchy of the society made manifest," he argued (1982, p. 597). "The sense of social solidarity developed in the rites is one of subordination to the authorities who can be relied on to deal with the threat posed."

Like Carey, Elliot focused on the role of mass-mediated ritual in maintaining society in time, but his tone was critical rather than celebratory. And, like Douglas, he saw the *use* of ritual in practical politics, but he knew that in class-structured societies some groups have more power than others when it comes to "forcing one another to conform to something they have in mind." Thus, Elliot emphasized the intrinsic conservatism of ritual, but he also cited Turner's argument that within ritual—as within society itself—there is a tension between the pursuit of hierarchy and status, on the one hand, and the pursuit of *communitas* or common humanity, on the other. He also acknowledged that not all news media performances are structure-enforcing press rites. Indeed, some are "propaganda victories for the opposition . . . because they refer to anti-structure as well as structure" (1982, p. 599). Thus, Elliot recognized limits on the power of the media to legitimize the prevailing social order, but he clearly associated the notion of a "press rite" with exercise of that power.

Press Rites and Race Relations

The idea that press performance can assume the character of a ritualized public enactment is the point of departure for a study of events that had substantial significance for race relations and mayoral politics in the city of Chicago. These events, which in the spring of 1988 came to be called "the Cokely affair," began with news reports that Steve Cokely, an aide to Acting Mayor Eugene Sawyer, had made anti-Semitic remarks in speeches to black nationalist audiences. This revelation came only a few months after Sawyer had been appointed acting mayor upon the death of Harold Washington. Sawyer had become the city's second African-American mayor (Washington was the first), but his appointment had been engineered by white aldermen who had wanted to deny the appointment to an alderman with stronger support in the African-American community. Thus, Sawyer's political position within that community was problematic as he began planning his campaign for a full term in City Hall. The reports of Cokely's speeches created a crisis for Sawyer, who knew very well that he, like Washington before him, would need not only the overwhelming support of Chicago's African-American citizens but also the support of white liberals—many of them Jews—to retain office.

The four phases of Turner's social drama paradigm describe with impressive precision the course of interaction between Chicago's two "mainstream"—that is to say, "white"—daily newspapers and such institutions as the mayor's office, the city council, and community groups.[1] The press was instrumental in exposing (at the behest of certain community groups) Cokely's activities, in bringing the affair to a crisis that demanded action by the mayor, in defining acceptable redress, and in seeking to close the affair with a symbolic reintegration of African-Americans and Jews. In each phase, the press not only portrayed but participated in the struggle either to find rhetorical strategies and ritual forms that could meet the political need at hand or to counter the rhetoric or ritual of the moment. Thus, both the political judgment of "star groupers" and the news judgment of journalists were shaped by a "processual structure," in Turner's terms, that offered participants "a rhetoric, a mode of emplotment, and a meaning" for events as they unfolded (1980-1981, p. 149).

While Carey and Elliot provide a point of departure, their examples of mass-mediated ritual differ from the Cokely affair in significant ways. Carey's example highlighted the experience of the mass audience, while this example will highlight the action of "star groupers"—those individuals and institutions who actively participated in the social drama. The Cokely affair was probably the quintessential polysemic situation, with audience reactions ranging from renewed commitment to social justice, on the one hand, to exacerbated racism or anti-Semitism, on the other. The notion of mass-mediated ritual developed here, however, necessarily means that most of the audience will merely observe the dramatic interaction as it is played out among the star groupers (though that is not so very different from what happens in many unmediated rituals). In any case, this study decenters individual-level experiences and effects in order to privilege social-level enactments and performances. "Since I regard cultural symbols including ritual symbols as originating in and sustaining processes involving temporal changes in social relations, and not as timeless entities," wrote Turner (1974, p. 55), "I have tried to treat the crucial properties of ritual symbols as being involved in these dynamic developments. Symbols instigate social action."

In Elliot's examples of mass-mediated ritual, the British press consistently framed its stories as a clash between a "we" ("innocent citizens") whose moral claims were affirmed as legitimate and a "they" ("terrorists") whose claims were denied. In the Cokely affair, however, facile distinctions between "we" and "they" collapsed as the Chicago press gradually uncovered a social drama involving two groups, African-Americans and Jews, each with long-standing moral claims against the larger community that the press recognized as legitimate. Journalists were frequently obliged to reframe their stories as events unfolded. This study examines neither racism nor anti-Semitism per se and makes no attempt to adjudicate the claims of either group against the other or against American society. Rather, this study examines the role of press rites in the *mediation* (both in the sense of representation and attempted resolution) of a painfully discordant social drama. It shows how such rites may be a site of cultural and political struggle and suggests that the maintenance of social stability—whether characterized as Durkheimian solidarity or Gramscian hegemony—is not the only possible role for ritual.

Breach

A social drama begins when someone who intends to trigger a confrontation publicly breaches a norm governing social relations. "To flout such a norm," noted Turner, "is one obvious symbol of dissidence" (1974, p. 38). And in this regard, the Cokely affair displays an interesting, media-related variation on Turner's formulation. In breaching a norm of mainstream political discourse, Cokely's anti-Semitic speeches were acts of dissidence, of course, but they probably were not intended to trigger the sort of confrontation that they eventually did. The speeches would have remained known only to their small audience and to a few political insiders had not the city's two metropolitan dailies, the *Chicago Tribune* and the *Chicago Sun-Times*, intervened. By bringing the speeches to public attention, the press—not Cokely—created the *public* breach that triggered the confrontation between Mayor Sawyer and those who wanted Cokely removed from the city's payroll. "There is always something altruistic about such a symbolic breach," Turner continued (p. 38). "A dramatic breach may be made by an individual certainly, but he always acts, or believes he acts, on behalf of other parties, whether they are aware of it or not." And, indeed, this social drama began when the press sought to confront, presumably on behalf of Chicago's citizens, what it took to be improper behavior by a public servant.

The drama began with simultaneous stories in the *Tribune* and *Sun-Times* on May 1, 1988. The stories were very similar, thanks to someone who had tipped both papers to the existence of tape recordings of Cokely's speeches. The *Tribune*'s version (Lipinski & Baquet, 1988a), however, was a particularly fine example of the expose, a traditional journalistic genre for the exposure of a breach in norms by an official.[2] The basic element of this story form is the "discovery" of unambiguous wrongdoing—or at least discovery of something that reporters and editors assume will be widely accepted as wrongdoing. In this case, the wrongdoing was seen to be an outrageous attack not only on Jews but on revered African-American leaders as well. The story began:

> An aide to Mayor Eugene Sawyer who acts as the administration's link to community groups has delivered public lectures in which he contends that Jews are engaged in an international conspiracy for world control and has attacked Mayor Harold Washington and Jesse Jackson for having Jewish advisers. (p. 1)

As the genre requires, the story went on persuasively to substantiate the wrongdoing by detailing the content of Cokely's lectures. For example:

> In a series of tape-recorded lectures to followers of Nation of Islam leader Louis Farrakhan, Cokely further suggested that Jewish physicians have injected blacks with the AIDS virus. (p. 1)

Also as the genre requires, the story quoted spokespersons for the norms that have been violated by the wrongdoing. Among others, Msgr. John Egan, Director of Community Affairs for DePaul University, was enlisted to voice the moral outrage:

> "For any such person of whatever race or nationality to be employed by the City of Chicago is a travesty and is insulting to the mayor and citizens of our great city," Msgr. Egan said in an interview. (p. 27)

Finally, the story completed the basic requirements of the genre by presenting the wrongdoing as a situation that must be addressed by responsible officials. Several months before, mayoral advisers had learned of Cokely's "reputation for anti-Semitism," and four weeks before, members of the Anti-Defamation League (ADL) of B'nai B'rith had met with the mayor to describe Cokely's "invective." Neither the ADL representative, Michael Kotzin, nor the story itself seemed to blame the mayor for the situation, but Kotzin gave voice to the expectation that action would be taken soon:

> Kotzin, who has listened to Cokely's tape-recorded lectures and describes them as being fraught with "paranoid-style, conspiracy-haunted views," said he left the City Hall meeting with the impression that Sawyer would take some action. (p. 27)

The mayor's press secretary said that the mayor would ask Cokely to "tone down his rhetoric" but that the aide would not be fired. An unidentified mayoral adviser said that Sawyer "has been reluctant to sever Cokely, who is black, from the administration because he provides a link to Chicago's

black nationalist movement, a group that soured on Sawyer because he was
elected by a coalition of white ethnic aldermen." On his own behalf, Cokely
said little more than that he was not anti-Semitic and that his role was to
"provoke debate."

Thus, the social drama began with a familiar exercise in the mass-mediated affirmation of norms appropriate to public officials.[3] "I remember
thinking while writing the first story that Sawyer would fire Cokely right
away and cut his losses," said Ann Marie Lipinski, the *Tribune* reporter who
helped to break the story. At that point, she expected the situation to be off
the front page within two days. *Affirmation* of norms does not ensure *enforcement* of them, however, and the next morning both papers reported that the
mayor had continued to defend rather than fire his aide. The "second-day"
stories focused on the corrective action that seemed to be so clearly demanded by the well-documented wrongdoing—or rather, they focused on
the lack of such action. The *Tribune*'s version began:

> Despite criticism from aldermen and constituents, Mayor Eugene Sawyer
> said Sunday that he has no intention of firing an aide who has used racial
> and religious epithets during a series of lectures. (Devall, 1988, p. 1)

The story went on to report that the mayor told participants in a neighborhood meeting that Cokely "did not mean those things in his heart" and
that "God forgives." Both papers quoted the press secretary's attempt to
minimize Cokely's role in the administration, but they also quoted several
African-American aldermen who said that if Cokely were fired, the mayor
would lose a contact with certain activist groups. Both papers also quoted
several white aldermen who demanded that Cokely be fired immediately.

The next day, both papers reported that Sawyer still had not fired Cokely
but rather had taken another ritual tack: public apology. The mayor's office
had issued a statement in which Cokely said that he "humbly apologizes"
to those who were offended (Lipinski & Devall, 1988, p. 1; Sweet & Hanania,
1988a). But the stories went on to report that the outcry was unabated and
that the mayor himself had said that an apology might not suffice.[4] On their
editorial pages that day, both papers angrily rejected the apology as insincere
and demanded that Cokely be fired. The *Tribune* went on to throw some of
Sawyer's rhetoric back in his face:

> Even after The Tribune disclosed Cokely's ravings in its Sunday edi-
> tions, Mayor Sawyer couldn't bring himself to act responsibly—that is,
> to fire him. "He's indicated to me that he did not mean those things in
> his heart," said Sawyer. Oh that explains it: Steve Cokely is not a true
> racist demagogue, he's only a hypocritical racist demagogue. ("Sawyer
> Should Fire Racist Aide," 1988)

According to *Sun-Times* reporter Lynn Sweet, stories written in the first
days of the affair portrayed the mayor as maddeningly and, moreover,

inexplicably indifferent to the mounting outrage primarily because no acceptable sources (e.g., aldermen) were willing to defend Cokely publicly or even explain the mayor's political predicament. "Black community groups were not speaking out on the issue, nor were many black political leaders; and Steve wasn't talking to the press so it was hard to get 'the other side,' " recalled Sweet. Meanwhile, "the ADL and other groups publicly were demanding Steve's head." Reporters understood well enough the cause of the mayor's indecision, but while they *knew* it, they couldn't get their sources to *say* it.

In contrast to the "mainstream" press, the *Chicago Defender*, a daily oriented to African-American readers, framed the situation less as a normative breach than as a practical political problem for the mayor. "Once again," its second-day story began, "the controversial mayoral aide Steve Cokely is under fire from city and private sector Jews who are reportedly angered over his anti-Semitic and pro-Black Muslim remarks" (Strausberg, 1988a). The story went on to quote several Cokely supporters, none of whom was an elected official. "I hope the mayor doesn't castrate Steve for exercising his First Amendment right," said one. Thus, the *Defender*, with closer ties to the African-American community and differing conceptions of acceptable sources, provided an alternative interpretation—an interpretation, as it turned out, that presaged the themes of Cokely-as-political-problem and Cokely-as-potent-symbol that the *Tribune* and *Sun-Times* would soon be compelled to consider.

Crisis

"Unless the breach can be sealed off quickly within a limited area of social interaction," argued Turner (1974, p. 38), "there is a tendency for the breach to widen and extend until it becomes coextensive with some dominant cleavage in the widest set of relevant social relations to which the conflicting or antagonistic parties belong." In the Cokely affair, Mayor Sawyer perhaps could have sealed off the breach by firing his aide quickly. However, the mayor hesitated while both the *Tribune* and *Sun-Times* continued to give voice to expressions of moral indignation and calls for Cokely's dismissal. Soon the papers began to define the situation explicitly as a crisis (though, at first, more as a crisis for an inexperienced mayor than as a crisis in Chicago's race relations). Thus, the mayor's hesitation at a key moment, along with the media's attention to every move by the antagonistic parties, widened the breach and propelled the drama into and through its next phase—crisis.

By the third day after the initial exposé, "the situation had become an important issue on which to test the new mayor's character," recalled reporter Lynn Sweet. "What began as a racial story soon developed into a political story of an administration in crisis." The *Tribune*, for example, now saw the mayor as caught in the middle of a controversy, much as the *Defender* had suggested:

> Mayor Eugene Sawyer huddled with his top advisers Tuesday in an
> effort to resolve the burgeoning controversy over aide Steve Cokely
> while publicly describing his efforts to rehabilitate Cokely by buying
> him clothes and talking to him "as a father would with a son." (Lipinski
> & Strong, 1988a, p. 1)

The mayor was said to be "struggling to find a 'middle ground' to appease
predominantly Jewish community leaders demanding Cokely's firing and
members of the black community who have defended him." However, the
story still did not present this "burgeoning controversy" as having "another
side." The story reviewed once again some of Cokely's more outrageous
statements and quoted several demands for his dismissal, but it did not
identify any of those "members of the black community who have defended
him." And so, while aldermen made plans to strike Cokely's salary from the
city budget and the Anti-Defamation League played tapes of Cokely's
speeches for local and national media, the mayor merely "huddled."

The *Sun-Times* also framed the situation as a practical political problem
that the mayor was not handling well. It did, however, give a little more play
to Sawyer's attempt to cast Cokely as an errant son who should not be judged
too harshly for his misdeeds:

> Sawyer said he considered himself a "father" figure to the 37-year-old
> Cokely and asserted he was helping him change his views as well as his
> grooming. . . .
>   Expanding on his fatherly role to the aide who has enmeshed the
> mayor in controversy dealing with black-Jewish relations, Sawyer said,
> "I have been strongly making efforts to turn the young man around, to
> change his views, which I think I have done." (Sweet & Hanania, 1988b)

But while the *Sun-Times* news columns emphasized the mayor's attempt at
redress through rhetorical rehabilitation, the editorial page threw the
mayor's rhetoric back at him, much as the *Tribune* had done. "Mayor Sawyer
has undertaken a special project: He says he is trying to 'rehabilitate' his
special projects coordinator," wrote the editorialist, adding, "we have no
hope at all that the object of his compassion is salvageable" ("Cokely Isn't
Salvageable," 1988).

Meanwhile, under the rubric of "news analysis," the *Tribune* finally
attempted to make sense of the mayor's behavior. As suggested by the
headline "Why Mayor Treads Lightly on Cokely," the question to be answered was why Mayor Sawyer seemed so reluctant to do the right thing.
The explanation, according to the article, was, of course, politics: The mayor
had yet to carve out a voting constituency within the African-American
community. However, the mayor's problem was not really the small black
nationalist movement that might agree with Cokely but rather "divisions
within the black community and longstanding emotions arising from a
protect-our-own sense of justice" (Dold, 1988a, p. 1). In this context, "the

unusual phenomenon of Farrakhan" created problems for Sawyer just as it had for Jesse Jackson and Harold Washington:

> Jackson and Washington may have been less concerned about Farrakhan's small cadre of radicals than they were about the thousands of blacks who gathered at a South Side armory in 1984 to hear Farrakhan speak. Many were not Muslims and they may not have shared Farrakhan's more radical beliefs but they enjoyed hearing a black leader boldly and eloquently speak his mind. . . .
>
> After years of fighting to be heard, they're saying we want to cut somebody a little slack when they go off the deep end. (Dold, 1988a, p. 18)

This, the article concluded, explained why many African-American leaders who rejected Cokely's views had not spoken out. Having defined Cokely as part of a sociopolitical "phenomenon" (though not as part of a legitimate sociopolitical debate), the article finally gave voice to a few of Cokely's supporters, including a clergyman who said, "We're going to request that Mayor Sawyer not sell Stevie Cokely for 30 pieces of silver."

Now the press was struggling to see beyond the politics of the moment and to confront the meaning of these events as something more complex than an instance of bad behavior by a city employee or an episode in the next mayoral campaign. Nevertheless, both papers kept the heat on the next day. The *Tribune*'s version, headlined "Mayor's Silence Heating Cokely Crisis to a Boil," began:

> Mayor Eugene Sawyer, buffeted by increasing demands to decide the fate of an aide who has rocked his administration with racist remarks, broke promises to resolve the matter Wednesday, apparently unable to decide how best to unite warring community factions. (Lipinski & Strong, 1988b, p. 1)

In day-long negotiations, the mayor had asked Cokely to resign or accept reassignment, but the aide had refused. At 11:10 p.m., the mayor's press secretary had told waiting reporters that there would be no statement from the mayor that night. Meanwhile, another day of indecision had "provoked a new level of outrage" among those demanding dismissal, but now there was also talk of a march on City Hall in support of Cokely. And there were more voices heard on his behalf (if not exactly on behalf of his views). "There is a growing opinion among younger blacks, grassroots black people, that Jews are running things, that Jews are unfair, unloving," said a well-known clergyman. A community activist said, "I think it is certainly possible that Jews, not just Jews but whites, are in a conspiracy to rule the world" (Lipinski & Strong, 1988b, p. 22). The issue, as the story made clear, was no longer Cokely but "the delicate issue of black and Jewish relations in Chicago." Thus, just as Turner would have predicted, the initial breach had widened to coincide with the "dominant cleavage in the widest set of relevant social relations to which the conflicting or antagonistic parties belong" (1974, p. 38).

Redress

"In order to limit the spread of crisis," wrote Turner, "certain adjustive and redressive 'mechanisms,' . . . informal and formal, institutionalized or ad hoc, are swiftly brought into operation by leading or structurally representative members of the disturbed social system" (1974, p. 39). In the Cokely affair, Mayor Sawyer began the redressive phase of the drama by firing his aide and issuing "a call for healing." But these were not the only—and perhaps not even the most important—redressive actions. "It is in the redressive phase that both pragmatic techniques and symbolic action reach their fullest expression," Turner continued (p. 41). "Redress . . . has its liminal features, its being 'betwixt and between,' and, as such, furnishes a distanced replication and critique of the events leading up to and composing the 'crisis.' " In media-saturated industrialized societies, "distanced replication" is, of course, the domain of mass communication, and in Chicago, the press did struggle to provide a meaningful account of what, exactly, had happened in their city. Indeed, the third phase of this social drama might be characterized as an exercise in "redress through explanation."

The redressive phase began five days after the initial exposé, when both papers reported that the mayor had taken the only action open to him in the situation as defined by the press. The *Tribune*'s story began:

> Mayor Eugene Sawyer, struggling to resolve the worst political crisis of his short tenure, bowed to community pressure Thursday and fired a mayoral aide who accused Jews of engaging in an international conspiracy for world control. (Lipinski & Baquet, 1988b, p. 1)

The story's overall frame for the firing was that of an ineptly handled political problem. Despite Sawyer's statement that he "took time to listen to people who wanted to be heard," the mayor's actions were characterized as a "slow and risky course" that "appeared to harden his reputation . . . for having trouble making up his mind." However, the story did seem to take seriously the idea, first advanced in the news analysis article of a few days before, that African-Americans were less committed to the substance of Cokely's comments than to the symbol of—and the perceived threat to—"a black leader boldly and eloquently speak[ing] his mind." The second paragraph of the story developed this theme:

> Later in the evening, the fired aide, Steve Cokely, was enthusiastically received at an emotional West Side rally where residents supported what they said was his "right to freedom of speech."
>
> "He don't owe them an apology for nothing; if anything blacks are due an apology," Roy Brown, 82, of South Woodlawn Avenue, said at the rally. (p. 1)

At the same time, the story began to move the affair toward symbolic closure, as suggested by the subhead, "Somber mayor asks city to look beyond controversy." The fourth paragraph developed this theme using familiar news conference imagery:

> Surrounded by black and Jewish civic leaders at a late afternoon news conference, a somber and weary Sawyer said Cokely has been dismissed as the administration's community liaison and pleaded for Chicagoans to look beyond what he called "this unfortunate chapter."
>
> "I hope and pray that all Chicago listening to me today hears my call for healing," Sawyer said. "Progress will be born of this struggle." (p. 1)

The *Sun-Times*, on the other hand, was less ready to seek symbolic closure. Under the headline "Cokely Is Fired," a subhead reported, "Mayor's aide charges plot to force him out" (Sweet, 1988a, p. 1). The fourth and fifth paragraphs of this story were devoted not to the mayor's call for closure but rather to Cokely's denunciation of his dismissal as "a plot." This story did, however, note the mayor's promise to call a conference of community and religious leaders "to work together to heal our wounds."

With the deed done at last, press attention turned from daily developments to placing the whole affair in various psychological, political, and cultural contexts.[5] In a story headlined "Cokely's Fire Proved Too Hot for Sawyer's Ice," the *Tribune* provided a rather sympathetic profile of the fired aide and his relationship to the mayor:

> Cokely, 35, was a firebrand whose politics were too hot for establishment black civil-rights groups. He had an unlikely dual passion for black extremist politics and the ever-conciliatory Sawyer, but he lost his job when those passions couldn't mesh. . . .
>
> Sawyer "picked him up, and started him on schooling (at Kennedy-King College) and talked to him about his attitude and his dress," said the mayor's press secretary Monroe Anderson. "Steve dressed something like a street bum and he (Sawyer) bought him some clothes." (Dold, 1988b)

In their big Sunday editions, one week after breaking the story, both papers continued the project of trying to make sense of what had happened.[6] The *Sun-Times* located the events within the context of Sawyer's political psyche:

> Mayor Sawyer said he delayed firing aide Steve Cokely because he was haunted by memories of his 1987 election night when he was pressured to become mayor without a chance to consult community groups. . . .
>
> "I remember the night of Dec. 2," the mayor said, "I never again want to allow myself to be in a position where I would not listen to all parties." (Sweet, 1988b, p. 1)

This explanation was not accepted uncritically, however. The story pointed out that the mayor had known of Cokely's activities for some time before the story broke and had taken five days to deal with the crisis.

The *Tribune,* on the other hand, located the events of the past week within the context of Chicago's recent political history. Under the headline "Cokely Was a Burning Fuse," it noted Harold Washington's skillful creation of a coalition between African-Americans and Jews despite a recent history of tension between them. However:

> Sawyer did not command the same devotion from prominent Jewish members of the administration, and he did not have the personal force that enabled Washington to still the feeling among black activists that Jews had gained too much influence in the administration. Cokely was a strain on that black-Jewish alliance that was being stretched to the limit in the weeks after Washington's death. (Dold, 1988c, p. 14)

The article mentioned that Cokely had been "effective at dealing with community groups that had been angered by Sawyer's selection by a white-dominated coalition of aldermen," though it said little about what, exactly, Cokely had done. But whatever Cokely may once have been willing to do for the mayor, he had not been willing to resign. He was, according to a mayoral adviser, "in search of martyrdom."

In another article, the *Sun-Times* sought social and cultural explanations for what it took to be the worsening problem of black anti-Semitism (Gibbons, 1988). The Anti-Defamation League's Michael Kotzin set the frame for this story with the comment, "The unanswered question that needs to be examined is: 'How widespread is anti-Semitism in the black community?' " In search of the answer, the story quoted an African-American sociologist who said that the rift, in part, "stems from the U.S. government's financial commitment to Israel at a time when its commitment to the homeless and needy is being re-examined." The story also suggested that some resentment stems from a time when Jewish shopkeepers controlled a large share of commerce in Chicago's neighborhoods. The sociologist went on to say that very few African-Americans agree with the substance of Cokely's remarks but that "an awful lot of blacks have hostility and negative feelings about Jews who they think want to deny blacks self-determination." [7]

Vernon Jarrett, a *Sun-Times* columnist who regularly writes on minority concerns, diverged somewhat from his paper's news columns that day by casting Cokely's anti-Semitism not as the important problem to be explained but rather as an unfortunate diversion from a badly needed discussion of African-American grievances:

> Mr. Cokely's raging, inane, ridiculous "lectures" are now the talk of the town because the sensible people of Chicago have for years avoided honest and reasonable confrontations on the issues at hand. They have treated black-Jewish relations with a delicacy that borders on hypocrisy. (Jarrett, 1988a)

Jarrett continued the theme a few days later:

> For almost 30 years black leaders and some Jewish leaders have been at real loggerheads over a gamut of issues from South Africa to affirmative action, but here in Chicago we are clashing over an asinine statement made by an arrogant, loudmouthed, self-appointed "black revolutionary." (Jarrett, 1988b)

The "gamut of issues" cited by Jarrett included statements by New York Mayor Koch critical of Jesse Jackson and reports of Israeli arms sales to South Africa. Jarrett acknowledged a "widening ideological gap separating black goals from what appears to be establishment Jewish leadership," but he angrily denounced the idea "that there is deep hatred of Jews in the black community."

And so, in the first days after Cokely's dismissal, the press attempted to map the social fault lines that lay beneath the breach. But even as it plumbed the breach, the press enlisted in the symbolic attempt to close it.

Reintegration/Separation

"The final phase," according to Turner, "consists either of the *reintegration* of the disturbed social group or of the social recognition and legitimization of irreparable schism between the contesting parties" (1974, p. 41). Early in this drama, Mayor Sawyer and other civic leaders had begun to search for rhetorical strategies and ritual forms that could serve as rites of reconciliation and reintegration. After Cokely had been removed and explanations had been offered, the press at last was ready to take these rites seriously. In the midst of its appeals to the symbols of racial harmony, however, the press was forced to report new threats to that harmony. Finally, as the mayoral election drew near, the press was compelled to acknowledge that Harold Washington's political coalition had fractured irreparably. The election, that most sacred of political rituals, officially recognized and institutionalized the schism.

Before Cokely's dismissal, only the *Defender* had used what might be termed the "rites of reconciliation" as a story frame. In an interview, a prominent African-American clergyman had called for "a summit in an effort to 'heal' racial wounds" (Strausberg, 1988b).[8] But a few days after the dismissal, when the mayor enacted still another familiar political ritual—the appointment of a commission—both the *Tribune* and the *Sun-Times* were ready to take seriously the notion of "a religious task force . . . to soothe tensions" (Lehmann & Hanania, 1988). And when Joseph Cardinal Bernardin, who had been asked to chair the commission, issued the expected press release, his vague statement of "deep concern" received story treatment (Hirsley, 1988).

The rites of reconciliation could not, at this point, command front-page treatment, and the story slipped to the inside pages of both papers. But on May 12, one week after the dismissal, a bizarre subplot returned the story to the front page. Word had spread through City Hall that a painting in a student exhibition at the Art Institute of Chicago depicted the late Mayor Washington in women's underwear. Upon hearing of the painting, several African-American aldermen had marched to the museum, removed the painting, and ordered police officers to impound it. "The Jewish community tried to keep our people silent, [yet] we cannot speak out against an injustice," Alderman Alan Streeter was quoted as saying in response to criticism of his actions. "I don't feel it's a coincidence. I feel the [art student] is a Jewish person who is defaming the mayor that I love" (Camper & Lipinski, 1988, p. 1).

"This, then, is what Chicago's religious and civic leaders are up against as they set out to repair the damage done to black-Jewish relationships by events of the last two weeks," said the *Tribune* as it attempted another analysis of black anti-Semitism (Camper & Lipinski, 1988, p. 1). The article cited such respected African-American writers as Richard Wright and James Baldwin to argue that anti-Semitism has "deep roots in black culture," but it also cited a historian who argued that blacks were merely "taking on the dominant culture" when they embraced anti-Semitism. African-Americans and Jews had allied in the 1950s to fight discrimination by white, gentile society, but

> the coalition began to fall apart in the late 1960's as black leaders became increasingly determined to make it on their own, without the guidance of Jewish liberals, and Jewish leaders became more concerned about the survival of Israel than racial injustice.

The story went on to suggest that, locally, there might be some African-American hostility toward Jewish merchants and landlords but that, more generally, hostility toward Jews is one aspect of hostility toward whites—the hostility of the "have nots" toward the "haves." The article concluded that Harold Washington's winning coalition had been seriously damaged. "I think it will be a long time before some Jewish voters will go out of their way to support black empowerment," said one Jewish elected official.

Meanwhile, on the editorial page, the *Tribune* invoked a powerful civic memory. "When Harold Washington was mayor, he closed his ears and his administration to the racist raving of this city's Steve Cokelys," wrote an editorialist who went on to criticize several African-American leaders for failing to follow Washington's example ("Some Things We Should Never Forget," 1988). "There has been talk among some clergy of restoring harmony. But the voices of anger and distrust have so far drowned out those of love and trust." In conclusion the editorialist summoned the memory of the African-American and Jewish civil rights workers who died together in the summer of 1964. A few days later, a *Sun-Times* columnist, taking much the same stand, also invoked "the blood of the black and white martyrs who died in the struggle for civil rights" (Halevi, 1988).[9]

Now the rites of reconciliation became important news. A routine mayoral speaking engagement became a major story within the "healing-and-dialogue" story frame:

Speaking before an annual luncheon of regional members of the National Conference of Christians and Jews, Sawyer said "the process of healing is under way" and declared his opposition to bigotry and intolerance. . . .

"There may be a silver lining to the events of the past few weeks," Sawyer said. "The surface of civility has been scraped away, leaving the scars of racism and bigotry. But if these feelings lie below the surface, and we know they do, it will be healthy to reveal them and to face them head-on." (Strong, 1988, p. 1)

But the mayor's denunciation of "the infectious diseases" of animosity and suspicion was interspersed with a countertext: the statements of Alderman Streeter, who charged that he and others were on a Jewish "hit list" targeting them for defeat in the next election. Streeter said that he would not be part of any move to "silence or castrate another black person" and that the decision on Cokely should have been made by Mayor Sawyer alone. "Other groups should not be allowed to discipline us," he said. "They don't allow us to discipline them."

By the end of May, the story had once again slipped from the front page, although it continued to reverberate through the editorial and opinion pages. The Cokely affair became a cautionary tale about the perils of racial divisiveness told by editorialists for the presumed benefit of the city's African-American leadership. For example, the idea that a few politicians and activists had exploited racial divisions helped to frame the results of a *Tribune* poll conducted in July. Only 8 percent of Chicago's African-American citizens thought Cokely should have been allowed to keep his job, and only 30 percent thought the mayor had handled the situation properly. "Considering the lunatic appeals to racial divisions that have shaken up Chicago's City Hall in recent weeks," the *Tribune* said in an editorial about the results, "it's comforting evidence that the city residents are more intelligent about human relations and fairness than their elected officials" ("Voters Smarter Than Their Pols," 1988). Ordinary Chicagoans, it seemed, had not been as easily inflamed by racial rhetoric as feared.

But only days later, the rhetorical lid threatened to fly off the situation once again. A Chicago-based academic, Eugene Kennedy, wrote in the *New York Times* (1988) that "virulent anti-Semitism has gripped Chicago's black community" and that the silence of leaders such as Jesse Jackson allowed the problem to fester. The *Sun-Times* responded with an article headlined "Blacks, Jews Debunk 'Rift' " (Newman & Williams, 1988, p. 3) reporting that "few blacks have been taken in by the Cokely brand of hatred." Kennedy's column was, in the words of a civil rights activist, "an insult to both sides." On the *Sun-Times*'s opinion page, Vernon Jarrett likened Kennedy's rhetoric to Cokely's. He argued that Cokely's visibility in the city was, after all, due to "hysteria spread in the white-controlled media, with the help of Mayor Sawyer, a black who was handpicked by white politicians who are out to destroy the movement fashioned by Mayor Washington" (Jarrett, 1988c).

The *Tribune* responded to Kennedy's column with an equally angry but quite differently framed editorial:

> "Chicago's most prominent black anti-Semite is Steve Cokely," he writes.
>
> Oh? Rest easy, Chicago. Cokely, the fanatical aide who was fired by Mayor Eugene Sawyer more than two months ago for his paranoid prattlings, seems barely able to keep a grip on himself, let alone Chicago's black community. ("Chicago Takes Another Bum Rap," 1988)

The newspaper's defense of its community against this attack, in addition to dismissing the importance of the whole affair, was to counterattack with references to New York's own "racial turmoil . . . swirling around Howard Beach, Bernard Goetz and Tawana Brawley—not to mention the ever-present threat of combustion anywhere within earshot of Mayor Ed Koch." The editorial concluded that the city's "turbulent ethnic atmosphere" had less to do with raging hatred than with "cowardice, greed, confusion and unenlightened self-interest as its elected representatives grapple for control in the wake of Mayor Harold Washington's death." [10]

By mid-August the last angry opinions had been written, and attention returned to rituals of healing. For example, a group called "Black-Jewish Dialog" had begun to promote the idea of pulpit exchanges between African-American and Jewish congregations, and the first such exchange provided both papers with another story in the healing frame. According to the *Sun-Times*, the minister of Blackwell Memorial AME Zion Church reminded Congregation Kol Ami that both African-Americans and Jews had endured slavery. "Both of us have been excluded," he said, "but let's admit we don't have the same advantages now" (Jeter, 1988). [11]

The Cokely affair also returned to the news columns as the mayoral campaign got under way. Cardinal Bernardin and his commission completed their part in the ritual begun eight months earlier when they offered "their reflections on the city's mayoral election and their recommended agenda for the winner" ("Next Mayor Should Lead," 1989, p. 1). Their essay briefly reviewed a number of issues facing the city, including employment, health care, education, and housing, and provided some of the relatively rare media attention to "the issues" as opposed to "the horse race" in the course of campaign coverage.

The Cokely affair also came up from time to time in stories on the mayoral horse race. The Democratic mayoral primary ultimately came down to a race between Eugene Sawyer and Richard M. Daley, the son of legendary Mayor Richard J. Daley. The race was portrayed largely as a scramble to secure racially and ethnically defined constituencies. The wards fronting on Lake Michigan (some largely white and effluent, others integrated) were often portrayed as the site of the decisive confrontation (as, in fact, they had been in Harold Washington's victories). There, on the lakefront, the last chapter of the Cokely affair to be recounted here was written. This passage from a *Tribune* story headlined "Daley Turning Tide in Lakefront Wards" tells the story:

> Several politically prominent Jewish lakefront residents who supported Washington say they can't bring themselves to support a black candidate this time around.
>
> "I asked a friend, 'Why are you going to vote for Daley?' " said a former Washington adviser who is reluctantly backing Daley.
>
> "He said, 'C-o-k-e-l-y.' " (Dold, 1989, p. 8)

Despite the rituals of redress and reintegration, Eugene Sawyer could not hold the Washington coalition together. He lost the lakefront and, in turn, the primary election to Daley, who went on easily to win the general election. "C-o-k-e-l-y" had become the symbol at the end of a chapter in Chicago politics.

Conclusion

Overall, the Cokely affair provides a rich case study of daily journalism as a political and cultural process. As practical politics, the episode provides a vivid instance of institutional agenda setting. The press, in Cohen's famous phrase, "may not be successful much of the time in telling people what to think, but it is stunningly successful in telling its readers what to think *about*" (Cohen, 1963, p. 13). In this instance, the press brought a situation that had long been known to City Hall insiders into public view and, therefore, onto the mayor's agenda. Subsequent coverage moved the issue to the very top of the agenda and created expectations for immediate action. Further, the portrayal of the mayor's performance in the crisis raised an issue that he would face again in the mayoral campaign. But if journalism does not exactly tell its readers—whether political elites or private citizens—what to think, it does more than merely tell them what to think about. The press gives its readers guidance in *how* to think about issues as well as how to act upon them, and in doing so, the press helps to "contain," in Carey's term, the domain of the political within that of the cultural. In this case, the press ushered into the consciousness of individuals and onto the agenda of institutions the paradigm for social action that Turner calls social drama. This drama was not only portrayed by, but enacted within and through, the news media, which wove together many ritualistic elements into a single meaningful event—"the Cokely affair."

Anthropologists and historians might see the origin of this social drama as a familiar ritual that often marks social fault lines: the insult.[12] However, the press saw it as an unambiguous moral outrage—ethnic slurs by a public servant—that demanded immediate corrective action. Employing the journalistic genre of the exposé, the press created a fully public normative breach. Although neither the *Tribune* nor the *Sun-Times* ever defined Cokely's statements as anything other than a moral outrage, they soon found that the simple moralistic frame of wrongdoing by an individual could not completely enclose the story. As the politics of the situation began to emerge, the stories were reframed as a test of the mayor's skill and viability, a test in which he was seen to fare poorly. With their continuous coverage of demands for dismissal, both papers kept the heat on the mayor, and with their angry editorials, they rejected the attempts to apologize and to reform Cokely rhetorically. Thus, the press moved the drama toward its crisis by compelling the mayor to resolve the situation with the requisite gesture.

After the mayor took the only redressive step available—the familiar modern rite of public dismissal—the story was again reframed, this time as evidence of a phenomenon, black anti-Semitism, that demanded explanation. In the ensuing attempt at "redness through explanation," the biographies of Sawyer and Cokely, the history of politics in Chicago, the sociology of minority relations in the United States, and the tradition of anti-Semitism in Western culture were all consulted for answers. Finally, with the affirmation of symbols intended to reintegrate sundered groups, the press ascended from a therapeutic to a priestly role. Within the frame of "healing the wounds," the press appealed not only to the traditions of Judaism and Christianity but to such cherished myths of civil religion as the crusade for civil rights and the goodness of ordinary citizens despite the manipulations of cynical politicians.

No doubt Phillip Elliot would have recognized both cauterization and affirmation among the mass-mediated rituals enacted here. The press specified the acts of redress deemed necessary to close the wound and promoted healing with its attention to the rites of reconciliation offered by the mayor and others. And throughout the process, it affirmed the norm of racial harmony. Max Gluckman, upon whom Elliot draws extensively, argued that "ritual operates to cloak the fundamental conflicts" (1962, p. 40) and, to some extent, the newspapers did mystify race relations by cloaking them in a rhetoric of good will. Thus, it might be argued, the press moved to contain symbolically the damage to the body politic rather than to accomplish any sort of authentic reintegration that in this case would be progress, not simply in racial "harmony," but in real racial equality.

But that analysis, while accurate, would not exhaust the political and cultural complexity of the situation. These rituals were purposefully used by actors to enact a drama that did not—indeed, could not—simply affirm social solidarity. In the breach phase, the press itself opened a wound with the intent of directing the curative powers of public scrutiny toward what it saw as a particularly vicious outbreak of anti-Semitism. The display of moral indignation in the initial exposé was motivated not simply by the desire of Jewish groups to be rid of an offensive city employee but also by memories of the inflammatory racial rhetoric heard in previous mayoral campaigns. Many "star groupers" throughout the city, including the press itself, were anxious to treat quickly and thoroughly any threat of rhetorical reinfection. Thus, in the crisis phase, the press gave voice on the front page to those demanding

Cokely's dismissal and, speaking in its own official voice on the editorial page, it conducted a dialogue of sorts with the mayor concerning the necessity and urgency of that action.

When the press thought that it had located the cause of the crisis, the ensuing exercise in redress through explanation confronted—if only very briefly and incompletely—the claims of both African-Americans and Jews on the conscience of the community. That exercise, an example of what Turner calls a "distanced replication," reveals the firm grip of technical rationality on contemporary ritual, with its insistence that things must be, and ultimately can be, *explained*. Even so, there was a liminal moment as journalists spewed out all sorts of hypotheses and considered many modes of explanation that they would ordinarily exclude from political reportage.[13] Literature and, for that matter, psychology and sociology were momentarily taken far more seriously than usual. There was a brief opportunity to think *about* rather than merely *in* the powerful images—injection, castration, conspiracy, slavery, martyrdom, healing—that had been invoked throughout the drama. Nevertheless, attempts at redress and reintegration failed as others exploited the breach. Even as the press attended to rites of reconciliation, it was forced to mediate, as best it could, a scramble to seize still other images that could be used in the coming campaign: beloved memories of Harold Washington for some, bitter memories of C-o-k-e-l-y for others.

In sum, the Cokely affair illustrates a definition of mass-mediated ritual as something more conceptually complex and more politically volatile than the transmission of mythic tales to mass audiences. Following Turner, the affair may be seen as a progression of rituals organized within the social drama paradigm.[14] And following Elliot, that progression of rituals may also be seen to have been enacted within and through the press by other institutions of social power. Indeed, the progression was a veritable catalog of the means available to contemporary social institutions for the ritual cleansing of civic pollution: a journalistic exposé of official wrongdoing, a news release offering a public apology, editorials demanding action, a news conference announcing a dismissal, an exclusive interview offering self-justification, the appointment of a blue-ribbon commission, news analysis seeking technical explanations, a march on a public building, an interfaith religious service, a call by clergy for moral renewal, and, finally, an election.

Following Douglas, Lincoln, and Kertzer, however, these rituals may be seen to have served certain political interests and undermined others. While Turner wrote that the social drama is "a process of converting particular values and ends . . . into a system (which is always temporary and provisional) of shared or consensual meaning" (1980-1981, p. 152), the Cokely affair suggests that such consensual meanings may be worth no more than the newsprint on which they are written. On the other hand, the affair also suggests that the social drama is an important cultural resource both for waging and for narrating politics. Politicians draw upon it to frame their plans for "forcing one another to conform to something they have in mind," and journalists draw upon it to frame their mediation of those plans. Thus, the progression of political purification rituals was, at the same time, a progression of story frames: exposing misconduct, measuring competence, explaining phenomena, reconciling differences, monitoring flare-ups, assessing consequences. Indeed, within mass-mediated ritual, the narrating of politics and the waging of politics merge into a single process—the production of political reality.

In his classic essay Carey brought us to understand that ritual is not only a means of representation but a means of realization. Now we must come to understand that the reality produced within and through ritual can be conflictual as well as consensual. Ritual may serve as a cultural "control and container for human action," thereby ensuring "the maintenance of society in time," but it also allows individuals and institutions the "scope for using the situation to manipulate other people," thereby helping to "serve certain political interests and undermine others." Ritual holds the potential for outcomes ranging from reaction to revolution, but between these extremes of continuity and discontinuity are the everyday realities of life in a diverse, often discordant, society. "Social life proceeds somewhere between the imaginary extremes of absolute order, and absolute chaotic conflict and anarchic improvisation," wrote Moore and Myerhoff (1977, p. 3) in their analysis of secular rituals. "There is endless tension between the two, and also remarkable synchrony." The Cokely affair shows us how social life—complete with its grinding contradictions as well as its orderly sequences—can be produced within and through the process of mass-mediated ritual.

Notes

1. The news texts analyzed here were collected from the *Chicago Tribune* and the *Chicago Sun-Times* for the period between May 1, 1988, when the Cokely story broke, and February 28, 1989, when the mayoral primary election was held. Articles mentioning Cokely were located using the published indexes of both papers. These texts were supplemented with stories from the *Chicago Defender*, a paper oriented to African-Americans, and interviews with several journalists.

2. The *Sun-Times* framed its story less as an exposé of wrongdoing than as a reaction to it. Its story began, "Outraged religious leaders called Saturday for the firing of Steve Cokely," while the second paragraph reported that the mayor's press secretary thought the chances of that happening were "very, very remote" (Herrmann & O'Connor, 1988, p. 1).

3. For an analysis of investigative reporting as a form of ritualized moral discourse, see Ettema and Glasser (1988) and Glasser and Ettema (1989).

4. Two days after the Cokely story broke, Sawyer was obligated to attend a reception celebrating the fortieth anniversary of the founding of Israel—a definitive instance of bad political timing. It was at this reception, after several confrontations with Jewish community leaders, that the mayor said an apology might not suffice.

5. After the dismissal, Cokely said that he was sorry that the mayor had been "forced to bow to pressure to fire him" and that "his right to speak out as a black person without fear of apology was upper-most in the feelings of the black community" (Strong & Thornton, 1988). And, in one last enactment of his role as (what reporters called) "Sawyer's loyalty cop," Cokely attacked the alderman who was likely to be Sawyer's opponent in the mayoral election.

6. That Sunday was also a busy day on the op/ed pages. A *Sun-Times* editorial commended Sawyer for firing Cokely but argued that the episode revealed "a serious, perhaps even fatal, flaw in the mayor's leadership style" ("Better Late Than Never," 1988). The corresponding *Tribune* editorial said that Cokely had a right to freedom of speech but not a right to a job in city government, given what he had said ("Freedom to Speak," 1988). The *Sun-Time's* managing editor (Coffey, 1988) castigated Chicago's African-American leadership for not speaking out against "the demon's possessing Mr. Cokely." *Tribune* political writer Thomas Hardy (1988) found the mayor to be "politically hemorrhaging," and "this town smells blood."

7. Nearly all of the political analyses of the situation focused specifically on relations between African-Americans and Jews. Even a *Sun-Times* theater critic got into the act when, "amid all the shrill demagoguery," she "happily found sanctuary in the theater" with two "sane and thoughtful" plays about relationships between African-Americans and Jews— *Driving Miss Daisy* and, from South Africa, *Sophiatown* (Weiss, 1988, p. 51). One exception was an item on the *Tribune's* opinion page in which a political scientist argued that Reagan-era malign neglect of minority concerns was now yielding "a harvest of bitterness and resentment" (Weinstein, 1988).

8. This was the same clergyman who had said that many "grassroots blacks" thought that Jews were unloving. Interestingly, before the Cokely affair began this clergyman had been nominated by Mayor Sawyer to head the city's Human Rights Commission. Although both papers editorialized against the nomination after those remarks, the clergyman was eventually confirmed in the position. At that point, the *Tribune* published a rather sympathetic story that examined his behavior during the Cokely affair but also described his personal encounters with racial prejudice as a young man.

9. On the other hand, *Tribune* columnist Mike Royko (1988), whose politics can be described as cranky populism, mocked the notion of "a reaching out to each other" and castigated African-American officials, including the mayor, for failing to realize that they were supposed to be leading a large and diverse city. "What you have is a responsibility," he told them, "not an entitlement."

10. In a long letter to the *Tribune*, Nobel laureate Saul Bellow, a one-man Chicago cultural institution, criticized what he took to be the *Tribune's* excessive civic boosterism. "These 'nyeh-nyeh' civic rivalries are simply moronic," he wrote. "Few American cities are immune to such troubles" (Bellow, 1988). Citing the "grappling for control" acknowledged by the *Tribune's* editorialist, Bellow characterized the situation as an attempt by certain African-American politicians, who "are no more responsive to the real interests of their constituencies than their white counterparts were in the past," to "isolate and control" their constituencies.

11. Also in August, a large foundation, the Chicago Community Trust, organized a Human Relations Task Force "to study racial, ethnic and religious strife in Chicago and come up with a blueprint for change" (Cordts, 1988). The task force, which included a number of business and civic leaders, issued its report about a year later. The report contained analysis and recommendations for confronting a number of racially sensitive issues such as employment, housing, and education. The report also contained an earlier draft of this study.

12. See, for example, Garrioch (1987) and Gluckman (1963). For a relevant discussion of African-American rhetorical practices, see Kochman (1981), especially Chapter 3, "Fighting Words."

13. With a nod to Gregory Bateson, Turner argued that in the liminal suspension of daily reality during a ritual, a society may engage in metacommunication about itself. "A cyclical ritual is a frame within which members of a given group strive to see their own reality in new ways and to generate a language, verbal or nonverbal, that enables them to talk *about* what they normally talk" (1984, pp. 22, 23). In addition to cyclical rituals such as

seasonal rites of passage, social drama may also be an occasion for reflexivity. "If social drama regularly implies conflict of principles, norms, and persons, it also implies the growth of reflexivity: for if all principles and norms were consistent, and if all persons obeyed them, then, culture and society would be unself-conscious and innocent, untroubled by doubt. But few indeed are the human groups whose relationships are perpetually in equilibrium, and who are free from agonistic strivings" (p. 23).

14. The social drama is not a necessary element of mass-mediated ritual, although it is probably a very common component of such rituals. See, for example, Farrell's (1989) application of the concept to the Olympic Games—a ritual usually approached from a Durkheimian perspective.

References

Bellow, S. (1988, August 14). Bellow: Face truth of racial turmoil. *Chicago Tribune*, sec. 4, p. 2.

Better late than never on Cokely. (1988, May 8). *Chicago Sun-Times*, p. 12.

Camper, J., & Lipinski, A. M. (1988, May 15). Cokely furor ends the honeymoon between Chicago's blacks and Jews. *Chicago Tribune*, sec. 4, pp. 1, 4.

Carey, J. W. (1975). A cultural approach to communication. *Communication, 2*, 1-22.

Chicago takes another bum rap. (1988, July 30). *Chicago Tribune*, sec. 1, p. 10.

Coffey, R. R. (1988, May 8). Cokely's demons out among us. *Chicago Sun-Times*, p. 12.

Cohen, B. C. (1963). *The press and foreign policy.* Princeton, NJ: Princeton University Press.

Cokely isn't salvageable. (1988, May 5). *Chicago Sun-Times*, p. 54.

Cordts, M. (1988, August 28). 3rd group set up to study racial strife here. *Chicago Sun-Times*, p. 18.

Devall, C. (1988, May 2). Sawyer won't fire aide over ethnic slurs. *Chicago Tribune*, sec. 1, pp. 1, 8.

Dold, R. B. (1988a, May 4). Why mayor treads lightly on Cokely. *Chicago Tribune*, sec. 1, pp. 1, 18.

Dold, R. B. (1988b, May 6). Cokely's fire proved too hot for Sawyer's ice. *Chicago Tribune*, sec. 2, p. 4.

Dold, R. B. (1988c, May 8). Cokely was a burning fuse. *Chicago Tribune*, sec. 1, pp. 1, 14.

Dold, R. B. (1989, January 18). Daley turning tide in lakefront wards. *Chicago Tribune*, sec. 2, pp. 1, 8.

Douglas, M. (1975). *Implicit meanings: Essays in anthropology.* London: Routledge & Kegan Paul.

Elliot, P. (1982). Press performance as political ritual. In D. C. Whitney, E. Wartella, & S. Windahl (Eds.), *Mass communication review yearbook* (Vol. 3, pp. 583-619). Beverly Hills, CA: Sage.

Ettema, J. S., & Glasser, T. L. (1988). Narrative form and moral force: The realization of innocence and guilt through investigative journalism. *Journal of Communication, 38*(3), 8-26.

Farrell, T. B. (1989). Media rhetoric as social drama: The Winter Olympics of 1984. *Critical Studies in Mass Communication, 6*, 158-182.

Freedom to speak, yes, but not for us. (1988, May 8). *Chicago Tribune*, sec. 4, p. 2.

Garrioch, D. (1987). Verbal insults in eighteenth century Paris. In P. Burke & R. Porter (Eds.), *The social history of language* (pp. 104-119). Cambridge: Cambridge University Press.

Gibbons, T. (1988, May 8). Cokely flap spotlights old rift. *Chicago Sun-Times*, p. 8.

Glasser, T. L., & Ettema, J. S. (1989). Investigative journalism and the moral order. *Critical Studies in Mass Communication, 6*, 1-20.

Gluckman, M. (1962). Les rites de passage. In M. Gluckman (Ed.), *Essays on the ritual of social relations* (pp. 1-52). Manchester, UK: Manchester University Press.

Gluckman, M. (1963). Gossip and scandal. *Current Anthropology, 4,* 307-316.

Kennedy, E. (1988, July 26). Anti-Semitism in Chicago: A stunning silence. *New York Times,* sec. 1, p. 27.

Halevi, C. C. (1988, May 20). Cokely & company have badly wounded black-Jewish coalition. *Chicago Sun-Times,* p. 45.

Hardy, T. (1988, May 8). The week that was: A blood sport unfit for the squeamish. *Chicago Tribune,* sec. 4, p. 3.

Herrmann, A., & O'Connor, P. J. (1988, May 1). Mayor's aide's ouster sought. *Chicago Sun-Times,* pp. 1, 20.

Hirsley, M. (1988, May 11). Cardinal tells racial tension concern. *Chicago Tribune,* sec. 2, p. 6.

Jarrett, V. (1988a, May 8). When leaders leave vacuum, kooks fill void. *Chicago Sun-Times,* p. 13.

Jarrett, V. (1988b, May 12). Cokely blurs black-Jewish understanding. *Chicago Sun-Times,* p. 51.

Jarrett, V. (1988c, August 7). Prof causes more trouble than Cokely. *Chicago Sun-Times,* p. 13.

Jeter, J. (1988, August 20). Black-Jewish pulpit exchange begins. *Chicago Sun-Times,* p. 18.

Kertzer, D. I. (1988). *Ritual, politics, and power.* New Haven, CT: Yale University Press.

Kochman, T. (1981). *Black and white styles in conflict.* Chicago: University of Chicago Press.

Lehmann, D. J., & Hanania, R. (1988, May 12). 3 clerics seek calm in Cokely aftermath. *Chicago Sun-Times,* p. 20.

Lincoln, B. (1989). *Discourse and the construction of society.* New York: Oxford University Press.

Lipinski, A. M., & Baquet, D. (1988a, May 1). Sawyer aide's ethnic slurs stir uproar. *Chicago Tribune,* sec. 1, pp. 1, 27.

Lipinski, A. M., & Baquet, D. (1988b, May 6). Sawyer fires Cokely as aide. *Chicago Tribune,* sec. 1, p. 1; sec. 2, p. 4.

Lipinski, A. M., & Devall, C. (1988, May 3). Cokely's "sorry" fails to end fury. *Chicago Tribune,* sec. 1, pp. 1, 2.

Lipinski, A. M., & Strong, J. (1988a, May 4). Sawyer, top aides huddle on Cokely. *Chicago Tribune,* sec. 1, pp. 1, 9.

Lipinski, A. M., & Strong, J. (1988b, May 5). Mayor's silence heating Cokely crisis to a boil. *Chicago Tribune,* sec. 1, pp. 1, 22.

Moore, S. F., & Myerhoff, B. G. (1977). Secular ritual: Forms and meanings. In S. F. Moore & B. G. Myerhoff (Eds.), *Secular ritual* (pp. 3-24). Assen, The Netherlands: Van Gorcum.

Newman, M. W., & Williams, L. (1988, August 7). Blacks, Jews debunk "rift." *Chicago Sun-Times,* pp. 3, 22.

Next mayor should lead moral renaissance, clergy say. (1989, January 15). *Chicago Tribune,* sec. 4, pp. 1, 4.

Royko, M. (1988, May 18). Put up or shut up time in Chicago. *Chicago Tribune,* sec. 1, p. 3.

Sawyer should fire racist aide. (1988, May 3). *Chicago Tribune,* sec. 1, p. 18.

Slack, J. D. (1989, October). *Considering ritual in communication theory.* Paper presented at the Conference on Culture and Communication, Philadelphia.

Some things we should never forget. (1988, May 17). *Chicago Tribune,* sec. 1, p. 20.

Strausberg, C. (1988a, May 2). Sawyer swats stings over aide's words. *Chicago Defender,* p. 1.

Strausberg, C. (1988b, May 5). Rev. Martin seeks meeting to heal wounds over Cokely. *Chicago Defender,* p. 2.

Strong, J. (1988, May 19). Sawyer puts salve on racial wounds. *Chicago Tribune,* sec. 2, pp. 1, 6.

Strong, J., & Thornton, J. (1988, May 10). Cokely sorry mayor had to bow to pressure. *Chicago Tribune,* sec. 2, p. 3.

Sweet, L. (1988a, May 6). Cokely is fired. *Chicago Sun-Times,* pp. 1, 18.

Sweet, L. (1988b, May 8). Why mayor delayed on dismissal of Cokely. *Chicago Sun-Times,* pp. 1, 8.

Sweet, L., & Hanania, R. (1988a, May 3). Mayoral aide issues apology as furor grows. *Chicago Sun-Times*, p. 3.

Sweet, L., & Hanania, R. (1988b, May 4). Sawyer hedges on Cokely. *Chicago Sun-Times*, p. 3.

Turner, V. (1969). *The ritual process: Structure and anti-structure*. Chicago: Aldine.

Turner, V. (1974). *Dramas, fields, and metaphors*. Ithaca, NY: Cornell University Press.

Turner, V. (1980-1981). Social drama and stories about them. In W. J. T. Mithcell (Ed.), *On narrative* (pp. 137-167). Chicago: University of Chicago Press.

Turner, V. (1984). Liminality and the performance genres. In J. J. MacAloon (Ed.), *Rite, drama, festival, spectacle* (pp. 19-41). Philadelphia: Institute for the Study of Human Issues.

Voters smarter than their pols. (1988, July 7). *Chicago Tribune*, sec. 1, p. 16.

Weinstein, M. A. (1988, May 11). Malign neglect's harvest of bitterness and resentment. *Chicago Tribune*, sec. 1, p. 19.

Weiss, H. (1988, May 19). Easing tensions between blacks and Jews. *Chicago Sun-Times*, pp. 51, 54.

CHAPTER 30

Science, Technology and Risk Coverage of a Community Conflict

Cynthia-Lou Coleman

This article explores the news coverage of science, technology and risk when viewed through two distinct ideological lenses, one called scientific rationality, the other, cultural rationality (Plough and Krimsky, 1987). These constructs are used to illustrate how discourse is framed to legitimate some issues over others, some speakers over others, and some values over others. These views are traced to theoretical and practical approaches to risk communication. Plough and Krimsky (1987) note that risk assessment—the quantification of risk events—originates from a rational, scientific and technical world view that disregards values and other cultural elements. The authors note that risk communication, when derived from this framework, reflects top-down, one-way communication that attempts to bring public beliefs in line with expert views.

From *Media, Culture & Society*, 1995, Vol. 17, pp. 65-79. Copyright © 1995 Sage Publications, Ltd.

AUTHOR'S NOTE: The author thanks Roger Silverstone and Philip Schlesinger for their helpful comments on the manuscript; Carl Bybee for his critique of an earlier draft; and the Center for Environmental Communications and Education Studies at the University of Wisconsin for supporting her research.

Plough and Krimsky maintain that while *scientific rationality* ignores the issue of values, *cultural rationality* describes the view that the cultural context of risk embraces values, ethics, morality and qualitative judgements as critical to understanding risk communication. They note:

> Cultural rationality does not separate the context from the content of risk analysis. Technical rationality operates as if it can act independently of popular culture in constructing risk analysis, whereas cultural rationality seeks technical knowledge but incorporates it within a broader decision framework. (1987: 9)

One important avenue for examining how these world views shape public discourse is illustrated in news coverage of issues that embody technical and risk issues. One illuminating example is seen in the case of the Flambeau Copper Mine, which resulted in a great deal of news interest during 1990 and 1991. I examined coverage in 15 different newspapers, including the mainstream and advocacy presses, and weekly and daily newspapers, over an eighteen-month period, paying particular attention to the framing of the debate along scientific, technological and risk avenues. In all, 571 news stories were examined.

Before embarking on an explication of how discourse reflects scientific and cultural rationality, a brief history of the mine siting is presented.

Background of the Flambeau Mine

Wisconsin is no stranger to mineral mining. Its flag bears the figure of a miner, and the moniker "badger state" is derived from nineteenth-century lead miners who scooped out hillside living dens—badger-style—as temporary abodes (Reaves, 1988: 37-38). More recently, some 350,000 acres have been leased to various corporations (including Exxon, Kerr-McGee, Universal Oil Products, Amoco, Rayrock Mines, Western Nuclear, E. K. Lehman and Getty Oil, Kennecott, and American Copper and Nickel) for mineral exploration (Gedicks et al., 1982: 13-16). The Flambeau Copper Mine near Ladysmith is operated by the Salt Lake City-based Kennecott Corporation, whose parent organization is Rio Tinto Zinc (RTZ), based in London, England, and considered the world's largest mining company (*Wisconsin Treaties: What's the Problem?* n.d.: 9).

Kennecott made major efforts to establish itself as a community insider, opening a local office, donating money for a fire engine, establishing an adopt-an-eagle programme in the schools, and underwriting the cost of shipping homemade cakes to Gulf War soldiers. The company's newsletter, the *Flambeau News*, was distributed as a free insert in the local newspaper, the *Ladysmith News*, and both publications were mailed to servicemen and women from the region who were fighting the war. While the mining publication kept readers up-to-date on the progress of the mine, it additionally offered news of community interest including a "Good Neighbor Spot-light," a calendar of events, and a feature called "Letters and News From Home," addressed to Gulf War soldiers. In short, the newsletter also became a vehicle for embracing the United States' involvement in the Persian Gulf conflict.

Kennecott Corporation started the permit process in 1987 after filing an intent to begin mining, which was followed by a regulatory and environmental review. In Wisconsin, mining applicants are required to collect field data, submit various permits and ultimately develop a study of the environmental impacts. The official environmental document—the environmental impact statement—is officially authored by Department of Natural Resources (DNR) staff with literature provided by the mine company. The draft environmental impact statement is then made available to the public and a hearing ensues. In the case of the Flambeau Copper Mine, the final environmental impact report was released in 1990, followed by public hearings that summer.

The hearings, held in Ladysmith, drew statewide media attention and engendered heated debate over mining and the technical, political and legal process of approving the mine permit. Hearings were held throughout the summer, but the decision to approve the mine was not made until six months following the hearings. Examiner David Schwarz accepted the mining permit in January 1991, with construction scheduled to begin in July 1991.

Throughout the hearing process, the Lac Courte Oreilles band of the Ojibwa Indian nation maintained that the mine—which is located near the Flambeau River—would adversely impact upon natural resources in the region. One concern was the discharge of treated waste-water (effluent) from the mine into the river. Although the Indian band does not own the property or mineral rights, treaties with the U.S. government have guaranteed hunting, fishing and gathering access in the region. The Indians' lawyers had hoped to persuade the hearing examiner that mining would degrade the air, land and water, but they were unsuccessful.

Then, in May 1991, just months before mine construction was to begin, the Wisconsin DNR reported the discovery of endangered mollusks in the Flambeau River. Although discovery of the purple warty-back clams necessitated a revised study, the finding failed to halt pre-construction work at the mine site. Mine opponents were angered by the DNR's decision to explore the region for threatened and endangered species while the site was being prepared for mining, and brought court action.

The Sierra Club joined the Lac Courte Oreilles in filing a lawsuit to block construction, charging that the state had "improperly issued permits for the mine . . . [and] failed to do studies to support findings in the Environmental Impact Statement" ("Sierra Club, LCO File Suit," 1991). A judge enjoined the mine to desist from further construction until the DNR issued a revised environmental impact statement, and Kennecott was ordered to halt all work.

But the victory for the Sierra Club and the Ojibwa was short-lived. A second judge concluded in late 1991 that there was no basis to warrant further work stoppage. Construction resumed at the mine (C. Hammer, personal communication, 6 October 1992).

News Coverage and Framing

A number of events sparked off a plethora of news coverage of the Flambeau Mine. These included public hearings, a court injunction, the issuing of environmental impact reports and protest demonstrations. These events brought together sources with reporters, an intersection that provides the basis for the construction of news. Constructionists argue that the ability to define an issue is subject to the claims-maker's facility in forging social reality (Blumer, 1969; Hackett, 1984). And this social reality is more successful if it resonates with dominant cultural beliefs and values (Edelman, 1967/1985). More important, reporters take part in the construction of mediated reality by selecting which stories to pursue, which sources to interview, and which arguments to emphasize (Gitlin, 1980; Hartley, 1982).

Coverage of the Flambeau Mine was accomplished in three ways: (1) through direct quotes from news sources; (2) by positioning mine, DNR and government officials as arbiters of scientific, technical and factual information; and (3) construction of the dispute over the mine according to scientific and technical parameters determined, in part, by sources. In other words, who is selected to speak, the legitimacy accorded the speaker, and the type of arguments presented contributed to the construction of the mine discourse in news accounts.

Legitimacy Through Source Use and Framing

Sources set the tone and frame of discourse in media coverage. Particularly in the case of science and risk coverage, sources tend to be those who hold positions of authority, many of whom are scientists and government representatives (Lievrouw, 1990; Nelkin, 1989). This pattern is seen in the current case study, where 53 percent of all sources quoted during the eighteen-month period represented local, state and federal government sources, including scientists and technicians, and elected and appointed officials. Mining and business interests represented another 21 percent of all sources, while oppositional sources—Indians, environmentalists and protesters— accounted for 25 percent of those quoted. Sources are essential to the construction of news reality in that they are empowered to shape and frame discourse; moreover, a preponderance of one type of source can result in news coverage focused along narrow ideological lines (Berkowitz and Beach, 1993; Lasorsa and Reese, 1990; Molotch and Lester, 1975). "Framing" occurs when sources are allowed to set the parameters for debate by establishing the focal point of news and by setting boundaries for discourse. For example, Robert Ramharter, the DNR's supervisor of the mine, told a university audience that the decision to permit the mine was "not an ethical or moral or qualitative decision" (Center for Resource Policy Studies and Programs, 1991). Ramharter said staff members had "no position on mining" being "neither in favor nor against mining." Rather, the role of the DNR was defined by "mining statutes" and "administrative codes" (Department of Natural Resources, January, 1991). This view is an especially apt example of the scientific-technical rationality offered by Plough and Krimsky (1987). By establishing the mine permit decision as devoid of ethical or moral considerations, Ramharter implied that the issue was also value free. I argue, however, that cultural values are strikingly evident when viewing comments by government officials and others who embrace as values economic growth, progress and advancement through technology. One DNR document states that "following mining, if no other better use of the project area would be approved, the mining facilities would be dismantled and the land graded, vegetated and restored" (Department of Natural Resources, March 1991). The statement reveals a value that appropriate land use is development of the land, through industrial activities such as mining. Such values are underscored in arguments brought by mine company officials and local business owners in news accounts.

The preoccupation with growth and advancement is central to the metaphor-rich assertions by the mine company. The metaphor of "progress" resonates with Western cultural values and provides a pathway to enable the application of "modern technology" as a solution to environmental problems (Sjoberg, 1989). The slogan of the Flambeau Mine Company is "Partners in Progress," a recurrent theme heard at news conferences and found in the pages of company literature.

Progress is also used to distinguish the mine proponents (pro-progress) from those who do not share similar values. One resident's claim framed the mine opponents as primitive as well as anti-progress, noting, "they'll lead us back to the Stone Age" ("Use Extreme Caution," 1990). Metaphorically, progress is equated with the construction of the mine, which is construed as moving forward (positive value). Opponents are seen as restricting progress and moving backward (negative value) (Lakoff and Johnson, 1980).

Clearly, the arguments surrounding construction of the Flambeau Mine reflect a host of culturally based values, whether generated by scientists, engineers, Indians or politicians. Furthermore, the values that are expressed are central to the enactment of public policy that guides decisions that, in turn, reflect the value of industrial growth (Habermas, 1970). The values associated with scientific rationality—progress and economic rewards—guide the policy decisions enacted by the DNR.

Scientific Rationality and Meaning Construction

The overall structure of claims by mining proponents and opponents may be viewed as within the framework of scientific rationality, on the one hand, and that of cultural rationality, on the other. I first examine scientific rationality.

The value of progress is closely linked to the practice of finding technical solutions to scientific problems. We can distinguish technology from science in that technology applies science to solving problems. From this perspective, employees at the DNR (geologists, biologists, etc.) are technologists whose charge is to enable policy decisions within a technical, legal and political framework. Similarly engineers of the mining firm operate within the same legal-technical perspective. I argue that this framework or world view can be described as scientific rationality, borrowing from Plough and Krimsky's (1987) notion that this world view adopts a reductionist, rational and technical approach to social issues, while, at the same time, rejecting individual, qualitative, experiential and ethical approaches to solutions. Scientific rationality is an ideological perspective in which scientific information is regarded as factual, free of bias and bereft of emotion (Douglas, 1986; Habermas, 1970; Plough and Krimsky, 1987).

Yet scientific rationality is also a cultural concept in that it justifies, among other things, the dominion over nature through the use of technology, and thus secures power in the hands of scientists (Habermas, 1970). In turn, scientists are seen as hierarchically dominant over other actors, enjoying a privileged status in what Lievrouw (1990) called the knowledge culture. But power is also brokered by policymakers who similarly justify the control over nature by applying scientific rationality (Dornan, 1990). The hierarchy becomes visible in popular culture through the mass media, where technical solutions "become legitimized and contrasting models are then discarded as irrational" (Kawar, 1989: 739).

Mass media reflect the values of scientific and technical solutions (Hewitt, 1983; Schnaiberg, 1980). News media, in turn, accord science a privileged status. In this respect the news media system responds like other components of a social system (courts, government agencies, etc.) by regarding scientific solutions as paramount. Moreover, scientific values of objectivity and detachment strike a resonant chord with news values, providing a coupling of values—"objective" science with "objective" news reporting.

But science is hardly objective or free of social values. The rubric of scientific rationality has been used in support of countless political decisions, often under the guise of social progress. Witness, for example, news accounts of the western land movement in the United States throughout the nineteenth century. Progress was used to justify forced removal of indigenous natives in North America onto barren encampments (Deloria, 1974; Svensson, 1973). The allure of farming and grazing lands, and gold, silver, copper and crude oil prompted a takeover by European settlers of native territory that was justified as progress. Land use by Indians did not mesh with the values embraced by some settlers, a sentiment echoed in the statement by one pioneer's view of natives: "What is the right of a huntsman to the forest of a thousand miles over what he has accidentally ranged in quest of prey?" (Berkhofer, 1978: 138).

In similar vein, the notion of the frontier captures a metaphor used both in science and in legends of the "Old West." Nelkin (1989: 107) noted that when technology is associated with frontiers—maintained through the metaphor of battles or struggles—the "imagery of war implies that the experts should not be questioned, that new technology must go forward, and that limits are inappropriate." In North American cultures, the metaphor also conjures up clashes between Indians and encroaching Europeans.

I argue that the conflict over the Wisconsin copper mine was constructed against the backdrop of "appropriate" land use, progress and Indian-white relations. The mine company, politicians, business owners and technologists deemed mining to be a more appropriate use of the land than, for example, fishing, hunting and gathering, activities the Ojibwa people claim are not only more appropriate than mining, but are to be honoured under a nineteenth-century treaty signed by the Ojibwa and the United States governments (Center for Resource Policy Studies and Programs, 1991).

Thus, issues surrounding science and technology are enmeshed with values that reflect economic and political interests.

Technology, Control and Protection

Technology differs from science in that technology is the application of science to social problems (Schnaiberg, 1980). But technology is also a form of control. In the context of the copper mine, technology is the device used to inhibit pollution from mining waste-water and to stem seepage of chemicals into ground-water. Control can also be interpreted as control of nature via technological methods.

Moreover, control is interwoven with the metaphor of protection. In a broad sense, governments protect citizens through controls such as laws. In a more specific sense, controls at the Flambeau Copper Mine are interpreted as safeguards to protect wildlife, plant life and aquatic life: "Experts have found that the safeguards we have . . . will protect all the resources and all the wildlife in the area" (Associated Press, 1991c). The control over pollution is guaranteed by the application of technology: "Advanced technology . . . assure[s] that no pollution would reach the Flambeau River" (Associated Press, 1991b). Piloting the controls, however, is the mining company, and were it not for the mine in the first place, there would be no need for such technological measures.

For example, technological control was used to raise the value of mining. One mine proponent equated control with quality of life, noting: "Precisely because we have good environmental controls in place, mining should be embraced for its potential to improve the quality of life for many in Northern Wisconsin" (Mayers, 1991). The head of the local mining company remarked that improving the quality of life would benefit the entire community: "The bottom line here is that you can have mining and responsible environmental protection at the same time, and that's good news for everybody" (Mayers,

1990). The use of this phrasing successfully advances the pro-mining per-spective by universalizing a value held by some to a value shared by all, a technique commonly used to promote an ideological view (Eagleton, 1991).

Thus, arguments made by proponents of the Flambeau Copper Mine help illustrate the view that science and technology are accorded a higher status in social, political, legal and media arenas. The ideological perspective of scientific rationality is operationalized in the media discourse of the copper mine, where proponents and policymakers agree that mining em-braces social progress, appropriate and legitimate land use, improves the quality of life and benefits all. While such views are studded with cultural underpinnings, technologists and scientists deny that qualitative, ethical or moral considerations impact upon decision making. To do so would be subjective and unscientific.

When such views are presented in news accounts, the mass media are arguably seen as providing a clean canvas upon which contenders paint their claims. But, in the case of the Ladysmith mine, two aspects of coverage demonstrate that contenders and their claims are not accorded an equal share of legitimacy. First, scientific rationality appears to take the higher ground in the Flambeau mine discourse, where arguments forged by scientific rea-soning and technological promises are largely unquestioned by reporters, taken instead as bald facts. Second, the overall news discourse in the main-stream newspapers presented the copper mine issue as a war between opposing views. On a microsocial level, the battle was fought between pro-mine and anti-mine contenders, while, on a macrosocial level, the dis-pute illustrates differences arising from the scientific rationality perspective and the cultural rationality perspective.

Cultural Rationality and Meaning Construction

The flip side of the scientific rationality coin is cultural rationality. Recall the contention that cultural rationality is described by approaches to science, technology and risk using the very values that the DNR claimed are not applicable to the social discourse—morals, ethics, opinions and judgements (Plough and Krimsky, 1987). If *scientific rationality* provides the basis by which policy-making decisions embrace quantitative standards of risk, then *cultural rationality* provides the basis for individual, qualitative judgements of risk, what Douglas (1986: 8) called "standards of morality and decency."

Douglas's concept of culturally appropriate uses of technology can also be used to trace the distinction between risk assessment (quantitative im-pacts of risk) and risk acceptability (public responses to risk). The distinction is clearly illustrated in news accounts of the Flambeau Mine. Mine repre-sentatives and DNR officials frame risk around probabilistic impacts. While scientists reassure citizens that "standards" would "control" harmful risks, environmentalists question the efficacy of technology in addressing impacts, and the trustworthiness of the mine company and government technologists in carrying out risk abatement, otherwise termed "recreancy" (Freudenburg, 1993). Moreover, the context of risk, when viewed by supporters of the mine, is that health and environmental risks are offset by the benefits of jobs and tax revenue. One resident said he believed the mine to be necessary "even if there is some risk involved because it would help the economy" (Seely, 1991). Another citizen noted: "There's a risk in anything you do. The community needs to live" (Powers, 1991).

Yet mine opponents view risks in a different light. Some dispute the claim by mine and DNR representatives that the effects will be short term, noting that the company and community can never retreat to pre-mining conditions. One critic disputed the guarantee of "control," noting, "there is no way to put the poisons back in the bottle once they've escaped" (Hurrie, 1990). Others argued in a technological vein, saying that "the technology doesn't exist to clean up the contamination" ("Local Activists Blast," 1990). Another view questioned the ethics of the mine company, noting, "it's cheaper to pay a fine than it is to invest in abatement technology" (Swerkstrom, 1991).

Such views show a distrust of technology generally, and of the mine company and DNR specifically. Distrust was fueled by the discovery of endangered species after the mine permits were issued. Opponents charged that the DNR failed to explore the Flambeau region thoroughly for signs of such species, even though a staff biologist had recommended the action long before the permit was issued. Moreover, the DNR was accused of rubber-stamping the Flambeau Mine permit.

The discovery of endangered clams enabled mine opponents to call into question the role of the DNR in sanctioning the mine. According to one source, "the state's entire process was pre-judged, and designed [to] allow the project at all costs" ("Sierra Club, LCO File Suit," 1991). Others claimed "bad science," but such views were accorded little credence by the press. Instead, such claims tended to underscore the contention that mine opponents were behaving irrationally. A mining opponent equated science with witchcraft, accusing the DNR of engaging in "voodoo biology" (Rutlin, 1991). But even critics excuse scientists from having agendas: "The DNR is like a Dr. Jekyll and Mr. Hyde. They have scientists trying to do a good job and they have political handlers who are trying to handle a hot potato" (Associated Press, 1991a). The speaker equates scientists with the brilliant Dr. Jekyll and policymakers with the vile Mr. Hyde, ignoring the fact that many policymakers are, in fact, scientists.

The frame of cultural rationality enabled Ojibwa Indians to link science with values, although this viewpoint was limited in the media arena to nonmainstream Indian publications. An Indian biologist noted that "we have a moral obligation to future generations to protect our environment." She added:

> A system must be devised that not only takes into account the newest technologies, but also the understandings of culture beliefs. We must

look at the ecosystem as a whole when protecting the environment and its health. ("GLIFWC Biologist Questions," 1990)

The holistic viewpoint, that cultural beliefs are an important social complement in addressing environmental problems, is difficult to locate in the mainstream media discourse concerning the copper mine. Arguments tend to be reduced along dichotomous lines, driven asunder by the metaphor of war, this reducing the issue to simplistic, dualistic terms (Bennett, 1988: 21-64).

Conclusions

The distinction between ideological viewpoints characterized by scientific rationality and cultural rationality is illustrated in the Flambeau Copper Mine case study, where scientific claims, speakers and values are accorded greater legitimacy than cultural claims, speakers and values. "Scientific" sources from the DNR and mine company assert they are untouched by cultural constraints. These sources distanced cultural and moral concerns from scientific and technological ones, distinguishing objective facts from subjective beliefs. But by constructing a social reality that separates facts from feelings and assessments from perceptions, sources are disingenuous. Scientific judgements are not distinct from a cultural context. Risk assessment, for example, requires scientists and policymakers to make value judgements concerning the impacts of risks. These impacts typically reflect mortality (risk of death) which has been judged as having greater importance than morbidity (risk of disease). And impacts upon human health are judged hierarchically as more important than impacts upon wildlife. Thus, scientific rationality, which supposedly has no connection to a cultural context, is actually a revealing metaphor for discussing differing outlooks on social issues that embrace science.

Mass media reflect similar ideological views, endorsing the hierarchy of scientific rationality. We can witness this in news accounts of the copper mine coverage, where reporters support the belief that scientific and technological judgements are value free. Evidence for this is found in stories where views offered by scientists are unchallenged by other sources. In the case of the Flambeau mine, officials from government, science and industry are quoted more than any other sources, and their views are often used to establish the frame of the news story. Environmentalists and Indians "oppose" and "challenge" the dominant view and are characterized as the Other—outsiders—in mediated discourse. News reporters rarely looked beyond the claims of the mine company, the DNR, the courts or government officials, accepting their statements and claims at face value. And while those who opposed the established order were given a public platform to state their views, they were not accorded "equal time" with other sources, nor were they accorded equal legitimacy. Their claims tended to be disregarded as irrational, their opinions unscientific, in contrast to the "facts." The mining company seized ownership of the facts, noting "the facts speak for themselves," and that anyone who disagreed was "misinformed." Thus, news accounts approached the issue as a duel between facts and opinions, with scant attention paid to how facts became the purview of those with an interest in seeing the copper mine permit approved.

The mine news coverage demonstrates journalism's tendency to dichotomize news: The Wisconsin case was characterized as war between opposing sides, and the issues boiled down to rationality versus emotion, jobs versus clams, and democracy versus anarchy. By framing the issue as a war, the press implies that one side will emerge victorious. One powerful metaphor with historical overtones shows readers that battles between Indians and the U.S. government traditionally favour U.S. institutions. And with few exceptions, most battles between the two groups were lost by Native Americans. Contemporary press images of Indians still reflect antiquated stereotypes. Moreover, the relationship between the sovereign government of the Ojibwa Nation and the United States is far from equal. The U.S. government is the benefactor and protector of the Indian, just as the DNR protects the endangered clam. The Indian full-blood and the purple warty-back clam are portrayed as rare artifacts that necessitate protection by the powers of the state. In a similar vein, the mine company donned the mantle of protector and benefactor, thus elevating its status to that of the DNR and the state.

A reader of the small town *Ladysmith News*, for example, most likely saw a picture of the mining company as a friendly neighbour who promised financial prosperity to a poor community. And when the local newspaper was confronted with conflictive events, such as court hearings or public demonstrations, it tended to characterize these in scientific, technical or legal terms. The facts could then speak for themselves without seeming to engage in a battle over values. Rather than providing in-depth analyses of such issues as tribal rights or the controversial history of the mining company's operations in other communities, the newspaper covered events, such as court hearings. One of the few attempts at in-depth coverage was a long science story about the sex life of the endangered clam that required no exchange of ideas.

Such coverage in homogeneous communities like Ladysmith is probably functional. In a general sense, conflict may be viewed by editors and reporters as disruptive to the social fabric of the community (Olien et al., 1989). So newspapers protect the community by downplaying or reframing conflict. But conflict may also stimulate social change, and that requires reporting issues that might be viewed as threatening. Reporting social disputes, government ineptitude and clashes over values also has the potential for promoting social growth within communities by bringing these issues into the media arena for discussion. In order for this to occur, editors would need to see the newspaper's role as central to change, rather than a force for stability, cohesion and good feelings. Perhaps the framers of the document *A Free and Responsible Press* (Commission on Freedom of the Press, 1947) anticipated that newspapers might become overly concerned with maintaining social harmony and thus be blind to disputes or oppositional views that may appear to damage the social fabric. Perhaps because of the newspaper's proclivity for covering events and because of the characterization of the copper mine dispute as a battle, few reporters embarked on in-depth examination of views that question the very meaning of assumptions about values. Officials at the DNR quickly disassociated science from ethics, and as a result, reporters refrained from questioning or disputing scientific claims, thus illustrating the underlying persuasive power of the framework of scientific rationality. Similarly, policymakers claimed that their decisions were divorced from value judgements, and again, reporters failed to explore the value systems underlying such judgements. Ultimately, reporters failed to link these values with the organizations empowered to secure the interests of the full spectrum of the citizenry, as opposed to just securing the interests of those with economic investments in the copper mine. These so-called dominant interests are rooted in an ideological perspective that enables progress and financial growth through the extraction of minerals from the earth. Newspapers covering the Wisconsin mine reflect these values by their uncritical reporting practices.

Although dissenters outside the mainstream challenge the dominant view in their literature and through quotations in news stories, they are largely unsuccessful in setting the news frame. In the case of the Ladysmith copper mine, the viewpoints and values of the Flambeau Mining Company and the Department of Natural Resources resonated with culturally dominant beliefs such as appropriate land use, sanctity of science, efficacy of technology in problem solving, social progress and financial prosperity. And these beliefs are part and parcel of those who are empowered to effect policy decisions.

References

Associated Press (1991a) "Clam Protection Plan Announcement Today," *Wausau Daily Herald* (3 July): 3A.

Associated Press (1991b) "Mining Foe Takes Case to Firm's Doorstep," *Eau Claire Leader Telegram* (9 Aug.): 4B.

Associated Press (1991c) "Mining Firm to Appeal Order," *Superior Evening Telegram* (31 Aug.): 1.

Bennett, W. L. (1988) *News: The Politics of Illusion*. New York: Longman.

Berkhofer, R. F., Jr. (1978) *White Man's Indian: Images of the American Indian From Columbus to the Present*. New York: Vintage.

Berkowitz, D. and D. W. Beach (1993) "News Sources and News Context: The Effect of Routine News, Conflict and Proximity," *Journalism Quarterly*, 70(1): 4-12.

Blumer, H. (1969) *Symbolic Interactionism: Perspective and Method*. Berkeley: University of California.

Center for Resource Policy Studies and Programs (1991) Videotape series from lectures titled "Mining in Wisconsin." University of Wisconsin–Madison.

Commission on Freedom of the Press (1947) *A Free and Responsible Press.* Chicago: University of Chicago Press.

"Cumulative Impacts of Mining Development in Northern Wisconsin" (1991). Wisconsin Department of Natural Resources information sheet (Mar.).

Deloria, V. (1974) *The Indian Affair.* New York: Friendship.

Dornan, C. (1990) "Some Problems in Conceptualizing the Issue of Science and Media," *Critical Studies in Mass Communication,* 7: 48-71.

Douglas, M. (1986) *Risk Acceptability According to the Social Sciences.* London: Routledge.

Eagleton, T. (1991) *Ideology: An Introduction.* London: Verso.

Edelman, M. (1967/1985) *The Symbolic Uses of Politics.* Urbana: University of Illinois Press.

Freudenburg, W. (1993) "Risk and Recreancy: Weber, the Division of Labor and the Rationality of Risk Perceptions" *Social Forces,* 71(4): 909-932.

Gedicks, A., J. Clokey, R. Kennedy and M. Soref (1982) *Land Grab: The Corporate Theft of Wisconsin's Mineral Sources.* Madison, WI: Center for Alternative Mining Development Policy.

Gitlin, T. (1980) *The Whole World Is Watching: Mass Media in the Making and Unmaking of the New Left.* Berkeley: University of California Press.

"GLIFWC Biologist Questions Environmental Safety of Mine" (1990) *Masinaigan* (Fall): 20, 22.

Habermas, J. (1970) "Technology and Science as Ideology," pp. 81-127 in J. Habermas, *Toward a Rational Society.* Boston, MA: Beacon.

Hackett, R. (1984) "Decline of a Paradigm? Bias and Objectivity in News Media Studies," *Critical Studies in Mass Communication,* 1(3): 229-259.

Hartley, J. (1982) *Understanding News.* London: Routledge.

Hewitt, K. (1983) "The Idea of Calamity in a Technocratic Age," pp. 3-33 in K. Hewitt (ed.), *Interpretations of Calamity.* Boston, MA: Allen & Unwin.

Hurrie, W. (1990) "Mining Province of Wisconsin," *Green Net* (Apr.): 1, 3.

Kawar, A. (1989) "Issue Definition, Democratic Participation, and Genetic Engineering," *Policy Studies Journal,* 17(4): 714-744.

Lakoff, G. and M. Johnson (1980) *Metaphors We Live By.* Chicago: University of Chicago Press.

Lasorsa, D. L. and S. D. Reese (1990) "News Source Use in the Crash of 1987: A Study of Four National Media," *Journalism Quarterly,* 67(1): 60-71.

Lievrouw, L. A. (1990) "Communication and the Social Representation of Scientific Knowledge," *Critical Studies in Mass Communication,* 7(1): 1-10.

"Local Activists Blast Mining Plans at Rice Lake Forum Thursday" (1990) *Rice Lake Chronotype* (4 July): 1.

"Local Authority to Regulate Mining" (1991) Wisconsin Department of Natural Resources information sheet (Jan.).

Mayers, J. (1990) "Mine Raises Economic Issue Too Besides Environment, Is It Worth Change?" *Wisconsin State Journal* (10 June): 1F.

Mayers, J. (1991) "State Puts Toughness of Mining Laws to Test," *Wisconsin State Journal* (24 Mar.): 12A.

Molotch, H. and M. Lester (1975) "Accidental News: The Great Oil Spill as Occurrence and National Event," *American Journal of Sociology,* 81(2): 235-260.

Nelkin, D. (1989) "Communicating Technological Risk: The Social Construction of Risk Perception," *Annual Review of Public Health,* 10: 95-113.

Olien, C. N., P. J. Tichenor and G. A. Donohue (1989) "Media Coverage and Social Movements," pp. 139-163 in C. T. Salmon (ed.), *Information Campaigns: Balancing Social Values and Social Change.* Newbury Park, CA: Sage.

Plough, A. and S. Krimsky (1987) "The Emergence of Risk Communication Studies: Social and Political Context," *Science, Technology & Human Values,* 12(3, 4): 4-10.

Powers, P. (1991) "Some Are Sick and Tired of Protesters," *Eau Claire Leader Telegram* (7 July): 1.

Reaves, S. D. (1988) *Wisconsin: Pathways to Prosperity.* Northridge, CA: Windsor.

"Role of the Department of Natural Resources in Regulating Mining" (1991) Wisconsin Department of Natural Resources information sheet (Jan.).

Rutlin, T. (1991) "Endangered Species Has a PR Problem," *Wausau Daily Herald* (23 July): 1, 2.

Schnaiberg, A. (1980) *Environmental Intelligence: Constraints on Scientists and Technologists.* Oxford: Oxford University Press.

Seely, R. (1991) "Mining Company Donations: Generosity or Bribe?" *Wisconsin State Journal* (28 Mar.): 2A.

"Sierra Club, LCO File Suit to Block Open Pit Mines (1991) *Ladysmith News* (8 Aug.): 1A.

Sjoberg, L. (1989), "Global Change and Human Action: Psychological Perspectives," *International Social Science Journal* 121: 413-432.

Svensson, F. (1973) *The Ethnics in American Politics: American Indians.* Minneapolis, MN: Burgess.

Swerkstrom, B. (1991) "Mining Opponent Details Firm's Poor Track Record," *Superior Evening Telegram* (8 Aug.): 21.

"Use Extreme Caution Before Reneging on Mine Pact" (1990) *Ladysmith News* (4 Oct.): 1, 3.

Wisconsin Treaties: What's the Problem? (n.d.) Midwest Treaty Network brochure.

Epilogue
Applying the Tools to Study News

Altogether, the 30 readings in this book have shown how news is a social product shaped by several levels of social aggregation, particularly the professional, the organizational, the institutional, and the societal. This perspective brings many implications for the study of news and newsmaking. It leads toward vastly different answers to the question, "What is news?" The perspective also leads away from questions that ask whether news is good or bad, or if journalists have done the right thing. In sum, the value of this book's approach is that it moves away from normative evaluations of news and newswork and toward an understanding of why news turns out as it does.

To accomplish this, the collective body of readings here has contradicted the ideology of journalism by showing that in the larger picture, the opinions and beliefs of individual journalists will not have a great effect on the news: Their organization, their profession, their work processes, and society all impose constraints and expectations on *what* can be done and *how* it can be done. Similarly, media organizations will not have a great amount of autonomy from the rest of society, simply because their continued existence requires that they play by society's rules for selling a marketable product and remaining economically viable.

From an even bigger picture, the readings contained here show how news cannot stray too far from what news has been, because news stories must be resonant with the stories that society believes about itself. In essence, rather than working toward change, news tends to reproduce the existing social structure. For example, news stories cannot reinvent the social balances among social actors and social institutions and still be seen as accurate. To do so would make the news look "wrong," which would challenge the credibility of reporters and their media organization.

Applying the Tools

At this point, it becomes useful to move from describing the utility of a social approach toward news to applying some of the tools that have been introduced to examine specific news stories and situations. The three examples that are introduced move from a more microlevel—the effect of journalists on the news—to more macrolevels that consider the effect of society and the media institution.

The first example reassesses the effect of journalists on the news by applying the concept of *level of analysis*. In April 1996, a report from the Freedom Forum presented results from a survey about political beliefs of reporters and editors. The report triggered a string of news articles and opinion pieces asserting that the media reflect a liberal bias favoring the Democratic party (Povich, 1996). Much of this assertion was based on survey results showing that 89% of reporters and 60% of editors voted for Bill Clinton in the 1992 presidential election—much higher proportions than the 43% of all voters who did so. In other words, the articles argued that because individual journalists tended to be Democrats, the news would be slanted in favor of the Democratic party and its candidates.

From a social meanings of news perspective, though, the connection between an individual reporter's political leaning and that reporter's ability to get an intentionally biased story into print or on the air is questionable. At the societal level, news content must appear neutral enough to be accepted by the bulk of the audience. At the organizational level, publishers—in contrast to journalists—tend to be conservative and affiliate with the Republican party. Furthermore, unofficial newsroom policy tends to set the boundaries for acceptable slants a story can take.

Sociologist Herbert Gans addressed this ongoing debate about news slant in a 1985 *Columbia Journalism Review* article, "Are U.S. Journalists Dangerously Liberal?" Gans rebutted research by Stanley Rothman, S. Robert Lichter, and Linda Lichter that linked journalists' political leaning with production of biased news. As Gans explained, most other levels of analysis substantially cancel intentional news bias:

> The news is mainly shaped by the size of the newshole, news organization budgets, information available from news sources and newsmakers, and by "media considerations"—for example, television's need for dramatic tape or film. (Gans, 1985)

In other words, Gans argues that individual-level variability of the news is limited by organizational constraints, by news sources, and by conventions of the media institution in a marketplace press system. His assertion is clearly supported by the studies in this book, especially those concerning the effect of the news organization and of the news profession.

The second example applies the concepts of news as narrative and news as ideology to an incident where Charles Stuart, a white male, claimed that a black stranger had shot and killed (and also shot him) his pregnant wife,

Carol, while their car was stopped in city traffic. As the story unfolded, Stuart's brother revealed that he had been asked to dispose of a gun as part of what Charles Stuart called an insurance fraud scheme. Eventually, though, it dawned on the brother that Charles had used the gun to kill Carol Stuart and wound himself. Shortly after this revelation, Charles Stuart committed suicide. Until the real story came out, however, news reports continued to focus on crimes by blacks against whites. Afterward, black communities expressed concern that the mainstream media had accepted this socially stereotyped story so readily.

The Stuart case illustrates how news represents stories that society tells about itself, stories that tend to reflect key ideological beliefs of society. In this case, those beliefs concerned the connection between race and crime. As the *Washington Post*'s Richard Cohen explained:

> Credit Charles Stuart with something. He knew his country. When he wanted to frame someone for his wife's murder, he chose a whole category—young black men. We all—blacks and whites—believed his story until the lie was exposed. (Cohen, 1990, p. 1c)

Another news item in this case study suggests that mystery writers saw the Stuart story differently from the start. In part, this difference can be accounted for by journalists' beliefs about reporting the news rather than making it. Writers of fiction, however, do not subscribe to this professional ideology and are able to see the story differently. "It's not a terribly exotic idea for a man to want to kill his spouse and pretend it was done by a third party," explained Robert Parker, author of the "Spenser" mysteries, in a *Boston Globe* article. *Globe* reporter Chris Black's article further explained why the socially resonant occurrence was so readily accepted:

> The Stuart case has captured the imagination of the public precisely because it is an example of life imitating art, with all the malevolence and horror, all the unexpected twists and turns of a best-selling potboiler. (Black, 1990, p. A21)

Black went on to quote thriller novelist John Katzenbach's interpretation of the story:

> The essential thing that Chuck Stuart did that is truly intriguing, was to . . . make society think that it was guilty and that he was the victim.

In essence, if news tells stories about society the way we expect them to be told, those stories will be believed even if they are incorrect. Only after the real story is exposed will the story be revised. This point comes through clearly in the "Telling News" and "Ideology and News" sections in this book. Chapters in the section "Professionalizing News," such as Tuchman's "Making News by Doing Work" and Fishman's "News and Nonevents," also show

how reporters typify how occurrences are "supposed to go" to facilitate the predictable accomplishment of work.

A third and final application of a socially based analytic framework applies what Reese ("The News Paradigm and the Ideology of Objectivity") and others[1] have referred to as "paradigm repair": a process that attempts to show that despite an isolated instance that has occurred, the professional practices incorporated into the journalistic paradigm really do work to provide an objective rendering of reality.

Paradigm repair is often accomplished by showing how the "rules" of the paradigm were violated, so that the paradigm produced results other than what it should have. In Reese's case, a well-known journalist at the *Wall Street Journal* was found to have been an active socialist—journalists are not supposed to be able to participate actively in politics and retain their objectivity. In another study of paradigm repair, a television news crew was blamed for covering a story where a man waited for the crew to show up and then lit himself on fire when the cameraman began filming him. Most simply, the crew was seen as participating in the news instead of passively recording it.

Often in paradigm repair, the media institution accomplishes its task by engaging in a series of editorials and opinion pieces identifying a scapegoat and explaining how the wrongdoing occurred. This paradigm repair appears in another example, where a seven-year-old girl died while trying to be the youngest pilot to fly across the United States.

As Jessica Dubroff prepared for her transcontinental flight, news stories were filled with excitement—a world record was about to be broken by a spirited, adventurous youngster. Reporters wrote in highly positive terms, exalting the feat. "Young Pilot to Make History," one headline read (Associated Press, 1996). "They have a great American spirit," her mother was quoted as saying about Jessica and her brother Joshua.

But then tragedy struck. Taking off from Cheyenne, Wyoming, in bad weather, Jessica's plane nose-dived into the ground, killing her, her instructor, and her father. By its enthusiasm to applaud the "American spirit," the media institution quickly realized it had failed to serve the watchdog role embedded in journalistic ideology. Catching the problem, print media attempted paradigm repair by blaming broadcast media for sensationalizing the story, encouraging the events that led to Jessica's death. "What kind of media treat it as a legitimate news story? The answer to this couldn't be more depressing—all kinds of them did," wrote one newspaper columnist (Simon, 1996, p. 1D). Commenting on the media's sudden switch from jubilation to dubbing the flight "ill advised," another columnist admonished:

> Unfortunately, concerns about the wisdom of her attempt didn't stop newscasters from doing happy-face pre-flight interviews, or from setting up satellite trucks at her destination, or . . . from putting a camera in the cockpit. (Bianco, 1996, p. B-6)

Yet other headlines quickly placed the blame on society rather than the media. "What the hell were her parents doing?" read the title over a column by Eileen McNamara in the *Boston Globe* (McNamara, 1996, p. 18). "What on earth were they thinking when they let that little fresh-faced child, 7 years old, fly an airplane so far?" echoed the *Hartford Courant* (Horgan, 1996, p. A2). "Parental pride will not be listed as the cause of death," chided Steve Wilson in the *Arizona Republic*, "but it surely contributed to the crash that killed Jessica, her dad and flight instructor Joe Reid (Wilson, 1996, p. A2).

Another paradigm repair tactic in this incident was to focus on failings of Federal Aviation Administration pilot regulations. "A 7-year-old is not a pilot by any means," an FAA spokesman was quoted as saying in *Newsday* (Terrazzano, 1996, p. A4). That article further pointed out that the Dubroff incident caused the FAA to review rules governing flying by unlicensed pilots. The *Boston Globe* also dug into the regulation angle, asserting that "the Federal Aviation Administration historically has looked the other way whenever children climb into the cockpit in search of a record (Brelis, 1996, p. 16). There, an unnamed former FAA official condemned the record-setting effort as "patently stupid," and a spokesperson for the Aircraft Owner and Pilot's Association called it a "stunt flight" attempting to set a "pseudo-record."

This example shows how the news media—after realizing that the news paradigm had been violated by becoming part of the occurrence—began working to demonstrate that the general case of the paradigm really was reliable but that media enthusiasm over the flight was a fluke that violated the rules of an otherwise reliable paradigm. In all, paradigm repair becomes a way for the media institution to justify its existence within its current system of operation.

Combined, these examples have applied the book's concepts to show how they can be used to analyze and understand the news. For many readers, this approach will represent a new beginning, a way of seeing news in a fresh way that helps move from discussions about journalistic norms and ethics— shoulds and oughts—toward discussions that provide understanding and explanation. For other readers, this approach will not introduce new ideas but instead an organized way of thinking about what has become intuitive but not necessarily grounded in a conceptually cohesive way.

In either case, the hope here is that this book will lead readers on a more informed exploration of the social meanings of news.

Note

1. For example, see Bennett, W. L., Gressett, L. A., & Haltom, W. (1985). Repairing the news: A case study of the news paradigm. *Journal of Communication, 35*, 50-68.

References

Associated Press. (1996, April 8). 7-year-old girl plans to fly cross-country, back. *Chicago Tribune*, Sports section, p. 8.

Bianco, R. (1996, April 16). The media egged on Jessica with gee-whiz color stories. *Pittsburgh Post-Gazette*, p. B-6.

Black, C. (1990, January 14). Surprise ending in Boston case not so shocking to mystery writers. *Boston Globe*, p. A21.

Brelis, M. (1996, April 12). FAA to review child-pilot rules: Foul-weather flight questioned by some in wake of crash. *Boston Globe*, National section, p. 16.

Cohen, R. (1990, January 14). False accusation against black dupes nation. *Des Moines Register*, p. 1C.

Gans, H. J. (1985, November/December). Are U.S. journalists dangerously liberal? *Columbia Journalism Review, 24*, 29-33.

Horgan, D. (1996, April 12). A 7-year-old girl is dead, and for a foolhardy reason. *Hartford Courant*, p. A2.

McNamara, E. (1996, April 12). What the hell were her parents doing? *Boston Globe*, National section, p. 18.

Povich, E. (1996). *Partners and adversaries: The contentious connection between Congress and the media*. Arlington, VA: Freedom Forum.

Simon, J. (1996, April 16). A little girl sacrificed to feed the media monster. *Buffalo News*, p. 1D.

Terrazzano, L. (1996, April 12). Question: How old is too young? *Newsday*, p. A4.

Wilson, S. (1996, April 12). Dad's dream for girl can be called factor in plane crash. *Arizona Republic*, p. A2.

Name Index

Subject Index

About the Editor

Dan Berkowitz (B.S., Humboldt State University; M.S., University of Oregon; Ph.D., Indiana University) is Associate Professor of Journalism and Mass Communication at the University of Iowa. His research centers on the study of news, including the work of journalists, the role of news sources, the nature of local television news, and the relationship between community and local media. He has published his research in *Journal of Broadcasting & Electronic Media, Journal of Communication, Journalism Quarterly, Journal of Public Relations Research,* and *International Journal of Public Opinion Research.*

List of Authors

J. Herbert Altschull, Visiting Professor, Department of Writing Seminars, Johns Hopkins University

Roberta C. Baade, Vice President, Corporate Human Resources, Sunrise Medical, Carlsbad, California

Charles R. Bantz, Vice Provost, Arizona State University

S. Elizabeth Bird, Professor, Department of Sociology and Anthropology, University of Minnesota, Duluth

Glen L. Bleske, Assistant Professor, Department of Journalism, California State College, Chico

Warren Breed, formerly at Tulane University, now retired and living in Walnut Creek, California

Cynthia-Lou Coleman, Assistant Professor, School of Journalism and Communication, University of Oregon

Bryan K. Crow, Associate Professor, Department of Speech Communication, Southern Illinois University–Carbondale

Robert W. Dardenne, Associate Professor, School of Mass Communication, University of South Florida

Dennis K. Davis, Professor, College of Communications, Pennsylvania State University

G. A. Donohue, Professor Emeritus, Department of Sociology, University of Minnesota

EDITOR'S NOTE: This listing is current at the time of publication.

Sharon Dunwoody, Professor, School of Journalism and Mass Communication, University of Wisconsin–Madison

Matthew C. Ehrlich, Assistant Professor, Department of Journalism, University of Illinois, Urbana–Champaign

Nina Eliasoph, Assistant Professor, Department of Sociology, University of Wisconsin–Madison

James Stewart Ettema, Professor, Department of Communication Studies, Northwestern University

Mark Fishman, Associate Professor, Department of Sociology, Brooklyn College, City University of New York

Marilyn Lester, Ph.D. graduate of University of California, Santa Barbara

Jack Lule, Associate Professor, Department of Journalism, Lehigh University

Suzanne McCorkle, Interim Associate Dean, College of Social Sciences and Public Affairs, previously with the Department of Communication, Boise State University

John H. McManus, Assistant Professor, Department of Communications, St. Mary's College of California

Marian Meyers, Assistant Professor, Department of Communication, Georgia State University, Atlanta

Harvey Molotch, Professor, Department of Sociology, University of California, Santa Barbara

C. N. Olien, Professor Emeritus, Extension and Rural Sociology, University of Minnesota

Stephen D. Reese, Professor, Department of Journalism, University of Texas at Austin

Michael Schudson, Professor, Department of Communication, University of California, San Diego

Pamela J. Shoemaker, Professor, S. I. Newhouse School of Public Communication, Syracuse University

Robert Rutherford Smith, Professor, School of Communication and Theater, Temple University

John Soloski, Professor, School of Journalism and Mass Communication, University of Iowa

P. J. Tichenor, Professor Emeritus, School of Journalism and Mass Communication, University of Minnesota

Gaye Tuchman, Professor, Department of Sociology, University of Connecticut, Storrs

Richard C. Vincent, Associate Professor, Department of Communication, University of Hawaii at Manoa

Daniel B. Wackman, Professor, School of Journalism and Mass Communication, University of Minnesota, Minneapolis

David Manning White, Boston University and Virginia Commonwealth University—deceased

D. Charles Whitney, Professor, Department of Journalism, University of Texas at Austin

Barbie Zelizer, Assistant Professor, Annenberg School of Communication, University of Pennsylvania

Printed in the United States
33630LVS00003B/28-36

9 780761 900764